# FINAL FANTASY.X-2

## OFFICIAL STRATEGY GUIDE

D0907696

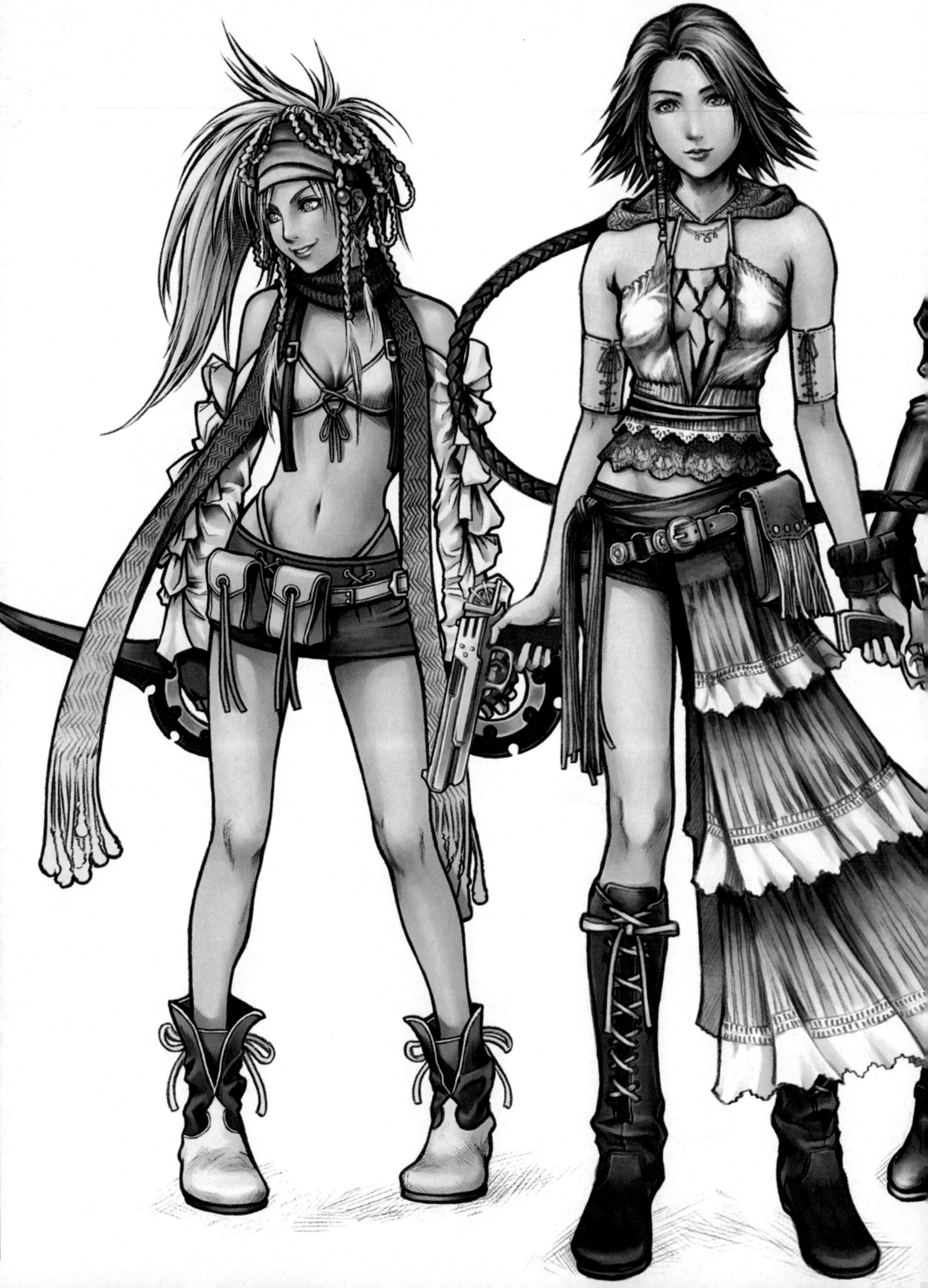

# THE GULLWINGS

For 1000 years, the world of Spira was held in the grip of terror as the great monster Sin punished its citizens for using the forbidden machina in the great wars. To combat Sin, powerful summoners would make a pilgrimage to Zanarkand, the ruins of what was once the greatest city in Spira. Able to call and control the devastating manifestations of the fayth, aeons, into battle, these summoners would sacrifice their lives and the life of a chosen guardian, to defeat Sin for a temporary period of time called the "Calm." Unfortunately, the Calm would end and Sin would eventually return, forcing a new summoner to forfeit their life to bring peace to Spira once again.

This cycle of life and death continued in Spira for untold generations, until one summoner stood against the teachings of Yevon and sought a new means by which to defeat Sin—permanently. The summoner's name was Yuna, and along with her guardians, went against the order of Yevon and fought enemies on all sides. In a last ditch effort, Yuna and her guardians took on Sin and defeated it forever, bringing forth a time that would be referred to as the "Eternal Calm." Although peace would finally last forever, Yuna was forced to say goodbye to someone whom she cared for very much. The young man named Tidus had been a dream of the Fayth, and when the Fayth were defeated during the attack on Sin, their dream faded.

Yuna thought that the love of her life had vanished alongside the last remaining traces of Sin. But two years later, Rikku appeared in Besaid Village and delivered a sphere found by Kimahri, Yuna's former guardian and the new Elder of the Ronso tribe of Mt. Gagazet. This sphere contained images of a young man who resembled Tidus so closely that Yuna was compelled to leave Besaid and begin a new search for more spheres that might lead her closer to the truth. This is her story.

YUNA

The daughter of Lord Braska, Yuna is the high summoner who defeated Sin and brought about the Eternal Calm. She lived most of her life by a strict code of ethics directed by the teachings of Yevon. She always believed that she would one day sacrifice herself to defeat Sin, but through the love and faith of her guardian she realized that it was possible to deliver to the people of Spira, an even greater gift by defeating Sin forever. After this great victory, Yuna is now attempting to explore and enjoy the life she thought she would have to forsake. Along with her cousin Rikku and the Gullwings—a group of Al Bhed sphere hunters—she scours Spira in search of valuable spheres containing records of the long forgotten history before Sin. While her main desires are to explore the world, meet new people, and have fun, Yuna also seeks to answer the mysteries surrounding the recordings of the strange sphere.

RIKKU

Rikku is Yuna's cousin and an Al Bhed. The Al Bhed are a race of people in Spira who speak a different language, which can be deciphered by obtaining the Al Bhed Primers. Al Bhed enjoy tinkering with machines, or "machina," and they have started an excavation in Bikanel Desert to unearth ancient machina to study in hopes of improving their current use and one day make their own. The Gullwings' airship, the Celsius, is a unique piece of machina. Rikku and her brother, appropriately named "Brother," have turned the machina into a first-class flying machine. Rikku was one of Yuna's guardians in the fight against Sin and aided her in bringing about the Eternal Calm. Now that Yuna has left her village in search of fun and adventure, Rikku is dedicated to helping her cousin find excitement, even at the risk of getting into trouble!

PAINE

The mysterious female warrior called Paine, joined the Gullwings before Yuna came along. No one knows much about her, except that she is rather quiet and generally keeps to herself. Paine is extremely tough and loves a good fight, but she is also reasonable enough to smell trouble a mile away. Paine reveals little about her past, except that she has always wanted to fly on an airship and hunt for spheres containing records of Spira's past. No one knows if perhaps some of these spheres may contain records that are personal to her…

*FINAL FANTASY X-2* features a new, unique system of character development and combat called the dressphere system. Dresspheres are small spheres that fit into a Garment Grid. When a character equips a Garment Grid, she can then equip any of the dresspheres placed on the grid. A character can also perform a "spherechange" during battle. Each dres-

sphere enables the character to play a unique role in the party. While a character has a dressphere equipped, she will learn a special set of abilities tailored to the functions of the dressphere. Upon learning all the abilities of a dressphere, the character is said to have "Mastered" the dressphere.

## EQUIPPING GARMENT GRIDS AND DRESSPHERES

For a character to use dresspheres, you must first equip a Garment Grid. To equip a Garment Grid, at least one node on the grid must be set with a dressphere. To prepare a Garment Grid for use, press the Triangle button to open the main menu. Open the "Garment Grids" sub-screen and select a grid from the list of acquired Garment Grids.

A list of available dresspheres appears on the left side of the screen. Select dresspheres and set them in the nodes on the Garment Grid. You can speed up this process by using the "Auto" option at the bottom of the list to automatically place a set of dresspheres on the grid. The "Rearrange" option enables you to switch the location of any spheres already placed

on the grid. To remove a dressphere and leave an empty node, move the cursor to the dressphere and press the Triangle button. The "Remove All" option enables you to instantly clear a Garment Grid. This is a handy option if you want to reset the grid with all new dresspheres, or if you no longer want to use the Garment Grid and want it to be grayed out when equipping your characters.

When you change the dresspheres on a Garment Grid that is already in use by one or more characters, you must then equip the characters with a dressphere from the new configuration. If you equip a character with a different Garment Grid, you must also choose a dressphere before exiting the menu. Each character must always be equipped with a Garment Grid and a dressphere.

## SPHERECHANGE

When battle begins, a character appears dressed according to the dressphere she is equipped with. During battle, you can use a character's combat turn to perform a "spherechange." Press the L1 button to access the character's Garment Grid. Use the cursor to select the dressphere you want to change into, then press the X button. After doing so, the character changes from the previous dressphere to the new one with a spectacular transformation sequence. If you don't want to view the transformation sequence, or if you prefer to view a shortened version, you can set such preferences in the "Config" sub-screen of the main menu. Regardless of this setting, the full transformation sequence will play whenever the player changes into a dressphere they haven't used before.

Spherechange is a strategic move to use in battle. For instance, once a Thief steals items and pilfers gil from an enemy, you may want to switch to a dressphere that will be more useful in defeating the enemy. Likewise, if a Black Mage runs out of MP and doesn't know the "MP Drain" ability, it's best to switch that character to a dressphere in which they can perform physical attacks that do not require MP.

*You can only change to a dressphere that is connected to the currently equipped dressphere by a single line on the Garment Grid.*

## GATES

When a character switches from one dressphere to another, a glowing, blue line is drawn between the two dresspheres on the Garment Grid. If this glowing line passes through a colored gate, the character gains an added ability or status bonus. Such effects can include the ability to cast a spell or a Strength

increase. Note, however, that the effect only lasts until the end of the current battle. Check the description of each Garment Grid to determine what effect a gate on the grid will provide when you pass through it during a spherechange.

## SPECIAL DRESSPHERES

By completing certain objectives or quests during the game, the party will find special dresspheres that can only be utilized by one of the three characters. Yuna's special dressphere is Floral Fallal, Rikku's is Machina Maw, and Paine's is Full Throttle. Special dresspheres are not equipped on Garment Grids. The character can always transform into a special dressphere no matter which Garment Grid is equipped.

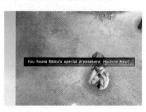

For a character to spherechange into a special dressphere, you must change to every dressphere on the Garment Grid during a battle. After changing into every dressphere on a fully loaded Garment Grid all the dresspheres on the grid should be connected by blue lines. Press the L1 button to access the spherechange menu, then press the R1 button to access the character's special dressphere command and press X. A special dressphere change can only be made if the player changes into all the dresspheres on a Garment Grid. This means that a dressphere must be placed in every node on the grid. A Garment Grid with fewer nodes, such as Unerring Path, makes transforming to the special dressphere much easier during combat.

When a character transforms into her special dressphere, the other two characters leave the battlefield. Each special dressphere consists of three sections, each of which receives a combat turn to perform an action. In essence, it's still like a three-character party. Special dresspheres acquire AP just like normal

dresspheres, and the character will learn new abilities and become more formidable in combat while wearing a special dressphere. However, unlike normal dresspheres, the special dresspheres require "key items" to be fully mastred.

# LEARNING ABILITIES

Each time a character takes a valid action on the battlefield, that character earns Ability Points (AP) that accumulate toward learning a new ability. To determine which ability the character will learn next, open the main menu and select the Abilities command. Select a character, then press the X button. The character's status and a list of all available dresspheres are displayed on the Abilities sub-screen. The currently equipped dressphere is highlighted by the cursor. Press the L1 or R1 buttons to cycle through the other characters in the party.

After choosing a dressphere, a list of all the abilities that the character has learned, or can learn, appears. The ability that will be learned next is highlighted in yellow. To select a different ability, move the cursor down the list and choose a new ability. Press the L1 or R1 buttons to cycle through the other dresspheres available to the character. As a character learns abilities, new ones may be added to this list. For more detailed information on learning new abilities, refer to the "Dresspheres" section in this chapter.

# GARMENT GRIDS

## FIRST STEPS

| Nodes | 6 |
|-------|---|
| Equip | No effect |
| Gates | None |

## VANGUARD

| Nodes | 5 |
|-------|---|
| Equip | Strength +5, Magic +5 |

- Strength +5
- Magic +5
- Strength +5
- Magic +5

## BUM RUSH

| Nodes | 5 |
|-------|---|
| Equip | Strength +10, Magic +10 |

- Strength +10
- Magic +10
- Strength +10
- Magic +10

## UNDYING STORM

| Nodes | 5 |
|-------|---|
| Equip | Strength +15, Magic +15 |

- Strength +15
- Magic +15
- Strength +15
- Magic +15

## FLASH OF STEEL

| Nodes | 5 |
|-------|---|
| Equip | Strength +20, Magic +20 |

- Strength +20
- Magic +20
- Strength +20
- Magic +20

## PROTECTION HALO

| Nodes | 5 |
|-------|---|
| Equip | Defense +5, Magic Defense +5 |

- Defense +5
- Magic Defense +5
- Defense +5
- Magic Defense +5

## HOUR OF NEED

| Nodes | 5 |
|-------|---|
| Equip | Defense +10, Magic Defense +10 |

- Defense +10
- Magic Defense +10
- Defense +10
- Magic Defense +10

## UNWAVERING GUARD

| Nodes | 5 |
|-------|---|
| Equip | Defense +15, Magic Defense +15 |

- Defense +15
- Magic Defense +15
- Defense +15
- Magic Defense +15

## VALIANT LUSTRE

| Nodes | 5 |
|-------|---|
| Equip | Defense +20, Magic Defense +20 |

- Defense +20
- Magic Defense +20
- Defense +20
- Magic Defense +20

Characters

1

Garment Grids & Dresspheres

2

Battle System

3

Accessories

4

Items and Item Shops

5

Walkthrough

6

Mini-Games

7

Fiends and Enemies

8

GARMENT GRIDS & DRESSPHERES

## HIGHROAD WINDS

| Nodes | 4 |
|---|---|
| Equip | First Strike |

- Slowproof
- Stopproof
- Use Haste
- SOS Haste

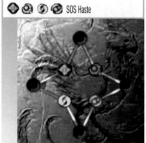

## MOUNTED ASSAULT

| Nodes | 4 |
|---|---|
| Equip | First Strike |

- Slowproof
- Stopproof
- Use Hastega
- Auto-Haste

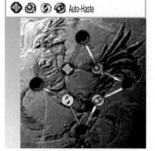

## HEART OF FLAME

| Nodes | 3 |
|---|---|
| Equip | Fire Eater, Use Fire |

- Firestrike
- Use Fira
- Use Firaga

## ICE QUEEN

| Nodes | 3 |
|---|---|
| Equip | Ice Eater, Use Blizzard |

- Icestrike
- Use Blizzara
- Use Blizzaga

## THUNDER SPAWN

| Nodes | 3 |
|---|---|
| Equip | Lightning Eater, use Thunder |

- Lightning Strike
- Use Thundara
- Use Thundaga

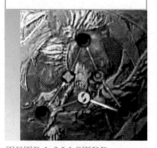

## MENACE OF THE DEEP

| Nodes | 3 |
|---|---|
| Equip | Water Eater, use Water |

- Waterstrike
- Use Watera
- Use Waterga

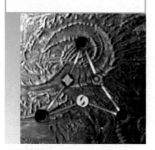

## DOWNTRODDER

| Nodes | 3 |
|---|---|
| Equip | Gravity Eater |

- Gravitystrike
- Use Demi
- Double HP

## SACRED BEAST

| Nodes | 4 |
|---|---|
| Equip | Holy Eater |

- Holystrike
- Use Holy

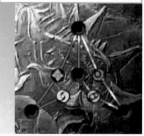

## TETRA MASTER

| Nodes | 5 |
|---|---|
| Equip | Tetrastrike |

- Fire Eater
- Ice Eater
- Lightning Eater
- Water Eater

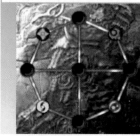

## RESTLESS SLEEP

| Nodes | 5 |
|---|---|
| Equip | Use Sleep & Bio |

- Sleepproof
- Sleeptouch
- Poisonproof
- Poisontouch

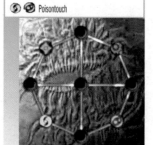

## STILL OF NIGHT

| Nodes | 5 |
|---|---|
| Equip | Use Silence & Blind |

- Silenceproof
- Silencetouch
- Darkproof
- Darktouch

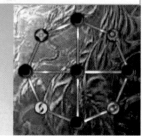

## MORTAL COIL

| Nodes | 5 |
|---|---|
| Equip | Itchproof |

- Curseproof
- Stoneproof
- Stonetouch
- Use Break

## RAGING GIANT

| Nodes | 5 |
|---|---|
| Equip | Use Confuse |

- Confuseproof
- Confusetouch
- Berserkproof
- Berserktouch

## BITTER FAREWELL

| Nodes | 5 |
|---|---|
| Equip | Use Death & Doom |

- Deathproof
- Deathtouch
- Doomproof
- Doomtouch

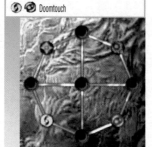

## SELENE GUARD

| Nodes | 4 |
|---|---|
| Equip | SOS Shell, Use Shell |

- Auto-Shell

## HELIOS GUARD

| Nodes | 4 |
|---|---|
| Equip | SOS Protect, Use Protect |

- Auto-Protect

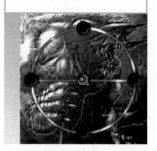

## SHINING MIRROR

| Nodes | 4 |
|---|---|
| Equip | Piercing Magic, Use Reflect |

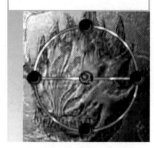 Auto-Reflect

## COVETOUS

| Nodes | 3 |
|---|---|
| Equip | No effect |

 Use Drain
 Use Osmose

## DISASTER IN BLOOM

| Nodes | 5 |
|---|---|
| Equip | No effect |

Sleeptouch
Silencetouch
Darktouch
Poisontouch
Stonetouch

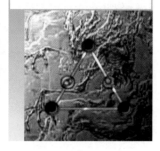

## SCOURGEBANE

| Nodes | 5 |
|---|---|
| Equip | No effect |

Sleepproof, Poisonproof
Silenceproof, Darkproof
Confuseproof, Berserkproof
Curseproof, Itchproof

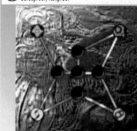

## HEALING WIND

| Nodes | 3 |
|---|---|
| Equip | Use Cure |

Use Cura
Use Curaga

## HEART REBORN

| Nodes | 3 |
|---|---|
| Equip | Use Life & Cure |

Use Cura
Use Curaga

## HEALING LIGHT

| Nodes | 4 |
|---|---|
| Equip | Use Cure |

Use Cura
Use Life
Use Curaga
Use Full-Cure

## IMMORTAL SOUL

| Nodes | 4 |
|---|---|
| Equip | Use Life & Cure |

Use Cura
Use Curaga
Use Full-Life

## WISHBRINGER

| Nodes | 5 |
|---|---|
| Equip | HP Stroll, use Regen |

Use Curaga
Auto-Regen

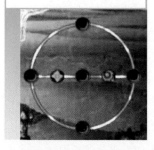

## STRENGTH OF ONE

| Nodes | 4 |
|---|---|
| Equip | Strength +10 |

Strength +15
Strength +15
Strength +15
Strength +15

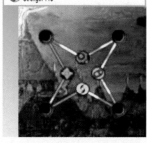

## SEETHING CAULDRON

| Nodes | 4 |
|---|---|
| Equip | Magic +10 |

Magic +15
Magic +15
Magic +15
Magic +15

## STONEHEWN

| Nodes | 4 |
|---|---|
| Equip | Defense +10 |

Defense +15
Defense +15
Defense +15
Defense +15

Characters

 1

Garment Grids & Dresspheres

 2

Battle System

 3

Accessories

 4

Items and Item Shops

 5

Walkthrough

 6

Mini-Games

 7

Fiends and Enemies

 8

## ENIGMA PLATE

| Nodes | 4 |
|---|---|
| Equip | Magic Defense+10 |

- Magic Defense+15
- Magic Defense+15
- Magic Defense+15
- Magic Defense+15

## HOWLING WIND

| Nodes | 4 |
|---|---|
| Equip | Agility +5 |

- Agility +5
- Agility +5
- Agility +5
- Agility +5

## RAY OF HOPE

| Nodes | 6 |
|---|---|
| Equip | Luck +30 |

- Luck +30
- Luck +30
- Luck +30
- Luck +30

## PRIDE OF THE SWORD

| Nodes | 6 |
|---|---|
| Equip | Use Swordplay abilities |

- Strength +15
- Strength +15
- Strength +15
- Strength +15
- Swordplay wait down

## SAMURAI'S HONOR

| Nodes | 6 |
|---|---|
| Equip | Use Bushido abilities |

- Strength +15
- Strength +15
- Strength +15
- Strength +15
- Bushido wait down

## BLOOD OF THE BEAST

| Nodes | 6 |
|---|---|
| Equip | Use Instinct abilities |

- Strength +15
- Strength +15
- Strength +15
- Strength +15
- Instinct wait down

## CHAOS MAELSTROM

| Nodes | 6 |
|---|---|
| Equip | Use Arcana abilities |

- Magic +15
- Magic +15
- Magic +15
- Magic +15
- Arcana wait down

## WHITE SIGNET

| Nodes | 6 |
|---|---|
| Equip | Use White Magic abilities |

- Magic +15
- Magic +15
- Magic +15
- Magic +15
- White Magic wait down

## BLACK TABARD

| Nodes | 6 |
|---|---|
| Equip | Use Black Magic abilities |

- Magic +15
- Magic +15
- Magic +15
- Magic +15
- Black Magic wait down

## MERCURIAL STRIKE

| Nodes | 6 |
|---|---|
| Equip | No effect |

- Swordplay wait down
- Bushido wait down
- Instinct wait down

## TRICKS OF THE TRADE

| Nodes | 6 |
|---|---|
| Equip | No effect |

- Black Magic wait down
- White Magic wait down
- Arcana wait down

## HORN OF PLENTY

| Nodes | 5 |
|---|---|
| Equip | Use Nab Gil |

- Gillionaire

## TREASURE HUNT

| Nodes | 5 |
|-------|---|
| Equip | Use Mug |

 Double Items

## TEMPERED WILL

| Nodes | 5 |
|-------|---|
| Equip | No effect |

 Double HP
 Double MP

## COVENANT OF GROWTH

| Nodes | 5 |
|-------|---|
| Equip | No effect |

 Double AP
 Double EXP

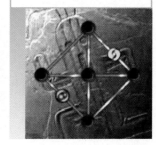

## SALVATION PROMISED

| Nodes | 4 |
|-------|---|
| Equip | Use White Magic abilities |

 Use Auto-Life

## CONFLAGRATION

| Nodes | 4 |
|-------|---|
| Equip | Use Black Magic abilities |

 Use Flare

## SUPREME LIGHT

| Nodes | 5 |
|-------|---|
| Equip | Use White Magic abilities |

 Use Auto-Life
 Use Holy

## MEGIDDO

| Nodes | 5 |
|-------|---|
| Equip | Use Black Magic abilities |

 Use Flare
 Use Ultima

## UNERRING PATH

| Nodes | 2 |
|-------|---|
| Equip | No effect |
| Gates | None |

## FONT OF POWER

| Nodes | 4 |
|-------|---|
| Equip | Half MP Cost |

 Magic +15
 Magic +15
 Magic +15
 One MP Cost

## HIGHER POWER

| Nodes | 5 |
|-------|---|
| Equip | Break HP Limit |

 Break Damage Limit

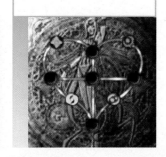

## THE END

| Nodes | 5 |
|-------|---|
| Equip | Break HP Limit |

 Break Damage Limit
 Use Finale

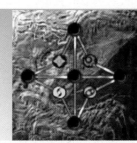

Characters

1

Garment Grids & Dresspheres

2

Battle System

3

Accessories

4

Items and Item Shops

5

Walkthrough

6

Mini-Games

7

Fiends and Enemies

8

# DRESSPHERES

## GUNNER

### MAIN COMMANDS

| |
|---|
| Attack |
| Trigger Happy |
| Gunplay |
| Item |

The Gunner uses firearms to attack enemies. Range isn't a problem and a Gunner's attacks are very effective against flying or airborne enemies. The "Trigger Happy" attack enables you to assail a single foe with a barrage of lower-powered chain attacks (quickly tap the R1 button) during the time allotted. You can even extend the time for "Trigger Happy" by leveling up the ability. At first, a Gunner's attacks won't deal much damage. But as a character gains levels, the Gunner dressphere becomes a powerful tool for quickly disposing of enemies. "Gunplay" abilities feature special shots that require MP to execute. However, unlike most skills and spells, "Gunplay" abilities are immediately performed by the Gunner, similar to physical attacks.

In combat, the Gunner's main job is to attack and destroy enemies. At the start of the game, the Gunner is quite effective at this job. Equip a Gunner with accessories and Garment Grids to boost Strength and Accuracy to inflict more damage. As the character donning the Gunner dressphere gains experience levels and grows in strength, her attacks become more devastating with a higher frequency of critical hits.

## GUNNER ABILITIES

| NAME | AP | MP | DESCRIPTION | REQUIRED ABILITIES |
|---|---|---|---|---|
| Attack | 0 | 0 | Attack one enemy. | None |
| Trigger Happy | 0 | 0 | Press R1 repeatedly during allotted time for multiple hits. | None |
| Potshot | 20 | 8 | Damage one enemy. | None |
| Cheap Shot | 30 | 8 | Damage one enemy regardless of its Defense. | Potshot |
| Enchanted Ammo | 30 | 8 | Inflict magical damage on one enemy. | None |
| Target MP | 30 | 8 | Inflict damage on one enemy's MP. | Enchanted Ammo |
| Quarter Pounder | 40 | 8 | Reduce one enemy's HP by one-fourth. | Target MP |
| On the Level | 40 | 12 | Damage one enemy according to the user's EXP level. | Target MP |
| Burst Shot | 60 | 12 | Critically damage one enemy. | None |
| Tableturner | 60 | 8 | Deal greater damage to enemies with high defense. | Potshot |
| Scattershot | 80 | 8 | Damage all enemies. | Burst Shot |
| Scatterburst | 120 | 36 | Critically damage all enemies | Scattershot |
| Darkproof | 30 | 0 | Guards against **Darkness**. | None |
| Sleepproof | 30 | 0 | Guards against **Sleep**. | Darkproof |
| Trigger Happy Lv.2 | 80 | 0 | Extends the time allotted for **Trigger Happy**. | None |
| Trigger Happy Lv.3 | 150 | 0 | Extends the time allotted for **Trigger Happy**. | Trigger Happy Lv.2 |

# THIEF

## MAIN COMMANDS

| |
|---|
| Attack |
| Steal |
| Flimflam |
| Flee |
| Item |

Characters

1

Garment Grids & Dresspheres

2

Battle System

3

Accessories

4

Items and Item Shops

5

Walkthrough

6

Mini-Games

7

Fiends and Enemies

8

While most enemies will drop items and small amounts of gil after each battle, a Thief can steal additional items, gil, HP, and MP from enemies during combat. While a Thief is neither strong nor sturdy like some of the typical "attacker" types, the Thief's high Agility and Evasion makes it easier to sidestep many physical attacks. By stealing items and using the "Pilfer Gil" ability during every battle, a Thief helps the party to amass an overwhelming supply of medicines, bombs, consumables and accessories, as well as plenty of gil. Stealing is one of the best methods to gain powerful equipment early in the game. The "First Strike" ability of a Thief enables her to get the first turn in combat.

During combat, spend the first few turns stealing items and gil from each enemy on the battlefield. If enemies are reluctant to give up items and your Thief continuously comes up empty-handed, use the "Sticky Fingers" ability to pry the items loose. In particular, bosses usually hold powerful accessories that can only be gained by stealing, so keep a Thief in the party at all times. Help out your fellow party members by halting enemy advancement with "Borrowed Time," or enable the entire party to run simultaneously with the "Flee" ability in case of an emergency.

## THIEF ABILITIES

| NAME | AP | MP | DESCRIPTION | REQUIRED ABILITIES |
|---|---|---|---|---|
| Attack | 0 | 0 | Attack one enemy. | None |
| Steal | 0 | 0 | Steal items from one enemy. | None |
| Pilfer Gil | 30 | 2 | Steal gil from one enemy. | None |
| Borrowed Time | 100 | 16 | Inflict Stop on one enemy. | None |
| Pilfer HP | 60 | 10 | Steal HP from one enemy. | Pilfer Gil |
| Pilfer MP | 60 | 0 | Steal MP from one enemy. | Pilfer HP |
| Sticky Fingers | 120 | 20 | Always steal items from one enemy. | Pilfer HP |
| Master Thief | 140 | 20 | Steal rare items from one enemy. | Sticky Fingers |
| Soul Swipe | 160 | 12 | Inflict Berserk on one enemy. | Pilfer HP |
| Steal Will | 160 | 18 | Cause one enemy to flee from battle. | Soul Swipe |
| Flee | 10 | 0 | Aid the party's escape from battle. | None |
| Item Hunter | 60 | 0 | Improves the odds of enemies dropping items. | None |
| First Strike | 40 | 0 | Act at the beginning of battle. | None |
| Initiative | 60 | 0 | Raises the party's chance of a preemptive strike. | First Strike |
| Slowproof | 20 | 0 | Guards against Slow. | Item Hunter |
| Stopproof | 40 | 0 | Guards against Stop. | Slowproof |

# GUN MAGE

## MAIN COMMANDS

| Attack |
|---|
| Blue Bullet |
| Fiend Hunter |
| Scan |
| Item |

The Gun Mage serves a variety of purposes on the battlefield, which adds up to one deadly combination. A Gun Mage can expose the weaknesses and current status ailments or benefits of a single enemy or ally with the "Scan" ability. Gun Mages learn a variety of "Fiend Hunter" skills that enable them to deal greater damage to certain types of enemies more easily. When dealing with Machina, Mechs, Helms, and Drakes in the early stages of the game, a Gun Mage who has learned the applicable skills will make quick work of these fights. Gun Mages also have the unique ability to learn the special attacks of enemies and use them in battle. When an enemy uses a special ability to attack a Gun Mage during combat, there is a chance that an active Gun Mage will learn the enemy's skill right on the spot. The only problem is whether or not the Gun Mage will survive the attack afterward!

In battle, use "Scan" on unknown enemies to reveal elemental or status weaknesses. For the rest of the battle, attack or perform "Fiend Hunter" abilities, if the types of fiends that the Gun Mage can affect are present. Always bring a Gun Mage if you want to learn new "Blue Bullet" abilities.

## GUN MAGE ABILITIES

| NAME | AP | MP | DESCRIPTION | REQUIRED ABILITIES |
|---|---|---|---|---|
| Attack | 0 | 0 | Attack one enemy. | None |
| Blue Bullet | 0 | 0 | Attack with bullets containing fiend skills. | None |
| Scan | 20 | 0 | View detailed information about one enemy. | None |
| Shell Cracker | 20 | 3 | Deal quadruple damage to Helms. | None |
| Anti-Aircraft | 20 | 3 | Deal quadruple damage to Birds and Wasps. | None |
| Silver Bullet | 20 | 3 | Deal quadruple damage to Lupines. | None |
| Flan Eater | 20 | 3 | Deal quadruple damage to Flans. | None |
| Elementillery | 20 | 3 | Deal quadruple damage to Elementals. | Flan Eater |
| Killasaurus | 20 | 3 | Deal quadruple damage to Reptiles. | None |
| Drake Slayer | 20 | 3 | Deal quadruple damage to Drakes. | Killasaurus |
| Dismantler | 20 | 3 | Deal quadruple damage to Machina. | None |
| Mech Destroyer | 20 | 3 | Deal quadruple damage to Mechs. | Dismantler |
| Demon Muzzle | 20 | 3 | Deal quadruple damage to Imps and Evil Eyes. | Anti-Aircraft |
| Fiend Hunter Lv.2 | 30 | 0 | Cuts the time required for Fiend Hunter by 40%. | None |
| Scan Lv.2 | 20 | 0 | Allows user to rotate targets when casting Scan. | None |
| Scan Lv.3 | 100 | 0 | Allows user to target party members with Scan. | Scan Lv.2 |

## BLUE BULLET ABILITIES

| ABILITY | MP | DESCRIPTION | LEARNED FROM |
|---|---|---|---|
| Fire Breath | 28 | Deal fire damage to all enemies. | Balivarha |
| Seed Cannon | 28 | Damage one enemy. | Leucophylla, Cephalotus |
| Stone Breath | 32 | Petrify all enemies. | Tomb, Monolith, Dolmen, Epitaph |
| Absorb | 3 | Absorb HP and MP from one enemy. | Protochimera, Haizhe, Baralai (CH. 2), Flan Azabache, Jahi, Cindy, Vegnagun |
| White Wind | 16 | Restore some HP to the party and cure status ailments. | Bully Cap, Coeurl, Queen Coeurl, Mycotoxin, Ms. Goon |
| Bad Breath | 64 | Inflict status ailments on all enemies. | Malboro, Great Malboro |
| Mighty Guard | 32 | Cast **Shell** and **Protect** on the party. | Haizhe, Garik Ronso |
| Supernova | 70 | Damage all enemies. | Ultima Weapon, Paragon |
| Cry in the Night | 80 | Damage all enemies. | Mega Tonberry |
| Drill Shot | 32 | Damage one enemy. | Baralai (CH. 5) |
| Mortar | 99 | Damage all enemies. | Gippal |
| Annihilator | 48 | Damage all enemies. | Experiment |
| Heaven's Cataract | 22 | Damage all enemies and lower Defense and Magic Defense. | Kukulcan, Gucumatz, Chac |
| 1000 Needles | 24 | Damage one enemy. | Cactuar |
| Storm Cannon | 38 | Damage all enemies. | Ironside |
| Blaster | 30 | Damage one enemy. | Coeurl, Queen Coeurl |

*Note that some abilities can only be learned when the monster is or isn't oversouled.

Characters

1

Garment Grids & Dresspheres

2

Battle System

3

Accessories

4

Items and Item Shops

5

Walkthrough

6

Mini-Games

7

Fiends and Enemies

8

# WARRIOR

| MAIN COMMANDS |
|---|
| Attack |
| Swordplay |
| Assault |
| Sentinel |
| Item |

GARMENT GRIDS & DRESSPHERES

The Warrior, Paine's initial dressphere, is the first of many strong "attacker" dblebspheres in the game. The main function of a Warrior is to hit enemies hard and bring down large amounts of enemy HP with each strike. A Warrior benefits from a lot of HP, but lacks a respectable amount of MP. A Warrior's "Swordplay" skills are all low MP-cost abilities that fuse magic with metal in a powerful attack designed to exploit enemy weaknesses. A Warrior can also make many enemies easier to defeat by lowering their attacking power, defense, and spell casting abilities. Additionally, a Warrior can also delay the action of an enemy with "Delay Attack" and "Delay Buster."

During battles, if an enemy is taking less than the normal amount of damage from a Warrior's attack, use "Swordplay" abilities to exploit elemental weaknesses or inflict status ailments on it. Without restorative abilities, a Warrior must depend on others to regain lost HP.

Characters

1

Garment Grids
& Dresspheres

2

Battle System

3

Accessories

4

Items and
Item Shops

5

Walkthrough

6

Mini-Games

7

Fiends and
Enemies

8

## WARRIOR ABILITIES

| NAME | AP | MP | DESCRIPTION | REQUIRED ABILITIES |
|------|-----|-----|-------------|--------------------|
| Attack | 0 | 0 | Attack one enemy. | None |
| Sentinel | 20 | 0 | Take less physical damage until next turn. | None |
| Flametongue | 20 | 4 | Deal fire damage to one enemy. | None |
| Ice Brand | 20 | 4 | Deal ice damage to one enemy. | None |
| Thunder Blade | 20 | 4 | Deal lightning damage to one enemy. | None |
| Liquid Steel | 20 | 4 | Deal water damage to one enemy. | None |
| Demi Sword | 60 | 6 | Deal gravity damage to one enemy. | Flametongue, Ice Brand, Thunder Blade, Liquid Steel |
| Excalibur | 120 | 24 | Deal holy damage to one enemy. | Demi Sword |
| Power Break | 30 | 4 | Damage one enemy and lower its Strength. | None |
| Armor Break | 30 | 4 | Damage one enemy and lower its Defense. | None |
| Magic Break | 30 | 4 | Damage one enemy and lower its Magic. | None |
| Mental Break | 30 | 4 | Damage one enemy and lower its Magic Defense. | Magic Break |
| Delay Attack | 100 | 10 | Damage one enemy and delay its action. | Armor Break |
| Delay Buster | 120 | 16 | Damage one enemy and greatly delay its action. | Delay Attack |
| Assault | 100 | 0 | Cast Berserk, Haste, Shell, and Protect on the party. | Sentinel |
| SOS Protect | 20 | 0 | Casts Protect when HP is low. | Sentinel |

# ALCHEMIST

## MAIN COMMANDS

| |
|---|
| Attack |
| Mix |
| Stash |
| Item |

An Alchemist has the ability to help the party make the most of their items. The "Mix" ability enables an Alchemist to combine any two items for greater effect. For example, a Potion and a Hi-Potion can be combined to achieve the effect of a Mega-Potion, which restores 2000 HP to each party member simultaneously. It's easy to see that the "Mix" ability makes it possible to use items you don't have by combining two lesser items. An Alchemist can also learn to create extra items and use them during a battle. Since an Alchemist can also attack, equip your party's main "healer" with this dressphere in the latter half of the game.

In any battle, have an Alchemist attack until a need for mixing or healing arises. If all the enemies can be affected by some status ailment, then mix up the appropriate bomb and launch it at them. If your party gets into trouble, have an Alchemist mix up restorative items or create new items by using her "Stash" skills.

### ATTACK TYPE

| # | Name |
|---|---|
| 1 | Pineapple |
| 2 | Potato Masher |
| 3 | Cluster Bomb |
| 4 | Sunburst |
| 5 | Blaster Mine |
| 6 | Hazardous Shell |
| 7 | Soul Spring |
| 8 | Soul Sea |
| 9 | Heat Blaster |
| 10 | Firestorm |
| 11 | Burning Soul |
| 12 | Brimstone |
| 13 | Abaddon Flame |
| 14 | Snow Flurry |
| 15 | Icefall |
| 16 | Winter Storm |
| 17 | Black Ice |
| 18 | Krysta |
| 19 | Thunderbolt |
| 20 | Rolling Thunder |
| 21 | Lightning Bolt |
| 22 | Electroshock |
| 23 | Thunderblast |
| 24 | Waterfall |
| 25 | Flash Flood |
| 26 | Tidal Wave |
| 27 | Aqua Toxin |
| 28 | Dark Rain |
| 29 | Nega Burst |
| 30 | Black Hole |
| 31 | Tallboy |
| 32 | Grand Slam |
| 33 | Archangel |
| 34 | White Hole |

### RECOVERY TYPE

| # | Name |
|---|---|
| 35 | Hi-Potion |
| 36 | Mega-Potion |
| 37 | Ultra Potion |
| 38 | Remedy |
| 39 | Panacea |
| 40 | Ultra Cure |
| 41 | Final Elixir |
| 42 | Mega Phoenix |
| 43 | Final Phoenix |
| 44 | Fantasy Phoenix |

### SUPPORT TYPE

| # | Name |
|---|---|
| 45 | Mega Vitality |
| 46 | Mega Mana |
| 47 | Mega Cocktail |
| 48 | Chocobo Wing |
| 49 | Wall |
| 50 | Hi-Wall |
| 51 | Final Wall |
| 52 | Hero Drink |
| 53 | Miracle Drink |

### Mix Combinations (First Item × Second Item)

| First Item \ Second Item | Potion | Hi-Potion | X-Potion | Mega-Potion | Ether | Turbo Ether | Phoenix Down | Mega Phoenix | Elixir | Megalixir | Antidote | Soft | Eye Drops | Echo Screen |
|---|---|---|---|---|---|---|---|---|---|---|---|---|---|---|
| Potion | 35 | 36 | 37 | | 36 | 37 | 42 | 43 | 37 | 41 | 35 | | | |
| Hi-Potion | | | | | | | | 43 | | | 36 | | | |
| X-Potion | 37 | | | | | | | | | | 37 | | | |
| Mega-Potion | | | | | | | | | | | | | | |
| Ether | 36 | | | | 36 | | | | | | 36 | | | |
| Turbo Ether | 37 | | | | | | | | | | 37 | | | |
| Phoenix Down | 42 | 43 | | | | | 42 | | | 44 | 42 | | | |
| Mega Phoenix | 43 | | | | | | | | | | 43 | | | |
| Elixir | 37 | | | | | | | | 37 | 41 | 37 | | | |
| Megalixir | 41 | | | | | | | | 44 | 41 | | | | |
| Antidote | 38 | 36 | 37 | | 36 | 37 | 38 | 43 | 37 | | 38 | | | |
| Soft | | | | | | | | | | | | | | |
| Eye Drops | | | | | | | | | | | | | | |
| Echo Screen | | | | | | | | | | | | | | |
| Holy Water | 33 | | | | 33 | | | | | | 33 | | | |
| Remedy | 39 | | | 39 | 39 | | | | | | 39 | | | |
| Budget Grenade | 1 | 36 | | | 36 | | 1 | 43 | | | 1 | | | |
| Grenade | 2 | | | 2 | | | 2 | | | | 2 | | | |
| S-Bomb | | | | | | | | | | | | | | |
| M-Bomb | | | | | | | | | | | | | | |
| L-Bomb | 3 | | | | | | | | | | 3 | | | |
| Sleep Grenade | 5 | | 37 | | 5 | 37 | 5 | | 37 | | 5 | | | |
| Silence Grenade | | | | | | | | | | | | | | |
| Dark Grenade | | | | | | | | | | | | | | |
| Petrify Grenade | | | | | | | | | | | | | | |
| Bomb Fragment | 9 | 36 | | | 36 | | 9 | 43 | | | 9 | | | |
| Bomb Core | 10 | | | | 10 | | 10 | | | | 10 | | | |
| Fire Gem | 11 | | | | | | | | | | 11 | | | |
| Antarctic Wind | 14 | 36 | 37 | | 36 | 37 | 14 | 43 | 37 | | 14 | | | |
| Arctic Wind | 15 | | | | 15 | | 15 | | | | 15 | | | |
| Ice Gem | 16 | | | | | | | | | | 16 | | | |
| Electro Marble | 19 | 36 | 37 | | 36 | 37 | 19 | 43 | 37 | | 19 | | | |
| Lightning Marble | 20 | | | | 20 | | 20 | | | | 20 | | | |
| Lightning Gem | 21 | | | | | | | | | | 21 | | | |
| Fish Scale | 24 | 36 | 37 | | 36 | 37 | 24 | 43 | 37 | | 24 | | | |
| Dragon Scale | 25 | | | | 25 | | 25 | | | | 25 | | | |
| Water Gem | 26 | | | | | | | | | | 26 | | | |
| Shadow Gem | 29 | 36 | 37 | | 36 | 37 | 29 | | 37 | | 29 | | | |
| Shining Gem | 3 | | | | | | | | | | 3 | | | |
| Blessed Gem | 34 | | | | | | | | | | 34 | | | |
| Supreme Gem | 4 | | | | | | | | | | | | | |
| Poison Fang | 5 | 36 | 37 | | 36 | 37 | 5 | 43 | 37 | 41 | 5 | | | |
| Silver Hourglass | | | | | 5 | | | | | | | | | |
| Gold Hourglass | 6 | | | | | | | | | | 6 | | | |
| Candle of Life | 5 | 36 | 37 | | 36 | 37 | 5 | 43 | 37 | | 5 | | | |
| Farplane Shadow | | | | | 5 | | | | | | | | | |
| Dark Matter | 53 | | | | | | | | | | | | | |
| Chocobo Feather | 48 | | 37 | | 48 | 37 | 48 | | 37 | 41 | 48 | | | |
| Chocobo Wing | 51 | | | | | | | | | | | | | |
| Lunar Curtain | 49 | | 37 | | 49 | 37 | 49 | | 37 | 41 | 49 | | | |
| Light Curtain | | | | | | | | | | | | | | |
| Star Curtain | 50 | | | | 50 | | 50 | | | | 50 | | | |
| Healing Spring | 37 | | | | | | | 43 | | | 37 | | | |
| Mana Spring | 7 | 36 | | | 36 | | 7 | | | | 7 | | | |
| Stamina Spring | | | | | | | | | | | | | | |
| Soul Spring | | | | | 7 | | | | | | | | | |
| Dispel Tonic | 40 | | | | | | | | | | 40 | | | |
| Stamina Tablet | 45 | | | | | | | | | | 45 | | | |
| Mana Tablet | 46 | | | | | | | | | | 46 | | | |
| Stamina Tonic | 47 | | | | | | | | | | | | | |
| Mana Tonic | | | | | | | | | | | | | | |
| Twin Stars | 30 | | | | | | | | | 41 | 30 | | | |
| Three Stars | | | | | | | | | | | | | | |
| Hero Drink | 52 | 36 | 37 | | 36 | 37 | 52 | 43 | 37 | | 52 | | | |
| Gysahl Greens | 36 | | | | | | | 43 | | | 36 | | | |
| Sylkis Greens | | | | | | | | | | | | | | |
| Mimett Greens | | | | | | | | | | | | | | |
| Pahsana Greens | | | | | | | | | | | | | | |

## ALCHEMIST ABILITIES

| NAME | AP | MP | DESCRIPTION | REQUIRED ABILITIES |
|---|---|---|---|---|
| Attack | 0 | 0 | Attack one enemy. | None |
| Mix | 0 | 0 | Combine two items for various results. | None |
| Potion | 10 | 0 | Use a spare Potion that you tucked away. | None |
| Hi-Potion | 40 | 0 | Use a spare Hi-Potion that you tucked away. | Potion |
| Mega-Potion | 120 | 0 | Use a spare Mega-Potion that you tucked away. | Hi-Potion |
| X-Potion | 160 | 0 | Use a spare X-Potion that you tucked away. | Mega-Potion |
| Remedy | 20 | 0 | Use a spare Remedy that you tucked away. | None |
| Dispel Tonic | 20 | 0 | Use a spare Dispel Tonic that you tucked away. | Remedy |
| Phoenix Down | 30 | 0 | Use a spare Phoenix Down that you tucked away. | None |
| Mega Phoenix | 200 | 0 | Use a spare Mega Phoenix that you tucked away. | Phoenix Down |
| Ether | 400 | 0 | Use a spare Ether that you tucked away. | Dispel Tonic |
| Elixir | 999 | 0 | Use a spare Elixir that you tucked away. | Ether |
| Items Lv.2 | 30 | 0 | Cuts the time required to use Items by 80%. | None |
| Chemist | 40 | 0 | Doubles the potency of recovery items. | None |
| Elementalist | 80 | 0 | Doubles the potency of elemental items. | None |
| Physicist | 100 | 0 | Doubles the potency of non-elemental items. | Elementalist and Chemist |

Garment Grids
& Dresspheres

Battle System

Accessories

4

Items and
Item Shops

5

Walkthrough

Mini-Games

7

Fiends and
Enemies

8

# SAMURAI

| MAIN COMMANDS |
|---|
| Attack |
| Bushido |
| Spare Change |
| Zantetsu |
| Item |

Another strong "attacker" type of dressphere, the Samurai inflicts large amounts of damage with a huge sword. The Samurai is surprisingly agile in spite of this heavy weapon and evades many attacks with surprising ease. However, the weight of the weapon makes it more difficult to hit flying or evasive targets. While many of the Samurai's abilities revolve mainly around striking non-elemental damage against one or more foes, this dressphere also bestows the user with many talents for reducing the magical enhancements of enemies while boosting the Samurai's own ability to fight. Thus, a Samurai specializes in creating a level playing field where honor can be maintained during combat.

During combat, use a Samurai to strike enemies and cause massive damage. If the enemies show unusually high defense or if they cast beneficial status-raising spells, use the Samurai's "Fingersnap," "Nonpareil," and "No Fear" abilities to elevate the Samurai to the fiends' level. Even with the "Clean Slate" ability, a Samurai must still depend on others to regain lost HP

Characters

1

Garment Grids
& Dresspheres

2

Battle System

3

Accessories

4

Items and
Item Shops

5

Walkthrough

6

Mini-Games

7

Fiends and
Enemies

8

## SAMURAI ABILITIES

| NAME | AP | MP | DESCRIPTION | REQUIRED ABILITIES |
|------|----|----|-------------|--------------------|
| Attack | 0 | 0 | Attack one enemy. | None |
| Spare Change | 0 | 0 | Attack by throwing gil. | None |
| Mirror of Equity | 30 | 16 | Attack one enemy, dealing greater damage when HP is low. | None |
| Magicide | 30 | 4 | Inflict damage on one enemy's MP. | None |
| Dismissal | 30 | 10 | Halt the pending action of one enemy. | Magicide |
| Fingersnap | 40 | 10 | Revert one enemy's attributes to normal levels. | Dismissal |
| Sparkler | 40 | 12 | Damage one enemy. | None |
| Fireworks | 60 | 18 | Damage all enemies. | Sparkler |
| Momentum | 60 | 10 | Deal increasing damage as you defeat more enemies. | Sparkler |
| Shin-Zantetsu | 100 | 32 | Instantly defeat all enemies. Sometimes fails. | Momentum |
| Nonpareil | 20 | 10 | Raise the user's Strength and Accuracy. | None |
| No Fear | 30 | 12 | Cast Shell and Protect on the user. | Nonpareil |
| Clean Slate | 40 | 16 | Restore HP and cure user of status ailments. | No Fear |
| Hayate | 60 | 20 | Raise Evasion and cast Haste on the user. | Clean Slate |
| Zantetsu | 140 | 0 | Instantly defeat one enemy. Sometimes fails. | Shin-Zantetsu |
| SOS Critical | 80 | 0 | Always inflict critical hits when HP is low. | Fireworks |

# DARK KNIGHT

## MAIN COMMANDS

Attack

Darkness

Arcana

Charon

Item

A death-dealer born of shadow, the Dark Knight infuses the crafts of the Underworld to deal massive damage to enemies on the battlefield. As is the law in the nether realms, the Dark Knight can sacrifice HP or her own life to defeat enemies. With the "Darkness" attack, a Dark Knight can sacrifice 1/8 of her total HP to inflict exorbitant amounts of damage to the entire enemy party. On the next turn, the Dark Knight can regain some of the HP sacrificed by using the "Drain" ability. The "Charon" ability enables a Dark Knight to sacrifice herself to inflict heavy damage on a single foe. However, the Dark Knight is removed from your party for the rest of the battle, and will not gain EXP following a victory. Use "Charon" only as a last resort. The Dark Knight can also make herself immune to many status ailments by learning a complete set of auto-abilities.

During battle, have a Dark Knight use "Darkness" to damage all of the enemies at once, followed by a regular attack on a single foe. If some enemies prove difficult to defeat, try casting "Black Sky." While a Dark Knight can recover small amounts of lost HP by draining it from enemies, it is wiser and more beneficial for a Dark Knight to work in conjunction with a good "healer" type, such as a White Mage or an Alchemist.

Characters

Garment Grids
& Dresspheres

Battle System

Accessories

Items and
Item Shops

Walkthrough

Mini-Games

## DARK KNIGHT ABILITIES

| NAME | AP | MP | DESCRIPTION | REQUIRED ABILITIES |
|------|-----|-----|-------------|--------------------|
| Attack | 0 | 0 | Attack one enemy. | None |
| Darkness | 0 | 0 | Sacrifice HP to damage all enemies. | None |
| Drain | 20 | 8 | Absorb HP from one enemy. | None |
| Demi | 20 | 10 | Reduce the HP of all enemies by 1/4. | None |
| Confuse | 30 | 12 | Confuse one enemy. | Demi |
| Break | 40 | 20 | Petrify one enemy. | Confuse |
| Bio | 30 | 16 | Poison one enemy. | None |
| Doom | 20 | 18 | Doom one enemy. Enemy is KO'd when the count reaches 0. | Bio |
| Death | 50 | 24 | Instantly defeat one enemy. Sometimes fails. | Doom |
| Black Sky | 100 | 80 | Randomly damages enemies. | Death |
| Charon | 20 | 0 | Sacrifice life to heavily damage one enemy. | None |
| Poisonproof | 30 | 0 | Guards against Poison. | None |
| Stoneproof | 30 | 0 | Guards against Petrification. | Poisonproof |
| Confuseproof | 30 | 0 | Guards against Confusion. | Stoneproof |
| Curseproof | 30 | 0 | Guards against Curse. | None |
| Deathproof | 40 | 0 | Guards against Death. | Curseproof |

# BERSERKER

## MAIN COMMANDS

| |
|---|
| Attack |
| Berserk |
| Instinct |
| Howl |
| Item |

The Berserker dressphere is quick and attacks with furious abandon. The Berserker strikes with its razor-sharp claws, inflicting damage to a single foe. The damage inflicted can increase when the user casts "Berserk" on herself. While in this state, a Berserker attacks automatically. Once a Berserker has learned hard-to-obtain auto-abilities (such as "Counterattack," "Magic Counter" and "Evade & Counter"), the character can strike back automatically multiple times per turn based on the enemies' actions. Couple this with the "Auto-Regen" ability and the Berserker becomes an independent killing machine with little need for help from the other party members.

Start each battle by doubling a Berserker's HP with the "Howl" ability, then determine your strategy and cast "Berserk" if all you need to do is attack. While doing all of this causes a Berserker to stay out of the battle for the first few rounds, the result is devastating to the enemy party.

Characters

1

Garment Grids
& Dresspheres

2

Battle System

3

Accessories

4

Items and
Item Shops

5

Walkthrough

6

Mini-Games

7

Friends and
Enemies

8

## BERSERKER ABILITIES

| NAME | AP | MP | DESCRIPTION | REQUIRED ABILITIES |
|---|---|---|---|---|
| Attack | 0 | 0 | Attack one enemy. | None |
| Berserk | 0 | 0 | Boost the user's Strength but lose control of her actions. | None |
| Cripple | 20 | 6 | Halve one enemy's HP. | None |
| Mad Rush | 30 | 6 | Heavily damage one enemy. Often fails. | Cripple |
| Crackdown | 30 | 6 | Damage one enemy and nullify Shell, Protect, and Reflect. | None |
| Eject | 40 | 8 | Instantly defeat one enemy. Sometimes fails. | Mad Rush |
| Unhinge | 40 | 8 | Damage one enemy and lower its Accuracy and Evasion. | Crackdown |
| Intimidate | 50 | 8 | Inflict damage and Slow on one enemy. | Unhinge |
| Envenom | 30 | 10 | Inflict damage and Poison on one enemy. | None |
| Hurt | 60 | 10 | Damage one enemy according to the user's current HP. | Envenom |
| Howl | 80 | 0 | Double the user's max HP. | Mad Rush |
| Itchproof | 20 | 0 | Guards against Itchy. | Cripple |
| Counterattack | 180 | 0 | Strike back after being physically attacked. | None |
| Magic Counter | 300 | 0 | Strike back after being attacked with magic. | Counterattack |
| Evade & Counter | 400 | 0 | Evade physical attacks and strike back. | Magic Counter |
| Auto-Regen | 80 | 0 | Automatically casts Regen. | Hurt |

# SONGSTRESS

## MAIN COMMANDS

Dance

Sing

Item

The Songstress dressphere transforms its user into a singing sensation who uses music and dance to distract the enemies from damaging the party. By learning the various "Dance" moves available, a Songstress can inflict status ailments on the enemy party with a 100% success rate (except in cases where enemies are immune to the status ailments). For example, while a Songstress is present, you can blind the entire enemy party to prevent them from striking with physical attacks, or even stop them completely to make them easier targets. The Songstress has no ability to attack or heal unless she is equipped with the proper Garment Grids or accessories. While equipping and mastering this dressphere, it's a good idea to equip accessories or Garment Grids that allow you to use the attack or healing abilities of another dressphere, so that the Songstress can adapt to emergency situations.

During combat, use "Dance" abilities to negate the enemies' combat abilities, or throw the whole party into a frenzy by casting "Jitterbug." A Songstress won't get another turn until the effects of the previous dance have ended. If a Songstress can't inflict status ailments on an enemy due to immunities, use "Sing" abilities to boost the attributes of allies.

## THE BOOKS OF MAGICAL DANCES

To learn "MP Mambo" and "Magical Masque," you must acquire two key items: **Magical Dances, Vol. I** and **Magical Dances, Vol. II**. Volume I is obtained by defeating the boss enemies inside the Den of Woe at Mushroom Rock. Volume II is obtained by defeating the Experiment machine at Djose Temple during Chapter 5, when the boss's Attack, Defense, and Special parameters are all at level 5.

Characters

1

Garment Grids & Dresspheres

2

Battle System

3

Accessories

4

Items and Item Shops

5

Walkthrough

6

Mini-Games

7

Fiends and Enemies

8

## SONGSTRESS ABILITIES

| NAME | AP | MP | DESCRIPTION | REQUIRED ABILITIES |
|---|---|---|---|---|
| Darkness Dance | 0 | 0 | Inflict Darkness on all enemies while dancing. | None |
| Samba of Silence | 20 | 0 | Inflict Silence on all enemies while dancing. | None |
| MP Mambo | 20 | 0 | Reduce the party's MP cost to 0 while dancing. | Magical Dances, Vol I key item |
| Magical Masque | 20 | 0 | Nullify magical attacks against the party while dancing. | Magical Dances, Vol II key item |
| Sleepy Shuffle | 80 | 0 | Inflict Sleep on all enemies while dancing. | None |
| Carnival Cancan | 80 | 0 | Double the party's max HP while dancing. | Sleepy Shuffle |
| Slow Dance | 60 | 0 | Inflict Slow on all enemies while dancing. | None |
| Brakedance | 120 | 0 | Inflict Stop on all enemies while dancing. | Slow Dance |
| Jitterbug | 120 | 0 | Sustain a Haste effect on the party while dancing. | Slow Dance |
| Dirty Dancing | 160 | 0 | The party inflicts critical hits while you dance. | Carnival Cancan |
| Battle Cry | 10 | 4 | Raise the party's Strength. | None |
| Cantus Firmus | 10 | 4 | Raise the party's Defense. | Battle Cry |
| Esoteric Melody | 10 | 4 | Raise the party's Magic. | None |
| Disenchant | 10 | 4 | Raise the party's Magic Defense. | Esoteric Melody |
| Perfect Pitch | 10 | 4 | Raise the party's Accuracy. | None |
| Matador's Song | 10 | 4 | Raise the party's Evasion. | Perfect Pitch |

# BLACK MAGE

## MAIN COMMANDS

| |
|---|
| Black Magic |
| Focus |
| MP Absorb |
| Item |

Utilizing the forces of elemental magic, the Black Mage focuses power to attack enemies with incredible spells. Control of such energy weighs heavily upon the physical frame, so characters equipping the Black Mage dressphere will have higher MP but lower HP and high Magic and Magic Defense, but low Strength and Defense. Protect Black Mages by equipping accessories and Garment Grids that raise HP and Defense. Without the ability to perform physical attacks, the Black Mage becomes useless on the battlefield once her MP is depleted. Since the learning of spell abilities is a gradual process requiring lots of battles, start by learning to bolster the magic at your disposal by learning the "Focus" and "MP Drain" abilities. By raising your Black Magic Level, you can assure shorter casting times. During the latter stages of the game, many enemies will be more difficult to defeat due to their higher Magic Defense. When placing the Black Mage dressphere on a character's Garment Grid, complement it with a dressphere that focuses on physical attacks. This should enable your character to remain useful even after MP is depleted or enemies become resistant to magic.

On the battlefield, the Black Mage depends on the defense of "attacker" types and the support of "healer" types. Never allow more than one character to equip a Black Mage dressphere at a time to avoid throwing off the balance of the party. Begin each battle by using "Focus" for stronger spell casting, then target spells at one or multiple enemies. When MP gets low, drain power from enemies instead of consuming Ethers.

## BLACK MAGE ABILITIES

| NAME | AP | MP | DESCRIPTION | REQUIRED ABILITIES |
|---|---|---|---|---|
| Fire | 0 | 4 | Deal fire damage to one or all enemies. | None |
| Blizzard | 0 | 4 | Deal ice damage to one or all enemies. | None |
| Thunder | 0 | 4 | Deal lightning damage to one or all enemies. | None |
| Water | 0 | 4 | Deal water damage to one or all enemies. | None |
| Fira | 40 | 12 | Deal fire damage to one or all enemies. | None |
| Blizzara | 40 | 12 | Deal ice damage to one or all enemies. | None |
| Thundara | 40 | 12 | Deal lightning damage to one or all enemies. | None |
| Watera | 40 | 12 | Deal water damage to one or all enemies. | None |
| Firaga | 100 | 24 | Deal fire damage to one or all enemies. | Fira |
| Blizzaga | 100 | 24 | Deal ice damage to one or all enemies. | Blizzara |
| Thundaga | 100 | 24 | Deal lightning damage to one or all enemies. | Thundara |
| Waterga | 100 | 24 | Deal water damage to one or all enemies. | Watera |
| Focus | 10 | 0 | Raise the user's Magic. | None |
| MP Absorb | 10 | 0 | Absorb MP from one enemy. | Focus |
| Black Magic Lv.2 | 40 | 0 | Cuts the time required for Black Magic by 30%. | MP Absorb |
| Black Magic Lv.3 | 60 | 0 | Cuts the time required for Black Magic in half. | Black Magic Lv.2 |

# WHITE MAGE

## MAIN COMMANDS

| |
|---|
| Pray |
| Vigor |
| White Magic |
| Item |

Characters

1

Garment Grids & Dresspheres

2

Battle System

3

Accessories

4

Items and Item Shops

5

Walkthrough

6

Mini-Games

7

Fiends and Enemies

8

While actively equipped by a party member, the White Mage dressphere enables a character to provide constant healing and support to all allies. Unable to attack under normal circumstances, the White Mage works to prevent the other characters from falling into KO status and to remove harmful status ailments affecting allies. Protective spells, such as "Protect" and "Shell," enable a White Mage to reduce the damage inflicted on the party. Abilities such as "Dispel" enable a White Mage to level the battlefield by removing status benefits an enemy may be using on itself, and "Reflect" causes most magic spells cast on the party to be bounced back at the enemy who attempted to cast it. While the presence of a White Mage limits the amount of damage the party can inflict on the enemy, it also enables the party to survive battles much easier. White Magic abilities learned through this dressphere will be useful throughout the game.

During combat, use the "Pray" ability during each combat turn to restore small amounts of HP to the entire party, even if such restoration is not required at the time. If the party is sustaining heavy damage, use "Cure," "Cura" or "Curaga" spells to cure one or all party members at once. Cast "Protect" to diminish physical damage, or "Shell' to reduce damage from magic.

## WHITE MAGE ABILITIES

| NAME | AP | MP | DESCRIPTION | REQUIRED ABILITIES |
|---|---|---|---|---|
| Pray | 0 | 0 | Restore a little HP to the party. | None |
| Vigor | 20 | 0 | Restore some HP to the user. | None |
| Cure | 20 | 4 | Restore a little HP to one or all party members. | None |
| Cura | 40 | 10 | Restore some HP to one or all party members. | None |
| Curaga | 80 | 20 | Restore a lot of HP to one or all party members. | Cura |
| Regen | 80 | 40 | Gradually restore one character's HP over time. | Curaga |
| Esuna | 20 | 10 | Cure one character's status ailments. | None |
| Dispel | 30 | 12 | Negate all spell effects on one enemy. | Esuna |
| Life | 30 | 18 | Revive one KO'd character. | None |
| Full-Life | 160 | 60 | Revive one KO'd character and fully restore HP. | Life |
| Shell | 30 | 10 | Reduce magical damage inflicted on the party. | None |
| Protect | 30 | 12 | Reduce physical damage inflicted on the party. | Shell |
| Reflect | 30 | 14 | Deflect spells cast at the party back at the enemy. | Protect |
| Full-Cure | 80 | 99 | Fully restore one character's HP and cure status ailments. | Regen |
| White Magic Lv.2 | 40 | 0 | Cuts the time required for White Magic by 30%. | Vigor |
| White Magic Lv.3 | 60 | 0 | Cuts the time required for White Magic in half. | White Magic Lv.2 |

# LADY LUCK

## MAIN COMMANDS

| Attack |
| --- |
| Gamble |
| Tantalize |
| Bribe |
| Item |

The Lady Luck dressphere transforms a character into a seductive and deceptive vixen who can use her feminine wiles to take enemies for all they're worth. Since the regular attack power of this dressphere is somewhat low, the effectiveness of Lady Luck is heavily dependent on a roll of the dice or a spin of the reels. The "Two Dice" ability enables Lady Luck to roll 2 dice that determine the number of quick, non-elemental attacks that the target foe will suffer. "Four Dice" is essentially the same attack against an entire party of foes, except 4 dice are rolled instead of 2. These are the skills that Lady Luck must resort to when a foe is resilient against normal attacks. The various "Reels" abilities provide further control over the forces of chance, since you can form Lady Luck's attack by stopping the reels on three identical icons. However, if you fail to stop the reels on an exact trio, the results can be devastating to your allies instead of the enemies. An auto-ability like "Double EXP" is sure to carry a Lady Luck character to level 99 in no time, while "Double Items" and "Gillionaire" will have the entire party rolling in gil and items.

During each combat turn, practice any form of reels and go for the best results possible. Stop the first reel on any icon, then try to stop the remaining reels on the exact same picture. If the results are disastrous, simply perform only physical attacks for the rest of the battle or try again. By doing so, the other characters can help the party recover before Lady Luck stumbles into another blunder.

## LADY LUCK ABILITIES

| NAME | AP | MP | DESCRIPTION | REQUIRED ABILITIES |
| --- | --- | --- | --- | --- |
| Attack | 0 | 0 | Attack one enemy. | None |
| Bribe | 40 | 0 | Offer gil to persuade one enemy to leave the battle. | None |
| Two Dice | 20 | 4 | Damage one enemy by rolling two dice. | None |
| Four Dice | 100 | 8 | Damage all enemies by rolling four dice. | Two Dice |
| Attack Reels | 60 | 0 | Spin slots to deal physical damage. | None |
| Magic Reels | 70 | 0 | Spin slots to deal magical damage. | None |
| Item Reels | 80 | 0 | Spin slots to trigger various item skills. | Magic Reels |
| Random Reels | 120 | 0 | Spin slots to trigger various skills. | Item Reels |
| Luck | 30 | 8 | Raise the user's Luck. | None |
| Felicity | 40 | 8 | Raise the party's Luck. | Luck |
| Tantalize | 60 | 0 | Inflict Confusion on all enemies. | None |
| Critical | 160 | 0 | Always inflict critical hits. | Felicity |
| Double EXP | 80 | 0 | Doubles the amount of EXP earned after battle. | None |
| SOS Spellspring | 30 | 0 | Reduces MP cost to 0 when HP is low. | Four Dice |
| Gillionaire | 100 | 0 | Doubles the amount of gil earned after battle. | Double EXP |
| Double Items | 100 | 0 | Doubles the number of items earned after battle. | Gillionaire |

Characters

1

Garment Grids
& Dresspheres

2

Battle System

3

Accessories

4

Items and
Item Shops

5

Walkthrough

6

Mini-Games

7

Fiends and
Enemies

8

## ATTACK REELS

These attacks come with different special effects. The reels rotate in the order shown below. Note, however, that the start position of the reel changes randomly.

**Shin-Zantetsu**
Instantly defeat all enemies.

**Excalibur**
Deal holy damage to one enemy.

**Cripple**
Halve one enemy's HP.

**Delay Buster**
Greatly delay one enemy's action.

**Fireworks**
Damage all enemies.

**Intimidate**
Inflict Slow on one enemy.

**Clean Slate**
Restore HP and cure user of status ailments.

**Power Break**
Lower one enemy's Strength by 2.

**Magicide**
Inflict damage on one enemy's MP.

**Eject**
Blow one enemy away.

**Armor Break**
Lower one enemy's Defense by 2.

**Dud**
Reduce the party's HP by 3/4.

## MAGIC REELS

This includes both attack and healing effects. The reels rotate in the positions noted below. Note, however, that the start position of the reel changes randomly.

**Ultima**
Damage all enemies.

**Black Sky**
Deal 10 consecutive attacks.

**Flare**
Damage one enemy.

**Demi**
Reduce the HP of all enemies by 1/4.

**Firaga**
Deal fire damage to all enemies.

**Auto-Life**
Ally is automatically revived once when KO'd.

**Bio**
Poison all enemies.

**Break**
Petrify one enemy.

**Thundara**
Deal lightning damage to all enemies.

**Esuna**
Cure one ally's status ailments.

**Cura**
Restore some HP to the party.

**Dud**
Reduce the party's HP by 3/4.

## ITEM REELS

Healing and support types are common among these results. As was the case with the Attack Slot, the reel rotates in the following order, but the start position changes randomly.

**Megalixir+**
Fully restore the party's HP and MP.

**Mighty Guard+**
Create multiple defensive effects on the party.

**Supreme Gem**
Damage all enemies.

**Megalixir**
Fully restore the party's HP and MP.

**Blessed Gem**
Deal 8 consecutive holy attacks.

**Mighty Guard**
Cast Shell and Protect on the party.

**Mega-Ether**
Restore the party's MP.

**Ether**
Restore MP to one ally.

**L-Bomb**
Damage all enemies.

**Lunar Curtain+**
Cast Shell on the party.

**Light Curtain+**
Cast Protect on the party.

**Dud**
Reduce the party's HP by 3/4.

## RANDOM REELS

This reel enables the user to use abilities with a variety of effects. As with the others, the reel rotates as shown below, but the reel's starting position changes randomly.

**CONGRATS!**
Eliminate opposition and steals gil and more.

**Mega-Potion**
Restore the party's HP.

**Blizzaga**
Deal ice damage to all enemies.

**Cry in the Night**
Damage all enemies.

**Dark Matter**
Damage all enemies.

**Quartet Knife**
Lower attributes of one enemy.

**Mental Break**
Lower one enemy's Magic Defense by 2.

**Cure**
Restore the party's HP.

**Primo Grenade**
Damage all enemies.

**Hi-Potion**
Restore HP to one character.

**Potion**
Restore HP to one character.

**Dud**
Reduce the party's HP by 3/4.

# TRAINER

## MAIN COMMANDS

| Attack |
| Pet |
| Item |

When equipped in combat, the Trainer dressphere calls a sacred animal into action. As the Trainer fights and learns abilities, the pet becomes capable of a wide variety of spells and actions to be used during battle. The abilities for each character are specific to the personality of each trainer: Yuna's dog, Kogoro, learns a variety of spells that inflict a combination of elemental damage and status ailments on an enemy. Rikku's pet monkey, Ghiki, helps steal items and gil from enemies. Paine's pheasant, Flurry, allows her to attack enemies with powerful blows that can inflict status ailments or instantly KO foes. Each character learns some form of Cure and Esuna spell, just like a White Mage. All of the characters also learn some kind of special attack and several beneficial auto-abilities that help restore HP and MP outside of battle. If you think about it, a party of three Trainers is actually a very balanced crew, capable of attacking, defeating enemies, and casting most types of spells!

During battle, have a Trainer attack foes to cause damage. When the Trainer's HP drops or if she becomes inflicted with status ailments, use special skills to recover. Use the next round to cast protective spells to prevent damage or status impairments. Between battles, auto-abilities (such as "HP Stroll" and "MP Stroll") will cause a character's HP and MP to recover depending on how much you walk, so that healing between battles is less necessary.

## YUNA TRAINER ABILITIES

| NAME | AP | MP | DESCRIPTION | REQUIRED ABILITIES |
|---|---|---|---|---|
| Attack | 0 | 0 | Attack one enemy. | None |
| Holy Kogoro | 0 | 18 | Deal holy damage to one enemy. | None |
| Kogoro Blaze | 40 | 4 | Inflict fire damage and sometimes Darkness on one enemy. | None |
| Kogoro Freeze | 40 | 4 | Inflict ice damage and sometimes Stop on one enemy. | None |
| Kogoro Shock | 40 | 4 | Inflict lightning damage and sometimes Berserk on one enemy. | None |
| Kogoro Deluge | 40 | 4 | Inflict water damage and sometimes Sleep on one enemy. | None |
| Kogoro Strike | 80 | 5 | Instantly defeat one enemy. Sometimes fails. | None |
| Doom Kogoro | 80 | 6 | Inflict damage and Doom on one enemy. | Kogoro Strike |
| Kogoro Cure | 30 | 10 | Restore HP to one character. | None |
| Kogoro Remedy | 40 | 10 | Cure one character of all status ailments. | Kogoro Cure |
| Pound! | 100 | 24 | Call Kogoro's friends to gang up on one enemy. | Doom Kogoro |
| Half MP Cost | 200 | 0 | Reduces MP cost by one-half. | MP Stroll |
| HP Stroll | 20 | 0 | Automatically restores HP while walking. | None |
| MP Stroll | 20 | 0 | Automatically restores MP while walking. | HP Stroll |
| Kogoro Lv.2 | 80 | 0 | Cuts the time required for Kogoro to attack by 30%. | None |
| Kogoro Lv.3 | 100 | 0 | Cuts the time required for Kogoro to attack in half. | Kogoro Lv.2 |

## RIKKU TRAINER ABILITIES

| NAME | AP | MP | DESCRIPTION | REQUIRED ABILITIES |
|---|---|---|---|---|
| Attack | 0 | 0 | Attack one enemy. | None |
| Sneaky Ghiki | 0 | 12 | Steal gil and damage one enemy. | None |
| Ghiki Gouge | 40 | 8 | Inflict damage and Darkness on one enemy. | None |
| Ghiki Gag | 80 | 8 | Inflict damage and Silence on one enemy. | None |
| Mugger Ghiki | 40 | 12 | Steal items and damage one enemy. | None |
| Pesky Ghiki | 100 | 8 | Inflict damage and Berserk on one enemy. | None |
| Bully Ghiki | 100 | 8 | Inflict damage and delay the actions of one enemy. | Pesky Ghiki |
| Ghiki Meds | 40 | 10 | Cure one character of all status ailments. | Ghiki Pep |
| Ghiki Pep | 30 | 10 | Restore HP to one character. | None |
| Ghiki Cheer | 80 | 12 | Raise one character's Strength and Defense. | None |
| Swarm, Swarm! | 100 | 24 | Call Ghiki's friends to gang up on one enemy. | Bully Ghiki |
| Half MP Cost | 200 | 0 | Reduces MP cost by one-half. | MP Stroll |
| HP Stroll | 20 | 0 | Automatically restores HP while walking. | None |
| MP Stroll | 20 | 0 | Automatically restores MP while walking. | HP Stroll |
| Ghiki Lv.2 | 80 | 0 | Cuts the time required for Ghiki to attack by 30%. | None |
| Ghiki Lv.3 | 100 | 0 | Cuts the time required for Ghiki to attack in half. | Ghiki Lv.2 |

## PAINE TRAINER ABILITY

| NAME | AP | MP | DESCRIPTION | REQUIRED ABILITIES |
|---|---|---|---|---|
| Attack | 0 | 0 | Attack one enemy. | None |
| Carrier Flurry | 0 | 8 | Instantly defeat one enemy. Sometimes fails. | None |
| Poison Flurry | 40 | 4 | Inflict damage and Poison on one enemy. | None |
| Stone Flurry | 60 | 16 | Inflict damage and Petrification on one enemy. | Poison Flurry |
| Death Flurry | 60 | 20 | Instantly defeat one enemy. Sometimes fails. | Stone Flurry |
| Flurry Guard | 60 | 10 | Restore one character's HP and cast Protect. | Flurry Speed |
| Flurry Speed | 60 | 10 | Restore one character's HP and cast Haste. | None |
| Flurry Shield | 60 | 10 | Restore one character's HP and cast Shell. | Flurry Speed |
| HP Flurry | 30 | 10 | Restore some HP to the party. | None |
| Recovery Flurry | 40 | 10 | Cure one character of all status ailments. | None |
| Maulwings! | 100 | 24 | Call Flurry's friends to gang up on one enemy. | Death Flurry |
| Half MP Cost | 200 | 0 | Reduces MP cost by one-half. | MP Stroll |
| HP Stroll | 20 | 0 | Automatically restores HP while walking. | None |
| MP Stroll | 20 | 0 | Automatically restores MP while walking. | HP Stroll |
| Flurry Lv.2 | 80 | 0 | Cuts the time required for Flurry to attack by 30%. | None |
| Flurry Lv.3 | 100 | 0 | Cuts the time required for Flurry to attack in half. | Flurry Lv.2 |

Characters

1

Garment Grids & Dresspheres

2

Battle System

3

Accessories

4

Items and Item Shops

5

Walkthrough

6

Mini-Games

7

Fiends and Enemies

8

# MASCOT

**MAIN COMMANDS**

| |
|---|
| Attack |
| (Mascot) |
| (Secondary Attack Abilities) |
| (Secondary Magic Abilities) |
| Item |

The Mascot dressphere is a special sphere gained by acquiring "Episode Complete" in every area during Chapter 5 except for Bevelle. Upon achieving all the Episode Completes, an extra scene will occur where the Gullwings return to the bridge of the Celsius and obtain the Mascot dressphere. However, if Zanarkand is the last Episode Complete acquired, you will not gain the Masot dressphere for some reason. Make sure that Zanarkand Ruins is not the last place you visit, or you will be unable to acquire this valuable dressphere.

When equipping the Mascot dressphere, each character wears a costume modeled after the cuter, cuddlier creatures in the game. In spite of the humorous appearance, the Mascot dressphere is definitely one of the best. In addition to learning a whole series of unique abilities with multiple effects, each character can also gain the ability to use the abilities of two other dresspheres. The Mascot enables all three characters to be devastating and helpful at the same time, all while defeating enemies in the process.

During combat, cast spells and use Mascot abilities to boost the party and weaken the enemies, then use normal attacks or the special attacks of other dresspheres to defeat enemies. If your allies get into trouble, use restorative and curative abilities to bring them back up to speed. Any party will rely heavily on the Mascot to keep them going in the face of tough enemies; that is, unless you equip *every* character with the Mascot dressphere.

## YUNA'S MOOGLE ABILITIES

| NAME | AP | MP | DESCRIPTION | REQUIRED ABILITIES |
|---|---|---|---|---|
| Attack | 0 | 0 | Attack one enemy. | None |
| Moogle Jolt | 40 | 0 | Restore MP to one character. | None |
| Moogle Cure | 0 | 10 | Cure one character of status ailments and restore HP. | None |
| Moogle Regen | 0 | 18 | Cast Haste and Regen on one character. | None |
| Moogle Wall | 0 | 18 | Cast Shell and Protect on one character. | None |
| Moogle Life | 0 | 40 | Revive one KO'd character and fully restore HP and MP. | None |
| Moogle Curema | 40 | 15 | Restore HP and cure the party's status ailments. | None |
| Moogle Regenja | 40 | 24 | Cast Haste and Regen on the party. | None |
| Moogle Wallja | 40 | 24 | Cast Shell and Protect on the party. | None |
| Moogle Lifeja | 40 | 60 | Revive all party members and fully restore HP and MP. | None |
| Moogle Beam | 80 | 99 | Damage one enemy. | * |
| Ribbon | 999 | 0 | Guards against all status ailments. | * |
| Auto-Shell | 80 | 0 | Automatically casts Shell. | None |
| Auto-Protect | 80 | 0 | Automatically casts Protect. | Auto-Shell |
| Swordplay | 80 | 0 | Use Warrior skills. | None |
| Arcana | 80 | 0 | Use Dark Knight skills. | None |

*\* Must know Warrior's SOS Protect ability to learn.*

## RIKKU'S CAIT SITH ABILITIES

| NAME | AP | MP | DESCRIPTION | REQUIRED ABILITIES |
|---|---|---|---|---|
| Attack | 0 | 0 | Attack one enemy. | None |
| Cait Fire | 0 | 12 | Fire damage to enemies. Sometimes Poison/Petrification. | None |
| Cait Thunder | 0 | 12 | Lightning damage to enemies. Sometimes Poison/Petrification. | None |
| Cait Blizzard | 0 | 12 | Ice damage to enemies. Sometimes Poison/Petrification. | None |
| Cait Water | 0 | 12 | Water damage to enemies. Sometimes Poison/Petrification. | None |
| Power Eraser | 40 | 12 | Lower Strength of all enemies. | None |
| Armor Eraser | 40 | 12 | Lower Defense of all enemies. | None |
| Magic Eraser | 40 | 12 | Lower Magic of all enemies. | None |
| Mental Eraser | 40 | 12 | Lower Magic Defense of all enemies. | None |
| Speed Eraser | 40 | 12 | Lower Evasion of all enemies. | None |
| PuPu Platter | 80 | 48 | Instantly defeat all enemies. Sometimes fails. | * |
| Ribbon | 999 | 0 | Guards against all status ailments. | * |
| Auto-Shell | 80 | 0 | Automatically casts Shell. | None |
| Auto-Protect | 80 | 0 | Automatically casts Protect. | Auto-Shell |
| Instinct | 80 | 0 | Use Berserker skills. | None |
| White Magic | 80 | 0 | Cast white magic spells. | None |

*\* Must know Warrior's SOS Protect ability to learn.*

## PAINE'S TONBERRY ABILITIES

| NAME | AP | MP | DESCRIPTION | REQUIRED ABILITIES |
|---|---|---|---|---|
| Attack | 0 | 0 | Attack one enemy. | None |
| Dark Knife | 0 | 10 | Inflict damage and Darkness on one enemy. | None |
| Silence Knife | 0 | 10 | Inflict damage and Silence on one enemy. | None |
| Sleep Knife | 0 | 10 | Inflict damage and Sleep on one enemy. | None |
| Berserk Knife | 0 | 10 | Inflict damage and Berserk on one enemy. | None |
| Poison Knife | 0 | 10 | Inflict damage and Poison on one enemy. | None |
| Stone Knife | 0 | 10 | Inflict damage and Petrification on one enemy. | None |
| Stop Knife | 0 | 10 | Inflict damage and Stop on one enemy. | None |
| Quartet Knife | 0 | 10 | Lower one enemy's Strength, Defense, Magic, and Magic Defense. | None |
| Arsenic Knife | 0 | 10 | Instantly defeat one enemy. Sometimes fails. | None |
| Cactling Gun | 80 | 99 | Inflict heavy damage on one enemy. | * |
| Ribbon | 999 | 0 | Guards against all status ailments. | * |
| Auto-Shell | 80 | 0 | Automatically casts Shell. | None |
| Auto-Protect | 80 | 0 | Automatically casts Protect. | Auto-Shell |
| Bushido | 80 | 0 | Use Samurai skills. | None |
| Black Magic | 80 | 0 | Cast black magic spells. | None |

*\* Must know Warrior's SOS Protect ability to learn.*

Characters

1

Garment Grids & Dresspheres

2

Battle System

3

Accessories

4

Items and Item Shops

5

Walkthrough

6

Mini-Games

7

Fiends and Enemies

8

# FLORAL FALLAL

| FLORAL FALLAL MAIN COMMANDS |
| --- |
| Attack |
| Fallalery |
| Great Whirl |
| Libra |

| RIGHT PISTIL MAIN COMMANDS |
| --- |
| Right Stigma |
| Right Pistilplay |

| LEFT PISTIL MAIN COMMANDS |
| --- |
| Left Stigma |
| Left Pistilplay |

You get Yuna's special dressphere during Chapter 2 while traveling the Djose Highroad just south of the temple during the mission to obtain three Leblanc Syndicate uniforms. The three portions of Floral Fallal act as a three-member party. Some portions can cast protective spells on the other parts, and each can inflict devastating magic attacks on enemies. To use Floral Fallal more often, equip Yuna with the Unerring Path Garment Grid, which only has two dressphere nodes. This makes switching into Yuna's special dressphere much faster, since she only needs to change once before transforming into Floral Fallal.

It takes two key items to enable the "Break HP Limit" and "Break Damage Limit" abilities on Floral Fallal: **Aurora Rain** and **Twilight Rain**. Aurora Rain is contained in a treasure chest inside the cave at the bottom of the gorge at the Calm Lands during Chapter 5. Twilight Rain is found in a treasure chest below the waterfalls at Besaid Island during Chapter 5.

## YUNA, FLORAL FALLAL ABILITIES

| NAME | AP | MP | DESCRIPTION | REQUIRED ABILITIES |
|------|----|----|-------------|-------------------|
| Attack | 0 | 0 | Attack one enemy. | None |
| Libra | 4 | 0 | View detailed information about one enemy. | None |
| Heat Whirl | 0 | 0 | Unleash a chain of fire attacks on all enemies. | None |
| Ice Whirl | 0 | 0 | Unleash a chain of ice attacks on all enemies. | None |
| Electric Whirl | 0 | 0 | Unleash a chain of lightning attacks on all enemies. | None |
| Aqua Whirl | 0 | 0 | Unleash a chain of water attacks on all enemies. | None |
| Barrier | 20 | 36 | Guard fully against magical attacks. | None |
| Shield | 20 | 36 | Guard fully against physical attacks. | Barrier |
| Flare Whirl | 24 | 64 | Unleash a chain of non-elemental attacks on all enemies. | None |
| Great Whirl | 30 | 0 | Inflict heavy damage on all enemies. | Flare Whirl |
| All-Life | 8 | 70 | Revive the party from KO. | None |
| Ribbon | 0 | 0 | Guards against all status ailments. | None |
| Double HP | 20 | 0 | Doubles max HP. | None |
| Triple HP | 30 | 0 | Triples max HP. | Double HP |
| Break HP Limit | 20 | 0 | Allows max HP to exceed 9999. | Aurora Rain key item |
| Break Dmg. Limit | 20 | 0 | Allows max damage to exceed 9999. | Twilight Rain key item |

## YUNA, RIGHT PISTIL ABILITIES

| NAME | AP | MP | DESCRIPTION | REQUIRED ABILITIES |
|------|----|----|-------------|-------------------|
| White Pollen | 0 | 0 | Restore the party's HP. | None |
| White Honey | 10 | 0 | Gradually restore the party's HP over time. | None |
| Hard Leaves | 0 | 0 | Reduce the magical damage inflicted on the party. | None |
| Tough Nuts | 0 | 0 | Reduce physical damage inflicted on the party. | None |
| Mirror Petals | 0 | 0 | Deflect spells cast at the party back at the enemy. | None |
| Floral Rush | 20 | 0 | Cast Haste on the party. | White Honey |
| Floral Bomb | 0 | 0 | Damage all enemies and lower their Strength. | None |
| Fallal Bomb | 10 | 0 | Damage all enemies and lower their Defense. | None |
| Floral Magisol | 10 | 0 | Damage all enemies and lower their Magic. | Fallal Bomb |
| Fallal Magisol | 10 | 0 | Damage all enemies and lower their Magic Defense. | Floral Magisol |
| Right Stigma | 20 | 0 | Damage one enemy. | Fallal Magisol |
| Ribbon | 0 | 0 | Guards against all status ailments. | None |
| Double HP | 20 | 0 | Doubles max HP. | None |
| Triple HP | 30 | 0 | Triples max HP. | Double HP |
| Break HP Limit | 20 | 0 | Allows max HP to exceed 9999. | Aurora Rain key item |
| Break Dmg. Limit | 20 | 0 | Allows max damage to exceed 9999. | Twilight Rain key item |

## YUNA, LEFT PISTIL ABILITIES

| NAME | AP | MP | DESCRIPTION | REQUIRED ABILITIES |
|------|----|----|-------------|-------------------|
| Dream Pollen | 0 | 0 | Inflict damage and Sleep on all enemies. | None |
| Mad Seeds | 0 | 0 | Inflict damage and Berserk on all enemies. | None |
| Sticky Honey | 0 | 0 | Inflict damage and Slow on all enemies. | None |
| Halfdeath Petals | 0 | 0 | Halve the HP of all enemies. | None |
| Poison Leaves | 10 | 0 | Inflict damage and Poison on all enemies. | None |
| Death Petals | 10 | 0 | Instantly defeat one enemy. Sometimes fails. | Poison Leaves |
| Silent White | 0 | 0 | Inflict damage, Silence, and Darkness on all enemies. | None |
| Congealed Honey | 20 | 0 | Inflict damage and Stop on all enemies. | None |
| Panic Floralysis | 10 | 0 | Inflict damage and Confusion on all enemies. | Congealed Honey |
| Ash Floralysis | 10 | 0 | Inflict damage and Petrification on all enemies. | Panic Floralysis |
| Left Stigma | 20 | 0 | Damage one enemy. | None |
| Ribbon | 0 | 0 | Guards against all status ailments. | None |
| Double HP | 20 | 0 | Doubles max HP. | None |
| Triple HP | 30 | 0 | Triples max HP. | Double HP |
| Break HP Limit | 20 | 0 | Allows max HP to exceed 9999. | Aurora Rain key item |
| Break Dmg. Limit | 20 | 0 | Allows max damage to exceed 9999. | Twilight Rain key item |

Characters

Garment Grids & Dresspheres

Battle System

Accessories

Items and Item Shops

Walkthrough

Mini-Games

Fiends and Enemies

# MACHINA MAW

| MACHINA MAW MAIN COMMANDS |
| --- |
| Attack |
| Machinations |
| Revival |
| Vajra |

| SMASHER-R MAIN COMMANDS |
| --- |
| Homing Ray |
| Smash |
| HP Repair |
| MP Repair |

| CRUSHER-L MAIN COMMANDS |
| --- |
| Homing Ray |
| Crush |
| HP Repair |
| MP Repair |

GARMENT GRIDS & DRESSPHERES

You get Rikku's special dressphere during Chapter 2 while investigating the Oasis at Bikanel Desert during the mission to obtain three Leblanc Syndicate uniforms. The three portions of Machina Maw act as a three-member party. Each portion can cast protective spells on the other parts, and each can inflict devastating physical attacks and status impairments on enemies. To use Machina Maw more often, equip Rikku with the Unerring Path Garment Grid, which has only two dressphere nodes. This makes switching to Rikku's special dressphere must faster, since she only needs to change once before transforming into Machina Maw.

To enable the "Break HP Limit" and "Break Damage Limit" abilities, you must obtain the **Machina Reactor** and **Machina Booster** key items. The Machina Booster is found in a treasure chest near the lift up to the Youth League headquarters at Mushroom Rock Road during Chapter 5. In order to obtain Machina Reactor, you must dispatch level 1, 2, 3, 4 and 5 chocobos three times each from Clasko's Chocobo Ranch at the Calm Lands out into Spira looking for items. In addition, all of your Choco-Runners must be level 5. When you return to the ranch later, Clasko reports that the chocobos found a secret dungeon at the Calm Lands. The item is contained in a chest inside the dungeon.

## RIKKU, MACHINA MAW ABILITIES

| NAME | AP | MP | DESCRIPTION | REQUIRED ABILITIES |
|------|----|----|-------------|--------------------|
| Attack | 0 | 0 | Attack one enemy. | None |
| Revival | 10 | 0 | Revive one KO'd character. | None |
| Death Missile | 0 | 12 | Instantly defeat one enemy. Sometimes fails. | None |
| Bio Missile | 0 | 12 | Inflict damage and Poison on one enemy. | None |
| Break Missile | 0 | 12 | Inflict damage and Petrification on one enemy. | None |
| Berserk Missile | 10 | 12 | Inflict damage and Berserk on one enemy. | None |
| Stop Missile | 10 | 12 | Inflict damage and Stop on one enemy. | Berserk Missile |
| Confuse Missile | 10 | 12 | Inflict damage and Confusion on one enemy. | Stop Missile |
| Shockwave | 20 | 36 | Damage all enemies. | None |
| Shockstorm | 20 | 36 | Damage all enemies and delay their actions. | Shockwave |
| Vajra | 30 | 0 | Damage all enemies. | Shockstorm |
| Ribbon | 0 | 0 | Guards against all status ailments. | None |
| Double HP | 20 | 0 | Doubles max HP. | None |
| Triple HP | 30 | 0 | Triples max HP. | Double HP |
| Break HP Limit | 20 | 0 | Allows max HP to exceed 9999. | Machina Reactor key item |
| Break Dmg. Limit | 20 | 0 | Allows max damage to exceed 9999. | Machina Booster key item |

## RIKKU, SMASHER-R ABILITIES

| NAME | AP | MP | DESCRIPTION | REQUIRED ABILITIES |
|------|----|----|-------------|--------------------|
| Howitzer | 0 | 12 | Damage one enemy. | None |
| Sleep Shell | 10 | 12 | Inflict damage and Sleep on one enemy | None |
| Slow Shell | 10 | 12 | Inflict damage and Slow on one enemy | Sleep Shell |
| Anti-Power Shell | 10 | 12 | Damage one enemy and lower its Strength. | Slow Shell |
| Anti-Armor Shell | 10 | 12 | Damage one enemy and lower its Defense. | Anti-Power Shell |
| Scan | 10 | 0 | View detailed information about one enemy. | None |
| Shellter | 20 | 10 | Cast Shell on the party. | None |
| Protector | 20 | 10 | Cast Protect on the party. | Shellter |
| HP Repair | 0 | 0 | Restore HP to one character. | None |
| MP Repair | 0 | 0 | Restore MP to one character. | None |
| Homing Ray | 0 | 0 | Damage one enemy. | None |
| Ribbon | 0 | 0 | Guards against all status ailments. | None |
| Double HP | 20 | 0 | Doubles max HP. | None |
| Triple HP | 30 | 0 | Triples max HP. | Double HP |
| Break HP Limit | 20 | 0 | Allows max HP to exceed 9999. | Machina Reactor key item |
| Break Dmg. Limit | 20 | 0 | Allows max damage to exceed 9999. | Machina Booster key item |

## RIKKU, CRUSHER-L ABILITIES

| NAME | AP | MP | DESCRIPTION | REQUIRED ABILITIES |
|------|----|----|-------------|--------------------|
| Howitzer | 0 | 12 | Damage one enemy. | None |
| Blind Shell | 10 | 12 | Inflict damage and Darkness on one enemy | None |
| Silence Shell | 10 | 12 | Inflict damage and Silence on one enemy | Blind Shell |
| Anti-Magic Shell | 10 | 12 | Damage one enemy and lower its Magic. | Silence Shell |
| Anti-Mental Shell | 10 | 12 | Damage one enemy and lower its Magic Defense. | Anti-Magic Shell |
| Booster | 20 | 30 | Cast Haste on the party. | None |
| Offense | 20 | 10 | Raise one character's Strength. | None |
| Defense | 20 | 10 | Raise one character's Defense. | Offense |
| HP Repair | 0 | 0 | Restore HP to one character. | None |
| MP Repair | 0 | 0 | Restore MP to one character. | None |
| Homing Ray | 0 | 0 | Damage one enemy. | None |
| Ribbon | 0 | 0 | Guards against all status ailments. | None |
| Double HP | 20 | 0 | Doubles max HP. | None |
| Triple HP | 30 | 0 | Triples max HP. | Double HP |
| Break HP Limit | 20 | 0 | Allows max HP to exceed 9999. | Machina Reactor key item |
| Break Dmg. Limit | 20 | 0 | Allows max damage to exceed 9999. | Machina Booster key item |

Characters

Garment Grids
& Dresspheres

Battle System

Accessories

Items and
Item Shops

Walkthrough

Mini-Games

Fiends and
Enemies

# FULL THROTTLE

| FULL THROTTLE MAIN COMMANDS | DEXTRAL WING MAIN COMMANDS | SINISTRAL WING MAIN COMMANDS |
| --- | --- | --- |
| Attack | Dextral Arts | Sinistral Arts |
| Throttle | Stamina | Stamina |
| Fright | Mettle | Mettle |
| Sword Dance | Reboot | Reboot |

Your first chance to obtain Paine's special dressphere is in Chapter 1. Find Tromell at Macalania Woods and speak to him four times and the dressphere is yours. The three portions of Full Throttle act as a three-member party. Each portion is specialized. The main body has elemental attack abilities, the Dextral Wing can inflict status and damage on foes, and the Sinistral Wing enables you to cast status adjustments on Full Throttle as a whole, as well as on enemies. To use Full Throttle more often, equip Paine with the Unerring Path Garment Grid, which has only two dressphere nodes. This makes switching to Paine's special dressphere much faster, since she only needs to change once before transforming to Full Throttle.

To enable the "Break HP Limit" and "Break Damage Limit" abilities, you must obtain the **Victor Primoris** and **Corpus Invictus** key items. Victor Primoris is located on a ledge just over the side of the northernmost curve in the Mi'ihen Highroad. To reach the item, ride a chocobo to the spot and wait in the gap for a few seconds until the chocobo offers to go. First, the chocobo will fly up to open a different chest, but if you repeat the process, it will fly into the chasm to obtain the Victor Primoris. Corpus Invictus is located in one of the chests inside the secret dungeon of the Thunder Plains. During Chapter 5, go to the Thunder Plains and defeat all of the fiends attacking the lightning towers. Afterward, an Al Bhed man will offer to take you to the secret dungeon. After finding Cid in the dungeon, explore further and open secret stone walls to uncover the chest with Corpus Invictus inside.

## PAINE, FULL THROTTLE ABILITIES

| NAME | AP | MP | DESCRIPTION | REQUIRED ABILITIES |
|------|----|----|-------------|--------------------|
| Attack | 0 | 0 | Attack one enemy. | None |
| Fright | 20 | 0 | Damage and confuse one enemy, while delaying its actions. | Assoil |
| Aestus | 0 | 0 | Deal fire damage to one enemy. | None |
| Winterkill | 0 | 0 | Deal ice damage to one enemy. | None |
| Whelmen | 0 | 0 | Deal water damage to one enemy. | None |
| Levin | 0 | 0 | Deal lightning damage to one enemy. | None |
| Wisenen | 10 | 0 | Reduce one enemy's HP by 3/4. | None |
| Fiers | 20 | 0 | Deal critical damage to one enemy. | Wisenen |
| Deeth | 20 | 0 | Instantly defeat one enemy. Sometimes fails. | Fiers |
| Assoil | 20 | 0 | Deal holy damage to one enemy. | None |
| Sword Dance | 30 | 0 | Damage all enemies. | Fright |
| Ribbon | 0 | 0 | Guards against all status ailments. | None |
| Double HP | 20 | 0 | Doubles max HP. | None |
| Triple HP | 30 | 0 | Triples max HP. | Double HP |
| Break HP Limit | 20 | 0 | Allows max HP to exceed 9999. | Corpus Invictus key item |
| Break Dmg. Limit | 20 | 0 | Allows max damage to exceed 9999. | Victor Primoris key item |

## PAINE, DEXTRAL WING ABILITIES

| NAME | AP | MP | DESCRIPTION | REQUIRED ABILITIES |
|------|----|----|-------------|--------------------|
| Venom Wing | 0 | 12 | Inflict damage and Poison on one enemy. | None |
| Blind Wing | 0 | 12 | Inflict damage and Darkness on one enemy. | None |
| Mute Wing | 0 | 12 | Inflict damage and Silence on one enemy. | None |
| Rock Wing | 10 | 12 | Inflict damage and Petrification on one enemy. | None |
| Lazy Wing | 0 | 12 | Inflict damage and Sleep on one enemy. | None |
| Violent Wing | 10 | 12 | Inflict damage and Berserk on one enemy. | None |
| Still Wing | 10 | 12 | Inflict damage and Stop on one enemy. | None |
| Crazy Wing | 10 | 12 | Inflict damage and Confusion on one enemy. | Violent Wing |
| Stamina | 0 | 0 | Restore HP to one character. | None |
| Mettle | 0 | 0 | Restore MP to one character. | None |
| Reboot | 10 | 0 | Revive one KO'd character. | None |
| Ribbon | 0 | 0 | Guards against all status ailments. | None |
| Double HP | 20 | 0 | Doubles max HP. | None |
| Triple HP | 30 | 0 | Triples max HP. | Double HP |
| Break HP Limit | 20 | 0 | Allows max HP to exceed 9999. | Corpus Invictus key item |
| Break Dmg. Limit | 20 | 0 | Allows max damage to exceed 9999. | Victor Primoris key item |

## PAINE, SINISTRAL WING ABILITIES

| NAME | AP | MP | DESCRIPTION | REQUIRED ABILITIES |
|------|----|----|-------------|--------------------|
| Steel Feather | 0 | 12 | Raise the party's Strength. | None |
| Diamond Feather | 0 | 12 | Raise the party's Defense. | None |
| White Feather | 0 | 16 | Lower the Strength of all enemies. | None |
| Buckle Feather | 0 | 16 | Lower the Defense of all enemies. | None |
| Cloudy Feather | 10 | 16 | Lower the Magic of all enemies. | None |
| Pointed Feather | 10 | 16 | Lower the Magic Defense of all enemies. | Cloudy Feather |
| Pumice Feather | 10 | 38 | Cast Haste on the party. | None |
| Ma'at's Feather | 10 | 0 | View detailed information about one enemy. | None |
| Stamina | 0 | 0 | Restore HP to one character. | None |
| Mettle | 0 | 0 | Restore MP to one character. | None |
| Reboot | 10 | 0 | Revive one KO'd character. | None |
| Ribbon | 0 | 0 | Guards against all status ailments. | None |
| Double HP | 20 | 0 | Doubles max HP. | None |
| Triple HP | 30 | 0 | Triples max HP. | Double HP |
| Break HP Limit | 20 | 0 | Allows max HP to exceed 9999. | Corpus Invictus key item |
| Break Dmg. Limit | 20 | 0 | Allows max damage to exceed 9999. | Victor Primoris key item |

Characters

Garment Grids
& Dresspheres

Battle System

Accessories

Items and
Item Shops

Walkthrough

Mini-Games

Fiends and
Enemies

# BATTLE SYSTEM

*FINAL FANTASY X-2* features combat and exploration systems that are easy to grasp, yet deep in management and customization. This chapter contains full explanations of the systems you must learn and master to win the game. By reading this section thoroughly, you will become better prepared to dive into the exciting fantasy world presented in this game.

## CONTROLLER FUNCTIONS

| FIELD CONTROLS | |
|---|---|
| D-pad/Left Stick | Move character |
| X | Speak to person/Search/Action |
| Circle | Jump or climb raised or cliff surface |
| Square | Speak to person (Special Events) |
| Triangle | Open menu |
| START | Pause |

| MENU CONTROLS | |
|---|---|
| D-pad/Left Stick | Move cursor |
| X | Select/Confirm |
| Circle | Cancel/Exit Menu |
| R1 | Next Character (Equip screens) |
| L1 | Previous Character (Equip screens) |
| R2 | Scroll to next screen (Item, accessory, and other lists) |
| L2 | Scroll to the previous screen (Item, accessory, and other lists) |

| BATTLE CONTROLS | |
|---|---|
| D-pad/Left Stick | Move cursor/target ally, enemy, groups |
| X | Confirm command or highlighted item |
| Circle | Cancel |
| Triangle | Skip character turn |
| R1 | Special Attack (e.g., Trigger Happy) |
| L1 | Change dresspheres |
| R2 | Scroll to next screen (Item and ability lists) |
| L2 | Scroll to previous screen (Item and ability lists) |

## MAIN MENU FUNCTIONS

Press Triangle to open the main menu while the party is standing in the field. The menu is not available during combat or cinematic events.

## ITEMS

Enables you to view, sort, and use items and view key items. Refer to the "Items and Items Shops" chapter for further information on the procurement and use of items.

## WHITE MAGIC

Spells and Abilities learned by equipping the White Mage dressphere can be used outside of combat to restore HP, heal status ailments, and recover fallen characters. This command only becomes available once the White Mage dressphere is obtained. See the "Garment Grids & Dresspheres" chapter for details on White Magic abilities.

## EQUIP

Equip or change the equipment of any character. Choose the Equip command, then choose a character to equip. While in the Equip sub-screen, press the R1 or L1 button to switch to the next or the previous character. The Equip sub screen presents a full status display for the character, whereupon you can view a complete list of statistics (such as a character's current HP, MP, Level, Strength, Magic, Defense, etc). You can also see the total experience gained and the amount required before a character will reach the next level. The selected character's current combat commands and auto-abilities are displayed in the lower-right corner of the screen. When you change a character's dressphere and accessories, the status, commands and auto-abilities possessed by the character may change. Decrease in status is indicated when any attribute turns red; an increase is indicated by blue colored attribute.

## GARMENT GRIDS

The Garment Grid sub-screen enables you to place dresspheres on Garment Grids. Select the Garment Grid to arrange, then choose dresspheres to insert in the nodes on the Garment Grid. In the lower-right corner of the Garment Grid sub-screen, the description of the garment grid is displayed. The description also contains information on any abilities or auto-abilities gained by the character when the garment grid is equipped. Blue, red, yellow and green symbols on Garment Grids indicate the locations of gates. When a character performs a spherechange during combat, the line between the previous dressphere and the next one begins to glow. If a gate is located along this line, the character gains the associated ability or benefit listed in the description. Select the Auto command and the game will automatically place a set of dresspheres on the Garment Grid. Use the Rearrange option to move one dressphere or switch two dresspheres already set on the Garment Grid. Remove All clears all dresspheres from the grid. Please refer to the "Garment Grids & Dresspheres" chapter for more detailed information on using Garment Grids and gates.

# ABILITIES

This menu allows you to change the abilities that a character will learn while using a certain dressphere. Select the Abilities command, then choose a character. The sub screen displays a list of all available dresspheres and the character's progress percentage toward mastering each. Also displayed are the character's status, battle commands, and auto-abilities. Move the cursor down the list of available dresspheres, and the character's status and commands will change to show how each dressphere alters the character's status when equipped. While on this screen, you can switch to the next or previous character by pressing the R1 or L1 buttons.

To select abilities to learn, highlight a dressphere and press the X button. On the list of abilities, highlight the ability you want to learn next while the dressphere is equipped and press the X button. Doing so highlights the ability in a swirling yellow color. Any Ability Points (AP) gained while the dressphere is in use will then be applied to the selected ability. While viewing this screen, press the R1 or L1 buttons to scroll to the next or previous dressphere. Read the "Garment Grids & Dresspheres" chapter to learn more about the various functions of the abilities of all the dresspheres.

# ACCESSORIES

View and sort the accessories possessed by the party. Accessories are equipped by using the Equip sub-screen. This screen enables you to view the descriptions of each accessory and to sort the inventory. For more information and a full listing of accessories, read the "Accessories" chapter.

# DRESSPHERES

This option enables you to view the dresspheres in your possession and read detailed descriptions of the abilities each one bestows on a character equipping it.

# CONFIG

The Config menu features several options that enable you to alter the gameplay experience in various ways.

**Spherechanges:** When a character changes dresspheres during battle, the battle changes briefly to "Wait" mode and a short transformation cinema plays. This option allows you to change the length of the cinema. When the function is set to "OFF," each transformation is shown only once in its entirety. Thereafter, the character transformation is instantaneous.

**ATB Mode:** When set to "Active," this function allows enemies to attack continuously regardless of what you're doing. When set to "Wait," time pauses while you choose abilities or items to use.

**ATB Speed:** Battle timer gauges will charge more quickly or more slowly depending on how this option is set. The change also affects Enemy turns, for better or worse. Slowing down battles allows for more time to enter combat commands for each character.

**Cursor:** In the "Default" setting, this option resets the cursor to the top option of each battle menu, item listing, and ability listing, but when set to Memory, the cursor is set to the last command issued or the last item or ability used. The Memory function makes it faster and easier to repeatedly cast the same spell or use the same ability.

**Battle Help:** The help window displayed at the top of the screen during a battle can be toggled on or off.

**Vibration:** The vibrating function of the controller can be turned on or off.

**Subtitles:** The subtitles that appear at the bottom of the screen during scenes can be turned on or off.

**Subtitle Names:** Shows or hides the name of the speaker when each subtitle is displayed during scenes of dialogue.

**Guide Map:** Toggles the guide map normally displayed in the upper-left corner of the screen during field mode on or off. The on-screen map provides an outline shape of the surrounding area, making it easier to spot side areas, entrances, and exits.

**Sound:** Changes the quality of sound to best suit televisions with stereo or monaural sound.

**Screen Position:** Corrects screen position errors that may occur on some smaller televisions. Move the cursor to highlight the Adjust option, then hold the Square button and use the D-pad to adjust the centering of the screen image. To return to the default position, highlight the position and press the Square button.

Characters

Garment Grids & Dresspheres

Battle System

Accessories

Items and Item Shops

Walkthrough

Mini-Games

Fiends and Enemies

# BASIC GAME PROGRESSION

Beginning a game of *FINAL FANTASY X-2*, the player assumes the awesome challenge of guiding a group of three especially talented ladies through a spectacular fantasy world. The story begins with the entertaining premise that the summoner who defeated Sin in the previous game has shed her robes to become a sphere hunter. A sphere hunter is an adventurer who travels Spira in search of rare spheres that bestow new abilities on the user and sometimes contain ancient recordings from the world's mysterious past. However, as strange events begin to occur and the political climate of Spira changes, the heroines' quest becomes deeper and more intense.

Throughout this journey, your job is to guide the player character group, or party, from location to location, searching for items that will aid you in battle or enable new abilities in combat. As you pass through areas, the screen may suddenly freeze and shatter as enemies appear and attack the party. Such random battles are called "encounters." As you conquer enemies, the characters gain Experience Points (EXP) and Ability Points (AP) that enable them to learn new skills and fight with greater speed and prowess. When certain events are triggered, the party must fight and defeat one or more unique enemies of superior strength and attack abilities, referred to as "bosses." Each boss defeated brings you one step closer to the conclusion of the quest.

## STORY COMPLETION

Progression through *FINAL FANTASY X-2* is also measured by a new story completion system. As the party visits various locations in Spira, scenes can be triggered by moving to certain spots or by speaking to certain non-player characters, or NPCs. During some scenes, the game awards completion percentage points. These points are displayed whenever you save or load your game, and enable you to track the total amount of the game that you have experienced. Completion points factor into the ending you will view at the end of the game.

## CHAPTERS

Another new method *FINAL FANTASY X-2* uses to track progress is the "Chapter" system. When the game begins, you start Chapter 1. After visiting a few key locations, marked on the airship Celsius's maps as "Hotspots," the story will progress to the point where visiting additional locations will enable you to advance through the chapter. Once a chapter is completed, new events, items and enemies become available in all areas of Spira. Thus, you can complete a chapter very quickly or very slowly, whichever you prefer. Be warned, however, that if you jump from Hotspot to Hotspot without visiting other locations in between, the game's difficulty will increase dramatically.

## COMPLETING THE GAME

As you complete chapters and engage in the events of Chapter 5, which features some of the most powerful boss monsters in the game, you will draw closer to the final confrontation with the enemy known as the final boss. If victorious against this enemy, the story completion percentage points are tallied and weighed against various decisions made at crucial points in the game. Thereafter, you will view one of many endings that best reflects your progress and choices during the game. *FINAL FANTASY X-2* is a game in which you cannot experience every event in a single game, due to the fact you must make choices that affect certain scenes. However, with diligent exploration and completion of certain side quests, it is possible to accumulate all 100% story completion in a single game. These are all aspects of the game that you must keep in mind while playing.

## EXPLORATION

Throughout the game, you must navigate the main character, Yuna, through various areas in search of items to aid in this quest. Yuna represents the position of the entire party on the map. The rest of the party, Rikku and Paine, will not appear on-screen until a cutscene or a battle is triggered.

Characters

1

Garment Grids
& Dresspheres

2

Battle System

3

Accessories

4

Items and
Item Shops

5

Walkthrough

6

Mini-Games

7

Fiends and
Enemies

8

Knowing how to search wisely and efficiently can reduce game time. Items that you can find are contained in treasure chests. Some treasure chests are positioned in obvious locations and are easy to locate. Other chests are cleverly tucked behind obstacles that make them difficult to see. As you move the player character around some areas, you'll notice that the camera moves relative to the character's position on-screen. Sometimes if you move to the forward portion or rear of an area, the camera will switch to a new position, enabling a different view that reveals the location of a hidden or obscure treasure chest or item. For this reason, it is important to move the player character all around a map as you cross through any area.

As you progress from one chapter to the next, each area becomes refilled with all new treasure chests. Sometimes the exact same chests become refilled with new items. Other chests will disappear at the end of a certain chapter, whether they've been opened or not, and new chests will appear in completely different locations on the map. For this reason, it is important to revisit every location in every chapter. With this method, you can supply the characters with enough items and accessories to carry them through any battle.

While exploring areas and defeating enemies, it's important to touch the blue, glowing Save Spheres scattered throughout Spira. Not only does a Save Sphere enable you to preserve your game progress, it also restores the entire party to full HP and MP and heals status ailments. Save Spheres enable your party to remain strong even while passing through dangerous areas where random encounters are frequent and draining on the characters' health.

# NON-PLAYER CHARACTERS

During your exploration of Spira, speak to local citizens and shop clerks standing or walking around the area. These NPCs include any character who does not become an active fighter that you can control in the combat party. Therefore, NPC refers to every person in the game except for Yuna, Rikku, and Paine.

By speaking to NPCs in every location, you may come to understand the history and purpose of each region. If the person is an important or key NPC, you may actually trigger a dialogue event by speaking with them. Dialogue events may divulge clues as to what tasks you should be performing to benefit the region or your party. These scenes may also signal the start of important missions. By completing missions assigned to you by NPCs, you will develop stronger relationships with these characters that should prove mutually beneficial to your party in terms of gaining new items, dresspheres, accessories, and Garment Grids. So don't hesitate to help out strangers you meet in the wilderness, because good deeds shine back on you even if it may take a while.

# MANAGING THE PARTY

During combat and while walking in the field, your job is to keep Yuna, Rikku, and Paine healthy and equipped in preparation for the next encounter. Press the Triangle button to open the main menu and use the options to consume items for the restoration of Hit Points (HP) and Magic Points (MP), or to remove status ailments inflicted on your characters by enemies, which sometimes linger after battle. Equip your characters with Garment Grids that benefit your characters with additional abilities and auto-abilities. Each character can also be fitted with up to two additional accessories that enable abilities and beneficial auto-abilities for use in combat.

Perform such management activities continuously as you progress in the game to ensure that all of your characters are prepared for any sudden encounters with fiends or foes that are difficult to defeat.

# BALANCING THE PARTY

Garment Grids have nodes whereupon you can set dresspheres. Each character can equip one dressphere at a time. You can change the dressphere equipped by the character between battles using the menu, or in the midst of battle by pressing the L1 button during the character's combat turn. While a character has a dressphere equipped, she can learn and perform a certain set of abilities.

Each dressphere bestows the character who equips it with amazing combat skills, but also limitations. For instance, a White Mage can heal the entire party every single round without consuming MP, but is incapable of attacking the enemy. A Black Mage can perform powerful spells that inflict damage on enemies, but is normally incapable of performing physical attacks. A Warrior can use physical attacks as well as magically-charged sword skills, but cannot cast spells like a Black Mage nor heal like a White Mage. A Thief has the ability to steal items and money, called gil, from enemies. However, the physical attacks of a Thief are far less damaging than those of a Warrior.

Due to these strengths and weaknesses of all dresspheres, it's important to equip your characters so that the three can combine their abilities in ways that compliment one another. One of the better combinations of dresspheres to equip for any boss battle is Black Mage, White Mage, and Thief. With this trio, the White Mage will keep the party healthy while the Black Mage damages the boss for massive amounts of HP with spells. Once the Thief steals rare or normal items from the boss, she can assist the Black Mage in defeating the boss. This is just one example of how dresspheres can be equipped among the three characters to balance the abilities of the party for greater combat efficiency.

Because any character can change to a more suitable dressphere in the middle of combat, there is no reason to remain tied to one particular set of abilities. For instance, if a Black Mage runs out of MP and does not have the means to recover spell casting points, change to a dressphere such as Warrior so that the character can continue to attack every round without need for MP. To be best prepared to change your characters' dresspheres during combat, pay attention to the placement of dresspheres on each of the character's Garment Grids.

# BATTLES

Combat is the key to character development and game progression. Battles occur randomly as you cross through areas, or they can be triggered by certain events or by contact with certain characters. Random battles usually involve weaker enemies. All enemies are listed in the "Fiends and Enemies" chapter with statistics detailing their strengths and weaknesses. By using an enemy's weaknesses against it, you should become able to defeat most enemies easily.

Unique enemies of particularly powerful strength and little weakness that are encountered through events are called boss monsters. Such enemies are also detailed in the "Fiends and Enemies" chapter. However, the "Chapters" walkthrough section also contains detailed strategies for overcoming such foes.

# INSIDE THE BATTLE!

The rest of this section describes, step by step, how to fight a battle and adjust your strategy to overcome enemies in a quick and efficient manner every time. Turn by turn, we'll describe how to enter a battle, how to observe enemy behavior, and how to rise to the challenge.

# THE BATTLE SCREEN

## COMBAT TURNS AND ROUNDS

When combat begins, the flow of battle commences in turns and rounds. Each character's ATB Gauge is displayed in the lower-right corner of the combat menu. When the timer gauge fills completely, the character becomes entitled to a combat turn. On a character's turn, you can use her personalized menu to enter commands to be executed. When an enemy attacks or performs an action, it is also referred to as their turn. Due to the ATB system, some characters or enemies can have multiple turns before the end of one combat round.

## INITIAL ACTIONS

During a character's turn, the command menu is displayed in the lower-left corner of the screen. The command menu is tailored to the abilities of the dressphere that the character is equipped with. Use the D-pad or analog stick to highlight a command, and press the X button to select it. The character will then execute the command chosen.

Most dresspheres enable the user to perform a simple physical Attack. Start the battle by attacking an enemy, and watch the results.

If the enemy sidesteps your first attack and you see the word "MISS" appear on-screen, it may just be luck on the enemy's part. Try another attack on your next turn, and see if you can cause some damage this time. If the attack misses the enemy again, it may be that the foe possesses a high Evasion. In that case, you should resort to using magic spells to attack, because they rarely miss. If spells are not at your disposal, there are abilities with status effects available on certain dresspheres that enable you to slow down an enemy or reduce its Evasion. If such an ability proves effective, you should be able to attack the enemy and land a hit.

If your physical attacks land on the foe, but the enemy suffers minimal damage, it may be that the enemy bears a high Defense. Again, you should switch to magical attacks to compensate for the enemy's high Defense. If you can't hurt foes one way, you can surely hurt them another way.

## CASTING MAGIC

If you've determined that an enemy is invulnerable to physical damage, it's time to switch to magic. You can't cast magic until you find suitable dresspheres such as White Mage and Black Mage. Both of these dresspheres are obtained by completing missions in Chapter 1. If a character is not already equipped with the Black Mage dressphere at the start of the battle, use the spherechange command to change dresspheres. During a character's turn, press the L1 button to access the character's spherechange menu. You can select and transform into a dressphere that is one node away from the one currently equipped. Change to a Black Mage, who can use attack magic.

Once the transformation is complete, a Black Mage should be immediately ready to cast spells. On her turn, open the Black Magic menu and select a spell to cast. When using magic, you can target one foe or all foes. To target the entire enemy party with a spell, move the analog stick left until flashing arrows appear next to the names of all the enemies. Targeting a spell at multiple enemies will reduce the effect of the magic, causing less damage to foes.

Casting a spell requires additional time to prepare. Once you've chosen a spell and commanded your character to perform this action on her turn, a second gauge appears next to her name on-screen. When this gauge fills, your character will unleash the magic you desire. Unfortunately, enemies have the ability to affect the time required for a Black Mage to cast a spell. If an enemy attacks a Black Mage, the timer gauge will stop filling for the time it takes for your character to recover her posture following the force of the blow. If a mage's gauge is full and the enemy attacks at the moment your character tries to cast the spell, this can delay your action for another full second. You can reduce the time required to cast spells by learning abilities such as Black Magic Lv.2 and Black Magic Lv.3.

When the Black Mage finally casts a spell, watch the effects. If the enemy or enemies suffer significant damage as a result of the spell, then magic use may be a more suitable strategy than physical attacks.

Characters

Garment Grids & Dresspheres

Battle System

Accessories

Items and Item Shops

Walkthrough

Mini-Games

Fiends and Enemies

1
2
3
4
5
6
7
8

# ELEMENTAL PROPERTIES OF MAGIC

Black Magic spells and other abilities that use the powers of Fire, Blizzard, Thunder, and Water all operate on elemental properties. As long as a foe does not have any inherent resistance to a spell, this doesn't affect a character's ability to damage it with magic. However, some enemies have the ability to halve damage from certain types of magic, or they may even be immune to the effects of a certain element. Enemies may even be able to *absorb* certain elements, thereby receiving healing effects from the spell!

For all these reasons, it's important to understand the elemental strengths and weaknesses of your foes ahead of time and use magic wisely. A Gun Mage can use the Scan ability to determine the elemental strengths and weaknesses of any unknown creature, so it is extremely helpful to have a Gun Mage present when using Black Magic.

# MAGICAL PROTECTION

If neither magic spells nor physical attacks are causing normal amounts of damage to a foe, it is very likely that the enemy just has high Defense and Magical Defense. You can check this by using a Gun Mage's Scan ability. Any status effects that the enemy is currently benefiting from will be displayed directly under its main data in the upper right-hand window. If these benefits are the result of a spell or special ability, then you can remove these effects with a White Mage's Dispel spell, a Dispel Tonic, or other items and abilities that allow the user some form of Dispel.

However, some enemies benefit from these status effects permanently. For example, a foe may be in a constant state of Haste, or may be sheltered by a constant Protect effect. Use the strategies described below to counter whatever beneficial status the enemy has.

## PROTECT

Reduces the amount of damage received from physical attacks. Use Dispel or cast spells to increase Strength.

## SHELL

Reduces the amount of damage received from magic spells. Use Dispel or cast spells to raise Magic.

## REGEN

Regenerates small amounts of HP gradually. Use Dispel or attempt to inflict Poison status.

## REFLECT

Spells will bounce back to the opposing side. Spells can only be reflected once, so cast Reflect on your own party members. Target your spells at your party, and the spell will bounce off to damage the enemy. You can also cast Dispel on the enemy.

## HASTE

The speed of the enemy is raised to such a degree that it attacks more frequently during battle. This can be nullified by casting Dispel on the enemy. Another tactic would be to cast Slow on the enemy, which replaces the enemies' Haste effect with the Slow effect.

# CHAIN ATTACKS

If two or more characters in the party execute their attacks, spells, or abilities consecutively, a "chain attack" is formed. Chain attacks cause greater damage to the enemy than usual, and provide a way to maximize physical attacks. Each chain attack causes slightly more damage than the last. Thus, if you can string together a series of consecutive attacks, the damage will increase more than the normal amount of damage inflicted by a lone attack. The easiest way to do this is with a Gunner's Trigger Happy ability. With three Gunners in the party, you may be able to execute three consecutive Trigger Happy attacks and never let the enemy have a turn!

Attacks do not have to strike the target at the exact same time. A chain attack will occur as long as the second attack occurs before the enemy fully recovers its normal posture after the first attack.

Enemies are also capable of using chain attacks against your characters. If one or more enemies are attempting a prolonged chain against one of your characters, try to break the chain by attacking the enemy. But remember, some enemy chains cannot be interrupted.

# RECOVERY

After an attack, damage has usually been done to your party. Hit Points can be recovered by using the Pray or Cure abilities of a White Mage or by consuming Potions, Hi-Potions, X-Potions, Mega-Potions, or Megalixirs.

Using either spells or potions to recuperate requires extra time to prepare and execute, so don't let your characters drop to low HP before healing them. When characters drop below 25% of their maximum HP, their HP display turns yellow and they stumble in pain. Administer recovery spells or items immediately to avoid a "KO." Casting Life magic or using Phoenix Down items can revive fallen characters, but you'll need to use one turn to revive and yet

another turn to heal, because a character rarely comes back to life in good condition. Avoid the hassle of KO by staying above critical status.

Stronger restorative items should be reserved for the latter stages of the game, where many enemies have the ability to take down lots of HP with single attacks. Unless the enemies are reducing the HP of your characters close to zero during every single round, there is no reason to recover HP until an emergency situation arises. Use your combat turns to attack enemies, and tend to the matter of healing characters and removing status ailments between battles.

# STATUS AILMENTS

Enemies are capable of affecting the combat abilities of the characters by using attacks or spells that inflict status ailments. Once a character is affected by a status, achieving victory is more difficult. Once afflicted with a status ailment, icons will appear over the characters' heads. Characters may also flash in strange colors to indicate some kind of affliction.

If a character becomes partially disabled by status, use the affected character's next turn to consume a curative item or cast an Esuna spell. An Esuna spell will remove most status ailments from a character, but the MP cost and extra time required to cast the spell make this a less attractive option in the heat of fast-paced battles.

Items can be used to cure status ailments more rapidly but also take a certain amount of time to use in battle. A Remedy item takes care of all the same status impairments as an Esuna spell. However, Remedy potions cannot be purchased and are difficult to find in the early stages of the game. You can easily purchase status-specific cures such as Antidotes, Eye Drops, Echo Screens, etc. at most shops to remove what ails your party.

If you determine that an enemy is susceptible to any type of status ailment, don't hesitate to inflict the enemy with some ailment if possible.

| CURABLE STATUS AILMENTS | | |
|---|---|---|
| **STATUS** | **DESCRIPTION** | **CURE** |
| Poison | Suffers damage at set intervals. | Antidote, Remedy, Esuna |
| Darkness | Reduced accuracy of physical attacks. | Eye Drops, Remedy, Esuna |
| Silence | Cannot cast spells or sing. | Echo Screen, Remedy, Esuna |
| Sleep | Cannot participate in battle. | Physical attack, Remedy, Esuna |
| Petrification | Cannot participate in battle. | Soft, Remedy, Esuna |
| Confusion | Actions are unpredictable and uncontrollable. | Physical attack, Remedy, Esuna |
| Berserk | Increased Strength, but attacks enemies impulsively and uncontrollably. | Remedy, Esuna |
| Pointless | No AP is earned during battle, and no EXP is earned after battle. | Holy Water, Remedy, Esuna |
| Curse | Cannot spherechange. | Holy Water, Remedy, Esuna |
| Itchy | Cannot use any command but spherechange. | Holy Water, Remedy, Esuna, Spherechange to new dressphere |
| Slow | ATB gauge takes longer to fill. | Remedy, Esuna, wears off |
| Stop | ATB gauge stops. | Remedy, Esuna, wears off |
| KO | Cannot participate in battle. | Phoenix Down, Life magic |
| INCURABLE STATUS AILMENTS | | |
| **STATUS** | **DESCRIPTION** | |
| Auto-Life | The ally or enemy recovers from KO status automatically. | |
| Doom | The target dies after three combat rounds. | |
| Eject | An ally or enemy is permanently removed from a battle. | |
| Invincible | Cannot suffer damage. | |
| Null Magic | Cannot suffer damage or status ailment via magic. | |
| Null Physical | Cannot suffer damage or status ailment via physical attack. | |

Characters

1

Garment Grids & Dresspheres

2

Battle System

3

Accessories

4

Items and Item Shops

5

Walkthrough

6

Mini-Games

7

Fiends and Enemies

8

In addition to a Garment Grid and a Dressphere, each Gullwing can equip two accessories from the Equip sub-screen. Accessories are a type of equipment that benefit the character wearing them, either by raising status attributes (such as HP, MP, Strength, Defense, etc.), or by preventing status ailments inflicted by fiends. Some accessories can also add the benefit of casting spells or using additional abilities. When using accessories, be sure to check what abilities they grant as they can be very helpful throughout the game.

## OBTAINING ACCESSORIES

The unique and tough opponents known as "bosses" usually drop accessories. Sometimes, however, a character can steal accessories from certain fiends. Accessories are found in many of the treasure chests located throughout Spira. Basic accessories are sold at most shops throughout Spira, also. As you progress through the game, better shops begin to sell better accessories. However, it's also a matter of keeping in touch with the right merchants...

## VIEWING ACCESSORIES

After acquiring some accessories, press the Triangle button to enter the Main Menu and open the Accessories sub-screen. Highlight any accessory on the list to view its description. While an accessory's description provides some insight into its function, there are sometimes hidden benefits or penalties that come with equipping an accessory. You can even sort the accessories manually or automatically. To sort accessories manually, press the X button. One cursor stays at the accessory you choose to move and another cursor appears on-screen. Move the second cursor to the accessory or the slot where you want to place the accessory within the list. Press the X button again to move the accessory. To sort automatically, cancel out of the Examine option and choose Sort. The accessories are then reorganized based on function and value.

Another way to view accessories is to equip them on a character in the Equip sub-screen. To get a better idea of how an accessory will affect a character's status, highlight an empty accessory slot and scroll through the list of available accessories. The description of the accessory appears at the top of the screen. Any auto-abilities that the accessory adds are displayed in the blue window in the lower-right corner of the Equip sub-screen. Additionally, watch for changes in the character's statistics, such as HP, MP, Strength, Defense, etc. When a stat turns blue, it means the accessory increases the stat. If a stat turns red, equipping the accessory actually lowers it. When equipping accessories, it's extremely important to consider all of the positive and possibly negative effects the accessory will have on a character.

| LIST KEY | |
| --- | --- |
| Name | The name of the accessory as it appears in the game. |
| Description | The use of the item. |
| Buy | The accessory can be purchased at a shop for the amount of gil listed. Accessories without a number cannot be bought; they can only be found or stolen. |
| Sell | The amount of gil an accessory can be sold for at any shop. |

| NAME | DESCRIPTION | EFFECT | BUY | SELL |
| --- | --- | --- | --- | --- |
| Adamantite | Provides incredible defense but is miserably heavy. | HP +100%, Defense +120, Magic +120, Agility −30, Auto-Wall | NA | 10 |
| Amulet | Raises Magic by 10. | Magic +10 | 1000 | 250 |
| Angel Earrings | Guards against Death. | Defense +5, Magic Defense +5, Deathproof | 5000 | 1250 |
| AP Egg | Triples the amount of AP earned. | Luck +15, Triple AP | NA | 10 |
| Arcane Lore | Use **Arcana** abilities learned as a Dark Knight. | Magic +12 | 50000 | 12500 |
| Arcane Tome | Cuts the time required for Arcana by 40%. | MP +10%, Agility +5, Turbo Arcana | NA | 10 |
| Beaded Brooch | Guards against Silence and Darkness. | Defense +8, Magic Defense +8, Sense Preserver | 10000 | 2500 |
| Black Belt | Raises Strength and Defense by 20. | Strength +20, Defense +20 | NA | 2000 |
| Black Choker | Guards against Confusion. | Defense +4, Magic Defense +4, Confuseproof | 4000 | 1000 |

| NAME | DESCRIPTION | EFFECT | BUY | SELL |
|------|-------------|--------|-----|------|
| Black Lore | Use **Black Magic** abilities learned as a Black Mage. | Magic +12 | 50000 | 12500 |
| Black Ring | Nullifies gravity damage. User can cast Demi. | HP +10%, MP +10%, Gravityproof | NA | 2500 |
| Black Tome | Black Magic requires 40% less time. User can cast Osmose. | MP +10%, Agility +5, Turbo Black Magic | NA | 10 |
| Blind Shock | Adds Darkness to attacks and skills. User can cast Blind. | Strength −5, Magic +3, Darktouch | 15000 | 3750 |
| Bloodlust | Horrific invention said to make its bearer fight to the death. | HP −40%, MP −40, Strength +60, Magic −50, Magic Defense −50, Kijo's Soul (generates a constant Poison and Berserk status on character during battle) | NA | 10 |
| Blue Ring | Halves water damage. User can cast Water. | Magic +4, Water Ward | 3000 | 750 |
| Bushido Lore | Use **Bushido** abilities learned as a Samurai. | Strength +12 | 50000 | 12500 |
| Bushido Tome | Cuts the time required for Bushido by 40%. | HP +10%, Agility +5, Turbo Bushido | NA | 10 |
| Cat Nip | A seemingly ordinary jewel, but when the going gets tough… | SOS ???? (character strikes for 9999 damage when HP is low) | NA | 10 |
| Cat's Bell | Automatically recover HP while walking. | HP +15%, HP Stroll | NA | 10 |
| Cerulean Ring | Converts water damage to HP. User can cast Waterga. | Magic +10, Water Eater | 10000 | 2500 |
| Champion Belt | Raises Strength and Defense by 40. | Strength +40, Defense +40 | NA | 2500 |
| Chaos Shock | Adds Confusion to attacks & skills. User can cast Confuse. | Strength −5, Magic +5, Confusetouch | 15000 | 3750 |
| Charm Bangle | Eliminates random enemy encounters. | Luck +10, No Encounters | NA | 10 |
| Circlet | Raises Magic and Magic Defense by 10. | Magic +10, Magic Defense +10 | 4000 | 1000 |
| Crimson Ring | Converts fire damage to HP. User can cast Firaga. | Magic +10, Fire Eater | 10000 | 2500 |
| Crystal Ball | Raises Magic by 50. | Magic +50 | NA | 3000 |
| Crystal Bangle | Raises max HP by 100%. | HP +100% | NA | 2000 |
| Crystal Gloves | Raises Defense by 60. | Defense +60 | NA | 2000 |
| Defense Bracer | Generates constant Shell and Protect effects. | Auto-Wall | NA | 10 |
| Defense Veil | Raises Magic Defense by 20. | Magic Defense +20 | 1000 | 250 |
| Diamond Gloves | Raises Defense by 40. | Defense +40 | 6000 | 1500 |
| Dragonfly Orb | Guards against Stop. | Defense +4, Magic Defense +4, Stopproof | 4000 | 1000 |
| Dream Shock | Adds Sleep to attacks and skills. User can cast Sleep. | Strength −5, Magic +3, Sleeptouch | 15000 | 3750 |
| Electrocutioner | Adds lightning and water elements to attacks and skills. | Strength +10, Lit./Water Strike | NA | 10 |
| Enterprise | Insignia of health. Allows max HP to exceed 9999. | Break HP Limit | NA | 10 |
| Faerie Earrings | Guards against Confusion and Berserk. | Defense +8, Magic Defense +8, Sanity Preserver | 10000 | 2500 |
| Favorite Outfit | Guards against Itchy. | Evasion +10, Luck +10, Itchproof | 4000 | 1000 |
| Fiery Gleam | Adds fire element to attacks and skills. | Strength +8, Firestrike | 3000 | 750 |
| Force of Nature | Adds all elements to attacks. Turns elemental damage to HP. | Omnistrike | NA | 10 |
| Freezerburn | Adds fire and ice elements to attacks and skills. | Strength +10, Fire/Ice Strike | NA | 10 |
| Fury Shock | Adds Berserk to attacks and skills. User can cast Berserk. | Strength −5, Magic +5, Berserktouch | 15000 | 3750 |
| Gauntlets | Raises Strength and Defense by 5. | Strength +5, Defense +5 | 2500 | 625 |
| Glass Buckle | Guards against Poison and Sleep. | Defense +8, Magic Defense +8, Health Preserver | 10000 | 2500 |
| Gold Anklet | Guards against Petrification. | Defense +4, Magic Defense +4, Stoneproof | 5000 | 1250 |
| Gold Bracer | Raises max MP by 60%. | MP +60% | 4000 | 1000 |
| Gold Hairpin | Halves MP cost during battle. | Magic +20, Half MP Cost | NA | 10 |
| Gris-Gris Bag | Guards against Curse. | Defense +4, Magic Defense +4, Curseproof | 4000 | 1000 |
| Haste Bangle | Casts Haste when HP is low. | SOS Haste | NA | 750 |
| Heady Perfume | Leblanc's secret weapon. Dated, but still good for a high. | MP +20%, Magic +5, Defense +10, Magic Defense +10, Agility +2, Luck +10, HP/MP Stroll | NA | 10 |
| Hyper Wrist | Raises Strength by 30. | Strength +30 | NA | 2000 |
| Hypno Crown | Raises Magic and Magic Defense by 20. | Magic +20, Magic Defense +20 | NA | 2000 |
| Icy Gleam | Adds ice element to attacks and skills. | Strength +8, Icestrike | 3000 | 750 |
| Invincible | Insignia of destruction. Allows max damage to exceed 9999. | Break Dmg. Limit | NA | 10 |
| Iron Bangle | Raises max HP by 20%. | MP +20% | 500 | 125 |
| Iron Duke | Forged in the belief that power is but a number. | HP +100%, MP +100%, Strength +100, Magic +100, Defense +100, Magic Defense +100, Agility +10, Accuracy +100, Evasion +100, Luck +50 | NA | 10 |

Characters

Garment Grids & Dresspheres

Battle System

Accessories

Items and Item Shops

Walkthrough

Mini Games

Fiends and Enemies

| NAME | DESCRIPTION | EFFECT | BUY | SELL |
|------|-------------|--------|-----|------|
| Kaiser Knuckles | Raises Strength by 50. | Strength +50 | NA | 3000 |
| Key to Success | Tobli's guide to getting all one's desires at twice the speed. | HP +100%, MP +100%, Luck +100, Double All (doubles AP, EXP, gil & items earned, and general effectiveness of recovery, elemental, & non-elemental items) | NA | 10 |
| Kinesis Badge | Guards against Slow and Stop. | Defense +8, Magic Defense +8, Time Preserver | 10000 | 2500 |
| Lag Shock | Adds Slow to attacks and skills. | Strength −5, Slowtouch | 15000 | 3750 |
| Lightning Gleam | Adds lightning element to attacks and skills. | Strength +8, Lightningstrike | 3000 | 750 |
| Lure Bracer | Raises the frequency of random enemy encounters. | Strength +15, More Encounters | NA | 10 |
| Minerva's Plate | Dramatically increases magic power... but what's the point? | MP +100%, Strength −80, Magic +100, Turbo Black Magic, Gain 0 AP, Gain 0 EXP, use any Black Magic already learned. | NA | 10 |
| Moon Bracer | Generates constant Shell effect. | Auto-Shell | NA | 10 |
| Mortal Shock | Adds Death to attacks and skills. User can cast Death. | Strength −6, Magic +5, Deathtouch | NA | 10 |
| Muscle Belt | Raises Strength and Defense by 10. | Strength +10, Defense +10 | 4000 | 1000 |
| Mute Shock | Adds Silence to attacks and skills. User can cast Silence. | Strength −5, Magic +3, Silencetouch | 15000 | 3750 |
| Mystery Veil | Raises Magic Defense by 40. | Magic Defense +40 | 6000 | 1500 |
| Mythril Bangle | Raises max HP by 60%. | HP +60% | NA | 1500 |
| Mythril Gloves | Raises Defense by 20. | Defense +20 | 1000 | 250 |
| Nature's Lore | Use **Instinct** abilities learned as a Berserker. | Strength +12 | 50000 | 12500 |
| Nature's Tome | Cuts the time required for Instinct by 40%. | HP +10%, Agility +5, Turbo Instinct | NA | 10 |
| NulBlaze Ring | Nullifies fire damage. User can cast Fira. | Magic +6, Fireproof | 8000 | 2000 |
| NulFrost Ring | Nullifies ice damage. User can cast Blizzara. | Magic +6, Iceproof | 8000 | 2000 |
| NulShock Ring | Nullifies lightning damage. User can cast Thundara. | Magic +6, Lightningproof | 8000 | 2000 |
| NulTide Ring | Nullifies water damage. User can cast Watera. | Magic +6, Waterproof | 8000 | 2000 |
| Oath Veil | Raises Magic Defense by 60. | Magic Defense +60 | NA | 2000 |
| Ochre Ring | Converts lightning damage to HP. User can cast Thundaga. | Magic +10, Lightning Eater | 10000 | 2500 |
| Pearl Necklace | Guards against Pointless. | Defense +4 , Magic Defense +4, Pointlessproof | 4000 | 1000 |
| Pixie Dust | Raises Magic by 40. | Magic +40 | NA | 2500 |
| Potpourri | Guards against Berserk. | Defense +4 , Magic Defense +4, Beserkproof | 4000 | 1000 |
| Power Gloves | Raises Strength by 40. | Strength +40 | NA | 2500 |
| Power Wrist | Raises Strength by 20. | Strength +20 | 6000 | 1500 |
| Pretty Orb | Guards against Slow. | Defense +4, Magic Defense +4, Slowproof | 4000 | 1000 |
| Rabite's Foot | Raises Luck by 100. | Luck +100 | NA | 10 |
| Ragnarok | Insignia of magic. Reduces MP cost to zero during battle. | Spellspring | NA | 10 |
| Recovery Bracer | Generates constant Regen effect. | Auto-Regen | NA | 10 |
| Red Ring | Halves fire damage. User can cast Fire. | Magic +4, Fire Ward | 3000 | 750 |
| Regal Crown | Raises Magic and Magic Defense by 40. | Magic +40, Magic Defense +40 | NA | 2500 |
| Regen Bangle | Casts Regen when HP is low. | SOS Regen | 3000 | 750 |
| Ribbon | Guards against all status ailments. | Ribbon | NA | 10 |
| Rune Bracer | Raises max MP by 100%. | MP +100% | NA | 1500 |
| Safety Bit | Guards against Petrification and Death. | Defense +12, Magic Defense +12, Life Preserver | 10000 | 2500 |
| Shining Bracer | Generates constant Protect effect. | Auto-Protect | NA | 10 |
| Shmooth Shailing | Protects against all status ailments, but it's Hypello, so... | Defense +30, Magic Defense +30, Super Ribbon (generates a constant Slow effect on character) | NA | 10 |
| Short Circuit | Converts lightning and water damage to HP. | Magic +10, Magic Defense +10, Lit./Water Eater | NA | 10 |
| Silver Bracer | Raises max MP by 40%. | MP +40% | 500 | 125 |
| Silver Glasses | Guards against Darkness. | Defense +4, Magic Defense +4 | 3000 | 750 |
| Snow Ring | Converts ice damage to HP. User can cast Blizzaga. | Magic +10, Ice Eater | 10000 | 2500 |
| Soul of Thamasa | Strengthens spells but doubles their MP cost. | Magic +15, Magic Booster (increases spell's effectiveness 1.5x normal amount) | NA | 10 |

| NAME | DESCRIPTION | EFFECT | BUY | SELL |
|------|-------------|--------|-----|------|
| Speed Bracer | Generates constant Haste effect. User can cast Hastega. | Auto-Haste | NA | 10 |
| Sprint Shoes | Act at the beginning of battle. User can cast Haste. | Agility +10, First Strike | NA | 10 |
| Star Bracer | Generates constant Reflect effect. | Auto-Reflect | NA | 10 |
| Star Pendant | Guards against Poison. | Defense +4, Magic Defense +4, Poisonproof | 4000 | 1000 |
| Stone Shock | Adds Petrification to attacks & skills. User can cast Break. | Strength −5, Magic +4, Stonetouch | NA | 10 |
| Silver Glasses | Guards against Darkness. | Defense +4, Magic Defense +4 | 3000 | 750 |
| Snow Ring | Converts ice damage to HP. User can cast Blizzaga. | Magic +10, Ice Eater | 10000 | 2500 |
| Soul of Thamasa | Strengthens spells but doubles their MP cost. | Magic +15, Magic Booster (increases spell's effectiveness 1.5x the normal amount) | NA | 10 |
| Speed Bracer | Generates constant Haste effect. User can cast Hastega. | Auto-Haste | NA | 10 |
| Sprint Shoes | Act at the beginning of battle. User can cast Haste. | Agility +10, First Strike | NA | 10 |
| Star Bracer | Generates constant Reflect effect. | Auto-Reflect | NA | 10 |
| Star Pendant | Guards against Poison. | Defense +4, Magic Defense +4, Poisonproof | 4000 | 1000 |
| Stone Shock | Adds Petrification to attacks & skills. User can cast Break. | Strength −5, Magic +4, Stonetouch | NA | 10 |
| Sublimator | Converts fire and ice damage to HP. | Magic +10, Magic Defense +10, Fire/Ice Eater | NA | 10 |
| Sword Lore | Use **Swordplay** abilities learned as a Warrior. | Strength +12 | 50000 | 12500 |
| Sword Tome | Cuts the time required for Swordplay by 40%. | HP +10%, Agility +5, Turbo Swordplay | NA | 10 |
| System Shock | Adds Stop to attacks and skills. | Strength −10, Stoptouch | 15000 | 3750 |
| Talisman | Raises Magic by 30. | Magic +30 | NA | 2000 |
| Tarot Card | Raises Magic by 20. | Magic +20 | 6000 | 1500 |
| Tetra Band | Reduces fire, ice, lightning, and water damage by half. | Defense +10, Magic Defense +10, Tetra Ward | NA | 10 |
| Tetra Bracelet | Converts fire, ice, lightning, and water damage to HP. | Defense +20, Magic Defense +20, Tetra Eater | NA | 10 |
| Tetra Gloves | Adds fire, ice, lightning, and water to attacks and skills. | Strength +12, Magic +12, Tetrastrike | NA | 10 |
| Tetra Guard | Nullifies fire, ice, lightning, and water damage. | Defense +15, Magic Defense +15, Tetraproof | NA | 10 |
| Tiara | Raises Magic and Magic Defense by 5. | Magic +5, Magic Defense +5 | 2500 | 625 |
| Titanium Bangle | Raises max HP by 40%. | HP +40% | 3000 | 750 |
| Twist Headband | Guards against Sleep. | Defense +4, Magic Defense +4 | 3000 | 750 |
| Venom Shock | Adds Poison to attacks and skills. User can cast Bio. | Strength −5, Magic +3, Poisontouch | 15000 | 3750 |
| Wall Ring | Casts Shell and Protect when HP is low. | SOS Wall | 10000 | 2500 |
| Watery Gleam | Adds water element to attacks and skills. | Magic +8, Waterstrike | 3000 | 750 |
| White Cape | Guards against Silence. | Defense +4, Magic Defense +4, Silenceproof | 3000 | 750 |
| White Lore | Use **White Magic** abilities learned as a White Mage. | Magic +12 | 50000 | 12500 |
| White Ring | Halves ice damage. User can cast Blizzard. | Magic +4, Ice Ward | 3000 | 750 |
| White Tome | White Magic requires 40% less time. User can cast Osmose. | Agility +5, MP +10%, Turbo White Magic | NA | 10 |
| Wizard Bracelet | Automatically recover MP while walking. | MP +20%, MP Stroll | NA | 10 |
| Wring | From an ancient war. Makes its user a spellcasting machine. | HP −40%, Magic +80, Defense −20, Majo's Soul (generates a constant Poison & Haste effect on character; Black Magic spells require 50% less time to cast); use any Black Magic already learned. | NA | 10 |
| Wristband | Raises Strength by 10. | Strength +10 | 1000 | 250 |
| Yellow Ring | Halves lightning damage. User can cast Thunder. | Magic +4, Lightning Ward | 3000 | 750 |

Characters

Garment Grids & D>spheres

Battle System

Accessories

Items and Item Shops

Walkthrough

Mini Games

Fiends and Enemies

# ITEMS AND ITEM SHOPS

The term "item" refers to any object that is obtained during the game that can be used during combat or in the field to benefit your party. Dozens of items are tucked inside treasure chests located in various cities, dungeons, and wilderness areas. You can purchase many of these items from shops and merchants throughout Spira. Monsters and enemies leave behind items when defeated in battle, and additional items can be snatched from enemies by using the Thief's Steal or Mug abilities. To view item descriptions and their use in the field, access the Items sub-screen.

Key Items are required in order to trigger certain events that advance the story of the game, to access new areas, or to decode the letters of the Al Bhed language. They are displayed in a separate menu within the Items sub-screen.

## ITEM TYPES

| ICON | TYPE | FIELD USE | BATTLE USE | USAGE |
|---|---|---|---|---|
| (icon) | Recovery | Yes | Yes | Restore HP, MP, cure ailments . |
| (icon) | Attack Item | No | Yes | Damage enemies, inflict ailments. |
| (icon) | Support Item | No | Yes | Cast beneficial effects on party. |
| (icon) | "Greens" | No | Yes | Capture and feed chocobos. |

# CONSUMABLE ITEMS

Items are generally consumable goods that benefit the party in some manner, during combat or in the field. Recovery Items can be used in the field or during battle to restore lost Hit Points or Magic Points, to remove detrimental status ailments, or to revive characters who have fallen in combat. Some items that fall under the recovery category are Potions which are items used to recover a character's HP. Attack items can be used to attack enemies and inflict status ailments to reduce the combat abilities of monsters. Status items are used to raise the combat abilities of your characters to improve the chances of success in battle.

# USING ITEMS

To use items in the field press the Triangle button to open the menu. Chose the "Item" option in the menu, move the cursor to highlight the appropriate item, and press the X button. When the character choice sub-menu appears, move the cursor to highlight the character who needs the item, and press the X button again. If the character does not need the benefits of the item, a buzzer will sound. If an item is designed to benefit the entire party, flashing cursors will point to all three characters.

To use items during combat, select the Item command from a character's battle menu. Scroll up or down to the desired item, then press the X button to use the item.

Using an item during combat requires one full turn, and the character who selects the item cannot act again until the next combat round.

## FAST ITEM MENU SCROLLING

*When your party carries many items, scrolling through the item list line by line takes longer. In the fast-paced battles of FINAL FANTASY X-2, this can become detrimental to your characters' survival. Whether you're in the Items sub-screen of the menu or the Item menu during combat, press the R2 button to scroll down one entire screen. Press the L2 button to scroll up one entire screen. Hold down either button to rapidly scroll through the entire list.*

# SORTING ITEMS

Items are stored in the Items sub-screen in the order in which they are received. To arrange items in a manner that makes them easier to find and use, such as during the hurried pace of a battle, cancel out of the Use function and select the Sort function. Items can be sorted by Manual or Auto methods. The Auto option arranges all items in the order predetermined by the game's design. The item lists in this chapter are arranged by the sorting of the Auto method.

If you want to make a certain item handier during combat, use the Manual method. Select the item you want to move to a new location. When the item is selected, a second cursor appears. Move the second cursor to the slot on the menu where you want to relocate the item and press the X button to move the item manually. Using this method, you can move items to blank slots or switch the locations of any two items.

| Name | The name of the item as it appears in the game. |
| Description | The use of the item. |
| Buy | The item can be purchased at a shop for the amount of gil listed. Items without a number cannot be bought; they can only be found or stolen. |
| Sell | The amount of gil an item can be sold for at any shop. |
| Target | Single: The item affects one ally or enemy; All: The item affects all allies or all enemies simultaneously; Random: The item selectively affects all allies or enemies. |

## CONSUMABLE ITEMS LIST

| ITEM NAME | DESCRIPTION | BUY | SELL | TARGET |
|---|---|---|---|---|
| Potion | Restores 200 HP to one character. | 50 | 12 | Single |
| Hi-Potion | Restores 1000 HP to one character. | 500 | 125 | Single |
| X-Potion | Fully restores HP to one character. | NA | 250 | Single |
| Mega-Potion | Restores 2000 HP to each character. | NA | 375 | All |
| Ether | Restores 100 MP to one character. | NA | 250 | Single |
| Turbo Ether | Restores 500 MP to one character. | NA | 750 | Single |
| Phoenix Down | Revives one character from KO. | 100 | 25 | Single |
| Mega Phoenix | Revives the party from KO. | NA | 1000 | All |
| Elixir | Fully restores one character's HP and MP. | NA | 1250 | Single |
| Megalixir | Fully restores the party's HP and MP. | NA | 5000 | All |
| Antidote | Cures **Poison**. | 50 | 12 | Single |
| Soft | Cures **Petrification**. | 50 | 12 | Single |
| Eye Drops | Cures **Darkness**. | 50 | 12 | Single |
| Echo Screen | Cures **Silence**. | 50 | 12 | Single |
| Holy Water | Cures **Curse**, **Itchy**, and **Pointless**. | 300 | 75 | Single |
| Remedy | Cures all status ailments. | NA | 375 | Single |
| Budget Grenade | Damages all enemies. | NA | 12 | All |
| Grenade | Damages all enemies. | NA | 25 | All |
| S-Bomb | Damages all enemies. | NA | 50 | All |
| M-Bomb | Damages all enemies. | NA | 75 | All |
| L-Bomb | Damages all enemies. | NA | 100 | All |
| Sleep Grenade | Inflicts damage and **Sleep** on all enemies. | NA | 50 | All |
| Silence Grenade | Inflicts damage and **Silence** on all enemies. | NA | 37 | All |
| Dark Grenade | Inflicts damage and **Darkness** on all enemies. | NA | 37 | All |
| Petrify Grenade | Inflicts damage and **Petrification** on all enemies. | NA | 50 | All |
| Bomb Fragment | Deals fire damage to one enemy. | NA | 25 | Single |
| Bomb Core | Deals fire damage to one enemy. | NA | 50 | Single |
| Fire Gem | Deals fire damage to all enemies. | NA | 75 | Random |
| Antarctic Wind | Deals ice damage to one enemy. | NA | 50 | Single |
| Arctic Wind | Deals ice damage to one enemy. | NA | 50 | Single |
| Ice Gem | Deals ice damage to all enemies. | NA | 75 | Random |
| Electro Marble | Deals lightning damage to one enemy. | NA | 25 | Single |
| Lightning Marble | Deals lightning damage to one enemy. | NA | 50 | Single |
| Lightning Gem | Deals lightning damage to all enemies. | NA | 75 | Random |
| Fish Scale | Deals water damage to one enemy. | NA | 25 | Single |
| Dragon Scale | Deals water damage to one enemy. | NA | 50 | Single |
| Water Gem | Deals water damage to all enemies. | NA | 75 | All |
| Shadow Gem | Reduces HP of all enemies by 1/4. | NA | 50 | Random |
| Shining Gem | Deals non-elemental damage to one enemy. | NA | 75 | Single |
| Blessed Gem | Deals holy damage to one enemy. | NA | 125 | Single |
| Supreme Gem | Deals non-elemental damage to all enemies. | NA | 250 | All |
| Poison Fang | Inflicts damage and **Poison** on one enemy. | NA | 25 | Single |
| Silver Hourglass | Delays the actions of one enemy. | NA | 25 | Single |
| Gold Hourglass | Delays the actions of all enemies. | NA | 37 | All |

Characters

Garment Grids & D…spheres

Battle System

Accessories

Items and Item Shops 5
Consumable Items

Key Items

Shops

Walkthrough

Mini-Games

Fiends and Enemies

## CONSUMABLE ITEMS LIST (continued)

| ITEM NAME | DESCRIPTION | BUY | SELL | TARGET |
|---|---|---|---|---|
| Candle of Life | Casts **Doom** on one enemy. | NA | 50 | Single |
| Farplane Shadow | Sometimes inflicts **Death** on one enemy. | NA | 75 | Single |
| Dark Matter | Deals major damage to all enemies. | NA | 7500 | All |
| Chocobo Feather | Casts **Haste** on one character. | NA | 40 | Single |
| Chocobo Wing | Casts **Haste** on the party. | NA | 50 | All |
| Lunar Curtain | Casts **Shell** on the party. | NA | 45 | All |
| Light Curtain | Casts **Protect** on the party. | NA | 45 | All |
| Star Curtain | Casts **Reflect** on the party. | NA | 45 | All |
| Healing Spring | Casts **Regen** on the party. | NA | 150 | All |
| Mana Spring | Absorbs MP from one enemy. | NA | 75 | Single |
| Stamina Spring | Absorbs HP from one enemy. | NA | 75 | Single |
| Soul Spring | Absorbs HP and MP from one enemy. | NA | 100 | Single |
| Dispel Tonic | Negates all spell effects on one enemy. | NA | 70 | Single |
| Stamina Tablet | Doubles the max HP of one character. | NA | 200 | Single |
| Mana Tablet | Doubles the max MP of one character. | NA | 300 | Single |
| Stamina Tonic | Doubles the party's max HP. | NA | 400 | All |
| Mana Tonic | Doubles the party's max MP. | NA | 400 | All |
| Twin Stars | Reduces the MP cost of one character to 0. | NA | 200 | Single |
| Three Stars | Reduces the party's MP cost to 0. | NA | 1250 | All |
| Hero Drink | Makes one character invincible. | NA | 25 | Single |
| Gysahl Greens | If you give it to a chocobo…; restores 100 HP (Feed/capture chocobo) | NA | 25 | Single |
| Sylkis Greens | If you give it to a chocobo…; restores 100 HP (Feed chocobo) | NA | 25 | Single |
| Mimett Greens | If you give it to a chocobo…; restores 100 HP (Feed chocobo) | NA | 25 | Single |
| Pahsana Greens | If you give it to a chocobo…; restores 100 HP (Feed chocobo) | NA | 25 | Single |

# KEY ITEMS

Key items are displayed in the Key Items menu of the Items sub-screen. All Key Items are obtained by completing certain objectives or triggering special events. Crimson Spheres contain short movies relating to the fate of the Crimson Guard squad of the Crusaders. Al Bhed Primers decode the language spoken by Al Bhed citizens. During conversations in Al Bhed, letters of the subtitles are converted to the common tongue if you have an Al Bhed Primer in your possession that translates one or more letters. Spheres contain short movies that help to unravel the mystery of the familiar looking stranger. You can review movie spheres at any time by speaking to Shinra on the bridge of the airship Celsius. Keys and objects enable you to unlock various chests and doors and explore areas previously unreachable.

## KEY ITEMS LIST

| KEY ITEM NAME | DESCRIPTION | KEY ITEM NAME | DESCRIPTION |
|---|---|---|---|
| Crimson Sphere 1 | Appears to be part of some kind of record. | Al Bhed Primer XIV | Teaches the letter "N" in Al Bhed. |
| Crimson Sphere 2 | Appears to be part of some kind of record. | Al Bhed Primer XV | Teaches the letter "O" in Al Bhed. |
| Crimson Sphere 3 | Appears to be part of some kind of record. | Al Bhed Primer XVI | Teaches the letter "P" in Al Bhed. |
| Crimson Sphere 4 | Appears to be part of some kind of record. | Al Bhed Primer XVII | Teaches the letter "Q" in Al Bhed. |
| Crimson Sphere 5 | Appears to be part of some kind of record. | Al Bhed Primer XVIII | Teaches the letter "R" in Al Bhed. |
| Crimson Sphere 6 | Appears to be part of some kind of record. | Al Bhed Primer XIX | Teaches the letter "S" in Al Bhed. |
| Crimson Sphere 7 | Appears to be part of some kind of record. | Al Bhed Primer XX | Teaches the letter "T" in Al Bhed. |
| Crimson Sphere 8 | Appears to be part of some kind of record. | Al Bhed Primer XXI | Teaches the letter "U" in Al Bhed. |
| Crimson Sphere 9 | Appears to be part of some kind of record. | Al Bhed Primer XXII | Teaches the letter "V" in Al Bhed. |
| Crimson Sphere 10 | Appears to be part of some kind of record. | Al Bhed Primer XXIII | Teaches the letter "W" in Al Bhed. |
| Al Bhed Primer I | Teaches the letter "A" in Al Bhed. | Al Bhed Primer XXIV | Teaches the letter "X" in Al Bhed. |
| Al Bhed Primer II | Teaches the letter "B" in Al Bhed. | Al Bhed Primer XXV | Teaches the letter "Y" in Al Bhed. |
| Al Bhed Primer III | Teaches the letter "C" in Al Bhed. | Al Bhed Primer XXVI | Teaches the letter "Z" in Al Bhed. |
| Al Bhed Primer IV | Teaches the letter "D" in Al Bhed. | New Beginnings Sphere | Led Yuna to become a sphere hunter. |
| Al Bhed Primer V | Teaches the letter "E" in Al Bhed. | Gagazet Sphere | Found in the Floating Ruins at Gagazet. |
| Al Bhed Primer VI | Teaches the letter "F" in Al Bhed. | Sphere Fragment | Half of a sphere, found in the Zanarkand Ruins. |
| Al Bhed Primer VII | Teaches the letter "G" in Al Bhed. | Awesome Sphere | Formerly hidden away in Kilika Temple. |
| Al Bhed Primer VIII | Teaches the letter "H" in Al Bhed. | Leblanc's Sphere | Left behind by Leblanc's gang. |
| Al Bhed Primer IX | Teaches the letter "I" in Al Bhed. | Reassembled Sphere | Composed of two sphere fragments. |
| Al Bhed Primer X | Teaches the letter "J" in Al Bhed. | Logos's Sphere | Recorded by Logos in the Bevelle Underground. |
| Al Bhed Primer XI | Teaches the letter "K" in Al Bhed. | | |
| Al Bhed Primer XII | Teaches the letter "L" in Al Bhed. | Ormi's Sphere | Recorded by Ormi in the Bevelle Underground. |
| Al Bhed Primer XIII | Teaches the letter "M" in Al Bhed. | Gaol Sphere | Found by Logos in the Bevelle Underground. |

| KEY ITEM NAME | DESCRIPTION |
|---|---|
| Nooj's Sphere | A sphere from Lucil. |
| Gippal's Sphere | A sphere from Rin. |
| Baralai's Sphere | Found in Guadosalam. |
| Paine's Sphere | Found inside Paine's sphere recorder. |
| War Buddy Sphere | A sphere from Beclem. |
| Besaid Sphere | Found on Besaid Island. |
| Syndicate Uniform (S) | Courtesy of Leblanc's goons. |
| Syndicate Uniform (M) | Courtesy of Leblanc's goons. |
| Syndicate Uniform (L) | Courtesy of Leblanc's goons. |
| Letter of Introduction | Letter from Gippal to Nhadala. |
| How to Repair with Soul | May be useful for repairing machines. |
| The Spirit of Recycling | May be useful for repairing machines. |
| The ABCs of Repair | May be useful for repairing machines. |
| Repairing for Dummies | May be useful for repairing machines. |
| Everyman's Repair Manual | May be useful for repairing machines. |
| Besaid Key | Engraved with the emblem of Besaid. |
| Desert Key | Found in the desert. |
| Twilight Rain | Enables Floral Fallal to learn Break Damage Limit. |

| KEY ITEM NAME | DESCRIPTION |
|---|---|
| Aurora Rain | Enables Floral Fallal to learn Break HP Limit. |
| Machina Booster | Enables Machina Maw to learn Break Damage Limit. |
| Machina Reactor | Enables Machina Maw to learn Break HP Limit. |
| Victor Primoris | Enables Full Throttle to learn Break Damage Limit. |
| Corpus Invictus | Enables Full Throttle to learn Break HP Limit. |
| Calm Lands Discount Pass | Allows bearer to ride hovers at a reduced fare. |
| Calm Lands Free Pass | Allows bearer to ride hovers free of charge. |
| Book of Magical Dances I | Enables Songstress to learn MP Mambo. |
| Book of Magical Dances II | Enables Songstress to learn Magical Masque. |

# SHOP LISTS

The shops throughout Spira sell supplies and accessories to daring young adventurers. During Chapter 1, all shops offer a minimum assortment of goods. As you progress through the game to higher Chapters, especially Chapter 3, shops begin to sell better items.

> To determine when the shops will sell items, refer to the bar underneath the shop screenshot. The blue highlighted chapter number indicates the shop is available; the lighter color signifies it isn't available. CH3+ means it's available starting in Chapter 3, throughout the rest of the game

## CALM LANDS TRAVEL AGENCY

| ITEM | COST |
|---|---|
| Potion | 50 |
| Hi-Potion | 500 *CH3+ |
| Phoenix Down | 100 |
| Antidote | 50 |
| Eye Drops | 50 |
| Echo Screen | 50 |
| Soft | 50 |
| Holy Water | 300 |
| Iron Bangle | 500 *CH1-2 |
| Silver Bracer | 500 *CH1-2 |
| Wristband | 1000 *CH1-2 |
| Amulet | 1000 *CH1-2 |
| Titanium Bangle | 3000 *CH3+ |
| Gold Bracer | 4000 *CH3+ |
| Power Wrist | 6000 *CH3+ |
| Tarot Card | 6000 *CH3+ |

**CHAPTERS** CH1 CH2 CH3 CH4 CH5

## BESAID ISLAND

| ITEM | COST |
|---|---|
| Potion | 50 |
| Hi-Potion | 500 *CH3+ |
| Phoenix Down | 100 |
| Antidote | 50 |
| Eye Drops | 50 |
| Echo Screen | 50 |
| Soft | 50 |
| Holy Water | 300 |
| Watery Gleam | 3000 |
| Blue Ring | 3000 |
| NulTide Ring | 8000 *CH3+ |
| Besaid Key | 9000 *CH1&2 |

**CHAPTERS** CH1 CH2 CH3 CH4 CH5

## FARPLANE, DEPTHS

| ITEM | COST |
|---|---|
| Potion | 50 |
| Hi-Potion | 500 |
| Phoenix Down | 100 |
| Antidote | 50 |
| Eye Drops | 50 |
| Echo Screen | 50 |
| Soft | 50 |
| Holy Water | 300 |

**CHAPTERS** CH1 CH2 CH3 CH4 CH5

*Must speak to Leblanc.*

## O'AKA THE MERCHANT, AIRSHIP CELSIUS

| ITEM | COST |
|---|---|
| Potion | 5 |
| Hi-Potion | 50 |
| Phoenix Down | 10 |
| Antidote | 5 |
| Eye Drops | 5 |
| Echo Screen | 5 |
| Soft | 5 |
| Holy Water | 30 |

*Debt Paid

**CHAPTERS** CH1 CH2 CH3 CH4 CH5

Characters

1

Garment Grids & Dresspheres

2

Battle System

3

Accessories

4

Items and Item Shops 5
Consumable Items

Key Items

Shops

Walkthrough

6

Mini-Games

7

Fiends and Enemies

8

## KILIKA ISLAND, PORT MERCHANT

| ITEM | COST |
|---|---|
| Potion | 50 |
| Hi-Potion | 500 *CH3+ |
| Phoenix Down | 100 |
| Antidote | 50 |
| Eye Drops | 50 |
| Echo Screen | 50 |
| Soft | 50 |
| Holy Water | 300 |
| Twist Headband | 3000 |
| White Cape | 3000 |
| Silver Glasses | 3000 |
| Star Pendant | 4000 |
| Beaded Brooch | 10000 *CH3+ |
| Glass Buckle | 10000 *CH3+ |

**CHAPTERS**
CH1 CH2 CH3 CH4 CH5

## ZANARKAND RUINS DOME MERCHANT

| ITEM | COST |
|---|---|
| Potion | 50 |
| Hi-Potion | 500 *CH3+ |
| Phoenix Down | 100 |
| Antidote | 50 |
| Eye Drops | 50 |
| Echo Screen | 50 |
| Soft | 50 |
| Holy Water | 300 |
| Iron Bangle | 500 *CH1, 2 |
| Silver Bracer | 500 *CH1, 2 |
| Mythril Gloves | 1000 *CH1, 2 |
| Defense Veil | 1000 *CH1, 2 |
| Titanium Bangle | 3000 *CH3+ |
| Gold Bracer | 4000 *CH3+ |
| Diamond Gloves | 6000 *CH3+ |
| Mystery Veil | 6000 *CH3+ |

**CHAPTERS**
CH1 CH2 CH3 CH4 CH5

## MI'IHEN HIGHROAD TRAVEL AGENCY

| ITEM | COST |
|---|---|
| Potion | 50 |
| Hi-Potion | 500 *CH3+ |
| Phoenix Down | 100 |
| Antidote | 50 |
| Eye Drops | 50 |
| Echo Screen | 50 |
| Soft | 50 |
| Holy Water | 300 |
| Iron Bangle | 500 *CH1-2 |
| Silver Bracer | 500 *CH1-2 |
| Gauntlets | 2500 *CH1-2 |
| Tiara | 2500 *CH1-2 |
| Titanium Bangle | 3000 *CH3+ |
| Gold Bracer | 4000 *CH3+ |
| Muscle Belt | 4000 *CH3+ |
| Circlet | 4000 *CH3+ |

**CHAPTERS**
CH1 CH2 CH3 CH4 CH5

## KILIKA ISLAND, TEMPLE MERCHANT

| ITEM | COST |
|---|---|
| Potion | 50 |
| Hi-Potion | 500 |
| Phoenix Down | 100 |
| Antidote | 50 |
| Eye Drops | 50 |
| Echo Screen | 50 |
| Soft | 50 |
| Holy Water | 300 |

**CHAPTERS**
CH1 CH2 CH3 CH4 CH5

## THUNDER PLAINS TRAVEL AGENCY

| ITEM | COST |
|---|---|
| Potion | 50 |
| Hi-Potion | 500 *CH3+ |
| Phoenix Down | 100 |
| Antidote | 50 |
| Eye Drops | 50 |
| Echo Screen | 50 |
| Soft | 50 |
| Holy Water | 300 |
| Lightning Gleam | 3000 |
| Yellow Ring | 3000 |
| NulShock Ring | 8000 *CH3+ |

**CHAPTERS**
CH1 CH2 CH3 CH4 CH5

## GUADOSALAM

| ITEM | COST |
|---|---|
| Potion | 50 |
| Antidote | 50 |
| Eye Drops | 50 |
| Echo Screen | 50 |
| Soft | 50 |
| Holy Water | 300 |

**CHAPTERS**
CH1 CH2 CH3 CH4 CH5

### ACCESSORIES CHAPTERS 1 & 2

| ITEM | COST |
|---|---|
| Pearl Necklace | 4000 |
| Angel Earrings | 5000 |
| Gold Anklet | 5000 |
| Kinesis Badge | 10000 |
| Mute Shock | 15000 |
| Venom Shock | 15000 |

### ACCESSORIES CHAPTER 3

| ITEM | COST |
|---|---|
| Gris-Gris Bag | 4000 |
| Favorite Outfit | 4000 |
| Regen Bangle | 3000 |
| Wall Ring | 10000 |
| Dream Shock | 15000 |
| Venom Shock | 15000 |

### ACCESSORIES CHAPTERS 5

| ITEM | COST |
|---|---|
| Pearl Necklace | 4000 |
| Favorite Outfit | 4000 |
| Angel Earrings | 5000 |
| Gold Anklet | 5000 |
| Mute Shock | 15000 |
| Dream Shock | 15000 |
| Blind Shock | 15000 |
| Venom Shock | 15000 |

## BIKANEL DESERT MERCHANT

| ITEM | COST |
|------|------|
| Potion | 50 |
| Hi-Potion | 500 *CH3+ |
| Phoenix Down | 100 |
| Antidote | 50 |
| Eye Drops | 50 |
| Echo Screen | 50 |
| Soft | 50 |
| Holy Water | 300 |
| Fiery Gleam | 3000 |
| Red Ring | 3000 |
| NulBlaze Ring | 8000 *CH3+ |

**CHAPTERS**

| CH1 | CH2 | CH3 | CH4 | CH5 |
|-----|-----|-----|-----|-----|

## MACALANIA LAKE TRAVEL AGENCY

| ITEM | COST |
|------|------|
| Faerie Earrings | 10000 |
| Kinesis Badge | 10000 |
| Safety Bit | 10000 |
| Beaded Brooch | 10000 |
| Crimson Ring | 10000 |
| Snow Ring | 10000 |
| Ochre Ring | 10000 |
| Cerulean Ring | 10000 |
| Chaos Shock | 15000 |
| Fury Shock | 15000 |
| Lag Shock | 15000 |
| System Shock | 15000 |

**CHAPTERS**

| CH1 | CH2 | CH3 | CH4 | CH5 |
|-----|-----|-----|-----|-----|

*Must speak to Wantz.*

## O'AKA THE MERCHANT, AIRSHIP CELSIUS

| ITEM | COST |
|------|------|
| Potion | 49 |
| Hi-Potion | 490 |
| Phoenix Down | 98 |
| Antidote | 49 |
| Eye Drops | 49 |
| Echo Screen | 49 |
| Soft | 49 |
| Holy Water | 294 |

**CHAPTERS**

| CH1 | CH2 | CH3 | CH4 | CH5 |
|-----|-----|-----|-----|-----|

*\*Starting prices.*

## THE GULLSTORE

| ITEM | COST |
|------|------|
| Potion | 50 |
| Hi-Potion | 500 *CH3+ |
| Phoenix Down | 100 |
| Antidote | 50 |
| Eye Drops | 50 |
| Echo Screen | 50 |
| Soft | 50 |
| Holy Water | 300 |
| Twist Headband | 3000 |
| White Cape | 3000 |
| Silver Glasses | 3000 |
| Star Pendant | 4000 |

**CHAPTERS**

| CH1 | CH2 | CH3 | CH4 | CH5 |
|-----|-----|-----|-----|-----|

## MACALANIA LAKE TRAVEL AGENCY

| ITEM | COST |
|------|------|
| Potion | 50 |
| Hi-Potion | 500 *CH3+ |
| Phoenix Down | 100 |
| Antidote | 50 |
| Eye Drops | 50 |
| Echo Screen | 50 |
| Soft | 50 |
| Holy Water | 300 |
| Icy Gleam | 3000 |
| White Ring | 3000 |
| NulFrost Ring | 8000 *CH3+ |

**CHAPTERS**

| CH1 | CH2 | CH3 | CH4 | CH5 |
|-----|-----|-----|-----|-----|

*This is the Al Bhed version.*

## BIKANEL DESERT OASIS CARAVAN

| ITEM | COST |
|------|------|
| Black Choker | 4000 |
| Potpourri | 4000 |
| Gris-Gris Bag | 4000 |
| Pearl Necklace | 4000 |
| Pretty Orb | 4000 |
| Dragonfly Orb | 4000 |
| Chaos Shock | 15000 |
| Fury Shock | 15000 |
| Lag Shock | 15000 |
| System Shock | 15000 |

**CHAPTERS**

| CH1 | CH2 | CH3 | CH4 | CH5 |
|-----|-----|-----|-----|-----|

## MACALANIA LAKE TRAVEL AGENCY

| ITEM | COST |
|------|------|
| Faerie Earrings | 10000 |
| Kinesis Badge | 10000 |
| Safety Bit | 10000 |
| Sword Lore | 50000 |
| Bushido Lore | 50000 |
| Arcane Lore | 50000 |
| Nature's Lore | 50000 |
| Black Lore | 50000 |
| White Lore | 50000 |
| Crimson Ring | 10000 |
| Snow Ring | 10000 |
| Ochre Ring | 10000 |
| Cerulean Ring | 10000 |

**CHAPTERS**

| CH1 | CH2 | CH3 | CH4 | CH5 |
|-----|-----|-----|-----|-----|

*Must speak to O'aka.*

Characters

1

Garment Grids & Dresspheres

2

Battle System

3

Accessories

4

**Items and Item Shops 5**
Consumable Items

Key items

Shops

Walkthrough

6

Mini-Games

7

Fiends and Enemies

8

# CHAPTERS

*FINAL FANTASY X-2* uses a very different advancement system than its predecessor, which featured a gradual approach to exploring the world of Spira. This time out, Yuna and the ladies of the Gullwings have an airship and the ability to jump to any location in Spira with the greatest of ease. This chapter indicates when events occur and how to complete them; it also illustrates how to experience interesting features of the game that you might overlook on your own.

## CHAPTER SYSTEM

The game takes place in five "chapters." When the game begins, you automatically start in Chapter 1. After completing several key missions, you progress to Chapter 2. You do *not* have to visit every location to complete a chapter. This means that progression through the game can be very fast or very slow, whichever method you prefer.

## MISSIONS AND VISITING LOCATIONS

The first two missions in the game, "Luca" and "Mt. Gagazet—Floating Ruins," are mandatory introductory scenarios that must be completed to advance in the game. After clearing these two missions, the airship Celsius becomes yours to command and the crew will fly you wherever you want to visit. To fly to a certain location, speak to Buddy who sits to the left of Brother. After Buddy makes one or two comments, the navigation maps appear. The towns and major locations of the world of Spira are listed on the map in the same order they were visited in the original *FINAL FANTASY X*. After choosing a location, the Celsius crew will drop off the Gullwings at a Save Sphere in a relatively safe spot in the town or location of your choice. To return to the Celsius, examine a Save Sphere and choose the "Board airship" option. If you cannot board the Celsius from your current location, this option will not appear on the Save Sphere menu.

As much as possible, this walkthrough is organized according to the order of locations as listed on the Celsius's navigation map. This organization is most beneficial, because with the exception of Besaid Island, Kilika Island and Bikanel Desert, you can travel from location to location on foot, without need to return to the airship.

To take control of the airship, speak to Buddy.

Select one of the locations from the navigational map.

The airship crew automatically flies to the location and drops the Gullwings off at a Save Sphere.

If the navigation map does not appear when you speak to Buddy, it means you still have duties to attend to on the Celsius before you can leave.

## "HOTSPOTS"

As you complete missions in the game, certain "Hotspots" appear on the navigation map. These are key locations where new story advancements will take place. Visiting these locations and completing missions will bring you closer to the end of chapters and, eventually, the conclusion of the game. However, if you jump from Hotspot to Hotspot without visiting other areas in between, you'll miss out on beneficial events that occur in unmarked areas. Each Hotspot is more difficult than the last, due to the fiends and boss monsters in each location. *Take your time and visit other locations between trips to Hotspots!*

## STORY PERCENTAGE

Each time you save your game at a Save Sphere or during events, you'll notice a percentage marked "COMPLETED x%." The total amount of "COMPLETED x%" accumulated by the end of the game dictates whether or not you see a bonus ending at Zanarkand Ruins.

Throughout the walkthrough, specific situations are discussed and the effect on the game's story percentage is explained. The percentage points

gained for completing each mission are listed at the start of each location's description in the walkthrough. For a complete analysis on how your actions and decisions affect your game percentage, please reference the *100% Completion Guide* section at the end of the walkthrough.

## CHECKLISTS

Each portion of the walkthrough begins with three "checklists." If there is no information in one of the checklists, it's only because there are no fiends or items in that location.

The "Wandering Fiends" list warns you about the fiends that appear during random encounters in an area. Cross-reference these lists with the information in the "Fiends and Enemies" chapter in this guide for a better understanding of the strengths and weaknesses of the enemies.

A fiend name marked in yellow indicates that the foe is a "Boss." Bosses are tough foes encountered only once during a mission; they do not appear in random encounters. The walkthrough chapter also includes statistics and notes to help you defeat these foes. Statistics presented in the walkthrough represent only the essentials. More extensive status information and details on each boss are also included in the "Fiends and Enemies" chapter.

## BOSS STATISTICS EXPLANATION

| Name | The name of the boss. You may fight more than one boss simultaneously. |
|---|---|
| HP | Total Hit Points of the enemy. Damage inflicted to the enemy lowers HP. When HP reaches zero, the boss is defeated. |
| MP | Total Magic Points of the enemy. MP is used to cast spells or perform special attacks. When MP reaches zero, the enemy cannot cast any more spells. |
| EXP | Total Experience Points gained by each surviving character who assists in defeating the enemy. |
| AP | Ability Points earned by each surviving character who assists in defeating the enemy. |
| Gil Dropped | The amount of money gained when the enemy is defeated. |
| Pilfer Gil | The amount of money that might be obtained from an enemy by using the Pilfer Gil or equivalent abilities during combat. The amount pilfered will range anywhere between 50% to 100% of the number listed. |
| Steal | Items that can be stolen from enemies using the Steal ability during combat. Quantities range anywhere from 50% to 100% of the number listed. Normal items have a 3/4 chance of being stolen; rare items have a 1/4 chance. |
| Drop | Items that may be left behind by defeated enemies when the battle ends. Normal items have a 7/8 chance of appearance; rare items have a 1/8 chance. |

Each area's "Item Checklist" reveals the items found in treasure chests, as well as key items given to the party during events. Items marked with an ⬤ icon are things not found in chests. Instead, they are gained through story events.

The "Action Checklist" section depicts a shot-by-shot series of actions to take to complete the objectives in an area. Naturally, these images and captions cannot explain certain events of the game half as well as needed. The information within the walkthrough is written to support the "Action Checklist," or basically, to provide additional information needed to progress to the next chapter. Refer to both the "Action Checklist" and the contextual paragraphs in each section to fully understand events in the game.

### ACTION CHECKLIST

*Defeat the impostor at the concert.*

*Follow her to the third dock outside the stadium*

*Defeat Leblanc and her henchmen.*

**COMPLETION: +1.6%**

## WANDERING FIENDS

**GOON**
HP: 29 | AP: 1 | Gil: 30
Steal: Budget Grenade
Drop: Potion

**SHE-GOON**
HP: 7 | AP: 1 | Gil: 30
Steal: Budget Grenade
Drop: Potion

**????**
HP: 82 | AP: 1 | Gil: 100
Steal: Hi-Potion
Drop: Phoenix Down (x2)

**LOGOS**
HP: 86 | AP: 1 | Gil: 60
Steal: Silver Glasses
Drop: Potion

**ORMI**
HP: 97 | AP: 1 | Gil: 60
Steal: Iron Bangle
Drop: Potion

**LEBLANC**
HP: 130 | AP: 2 | Gil: 180
Steal: Silver Bracer
Drop: Hi-Potion

Characters

1

Garment Grids & Dresspheres

2

Battle System

3

Accessories

4

Items and Item Shops

5

Walkthrough
Chapter 1
Chapter 2
Chapter 3
Chapter 4
Chapter 5

Mini-Games

7

Fiends and Enemies

8

# TAKE BACK THE GARMENT GRID!

All of the enemies in this introductory mission can be easily defeated with just a few ordinary attacks. Choose the Attack option for Rikku and Paine in quick succession to score Chain attacks that will cause more damage. Once the action shifts to the Luca docks, follow the impostor around the circular promenade. Goons and She-Goons of the Leblanc Syndicate will approach, and physical contact with any of them triggers battles. Upon reaching the third dock, the boss fights with Ormi, Logos, and Leblanc occur in quick succession and the first mission ends. Refer to the boss strategies for help, if needed.

By fighting multiple battles in the docks area, Rikku and Paine can learn abilities.

For healing, find the person in the Moogle suit who is cringing in fear on the second dock. Stand near the costumed individual and press X to completely restore HP and MP to Paine and Rikku.

Touch the person in the moogle suit at least once to receive a small amount of story completion percentage.

## ???? BOSS FIGHT

Yuna's impersonator can be defeated with normal Attack commands. Issue the commands for Rikku and Paine in rapid succession to strike chain attacks for greater damage in one turn. Take out the two Goons first, then wait for both characters' battle gauges to fill completely and enter the attack commands in rapid succession to ensure a chain attack on the impostor.

Use Rikku's Steal ability to pilfer items from each foe before annihilating them. Rikku can usually steal a Budget Grenade from a Goon. After successfully stealing a grenade, use it on your next turn to damage the entire enemy party in a single attack. To use a Budget Grenade, choose the Items command and select the Budget Grenade item from the list. A single Budget Grenade will nearly kill both Goons in a single attack and cause heavy damage to "????". Use this strategy as you fight through the Luca docks area as well. Also, try stealing a Hi-Potion from "????" before finishing the battle, especially since these powerful restorative items aren't easy to purchase yet.

**HP: 82  MP: 9999  EXP: 3  AP: 1**

**GIL DROPPED:** 100
**PILFER GIL:** 300

**STEAL:** Normal: Hi-Potion  Rare: Hi-Potion
**DROP:** Normal: Phoenix Down  Rare: Phoenix Down (x2)

## LOGOS, ORMI BOSS FIGHT

**HP: 86  MP: 18  EXP: 3  AP: 1**

**GIL DROPPED:** 60
**PILFER GIL:** 200

**STEAL:** Normal: Silver Glasses  Rare: Silver Glasses
**DROP:** Normal: Potion  Rare: Phoenix Down

**HP: 86  MP: 18  EXP: 3  AP: 1**

Steal from Logos and Ormi for a chance to gain valuable accessories, then focus your attacks on Logos and take him out of the battle first. Logos's gun attacks are quick and cause a lot of damage, whereas Ormi's shield attacks take longer to prepare, but inflict more damage. Logos occasionally uses a Potion on himself or Ormi, so the Syndicate gunner should be eliminated first. Once the boisterous Ormi is alone, use Chain Attacks to take him down quickly.

**GIL DROPPED:** 60
**PILFER GIL:** 200

**STEAL:** Normal: Iron Bangle  Rare: Iron Bangle
**DROP:** Normal: Potion  Rare: Phoenix Down

LUCA

# LEBLANC BOSS FIGHT

This battle mainly serves as a tutorial on changing dresspheres during battle. Press L1 and change Yuna to the Songstress dressphere to proceed. Thereafter, cast Darkness Dance on Leblanc to blind her. An enemy inflicted with the Darkness status ailment suffers a severe reduction in accuracy. As a result, most of Leblanc's physical attacks will miss. Recast Darkness Dance on Leblanc each time Yuna gets a turn to maintain the advantage during the battle. Steal from Leblanc and perform chain attacks to take her down. Rikku and Paine also have the ability to change to other dresspheres during this battle, if you so desire.

**HP:** 130 **MP:** 101 **EXP:** 8 **AP:** 2

**GIL DROPPED:** 180
**PILFER GIL:** 500
**STEAL:** Normal: Silver Bracer   Rare: Silver Bracer
**DROP:** Normal: Hi-Potion   Rare: Phoenix Down

ACTION CHECKLIST

1. Speak to Paine, Rikku, Brother, and Shinra on the bridge.

2. Ride the elevator to the Cabin level.

3. Speak to Barkeep and choose "Rest."

4. Ride the elevator to the Bridge.

5. Direct the Celsius to travel to Mt. Gagazet.

COMPLETION: +1.8%

## ITEM CHECKLIST

*Al Bhed Primer 🅔            *Al Bhed Primer 🅔            Remedy (x3)
*Al Bhed Primer 🅔            Phoenix Down (x4)            Potion (x4)
*Al Bhed Primer 🅔            Ether                       Vanguard Garment Grid 🅔

**\*Only if you haven't mastered Al Bhed.**

Characters

1

Garment Grids & Dresspheres

2

Battle System

3

Accessories

4

Items and Item Shops

5

Walkthrough 6
Chapter 1
Chapter 2
Chapter 3
Chapter 4
Chapter 5

Mini-Games

7

Fiends and Enemies

8

67

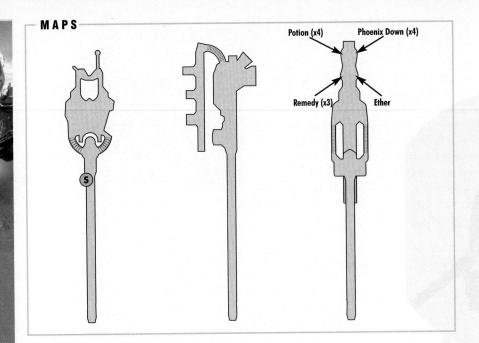

Potion (x4)  Phoenix Down (x4)

Remedy (x3)  Ether

# ALL ABOARD!

Following the initial scenes, direct Yuna around the Bridge area and speak to Paine and Rikku for backstory. Speaking to Brother nets you three Al Bhed Primers, which enable you to decipher letters in the subtitles that appear whenever someone is speaking the Al Bhed language. Speak to Buddy to obtain an **Al Bhed Primer**, and talk to Shinra to learn what he knows. Navigate Shinra's menus to view information on the combat system, the menus, and a variety of other topics. If you want to know why Yuna has embarked upon this quest and whom she is speaking to in her private thoughts, select the "Treasure Spheres" option to view the sphere titled "Journey's Start." Complete the Garment Grid tutorial to receive the **Vanguard Garment Grid**.

Speak to Shinra to learn about the game system, to view the images stored on treasure spheres, to read bios on main characters, and to view analysis data of fiends.

# RAID THE SUPPLIES

Exit the control room area and use the Save Sphere in the corridor if you desire. Proceed further down the corridor onto the elevator, and use the control panel to ride down to the Engine Room. There are four chests in the engine room that are restocked at the start of each new chapter. In Chapter 1, these chests contain the following: **Phoenix Down (x4)**, **Ether**, **Remedy (x3)**, and **Potion (x4)**.

The elevator transports you to any part of the ship.

Remember to return to the Engine Room each time a new chapter begins to find all four chests restocked.

# A LITTLE SHOPPING BEFORE NAPTIME

Ride the elevator to the Cabin area and speak to Barkeep, the Hypello creature behind the bar. Barkeep sells basic items for use in combat, as well as a few decent accessories. For the time being, purchase some items that guard against status ailments like Antidotes, Eye Drops, Echo Screens, and Softs. Save the rest of your gil for bigger purchases. When finished shopping, speak to Barkeep again and select the "Rest" option. After resting, head back toward the elevator to hear an announcement from the Bridge.

Barkeep takes care of all your needs onboard the Celsius airship.

## REQUIRED REST

Remember to rest at least once in the Cabin area during every chapter. During Chapter 5, you will only be able to witness certain events on the Celsius if you rested during each chapter.

| THE GULLSTORE | |
|---|---|
| ITEM | COST |
| Potion | 50 |
| Phoenix Down | 100 |
| Antidote | 50 |
| Eye Drops | 50 |
| Echo Screen | 50 |
| Soft | 50 |
| Holy Water | 300 |
| Twist Headband | 3000 |
| White Cape | 3000 |
| Silver Glasses | 3000 |
| Star Pendant | 4000 |

# MT. GAGAZET - FLOATING RUINS

## ACTION CHECKLIST

**1** Jump and climb across the ledges.

**2** Press the elevator button.

**3** Defeat the combined Leblanc Syndicate.

**4** Race to the top of the Floating Ruins before time expires.

**5** Defeat Boris to obtain the sphere.

**6** Exit the treasure sphere chamber.

**COMPLETION: +3.2%**

## WANDERING FIENDS

**AHRIMAN**
HP: 99  AP: 1  Gil: 20
Steal: Potion
Drop: Eye Drops

**BOMB**
HP: 140  AP: 1  Gil: 30
Steal: Potion
Drop: Potion

**QUADRICORN**
HP: 188  AP: 1  Gil: 13
Steal: Echo Screen
Drop: Potion

**RECOIL**
HP: 38  AP: 1  Gil: 10
Steal: Budget Grenade
Drop: Potion

**SHE-GOON**
HP: 7  AP: 1  Gil: 30
Steal: Budget Grenade
Drop: Potion

**YELLOW ELEMENTAL**
HP: 12  AP: 1  Gil: 24
Steal: Potion
Drop: Potion

**DIVEBEAK**
HP: 10  AP: 1  Gil: 12
Steal: Potion
Drop: Antidote

**GOON**
HP: 13  AP: 1  Gil: 30
Steal: Budget Grenade
Drop: Potion

**LEBLANC**
HP: 120  AP: 2  Gil: 250
Steal: Tiara
Drop: Hi-Potion

**LOGOS**
HP: 100  AP: 1  Gil: 80
Steal: White Cape
Drop: Potion

**ORMI**
HP: 130  AP: 1  Gil: 80
Steal: Gauntlet
Drop: Potion

**BORIS**
HP: 480  AP: 1  Gil: 300
Steal: Remedy
Drop: Star Pendant

## ITEM CHECKLIST

| | | | |
|---|---|---|---|
| Yellow Ring | Mega-Phoenix | Red Ring | Muscle Belt |
| Elixir | White Ring | Star Pendant | Black Mage Dressphere  |

Characters
1

Garment Grids & Dresspheres
2

Battle System
3

Accessories
4

Items and Item Shops
5

Walkthrough
Chapter 1
Chapter 2
Chapter 3
Chapter 4
Chapter 5
Mini-Games
7

Fiends and Enemies
8

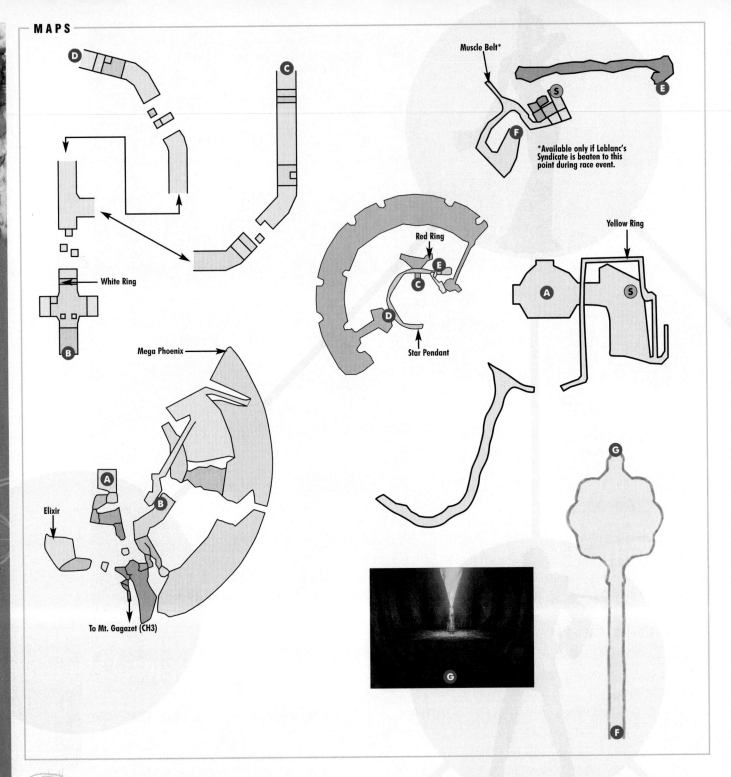

Muscle Belt*

*Available only if Leblanc's Syndicate is beaten to this point during race event.

White Ring

Red Ring

Yellow Ring

Mega Phoenix

Star Pendant

Elixir

To Mt. Gagazet (CH3)

# CLIFFS AND CRAGS

Follow the on-screen instructions to learn how to jump and climb up ledges. After leaping the first gap, follow the girls to a place where you can see a treasure chest below. Drop down to open the chest for a **Yellow Ring**. Move left and hold Circle to climb back up to the first ledge. Then run toward the ledge and hold Circle to leap across and join the other girls. Run down the stairs and use the Save Sphere. Take this opportunity to make sure everyone is equipped with an accessory, and then proceed.

When the girls reach a dead end, press the button on the wall to start the elevator. Reaching the bottom of the shaft, hop down the ledges until you reach the base of the waterfall. Move left in front of the waterfall and hop up the mountain ledge to find a chest containing an **Elixir**. Then hop back across the platforms until you reach the ruins of a suspended road.

*After grabbing the accessory, move to the ledge on the left and hold Circle to climb back up. Then run toward the ledge and hold Circle to jump the gap.*

*When you reach the bottom ledge, go left for an item and then go back to the right to continue.*

*Climb this ledge to initiate the boss fight.*

**HP:** 120 **MP:** 320 **EXP:** 20 **AP:** 2

**GIL DROPPED:** 250
**PILFER GIL:** 700
**STEAL:** Normal: Tiara Rare: Tiara
**DROP:** Normal: Hi-Potion Rare: Hi-Potion (x2)

A Thief will have a grand old time during this battle, considering all the accessories that are up for grabs from this trio. If your Thief has learned the Pilfer Gil ability, you can also gain lots of gil for the time being. Note that all enemies have more gil to steal during a battle than they will drop after a battle. Also, have a Songstress keep the enemy trio blinded with Darkness Dance while a Warrior or Gunner attacks. Concentrate your efforts to rob and eliminate Leblanc first, since her attacks damage the entire party. With her gone, take out Logos and Ormi.

**HP:** 100 **MP:** 25 **EXP:** 310 **AP:** 1

**GIL DROPPED:** 80
**PILFER GIL:** 280
**STEAL:** Normal: White Cape Rare: White Cape
**DROP:** Normal: Potion Rare: Phoenix Down

**HP:** 130 **MP:** 10 **EXP:** 10 **AP:** 1

**GIL DROPPED:** 80
**PILFER GIL:** 280
**STEAL:** Normal: Gauntlets Rare: Gauntlets
**DROP:** Normal: Potion Rare: Phoenix Down

## RACE TO THE PEAK

The on-screen timer indicates the time remaining before the Leblanc Syndicate reaches the treasure sphere at the top of the Floating Ruins. If you reach the top before the Syndicate, you get an opportunity to claim a great accessory. The timer stops during each random and event battle. It is possible to grab all the items in the ruins and reach the top before the Leblanc Syndicate, but only if you hurry! Ignore the tilted columns, which only lead to a dead end. Instead, hold the Circle button to climb over platforms to reach the door.

Run to the far end of the ruined high-way, where a chest contains a valuable **Mega Phoenix**.

Fight Logos's goon squad, then enter the temple.

### SNATCH BEFORE YOU CHOP

*You may encounter Divebeaks during some of the random encounters in the Floating Ruins. Although these bird-like monsters are easily dispatched with a single attack, a Thief can steal Ethers from them on occasion. Ethers are a difficult item to come by in the game, so attempt to steal one before finishing off these creatures.*

## TEMPLE INTERIOR

Just inside the entrance to the ruins, move left or right and climb up a ledge to find a mysterious switch on either side of the room. Pressing both switches lowers a column in a connecting corridor. However, this task is entirely optional.

The two switches lower a column in another hallway, but activating them is not necessary.

Head north from the entry point and drop into the first pit to find a chest containing a **White Ring**. Climb out of the pit and jump across the platforms heading north. At the intersection, go down the corridor to the right.

*Climb back out the way you came, then leap across the platform tops.*

If you pressed the mysterious switches in the first room of the ruins, this is where the column fell. As you can see, you can cross this room just as easily by dropping into the pit and climbing right out. This curving hallway emerges onto a ledge with a chest that has a **Red Ring** inside. Run back to the intersection, but this time take the other branch out to another ruined highway.

*Take the first right inside the ruins to reach the chest on this isolated platform.*

# REACHING THE TOP

Follow the road around the ruins until you're almost at the end. After Ormi orders some Recoils and She-Goons to attack, hop up a series of rocks floating just off the right side of the toppled pillar. Follow the curvy ribbon of ledge around the spire to a chest at the end, which contains a **Star Pendant**, then return to the slanted pillar, hop across the gap and quickly go after Leblanc before time runs out. If you beat Leblanc's Syndicate to the Save Sphere, you'll see them hanging from a ledge below a chest. Open the chest to obtain a **Muscle Belt**.

*Dash all the way around the tower to find this hidden chest.*

*Jump across this gap to reach the top.*

*If you fail to reach the top chest before time runs out, the chest will be empty. Either way, continue to climb the cliff ledges and go up the stairs.*

## BORIS

BOSS FIGHT

For the most part, Boris the spider presents a fairly straightforward brawl. Switch dresspheres (if needed) so that at least two characters can attack, while the third slips into the Songstress dressphere and casts Darkness Dance on the fiend every other round. A single attack by this powerful creature can cause about 50 HP damage, so immediately use a Potion on a character who drops below 70 HP. If Boris gets to use its Sticky End attack, check to see if anyone's battle gauge turns gray and stops. This indicates that the character has been inflicted with Stop status, and the only way to cure it at this point is to use a Remedy or wait for the ailment to go away. Otherwise, attack and blind Boris to win the battle.

**HP:** 480 **MP:** 0 **EXP:** 26 **AP:** 1

**GIL DROPPED:** 300
**PILFER GIL:** 700

**STEAL:** Normal: Remedy  Rare: Remedy (x2)
**DROP:** Normal: Star Pendant  Rare: Star Pendant

MT. GAGAZET

## HOTSPOT ALERT!

Back on the bridge of the Celsius, speak to Brother and choose the option "Comfort him," then speak to Shinra to view the contents of the sphere that was taken from the Floating Ruins. Although the images recorded on the device don't reveal much, the sphere turns out to be the **Black Mage Dressphere**. If you equip a character with this dressphere for the rest of Chapter 1, you will be satisfied with the results.

Afterward, Buddy reports new Hotspots for sphere activity. The Hotspots are Besaid Island and Zanarkand Ruins. If you go to Zanarkand after exploring Besaid Island, you will trigger the Kilika sphere hunt.

*Buddy won't allow you to navigate to any location until Shinra shows you the contents of the sphere.*

*Once you visit Zanarkand after exploring Besaid Island, you'll be on a collision course with the end of Chapter 1. Visit other locations first!*

Characters

1

Garment Grids & Dc:spheres

2

Battle System

3

4

Accessories

Items and Item Shops

5

Walkthrough

Chapter 1

Chapter 2

Chapter 3

Chapter 4

Chapter 5

Mini-Games

7

Fiends and Enemies

8

## HOTSPOTS ARE A FAST TRACK!

*If you go to Zanarkand after exploring Besaid Island and complete the mission, you're taken straight to Kilika for the final mission of Chapter 1. Consequently, you will miss all the extras that Chapter 1 offers, as well as a hefty amount of story completion percentage.*

*Hotspots do not disappear for any reason. The missions at Besaid and Zanarkand will remain until you visit every other location. This walkthrough is organized to help you visit every location in Spira before completing Chapter 1. Visit the locations in the order presented to get the most from the game.*

BESAID ISLAND

### ACTION CHECKLIST

**3** Return to Lulu's hut and rest.

**7** Input the four ciphers into the panel of the mysterious door.

**4** Exit the hut and find Lulu; agree to search for Wakka.

**8** Speak to Wakka inside the cave.

**1** Enter the village of Besaid and reunite with Wakka.

**5** Speak to the villagers to learn the order of the ciphers.

**9** Search the cave to find the White Mage dressphere.

**2** Enter Lulu's home and catch up on current events.

**6** Locate the four ciphers on Besaid Island.

**10** Talk to Wakka to receive the Besaid Sphere.

**COMPLETION: +2.2%**

## WANDERING FIENDS

**CHOCOBO**
HP: 368 | AP: 0 | Gil: 0
Steal: N/A
Drop: N/A

**COEURL**
HP: 320 | AP: 1 | Gil: 30
Steal: Phoenix Down
Drop: Potion (x2)

**COYOTE**
HP: 74 | AP: 1 | Gil: 10
Steal: Potion
Drop: Potion

**FLAN AZUL**
HP: 55 | AP: 1 | Gil: 20
Steal: Potion
Drop: Potion

**IRON GIANT**
HP: 222 | AP: 1 | Gil: 40
Steal: Budget Grenade
Drop: Budget Grenade

**PURPUREA**
HP: 196 | AP: 1 | Gil: 18
Steal: Echo Screen
Drop: Echo Screen

**SAHAGIN**
HP: 60 | AP: 1 | Gil: 7
Steal: Potion
Drop: Potion

**SALLET**
HP: 60 | AP: 1 | Gil: 10
Steal: Potion
Drop: Potion

**FLAME DRAGON**
HP: 980 | AP: 1 | Gil: 300
Steal: Hi-Potion
Drop: Red Ring

## ITEM CHECKLIST

Chocobo Wing (x2)
Hi-Potion
1000 gil

Potion (x2)
White Mage Dressphere
Besaid Sphere **E**

Protection Halo Garment Grid **E**
Ether

## MAPS

Chocobo Wing (x2)

Hi-Potion

1000 gil

To Chamber of the Fayth

White Mage Dressphere

Ether

Potion (x2)

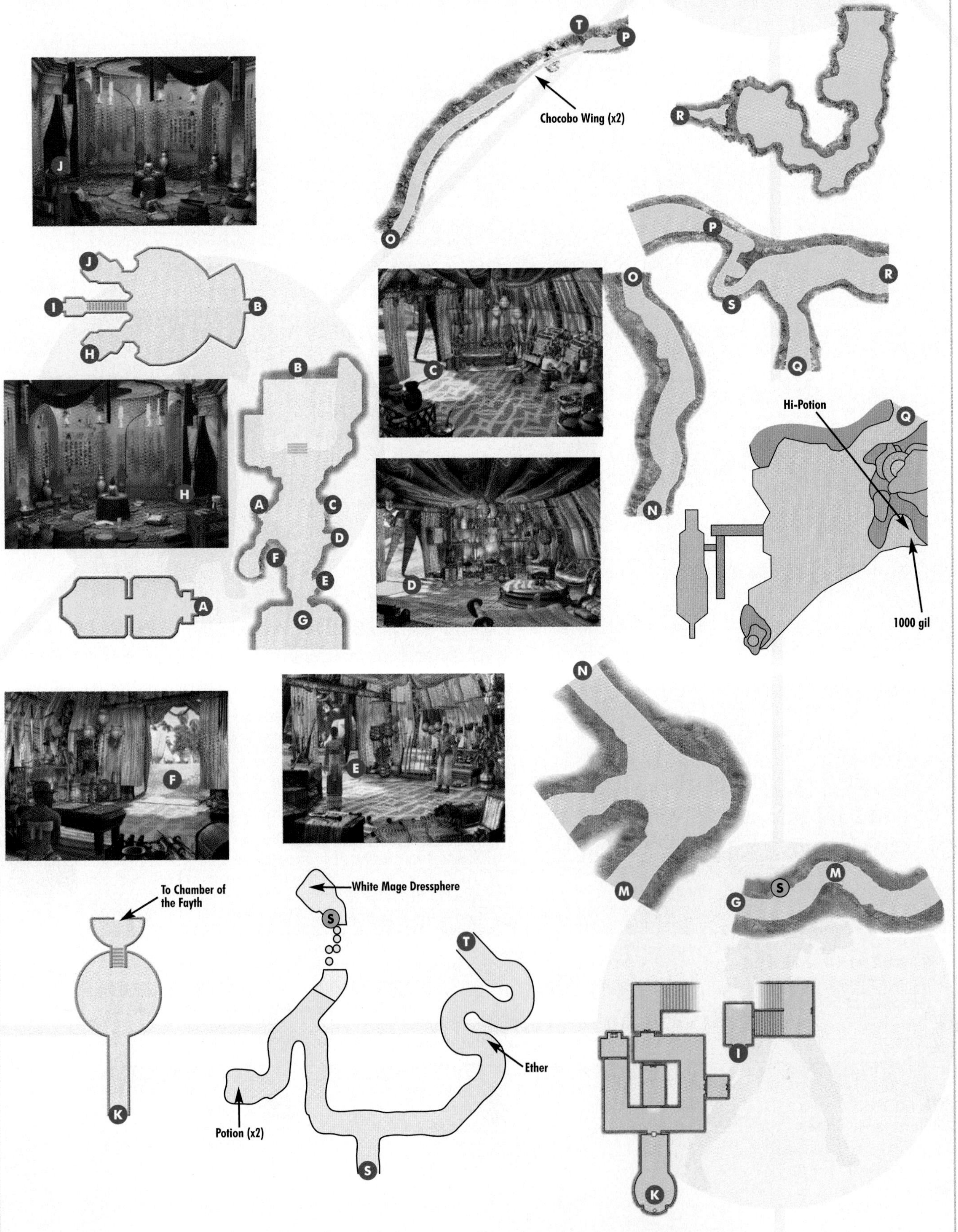

# HOMECOMING

Engage a series of scenes by following the first couple of steps in the Action Checklist section. After resting for the night at Wakka's place, exit the hut and speak to Lulu. Accept the "Where's Wakka?" mission, and speak to people around the village to get clues on the whereabouts of a mysterious cave. To penetrate the cave, you must locate four numbers hidden in various locations around the island and input them in the correct order into the security panel on the door barring the entrance of the cave. Collectively, the people of the village will tell you everything you need to know to complete this mission. After speaking to the appropriate people (see the following screenshots and captions), exit the village and follow the path to the beach area:

*The woman standing near the exit of town has the best clue regarding the location of the cave.*

*Jassu, behind the counter at the lodge, knows where cipher number one is located.*

*Datto, resting at the back of the lodge, indicates where to find cipher number four.*

*Speak to the man in shorts wandering around town to learn about the "Four Ciphers."*

*Talk with the young woman walking her dog to learn the locations of ciphers two and three of the four-number code.*

# THE FOUR CIPHERS

Head up the hill from the village to the second outdoor area. Check the on-screen map to find a purple beacon near the shrine at the cliff's edge. Examine the shrine to view a number. The number is randomly generated, so make a note of it. This number is the first of the four ciphers. Continue downhill into the ruins area. Climb up the first broken column on the left and search to find the last number of the four-digit combination.

*This is the first cipher of the four-digit code.*

*The cipher found atop this column is the last in the series.*

*Treasure chests sometimes rest in strange places.*

Keep moving uphill after Brother contacts the group. As you approach the bridge in the waterfall area, move to the left of the bridge to drop down to the rocky area at the bottom of the falls. A treasure chest on the rocks contains a **Chocobo Wing (x2)**. Exit the area by climbing out the way you dropped down.

---

*This is the door you seek to open. Just two more ciphers to go…*

Cross the bridge and continue into the overgrown area. Among the rough, move to the left side of the screen to notice some steps and a door with a number key lock. You don't yet have all of the numbers for the code, so continue down the slope and head toward the beach area.

At the beach, go back a few steps to the left to see a kid on a rock ledge higher up. Press Circle to hop up to the kid, then continue climbing up to the ruins. Check the flashing beacon to find another cipher, then move left across the ledge and jump across the gap to a grassy rise. Drop from the rise into a secret sandy cove, where two chests contain a **Hi-Potion** and **1000 gil**. To climb out of the cove, climb onto the cargo boxes stacked near the cliff face. Proceed across the beach, following the shoreline until you reach the grassy rocks at the far end. Climb up those rocks and check the beacon there to find the last number.

*The cipher that is third in the series is hidden amongst these ruins.*

*Leap from the backside of the ruins into this cove, open the two chests, and use the crates to climb out.*

Return to the cave entrance. When you have all of the ciphers, they will be displayed at the top of the screen in the correct order. Input the number combination into the panel beside the door and proceed into the cave.

*The second and last remaining cipher lies among these rocks at the far end of the beach.*

*If you didn't take the time to get clues from the villagers, just input the ciphers in the order described in the captions for all the screenshots above.*

# SECRET OF THE CAVE

After speaking to Wakka in the cave, move to the dead-end on the right to locate another panel for cipher input. Sorry, but the correct ciphers won't be revealed until later in the game. Follow the cave to the first intersection, where Brother checks up on Yuna yet again. Take the left branch to a chest containing a **Potion (x2)**, then return to the intersection and head the other way, jumping and climbing across some narrow rock platforms. Use the Save Sphere on the other side, then proceed into the chamber at the end and examine the sphere on the pedestal.

*Use the Save Sphere after jumping over these rocks.*

---

# FLAME DRAGON

The Flame Dragon is strong versus fire and weak versus cold. Use the Warrior's Ice Brand attack and the Black Mage's Blizzard spell to quickly break down this fiend. Meanwhile, a Songstress can successfully cast Darkness Dance, although the Flame Dragon seems capable of inflicting damage even while blinded. A much better use for a third character is to administer Potions. Be prepared to recoup each time the Flame Dragon breathes fire, which causes between 100-175 points of damage to each character. After bathing in the flames, use a full combat round to heal the entire party.

**HP:** 980 **MP:** 84 **EXP:** 60 **AP:** 1

**GIL DROPPED:** 300
**PILFER GIL:** 800

**STEAL:** Normal: Hi-Potion  Rare: Hi-Potion (x2)
**DROP:** Normal: Red Ring  Rare: Red Ring

## THE SECOND CIPHERS

The shop is in the first tent to the left as you enter the village of Besaid. The shop person sells rare items for large amounts of gil that you probably can't afford just yet. During Chapter 1, she offers a Besaid Key for 900,000 gil. This is the key that unlocks the treasure chest inside the north chamber inside Besaid Temple. If, by some very hard work, you've accumulated this much already, purchase the key and use it to unlock the chest in the north room of the temple to receive the **Search Sphere**, then speak to the man in the south chamber to determine how to use it.

*Got gil? Probably not…*  *…but if you do, this is where you'll find the Search Sphere.*

*Answer this man honestly for clues regarding the second four ciphers.*

If you intend to purchase the key but don't have the gil required, don't speak to the clerk until you're ready! Each time you visit the shop and inquire about the key, there is a 25% chance that the key will have been sold to a traveler. The chance for the clerk to sell the key to the traveler increases to 50% if you have spoken to the priest sitting cross-legged in the south chamber inside the temple of the fayth.

The Search Sphere enables you to find four more ciphers for the door inside the cave where Wakka was found. Along the path, you'll find a chest containing an **Ether**. This path eventually leads to a ledge high above the waterfall area, where an extra Garment Grid is located. For more details, refer to the section on Besaid Island in Chapter 3.

*Paying a high price for the Besaid Key now enables you to ransack this chest in Chapters 1 and 2, instead of having to wait until Chapter 3.*

Since you probably can't afford such exorbitant prices at this early stage of the game, return to the shop and speak to the clerk again in Chapter 3. At this later point in the game, the clerk will be desperately attempting to sell the key for a much lower price, and you can easily acquire and use the Search Sphere at that time.

| BESAID ISLAND SHOP | |
|---|---|
| **ITEM** | **COST** |
| Potion | 50 |
| Phoenix Down | 100 |
| Antidote | 50 |
| Eye Drops | 50 |
| Echo Screen | 50 |
| Soft | 50 |
| Holy Water | 300 |
| Watery Gleam | 3000 |
| Blue Ring | 3000 |

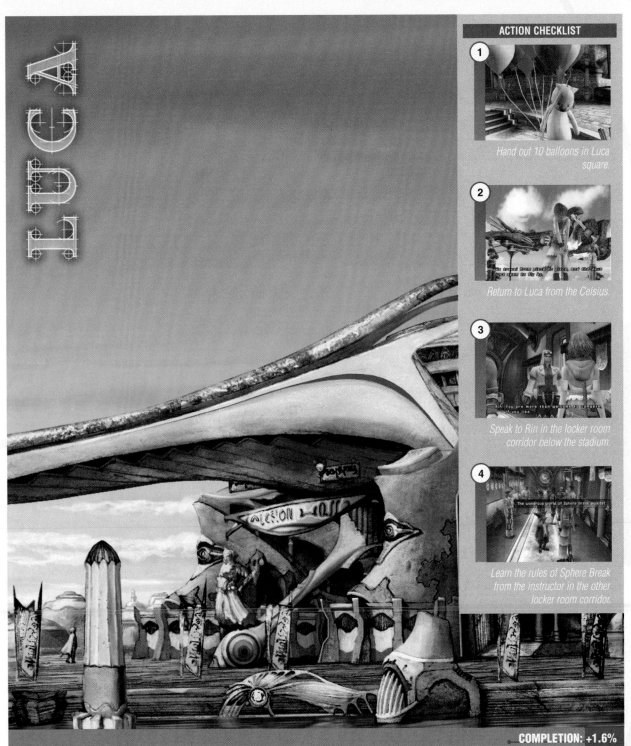

# LUCA

Characters

Garment Grids
& Dressspheres

Battle System

Accessories

Items and
Item Shops

Walkthrough

Chapter 1

Chapter 2

Chapter 3

Chapter 4

Chapter 5

Mini-Games

Fiends and
Enemies

## ACTION CHECKLIST

**1** Hand out 10 balloons in Luca square.

**2** Return to Luca from the Celsius.

**3** Speak to Rin in the locker room corridor below the stadium.

**4** Learn the rules of Sphere Break from the instructor in the other locker room corridor.

**COMPLETION: +1.6%**

## ITEM CHECKLIST

Healing Wind Garment Grid **E**

Lunar Curtain (x2)

*Al Bhed Primer **E**

Helm Coins (x5) **E**

Zurvan Coins (x5) **E**

Coyote Coins (x5) **E**

Flan Coins (x5) **E**

**\*Only if you haven't mastered Al Bhed.**

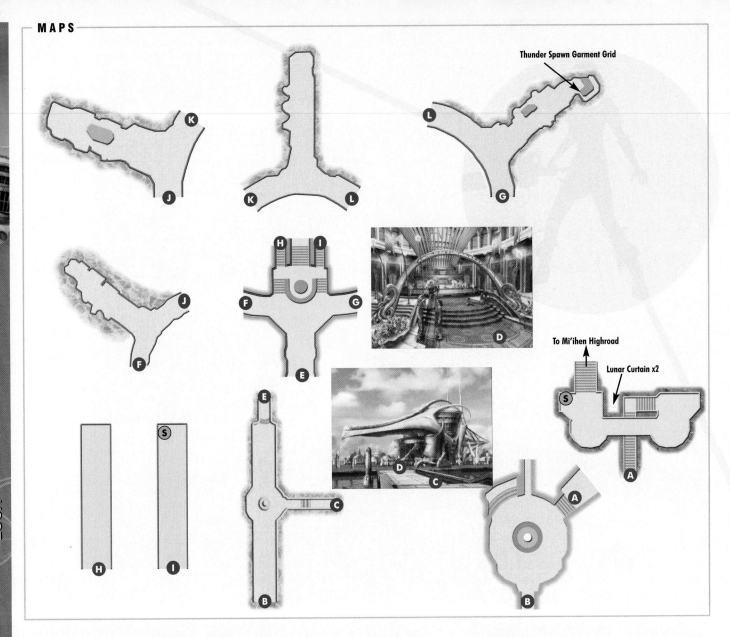

Thunder Spawn Garment Grid

To Mi'ihen Highroad

Lunar Curtain x2

# PROMOTING THE IMPOSTOR

Return to Luca for a little fanfare following the concert. Dressed as a moogle, Yuna must hand out 10 balloons in the plaza area. The child running in a circle and a man dressed in green will not accept balloons, but everyone else will. Give a balloon to the man standing near the door at the back of the red carpet area. Also, there are two people hidden behind a window near the café. Examine the window to open it. Give each person behind the shield a balloon. After completing this task, Yuna receives the **Healing Wind Garment Grid**. This Garment Grid enables the user to cast Cure. It also allows the user to cast Cura and Curaga by changing dressspheres during combat.

Open the window at the café in the back of the area.

Give balloons to these two guys, and everyone else in the square who will take one.

Give this hidden man a balloon as well.

# INTRODUCING SPHERE BREAK

After completing the first mission in Luca and returning to the Celsius, return to Luca again. Descend the stairs, and this time, notice a chest on a small islet just over the curb. Climb onto the curb and jump over the tree to the chest that contains a **Lunar Curtain (x2)** during Chapter 1. This chest reappears during different chapters, so check it out each time.

Climb onto the curb, then jump over the chest.

Rin also encourages your language studies by handing over **Al Bhed Primer XXII**.

Travel to the stadium and go down the stairs behind the information booth and to the right of the entrance to the stadium. Those who played *FINAL FANTASY X* will instantly recognize Rin of the Al Bhed Travel Agency. He is introducing Sphere Break, a mini-game that people can't stop playing in Luca.

To learn how to play Sphere Break, exit the corridor and head to the other locker room corridor to the left of the entrance to the stadium. Speak to the little person in blue standing at the front of the crowd and ask questions to learn about Sphere Break. The important question to ask is "Tell me the rules!" for which you receive **5 Helm Coins**, **5 Zurvan Coins**, **5 Coyote Coins**, and **5 Flan Coins**. You'll then learn how to play Sphere Break from start to finish. After reading all the tutorials, speak to the little blue person again to practice Sphere Break. Learn as much about Sphere Break as possible because there is a tournament in Luca during Chapter 3!

*This little person knows all the rules. Read the tutorials because your skills and knowledge of the game will be tested in Chapter 3's tournament.*

# MI'IHEN HIGHROAD

### ACTION CHECKLIST

1

*Yuna remembers her journey on the Mi'ihen Highroad.*

**COMPLETION: +0.2%**

## WANDERING FIENDS

**BULLY CAP**
HP: 94 | AP: 1 | Gil: 14
Steal: Eye Drops
Drop: Eye Drops

**DIVEBEAK**
HP: 10 | AP: 1 | Gil: 12
Steal: Potion
Drop: Antidote

**FLAN PALIDO**
HP: 188 | AP: 1 | Gil: 30
Steal: Potion
Drop: Potion

**FLY EYE**
HP: 258 | AP: 1 | Gil: 20
Steal: Phoenix Down
Drop: Phoenix Down

**IRON GIANT**
HP: 222 | AP: 1 | Gil: 40
Steal: Budget Grenade
Drop: Budget Grenade

**PURPUREA**
HP: 196 | AP: 1 | Gil: 18
Steal: Echo Screen
Drop: Echo Screen

**QUADRICORN**
HP: 188 | AP: 1 | Gil: 13
Steal: Echo Screen
Drop: Potion

**SHANTAK**
HP: 1130 | AP: 1 | Gil: 120
Steal: Remedy
Drop: Phoenix Down

**WILD WOLF**
HP: 185 | AP: 1 | Gil: 12
Steal: Potion
Drop: Potion

## ITEM CHECKLIST

| | | | | |
|---|---|---|---|---|
| Phoenix Down (x2) | Antidote (x2) | Iron Bangle | Phoenix Down (x2) | Echo Screen (x2) |
| 500 gil | Holy Water (x2) | Eye Drops (x2) | Budget Grenade (x2) | Soft (x2) |
| Circlet | Potion (x2) | Potion | Mana Spring | |

Characters

1

Garment Grids & Dresspheres

2

Battle System

3

Accessories

4

Items and Item Shops

5

Walkthrough
Chapter 1
Chapter 2
Chapter 3
Chapter 4
Chapter 5

6

Mini-Games

7

Fiends and Enemies

8

MI'IHEN HIGHROAD

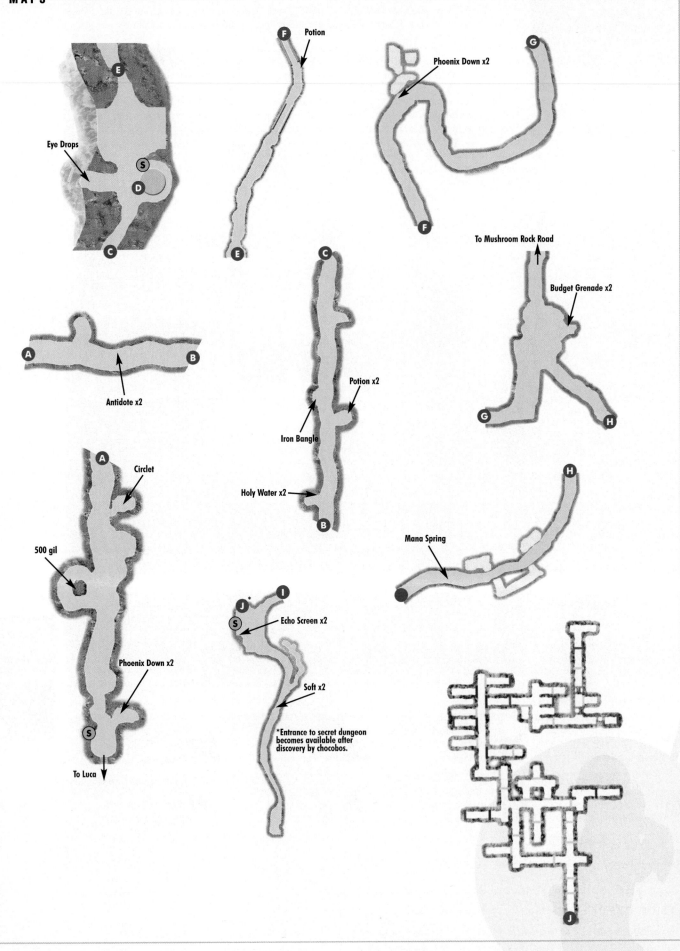

Potion

Phoenix Down x2

To Mushroom Rock Road

Budget Grenade x2

Eye Drops

Antidote x2

Potion x2

Iron Bangle

Holy Water x2

Circlet

500 gil

Mana Spring

Phoenix Down x2

Echo Screen x2

Soft x2

To Luca

*Entrance to secret dungeon
becomes available after
discovery by chocobos.

The Mi'ihen Highroad is just as populated as ever with interesting people.

Enter the Mi'ihen Highroad to gain a few story completion points. Speak to the people near the entrance if you desire. The guy by the stairs explains the benefits of riding a hover versus using a chocobo like in the old days. Speak to the person closer to the Save Sphere if you want to ride a hover to another destination; it only costs 30 gil. However, traveling up the Mi'ihen Highroad on foot is a great way to level up, learn abilities, and gain some items from chests.

## HIGHROAD TRAVEL AGENCY SHOP

| ITEM | COST |
|------|------|
| Potion | 50 |
| Phoenix Down | 100 |
| Antidote | 50 |
| Eye Drops | 50 |
| Echo Screen | 50 |
| Soft | 50 |
| Holy Water | 300 |
| Iron Bangle | 500 |
| Silver Bracer | 500 |
| Gauntlets | 2500 |
| Tiara | 2500 |

# MUSHROOM ROCK ROAD

## ACTION CHECKLIST

1. Speak with Yaibal.

2. Talk to Clasko.

3. Follow Leblanc's men into the ravine.

4. Confront Logos and Ormi at the Den of Woe.

5. Learn about the Den from Maroda.

6. Cross Mushroom Rock Road until Elma greets the party.

7. Ride the elevator to the higher level.

8. Speak to Lucil two times at the entrance of Youth League Headquarters.

9. Listen to Maechen's full story.

10. Return to the entrance and talk to Clasko. Agree to let him ride on the airship.

11. Aboard the Celsius, Shinra plays the contents of Crimson Sphere 9.

12. Check up on Clasko in the Cabin area.

COMPLETION: +4.6%

Characters

Garment Grids & Dresspheres

Battle System

Accessories

Items and Item Shops

Walkthrough
Chapter 1
Chapter 2
Chapter 3
Chapter 4
Chapter 5

Mini-Games

Fiends and Enemies

## WANDERING FIENDS

**BULLY CAP**
HP: 94 | AP: 1 | Gil: 14
Steal: Eye Drops
Drop: Eye Drops

**COYOTE**
HP: 74 | AP: 1 | Gil: 10
Steal: Potion
Drop: Potion

**RED ELEMENTAL**
HP: 99 | AP: 1 | Gil: 26
Steal: Potion
Drop: Potion

**TONBERRY**
HP: 9999 | AP: 2 | Gil: 300
Steal: Ether
Drop: Hi-Potion

## ITEM CHECKLIST

1000 gil

Turbo Ether

Phoenix Down

Hi-Potion

Crimson Sphere 9 **E**

Glass Buckle **E**

Heart of Flame Garment Grid **E**

Favorite Outfit

Restless Sleep Garment Grid

## MAPS

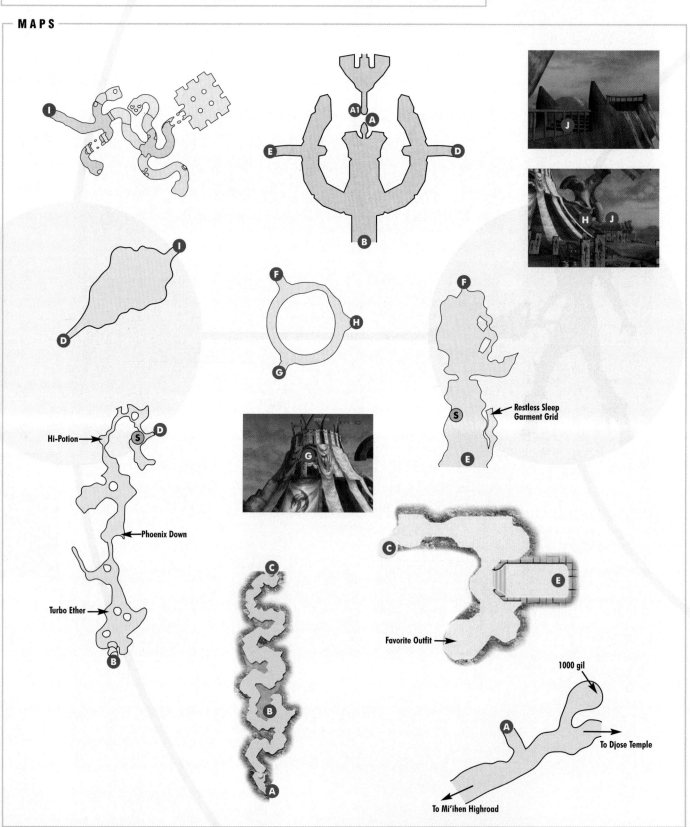

Hi-Potion

Phoenix Down

Turbo Ether

Restless Sleep Garment Grid

Favorite Outfit

1000 gil

To Djose Temple

To Mi'ihen Highroad

82

# YOUTH LEAGUE GREETINGS

Entering from the Mi'ihen Highroad, the girls spot Leblanc's cronies traveling ahead. Continue forward until Yaibal addresses Lady Yuna. Agree to destroy the fiends on the road, then speak to Clasko, a recognizable character from *FINAL FANTASY X*. Continue up the road to collect the **1000 gil** from the treasure chest near the statue of Mi'ihen, then return to the Youth League greeting party and head past them into the next area.

# FOGGY FIEND FRENZY

Follow Logos and Ormi into the ravine, and fight through the lower areas, collecting the items from the chests along the way. Upon reaching a Save Sphere, go inside a cave to confront the bandits. When they flee, Logos and Ormi leave behind the **Crimson Sphere 9** in their haste. Examine the strange door to see something weird and mysterious, then head toward the exit to speak with Maroda. Leave the cave and run back to the point where you dropped into the lower area.

## TONBERRY TERROR

*If you encounter a Tonberry, run away! These deceptively small creatures have 9999 HP and inflict tremendous damage to low-level characters. Only by casting your most powerful spells repeatedly will you defeat a Tonberry. Offering little EXP and AP, the only advantage to fighting a Tonberry is that they are added to Shinra's bestiary. Otherwise, you might steal Ethers and pilfer large amounts of gil from them. However, the chance to steal from them is very small. Unless you like taking extreme risks, command your party to escape after successfully robbing the monster.*

# MEETING WITH THE YOUTH LEAGUE

Continue across the upper part of Mushroom Rock to the north lift and ride it up to the elevator level. After speaking with Elma, the mission is complete. The party receives a **Glass Buckle** and the **Heart of Flame Garment Grid**. After the scene, move below the guards and open the treasure chest on the lower ledge to obtain **Favorite Outfit**. Get on the elevator and ride to the level above.

Move to the rear of the elevator and press X.

Hidden on a ledge just outside Youth League Headquarters is a chest containing the **Restless Sleep Garment Grid**.

Maechen reveals the entire backstory regarding New Yevon and the Youth League.

Go up to the entrance of the Youth League Headquarters building and speak to Lucil twice to view two different scenes. After speaking with Lucil, find Maechen off to the right. Speak to him and ask him to tell you a story. Use the "Please go on" option if you want to proceed, or use the "Enough, enough!" option to quit. Get through the entire story to understand past events that will come into play throughout the game, and to ensure you gain all the completion percentage possible.

# ENDING CLASKO'S MISERY

When you're finished, run through Mushroom Rock back to where Yaibal greeted the party. Continue down toward the Save Sphere and speak to Clasko, who is shaking his head in agony near the edge of the cliff. Allow him to ride onboard the airship by choosing the option, "The more the merrier!" Use the Save Sphere to return to the Celsius, speak to Shinra, and watch Crimson Report 1, which was on the sphere you found in the ravine. Then go down to the Cabin and speak to Clasko, who's standing on the upper level by the window.

Poor Clasko... Will he ever find his true calling? Perhaps you can help and benefit in the process.

Characters

Garment Grids & Dresspheres

Battle System

Accessories

Items and Item Shops

Walkthrough
Chapter 1
Chapter 2
Chapter 3
Chapter 4
Chapter 5

Mini-Games

Fiends and Enemies

# DJOSE TEMPLE

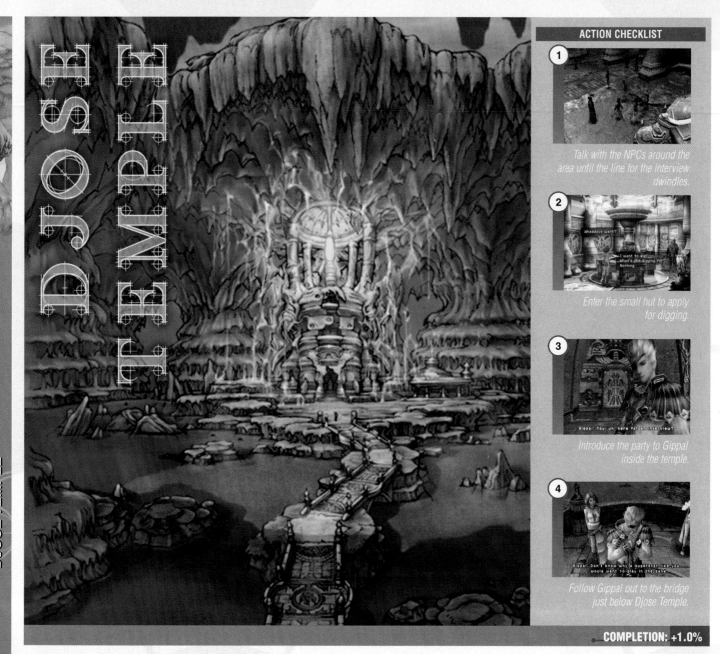

**ACTION CHECKLIST**

1. Talk with the NPCs around the area until the line for the interview dwindles.

2. Enter the small hut to apply for digging.

3. Introduce the party to Gippal inside the temple.

4. Follow Gippal out to the bridge just below Djose Temple.

**COMPLETION: +1.0%**

## WANDERING FIENDS

**AGAMA**
HP: 133 | AP: 1 | Gil: 16
Steal: Hi-Potion
Drop: Antidote

**CHOCOBO**
HP: 368 | AP: 0 | Gil: 0
Steal: N/A
Drop: N/A

**DEATH DAUBER**
HP: 78 | AP: 1 | Gil: 12
Steal: Potion
Drop: Potion

**SALLET**
HP: 60 | AP: 1 | Gil: 10
Steal: Potion
Drop: Potion

**BANDIT**
HP: 132 | AP: 1 | Gil: 30
Steal: Budget Grenade
Drop: Potion

**GOLD ELEMENTAL**
HP: 99 | AP: 1 | Gil: 25
Steal: Electro Marble
Drop: Electro Marble

## ITEM CHECKLIST

Phoenix Down
Echo Screen
Potion (x2)

*Al Bhed Primer **E**
Letter of Introduction **E**

*Only if you haven't mastered Al Bhed.

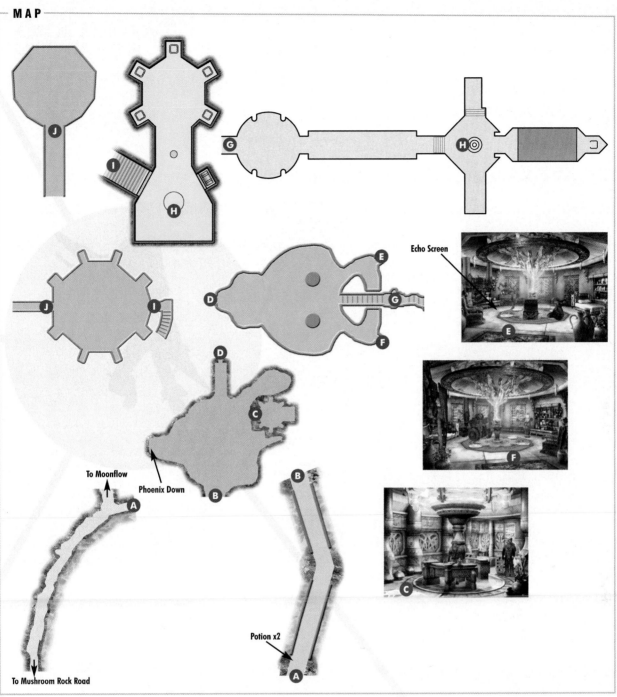

Echo Screen

To Moonflow

Phoenix Down

Potion x2

To Mushroom Rock Road

Characters

Garment Grids & Dresspheres

Battle System

Accessories

Items and Item Shops

Walkthrough

**Chapter 1**

Chapter 2

Chapter 3

Chapter 4

Chapter 5

Mini-Games

Fiends and Enemies

# GOTTA GET PAID!

Many people are gathered around the Djose Temple entrance waiting to be interviewed by Machine Faction leader Gippal. After the leader arrives, a line forms in front of the shop off to the right. Simply wait in this area until all of the other applicants go inside. To expedite the wait, sneak off to the far side of the area to find a chest containing a **Phoenix Down**, or spend some time speaking to the other people standing around the area.

*You can take Gippal's letter directly to Bikanel Desert, or you can explore this region further and cross the Moonflow for old time's sake.*

After all of the applicants have gone inside, enter and speak to the man at the counter. Tell him you want to dig, then exit the building and go inside the temple. After speaking with Gippal, you receive the **Al Bhed Primer IV**. Follow Gippal out of the temple. Leave the temple grounds and continue across the bridge. After expressing an interest in the job, Gippal will hand over the **Letter of Introduction**. After the scene, head across the bridge to find a chest with a **Potion (x2)** inside.

*Wait for the line to more forward.*

# MOONFLOW

COMPLETION: +0.6%

## WANDERING FIENDS

**AGAMA**
HP: 133 | AP: 1 | Gil: 16
Steal: Hi-Potion
Drop: Antidote

**BANDIT**
HP: 132 | AP: 1 | Gil: 140
Steal: Budget Grenade
Drop: Potion

**CHOCOBO**
HP: 368 | AP: 0 | Gil: 0
Steal: N/A
Drop: N/A

**FLAN AZUL**
HP: 55 | AP: 1 | Gil: 20
Steal: Potion
Drop: Potion

**PROTOCHIMERA**
HP: 420 | AP: 1 | Gil: 120
Steal: Potion
Drop: Phoenix Down

**QUADRICORN**
HP: 188 | AP: 1 | Gil: 13
Steal: Echo Screen
Drop: Potion

**SHELL SHOCKER**
HP: 4700 | AP: 1 | Gil: 780
Steal: Iron Bangle
Drop: Black Ring

**TAKOUBA**
HP: 984 | AP: 1 | Gil: 75
Steal: Phoenix Down
Drop: Phoenix Down

## ITEM CHECKLIST

Gun Mage Dressphere **E**
Circlet **E**
Helios Guard Garment Grid **E**

# CARAVAN BODYGUARDS

Enter the Moonflow via the navigation menu of the Celsius to trigger an extra scene. Then find a small person dressed in red running nervously around the area near the Moonflow Banks.

This is Tobli. He will reward you well for finding and protecting his caravan.

Head south from the banks of the Moonflow down the road toward Djose, and continue until a Hypello begs for help. For this mission, you must follow the wagon north on the Moonflow road. If any bandits steal any of the cargo, you must chase them down and get it back. Once you catch up to the bandit, press X to initiate a battle and defeat the bandits to retrieve the cargo. After doing so, move ahead of the caravan and the chocobo will begin to pull the wagon forward again.

*When the Hypello's wagon reaches a sharp bend in the road, move Yuna around the corner and the chocobo will resume travelling.*

When you reach the bank of the Moonflow, Tobli shows his appreciation to the Gullwings by offering the **Gun Mage dressphere**, a **Circlet**, and a **Helios Guard Garment Grid** as a reward! Ride the shoopuf across the Moonflow and race up the forest path to Guadosalam.

*Tobli proves to be a generous sort. It will benefit you greatly to assist him over and over again.*

## BANDIT THE BANDITS!

A Thief can steal lots of gil from bandits by using the Pilfer Gil ability. Talk about no honor among thieves!

COMPLETION: +0.4%

# LONGING FOR THE FARPLANE

The only thing to do in Guadosalam at this point is to gain a small amount of story completion by watching two scenes. After the initial cinema that occurs upon entering the town, move up the central ramp toward the Farplane entrance to view another scene. While you're here, stop at the item shop on the mid-level of town, which carries the best accessories you can purchase in Chapter 1. Afterwards, run back to the lower level and exit Guadosalam via the cave near the Save Sphere.

*Watch the second scene near the Farplane entrance to earn more completion %.*

| GUADOSALAM SHOP | |
|---|---|
| ITEM | COST |
| Potion | 50 |
| Antidote | 50 |
| Eye Drops | 50 |
| Echo Screen | 50 |
| Soft | 50 |
| Holy Water | 300 |
| Pearl Necklace | 4000 |
| Angel Earrings | 5000 |
| Gold Anklet | 5000 |
| Kinesis Badge | 10000 |
| Mute Shock | 15000 |
| Venom Shock | 15000 |

Characters

1

Garment Grids & Dresspheres

2

Battle System

3

Accessories

4

Items and Item Shops

5

Walkthrough

Chapter 1

Chapter 2

Chapter 3

Chapter 4

Chapter 5

Mini-Games

7

Fiends and Enemies

8

# THUNDER PLAINS

**COMPLETION: +0.2**

## WANDERING FIENDS

**BICOCETTE**
HP: 182　AP: 1　Gil: 18
Steal: Potion
Drop: Potion

**BOLT DRAKE**
HP: 623　AP: 1　Gil: 130
Steal: Lightning Marble
Drop: Hi-Potion

**CHOCOBO**
HP: 368　AP: 0　Gil: 0
Steal: N/A
Drop: N/A

**GOLD ELEMENTAL**
HP: 99　AP: 1　Gil: 25
Steal: Electro Marble
Drop: Electro Marble

**LESSER DRAKE**
HP: 577　AP: 1　Gil: 22
Steal: Potion
Drop: Potion

**OCHU**
HP: 1480　AP: 1　Gil: 133
Steal: Antidote
Drop: Antidote (x2)

**RED ELEMENTAL**
HP: 99　AP: 1　Gil: 25
Steal: Potion
Drop: Potion

**STALWART**
HP: 1240　AP: 1　Gil: 100
Steal: Phoenix Down
Drop: Phoenix Down (x2)

## ITEM CHECKLIST

Echo Screen (x3)
Potion (x2)
Black Choker
Phoenix Down
Grenade (x2)
Ether

## MAP

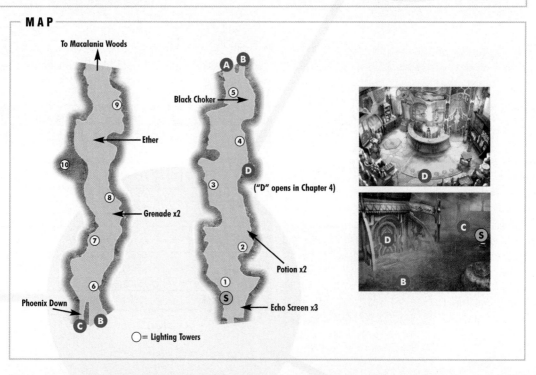

To Macalania Woods

Black Choker

("D" opens in Chapter 4)

Potion x2

Echo Screen x3

Ether

Grenade x2

Phoenix Down

○ = Lighting Towers

88

# HOME OF LIGHTNING

After Yuna's memoirs, move forward and speak to the Al Bhed near the entrance. Continue across the plains, gathering items and fighting fiends. Stop by the Travel Agency to use the Save Sphere and buy items. Continue through the area to Macalania Woods.

*Now that the lightning is under control, there's not much to do but cross the plains, fight, level up, and learn abilities!*

| THUNDER PLAINS TRAVEL AGENCY | |
|---|---|
| **ITEM** | **COST** |
| Potion | 50 |
| Phoenix Down | 100 |
| Antidote | 50 |
| Eye Drops | 50 |
| Echo Screen | 50 |
| Soft | 50 |
| Holy Water | 300 |
| Lightning Gleam | 3000 |
| Yellow Ring | 3000 |

**MACALANIA WOODS**

## ACTION CHECKLIST

**1** Speak to the three musicians at various locations in Macalania Woods.

**2** Converse four times with Tromell at the Sphere Spring.

**3** Visit the Al Bhed Travel Agency to learn that O'aka is in trouble.

**4** Chase O'aka back through the woods to the entrance point.

**5** Catch O'aka hiding in the tree.

**6** Give O'aka permission to come aboard the Celsius, or turn him in.

**COMPLETION: +2.2%**

## WANDERING FIENDS

**AMORPHOUS GEL**
HP: 973  AP: 1  Gil: 380
Steal: White Ring
Drop: Blue Ring

**CHOCOBO**
HP: 368  AP: 0  Gil: 0
Steal: N/A
Drop: N/A

**DEEP HAIZHE**
HP: 1030  AP: 1  Gil: 40
Steal: Gold Anklet
Drop: Hi-Potion

**GOLD ELEMENTAL**
HP: 99  AP: 1  Gil: 25
Steal: Electro Marble
Drop: Electro Marble

**HAIZHE**
HP: 653  AP: 1  Gil: 22
Steal: Phoenix Down
Drop: Potion

**RED ELEMENTAL**
HP: 99  AP: 1  Gil: 25
Steal: Potion
Drop: Potion

**SALLET**
HP: 60  AP: 1  Gil: 10
Steal: Potion
Drop: Potion

**WHITE ELEMENTAL**
HP: 77  AP: 1  Gil: 26
Steal: Antarctic Wind
Drop: Potion

**XIPHACTINUS**
HP: 77  AP: 1  Gil: 30
Steal: Fish Scale
Drop: Fish Scale

### ITEM CHECKLIST

Turbo Ether

White Ring

Full Throttle Dressphere ⓔ

Unerring Path Garment Grid ⓔ

*Al Bhed Primer ⓔ

Ice Queen Garment Grid ⓔ

**\*Only if you haven't mastered Al Bhed.**

MAP

Garment Grids & Dresspheres

2

Battle System

3

Accessories

4

Items and Item Shops

5

Walkthrough

Chapter 1

Chapter 2

Chapter 3

Chapter 4

Chapter 5

Mini-Games

7

Fiends and Enemies

8

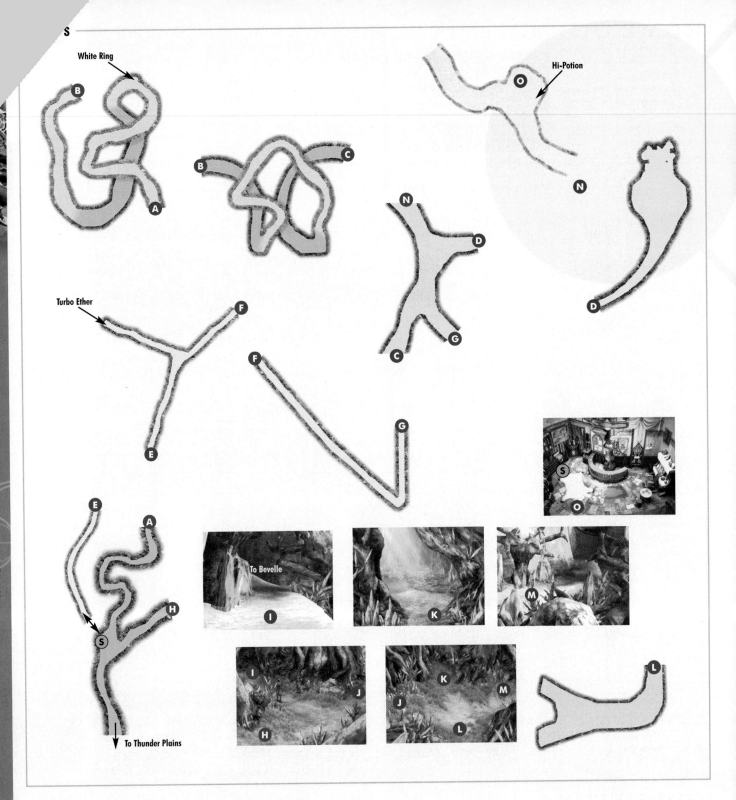

# FRIENDLY RESPONSES

Move toward the figure in blue standing at the foot of the tree branch path to trigger a scene wherein a musician goes to join some of his friends. Follow the path east of the Save Sphere, beyond where the Guado stands. Keep running past the two New Yevon guards into the next area. At the four-path intersection, follow the bottom path to the spring. Speak to Donga, the creature standing at the water's edge. Once Donga fades away, return to the Save Sphere and follow the tree branch path until you spot Pukutak. Speak to the small, brownish creature to initiate another scene. These actions let you accumulate a small amount of completion percentage. This storyline picks up again later in the game, but only if you trigger these mini-scenes.

Bayra is hard to miss as you're entering Macalania.

Donga stands near the spring's edge.

Pukutak stands on the tree branch path in the third section of Macalania Woods.

## FIGHTING AMORPHOUS GELS

*Amorphous Gels take very little damage from physical attacks, and these massive blobs have the ability to make themselves strong versus all elements—except one. The best method to defeat an Amorphous Gel is for a Gun Mage to use the Scan ability on the monster. Once you've determined the current weakness of the fiend, a Black Mage or a Warrior can use the proper abilities. However, keep a sharp eye on the creature just in case it uses the Barrier Shift ability to change its elemental weakness and absorption. Cast Scan on the monster again after each Barrier Shift to determine its new strengths and weaknesses.*

# FAITHFUL TROMELL

Follow the tree trunk path or the shimmering path until you reach a four-way split in the road. Going by the on-screen map, head up the top right fork. Proceed into the area until Yuna reunites with old acquaintance Tromell. Speak to him four times to trigger four separate dialogues. Eventually, he turns over the **Full Throttle** special dressphere for Paine and the **Unerring Path Garment Grid,** which makes transformation to special dresspheres very easy.

*Due to his regretful state, Tromell requires four conversations before he finally lightens up and hands over the goods.*

# O'AKA IN A PINCH

Return to the four-path fork area where the tree branch and shimmering paths converge, and head up the top left path to the Travel Agency area where a coup is in progress. The Al Bhed are hunting the new proprietor, O'aka, who apparently owes them a great deal of gil. After the first scene, you gain an **Al Bhed Primer,** and O'aka walks up behind the Gullwings. Speak to him, if you can, before he runs off. If you don't get a chance to do so, follow him back out of the area to begin the "Follow That O'aka!" mission.

The easiest way to find and catch O'aka is to use the glimmering path to return to the starting point of Macalania. Along the way, you'll see O'aka. When you reach the Save Sphere, head along the east path toward the spring. After just a few steps, O'aka can be seen dashing off again. Stay after him. Head past the two New Yevon guards to a path intersection. Using the on-screen map, take the top path to finally catch O'aka.

*O'aka XXIII has problems and you can benefit by helping him out.*

*The elder Guado on the right accidentally divulges O'aka's hiding spot.*

Speak to the elder Guado several times to get a clue as to O'aka's hiding spot, then move behind the tree to the left and search to spot O'aka in the tree. Speak to O'aka again after he's on ground level. By agreeing to hide him on the airship, he hands over the **Ice Queen Garment Grid**. Conversely, if you decide to turn O'aka over to the Al Bhed, his destiny takes a different path, but you still receive the garment grid. This is described in more detail later in the walkthrough.

If you choose to assist O'aka by letting him on the Celsius, return there and speak to the sketchy merchant in the Cabin. His debt to the Al Bhed appears on-screen. The gil amount purchased from him is subtracted from his 100,000 gil debt. If you don't repay the debt in your first game, the amount of debt remaining carries over to your New Game Plus with a 1,000 gil penalty. It is possible to pay down the debt in one game by merely using the Thief's Pilfer Gil ability on every enemy encountered. After erasing his debt, he begins to sell restorative items at next-to-nothing costs. In addition, if you can pay down his debt before the end of Chapter 3, he returns to Macalania Woods. There, he sets up a very valuable shop during Chapter 5.

*Buy 100,000 gil's worth of items and O'aka will treat you right.*

| O'AKA THE MERCHANT (STARTING PRICES) | | O'AKA THE MERCHANT (AFTER 100,000 GIL DEBT IS PAID) | |
|---|---|---|---|
| **ITEM** | **COST** | **ITEM** | **COST** |
| Potion | 49 | Potion | 5 |
| Hi-Potion | 490 | Hi-Potion | 50 |
| Phoenix Down | 98 | Phoenix Down | 10 |
| Antidote | 49 | Antidote | 5 |
| Eye Drops | 49 | Eye Drops | 5 |
| Echo Screen | 49 | Echo Screen | 5 |
| Soft | 49 | Soft | 5 |
| Holy Water | 29 | Holy Water | 30 |

Characters

1

Garment Grids & Dresspheres

2

Battle System

3

Accessories

4

Items and Item Shops

5

Walkthrough

Chapter 1
Chapter 2
Chapter 3
Chapter 4
Chapter 5

Mini-Games

7

Fiends and Enemies

8

# BIKANEL DESERT

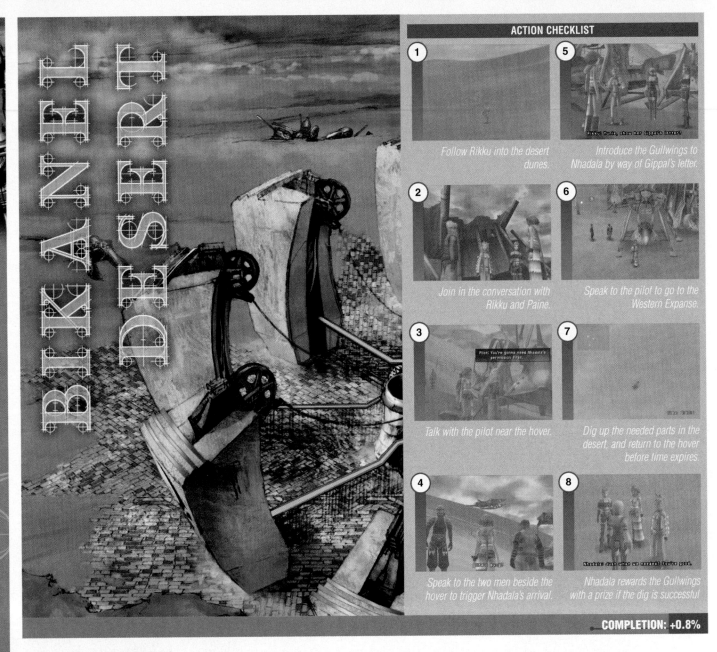

## ACTION CHECKLIST

**1** Follow Rikku into the desert dunes.

**2** Join in the conversation with Rikku and Paine.

**3** Talk with the pilot near the hover.

**4** Speak to the two men beside the hover to trigger Nhadala's arrival.

**5** Introduce the Gullwings to Nhadala by way of Gippal's letter.

**6** Speak to the pilot to go to the Western Expanse.

**7** Dig up the needed parts in the desert, and return to the hover before time expires.

**8** Nhadala rewards the Gullwings with a prize if the dig is successful

**COMPLETION: +0.8%**

## WANDERING FIENDS

**ANGRA MAINYU**
HP:333444 | AP:30 | Gil:5000
Steal: Megalixir
Drop: Ribbon

**BOLT DRAKE**
HP: 623 | AP: 1 | Gil: 130
Steal: Lightning Marble
Drop: Hi-Potion

**CHOCOBO**
HP: 368 | AP: 0 | Gil: 0
Steal: N/A
Drop: N/A

**FLY EYE**
HP: 258 | AP: 1 | Gil: 20
Steal: Phoenix Down
Drop: Phoenix Down

**HRIMTHURS**
HP: 552 | AP: 1 | Gil: 44
Steal: Phoenix Down
Drop: Phoenix Down

**KILLER HOUND**
HP: 202 | AP: 1 | Gil: 18
Steal: Potion
Drop: Potion

## ITEM CHECKLIST

*Al Bhed Primer **E**

Still of Night Garment Grid **E**

Elixir

***Only if you haven't mastered Al Bhed.**

**MAP**

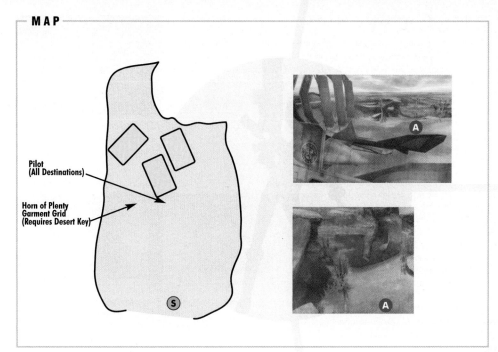

Pilot
(All Destinations)

Horn of Plenty
Garment Grid
(Requires Desert Key)

Characters

1

Garment Grids
& Dresspheres

2

Battle System

3

Accessories

4

Items and
Item Shops

5

Walkthrough 6
Chapter 1
Chapter 2
Chapter 3
Chapter 4
Chapter 5

Mini-Games

7

Fiends and
Enemies

8

# IN THE SANDS

Bikanel Desert becomes a Hotspot after you receive the **Letter of Introduction** from Gippal. Pilot the Celsius to Bikanel and follow Rikku into the desert. After some Al Bhed rescue the lost party, you receive an **Al Bhed Primer**. Speak to the man standing next to the Save Sphere if you want to buy items.

*The merchant calls you back if you attempt to leave the camp.*

| BIKANEL DESERT MERCHANT | |
|---|---|
| **ITEM** | **COST** |
| Potion | 50 |
| Phoenix Down | 100 |
| Antidote | 50 |
| Eye Drops | 50 |
| Echo Screen | 50 |
| Soft | 50 |
| Holy Water | 300 |
| Fiery Gleam | 3000 |
| Red Ring | 3000 |

# GET THIS DIG STARTED!

Follow the steps in the Action Checklist to initiate the first desert excavation for machine parts. Upon your arrival at the digging site, use the on-screen map as a guide and run to the yellow "X." When you reach the exact spot, Yuna automatically starts digging. After excavating the needed parts, you can return to the hover or attempt to dig at any of the other white "Xs" on the map. In some white "X" spots, it's possible to dig up useful items, Sphere Break coins, Al Bhed Primers, and accessories. Sometimes a white "X" marks a spot where enemies will ambush your party. Even if you don't get ambushed, random battles will occur.

*Whenever you dig, always go for the important item marked by the yellow "X" before chasing after other possible items.*

*You must touch the hover to complete or forfeit a dig.*

You may encounter competition while on an expedition. If another Al Bhed excavator beats you to a white "X", search somewhere else. Don't run too far from the hover, though. If you run out of time, the party suffers from water deprivation and the dig is scrapped. When the on-screen timer drops to roughly 12 seconds remaining, give up and head back to the hover if you've already excavated the yellow "X."

After you successfully complete a dig, you complete the mission and receive a 100 gil reward, the **Still of Night Garment Grid,** and an **Elixir**. At this point, you can return to the Celsius using the nearby Save Sphere, or you can dig some more. The only available location for digging in Chapter 1 is the Western Expanse. As you progress further into the game, more areas open up, and your gil reward for each excavation increases as you take promotion exams at Djose Temple. In addition, mastery of digging at an early stage may result in failure to complete certain events at Djose Temple very late in the game. More on this is explained in the "Chapter 5" section of the walkthrough. Until then, keep your digging to a minimum!

*Digging in Bikanel can be extremely rewarding to your pocketbook and your knowledge of the Al Bhed language.*

# REQUESTING HIGHER PAY

After each five to ten successful digs, return to Djose Temple and use the panel in the south chamber. The device offers a series of options, such as applying for a raise. If the device determines that you are eligible for a raise, you must answer a series of questions with the best attitude. If you score a certain number of points by answering questions, you'll receive a raise for digging. More information on excavation is included in the "Mini-Games" chapter, including the answers that will get you a raise!

Choosing the answers that best suit a professional digger isn't easy, since the answer isn't always what you might think.

# UNIDENTIFIED OBJECT APPROACHING!

Occurring randomly during your digging excursions, Picket may report something large heading your way. After a few moments, a large red arrow appears on the radar map and quickly converges on your location. If your yellow arrow touches the approaching red arrow, a battle against a truly ominous foe begins.

Angra Mainyu is a three-part monster. During Chapter 1, only the middle portion is active. Later, in Chapters 2 and 3, the right and left sub-monsters aid in the battle. The left and right subordinates cannot be targeted for attacks or spells right now. When only the center body is active, the sole attack of the creature is the Unnatural Selection attack, which flings the entire party off the battlefield, effectively ending combat. Angra Mainyu performs this attack after exactly 60 seconds or if its HP drops to a "bottom HP level" depending on the chapter you're currently playing. Refer to the table in this section for more details.

This monster proves extremely challenging to defeat, even for veteran RPG players.

Punching attacks from an active right or left arm reduces the party's ability to chain consecutive attacks during chapters after Chapter 1.

To defeat Angra Mainyu, use an item that accelerates one or all of the party members into Haste status, such as a Chocobo Feather or Chocobo Wing. Then chain together attacks in quick succession to prevent the monster from having a turn. If Angra Mainyu doesn't get a turn, it cannot perform Unnatural Selection. The best way to chain together rapid attacks is to transform all of the Gullwings into Thieves and attack in such a manner so that when one Thief attacks and causes the monster to stagger, the next Thief attacks before the creature can execute its turn. Another way to prevent it from having a turn is for all three party members to learn the Gunner's Trigger Happy Lv.3 ability, which greatly extends the time of the attack. Cast Haste on the party, wait until all three Gullwings are ready to have turns, then begin executing Trigger Happy one after another.

If Angra Mainyu manages to end the battle with the Unnatural Selection attack, its HP remains at the level where you left off. The next time you encounter this unique creature, it will be like picking up exactly where you left off. However, if you reduce the fiend's HP to the "bottom HP level" as shown in the following table, then Angra Mainyu recovers HP up to the "return HP" level before the next battle. For example, if you're fighting the fiend during Chapter 1 and lower its HP to 290,000 or less, the fiend returns with 300,099 HP when it is encountered again. If you reduce Angra Mainyu's HP to 240,000 during Chapter 2, it returns with 266,755 HP the next time you encounter it.

You will probably get blown out of battle several times before you actually defeat Angra Mainyu, but don't quit!

| ANGRA MAINYU'S HP BEHAVIOR—333,444 HP MAX | | | |
| --- | --- | --- | --- |
| CHAPTER | SUBORDINATES | BOTTOM HP | RETURN HP |
| 1 | None | 300,099 | 300,099 |
| 2 | Right Arm | 233,410 | 266,755 |
| 3 | Right Arm, Left Arm | 166,722 | 200,066 |

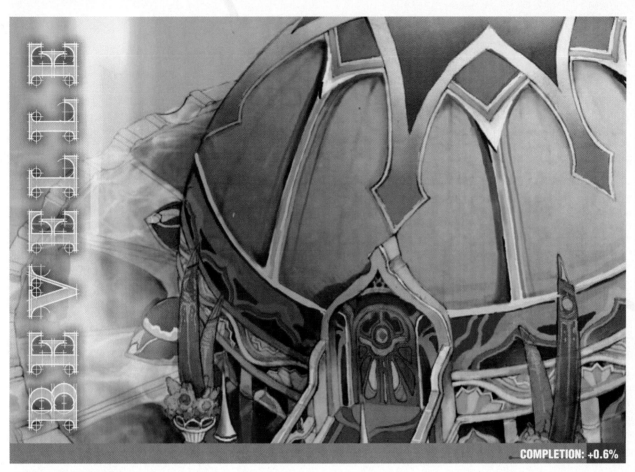

COMPLETION: +0.6%

**BEVELLE**

Characters

Garment Grids & Dressspheres

Battle System

Accessories

Items and Item Shops

Walkthrough
Chapter 1
Chapter 2
Chapter 3
Chapter 4
Chapter 5

Mini-Games

Fiends and Enemies

## ITEM CHECKLIST

Tiara 🅔

# UNEASY VISIT

When entering Bevelle from the Macalania Woods, use the Save Sphere on the left and speak to the old man on the right to ride the lift down the long path. In the next area, move Yuna forward until a woman greets the high summoner. Follow the young lady until a gentleman greets Yuna and goes to summon Praetor Baralai. After the scene, follow Baralai into New Yevon Headquarters. Ride the lift to the upper level and speak to Baralai again to receive a **Tiara**. Guards prevent access to other areas inside the HQ, so return to the Celsius.

*Chase after Baralai to get an item, not because he's cute.*

# CALM LANDS

**COMPLETION: +0.2%**

CALM LANDS

## WANDERING FIENDS

**AHRIMAN**
HP: 99 | AP: 1 | Gil: 20
Steal: Potion
Drop: Eye Drops

**AMORPHOUS GEL**
HP: 973 | AP:1 | Gil: 380
Steal: White Ring
Drop: Blue Ring

**CHOCOBO**
HP: 368 | AP: 0 | Gil: 0
Steal: N/A
Drop: N/A

**COEURL**
HP: 320 | AP: 1 | Gil: 30
Steal: Phoenix Down
Drop: Potion (x2)

**DEATH DAUBER**
HP: 78 | AP: 1 | Gil: 12
Steal: Potion
Drop: Potion

**DIVEBEAK**
HP: 10 | AP: 1 | Gil: 12
Steal: Potion
Drop: Antidote

**NASHORN**
HP: 482 | AP: 1 | Gil: 22
Steal: Potion
Drop: Potion

**WILD WOLF**
HP: 185 | AP: 1 | Gil: 12
Steal: Potion
Drop: Potion

## ITEM CHECKLIST

Ether    Phoenix Down    Chocobo Feather (x2)    Potion (x2)    Phoenix Down

## MAPS

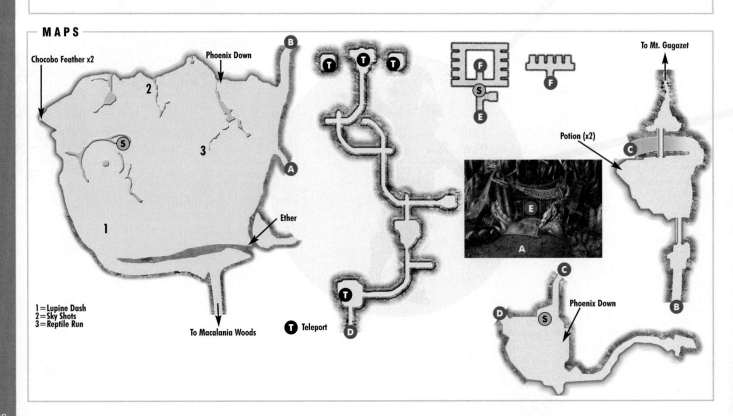

Chocobo Feather x2

Phoenix Down

To Mt. Gagazet

Potion (x2)

2

3

1

Ether

Phoenix Down

1 = Lupine Dash
2 = Sky Shots
3 = Reptile Run

To Macalania Woods

**T** Teleport

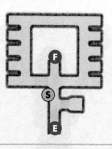

# THE MARKETING DEPARTMENT

The Calm Lands have become a tourist attraction, full of mini-games to play. Two companies are vying for dominance of the tourist trade: Open Air, Inc. and Argent, Inc. Thanks to Rikku and Paine, you have 100 credits to use at either agency. If you want to ride the hover to another part of the Calm Lands, pay the required 10 credits at either company.

To start the publicity campaign, speak to one company representative or the other at any hover, choose the "Publicity menu" option, then choose "Sign me up!" The company awards you publicity points for speaking to people all around Spira by pressing the Square button in an attempt to bolster and promote the company. Each person prefers to be pitched to in a different way. This quest is a game-long undertaking that will have you pitching your company to NPCs in every location during every chapter, so start talking it up!

*Return to the Calm Lands and speak to any representative to find out how your publicity campaign is going. Refer to the "Mini-Games" chapter for more information.*

# SPENDING CREDITS

Entering the Calm Lands from Macalania Woods, the first mini-game you should encounter is Lupine Dash, located in the southwest corner of the Calm Lands nearest to the starting point. Two people are standing near a hover. Speak to the person from Argent or the person from Open Air to start the game. If you need to purchase credits to play (you start with 100), purchase them for 10 gil apiece. Choose one or two winning hounds, and hope they win the race. The game pays out credits based on the odds of your hound winning.

*Across the field the lupines go, and who will win nobody knows.*

*Hope you scored high on Frogger, 'cause Reptile Run is twice as hard!*

Reptile Run is available from the people standing near the hover just northeast of the center of the Calm Lands. This game functions exactly like the classic arcade game "Frogger." Place a bet, then attempt to navigate your reptile through several lines of fiends. Use the line of spheres displayed on-screen to guide the reptile away from danger spots. If you get caught by a fiend, you lose. If you make it all the way to the other side, the game pays out your winnings based on the time it took for you to reach the finish line.

Sky Slots is the game being offered by the individuals standing near the hover close to the north edge of the Calm Lands. After placing a bet of one to five credits, you must attempt to line up three flying creatures of the same color. More information on all the games at the Calm Lands is covered in the "Mini-Games" chapter.

*Try to line up three flying creatures of the same color. Go ahead, just try!*

# A DECENT PROPOSAL

At the Travel Agency near the center of the massive plain is a man who's looking for a wife for his son. Whether you agree to be his wife or not, you can undertake a mission to find a wife for the young man. Approach women throughout Spira and press the Square button to talk to ladies about marrying the man's son. The "Matrimony" mission goes hand-in-hand with the "Publicity" mission. It's a wise idea to undertake both missions simultaneously if you are going to do them.

| CALM LANDS TRAVEL AGENCY ||
| --- | --- |
| **ITEM** | **COST** |
| Potion | 50 |
| Phoenix Down | 100 |
| Antidote | 50 |
| Eye Drops | 50 |
| Echo Screen | 50 |
| Soft | 50 |
| Holy Water | 300 |
| Iron Bangle | 500 |
| Silver Bracer | 500 |
| Wristband | 1000 |
| Amulet | 1000 |

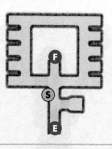

# MT. GAGAZET

## ACTION CHECKLIST

**1** Reunite with Kimahri.

**2** Answer the complaints of the Ronso in an attempt to unite the tribe.

**COMPLETION: +0.4%**

## WANDERING FIENDS

**AHRIMAN**
HP: 99 | AP: 1 | Gil: 20
Steal: Potion
Drop: Eye Drops

**BICOCETTE**
HP: 182 | AP: 1 | Gil: 18
Steal: Potion
Drop: Potion

**BULLY CAP**
HP: 94 | AP: 1 | Gil: 14
Steal: Eye Drops
Drop: Eye Drops

**FLAN PALIDO**
HP: 188 | AP: 1 | Gil: 30
Steal: Potion
Drop: Potion

**FLY EYE**
HP: 258 | AP: 1 | Gil: 20
Steal: Phoenix Down
Drop: Phoenix Down

**PROTOCHIMERA**
HP: 420 | AP: 1 | Gil: 120
Steal: Potion
Drop: Phoenix Down

**TAKOUBA**
HP: 984 | AP: 1 | Gil: 75
Steal: Phoenix Down
Drop: Phoenix Down

**WHITE FANG**
HP: 378 | AP: 1 | Gil: 48
Steal: Potion
Drop: Potion

## DISHARMONY IN THE TRIBE

After conversing briefly with beleaguered Ronso Elder Kimahri, Kimahri's rival Garik leaps in to deliver a few critical words. Your responses affect whether or not the Ronso Tribe reunites under their new elder. Choose the appropriate answers from the list that follows to build a better relationship with the Ronso.

Speak to the Ronso in the area and respond to their concerns. Your responses add or subtract points from the amount that the Ronso trust Yuna. The level of trust you build affects how the Ronso act throughout the game. This will especially come into play during the events at Gagazet during Chapter 3 and Chapter 5. Work to build a strong relationship between Yuna and the tribe by giving the best answers now and in Chapter 2. If you want to know exactly how these answers affect your relationship with the Ronso, refer to the Mt. Gagazet sections in their respective chapters.

If you speak to Kimahri again, he says "Ronso youth grown horns of hatred for Guado," and he expects a response. Your response to Kimahri does not affect events at Mt. Gagazet; it only affects your ability to gain the Trainer dressphere at a later point in the game. **Hint:** Pick the middle option!

*Your answers here have far-reaching political consequences that affect a future boss fight and heavy changes at Gagazet.*

**MAP**

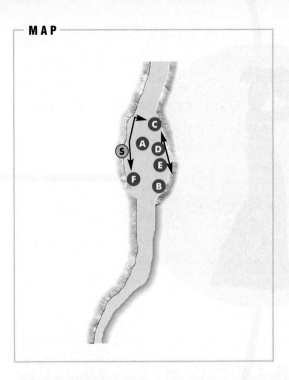

| RONSO CONCERNS AND ANSWERS, CHAPTER 1 | | | | |
|---|---|---|---|---|
| **MAP LETTER** | **RONSO** | **CONCERN** | **YUNA'S ANSWERS** | **TRUST** |
| A | Woman standing beside Kimahri. | Must ask High Summoner Yuna: Find Lian and Ayde. | Leave it to the Gullwings!<br>Please help Kimahri.<br>I can't promise anything. | +1<br>0<br>-1 |
| B | Garik (Conversation starts automatically the first time you enter.) | Garik know Yuna save Spira, but Ronso not saved yet. | That's a really nice horn.<br>We'll take care of Lian and Ayde.<br>Try and be nice to Kimahri. | 0<br>+1<br>-1 |
| C | Male walking around near exit to the snowy slopes area. | Many Ronso lost lives in battle to defend High Summoner Yuna. | Yes, many Ronso died...<br>I will never forget their sacrifice.<br>What am I supposed to do about it? | 0<br>+1<br>-1 |
| D | Female on right side of screen at entrance to Mt. Gagazet. | Guado leave Guadosalam. Guado plan dark schemes! | You're just making that up!<br>I'm sure you're right.<br>Hrm. | -1<br>+1<br>0 |
| E | Male standing near Garik. | Many friends and kin die two years ago. Ronso grief deeper than mountain snow. | You have to try not to be so sad!<br>I can imagine how you must feel...<br>Tough breaks, huh. | 0<br>+1<br>-1 |
| F | Male in red armor with green hair on left side of screen at entrance to Mt. Gagazet. | Never forgive Seymour, never forgive Guado! | Hatred won't solve anything!<br>I wouldn't forgive them either.<br>Do what you want. | -1<br>+1<br>0 |
| G | Guard near stairs in mountain cave of Mt. Gagazet. | Power of the fayth wane, cave water disappears. Change will come to Ronso, too. | The cave and the Ronso aren't connected.<br>A change for the better, I hope.<br>I... see. | 0<br>+1<br>-1 |

Characters

Garment Grids & Dresspheres

Battle System

Accessories

Items and Item Shops

Walkthrough

Chapter 1

Chapter 2

Chapter 3

Chapter 4

Chapter 5

Mini-Games

Fiends and Enemies

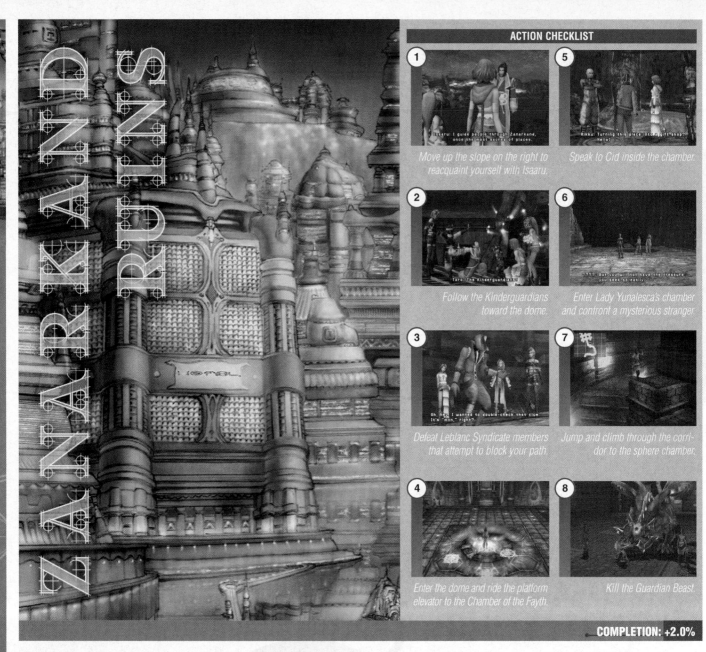

# ZANARKAND RUINS

**1** Move up the slope on the right to reacquaint yourself with Isaaru.

**2** Follow the Kinderguardians toward the dome.

**3** Defeat Leblanc Syndicate members that attempt to block your path.

**4** Enter the dome and ride the platform elevator to the Chamber of the Fayth.

**5** Speak to Cid inside the chamber.

**6** Enter Lady Yunalesca's chamber and confront a mysterious stranger.

**7** Jump and climb through the corridor to the sphere chamber.

**8** Kill the Guardian Beast.

**COMPLETION: +2.0%**

## WANDERING FIENDS

**BEHEMOTH**
HP: 1420 AP: 1 Gil: 80
Steal: Phoenix Down
Drop: Circlet

**FLAK PYTHON**
HP: 152 AP: 1 Gil: 10
Steal: Budget Grenade
Drop: Potion

**GECKO**
HP: 228 AP: 1 Gil: 18
Steal: Antidote
Drop: Antidote

**MR. GOON**
HP: 120 AP: 1 Gil: 30
Steal: Budget Grenade
Drop: Potion

**MS. GOON**
HP: 80 AP: 1 Gil: 30
Steal: Budget Grenade
Drop: Potion

**NASHORN**
HP: 482 AP: 1 Gil: 22
Steal: Potion
Drop: Potion

**WHITE ELEMENTAL**
HP: 77 AP: 1 Gil: 26
Steal: Antarctic Wind
Drop: Potion

**GUARDIAN BEAST**
HP: 2886 AP: 1 Gil: 200
Steal: Defense Veil
Drop: Amulet

## ITEM CHECKLIST

Mega Phoenix
Phoenix Down
Remedy (x2)

Remedy
Ether
Elixir

Phoenix Down
Hi-Potion
Heart Reborn Garment Grid **G**

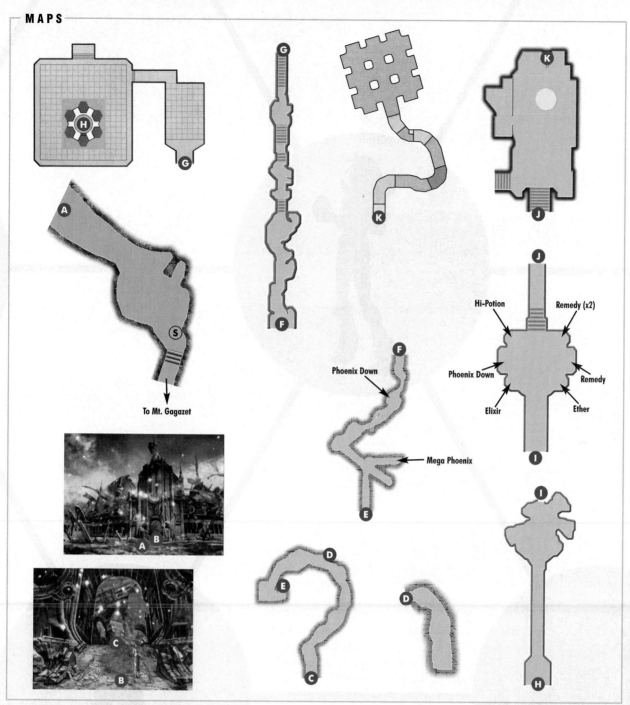

Characters

Garment Grids & Dresspheres

Battle System

Accessories

Items and Item Shops

Walkthrough
Chapter 1
Chapter 2
Chapter 3
Chapter 4
Chapter 5

Mini-Games

Fiends and Enemies

To Mt. Gagazet

Phoenix Down

Mega Phoenix

Hi-Potion

Remedy (x2)

Phoenix Down

Remedy

Elixir

Ether

# TOURISTS IN THE CITY OF THE DEAD

After Yuna's sad memories, talk to the people in the crowd. The tourists are so thick here that you can't move through them; therefore, head up the slope and speak to Isaaru. After doing so, the crowd below thins out enough that you can finally proceed toward the dome.

Inside the dome, the Gullwings overhear Pacce instructing the Kinderguardians. Speak to the woman on the left to purchase items, if you desire, then follow the Kinderguardians to the next area.

*The tour guide won't let you enter the area until you go up the nearby slope.*

| ZANARKAND DOME MERCHANT | |
|---|---|
| ITEM | COST |
| Potion | 50 |
| Phoenix Down | 100 |
| Antidote | 50 |
| Eye Drops | 50 |
| Echo Screen | 50 |
| Soft | 50 |
| Holy Water | 300 |
| Iron Bangle | 500 |
| Silver Bracer | 500 |
| Mythril Gloves | 1000 |
| Defense Veil | 1000 |

### WHY, YOU LITTLE THIEF!

*Avoid the monkey to the left just inside the dome. If you attempt to interact with it, the little creature steals some gil!*

*After speaking to Cid, speak to the man that Cid was talking to. This causes the monkeys to disperse from in front of Lady Yunalesca's former haunt.*

*In the large round chambers, open the chests while avoiding the monkeys.*

## ROAD TO THE DOME

Follow the kids into the next area, then speak to Pacce and his gang. Proceed up the hill thereafter to overhear a Syndicate Goon with a big mouth. After fighting the Syndicate enemy party, head through the next intersection to find a chest containing a **Mega Phoenix**, then continue down the slope. Continue defeating Syndicate members as you work your way to the dome.

*Even if you try to slip past Ms. Goon standing by the circular portal, she will call you back!*

## REVERSING ISAARU'S PRANK

Inside the spiritual chamber, follow Rikku and Paine onto the platform until Isaaru plays a mean prank on them. When five choices are offered, choose the bottom one (Is that you, Isaaru?). With the right choice, Isaaru hands over the **Heart Reborn Garment Grid**. When the former summoner leaves, head down the steps at the far end of the platform.

Climb and jump through the winding corridor to the room at the end. When you spot the sphere at the end of the passage, it's time to take on another boss.

*Don't play Isaaru's game to make him hand over a Garment Grid.*

## CHIDING CID

Tourists have opened all the chests and emptied them. Continue to the top of the stairs and through the door. Move past the dancing woman in the square room into the larger chamber. Navigate onto the center lift and ride it down to the level below. Use the Save Sphere if needed, then proceed into the next chamber and speak to the bald man, who is Cid. During the conversation, tell Cid that you do indeed have a bone to pick with him by saying, "You bet I do!" Your choice here affects later events on the Thunder Plains.

## GUARDIAN BEAST

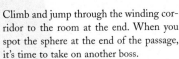

A quick scan of the Guardian Beast by a Gun Mage reveals that it is weak against all forms of elemental magic, except Gravity. While a Black Mage casts second or third level elemental spells on the beast, a Songstress can reduce the accuracy of the monster with Darkness Dance. It's wise to have a White Mage present as well to restore HP from this creature's massive blows. Target the entire party with a Cure or Cura spell after the beast performs its Damocles Photon attack. Cast Esuna or use Remedy items to cure Curse status.

**HP:** 2886  **MP:** 1000  **EXP:** 170  **AP:** 1

**GIL DROPPED:** 200
**PILFER GIL:** 1500

**STEAL:** Normal: Defense Veil  Rare: Defense Veil
**DROP:** Normal: Amulet  Rare: Amulet

## HALF A SPHERE?!

Following the battle, the Gullwings gain a measly half a sphere and regroup onboard the Celsius. Brother receives reports of an "awesome sphere" in Kilika. Afterwards, proceed to the final destination of Chapter 1…

*Your stay aboard the Celsius is short.*

# KILIKA ISLAND

Characters

1

Garment Grids & D005paces

2

Battle System

3

Accessories

4

Items and Item Shops

5

Walkthrough

Chapter 1

Chapter 2

Chapter 3

Chapter 4

Chapter 5

Mini-Games

7

Fiends and Enemies

8

## ACTION CHECKLIST

**1** Stop by Lady Dona's place to say hello.

**2** Head through the gates to the Youth League rally.

**3** Follow Nooj and his group into the forest.

**4** Navigate through the woods using the path that isn't guarded by New Yevon.

**5** Speak the correct passwords to fool the guards.

**6** Deactivate the YSLS-Zero.

**COMPLETION: +1.6%**

## WANDERING FIENDS

**DEATH DAUBER**
HP: 78 | AP: 1 | Gil: 12
Steal: Potion
Drop: Potion

**LEAGUE DEFENDER**
HP: 186 | AP: 1 | Gil: 40
Steal: Budget Grenade
Drop: Potion

**LEAGUE FIGHTER**
HP: 1730 | AP: 1 | Gil: 140
Steal: Holy Water
Drop: Hi-Potion

**PROTOCHIMERA**
HP: 420 | AP: 1 | Gil: 120
Steal: Potion
Drop: Phoenix Down

**RED ELEMENTAL**
HP: 99 | AP: 1 | Gil: 26
Steal: Potion
Drop: Potion

**STALWART**
HP: 1240 | AP: 1 | Gil: 100
Steal: Phoenix Down
Drop: Phoenix Down (x2)

**YEVON GUARD**
HP: 1722 | AP: 1 | Gil: 140
Steal: Holy Water
Drop: Hi-Potion

## ITEM CHECKLIST

| | | | |
|---|---|---|---|
| Ether | 1500 gil | Holy Water (x2) | Turbo Ether 🅔 |
| Antidote (x2) | Lunar Curtain | Megalixir | Menace of the Deep Garment Grid |
| Eye Drops (x2) | Star Curtain | Hi-Potion 🅔 | |
| Phoenix Down | Light Curtain | Ether 🅔 | |

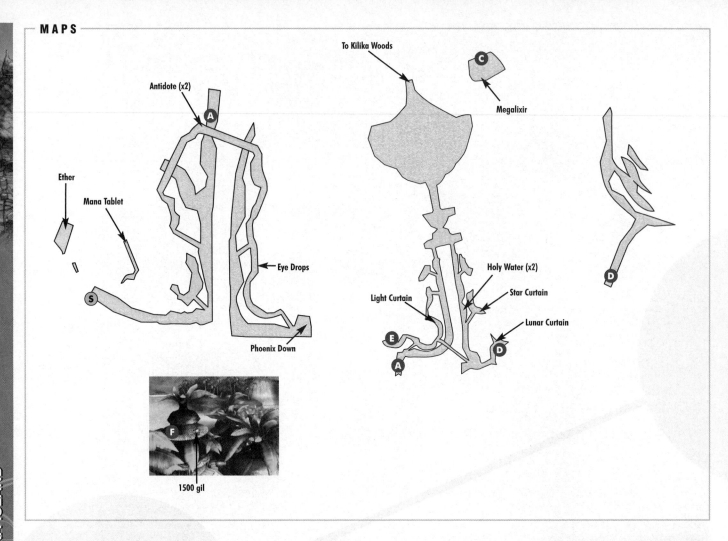

Antidote (x2)

To Kilika Woods

C

Megalixir

Ether

Mana Tablet

A

Eye Drops

S

Holy Water (x2)

Star Curtain

Light Curtain

D

Lunar Curtain

E

D

A

Phoenix Down

F

1500 gil

# UNDERSTANDING THE LAYOUT

Kilika port has been rebuilt since its sad destruction in *FINAL FANTASY X*, and now it is a confusing mass of connecting docks and bridges. For that reason, refer to the following section to make navigation much easier:

*1. From the starting point, jump off the dock onto a canoe and, from there, to an isolated chest on a dock which contains an **Ether**.*

*2. Jump from the dock to the right of the Save Sphere to another canoe and from there to a partially hidden platform where a chest contains a **Mana Tablet**.*

*3. Move up the dock and go up the second set of stairs. Cross a bridge and open the chest to get an **Antidote (x2)**.*

*4. Cross the canal and move across the upper platforms to reach chests containing **Eye Drops (x2)** and a **Phoenix Down**.*

*5. A woman near a red tent under the bridge in the first area sells items.*

| KILIKA PORT MERCHANT | |
|---|---|
| **ITEM** | **COST** |
| Potion | 50 |
| Phoenix Down | 100 |
| Antidote | 50 |
| Eye Drops | 50 |
| Echo Screen | 50 |
| Soft | 50 |
| Holy Water | 300 |
| Twist Headband | 3000 |
| White Cape | 3000 |
| Silver Glasses | 3000 |
| Star Pendant | 4000 |

# DONA'S TYRANNY

Head back to the stairs on the other side of the canal, then move up the dock until a short scene occurs with Yuna and Rikku. Arriving in the second area, head up the first set of stairs and move left up the ramp and around the hut until Barthello comes out screaming. Go inside the hut and speak to old acquaintance Lady Dona.

Dona drives her man out the door.

Up the stairs in Dona's house, open the chest on the patio to find **1500 gil**.

# HIDDEN MONKEYS OF KILIKA

Speak to the woman dressed in blue on the east side of the docks in the first area of Kilika Port. She and some children are playing with a Squatter Monkey. Speak to her a second time, and she asks you to search the Kilika Forest to find more Squatter Monkeys in hiding. There are 13 monkeys hidden here (see the following map). Once you gain access to the Kilika Forest area after the next events in the game, find all of the monkeys. However, you won't be able to report back to the woman dressed in blue for your reward until Chapter 3. At that time, speak to her again and show her that you found all 13 monkeys. In return, she hands over the **Chaos Maelstrom Garment Grid**.

Speak to the woman in blue to undertake the Squatter Monkey finding quest. She also reports how many monkeys you've found thus far.

## MAP

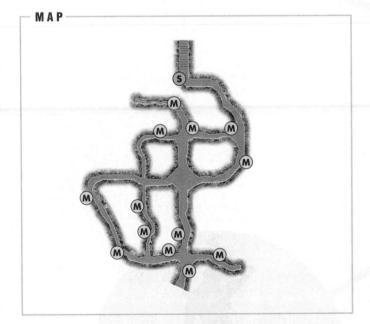

# YOUTH LEAGUE UPRISING

Proceed to the top of the second section of town, and the guards will open the gate for Yuna. After the speech by Meyvan Nooj, the Gullwings appear just outside Kilika Forest. Follow Nooj into the trees.

After another scene, backtrack to use the Save Sphere near the entrance and fight through the woods. You can't go directly up the center, and Yevon guards block off several of the paths. From the Save Sphere near the entrance, head down the left path. A short cinema of people running through the trees takes you right past the trail you must follow. Go back a few steps and up the trail, coming out behind a group of Yevon guards. Continue up the obscure trail around a curve to reach the central path.

Navigate through the area using the least obvious path.

Characters

Garment Grids & Dresspheres

Battle System

Accessories

Items and Item Shops

Walkthrough

Chapter 1

Chapter 2

Chapter 3

Chapter 4

Chapter 5

Mini-Games

Fiends and Enemies

# DETERMINING THE PASSWORDS

Upon reaching the central path, head upward until you hear voices through the trees. Listen in on the conversation, as the Yevon guards divulge passwords you'll need later. If the number of guards at a checkpoint is odd, the password is "Carved Monkey." But keep watching the conversation, because if the number of checkpoint guards is even, then the password changes to "Craven Monkey." If you don't remember the passwords, return to the peeking point and watch the conversation again.

Move toward the top center of the area to overhear the passwords.

# GIVING THE PASSWORDS

Follow the outside circular path to the Save Sphere, then approach the guards at the guard checkpoint. Say the appropriate password based on how many guards are standing there. If you give the correct password, they will leave and possibly give you an item. If you give the incorrect password, you're forced to fight them. The final group attempts to trick you by adding two more members and asking for the exact same password again. If you answer all guard groups with the correct password, you receive the **Menace of the Deep Garment Grid**.

The camera switches frantically in an attempt to throw you off.

## ONE HARD-TO-FIND LEDGE

*Head to the right along the path, then move downward against two greenish trees. When the Circle button appears on screen, jump to a secret ledge where a chest contains a **Megalixir**.*

### NEW YEVON GUARD GROUP NUMBERS, PASSWORDS AND REWARDS

| GROUP | # GUARDS | PASSWORD | ITEM |
|---|---|---|---|
| 1 | 4 | Craven Monkey | None |
| 2 | 3 | Carved Monkey | Hi-Potion |
| 3 | 4 | Craven Monkey | Ether |
| 4 | 3 | Carved Monkey | Turbo Ether |
| 4 (2nd) | 5 | Carved Monkey | Menace of the Deep Garment Grid |

# YSLS-ZERO

## BOSS FIGHT

Have a Gun Mage use Mech Destroyer on the metal brute, and command a Songstress to cast Darkness Dance round after round to prevent as many of its hits as possible. If your Gun Mage doesn't know Mech Destroyer yet, change someone into a knowledgeable Black Mage and cast your strongest spells against it. The other party member should keep everyone healthy as a White Mage. Be ready to cast Cure or Cura on all party members at once, especially if everyone's HP gets below 100 points. A single blow from this brute can KO a person with less than 100 HP. Fight hard because after the battle, Chapter 1 is complete!

HP: 1935   MP: 0   EXP: 350   AP: 1

| | |
|---|---|
| **GIL DROPPED:** 1000 | **STEAL:** Normal: Mythril Gloves   Rare: Mythril Gloves |
| **PILFER GIL:** 1400 | **DROP:** Normal: Wristband   Rare: Wristband |

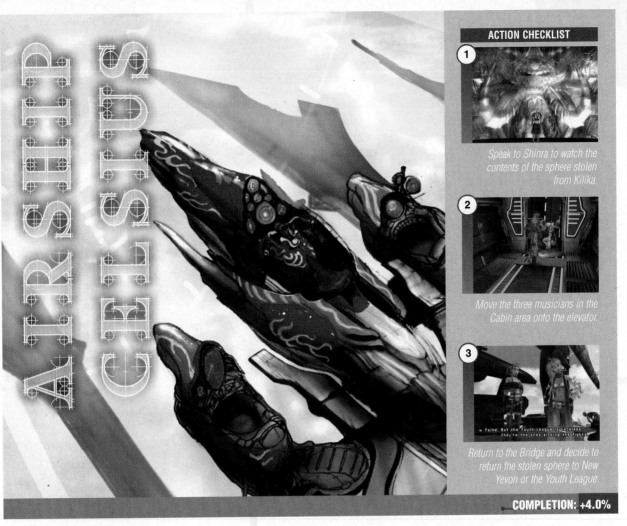

# AIRSHIP CELSIUS

Characters

1

Garment Grids & Dresspheres

2

Battle System

3

Accessories

4

Items and Item Shops

5

Walkthrough

Chapter 1

Chapter 2

Chapter 3

Chapter 4

Chapter 5

Mini-Games

7

Fiends and Enemies

8

## ACTION CHECKLIST

1

Speak to Shinra to watch the contents of the sphere stolen from Kilika.

2

Move the three musicians in the Cabin area onto the elevator.

3

Paine: But the Youth League is reckless. They're the ones picking the fights.

Return to the Bridge and decide to return the stolen sphere to New Yevon or the Youth League.

**COMPLETION: +4.0%**

## ITEM CHECKLIST

*Al Bhed Primer ⓔ
Phoenix Down (x5)
Ether (x2)

Remedy (x4)
Potion (x8)
Leblanc's Sphere ⓔ

**\*Only if you haven't mastered Al Bhed.**

## MAPS

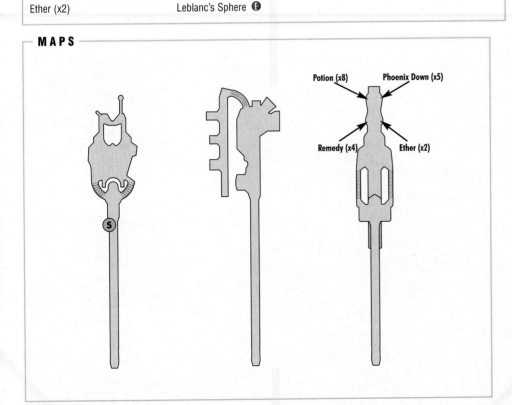

Potion (x8)     Phoenix Down (x5)

Remedy (x4)     Ether (x2)

# PRIVATE CONCERT

Shinra plays the movie stored on the sphere that was stolen from Kilika. He will replay the haunting images if you speak to him again after the conversations onboard the Bridge. Afterward, head down to the Engine Room to collect the new items in the four chests. Ride the lift to the Cabin area, where three musicians are practicing in the corridor. Speak to the third musician, Daraya, and start pushing all three of them onto the lift. Position Yuna behind each musician, and move toward the lift. Yuna will guide each musician by collision. You can also get a bonus accessory by pushing Tobli into the elevator. If you want to quit this task, speak to Barkeep at the top of the corridor. Once all three are onboard the lift, Yuna delights the crew with a concert on the deck outside the ship.

*If you allowed Clasko and O'aka to join the crew, they will attend the concert.*

# A WEIGHTY DECISION

*FINAL FANTASY X-2 is certainly a game worth replaying, since you can make different choices each time you undertake the adventure.*

After Yuna's awesome spectacle, follow Rikku and Paine from the Cabin area up to the Bridge. You must now decide whether to give the sphere that was stolen from Kilika to either the Youth League or to New Yevon. If you give the sphere to the Youth League, you can acquire 100% story completion in a single game. However, if you give the sphere to New Yevon, the highest percentage you can achieve is 99%. Your choice affects the scene that occurs afterward and many other dialogues and conversations throughout the game.

If you give the sphere to the Youth League, the Gullwings fly to Mushroom Rock Road and receive a grand reception from Lucil, Elma, and Nooj. Wherever you travel in Spira, Youth League members will welcome you with respect and thanks. However, New Yevon members will scorn your presence and if you attempt to enter Bevelle, the Gullwings will be forced to fight several sets of soldiers and machina.

*The opening events of Chapter 2 change depending on your decision.*

*Allying yourself with the Youth League is the only way to accumulate 100% completion in a single game.*

If you give the sphere to New Yevon, the crew of the Celsius has a conference with the grateful Praetor Baralai. Youth League members will look down upon the Gullwings, and if you attempt to enter Mushroom Rock Road, you're forced to complete an extra mission in which the girls fight Youth League warriors, culminating in a battle against Elma.

# ROBBED!

After choosing a side and handing over the sphere, the Gullwings are called back to the Celsius. Looks like Leblanc is back, and she's up to no good. She, Logos, and Ormi stole the broken sphere found at Zanarkand, leaving behind **Leblanc's Sphere**. For the main portion of Chapter 2, your quest is to find Leblanc Syndicate members (located at Djose Temple, Bikanel Desert, and Mt. Gagazet), defeat them, and steal three uniforms. The order in which you visit these locations and obtain the Syndicate Uniforms is not important. Upon acquiring all three uniforms, the option to fly the Gullwings to Guadosalam to infiltrate Leblanc's chateau will be available.

*While searching for opportunities to steal Syndicate Uniforms, be sure to revisit every other location in Spira to undertake a variety of vital missions and side quests.*

BESAID ISLAND

**ACTION CHECKLIST**

1

*Speak to the Aurochs to learn about their new trainer.*

2

*Run the Gunner's Gauntlet and earn 500 points.*

**COMPLETION: +0.8%**

## WANDERING FIENDS

### BARBUTA
HP: 562 | AP: 1 | Gil: 33
Steal: Lunar Curtain
Drop: Light Curtain

### CHOCOBO
HP: 368 | AP: 0 | Gil: 0
Steal: N/A
Drop: N/A

### COEURL
HP: 320 | AP: 1 | Gil: 30
Steal: Phoenix Down
Drop: Potion (x2)

### COYOTE
HP: 74 | AP: 1 | Gil: 10
Steal: Potion
Drop: Potion

### FLAN AZUL
HP: 55 | AP: 1 | Gil: 30
Steal: Potion
Drop: Potion

### IRON GIANT
HP: 222 | AP: 1 | Gil: 40
Steal: Budget Grenade
Drop: Budget Grenade

### LESSER DRAKE
HP: 577 | AP: 1 | Gil: 22
Steal: Potion
Drop: Potion

### PURPUREA
HP: 196 | AP: 1 | Gil: 18
Steal: Echo Screen
Drop: Echo Screen

### SAHAGIN
HP: 60 | AP: 1 | Gil: 7
Steal: Potion
Drop: Potion

### SALLET
HP: 60 | AP: 1 | Gil: 10
Steal: Potion
Drop: Potion

## ITEM CHECKLIST

Wall Ring

Potion (x3)

Hi-Potion (x2)

1500 gil

Enigma Plate Garment Grid **E**

## MAPS

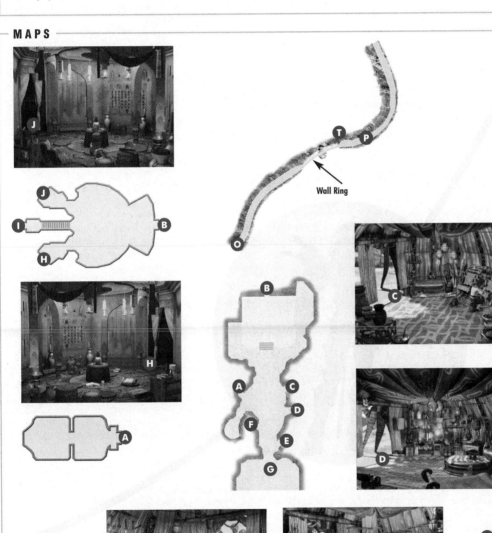

Wall Ring

To Chamber of the Fayth

Characters

1

Garment Grids & Dresspheres

2

Battle System

3

Accessories

4

Items and Item Shops

5

Walkthrough
Chapter 1
Chapter 2
Chapter 3
Chapter 4
Chapter 5

Mini-Games

7

Fiends and Enemies

8

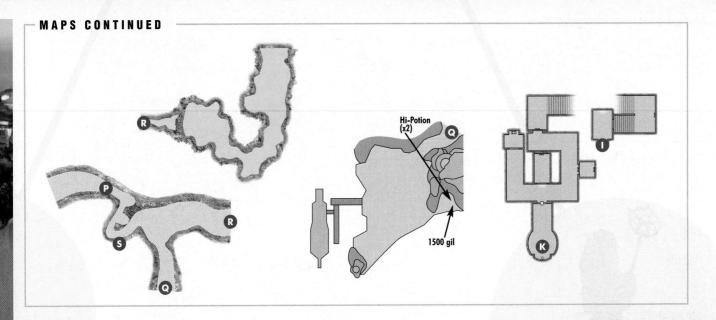

Hi-Potion (x2)

1500 gil

## BECLEM'S CHALLENGE

Return to Besaid and speak to any of the blitzball players standing near the Save Sphere. Beclem, of the Besaid Aurochs, is training new members for the Youth League. A drill sergeant, Beclem, from the Youth League is training the young men of Besaid—and not in a pleasant way. Yuna becomes incensed by Beclem's comments, resulting in an opportunity for you to undertake a challenging mini-game to put Beclem in his place. Complete the Gunner's Gauntlet mini-game with 500 points, reach the next level of the game, and gain the completion percentage available for visiting Besaid.

*Replay the Gunner's Gauntlet mini-game until you score high enough to put Beclem in his place!*

## GUNNING THROUGH THE GAUNTLET

*Take all the time you need to learn the mini-game because actually playing is a hectic experience.*

When the mission begins, tell Beclem "I need a tutorial first," or "Basic instructions" to learn how to play the mini-game. You start at a three-way junction and fight toward the beach. You must speak to Beclem at the shoreline before time expires with 500 points or more. When the mini-game begins, you begin in the area just outside the village with a small amount of normal ammo. The two Coyotes in the area remain stationary. Target them with the Circle button and shoot them with the X button. Press the Square button to cycle through targets. Switch ammunition types with the L1 and R1 buttons. Move Yuna toward a treasure chest dropped by the fiends to claim the ammo inside.

Quickly proceed toward the ruins and shoot the Coyotes coming down the hill. Frankly, this isn't the best area to gain points, simply because the camera angles make it more difficult to detect fiends coming down the slope. Blast through the ruins and get to the next area as soon as possible.

In the falls area, shoot the fiends emerging from the opposite end of the path. Continue fighting in this area until you have at least 500 points. Success in this

*Build up Yuna's chain gauge by taking out these easy targets before proceeding.*

*Tap the Circle button frequently while moving through the area to target fiends approaching from off-screen before they get too close.*

*Winning the mini-game in the time allotted requires maintaining a full chain bar while defeating roughly 20 or more fiends.*

mini-game is entirely dependent on playing the game without being attacked by the fiends. The more fiends you dispatch without taking a hit, the higher your chain multiplier will rise. The chain multiplier is displayed at the bottom of the screen. The yellow bar will extend farther as you defeat more enemies, and the points gained per kill will double. If the chain bar fills completely, each defeated fiend scores triple the usual points. To avoid hits from an enemy, tap the Circle button repeatedly to target fiends while they are still off-screen.

When you reach 500 points, look at the remaining time. Decide whether to continue playing to score even higher or to head to the beach. If less than a minute remains, it's time to call it quits. In the overgrown area with the cave entrance, a giant mech blocks Yuna's path. This opponent can be easily dispatched with a single Death bullet, if you have one remaining. Afterwards, continue out to the beach and head toward Beclem. If you played the game successfully, Beclem concedes victory. For completing the mission, you receive the **Enigma Plate Garment Grid**.

*Shooting the mech in the overgrown area rewards hefty bonus points if Yuna's chain bar is full.*

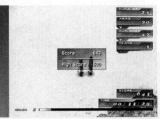

*To play this fun mini-game again, speak to Beclem either outside the village or on the beach.*

BESAID ISLAND

KILIKA ISLAND

COMPLETION: +0.2%

## ITEM CHECKLIST

Turbo Ether

# BARRED BY TROUBLES

You cannot visit Kilika during Chapter 2 because of the troubles between New Yevon and the Youth League. However, you can still jump to the chest beyond the canoe near the Save Sphere for a **Turbo Ether**.

*If you sided with New Yevon, Dona has even more choice words for you.*

Characters

1

Garment Grids & Dresspheres

2

Battle System

3

Accessories

4

Items and Item Shops

5

Walkthrough

Chapter 1
Chapter 2
Chapter 3
Chapter 4
Chapter 5

Mini-Games

7

Fiends and Enemies

8

COMPLETION: +0.8%

## ITEM CHECKLIST

Light Curtain (x2)

# SPOTLIGHT ON GULLWINGS

Luca is another location where very little is happening during Chapter 2. Still, there are easy completion points to gain simply by visiting. Enter the circular courtyard area to have a televised interview with Shelinda. Additionally, some of the folks in the locker room corridor (the one with the save sphere) are eager to play Sphere Break. Be careful, though, because you can actually lose coins during a real game. Run out of coins and you'll spend the rest of your day digging in the Bikanel Desert for more!

*During the interview with Shelinda, press R1 or L1 to switch cameras, adding an authentic newscast feel*

# MI'IHEN HIGHROAD

Characters

1

Garment Grids
& Dresspheres

2

Battle System

3

Accessories

4

Items and
Item Shops

5

Walkthrough

Chapter 1

Chapter 2

Chapter 3

Chapter 4

Chapter 5

Mini-Games

7

Fiends and
Enemies

8

## ACTION CHECKLIST

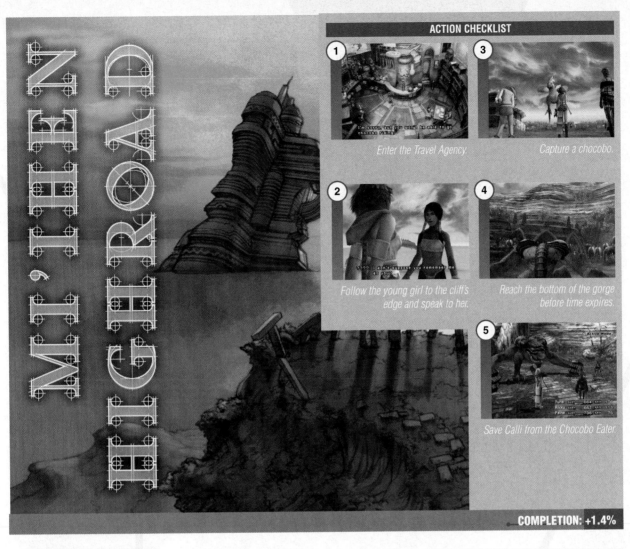

**1** Enter the Travel Agency.

**2** Follow the young girl to the cliff's edge and speak to her.

**3** Capture a chocobo.

**4** Reach the bottom of the gorge before time expires.

**5** Save Calli from the Chocobo Eater.

**COMPLETION: +1.4%**

## WANDERING FIENDS

**BULLY CAP**
HP: 94 | AP: 1 | Gil: 14
Steal: Eye Drops
Drop: Eye Drops

**DIVEBEAK**
HP: 10 | AP: 1 | Gil: 12
Steal: Potion
Drop: Antidote

**FLY EYE**
HP: 258 | AP: 1 | Gil: 20
Steal: Phoenix Down
Drop: Phoenix Down

**FLAN PALIDO**
HP: 188 | AP: 1 | Gil: 30
Steal: Potion
Drop: Potion

**IRON GIANT**
HP: 222 | AP: 1 | Gil: 40
Steal: Budget Grenade
Drop: Budget Grenade

**PEREGRINE**
HP: 735 | AP: 1 | Gil: 44
Steal: Hi-Potion
Drop: Hi-Potion

**PURPUREA**
HP: 196 | AP: 1 | Gil: 18
Steal: Echo Screen
Drop: Echo Screen

**QUADRICORN**
HP: 188 | AP: 1 | Gil: 13
Steal: Echo Screen
Drop: Potion

**SHANTAK**
HP: 1130 | AP: 1 | Gil: 120
Steal: Remedy
Drop: Phoenix Down

**WILD WOLF**
HP: 185 | AP: 1 | Gil: 12
Steal: Potion
Drop: Potion

**CHOCOBO EATER**
HP: 2350 | AP: 1 | Gil: 500
Steal: X-Potion
Drop: Wall Ring

## ITEM CHECKLIST

| | | | |
|---|---|---|---|
| Muscle Belt | Potion (x3) | Phoenix Down (x3) | Soft (x3) |
| 1000 gil | Silver Bracer | Grenade (x2) | Echo Screen (x3) |
| Phoenix Down (x3) | Holy Water (x3) | Ether | Selene Guard Garment Grid |
| Antidote (x3) | Eye Drops (x3) | Potion (x2) | |

MI'IHEN HIGHROAD

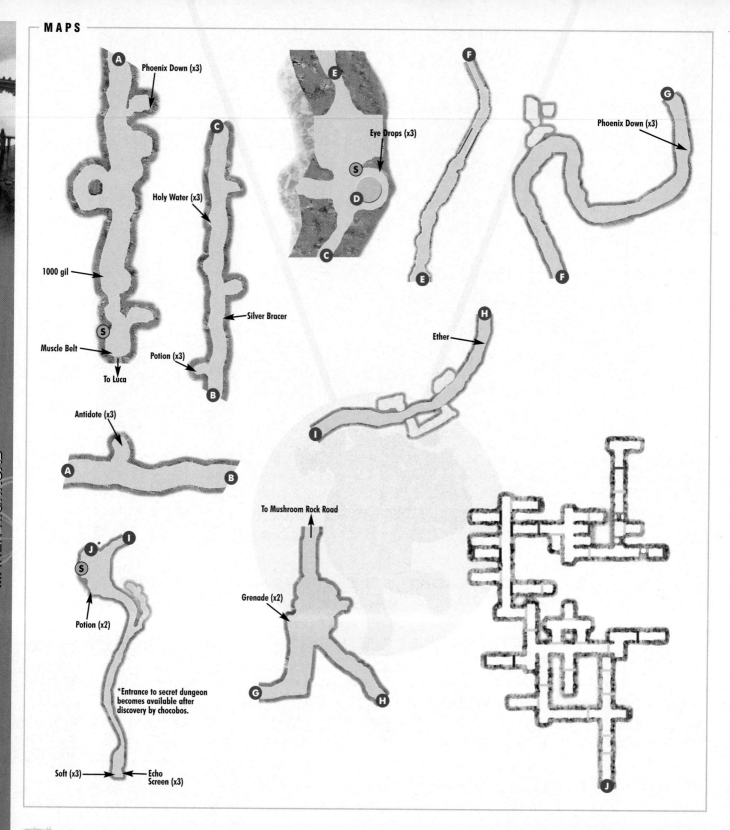

Phoenix Down (x3)

Holy Water (x3)

1000 gil

Silver Bracer

Muscle Belt

Potion (x3)

To Luca

Antidote (x3)

Eye Drops (x3)

Phoenix Down (x3)

Ether

To Mushroom Rock Road

Grenade (x2)

Potion (x2)

*Entrance to secret dungeon becomes available after discovery by chocobos.

Soft (x3)     Echo Screen (x3)

# SOMETHING OFF THE MENU

Enter the Highroad via the airship navigation map. Arriving at the Al Bhed Travel Agency, go inside just as a young woman is walking out. Follow her out of the shop and speak to her at the cliff's edge. The young lady turns out to be Calli, who certainly has grown up in the last two years. To help her out, you must corner and capture a wild chocobo running down the Mi'ihen Highroad.

Only the Gullwings can help Calli catch a chocobo on the Mi'ihen Highroad.

### BEFORE HELPING CALLI...

*Prior to speaking with Calli at the cliff's edge, complete any side quest obligations in this area, such as the Publicity and Matrimony quests. Also, raid the treasure chests and claim all the items possible. Once you capture the chocobo and rescue Calli from a tough opponent, certain areas of Mi'ihen will become inaccessible.*

# CATCH THAT CHOCOBO!

Rikku serves as your guide to capturing the chocobo. After your recent misadventures under Rikku's command in Bikanel Desert, you can probably imagine how this is going to turn out. Follow Rikku into the south section of the Highroad. After she spots the chocobo, follow very closely behind her. If you lag too far behind her, she will stop. An on-screen timer then appears and you must quickly run back toward Rikku for her to resume the chase.

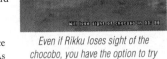

*Even if Rikku loses sight of the chocobo, you have the option to try again.*

While running down the Highroad, try to pick up feathers dropped by the chocobo in its haste. Once you grab a feather, run back and rejoin Rikku as quickly as possible before she loses sight of the bird. As you progress down the road, Rikku will suddenly stop and say that the chocobo has stopped in a side area. Unfortunately, Rikku is always wrong, but there is usually a chest in the side area that may contain a reward. As you run the full length of the Highroad's south section, Rikku points out three false chocobo sightings that turn out to be treasure chests. Each chest contains a reward based on the number of feathers you've picked up by the point at which you agreed to go search in the side area. However, you only get one reward in this manner. Therefore, run down the Highroad and gather as many feathers as possible.

When Rikku points into a side area for the third time, agree to investigate. This leads to a chest containing a reward for picking up feathers and cleaning the Highroad. After opening the chest to get the item, proceed to the next section of the Highroad to continue with the next leg of the event. Before leaving, you receive an additional item based on the total number of feathers that were picked up.

*Move over the yellow feathers on the path to pick them up.*

*When Rikku points at a side area, you have the option of sacrificing the chase to obtain an item.*

## NO EFFORT REQUIRED

*It's not important to pick up every feather for the best prize. Unless you're crazy about building your supply of Chocobo Wings and Chocobo Feathers (fairly common items in the game), just grab one of the feathers on the ground and race for the end of the area. The prize for leaving with few feathers is a **Gold Hourglass**, an item that delays the entire enemy party by one turn in battle. These are rare items, so get one early while you have the opportunity.*

| PRIZES FOUND IN CHESTS BY GATHERING FEATHERS | |
| --- | --- |
| FEATHERS RETRIEVED | ITEM IN CHEST |
| 0 | Empty |
| 1-3 | Chocobo Feather x2 |
| 4-14 | Chocobo Feather x3 |
| 15-17 | Chocobo Wing x2 |
| 18-21 | Chocobo Wing x3 |

| PRIZES GAINED UPON LEAVING THE AREA | |
| --- | --- |
| TOTAL FEATHERS | ITEM RECEIVED |
| 0 | None |
| 1-8 | Gold Hourglass |
| 9-15 | Chocobo Feather |
| 16-21 | Chocobo Feather (x2) |

# THE CHOCOBO RODEO

At the end of the Highroad, the girls decide to tackle the chocobo with a new strategy. Rikku and Paine stand at either end of a short section of the road to prevent the bird from escaping. Yuna's job is to corner the chocobo and block its escape.

When the creature gets trapped between Yuna and Rikku, you must guess which direction the chocobo will try to run and intercept it. After the short countdown, move Yuna left or right to catch the chocobo, or do nothing to protect the center. When done correctly, Yuna catches the chocobo and a chime sounds. Whether you are successful or not, run to the opposite end of the road and corner the chocobo again between Yuna and Paine.

*Once Rikku and Paine are set up, run down the path and chase the grazing chocobo to the end.*

*The first several attempts to predict the chocobo's direction of travel are merely guesswork. The task becomes much easier later.*

Continue running back and forth, attempting to catch the chocobo until you are successful at least two or three times. At this point, the chocobo becomes tired and actually faces the direction it intends to run. When it's time, move Yuna in the direction the chocobo is facing to intercept it. If the chocobo is facing Yuna, it intends to go straight. After three more successful captures, the chocobo escapes to the final section of Highroad.

*After the chocobo becomes tired, it faces the direction it will try to run.*

# WHERE DID THE CHOCOBO GO?

The third event in this exasperating chase involves leading Rikku to high ground areas so that she can spot the chocobo. Move down the Highroad, then turn into the first side area on the right side of the screen. When the chocobo is revealed, head down the path to that area. The chocobo flees again, but Rikku spots it further down the path. Continue down the Highroad and divert into the next side area on the right.

*The final leg of the chase involves nothing more than triggering a series of events.*

When the chocobo runs off yet again, follow it a short distance until Yuna says it's time to try something else. Instead of following it, run back toward the hover parked near the Highroad entrance from Luca and speak to the pilot. The pilot is indicated on the on-screen map by a white arrow. Speak to her twice and she offers to help catch the chocobo. When she blocks the Highroad with her massive transport, the chocobo chase is finally won!

*The hover near the entrance of Mi'ihen saves the day!*

# FIEND OF FEAST

After you catch the chocobo, word comes that Calli is in trouble. Use the Save Sphere at the Travel Agency, then follow Rikku and Paine to the bridge. Once the group spots Calli in danger, you must reach the bottom of the gorge before time runs out. Run north across the next bridge and follow the path to the entrance of Mushroom Rock. Run down the sloping path to the side, and continue until the party encounters the Chocobo Eater.

*Proceed directly to the bottom of the gorge. It's a long trek, and there's no time to spare!*

## CHOCOBO EATER — BOSS FIGHT

HP: 2350  MP: 230  EXP: 350  AP: 1

The predatory chocobo connoisseur is weak against fire, so use a Black Mage to cast a few Fira spells to end this battle quickly. A Songstress can cast Samba of Silence to prevent the Chocobo Eater's spell use. Have a Thief steal some gil and items before roasting this fiend.

**GIL DROPPED:** 500
**PILFER GIL:** 2000

**STEAL:** Normal: X-Potion  Rare: X-Potion (x2)
**DROP:** Normal: Wall Ring  Rare: Wall Ring

# MORE BORDERS

For helping Calli, you receive the **Selene Guard Garment Grid**. The girls return to the Celsius, so head straight back to the Mi'ihen Highroad and speak to Calli, who's standing with the chocobo by the exit to the north section. If you previously took Clasko onboard your airship, he's there too. Agree to let Calli and Clasko come back onboard.

A hover blocks the north path, so you can't head across the north section. You can enter the area from Mushroom Rock as usual, but several sections of Mi'ihen Highroad surrounding the site of the crash remain blocked off until Chapter 3. Return to the airship to find Calli and Clasko in the Cabin area. At this point, the Calm Lands become a Hotspot on the Celsius's navigation map because Clasko wants to be dropped off there.

*Return to Mi'ihen Highroad before you finish Chapter 2 if you want to bring Calli and Clasko onboard the Celsius.*

# MUSHROOM ROCK ROAD

Characters

Garment Grids
& Dresspheres

Battle System

Accessories

Items and
Item Shops

Walkthrough
Chapter 1
Chapter 2
Chapter 3
Chapter 4
Chapter 5

Mini-Games

Fiends and
Enemies

## ACTION CHECKLIST

**1** Follow or battle the Youth League members throughout Mushroom Rock.

**2** Sneak past the fiends if you want to avoid combat.

**3** Fight Elma, if necessary, near the second Mushroom Rock elevator.

**4** Ride the machina elevator to Youth League HQ.

**5** Speak to Elma and Lucil outside Youth League headquarters.

**COMPLETION: +1.0%**

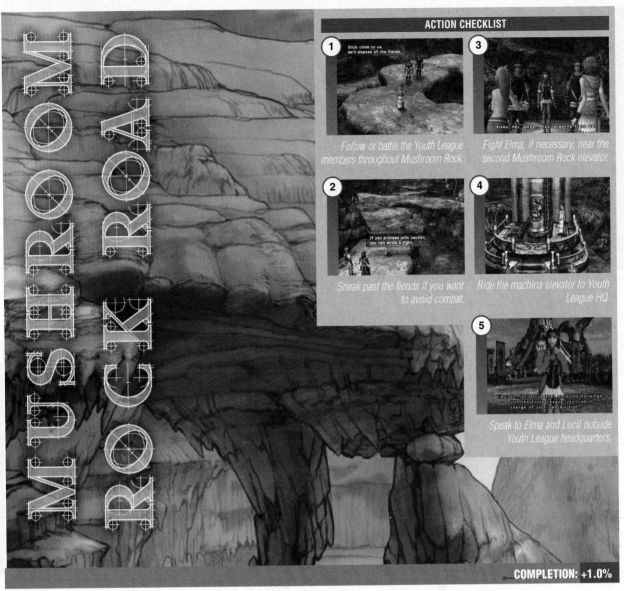

## WANDERING FIENDS

**BULLY CAP**
HP: 94 | AP: 1 | Gil: 14
Steal: Eye Drops
Drop: Eye Drops

**COYOTE**
HP: 74 | AP: 1 | Gil: 10
Steal: Potion
Drop: Potion

**DROWSY OCHU**
HP: 2484 | AP: 1 | Gil: 180
Steal: Remedy
Drop: Remedy (x2)

**LEAGUE RANGER***
HP: 230 | AP: 1 | Gil: 80
Steal: Phoenix Down
Drop: Potion

**LEAGUE SOLDIER***
HP: 178 | AP: 1 | Gil: 80
Steal: Grenade
Drop: Grenade

**LEAGUE TROOPER***
HP: 244 | AP: 1 | Gil: 60
Steal: Grenade
Drop: Grenade

**LEAGUE WARRIOR***
HP: 422 | AP: 1 | Gil: 120
Steal: Hi-Potion
Drop: Hi-Potion

**RED ELEMENTAL**
HP: 99 | AP: 1 | Gil: 25
Steal: Potion
Drop: Potion

**TONBERRY**
HP: 9999 | AP: 2 | Gil: 300
Steal: Ether
Drop: Hi-Potion

**ELMA***
HP: 1640 | AP: 2 | Gil: 230
Steal: Phoenix Down (x3)
Drop: Wall Ring

**\*Only if you gave the stolen sphere to New Yevon**

## ITEM CHECKLIST

| | | |
|---|---|---|
| Hi-Potion | Phoenix Down | Shining Bracer |
| 1500 gil | Ether | Mythril Bangle |
| Turbo Ether (x2) | Crimson Sphere 7 **E** | |

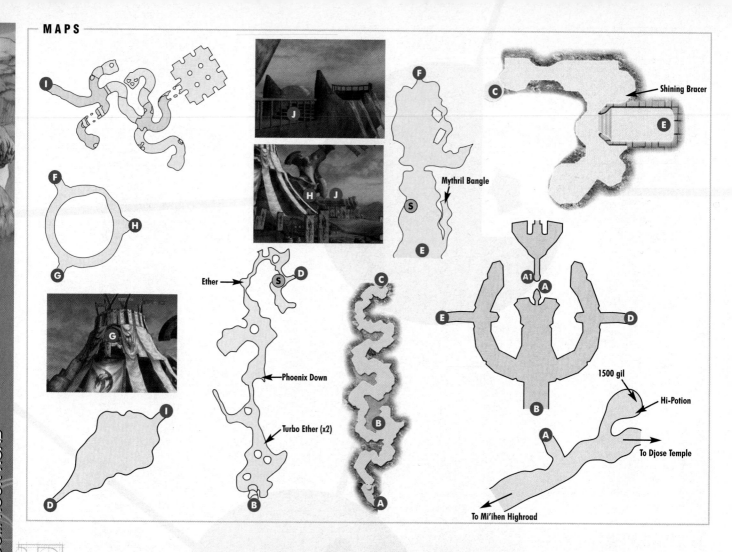

Shining Bracer

Mythril Bangle

Ether →

Phoenix Down

Turbo Ether (x2)

1500 gil

Hi-Potion

To Djose Temple

To Mi'ihen Highroad

# FRIENDLY WITH THE LEAGUE

Speak to the man near the hover to learn that he spotted the Leblanc Sydicate on the Djose Highroad. Head north to the statue of Mi'ihen and collect a **Hi-Potion** and **1500 gil**, then return to the entrance point and speak to Yaibal and his gang. The conversation changes depending on whether you chose to give the sphere to the Youth League or not. If you gave the sphere to the Youth League, the soldiers stationed along Mushroom Rock will prevent encounters with fiends as long as you run alongside the guards. If you fall too far behind or to the side, you'll have an encounter.

The guards at Mushroom Rock react to you differently depending on your allegiance.

After you hear a transmission from the Celsius regarding sphere waves, drop into the ravine. At the entrance of the Den of Woe, the girls encounter Nooj. He gives the group **Crimson Sphere 7** on the assumption that they will search for the missing spheres for the door.

If you visited here previously during Chapter 1, you should now have two of the spheres required to open the mysterious door.

Slipping past the fiends is as simple as strolling quietly on by.

Exit the Den of Woe and climb out of the ravine. As the Gullwings proceed toward New Yevon headquarters, two guards tell the girls to move quietly to avoid detection by the large Ochus positioned along the path. Press the analog stick very lightly to walk if you want to avoid a battle; if not, just run on through. If a fiend turns and spots the group, you're forced to fight a Drowsy Ochu. Once the guards move past the last Ochu and start running again, the girls can resume running too.

# ON THE BAD SIDE OF YOUTH

If you gave the stolen sphere to New Yevon near the beginning of Chapter 2, entering Mushroom Rock triggers an extra mission. Rather than receiving protection from each set of guards, you must battle them. When moving behind the Ochus, no one warns the Gullwings about walking slowly to avoid detection. The encounter with Nooj in the underground cave is terse, but he still hands over the **Crimson Sphere 7**. When you reach the mushroom-shaped elevator platform at the top of the road, you must fight Elma and two League Warriors.

Elma follows her good-humored chiding with an attempt to whip your behind.

# ELMA, LEAGUE WARRIOR (X2)

HP: 1640  MP: 450  EXP: 200  AP: 2

GIL DROPPED: 230
PILFER GIL: 800

STEAL: Normal: Phoenix Down (x3)  Rare: Mega-Phoenix (x2)
DROP: Normal: Wall Ring  Rare: Wall Ring

HP: 422  MP: 26  EXP: 70  AP: 1

The League Warriors are small fish to fry, so spend the first couple of turns taking them out of the battle. Elma uses items to put herself in Haste state, so she attacks quickly. She can be put to sleep, which is the best way to counter her Haste ability. While a Songstress puts her to sleep every round, have a Thief perform the Master Thief ability to make this battle against a long-time ally worthwhile.

GIL DROPPED: 120
PILFER GIL: 180

STEAL: Normal: Hi-Potion  Rare: Grenade (x2)
DROP: Normal: Hi-Potion  Rare: Grenade (x2)

## COMPLETION OTHERWISE

Ride the mushroom-shaped elevator up to the higher level. If you're currently in the mission to fight through the Youth League members, your mission ends here, and you receive a **Kinesis Badge** and the **Shining Mirror Garment Grid**. However, if you're on peaceful terms with the Youth League, ride the machina lift to headquarters. Elma runs out of headquarters and calls to the Gullwings. Before moving toward her, open the chest on the ledge to the right for a **Mythril Bangle**. After doing so, join Elma and Lucil for a brief conversation. After the scene, return to the Celsius and watch Crimson Sphere 7 for a few fractions of a completion point.

*Speak with Elma and Lucil if you're allied with the Youth League.*

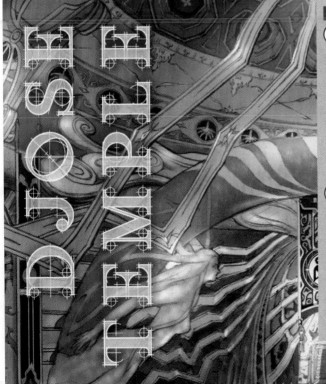

## DJOSE TEMPLE

### ACTION CHECKLIST

**1** Enter the Djose Highroad area from either the temple or Mushroom Rock Road.

**3** Search the Djose Highroad for the missing sphere.

**2** Proceed along the coastal highroad until the Gullwings overhear that the Fem-Goons lost something.

**4** Stand your ground against Ormi and Logos.

COMPLETION: +0.4%

Characters

1

Garment Grids & D{spheres

2

Battle System

3

Accessories

4

Items and Item Shops

5

Walkthrough
Chapter 1
Chapter 2
Chapter 3
Chapter 4
Chapter 5

Mini-Games

7

Fiends and Enemies

8

# WANDERING FIENDS

### AGAMA
HP: 133 | AP: 1 | Gil: 16
Steal: Hi-Potion
Drop: Antidote

### ASSASSIN BEE
HP: 233 | AP: 1 | Gil: 48
Steal: Antidote
Drop: Antidote

### CHOCOBO
HP: 368 | AP: 0 | Gil: 0
Steal: None
Drop: None

### DEATH DAUBER
HP: 78 | AP: 1 | Gil: 20
Steal: Potion
Drop: Potion

### DR. GOON
HP: 232 | AP: 1 | Gil: 50
Steal: Budget Grenade
Drop: Potion

### FEM-GOON
HP: 167 | AP: 1 | Gil: 70
Steal: Potion
Drop: Potion

### GOLD ELEMENTAL
HP: 99 | AP: 1 | Gil: 25
Steal: Electro Marble
Drop: Electro Marble

### LEAGUE RANGER*
HP: 230 | AP: 1 | Gil: 80
Steal: Phoenix Down
Drop: Potion

### LEAGUE SOLDIER*
HP: 178 | AP: 1 | Gil: 80
Steal: Grenade
Drop: Grenade

### LEAGUE TROOPER*
HP: 244 | AP: 1 | Gil: 60
Steal: Grenade
Drop: Grenade

### LEAGUE WARRIOR*
HP: 422 | AP: 1 | Gil: 120
Steal: Hi-Potion
Drop: Hi-Potion

### SALLET
HP: 133 | AP: 1 | Gil: 16
Steal: Hi-Potion
Drop: Antidote

### ORMI
HP: 1150 | AP: 3 | Gil: 120
Steal: X-Potion
Drop: Iron Bangle

### LOGOS
HP: 1030 | AP: 3 | Gil: 120
Steal: Mega-Potion
Drop: Silver Bracer

**\*Only if you gave the stolen sphere to New Yevon**

# ITEM CHECKLIST

Phoenix Down (x2)

Potion (x3)

Floral Fallal Dressphere

Syndicate Uniform **ⓔ**

# MAPS

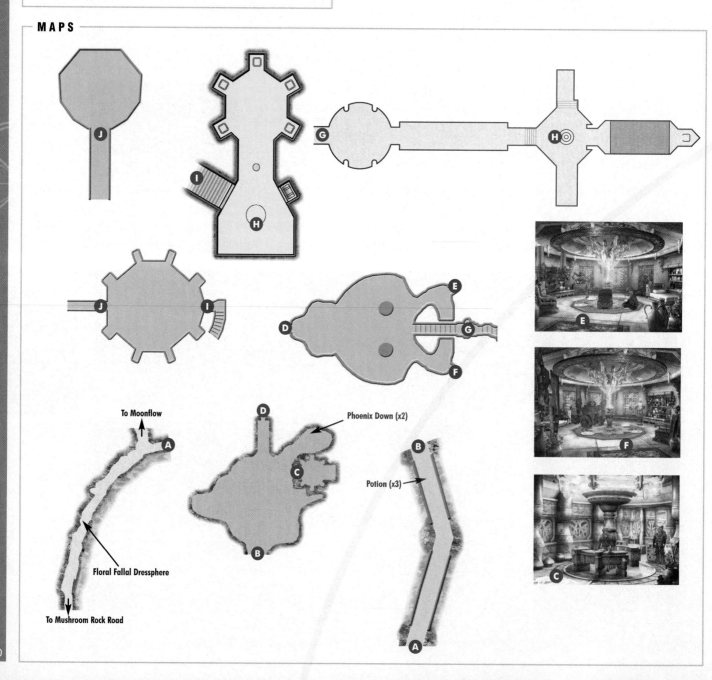

To Moonflow

Floral Fallal Dressphere

To Mushroom Rock Road

Phoenix Down (x2)

Potion (x3)

# EASY PICKINGS

Head south from the temple and proceed along the Djose Highroad until the girls spot some of Leblanc's Syndicate Goons standing near the hovers. Continue south to witness a scene in which two Fem-Goons let slip that they lost a sphere. Move south on the Djose Highroad, fighting Syndicate members in random battles. Halfway down the road, look for the **Floral Fallal Dressphere** (Yuna's special dressphere). Unfortunately, Ormi and Logos show up once again.

*The Syndicate won't allow you to ride the hovers until you defeat their leaders.*

# ORMI, LOGOS, FEM-GOON BOSS FIGHT

**HP:** 1150  **MP:** 22  **EXP:** 80  **AP:** 3

**GIL DROPPED:** 120  **STEAL:** Normal: X-Potion  Rare: Elixer
**PILFER GIL:** 380  **DROP:** Normal: Iron Bangle  Rare: Iron Bangle

Wipe out the Fem-Goon to cancel her magic casting, then take out Ormi and Logos as normal. To make the battle end quicker, use second-level elemental spells. Probably the main challenge of taking out the duo of Ormi and Logos at this stage of the game is using a Thief's Master Thief ability to successfully steal Elixirs from them before finishing them off.

**HP:** 1030  **MP:** 48  **EXP:** 80  **AP:** 3

**GIL DROPPED:** 120  **STEAL:** Normal: Mega-Potion  Rare: Elixer
**PILFER GIL:** 400  **DROP:** Normal: Silver Bracer  Rare: Silver Bracer

**HP:** 167  **MP:** 172  **EXP:** 10  **AP:** 1

**GIL DROPPED:** 70  **STEAL:** Normal: Potion  Rare: Potion (x2)
**PILFER GIL:** 200  **DROP:** Normal: Potion  Rare: Hi-Potion

Characters

1

Garment Grids & Dresspheres

2

Battle System

3

Accessories

4

Items and Item Shops

5

Walkthrough
Chapter 1
Chapter 2
Chapter 3
Chapter 4
Chapter 5

Mini-Games

7

Fiends and Enemies

8

# MOONFLOW

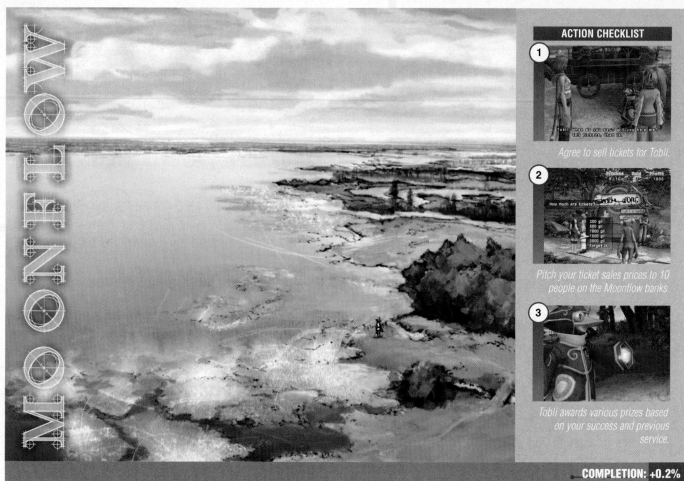

**1** Agree to sell tickets for Tobli.

**2** Pitch your ticket sales prices to 10 people on the Moonflow banks.

**3** Tobli awards various prizes based on your success and previous service.

**COMPLETION: +0.2%**

## WANDERING FIENDS

**AGAMA**
HP: 133 | AP: 1 | Gil: 16
Steal: Hi-Potion
Drop: Antidote

**BANDIT**
HP: 132 | AP: 1 | Gil: 30
Steal: Budget Grenade
Drop: Potion

**BLACKGUARD**
HP: 760 | AP: 1 | Gil: 42
Steal: Phoenix Down
Drop: Potion

**CHOCOBO**
HP: 368 | AP: 0 | Gil: 0
Steal: N/A
Drop: N/A

**FLAN BLANCO**
HP: 625 | AP: 1 | Gil: 72
Steal: Arctic Wind
Drop: Arctic Wind

**PROTOCHIMERA**
HP: 420 | AP: 1 | Gil: 120
Steal: Potion
Drop: Potion

**QUADRICORN**
HP: 188 | AP: 1 | Gil: 13
Steal: Echo Screen
Drop: Potion

**SHELL SHOCKER**
HP: 4700 | AP: 1 | Gil:1300
Steal: Iron Bangle
Drop: Black Ring

**TAKOUBA**
HP: 984 | AP: 1 | Gil: 110
Steal: Phoenix Down
Drop: Phoenix Down

### ITEM CHECKLIST

Gun Mage Dressphere 🅔

Seething Cauldron Garment Grid 🅔

Muscle Belt 🅔

Tobli, located near the wagon on the Moonflow banks, has a new request. He needs someone to sell tickets for his concert. By accepting this mission, you must approach people along both sides of the Moonflow and ask them if they want to buy tickets (press the Square button). You must sell at least six tickets to complete this mission.

You cannot pitch to everyone on the Moonflow. Also, you can only attempt 10 times before the event ends and your results are tallied.

You only get one shot per customer, so if the sale doesn't happen on the first attempt, it never will. The base price is 1000 gil, or 500 gil if you spoke to Tobli *before* completing the mission to protect the Hypello's caravan from the bandits during Chapter 1. If a customer is willing to pay any amount of money over the base price, you get to keep the difference as long as you sell more than five tickets. If you sell a ticket for less than the base price, the loss is subtracted from your profits.

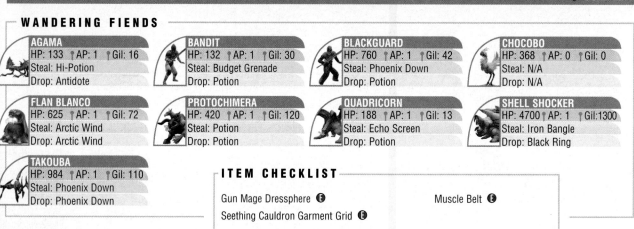

When pitching tickets to potential buyers, take a chance and try to sell for higher or lower prices.

Tobli awards prizes based on whether you make a profit and whether or not you completed the "Shave the Hypello?" mission in Chapter 1. Use the following table to sell to the right people for the right price. Play your cards right and you can make up to 11500 gil!

**MAPS**

Characters

1

Garment Grids & Dresspheres

2

Battle System

3

Accessories

4

Items and Item Shops

5

Walkthrough
Chapter 1
Chapter 2
Chapter 3
Chapter 4
Chapter 5

Mini-Games

7

Fiends and Enemies

8

## "YRP, THE SCALPERS THREE!" CUSTOMER BUYING RATES

| MAP LETTER | CUSTOMER | WILL PAY |
|---|---|---|
| A | Al Bhed Woman wearing pink near entrance. | Up to 1500 gil |
| B | Man wearing yellow and brown, standing in grass. | 200 gil |
| C | Woman wearing red headband, before reaching Tobli. | Up to 1500 gil |
| D | Woman standing beside child, after Tobli. | Up to 1000 gil |
| E | Woman wearing yellow and orange, standing across from Save Sphere. | Up to 1500 gil |
| F | Man wearing orange and green, sitting on bench. | Up to 1000 gil |
| G | Person wearing green sitting on dock stairs. | Up to 1500 gil |
| H | Person wearing green, standing next to dock. | Any gil amount |
| I | Child wearing white shirt, standing beside Hypello. | Up to 2000 gil |
| J | Person in yellow dress, standing at the top of the ramp. | Up to 2000 gil |
| K | Guard sleeping while standing. | Up to 500 gil |
| L | Woman in green standing across from bench. | Any gil amount |
| M | Man wearing blue and yellow, standing on the left side of the path. | Up to 1500 gil |
| N | Man speaking to elderly woman near entrance to Guadosalam. | Up to 500 gil |

## "YRP, THE SCALPERS THREE!" SALES REWARDS

| TICKETS SOLD | "SHAVE THE HYPELLO?" MISSION COMPLETE | MADE A PROFIT? | PRIZES GIVEN BY TOBLI |
|---|---|---|---|
| 0-5 | NA | NA | Nothing |
| 6-9 | Mission Complete | Yes | Profits, Seething Cauldron Garment Grid |
| | | No | Nothing |
| | Incomplete | Yes | Profits, Seething Cauldron Garment Grid, Gun Mage Dressphere |
| | | No | Gun Mage Dressphere |
| 10 | Mission Complete | Yes | Profits, Seething Cauldron Garment Grid, Muscle Belt |
| | | No | Seething Cauldron Garment Grid, Muscle Belt |
| | Incomplete | Yes | Profits, Seething Cauldron Garment Grid, Gun Mage Dressphere |
| | | No | Seething Cauldron Garment Grid, Gun Mage Dressphere |

# GUADOSALAM

**ACTION CHECKLIST**

1

Oh, look - the Dullwings.

Approach the Leblanc Syndicate Goons outside the Chateau.

**COMPLETION: +0.2%**

## SCOURING FOR LOCATION CLUES

Visit Guadosalam early in Chapter 2 because all of the citizens divulge clues to locations where the Leblanc Syndicate may be searching. These clues indicate where you can find three uniforms. While conversing with the citizens, approach the Syndicate Goons at the chateau doors to trigger a scene worth a few completion points.

Gotta wonder why Leblanc's goons would take off for the desert wearing stifling uniforms like that.

People in Guadosalam know where to find Leblanc Syndicate members and their uniforms.

## INFORMATION TRADE

The man behind the counter at the inn will sell some "valuable data" for 10,000 gil if you choose the "Got any data?" option. After your purchase, he provides a vague clue regarding the identity of the buyer. Speak to him a second time and choose the data option again to learn a second hint. You must sell the data to the *exact* person referenced in the clues. This person will buy the data for the amount of gil listed in the table on the following page. If you attempt to sell the data to the wrong person, the true buyer will lower the price he or she is willing to pay by 10,000 gil per wrong person spoken to.

That data sounds *juicy*! Tell me! Tell me!

Unravel the clues wisely before offering the data to anyone. Speaking to the wrong individual will decrease your take.

Actually, I'd be willing to pay 100000 gil for that data.

The man who sells you the data may be the one in the market for the information. If so, he will pay the most for it!

The data peddler is chosen randomly. Before speaking to the data peddler, save your game at the Save Sphere. The buyer who will pay the most for the data is, for some reason, the data peddler himself! If the clues given by the data peddler are not the ones that indicate that he is the buyer, reset your game, load your save, and try again. This is a great way to make 90,000 gil while barely lifting a finger.

Characters

1

Garment Grids & Dresspheres

2

Battle System

3

Accessories

4

Items and Item Shops

5

Walkthrough

Chapter 1

Chapter 2

Chapter 3

Chapter 4

Chapter 5

Mini-Games

7

Fiends and Enemies

8

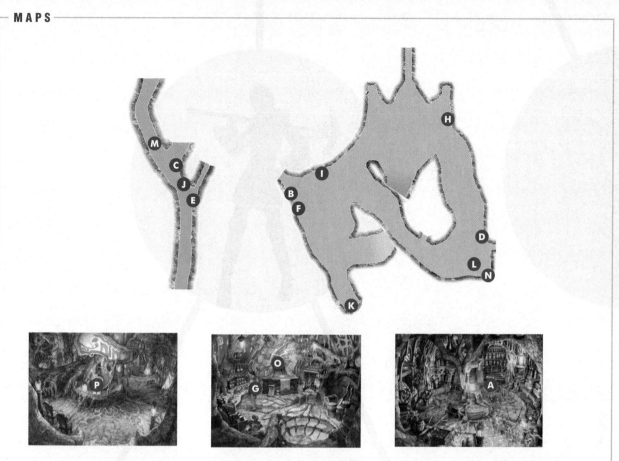

| LOCATION | HINT 1 | HINT 2 | PAYS |
|---|---|---|---|
| A | He is someone loafing about indoors. | It looks like this guy has some time to kill. Maybe he's housesitting? | 25000 gil |
| B | The person is a woman. | She would appear to enjoy speaking with other women. | 25000 gil |
| C | The guy you're after is just sitting around. | Step outside and you should find him easily. | 25000 gil |
| D | It's someone right next to a door. | I believe I saw them by the door to Tobli Productions. | 30000 gil |
| E | This man bears himself with confidence. | He should be just outside. | 30000 gil |
| F | It was someone rather young, yes. | Perhaps this person is watching to see when a certain . door will open | 30000 gil |
| G | This individual can be found indoors. | This person is one bad customer. | 30000 gil |
| I | It's someone sitting down. I wonder what he's doing there? | He's near the door that will not open. | 40000 gil |
| H | I believe it's someone interested in joining the Leblanc Syndicate. | She's not a man, which would make her a woman. | 40000 gil |
| J | It's a guy sitting down. | He's a rather little fellow. | 50000 gil |
| K | It's someone near the door that will not open. | He seemed concerned about relations between the Guado and the Ronso. | 50000 gil |
| L* | I haven't the slightest clue what this guy is doing. | He works for someone who never slows down. | 50000 gil |
| M | It's someone by the entrance to town. | He should still be by the road that leads to the Thunder Plains. | 60000 gil |
| N | It is a woman. | She often talks with the Hypello. | 70000 gil |
| O | This guy's in a place you wouldn't expect. | It seems he's gathering data for commercial reasons. | 80000 gil |
| P | It's the last person you'd expect, no question. | It's the closest person you can find. | 100000 gil |

**\*The Hypello moves all around the upper level of town; his position may vary.**

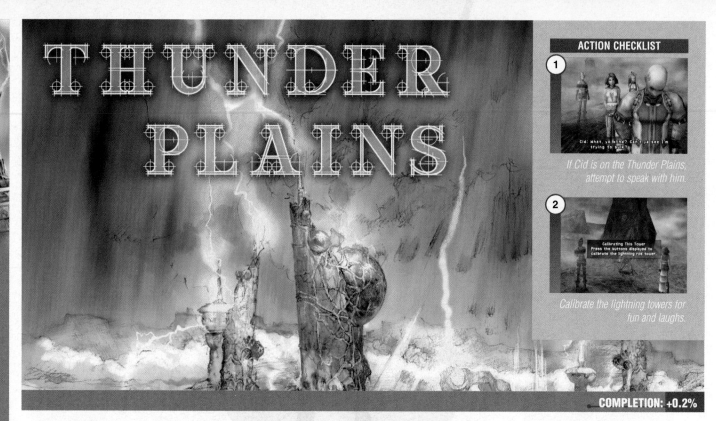

# THUNDER PLAINS

### ACTION CHECKLIST

**1** If Cid is on the Thunder Plains, attempt to speak with him.

**2** Calibrate the lightning towers for fun and laughs.

**COMPLETION: +0.2%**

## WANDERING FIENDS

**ARMET**
HP: 788 | AP: 1 | Gil: 74
Steal: Lunar Curtain
Drop: Light Curtain

**BICOCETTE**
HP: 182 | AP: 1 | Gil: 18
Steal: Potion
Drop: Potion

**BOLT DRAKE**
HP: 623 | AP: 1 | Gil: 130
Steal: Lightning Marble
Drop: Hi-Potion

**CHOCOBO**
HP: 368 | AP: 0 | Gil: 0
Steal: N/A
Drop: N/A

**GOLD ELEMENTAL**
HP: 99 | AP: 1 | Gil: 25
Steal: Electro Marble
Drop: Electro Marble

**LESSER DRAKE**
HP: 577 | AP: 1 | Gil: 22
Steal: Potion
Drop: Potion

**OCHU**
HP: 1480 | AP: 1 | Gil: 133
Steal: Antidote
Drop: Antidote (x2)

**RED ELEMENTAL**
HP: 99 | AP: 1 | Gil: 25
Steal: Potion
Drop: Potion

**STALWART**
HP: 1240 | AP: 1 | Gil: 100
Steal: Phoenix Down
Drop: Phoenix Down (x2)

## ITEM CHECKLIST

Echo Screen (x4)

Potion (x3)

Pearl Necklace

Silence Grenade (x2)

Ether (x2)

Phoenix Down (x2)

Samurai's Honor Garment Grid **E**

## MAPS

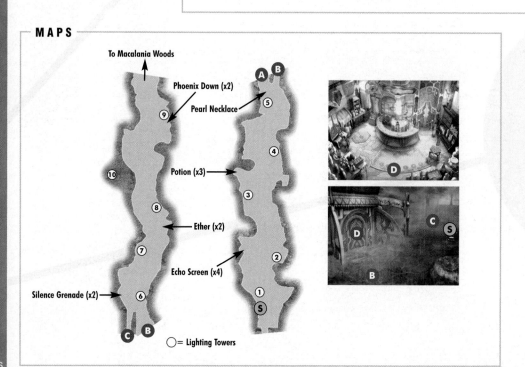

To Macalania Woods

Phoenix Down (x2)

Pearl Necklace

Potion (x3)

Ether (x2)

Echo Screen (x4)

Silence Grenade (x2)

○ = Lighting Towers

# POPS IS GRUMPY

During Chapter 1, if you told Cid that you weren't happy with the tourism at Zanarkand, he will be skulking around in the first area of the Thunder Plains. If you have trouble picking him out in the darkness, look for a red "X" on the on-screen map.

*Speaking with Cid accumulates a meager few completion points, but in the long run, it's worth it.*

# LIGHTNING TOWER CALIBRATION

The following describes a set of mini-games. These events do *not* count toward your completion percentage, but they're fun minigames and make a specific mission in Chapter 5 a bit easier. Upon entering the Thunder Plains during Chapter 2 from either entrance, an Al Bhed will be crouched down by a lightning tower attempting to calibrate it. Speak to the Al Bhed twice and offer to calibrate the towers. The Al Bhed retreats to the safety of the Travel Agency while the Gullwings set about their work. If you want to

*Talk to the Al Bhed technician to start calibrating lightning towers.*

know how well you're doing, or want further instructions, look for him inside the Travel Agency and ask to view your stats. After attempting to calibrate each tower at least once, whether you were successful or not, speak to the technician inside the Travel Agency to receive the **Samurai's Honor Garment Grid**.

Each lightning tower is calibrated via a challenging mini-game. For example, approach the lightning tower closest to the Save Sphere near the entrance from Guadosalam, and press X to start calibrating the tower. A series of PlayStation 2 controller buttons will appear. Memorize the buttons and their order. When the lightning tower is ready, press the controller buttons in the correct order. All of the towers feature mini-games based on pressing a series of buttons. As you score higher, the game becomes progressively faster and you're forced to input the answer more rapidly or the round will count as a miss. You must input the correct series of buttons 30 times to calibrate any tower.

*Calibration is a fun mini-game that tests your memory and reflexes.*

The towers closest to Guadosalam are the easiest to calibrate. The difficulty of the towers increases progressively as you get closer to the exit to Macalania Woods. There are ten lightning towers, nine

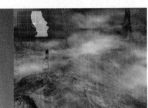

on the plains and a tenth one that stands outside the boundaries of the map. To calibrate the tower you cannot reach, search along the edge of the lake and press the X button.

*Press X at this location to calibrate the tower beyond the Thunder Plains.*

MACALANIA WOODS

## ACTION CHECKLIST

**3**

*Step inside the circles of blue butterflies to find the two missing musicians.*

**1** *Catch up with the Hypello to discover the problem.*

**4** *Speak to Bayra once more to rally the musicians to your cause.*

**2** *Find Bayra near the Sphere Spring deep in the woods.*

**5** *Contact the Hypello near the entrance to claim an extra prize.*

**COMPLETION: +1.4%**

Characters

1

Garment Grids & Dresspheres

2

Battle System

3

Accessories

4

Items and Item Shops

5

Walkthrough 6
Chapter 1
Chapter 2
Chapter 3
Chapter 4
Chapter 5

Mini-Games

7

Fiends and Enemies

8

## WANDERING FIENDS

**AMORPHOUS GEL**
HP: 999　AP: 1　Gil: 380
Steal: White Ring
Drop: Blue Ring

**BARBUTA**
HP: 562　AP: 1　Gil: 33
Steal: Lunar Curtain
Drop: Light Curtain

**CHOCOBO**
HP: 368　AP: 0　Gil: 0
Steal: N/A
Drop: N/A

**DEEP HAIZHE**
HP: 1030　AP: 1　Gil: 40
Steal: Gold Anklet
Drop: Hi-Potion

**FLAN AZUL**
HP: 55　AP: 1　Gil: 20
Steal: Potion
Drop: Potion

**GOLD ELEMENTAL**
HP: 99　AP: 1　Gil: 25
Steal: Electro Marble
Drop: Electro Marble

**HAIZHE**
HP: 653　AP: 1　Gil: 22
Steal: Phoenix Down
Drop: Potion

**RED ELEMENTAL**
HP: 99　AP: 1　Gil: 25
Steal: Potion
Drop: Potion

**SALLET**
HP: 60　AP: 1　Gil: 10
Steal: Potion
Drop: Potion

**WHITE ELEMENTAL**
HP: 77　AP: 1　Gil: 26
Steal: Antarctic Wind
Drop: Potion

**XIPHACTINUS**
HP: 773　AP: 1　Gil: 30
Steal: Fish Scale
Drop: Fish Scale

## ITEM CHECKLIST

Icy Gleam

Silver Bracer

Hi-Potion (x2)

Haste Bangle **E**

## MAPS

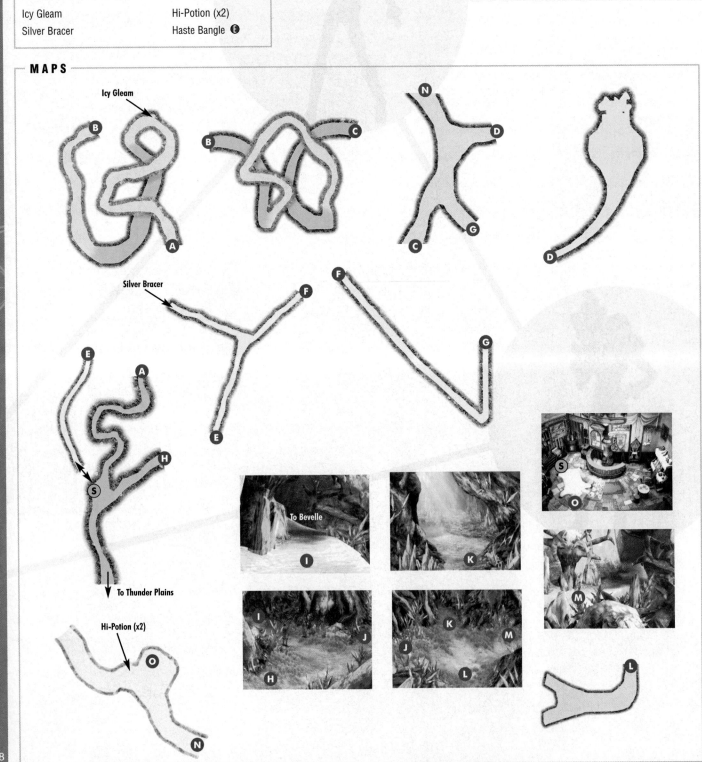

Icy Gleam

Silver Bracer

To Bevelle

To Thunder Plains

Hi-Potion (x2)

# REUNION OF THE DOOMED

Run a short distance up the tree branch path to intercept Tobli's assistant, Hypello, who is frantically waving his arms. The Hypello needs you to find the musicians that disappeared from the forest in Chapter 1.

Speak with the Hypello to get things started.

Donga is located at the intersection on the shimmering path.

Stepping inside the blue butterfly circle near the spring reveals Pukutak.

Follow the shimmering path that starts from the ground next to the Save Sphere. When you reach the four-way intersection deep in the woods, head along the top right path to the spring. Near the tree, speak to the musician in blue, Bayra. As he explains, you must step inside small circles of blue butterflies scattered throughout the forest to find the other two musicians.

When the two missing musicians are found, Yuna returns to the Sphere Spring automatically. Move forward and speak to Bayra again to complete the mission and receive a **Haste Bangle**. At this point, you can choose to return to the Celsius. Instead, head back to the Thunder Plains entrance of Macalania Woods and speak to the Hypello who asked you to complete the mission. He's hanging out by the Save Sphere near the entrance point. He gives you a **Bitter Farewell Garment Grid** as reward. If you completed the "Shave the Hypello?" mission during Chapter 1, the Hypello also generously bestows upon you a **Minerva's Plate**.

Don't return to the Celsius without claiming your reward from the Hypello.

## THERE'S ALWAYS TIME FOR TROMELL

*If you did not speak to Tromell during a visit to Macalania in Chapter 1, he will emerge from the forest as the musicians depart. Speak to him four times to get the **Full Throttle** dressphere for Paine!*

# AL BHED FOR BUSINESS

If you completed the mission "Follow That O'aka!" during Chapter 1 and chose to turn O'aka in to the Al Bhed, the Travel Agency near frozen Lake Macalania is now open. The Al Bhed sell a fairly common lot of items and accessories. However, you still have a chance to make amends with O'aka and help him return here to open the best accessory shop in the game.

Refer to the Bikanel Desert section of the Chapter 2 walkthrough to learn how to bring O'aka back here to open an excellent shop.

| MACALANIA TRAVEL AGENCY SHOP (AL BHED VERSION) | |
|---|---|
| **ITEM** | **COST** |
| Potion | 50 |
| Phoenix Down | 100 |
| Antidote | 50 |
| Eye Drops | 50 |
| Echo Screen | 50 |
| Soft | 50 |
| Holy Water | 300 |
| Icy Gleam | 3000 |
| White Ring | 3000 |

Characters

1

Garment Grids & Dresspheres

2

Battle System

3

Accessories

4

Items and Item Shops

5

Walkthrough

Chapter 1

**Chapter 2**

Chapter 3

Chapter 4

Chapter 5

Mini-Games

7

Fiends and Enemies

8

# BEVELLE

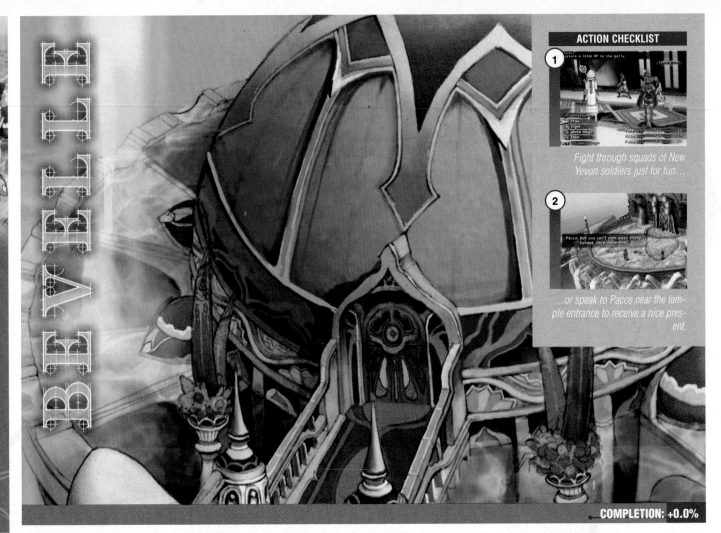

COMPLETION: +0.0%

**1**

Fight through squads of New Yevon soldiers just for fun...

**2**

...or speak to Pacce near the temple entrance to receive a nice present.

## WANDERING FIENDS

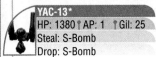
**YAC-13***
HP: 1380 | AP: 1 | Gil: 25
Steal: S-Bomb
Drop: S-Bomb

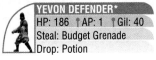
**YEVON DEFENDER***
HP: 186 | AP: 1 | Gil: 40
Steal: Budget Grenade
Drop: Potion

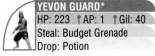
**YEVON GUARD***
HP: 223 | AP: 1 | Gil: 40
Steal: Budget Grenade
Drop: Potion

**\* Will only appear if you returned the sphere to the Youth League**

## ITEM CHECKLIST

Cat's Bell **E**

Coming here is somewhat pointless if you are allied with the Youth League.

# TWO RECEPTIONS

If you gave the stolen sphere to the Youth League and attempt to enter Bevelle during the mission to obtain three Syndicate Uniforms, each set of guards along the route will attack. If you reach the doors, the New Yevon forces attack you with machina. The Gullwings are then forced to retreat.

Pacce and the Kinderguardians are playing outside the temple.

However, if you gave the stolen sphere to New Yevon, then everyone here is happy to see the Gullwings. Proceed up the path and through the doors to the second area. You cannot gain access to the temple due to some crisis inside, but Pacce and the Kinderguardians are playing in the courtyard. Speak to Pacce to receive a **Cat's Bell**. This accessory allows the character who equips it to slowly recover HP while walking around a map.

# CALM LANDS

Characters

Garment Grids
& Dresspheres

Battle System

Accessories

Items and
Item Shops

Walkthrough
Chapter 1
Chapter 2
Chapter 3
Chapter 4
Chapter 5

Mini-Games

Fiends and
Enemies

## ACTION CHECKLIST

**3** Follow Clasko to the cave east of the Calm Lands.

**6** Protect Clasko from the final fiend.

**1** Find the two young Ronso near the Travel Agency.

**4** Agree to help Clasko chase the fiends out of the cave.

**7** Speak with Clasko to obtain greens for catching chocobos.

**2** If Clasko is a passenger on the Celsius, enter the Calm Lands via the airship's navigation panel.

**5** Defeat five sets of fiends in the ranch by determining which are real and which are illusions.

**8** Capture a chocobo by moving across the Calm Lands.

**COMPLETION: +0.8%**

## WANDERING FIENDS

**AHRIMAN**
HP: 99 AP: 1 Gil: 20
Steal: Potion
Drop: Eye Drops

**AMORPHOUS GEL**
HP: 999 AP: 1 Gil: 380
Steal: White Ring
Drop: Blue Ring

**ARMET**
HP: 788 AP: 1 Gil: 74
Steal: Lunar Curtain
Drop: Light Curtain

**BLUE ELEMENTAL**
HP: 363 AP: 1 Gil: 180
Steal: Dragon Scale
Drop: Dragon Scale

**CHOCOBO**
HP: 368 AP: 0 Gil: 0
Steal: N/A
Drop: N/A

**COEURL**
HP: 320 AP: 1 Gil: 30
Steal: Phoenix Down
Drop: Potion (x2)

**DEATH DAUBER**
HP: 78 AP: 1 Gil: 12
Steal: Potion
Drop: Potion

**DIVEBEAK**
HP: 10 AP: 1 Gil: 12
Steal: Potion
Drop: Antidote

**FLAN BLANCO**
HP: 625 AP: 1 Gil: 72
Steal: Arctic Wind
Drop: Arctic Wind

**NASHORN**
HP: 482 AP: 1 Gil: 22
Steal: Potion
Drop: Potion

**PEREGRINE**
HP: 735 AP: 1 Gil: 44
Steal: Hi-Potion
Drop: Hi-Potion

**QUEEN COEURL**
HP: 3270 AP: 1 Gil: 330
Steal: Phoenix Down,
Drop: Phoenix Down (x2)

**SKINK**
HP: 882 AP: 1 Gil: 78
Steal: Hi-Potion
Drop: Hi-Potion

**WILD WOLF**
HP: 185 AP: 1, Gil: 12
Steal: Potion
Drop: Potion

## ITEM CHECKLIST

Ether (x2)

Chocobo Wing (x2)

Phoenix Down (x2)

Phoenix Down (x2)

Alchemist Dressphere 🄴

Highroad Winds Garment Grid 🄴

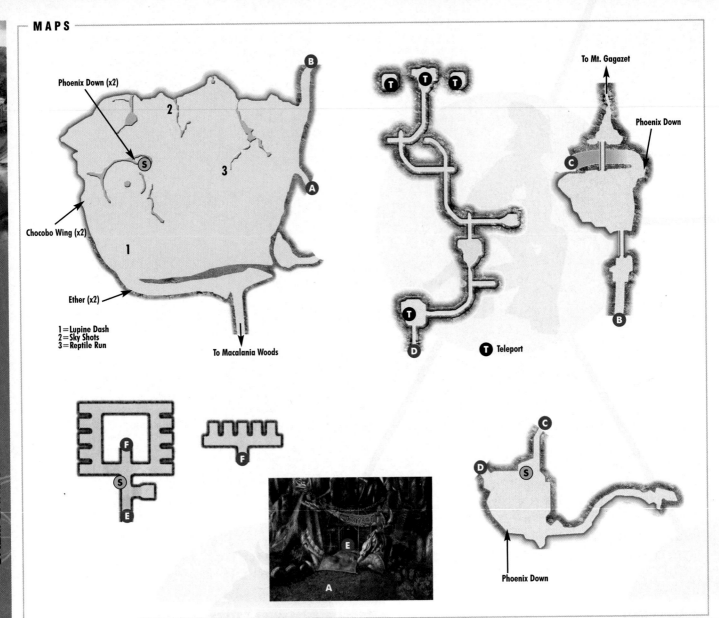

Phoenix Down (x2)

B

2

3

A

S

Chocobo Wing (x2)

1

Ether (x2)

1 = Lupine Dash
2 = Sky Shots
3 = Reptile Run

To Macalania Woods

T   T   T

T

T   Teleport

D

To Mt. Gagazet

Phoenix Down

C

B

F

F

S

E

C

D   S

A

E

Phoenix Down

# CLASKO'S DEATHTRAP FIXER-UPPER

If Clasko is onboard the Celsius, enter the Calm Lands via the airship navigation panel to trigger a scene with him. When Clasko takes off for the building where the old Monster Arena used to be, choose the option to follow him. The Gullwings find Clasko whining outside a small alcove. When he's through, talk him into letting you remove the pesky fiends from the place.

Clasko's dying to pursue his dreams in the Calm Lands.

To clear the fiends, move toward fiends visible on the map until a battle begins.

Yuna enters the ruins of the old Monster Arena, which is full of fiends. Use the Save Sphere near the entrance and use it again between each battle to restore your party. Down the short passage to the right is a fiend. Move toward the fiend until a battle with a Skink begins. After the battle, a counter displays the number of fiends remaining. You must kill five more fiends in the ruins, however, some of them are illusions.

All of the illusionary fiends are facing the real fiend. If you touch three illusions by mistake, the real fiend changes location and you must find the real fiend's new location. Judge the direction the fiends are facing, then head toward that side of the ruins. Go down the row of corrals until you find a fiend that is facing the opposite way of all the other fiends. The first fiend facing the wrong way is often the real fiend.

If you touch the wrong fiend a couple of times, helpful arrows will appear above the fiends to indicate the directions they are facing.

Protect the Gullwings against instant KO with accessories or by equipping Garment Grids if possible.

Be extremely careful around the Queen Coeurls. While their lesser counterparts can reduce a party member's HP to 1 with a single attack, a Queen Coeurl can instantly kill a character. Between each battle, run back and touch the Save Sphere to keep your party in optimum fighting shape.

After defeating five fiend parties in this manner, Clasko is found cringing near the entrance. Move up the short corridor to the right to find the fiend he is looking at. Touch the fiend to begin a battle with three Blue Elementals.

Unleash lightning elemental spells at the entire enemy party to easily defeat the Blue Elementals.

# BEGIN CATCHING CHOCOBOS!

After the sixth set of fiends dissolves, you receive the **Alchemist Dressphere** and the **Highroad Winds Garment Grid**. Talk to Clasko to get a number of **Gysahl Greens**, which are used to catch chocobos, and **Pahsana Green**s, which are used to raise them.

Clasko knows everything regarding the capturing, raising, and training of chocobos.

Chocobos are common on the Calm Lands.

A captured chocobo appears at Clasko's chocobo ranch, where you can view its stats.

Before the end of Chapter 3, you must catch a chocobo if you want to gain the full completion percentage. Once a chocobo appears among a group of enemies, use a Gysahl Green to keep the yellow bird from running off. After the battle, use another Gysahl Green to capture it. Don't issue too many attack commands when attempting to capture a chocobo. By doing so, a fiend might perish and a character with an attack command remaining will assault the chocobo and drive it off no matter how many greens you have fed it.

# LIAN AND AYDE

Before or after finishing the mission to aid Clasko, head for the Travel Agency in the western section of the Calm Lands to find the two Ronso youths standing off to the left. After speaking with the two youngsters, head to Mt. Gagazet on foot.

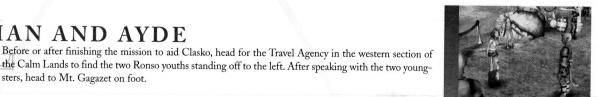

Lian and Ayde are the two young Ronso that Kimahri is worried about.

Characters

1

Garment Grids & Dresspheres

2

Battle System

3

Accessories

4

Items and Item Shops

5

Walkthrough
Chapter 1
Chapter 2
Chapter 3
Chapter 4
Chapter 5

Mini-Games

7

Fiends and Enemies

8

# MT. GAGAZET

## ACTION CHECKLIST

**1** Find out about Syndicate activities on Gagazet from Kimahri.

**5** Jump across the floating platforms inside the cave.

**2** Answer the concerns of the Ronso tribe near the entrance.

**6** Follow the Fem-Goon into the hot springs area, or ascend to the cliff high overhead.

**3** In the Fayth Scar area, the Gullwings spot a Fem-Goon escaping up the cliffs.

**7** Defeat Ormi and the Fem-Goon squad to obtain a Syndicate Uniform.

**4** Climb up the cliff faces to the top ledge and enter the cave.

**COMPLETION: +1.0%**

## WANDERING FIENDS

**AHRIMAN**
HP: 99 | AP: 1 | Gil: 20
Steal: Potion
Drop: Eye Drops

**BICOCETTE**
HP: 182 | AP: 1 | Gil: 18
Steal: Potion
Drop: Potion

**BULLY CAP**
HP: 94 | AP: 1 | Gil: 14
Steal: Eye Drops
Drop: Eye Drops

**DR. GOON**
HP: 232 | AP: 1 | Gil: 50
Steal: Budget Grenade
Drop: Potion

**FEM-GOON**
HP: 167 | AP: 1 | Gil: 70
Steal: Potion
Drop: Potion

**FLAN AMARILLO**
HP: 303 | AP: 1 | Gil: 42
Steal: Electro Marble (x2)
Drop: Electro Marble (x2)

**FLAN PALIDO**
HP: 188 | AP: 1 | Gil: 30
Steal: Potion
Drop: Potion

**FLY EYE**
HP: 258 | AP: 1 | Gil: 20
Steal: Phoenix Down
Drop: Phoenix Down

**PROTOCHIMERA**
HP: 420 | AP: 1 | Gil: 120
Steal: Potion
Drop: Potion

**SHANTAK**
HP: 1130 | AP: 1 | Gil: 120
Steal: Remedy
Drop: Phoenix Down

**TAKOUBA**
HP: 984 | AP: 1 | Gil: 110
Steal: Phoenix Down
Drop: Phoenix Down

**VIPER SNIPER**
HP: 256 | AP: 1 | Gil: 20
Steal: Phoenix Down
Drop: Budget Grenade

**WHITE FANG**
HP: 378 | AP: 1 | Gil: 48
Steal: Potion
Drop: Potion

**ORMI**
HP: 1350 | AP: 1 | Gil: 80
Steal: Gauntlet
Drop: Potion

## ITEM CHECKLIST

| | |
|---|---|
| Elixir | Phoenix Down |
| Hi-Potion | Syndicate Uniform |
| White Cape | Stonehewn Garment Grid |

**MAPS**

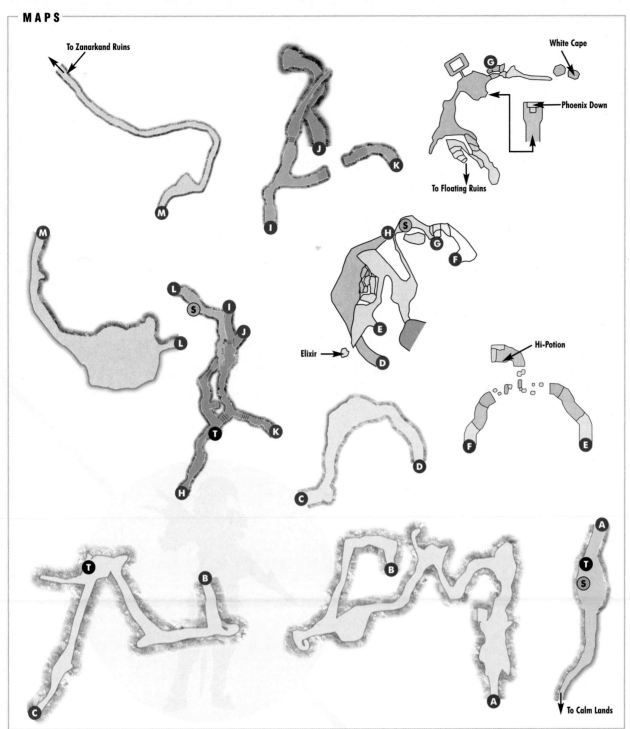

To Zanarkand Ruins

White Cape

Phoenix Down

To Floating Ruins

Elixir

Hi-Potion

To Calm Lands


Characters

1

Garment Grids
& Dspheres

2

Battle System

3

Accessories

4

Items and
Item Shops

5

Walkthrough
Chapter 1
Chapter 2
Chapter 3
Chapter 4
Chapter 5

Mini-Games

7

Fiends and
Enemies

8

# RONSO NEED MORE REASSURANCE

Speak to Kimahri and the Ronso gathered near the entrance of Mt. Gagazet and answer each of their concerns with the correct responses. You must talk to Kimahri twice: once to undertake the mission currently available at Gagazet and then a second time to appease his anxieties. If you correctly addressed the concerns of all the Ronso during Chapter 1, a certain boss fight becomes a little easier to deal with in Chapter 3. Also, you'll be well on your way to immortalizing Yuna in a way you never thought possible.

*Correctly addressing Kimahri's worries nets you a valuable prize later. Again, you must be firm with Kimahri and tell him to handle his own problems.*

135

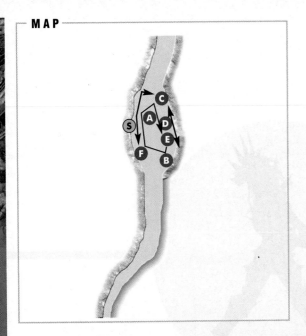

MT. GAGAZET

## RONSO CONCERNS AND ANSWERS, CHAPTER 2

| MAP LETTER | DESCRIPTION | CONCERN | YUNA'S ANSWERS | TRUST |
|---|---|---|---|---|
| A | Woman standing beside Kimahri. | Worry is great burden on Elder's shoulders. | He does seem very tired. | +1 |
| | | | You should help Kimahri! | 0 |
| | | | Of course - he's the elder. | -1 |
| B | Garik | Ronso youth grow strong, destroy hated Guado. Garik swear to mountain! Garik avenge murdered Ronso! | Have you talked with Kimahri about this? | -1 |
| | | | What if the Guado retaliate? | +1 |
| | | | That won't make anyone happy. | 0 |
| C | Male walking around near exit to the snowy slopes area. | Al Bhed, too, suffer at hands of Guado. Guado is source of much chaos! | It's not as simple as that. | -1 |
| | | | Maybe the Guado really are to blame. | +1 |
| | | | The Al Bhed have put revenge behind them. | 0 |
| D | Female on right side of screen at entrance to Mt. Gagazet. | Guado must die for Ronso future! | You have to cool off and think. | -1 |
| | | | And what of the Guado? | +1 |
| | | | What future will that bring? | 0 |
| E | Male walking around near entrance to Mt. Gagazet. | Garik will march, fight Ronso enemies. Fight Guado! | Can you think of nothing but fighting? | -1 |
| | | | Please, try to think about it some more. | +1 |
| | | | Will that make you satisfied? | 0 |
| F | Male in red armor with green hair on left side of screen at entrance to Mt. Gagazet. | Elder is weakling, Garik move too slow! Guado will escape us! | They have to think everything through. | -1 |
| | | | Then… there won't be anyone left to fight. | +1 |
| | | | There's nothing we can do about it. | 0 |
| G | Guard near stairs in mountain cave of Mt. Gagazet. | Many people come to sacred mountain uninvited. Sphere hunters are problem! | They're searching for the mountain's secrets. | 0 |
| | | | They should take better care of the mountain. | +1 |
| | | | That's the way things are now. | -1 |

# MOUNTAIN PURSUIT

Use the teleport pad near the entrance to quickly travel up to the Mountain Path area, then ascend the slope and follow the trail until the mission begins. Follow the Fem-Goon by climbing up the cliffs to the top ledge. Enter the cave off to the right side.

Keep an eye on the map in the upper-left corner to avoid missing side chambers.

Head through the cave and jump over the platforms. Keep an eye glued to the on-screen map, and take the side path to a small cave where a **Hi-Potion** awaits in a chest on a ledge. Return to the floating rock path and continue hopping and running toward the exit.

Look for a treasure chest on a rock platform floating off the side of the mountain ledge. To reach it, slowly WALK from the cave toward the edge and the platform won't rise. Jump to the platform to obtain the **Elixir** inside the chest.

# CHOICE OF EVENTS

Emerging from the other side of the cave, you should spot the Fem-Goon on the move again. If you follow her directly, you'll see the next scenario play out in short form.

*The low path takes you directly to the hot springs, but you'll miss some items and completion percentage.*

However, if you ascend up the cliffs to the highest ledge instead of following the Fem-Goon directly, the scenario is greatly extended. This series of events does award more completion percentage than the other, but it's fun to know that you can experience this series of events in two different ways.

*Inside a cave on the uppermost level is a chest containing a **Phoenix Down**.*

*Walk slowly up the narrow path east from the hot springs area so that the top rock platform doesn't rise. Hop across the two floating rocks to obtain a **White Cape**.*

*If you attempt to continue climbing the cliffs above the hot springs overlook, the winds blow too hard and the Gullwings must turn back.*

## Path A (Follow Fem-Goon Directly to Hot Springs)

- The Gullwings spot the Fem-Goons soaking in the hot springs.

- Ormi enters and stumbles onto the Gullwings.

- Boss Fight: Ormi

- Battle with Fem-Goon squad.

- Obtain Syndicate Uniform

- Mission Complete!

## Path B (Proceed to Top Cliff)

- The Gullwings spy on the Fem-Goons getting out of the hot springs.

- The cliff crumbles, spilling the Gullwings into the hot springs, frightening off Ormi and the Fem-Goons.

- Obtain Syndicate Uniform.

- The Gullwings bathe in the hot springs.

- Exit the hot springs; the Gullwings encounter the Fem-Goon squad.

- Boss Fight: Ormi

- Mission Complete!

## ORMI BOSS FIGHT

**HP: 1350  MP: 22  EXP: 180  AP: 1**

Ormi fights in the same manner as in previous battles, so use the same tactics against him here. Prevent Ormi from attacking by using items or dances that put him to sleep. Unleash a couple of chain attacks or second-level Black Mage spells, such as Fira or Blizzara, to end the battle.

**GIL DROPPED:** 200
**PILFER GIL:** 520

**STEAL:** Normal: X-Potion  Rare: Elixir
**DROP:** Normal: Beaded Brooch  Rare: Beaded Brooch

Characters

1

Garment Grids & Dresspheres

2

Battle System

3

Accessories

4

Items and Item Shops

5

Walkthrough

Chapter 1

Chapter 2

Chapter 3

Chapter 4

Chapter 5

Mini-Games

7

Fiends and Enemies

8

# ZANARKAND RUINS

## ACTION CHECKLIST

**1** Learn of Isaaru's problems by speaking to him just inside the dome.

**2** Match each monkey to its soul mate before the conclusion of Chapter 3

**COMPLETION: +0.4%**

## WANDERING FIENDS

**ANOLE**
HP: 734 | AP: 1 | Gil: 70
Steal: Hi-Potion
Drop: Hi-Potion

**BEHEMOTH**
HP: 1420 | AP: 1 | Gil: 80
Steal: Phoenix Down
Drop: Circlet

**GECKO**
HP: 228 | AP: 1 | Gil: 18
Steal: Antidote
Drop: Antidote

**NASHORN**
HP: 482 | AP: 1 | Gil: 22
Steal: Potion
Drop: Potion

**WHITE ELEMENTAL**
HP: 77 | AP: 1 | Gil: 26
Steal: Antarctic Wind
Drop: Potion

## ITEM CHECKLIST

- Dispel Tonic
- Phoenix Down (x2)
- Hi-Potion(x2)
- Grenade (x2)
- L-Bomb (x2)
- Remedy
- Lunar Curtain
- Mana Spring
- 1000 gil
- Light Curtain
- Remedy (x3)
- Remedy (x2)
- Ether (x2)
- Elixir (x2)
- Phoenix Down (x2)
- Hi-Potion (x2)
- Soul of Thamasa ⑤

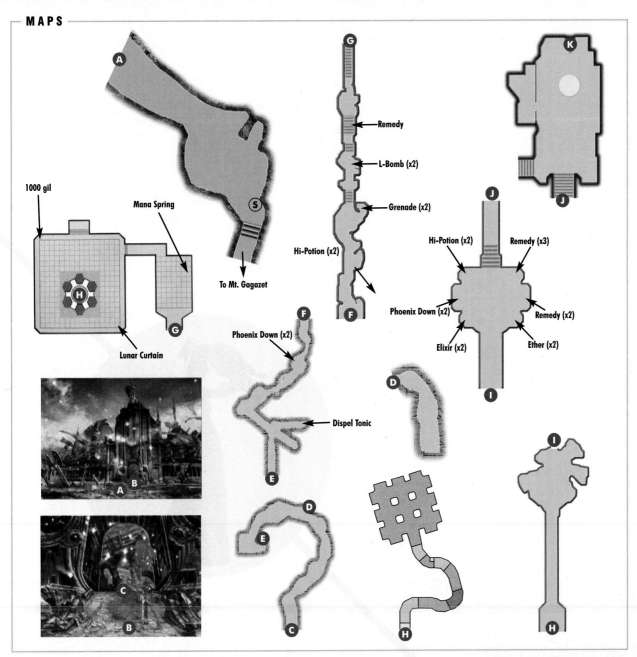

1000 gil

Mana Spring

To Mt. Gagazet

Lunar Curtain

Remedy

L-Bomb (x2)

Grenade (x2)

Hi-Potion (x2)

Phoenix Down (x2)

Dispel Tonic

Hi-Potion (x2)

Remedy (x3)

Phoenix Down (x2)

Remedy (x2)

Elixir (x2)

Ether (x2)

Characters

Garment Grids
& D. Dresspheres

Battle System

Accessories

Items and
Item Shops

Walkthrough
Chapter 1
Chapter 2
Chapter 3
Chapter 4
Chapter 5

Mini-Games

Fiends and
Enemies

# OPERATION: MONKEY!

The tourists seem to be leaving the treasure chests unopened, so enter the dome and speak to Isaaru to find out why. He is standing at the base of the stairs, wondering how he's going to prevent the monkeys that are infesting the ruins from driving off tourists. As Isaaru leaves, Rikku and Paine get the crazy idea of breeding the monkeys to increase their population, thus scaring away the tourist trade permanently.

*Isaaru is foolish to leave these three mischievous girls in the temple alone.*

To complete this short side quest, grab a monkey that is in love and offer it to the other monkeys inside the Zanarkand dome until you find the monkey's soul mate. When small hearts start emanating over a monkey's head, it means that it is ready for true love. Press the X button to grab a monkey. As Yuna is holding the lovey-dovey creature in front of her, move to other monkeys and check to see if they like the monkey that you're holding by pressing the X button. If the monkeys are a match, the two will instantly fall in love.

*The monkeys are connected by their names.*

The location of each monkey and its soul mate is marked on the following maps. Match a red numeral with its corresponding purple numeral to make a match. After matching up all twelve pairs of monkeys, you'll complete the mission and receive a **Soul of Thamasa** accessory.

*When Yuna is holding a monkey, move to other monkeys and check to see if they are interested in falling in love.*

*Remember, if you speak to the wrong monkey, it might swipe some gil!*

BIKANEL DESERT

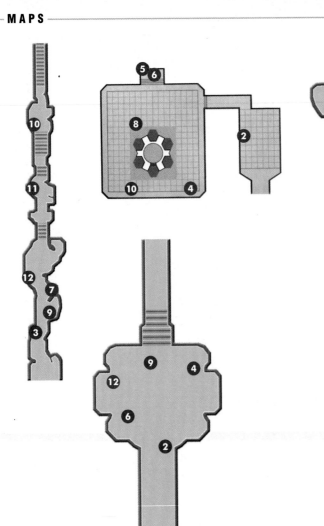

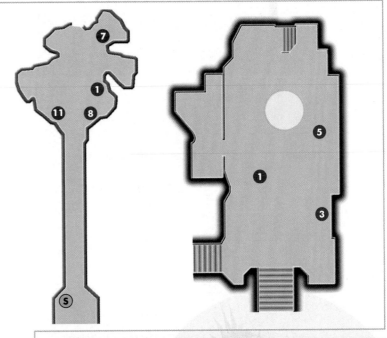

| OPERATION: MONKEY! MATCHES | | |
|---|---|---|
| **SET** | **LOVER** | **SOUL MATE** |
| 1 | Birch | Sequoia |
| 2 | Spring | Autumn |
| 3 | Dusky | Dawne |
| 4 | Rosemary | Thyme |
| 5 | Terran | Skye |
| 6 | Minni | Maxx |
| 7 | Summer | Winter |
| 8 | Peke | Valli |
| 9 | Canis | Felina |
| 10 | Arroh | Quivrr |
| 11 | Golde | Sylva |
| 12 | Luna | Sol |

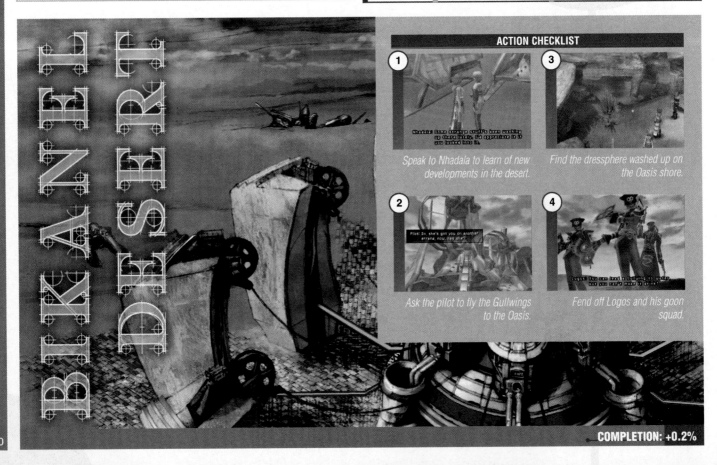

## ACTION CHECKLIST

**1** Speak to Nhadala to learn of new developments in the desert.

**2** Ask the pilot to fly the Gullwings to the Oasis.

**3** Find the dressphere washed up on the Oasis shore.

**4** Fend off Logos and his goon squad.

**COMPLETION: +0.2%**

Characters

1

Garment Grids & Dresspheres

2

Battle System

3

Accessories

4

Items and Item Shops

5

Walkthrough

Chapter 1

Chapter 2

Chapter 3

Chapter 4

Chapter 5

Mini-Games

7

Fiends and Enemies

8

## WANDERING FIENDS

**ANGRA MAINYU**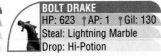
HP: 333444 ↑ AP: 30 ↑ Gil: 5000
Steal: Megalixir
Drop: Ribbon

**BOLT DRAKE**
HP: 623 ↑ AP: 1 ↑ Gil: 130
Steal: Lightning Marble
Drop: Hi-Potion

**CHOCOBO**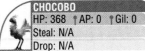
HP: 368 ↑ AP: 0 ↑ Gil: 0
Steal: N/A
Drop: N/A

**FLY EYE**
HP: 258 ↑ AP: 1 ↑ Gil: 20
Steal: Phoenix Down
Drop: Phoenix Down

**HRIMTHURS**
HP: 552 ↑ AP: 1 ↑ Gil: 44
Steal: Phoenix Down
Drop: Phoenix Down

**KILLER HOUND**
HP: 202 ↑ AP: 1 ↑ Gil: 18
Steal: Potion
Drop: Potion

**NASHORN**
HP: 482 ↑ AP: 1 ↑ Gil: 22
Steal: Potion
Drop: Potion

**LOGOS**
HP: 1220 ↑ AP: 1 ↑ Gil: 200
Steal: Mega-Potion
Drop: Lure Bracer

**FEM-GOON**
HP: 167 ↑ AP: 1 ↑ Gil: 70
Steal: Potion
Drop: Potion

## ITEM CHECKLIST

Machina Maw Dressphere **E**
Hour of Need Garment Grid **E**

# WATER WE DOING HERE?

Nhadala is worried about strange events and odd interlopers in the Oasis region. Talk to the pilot twice and ask him to fly to the Oasis for a look. Approaching the water's edge, Yuna finds Rikku's special Dressphere, the **Machina Maw**. Logos and the Leblanc Syndicate then ambush the Gullwings.

## BOSS FIGHT

# LOGOS, FEM-GOON (X2)

**HP: 1220 MP: 46 EXP: 160 AP: 1**

| GIL DROPPED: 200 | STEAL: Normal: Mega-Potion | Rare: Elixir |
| PILFER GIL: 460 | DROP: Normal: Lure Bracer | Rare: Lure Bracer |

Use the first few turns during the battle to eliminate Logos's companions, reducing the number of enemy turns per round. Logos unleashes a new attack during this battle, Hail of Bullets, wherein he shoots the entire party with a volley of shots. Logos also attempts to incapacitate the party with bombs that inflict Darkness or Silence. If his bomb tossing becomes a problem, have a Songstress tame the fierce gun master by casting Sleepy Shuffle. The **Hour of Need Garment Grid** is awarded for defeating the trio and completing this short mission.

**HP: 160 MP: 172 EXP: 10 AP: 1**

| GIL DROPPED: 70 | STEAL: Normal: Potion | Rare: Potion |
| PILFER GIL: 200 | DROP: Normal: Potion | Rare: Potion |

# O'AKA PAYS OFF HIS OWN DEBT

If for some reason you elected to turn O'aka over to the Al Bhed to pay off his own debt, he will be found in the desert toiling away! After taking care of business at the Oasis, return to the digger's camp and speak to the man in green standing beside the hover. It sounds like someone familiar is toiling away in the Southern Expanse. Ask the pilot to fly you to the Southern Expanse to look for O'aka.

*Rumors at the camp indicate O'aka is around.*

Repeatedly excavate treasures and machina in the Southern Expanse. During an excursion, a green "X" may appear on-screen. Head for it to find O'aka. He paid off his own debt and is now weary from his toils. Allow him to come aboard the Celsius.

Back onboard the Celsius, run down to the Cabin to visit the merchant. Ask to see his goods, which are all slightly cheaper than usual. He then begins to sell items at ridiculously cheap prices! In addition, he and his brother Wantz later reopen the Travel Agency at Macalania, selling some of the better accessories in the game!

*Agreeing to take O'aka onboard the Celsius counts as a failed dig, but this time, it's worth the trouble.*

# GUADOSALAM — LEBLANC'S CHATEAU

## ACTION CHECKLIST

**1** Approach the entrance of Leblanc's chateau in disguise.

**2** Speak to Logos and Ormi in the living room.

**3** Run upstairs to massage Leblanc.

**4** Push the secret switch at the back of the living room and penetrate the secret corridor of the chateau

**5** Fight Ormi after he discovers the Gullwings inside the hideout.

**6** Snatch the sphere inside Logos's and Ormi's room.

**7** Deactivate the booby traps in the deadly corridor.

**8** Enter Leblanc's room and confront the Syndicate leaders.

**COMPLETION: +4.0%**

## WANDERING FIENDS

**BATTLESNAKE**
HP: 252 | AP: 1 | Gil: 40
Steal: Phoenix Down
Drop: Potion

**DR. GOON**
HP: 232 | AP: 1 | Gil: 50
Steal: Budget Grenade
Drop: Potion

**FEM-GOON**
HP: 167 | AP: 1 | Gil: 70
Steal: Potion
Drop: Potion

**ORMI**
HP: 1640 | AP: 1 | Gil: 220
Steal: X-Potion
Drop: Black Choker

**LOGOS**
HP: 1432 | AP: 1 | Gil: 230
Steal: Mega-Potion
Drop: Favorite Outfit

**LEBLANC**
HP: 1380 | AP: 1 | Gil: 300
Steal: Elixir
Drop: Reassembled Sphere

## ITEM CHECKLIST

Heady Perfume or Gold Hairpin

Crimson Sphere 10 🅕

Healing Light Garment Grid 🅔

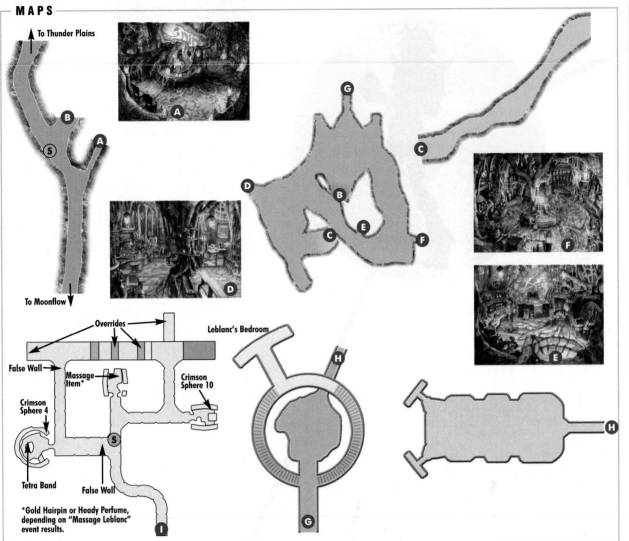

To Thunder Plains

G

C

B

A

S

A

D

B

C

E

F

To Moonflow

F

E

Overrides

Leblanc's Bedroom

False Wall

Massage Item*

Crimson Sphere 10

Crimson Sphere 4

S

H

Tetra Band

False Wall

*Gold Hairpin or Heady Perfume, depending on "Massage Leblanc" event results.

I

G

H

Characters

1

Garment Grids & Dressspheres

2

Battle System

3

Accessories

4

Items and Item Shops

5

Walkthrough

Chapter 1

Chapter 2

Chapter 3

Chapter 4

Chapter 5

Mini-Games

7

Fiends and Enemies

8

143

# THREE UNIFORMS COLLECTED

As you track down Leblanc Syndicate members and steal their uniforms, one by one the Gullwings on the bridge of the Celsius will

don the uniforms of their rivals. When the third uniform is obtained, the party automatically returns to the Celsius. For completing the mission to get three Syndicate Uniforms, you're awarded the **Bum Rush Garment Grid**.

*Once you have all three uniforms, the girls lounge around the bridge in Syndicate fashions.*

## DESTINATION: CHAPTER 3!

*With all three uniforms obtained, access to Leblanc's chateau in Guadosalam will be open. If you need to go somewhere else and complete any remaining side missions, be sure to do it before you change into the uniforms. Once you change into the uniforms at Guadosalam, you will be unable to return to the Celsius. After the mission inside the Syndicate's hideout, Brother automatically flies to Bevelle.*

# FAKING AND ENTERING

Approach the doors guarded by Leblanc Syndicate Goons. The girls automatically put on their uniforms and slip inside. After the

scene in the foyer, head through the door at the back of the first level. Proceed to the far side of the living room and receive your orders from Logos and Ormi. They need someone to go upstairs and massage the boss.

*Leblanc is a pushover for her Noojie-Woojie.*

Return to the foyer and ascend the stairs to the upper level, where Leblanc demands a massage at once. To massage her, move the heart-shaped icon to any point on the grid and press the X button. Not only does Leblanc react vocally, but the icon lights up a certain color:

- A red heart means you've hit the perfect spot. The grid resets, forcing you to look for the red spot in its new location.

- A yellow heart indicates that the perfect spot is just one square away, either to the left, the right, up, or down.

- A green heart means that the perfect spot is just one diagonal square away.

- A blue heart indicates that you're nowhere close to the satisfaction spot.

You must completely satisfy Leblanc within 15 rounds. A round concludes each time you attempt to massage a spot. Points are awarded based on the color of the heart icon revealed. The better the spot, the more points you receive. If you fail to score 32 points within 15 rounds on your first attempt, you're forced to do it again.

During your second attempt, Leblanc awards more points, but the item found in Ormi's bedroom within the secret corridor changes from the Gold Hairpin to the Heady Perfume. While the Heady Perfume raises a few stats, the Gold Hairpin cuts the MP cost of spells by half. If you don't satisfy Leblanc on the first try and want the other item, reset your game and try again.

## REVEALING THE SECRET PASSAGE

The secret switch is on the back wall of the living room on the first floor of the chateau, between the blue pedestal and the door. Once the girls are inside the secret corridor, proceed down the curving passage until Ormi discovers the group.

*Darn that Brother of Rikku's. Your cover is blown!*

# ORMI, FEM-GOON, DR. GOON — BOSS FIGHT

**HP: 1640    MP: 40    EXP: 220    AP: 1**

| | |
|---|---|
| **GIL DROPPED:** 220 | **STEAL:** Normal: X-Potion   Rare: Elixer |
| **PILFER GIL:** 560 | **DROP:** Normal: Black Choker   Rare: Black Choker |

Take out Ormi's sidekicks quickly, then use a few Black Mage spells on Ormi. Try to inflict more damage when Ormi holsters his shield in preparation for one of his special attacks. Ormi's Huggles attack inflicts several hits to one character, usually enough to KO her. Revive a fallen ally with a Phoenix Down, then use a Potion and continue your assault. Inflict Ormi with Poison or Darkness to give yourself an advantage.

**HP: 167    MP: 172    EXP: 10    AP: 1**

| | |
|---|---|
| **GIL DROPPED:** 70 | **STEAL:** Normal: Potion   Rare: Potion |
| **PILFER GIL:** 200 | **DROP:** Normal: Potion   Rare: Hi-Potion |

**HP: 232    MP: 41    EXP: 10    AP: 1**

| | |
|---|---|
| **GIL DROPPED:** 50 | **STEAL:** Normal: Budget Grenade   Rare: Grenade |
| **PILFER GIL:** 160 | **DROP:** Normal: Potion   Rare: Grenade |

# SNOOPING AROUND THE GOONS' QUARTERS

Proceed down the secret hallway and use the Save Sphere on the left. Continue past the Save Sphere and open the purple doors at the corner. Inside Ormi's room is the chest containing the item determined by your skill at massaging Leblanc—either the **Heady Perfume** or the **Gold Hairpin**.

The item found here changes depending on your massage technique.

Outside Ormi's chamber, continue down the next section of corridor and enter the next set of purple doors. Pick up the **Crimson Sphere 10** on Logos's bedside bookshelf.

Yuna and crew are discovered once again!

## ORMI, LOGOS — BOSS FIGHT

**HP:** 1840  **MP:** 42  **EXP:** 240  **AP:** 1

**GIL DROPPED:** 230  
**PILFER GIL:** 580

**STEAL:** Normal: X-Potion  Rare: Elixir  
**DROP:** Normal: Defense Veil  Rare: Defense Veil

Logos's attacks are more frequent and tend to interrupt your characters' attacks; focus on him first. Steal from him, then let a Black Mage douse him with spells. Logos occasionally performs Russian Roulette, a weak attack that tends to apply status ailments (such as Poison or KO). With Logos down, treat Ormi to some strong Black Mage spells but watch out for his devastating Huggles attack. Poison, Sleep, and Darkness can reduce the ability of either thug to attack.

**HP:** 1432  **MP:** 64  **EXP:** 240  **AP:** 1

**GIL DROPPED:** 230  
**PILFER GIL:** 580

**STEAL:** Normal: Mega-Potion  Rare: Elixer  
**DROP:** Normal: Favorite Outfit  Rare: Favorite Outfit

## DEACTIVATING THE SECURITY SYSTEM

Exit Logos's room, head down the corridor to its right, and climb to the top of the raised ledge. Rather than leap from ledge to ledge down the corridor, drop into the first pit. Within this pit, you'll discover one of three switches that overrides the security system. Activate the switch, then climb the next section and drop into the next pit. Turn on yet another override switch, then climb out and proceed to the end of the corridor.

The switches to override the security devices are tucked inside the pits of the long corridor.

The spikes are more threatening than harmful.

As you proceed toward the back wall, panels slide away to reveal sharp spikes. Turn and run down the corridor, leaping from ledge to ledge as quickly as possible. If you drop into a pit, climb out fast and continue. When you reach the bottom edge of the corridor, wait for the wall to catch up. In order to reach the alcove above the passageway, you must let the spikes catch up to you at this point. Doing so will trigger a short scene of the girls outrunning the spikes and jumping to the alcove above. Press the override in this corridor to finally deactivate the booby traps.

1

Garment Grids & Dresspheres

2

Battle System

3

Accessories

4

Items and Item Shops

5

Walkthrough

Chapter 1

**Chapter 2**

Chapter 3

Chapter 4

Chapter 5

Mini-Games

7

Fiends and Enemies

8

# UNCOVERING LEBLANC'S ROOM

With the booby traps in the long corridor disabled, run to the top of the corridor and press the switch that is now visible on the back wall. A section of the corridor on the left slides down to reveal a new portion of the passage. Head into the newly opened corridor and enter the first doorway—a circular portal with Leblanc's seal engraved upon it. Proceed a little ways into the room for the final showdown.

*The final encounter occurs in Leblanc's room.*

## RETURN TRIP REQUIRED

*Some additional items are located in Leblanc's room, but they'll have to wait until you have a chance to return here during Chapter 3.*

# ORMI, LOGOS, LEBLANC

**BOSS FIGHT**

**HP:** 1344 **MP:** 45 **EXP:** 260 **AP:** 2

**GIL DROPPED:** 240
**PILFER GIL:** 600

**STEAL:** Normal: X-Potion  Rare: Elixir
**DROP:** Normal: Twist Headband  Rare: Twist Headband

Leblanc and crew have been practicing a three-person combo attack for the girls. Since Logos has a surprisingly low amount of HP, dispose of him as quickly as possible with a second-level Black Mage spell. This negates the ability of the Syndicate trio to use their No Love Lost combo. If the trio executes the attack, use a Mega-Potion to recover if necessary.

**HP:** 989 **MP:** 70 **EXP:** 260 **AP:** 2

**GIL DROPPED:** 240
**PILFER GIL:** 640

**STEAL:** Normal: Mega-Potion  Rare: Elixir
**DROP:** Normal: Charm Bangle  Rare: Charm Bangle

Leblanc motivates her men by casting Shell, Protect, and Regen on them simultaneously. Therefore, Leblanc is the next target. Use a Dispel Tonic or a Dispel spell to get rid of the positive effects she casts on herself and Ormi. She is susceptible to Poison and Darkness, as are Ormi and Logos. After Leblanc is gone, finish up Ormi as quickly as possible. You will receive the **Healing Light Garment Grid** for completing this mission.

**HP:** 1380 **MP:** 460 **EXP:** 380 **AP:** 2

**GIL DROPPED:** 300
**PILFER GIL:** 1500

**STEAL:** Normal: Elixir  Rare: Elixir
**DROP:** Normal: Reassembled Sphere  Rare: Reassembled Sphere

# BEVELLE - SECRETS OF NEW YEVON

## ACTION CHECKLIST

**1**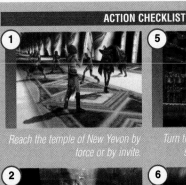
Reach the temple of New Yevon by force or by invite.

**5**
Turn the gaol on and off to reach some valuable accessories.

**2**
Activate the switch to change the direction of the lift.

**6**
Step on the glyphs to activate the lifts.

**3**
Ride the lift to the lower levels of the temple.

**7**
Confront Praetor Baralai at the heart of New Yevon's secrets.

**4**
Touch the panels on the security towers to create an exit.

**8**
Battle an aeon turned evil.

**COMPLETION: +2.6%**

## WANDERING FIENDS

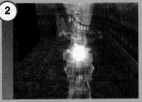 **FLAN AMARILLO**
HP: 303 | AP: 1 | Gil: 42
Steal: Electro Marble (x2)
Drop: Electro Marble (x2)

 **FLAN BLANCO**
HP: 625 | AP: 1 | Gil: 72
Steal: Arctic Wind
Drop: Arctic Wind

**KUKULCAN**
HP: 3220 | AP: 1 | Gil: 86
Steal: Soft (x2)
Drop: Soft (x2)

**SKINK**
HP: 882 | AP: 1 | Gil: 78
Steal: Hi-Potion
Drop: Hi-Potion

 **VERTIGO**
HP: 688 | AP: 1 | Gil: 36
Steal: Antidote (x2)
Drop: Antidote

**YAC-13**
HP: 1380 | AP: 1 | Gil: 25
Steal: S-Bomb
Drop: S-Bomb

**YAU-28**
HP: 1270 | AP: 1 | Gil: 25
Steal: Grenade
Drop: S-Bomb

**YEVON DEFENDER**
HP: 186 | AP: 1 | Gil: 40
Steal: Budget Grenade
Drop: Potion

 **YEVON GUARD**
HP: 223 | AP: 1 | Gil: 40
Steal: Budget Greande
Drop: Potion

**YSLS-ZERO**
HP: 1935 | AP: 1 | Gil: 100
Steal: Mythril Gloves
Drop: Wristband

**YSLS-99**
HP: 2775 | AP: 1 | Gil: 400
Steal: Mythril Gloves
Drop: Stamina Tablet

**PRECEPTS GUARD**
HP: 3680 | AP: 1 | Gil: 800
Steal: Mana Tablet
Drop: Regen Ring

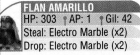 **GEORAPELLA**
HP: 4420 | AP: 1 | Gil:1000
Steal: Water Gem
Drop: NulTide Ring

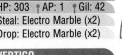 **BARALAI**
HP: 3380 | AP: 10 | Gil:1300
Steal: Charm Bangle
Drop: Pearl Necklace

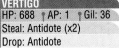 **BAHAMUT**
HP: 8400 | AP: 15 | Gil:1000
Steal: Mute Shock
Drop: Gris-Gris Bag

## ITEM CHECKLIST

| | | | |
|---|---|---|---|
| Remedy (x3) | Phoenix Down (x4) | Ribbon | Wring |
| Remedy (x3) | Chocobo Feather | Ether (x4) | Phoenix Down (x5) |
| 3000 gil | Pearl Necklace | Remedy (x4) | Hi-Potion |
| Hi-Potion (x4) | Glass Buckle | Downtrodder Garment Grid | Dark Knight Dressphere |
| Potion (x8) | 500 gil | Bloodlust | |

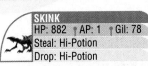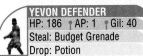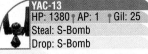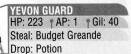

Characters 1
Garment Grids & Dresspheres 2
Battle System 3
Accessories 4
Items and Item Shops 5
Walkthrough 6
Chapter 1
Chapter 2
Chapter 3
Chapter 4
Chapter 5
Mini-Games
7
Fiends and Enemies 8

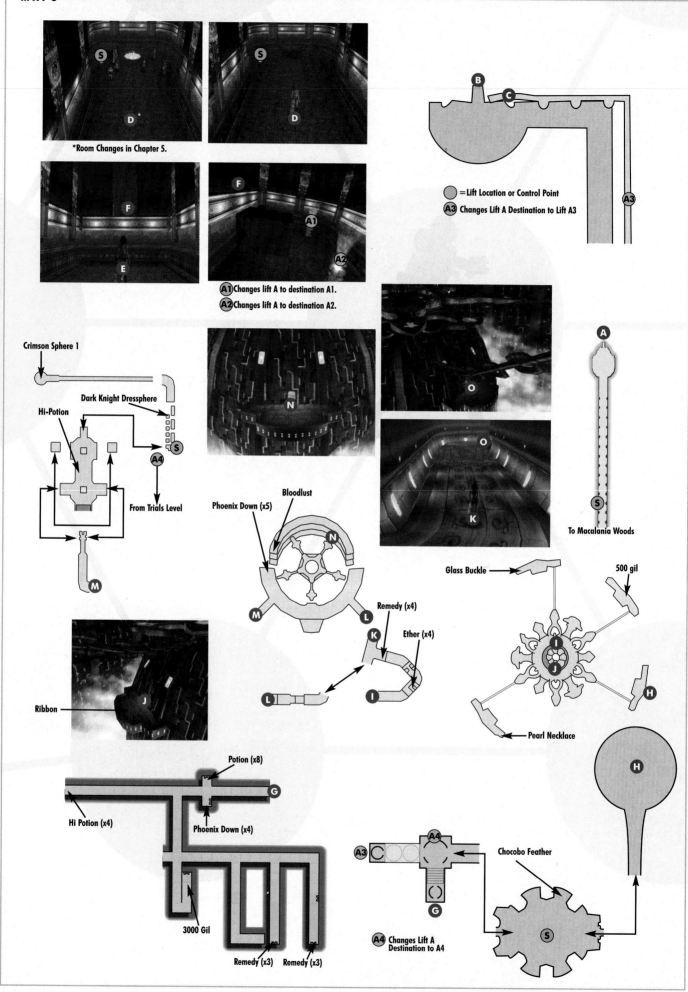

*Room Changes in Chapter 5.

A1 Changes lift A to destination A1.
A2 Changes lift A to destination A2.

= Lift Location or Control Point

A3 Changes Lift A Destination to Lift A3

Crimson Sphere 1

Dark Knight Dressphere

Hi-Potion

From Trials Level

To Macalania Woods

Bloodlust

Phoenix Down (x5)

Remedy (x4)

Ether (x4)

Glass Buckle

500 gil

Pearl Necklace

Ribbon

Potion (x8)

Hi Potion (x4)

Phoenix Down (x4)

3000 Gil

Remedy (x3)    Remedy (x3)

A4 Changes Lift A
Destination to A4

Chocobo Feather

# DEPENDING ON ALLIANCE

Leblanc and the Gullwings hatch out a plan to find Baralai, the New Yevon praetor, and make him reveal the ominous weapon Vegnagun. If the Gullwings allied with New Yevon at the beginning of Chapter 2, you will have no problems proceeding directly to the temple. Along the way, speak to NPCs in the area to find out that some strange events have been occurring in Bevelle recently and that no one has any idea where the praetor is.

Barkeep sets up shop near the first Save Sphere. He sells the same items as he does onboard the airship.

Take out soldiers with flamethrowers first to lessen any potential damage.

If the Gullwings gave the stolen sphere to the Youth League at the beginning of Chapter 2, each set of guards that identifies the Gullwings will move in to attack. Battle up the Highbridge and avoid speaking to NPCs who may yell for help.

# CHANGING LIFT DIRECTION

Whether you're allied with New Yevon or not, the events occurring inside the temple will be the same either way. Speak to the priests to learn more of the recent developments in Bevelle. The lift takes the group deep underground in the temple, but you must change its course. Follow the curving wall of the temple east toward the doorway. Inside the small room, climb onto the platform and step onto the seal. A doorway opens in another chamber. Exit the small room and head back through the temple area to the west side of the lift chamber.

Climb up to the new opening in the wall and drop into a secret chamber. The two pillars here control the direction of the lift. Examine the pillar closest to the screen to change the direction of the lift in the central area. Return to the central area where the priests congregate and ride the lift down to the core of the temple.

Step on raised square platforms to activate glyphs.

When the lift hologram drops, it means that the lift will descend to the lower levels.

# TRIAL OF FIENDS

Although this mobile pathway was once the home of a head-scratching puzzle, you can now move through the chamber freely and collect the items stored inside the chests. While random battles will not occur, fiends will materialize as you head for each chest. Proceed to the lift at the east end of the top level, and ride it to the stage above.

Fight for all the items in the temple before proceeding to the top level.

# BEVELLE SECURITY CORE

Barkeep's list of goods is identical to the ones he has onboard the airship.

Barkeep the Hypello moves to the antechamber to set up shop, so use this opportunity to stock up on goods. Grab the **Chocobo Feather** from the chest in the corner, then save your game at the Save Sphere. The next section of the game is extremely challenging combat-wise and may prove to be a strain on the entire party. Enter with nothing short of full HP and MP.

Proceed into the Chamber of the Fayth and leap into the large hole in the center of the room. The Gullwings find themselves in a massive, unknown chamber deep under Bevelle. Move along the platform toward the screen to find a machina pillar. Examine the pillar to receive a message regarding the security system inside this massive room. After doing so, return to the group and move to the edge of the platform. After the security shutdown begins, move toward the top of the platform to make Yuna slide down a chain to the massive security station below. Move forward a few steps and prepare to battle a set of YAC-13s.

Move upward along the edge of the platform to make Yuna automatically hop onto the chain.

## CONSERVE MP IN BEVELLE!

*If you normally depend on a Black Mage to vanquish your foes, you won't be able to rely on the same strategy here. Try to conserve MP for the bosses in this area, and enlist the aid of a skilled Gun Mage or two to take down all the machina and mechs in this area.*

*First, use the Scan ability on each robot to determine whether it is a machina or a mech. Then use Mech Destroyer or Dismantler to take down the sentries efficiently. YAC-13s are machina, while other machines (such as the YSLS-99s and YSLS-Zeros) are mechs.*

Characters

1

Garment Grids
& Dresspheres

2

Battle System

3

Accessories

4

Items and
Item Shops

5

Walkthrough

Chapter 1

**Chapter 2**

Chapter 3

Chapter 4

Chapter 5

Mini-Games

7

Fiends and
Enemies

8

## EATING ELEMENTS

Before undertaking the task of activating the security towers, it would be wise to equip your characters with Garment Grids such as Ice Queen, Heart of Flame, Thunder Spawn, or Menace of the Deep. These grids all have the ability to absorb a certain kind of elemental spell, which will prove invaluable against a particular boss monster encountered in the security tower room.

# THE WATCHTOWERS

After disposing of the first set of security drones, it's time to go about disabling the security towers. Yuna is standing in front of the first of three "blue towers." (Note the two blue lights positioned below the tower's steps are glowing brightly.) When the tower is activated, part of the security system shuts down. After a fight with a YSLS-Zero, a platform appears in the central pit.

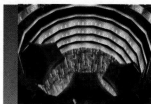

The lights outside a "blue tower" remain blue once it's activated.

Behind the third tower is a chain. Run up the chain to the platform against the side wall of the chamber. Defeat a YSLS-99 to clear the path to a chest containing a **Pearl Necklace**.

Ascend the chains in the north portion of the room to obtain a **Glass Buckle** and **500 gil**.

When you can move again, proceed in a clockwise fashion around the circular area. The next tower is a "red tower." The only indication that this is a red tower is that the twin lights in front of the tower steps are *not* glowing at all. When you ascend the steps and touch the control panel, the two lights in front of the tower glow red. This triggers a fight with another mech, and then a second platform appears in the central pit.

Continue to move around the circle, ascend the stairs of every tower, and touch the control panel. When you activate the three blue towers, you must fight the Precepts Guard. At this point, three of the platforms in the pit form a large stairway to the level below.

Upon activating all three of the red towers, you must fight the Georappella boss. You will notice that three additional platforms have emerged in the pit, but they don't seem to go anywhere… for the moment.

The lights outside a red tower change colors when activated.

Move to the edge of the pit to view the progress of the platforms.

# PRECEPTS GUARD

BOSS FIGHT

The Precepts Guard inflicts Poison status by casting Bio and drains HP and MP from your characters. Because the creature casts Demi to reduce the entire party's HP by a percentage, you must have a White Mage present to cast Pray or Cure every round. The Precepts Guard may also inflict party members with Slow status, and it also has a Death attack that causes instant KO. For all these reasons, you must assault this fiend with extreme speed and efficiency.

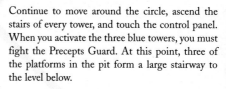

Cast your most powerful Black Mage spells to defeat the fiend in the shortest amount of time possible. This way, you don't allow the fiend the opportunity to use too many of its attacks. While a Black Mage is casting and a White Mage is healing, a Warrior can cause a good amount of damage with the Excalibur attack. Excalibur is the only Holy-based attack at your disposal for the moment.

**HP: 3680   MP: 9999   EXP: 700   AP: 1**

| | |
|---|---|
| GIL DROPPED: 800 | STEAL: Normal: Mana Tablet   Rare: Mana Tablet (x2) |
| PILFER GIL: 1600 | DROP: Normal: Regen Bangle   Rare: Regen Bangle |

# GEORAPELLA

Like the Precepts Guard, Georappella is also weak versus Holy. Therefore, the strategy for defeating the fiend is relatively the same. Use a White Mage to heal, have a Warrior attack with Excalibur, and use a Black Mage to cast powerful spells at the fiend.

HP: 4420   MP: 9999   EXP: 800   AP: 1

Georappella's sole means of attack is casting third-level black magic spells at the entire party. However, it can cast spells at an alarming frequency. Use Chocobo Feathers or a Chocobo Wing to thrust the Gullwings into Haste mode, which gives you more turns to deal with each spell attack. You can also let a Songstress cast Jitterbug every round. If your characters are low on MP, the boss has plenty to steal. A Black Mage can restore her MP with the MP Drain skill, and other characters can use Mana Springs for the same purpose.

**GIL DROPPED:** 1000   **STEAL:** Normal: Water Gem   Rare: Water Gem (x2)
**PILFER GIL:** 1300   **DROP:** Normal: NulTide Ring   Rare: NulTide Ring

## OBTAINING THE RIBBON

Before leaving the security tower room, there is an additional challenging task to undertake to reach an extremely useful accessory. Now that the security forces in the room have been deactivated, the blue towers have gained new functions. When you touch the control panel of a red tower and then the control panel of a blue tower, one of the lower three platforms in the pit will move. Referring to the labeling on the following map, refer to the steps below to obtain a **Ribbon** accessory.

*Once you have this item, you won't mind all the work required to obtain it. A Ribbon protects one character from all status ailments!*

**Steps to Align the Lower Platforms**

1. Touch the control panel of red tower D, then the control panel of blue tower A. The fourth platform from the top rotates to a new position.

2. At this point, you must fight a Precepts Guard or Georappella.

3. Touch the control panel of blue tower B. The fourth platform from the top moves to the opposite side of the pit.

4. Touch the control panel of red tower E, then touch the panel of blue tower B. These actions cause the fifth platform from the top to flip to the opposite side of the pit.

5. Touch the control panel of red tower F, then touch the panel of blue tower C. This causes the bottom platform in the pit to rotate to a new position.

6. At this point, you must fight another Precepts Guard or a Georappella.

7. Touch the control panel of blue tower B. The bottom platform in the pit flips to the opposite side. There is now a series of platforms to descend to reach the bottom level of the pit and go through the opening. On the ledge, you will find the chest containing the accessory.

**MAP**

## CONFUSING CORRIDORS

Proceed into the corridor and jump to the chest containing an **Ether (x4)**. Proceed to the next obstacle and climb up the column on the right. Grab a **Remedy (x4)** from the chest at the bottom of the ramp. At the t-shaped intersection, head to the right.

*Your party could probably use a little MP refresher, so use these items to regain some.*

Stepping on the center square causes the lift to appear.

Run to the edge and step on the center of the three squares. This causes the square to drop away and a lift to appear. Ride the lift across the gap and exit to a balcony where a chest holds a **Downtrodder Garment Grid**.

Climb up the side of the column where the glyph is lit.

Return to the t-intersection and head down the next corridor. Climb up either column to trigger a reaction on both sides of the chasm. Now climb the other column from the inside to make a bridge form across the gap.

# THE GAOL

At first glance, the giant machine in the next room doesn't exactly look like something that you would want to climb on. However, you can reach some really cool items with a little patience on your part and some teamwork from the Gullwings. Move to where Ormi and Logos are standing, then walk straight backward to find a giant switch on the floor of a lower ledge. Step on the switch to stop the piston. Notice that after the central mechanism stops, the pistons still settle to a certain level. In the future, you don't want to stop the machinery until the pistons have risen or fallen to their levels.

Unraveling the secrets of Bevelle involves solving many environmental puzzles.

When the piston falls to this position, step on the switch to stop the device.

Walk off the switch, then step on it again (if needed) to get the gaol mechanism rolling. Stay on the ledge and watch the pistons carefully. Wait until one of the pistons rotates into a position directly beside Logos and Ormi. If the piston falls downward so that the top of it is just above the level of the floor where the two Syndicate goons are standing, stop the device.

Jump from the opening in the circular walk to the piston head, and Yuna will leap to the top of the device. The cinema makes it readily apparent that you cannot climb on the device while it is active. Move toward the side of the machine and descend one of the curved arms. Jump from the piston head to the ledge on the back wall.

This puzzle can be mind boggling and challenging. It's all about timing and practice.

Rikku! Coming right up!

Rikku helps stop and start the gaol mechanism when you press the Square button.

At this point, press the Square button to make Rikku activate the machinery. Watch carefully as the pistons rotate, rise, and fall. When the pistons arrange in a position so that the rear piston on the left is high and the rear piston on the right is at Yuna's level, press the Square button again to make Rikku stop the device. With the pistons in the proper alignment, you can hop onto the machine, climb across to the west side of the room, and reach the treasure chest that contains the **Bloodlust** accessory.

Signal Rikku to start up the machinery again, and wait until the pistons are high enough to reach your current level and low enough to reach the lowest level. Cross the machinery again to the bottom level, then go through the doorway on the lower east level of the room. A chest on a ledge contains a **Wring** accessory.

You scored the accessory Wring!

Another great accessory is found hidden deep within Bevelle.

# LIFTS AND LEDGES

Step on the square beside either lift to board it.

The columns at the end of the corridor move aside for the high summoner. At the end of the path are three lifts and two switch pillars. The bluish-colored lift in the center doesn't work yet, so move onto the squares to either side to ride one of the side lifts to the upper level.

Open the chest to score a **Hi-Potion**, then move toward the bottom of the screen to jump off a ledge. Yuna drops back down to the area of the three lifts. With one lift gone, the middle lift now transports Yuna to a hidden ledge. Climb onto the square platform and move to the center. Activating this glyph causes two platforms to rise in the chamber near the Save Sphere. You've just taken the first step toward getting your next dressphere!

Activate the glyphs on these hidden platforms to obtain a dressphere.

Return to the platform where the two lifts are docked, and ride the side lift to the upper level. Move directly across the upper level to the lift docked on the other side, and ride it down to the level below. Now ride the middle lift to another square platform. Climb onto the second square and activate the glyph to raise the remaining two platforms in the other chamber.

At this point, you're ready to proceed. Return to the upper level and climb onto the raised square platform closest to the screen. A block falls away, unlocking the lift that floats over space. Climb on top of the raised square block nearest the lift, and a short bridge extends over space. Ride the lift to the next level.

*The two glyphs on the upper level activate the final lift.*

Jump across the platforms you raised to the chest suspended over space, which contains the **Dark Knight Dressphere**. Save your game before proceeding, because the path leads to two consecutive boss fights!

*With one lift gone, the blue lift takes Yuna to a hidden platform.*

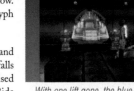

*Grab the dressphere from the chest before moving on.*

# BARALAI BOSS FIGHT

Baralai is one fast customer who attacks one or all party members in quick succession with his long, dual-edged weapon. Although he is susceptible to Poison and Darkness, there seems to be only a very slim chance that he will succumb to the toxin and he continues to hit with extreme accuracy even when blinded.

**HP:** 3380 **MP:** 540 **EXP:** 1000 **AP:** 10

Focus on raising the speed of the party with Chocobo Wings or the Jitterbug dance of a Songstress. Be warned, however, that Baralai tends to react to the presence of a Songstress by inflicting Stop status on that character. Use a Remedy or Esuna spell to keep a Songstress dancing with the beat. If he can't inflict Stop, Baralai pulls out a gun and fires an explosive bullet that causes lots of damage. A White Mage will be very busy during this battle, but if you can keep everyone healthy and in Haste mode, then a Black Mage can take him down swiftly with a few high-powered spells.

**GIL DROPPED:** 1300    **STEAL:** Normal: Charm Bangle   Rare: Charm Bangle
**PILFER GIL:** 2000    **DROP:** Normal: Pearl Necklace   Rare: Pearl Necklace

# BAHAMUT BOSS FIGHT

One character must be a White Mage throughout this battle for the group to recover with efficiency from Impulse and the other powerful attacks of Yuna's former aeon. Hit Bahamut with your strongest Black Mage spells and attacks, and cure Curse status with Holy Waters or Esuna. Once a countdown appears on-screen, you have only five turns to heal your characters to full health and prepare for Bahamut to fire Mega Flare.

If you cannot defeat Bahamut before it fires Mega Flare, use a Mega Phoenix just as the aeon gets ready to attack. If you issue the command with the proper timing, the item will be used even if your entire party perishes. However, don't rely on this trick and instead cast Haste on your entire party with a Chocobo Wing or a Songstress's Jitterbug dance. Act quickly to try and eliminate Bahamut with your strongest spells and attacks before the insanely powerful creature gets to use its most devastating attack.

**HP:** 8400 **MP:** 9999 **EXP:** 1300 **AP:** 15

**GIL DROPPED:** 1000    **STEAL:** Normal: Mute Shock   Rare: Mute Shock
**PILFER GIL:** 2200    **DROP:** Normal: Gris-Gris Bag   Rare: Gris-Gris Bag

Characters

1

Garment Grids & Dresspheres

2

Battle System

3

Accessories

4

Items and Item Shops

5

Walkthrough
Chapter 1
Chapter 2
Chapter 3
Chapter 4
Chapter 5

Mini-Games

7

Fiends and Enemies

8

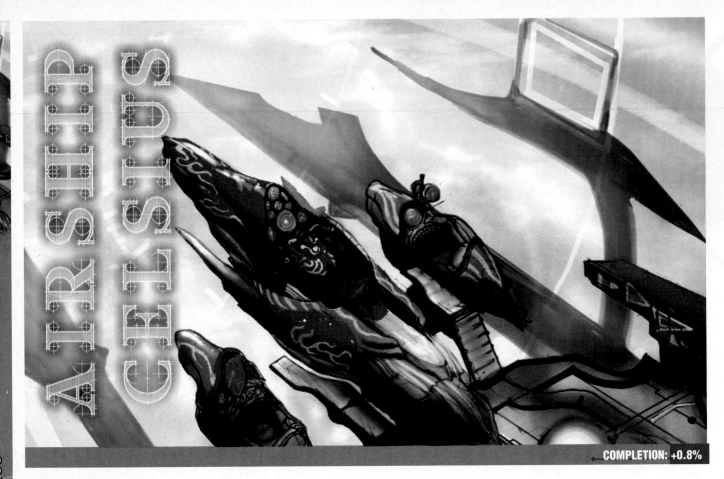

# AIRSHIP CELSIUS

**COMPLETION: +0.8%**

## ITEM CHECKLIST

Phoenix Down (x6)          Remedy (x5)

Ether (x3)                 Hi-Potion (x4)

## MAPS

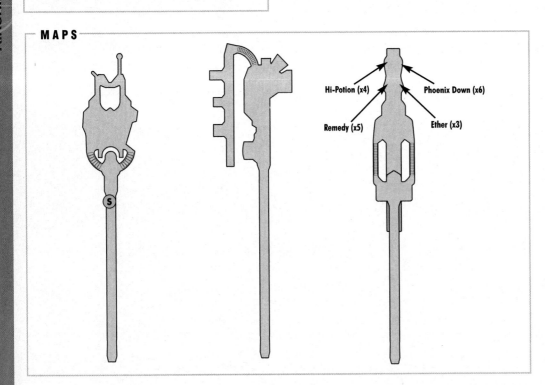

Hi-Potion (x4)

Phoenix Down (x6)

Remedy (x5)

Ether (x3)

# THE SCOURGE OF FIENDS

When fiends suddenly manifest in all the old temples, the girls decide to give up sphere hunting for a while to focus instead on protecting the citizens of Spira. Hotspots appear on the navigation map at Besaid Island and Kilika. If you gave the stolen sphere to the Youth League at the start of Chapter 2, Mushroom Rock Road will also be a Hotspot. However, if you sided with New Yevon, then there is extra business to take care of at Bevelle. When both the Kilika and Besaid missions are complete, the last mission of Chapter 3, at Djose Temple, becomes a Hotspot. Accumulate a few extra fractions of a percentage point by visiting Djose *before* it becomes a Hotspot.

*Be sure to visit every other location in Spira to gather minor completion points before heading to Kilika, Besaid, and then to Djose thereafter.*

Chapter 3 is the turning point of the game, as the fiends in every area become much more difficult. Many monsters now inflict instant KO or multiple status ailments. Make sure your characters are equipped with the best gear possible before proceeding. The shops sell better items, and you can even purchase Hi-Potions at most locations. If O'aka is onboard the ship and his debt is paid, he will leave and head for the Travel Agency at Lake Macalania.

## WATCHER ALERT!

*In many random battles, starting in Chapter 3, small enemies called Watchers appear alongside other fiends and foes. Watchers can cast magic attacks, but their function serves a far more sinister purpose. Throughout Chapters 3 and 4, Watchers will record your actions and report them to a particular boss encountered later in the game. Any action you take or any ability used in the presence of a Watcher may get locked out during this crucial and difficult battle. For this reason, it's important to eliminate Watchers before all other opponents, using only regular physical attacks.*

### THE GULLSTORE (CHAPTER 3)

| ITEM | COST |
|---|---|
| Potion | 50 |
| Hi-Potion | 500 |
| Phoenix Down | 100 |
| Antidote | 50 |
| Eye Drops | 50 |
| Echo Screen | 50 |
| Soft | 50 |
| Holy Water | 300 |
| Twist Headband | 3000 |
| White Cape | 3000 |
| Silver Glasses | 3000 |
| Star Pendant | 4000 |

### ACTION CHECKLIST

*1 — Enter the Sphere Break tournament.*

*2 — Challenge and defeat three players to qualify.*

*3 — Defeat the master Sphere Break player to win the tournament.*

**COMPLETION: +0.8%**

## ITEM CHECKLIST

Lunar Curtain (x3)

Reptile Coin (x5) 🅔

Bird Coin (x5) 🅔

Wasp Coin (x5) 🅔

Ahriman Coin (x5) 🅔

Lady Luck Dressphere 🅔

Characters

Garment Grids & D[r]esspheres

Battle System

Accessories

Items and Item Shops

Walkthrough
Chapter 1
Chapter 2
Chapter 3
Chapter 4
Chapter 5

Mini-Games

Fiends and Enemies

# THE SPHERE BREAK CHALLENGE

Upon entering Luca, the Gullwings enter the Sphere Break tournament. You must defeat three players to qualify. If you are defeated three times, you are disqualified.

Save your game before challenging any players, and also save each time you defeat an opponent. If you fail to defeat the Sphere Break champion, you can still acquire the dressphere later in Chapter 5. The champion's core sphere is so tricky that it will probably take a couple of attempts to beat him.

The easiest players to defeat include a guy in green and brown walking randomly around the square...

...an old person sitting on the bridge between the square and the stadium...

...and an intimidating woman in blue standing just inside the Blitzball dome.

# TAKING DOWN THE CHAMP

Upon winning your third match against any of the challengers positioned around Luca, you proceed directly to the championship round. The champ's core sphere has an extremely high quota of 50 coins, with only 45 seconds per round. The key to defeating the champ is to rack up a high "Echo Bonus." Complete a core using two or three coins, then continue to make core breaks using the same number of coins used in the previous turn to achieve an "Echo Bonus." This way, the number of coins in subsequent rounds is multiplied by 2, 3, 4, 5, 6, etc. For example, even if you core break with only 3 coins but you achieve an Echo Bonus for five consecutive turns, your total is multiplied to count as 6, 9, 12, and then 15 coins. After five rounds of 3 core breaks, you've already fulfilled the quota! The champ's core has a strong tendency to throw a 1, which means that any coin you pick during that turn will core break and end your Echo Bonus streak. If this occurs during the 14th or 15th round, start breaking the core with as many coins as possible.

Defeat the champ to receive the **Lady Luck dressphere**.

## SHINRA'S ITEM

*By using coins with the "Item" or "Rare" traits, you can occasionally gain an item from the person you are playing. In Shinra's case, you may win the **Treasure Hunt Garment Grid** (with some luck), which allows the user to perform the Mug ability during combat. With this Garment Grid equipped, any character can steal normal or rare items without equipping the Thief dressphere!*

MI'IHEN HIGHROAD

### ACTION CHECKLIST

**1** Run toward citizens in peril and destroy the machina attacking them.

**2** After defeating 13 sets of machina, the Gullwings collect a sizable reward!

**COMPLETION: +0.6%**

## WANDERING FIENDS

**BARBUTA**
HP: 562 | AP: 1 | Gil: 33
Steal: Lunar Curtain
Drop: Light Curtain

**CEPHALOTUS**
HP: 1830 | AP: 1 | Gil: 62
Steal: Echo Screen x2
Drop: Echo Screen x2

**FLAN ROJO**
HP: 1220 | AP: 1 | Gil: 125
Steal: Bomb Core
Drop: Bomb Core

**MACHINA RANGER**
HP: 2490 | AP: 1 | Gil: 22
Steal: S-Bomb
Drop: Darkness Grenade

**MYCOTOXIN**
HP: 810 | AP: 1 | Gil: 83
Steal: Antidote x2
Drop: Antidote x2

**PEREGGRINE**
HP: 735 | AP: 1 | Gil: 44
Steal: Hi-Potion
Drop: Hi-Potion

**QUEEN COEURL**
HP: 3270 | AP: 1 | Gil: 330
Steal: Phoenix Down
Drop: Phoenix Down x2

**SCOUT MACHINA**
HP: 3444 | AP: 1 | Gil: 48
Steal: S-Bomb
Drop: S-Bomb

**WATCHER-A**
HP: 624 | AP: 1 | Gil: 0
Steal: Potion
Drop: Potion

**WATCHER-R**
HP: 620 | AP: 1 | Gil: 0
Steal: Potion
Drop: Potion

**WATCHER-S**
HP: 620 | AP: 1 | Gil: 0
Steal: Potion
Drop: Potion

**ZU**
HP: 9338 | AP: 1 | Gil: 164
Steal: Phoenix Down
Drop: Phoenix Down x2

## ITEM CHECKLIST

- Phoenix Down (x4)
- 2000 gil
- Hypno Crown
- Hi-Potion (x2)

- Holy Water (x4)
- Hi-Potion (x4)
- Hi-Potion (x2)
- Eye Drops (x3)

- Soft (x4)
- Phoenix Down (x4)
- Ether (x2)
- 10000 gil ⓔ

- Undying Storm Garment Grid ⓔ
- Echo Screen (x4)
- Hi-Potion (x2)
- S-Bomb (x2)

## MAPS

Hypno Crown

2000 gil

Ⓢ

To Luca

Phoenix Down x4

Eye Drops x3

Ⓢ

Ⓓ

Soft x4

Phoenix Down x4

Echo Screen x4

Ⓢ

Hi-Potion x2

C

Hi-Potion x2

Holy Water x4

Hi-Potion x4

*Entrance to secret dungeon becomes available after discovery by chocobos.

Ether x2

Hi-Potion x2

To Mushroom Rock Road

S-Bomb x2

Characters

Garment Grids & D	Spheres

Battle System

Accessories

Items and Item Shops

Walkthrough
Chapter 1
Chapter 2
Chapter 3
Chapter 4
Chapter 5

Mini-Games

Fiends and Enemies

Although the Mi'ihen Highroad is not affected by the fiend invasion occurring all across Spira, the machina that usually protect travelers on the road have suddenly and inexplicably gone out of control. The Gullwings must run the full length of the highroad and descend into the gorge, defeating sets of rampant machina that are attacking the pedestrians. Sets of machina encountered in random battles do *not* count; only those destroyed in battles triggered by running toward pedestrians in trouble count toward the quota.

Machina such as this require that you leap to high ledges to rescue the civilians.

The Agency is thankful even if you do nothing.

However, there is also a team of skilled Al Bhed that is dismantling the rampaging machina. It is not required that you destroy more machina than the Al Bhed; in fact, you don't have to lift a finger, but in doing so you will miss out on a key item. Even if you do not destroy a single machina during this mission, a **10,000 gil** reward and the **Undying Storm Garment Grid** is turned over to the Gullwings regardless. But if you're feeling competitive, you can outfight the Al Bhed by not collecting any items along the route. Complete the mission, then return to Mi'ihen a second time and travel the highroad once again to collect items.

| STARTING CHAPTER 3 | |
|---|---|
| ITEM | COST |
| Potion | 50 |
| Hi-Potion | 500 |
| Phoenix Down | 100 |
| Antidote | 50 |
| Eye Drops | 50 |
| Echo Screen | 50 |
| Soft | 50 |
| Holy Water | 300 |
| Titanium Bangle | 3000 |
| Gold Bracer | 4000 |
| Muscle Belt | 4000 |
| Circlet | 4000 |

# MUSHROOM ROCK ROAD

COMPLETION: +0.4%

## ITEM CHECKLIST

2000 gil

# YOUTH LEAGUE FORTIFICATIONS

The Youth League has blocked the route through Mushroom Rock Road with hovers to hold off the fiends ravaging Spira. This area will be off-limits throughout Chapter 3. Check in with Yaibal, then continue your conversation with Lucil to gain a few fractions of a completion point.

Lucil wants to chat even if you haven't supported the Youth League in your previous actions.

# DJOSE TEMPLE

COMPLETION: +0.2%

Characters

1

Garment Grids & Dresspheres

2

Battle System

3

Accessories

4

Items and Item Shops

5

Walkthrough

Chapter 1

Chapter 2

Chapter 3

Chapter 4

Chapter 5

Mini-Games

7

Fiends and Enemies

8

159

## WANDERING FIENDS

| | | |
|---|---|---|
| **AGAMA** HP: 133 ∣ AP: 1 ∣ Gil: 16 Steal: Hi-Potion Drop: Antidote | **ARCHAEOTHYRIS** HP: 1332 ∣ AP: 1 ∣ Gil: 110 Steal: Eye Drops x2 Drop: Eye Drops x2 | **ASSASSIN BEE** HP: 233 ∣ AP: 1 ∣ Gil: 48 Steal: Antidote Drop: Antidote | **CHOCOBO** HP: 3890 ∣ AP: 0 ∣ Gil: 0 Steal: None Drop: None |
| **GOLD ELEMENTAL** HP: 99 ∣ AP: 1 ∣ Gil: 25 Steal: Electro Marble Drop: Electro Marble | **GREATER DRAKE** HP: 1819 ∣ AP: 1 ∣ Gil: 140 Steal: Fire Gem Drop: Fire Gem | **LEAGUE MAGE** HP: 1020 ∣ AP: 1 ∣ Gil: 130 Steal: Ether Drop: Hi-Potion | **LEAGUE RAIDER** HP: 293 ∣ AP: 1 ∣ Gil: 130 Steal: Phoenix Down Drop: Hi-Potion |
| **LEAGUE RANGER** HP: 230 ∣ AP: 1 ∣ Gil: 80 Steal: Phoenix Down Drop: Potion | **LEAGUE TROOPER** HP: 244 ∣ AP: 1 ∣ Gil: 60 Steal: Grenade Drop: Grenade | **LEAGUE WARRIOR** HP: 422 ∣ AP: 1 ∣ Gil: 120 Steal: Hi-Potion Drop: Hi-Potion | **RUKH** HP: 12850 ∣ AP: 1 ∣ Gil: 530 Steal: Phoenix Down x2 Drop: Phoenix Down x2 |
| **SKINK** HP: 882 ∣ AP: 1 ∣ Gil: 78 Steal: Hi-Potion Drop: Hi-Potion | **WATCHER-A** HP: 624 ∣ AP: 1 ∣ Gil: 0 Steal: Potion Drop: Potion | **WATCHER-R** HP: 620 ∣ AP: 1 ∣ Gil: 0 Steal: Potion Drop: Potion | **WATCHER-S** HP: 620 ∣ AP: 1 ∣ Gil: 0 Steal: Potion Drop: Potion |

## ITEM CHECKLIST

Hi-Potion (x3)

Phoenix Down (x3)

*Al Bhed Primer **E**

Wrist Band

Remedy

**\*Only if you haven't mastered Al Bhed.**

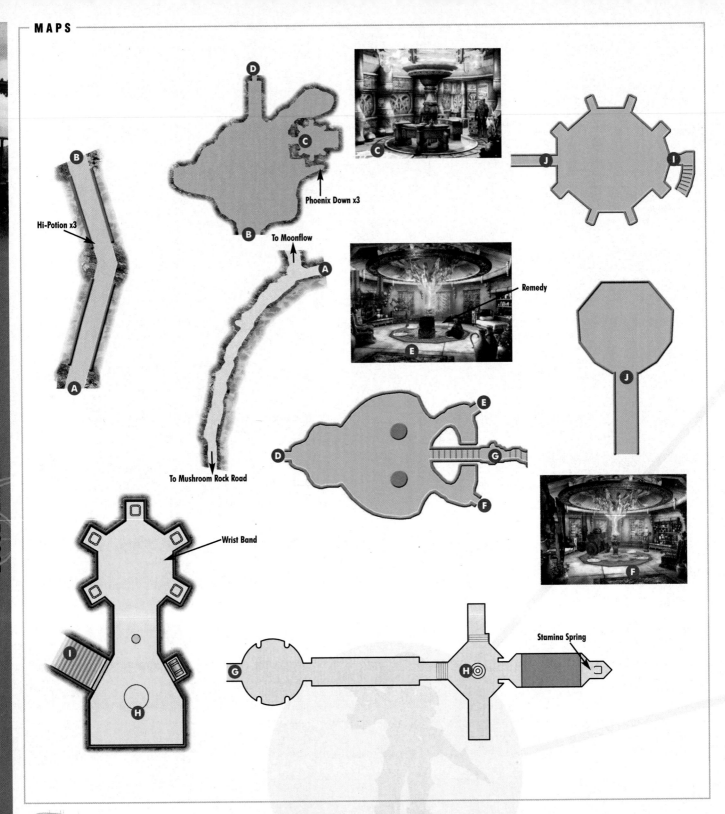

Hi-Potion x3

Phoenix Down x3

To Moonflow

Remedy

To Mushroom Rock Road

Wrist Band

Stamina Spring

# CHECKING UP ON THE MACHINE FACTION

If you proceed up the Djose Highroad from Mushroom Rock Road, go ahead and pay the Al Bhed near the entrance to drive the Gullwings up the path on a hover. A fiend called Rukh attacks pedestrians with some frequency along the highroad. Unless all of your characters are protected against Petrification, this monster could easily slay your entire

party and end your game. In addition, if you sided against the Youth League, then a variety of their soldiers will attack throughout this region.

At the temple, speak to Gippal standing just outside the building to obtain an **Al Bhed Primer** and a few fractions of a completion point. While the Machine Faction leader is confident and in control for now, the situation here will deteriorate near the end of Chapter 3.

*Rukhs will take advantage of unprotected characters by inflicting Petrification.*

*Stop by the Machine Faction HQ at Djose Temple to hear Gippal boast confidently.*

# MOONFLOW

**COMPLETION: +0.2%**

Characters

1

Garment Grids & Dresspheres

2

Battle System

3

Accessories

4

Items and Item Shops

5

Walkthrough

Chapter 1

Chapter 2

**Chapter 3**

Chapter 4

Chapter 5

Mini-Games

7

Fiends and Enemies

8

## WANDERING FIENDS

**AGAMA**
HP: 133 | AP: 1 | Gil: 16
Steal: Hi-Potion
Drop: Antidote

**ARCHAEOTHYRIS**
HP: 1332 | AP: 1 | Gil: 110
Steal: Eye Drops x2
Drop: Eye Drops x2

**BALIVARHA**
HP: 3688 | AP: 1 | Gil: 230
Steal: Hi-Potion x2
Drop: Fire Gem

**BANDIT**
HP: 132 | AP: 1 | Gil: 30
Steal: Budget Grenade
Drop: Potion

**BARBUTA**
HP: 562 | AP: 1 | Gil: 33
Steal: Lunar Curtain
Drop: Light Curtain

**BLACKGUARD**
HP: 760 | AP: 1 | Gil: 42
Steal: Phoenix Down
Drop: Potion

**CHOCOBO**
HP: 368 | AP: 0 | Gil: 0
Steal: None
Drop: None

**FLAN BLANCO**
HP: 625 | AP: 1 | Gil: 72
Steal: Arctic Wind
Drop: Arctic Wind

**PROTOCHIMERA**
HP: 420 | AP: 1 | Gil: 120
Steal: Potion
Drop: Potion

**SHELL SHOCKER**
HP: 4700 | AP: 1 | Gil: 780
Steal: Iron Bangle
Drop: Black Ring

**WATCHER-A**
HP: 624 | AP: 1 | Gil: 0
Steal: Potion
Drop: Potion

**WATCHER-R**
HP: 620 | AP: 1 | Gil: 0
Steal: Potion
Drop: Potion

**WATCHER-S**
HP: 620 | AP: 1 | Gil: 0
Steal: Potion
Drop: Potion

## CAN'T KEEP A TUNE

Speak to Tobli near the bandwagon to get a few fractions of a completion point. Even with the musicians from Macalania Woods, the show isn't going well. However, there's nothing that can be done at this point.

*Tobli's show is currently a bomb and debt collectors are looking for him in Guadosalam.*

## ACTION CHECKLIST

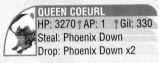

**1** Check in with the Syndicate.

**2** Try to cheer up Leblanc.

**3** Meet Logos in his room for a little "screening."

**4** Receive history lessons from Maechen.

**COMPLETION: +2.0%**

## WANDERING FIENDS

**ARCHAEOTHYRIS**
HP: 1332 | AP: 1 | Gil: 110
Steal: Eye Drops x2
Drop: Eye Drops x2

**BASCINET**
HP: 1342 | AP: 1 | Gil: 110
Steal: Hi-Potion
Drop: Hi-Potion

**BLUE ELEMENTAL**
HP: 363 | AP: 1 | Gil: 180
Steal: Dragon Scale
Drop: Dragon Scale

**QUEEN COEURL**
HP: 3270 | AP: 1 | Gil: 330
Steal: Phoenix Down
Drop: Phoenix Down x2

## ITEM CHECKLIST

Logos's Sphere **E**

Ormi's Sphere **E**

Gaol Sphere

Tetra Band

Crimson Sphere 4

## MAPS

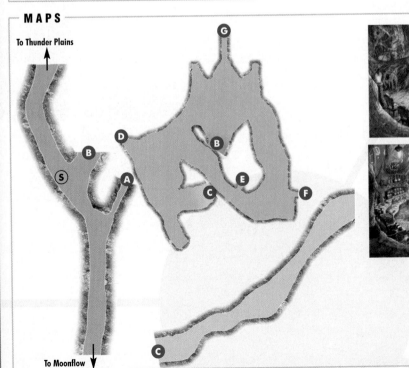

To Thunder Plains

G

D

B

B

S

A

E

C

F

To Moonflow

C

A

D

E

F

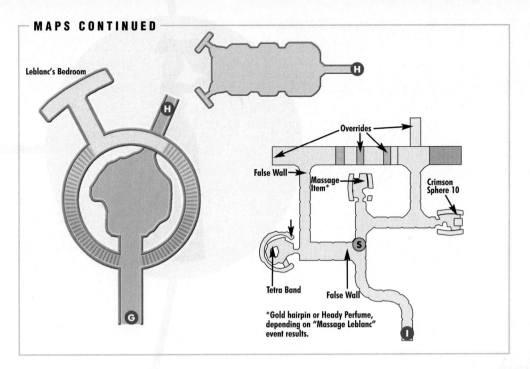

Leblanc's Bedroom

Overrides

False Wall

Massage Item*

Crimson Sphere 10

Tetra Band

False Wall

S

*Gold hairpin or Heady Perfume, depending on "Massage Leblanc" event results.

Speak to Logos and Ormi in the living room on the first floor, then head upstairs and try to talk to Leblanc. Confer with her henchmen again downstairs, and agree to meet in Logos's room. Head into the secret passage, which is still inhabited by fiends. Return to the room with Logos's guns decorating the wall above the bed to have him join you there. After viewing **Logos's Sphere** and **Ormi's Sphere**, move to the nightstand to the right side of the bed and examine the **Gaol Sphere**. Maechen then appears in the room. After the scene, speak to Maechen again to explore Spira's history further.

*Pick up the **Gaol Sphere** on the bookshelf.*

# FURTHER CHATEAU PLUNDERS

Before leaving the secret corridor, enter the room with the circular door where you fought the Syndicate trio during Chapter 2. The chest in the back of the room contains a **Tetra Band**. Against the top wall is a crate that Yuna can climb onto. From there, climb up to a partially hidden ledge that runs around the outside of the room. Follow this semi-circle to a chest containing **Crimson Sphere 4**. Return to the Celsius and view Crimson Record 4 from Shinra's list of Treasure Spheres.

*Climb up the crate against the side of the room, then climb up and explore the ledge above to find a hidden treasure sphere.*

| GUADOSALAM SHOP (CHAPTER 3 ONLY) | |
| --- | --- |
| ITEM | COST |
| Potion | 50 |
| Antidote | 50 |
| Eye Drops | 550 |
| Echo Screen | 50 |
| Soft | 50 |
| Holy Water | 300 |
| Gris-Gris Bag | 4000 |
| Favorite Outfit | 4000 |
| Regen Bangle | 3000 |
| Wall Ring | 10000 |
| Dream Shock | 15000 |
| Venom Shock | 15000 |

# THUNDER PLAINS

**ACTION CHECKLIST**

1 Lian: Lian and Ayde go there to look. Thank you, High Summoner!

*Advise Lian and Ayde.*

## WANDERING FIENDS

**ANOLE**
HP: 734 | AP: 1 | Gil: 70
Steal: Hi-Potion
Drop: Hi-Potion

**ARMET**
HP: 788 | AP: 1 | Gil: 74
Steal: Lunar Curtain
Drop: Light Curtain

**ASSASSIN BEE**
HP: 233 | AP: 1 | Gil: 48
Steal: Antidote
Drop: Antidote

**BARBUTA**
HP: 562 | AP: 1 | Gil: 33
Steal: Lunar Curtain
Drop: Light Curtain

**BOLT DRAKE**
HP: 623 | AP: 1 | Gil: 130
Steal: Lightning Marble
Drop: Hi-Potion

**CHOCOBO**
HP: 360 | AP: 0 | Gil: 0
Steal: None
Drop: None

**GEMINI**
HP: 2044 | AP: 1 | Gil: 153
Steal: Lunar Curtain x2
Drop: Light Curtain x2

**GUCUMATZ**
HP: 3720 | AP: 1 | Gil: 173
Steal: Soft (x2)
Drop: Soft (x2)

**MALBORO**
HP: 5877 | AP: 1 | Gil: 370
Steal: Hi-Potion
Drop: Remedy (x2)

**WATCHER-A**
HP: 624 | AP: 1 | Gil: 0
Steal: Potion
Drop: Potion

**WATCHER-R**
HP: 620 | AP: 1 | Gil: 0
Steal: Potion
Drop: Potion

**WATCHER-S**
HP: 620 | AP: 1 | Gil: 0
Steal: Potion
Drop: Potion

## ITEM CHECKLIST

Echo Screen (x5)
Hi-Potion (x2)
Safety Bit
Phoenix Down (x3)
Dark Grenade (x2)
Ether (x3)

## MAPS

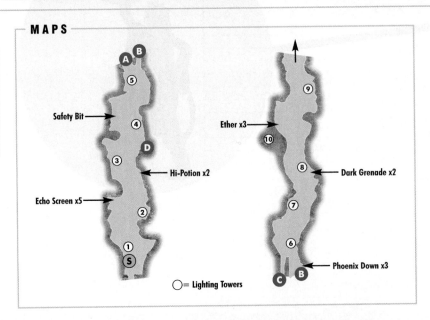

○ = Lighting Towers

164

# RELUCTANT ACQUIESCENCE

If during your visit to Zanarkand you expressed displeasure to Cid in the underground chamber of the fayth, you can find him on the Thunder Plains. Speak to him again if you desire.

*If Cid is doing his thinking on the Thunder Plains, he's ready to apologize.*

# HOW DO LIAN AND AYDE REPAIR THE ELDER'S HORN?

In the second section of the Thunder Plains, move under the old lightning shelter to find the two Ronso children, Lian and Ayde. The youths now want advice on where they might find a way to fix Kimahri's broken horn. The choices are Djose Temple, the Moonflow, and Kilika Island. The location you suggest does not affect your game much, except that the two young Ronso will appear in the location of your choice during Chapter 4.

*The Ronso youngsters need advice on where to find clues to repairing a lost horn.*

# MACALANIA WOODS

## ACTION CHECKLIST

**1** *Defeat the fiends attacking the Travel Agency by the lake.*

**2** *Learn the fate of the Al Bhed shopkeeper.*

COMPLETION: +0.8%

## WANDERING FIENDS

**AMORPHOUS GEL**
HP: 973 | AP: 1 | Gil: 380
Steal: White Ring
Drop: Blue Ring

**BARBUTA**
HP: 562 | AP: 1 | Gil: 33
Steal: Lunar Curtain
Drop: Light Curtain

**BLUE ELEMENTAL**
HP: 363 | AP: 1 | Gil: 180
Steal: Dragon Scale
Drop: Dragon Scale

**CHOCOBO**
HP: 360 | AP: 0 | Gil: 0
Steal: None
Drop: None

**DEEP HAIZHE**
HP: 1030 | AP: 1 | Gil: 40
Steal: Gold Anklet
Drop: Hi-Potion

**DINICTUS**
HP: 1873 | AP: 1 | Gil: 88
Steal: Water Gem
Drop: Water Gem

**FLAN BLANCO**
HP: 625 | AP: 1 | Gil: 72
Steal: Arctic Wind
Drop: Arctic Wind

**GOLD ELEMENTAL**
HP: 99 | AP: 1 | Gil: 25
Steal: Electro Marble
Drop: Electro Marble

**PROTEAN GEL**
HP: 6680 | AP: 1 | Gil: 380
Steal: Blue Ring
Drop: White Ring

**RHYOS**
HP: 4360 | AP: 1 | Gil: 310
Steal: Lightning Gem
Drop: Lightning Gem

**TENTACLES**
HP: 2530 | AP: 1 | Gil: 95
Steal: Phoenix Down
Drop: Phoenix Down

**VERTIGO**
HP: 688 | AP: 1 | Gil: 36
Steal: Antidote x2
Drop: Antidote

**WATCHER-A**
HP: 624 | AP: 1 | Gil: 0
Steal: Potion
Drop: Potion

**WATCHER-R**
HP: 620 | AP: 1 | Gil: 0
Steal: Potion
Drop: Potion

**WATCHER-S**
HP: 620 | AP: 1 | Gil: 0
Steal: Potion
Drop: Potion

Characters

1

Garment Grids & Dresspheres

2

Battle System

3

Accessories

4

Items and Item Shops

5

Walkthrough

Chapter 1

Chapter 2

Chapter 3

Chapter 4

Chapter 5

Mini-Games

7

Fiends and Enemies

8

## ITEM CHECKLIST

NulFrost Ring
Gold Bracer

Pride of the Sword Garment Grid **Ⓔ**
Berserker Dressphere **Ⓔ**

*Al Bhed Primer **Ⓔ**
X-Potion

**\*Only if you haven't mastered Al Bhed.**

## MAPS

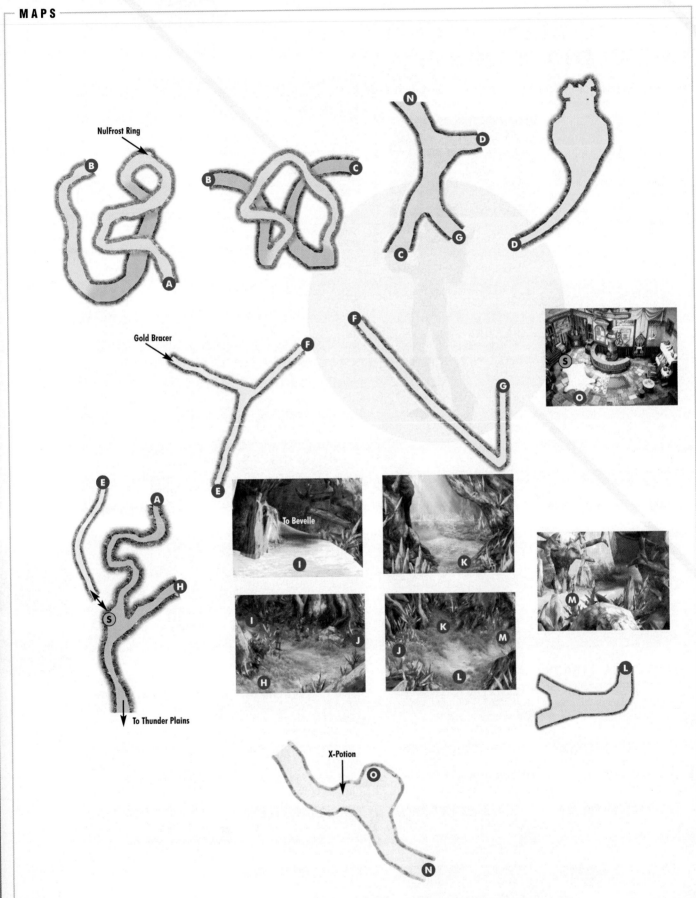

# ICE LAKE RESCUE

Make sure you've paid off O'aka's debt before taking on this mission. Head to Lake Macalania via the shimmering path shortcut. The Travel Agency has been overrun by fiends. The goal is to defeat six sets of fiends without a break in between. When fighting groups with Rhyos enemies, give it all you've got. While fighting lesser foes like Barbuta and Flan Blancos, remember to heal with spells or items before finishing the battle. This approach should keep your characters healthy throughout this series of battles.

In spite of the Gullwings' efforts, it's too late for the Al Bhed shopkeeper. Still, he's very grateful for their attempt.

After defeating all six sets, the Al Bhed inside the agency gives up the **Berserker Dressphere** and an **Al Bhed Primer**. If O'aka's debt is paid, he enters the agency, laments, and vows to set up his own shop here once again. His shop will sell some of the best accessories in all of Spira, but not until Chapter 5! For the remainder of Chapter 3, this shop remains closed. If, however, you have not paid off O'aka's debt or found him digging in Bikanel Desert, the Travel Agency at Macalania will reopen during Chapter 5 under Al Bhed management with only a normal list of items and accessories.

Between each battle, choose fight or flight.

## GREAT GRID!

The **Pride of the Sword Garment Grid**, awarded for defeating the fiends outside the Travel Agency, is a fantastic addition to any character who has mastered, or nearly mastered, the Warrior dressphere. With the Pride of the Sword equipped, a character can perform all the Warrior's Swordplay abilities they've learned, no matter what dressphere is currently equipped.

Characters

1

Garment Grids & Dresspheres

2

Battle System

3

Accessories

4

Items and Item Shops

5

Walkthrough

Chapter 1

Chapter 2

Chapter 3

Chapter 4

Chapter 5

Mini-Games

7

Fiends and Enemies

8

# BIKANEL DESERT

COMPLETION: +0.4%

## WANDERING FIENDS

**ACULEATE**
HP: 776 | AP: 1 | Gil: 72
Steal: Echo Screen (x2)
Drop: Echo Screen (x2)

**ANGRA MAINYU**
HP: 333444 | AP: 30 | Gil: 5000
Steal: Megalixir
Drop: Ribbon

**AQUILA**
HP: 1897 | AP: 1 | Gil: 55
Steal: Hi-Potion
Drop: Hi-Potion

**BOLT DRAKE**
HP: 623 | AP: 1 | Gil: 130
Steal: Lightning Marble
Drop: Hi-Potion

**CANIS MAJOR**
HP: 943 | AP: 1 | Gil: 67
Steal: Hi-Potion
Drop: Hi-Potion

**CHOCOBO**
HP: 3890 | AP: 0 | Gil: 0
Steal: None
Drop: None

**GIGAS**
HP: 2290 | AP: 1 | Gil: 180
Steal: Hi-Potion
Drop: None

**GUARD MACHINA**
HP: 2460 | AP: 1 | Gil: 40
Steal: Budget Grenade
Drop: Budget Grenade

**GUCUMATZ**
HP: 3720 | AP: 1 | Gil: 173
Steal: Soft (x2)
Drop: Soft (x2)

**HRIMTHURS**
HP: 552 | AP: 1 | Gil: 44
Steal: Phoenix Down
Drop: Phoenix Down

**KILLER HOUND**
HP: 202 | AP: 1 | Gil: 18
Steal: Potion
Drop: Potion

**MACHINA HUNTER**
HP: 1780 | AP: 1 | Gil: 30
Steal: Budget Grenade
Drop: Budget Grenade

**POP FRY**
HP: 4293 | AP: 1 | Gil: 100
Steal: Sleep Grenade
Drop: Sleep Grenade

**SAND WORM**
HP: 12722 | AP: 1 | Gil: 340
Steal: Phoenix Down
Drop: Mythril Bangle

**WATCHER-A**
HP: 624 | AP: 1 | Gil: 0
Steal: Potion
Drop: Potion

**WATCHER-R**
HP: 620 | AP: 1 | Gil: 0
Steal: Potion
Drop: Potion

**WATCHER-S**
HP: 620 | AP: 1 | Gil: 0
Steal: Potion
Drop: Potion

**ZU**
HP: 9338 | AP: 1 | Gil: 164
Steal: Phoenix Down
Drop: Phoenix Down (x2)

# EMISSARIES TO THE CACTUARS

Nhadala has another special assignment for the Gullwings. Marnela of the Cactuar Nation has summoned a diplomatic party and translator. Your job is to escort the translator, Benzo, to the Cactuar Nation and speak to the cacti growing there. When asked if you believe Marnela's story, you must agree that it "makes perfect sense" or things will not progress.

Afterward, you learn that a great menace is about to resurface in the desert. The cacti need you to search Spira and find 10 Cactuars who serve as the gatekeepers that can summon the Great Haboob.

*Marnela the cactus requires some reassurance that you're going to take her seriously.*

To start the search, look at the on-screen map. Marnela's position is marked with a pink "X." Speak with her again if you need further instruction. The cactus a short distance away is marked with a green square, so speak to it to learn clues that will help you find the

Cactuar Mothers awaken to provide clues to the 10 gatekeepers' whereabouts. More details are covered in Chapter 5, when you can find all 10 Cactuar critters.

first of the 10 gatekeepers. Once you find the gatekeeper and bring it back to its mother, another cactus in the area will awaken and begin to divulge clues as to another gatekeeper's whereabouts. During Chapter 3, you can only find the first six Cactuars. Subsequently, the remaining Cactuar's locations and full information for completing this mission can be found in the Chapter 5 portion of the walkthrough.

New digging areas include the Eastern Expanse and the Northern Expanse. A strange thing may occur in the Eastern Expanse. If you spot a green "X" on the on-screen map, you'll find a pile of machina in the sand. Unfortunately, the drones come to life and attack in waves. Eventually, the girls give up and it counts as a failed dig. The Northern Expanse is haunted by the Zu creatures. Before you can begin an excavation here, you *must* fight one of these creatures.

Powerful Zu enemies protect the Northern Expanse from greedy diggers.

A caravan of strange characters can be found at the Oasis selling cool accessories.

| BIKANEL DESERT MERCHANT (STARTING CHAPTER 3) | |
|---|---|
| ITEM | COST |
| Potion | 50 |
| Hi-Potion | 500 |
| Phoenix Down | 100 |
| Antidote | 50 |
| Eye Drops | 50 |
| Echo Screen | 50 |
| Soft | 50 |
| Holy Water | 300 |
| Fiery Gleam | 3000 |
| Red Ring | 3000 |
| NulBlaze Ring | 8000 |

| BIKANEL DESERT OASIS CARAVAN | |
|---|---|
| ITEM | COST |
| Black Choker | 4000 |
| Potpourri | 4000 |
| Gris-Gris Bag | 4000 |
| Pearl Necklace | 4000 |
| Pretty Orb | 4000 |
| Dragonfly Orb | 4000 |
| Chaos Shock | 15000 |
| Fury Shock | 15000 |
| Lag Shock | 15000 |
| System Shock | 15000 |

# CALM LANDS

## ACTION CHECKLIST

**1**
Agree to rescue the tourists trapped in the gorge cave.

**2**
Rescue tourists one at a time or en masse.

**3**
Lead the victims to the cave entrance to receive prizes or thanks.

**4**
Activate the teleport pads to rescue the last two tourists.

**5**
Teleport to the Chamber of the Fayth to confront a tricky aeon.

Characters

1

Garment Grids & Dresspheres

2

Battle System

3

Accessories

4

Items and Item Shops

5

Walkthrough
Chapter 1
Chapter 2
Chapter 3
Chapter 4
Chapter 5

Mini-Games

7

Fiends and Enemies

8

COMPLETION: +0.4%

## WANDERING FIENDS

### ADAMANTOISE
HP: 7850 | AP: 1 | Gil: 650
Steal: X-Potion
Drop: Hi-Potion (x4)

### AMORPHOUS GEL
HP: 973 | AP: 1 | Gil: 380
Steal: White Ring
Drop: Blue Ring

### ARMET
HP: 788 | AP: 1 | Gil: 74
Steal: Lunar Curtain
Drop: Light Curtain

### BALIVARHA
HP: 3688 | AP: 1 | Gil: 230
Steal: Hi-Potion (x2)
Drop: Fire Gem

### BLUE ELEMENTAL
HP: 363 | AP: 1 | Gil: 180
Steal: Dragon Scale
Drop: Dragon Scale

### CHOCOBO
HP: 368 | AP: 0 | Gil: 0
Steal: None
Drop: None

### DAEVA
HP: 3230 | AP: 1 | Gil: 90
Steal: Farplane Shadow
Drop: Phoenix Down

### FLAN BLANCO
HP: 625 | AP: 1 | Gil: 72
Steal: Arctic Wind
Drop: Arctic Wind

### FLAN ROJO
HP: 1220 | AP: 1 | Gil: 125
Steal: Bomb Core
Drop: Bomb Core

### GRIM GAZE
HP: 1720 | AP: 1 | Gil: 130
Steal: Phoenix Down
Drop: Phoenix Down

### HAUNT
HP: 813 | AP: 1 | Gil: 120
Steal: Arctic Wind
Drop: Water Ring

### LEUCOPHYLLA
HP: 2234 | AP: 1 | Gil: 86
Steal: Hi-Potion
Drop: Remedy

### PAIRIKA
HP: 1130 | AP: 1 | Gil: 100
Steal: Lightning Marble
Drop: Stamina Spring

### PEREGRINE
HP: 735 | AP: 1 | Gil: 44
Steal: Hi-Potion
Drop: Hi-Potion

### PROTEAN GEL
HP: 6680 | AP: 1 | Gil: 380
Steal: Blue Ring
Drop: White Ring

### QUEEN COEURL
HP: 3270 | AP: 1 | Gil: 330
Steal: Phoenix Down
Drop: Phoenix Down (x2)

### RHYOS
HP: 4360 | AP: 1 | Gil: 310
Steal: Lightning Gem
Drop: Lightning Gem

### SKINK
HP: 882 | AP: 1 | Gil: 78
Steal: Hi-Potion
Drop: Hi-Potion

### TOMB
HP: 4820 | AP: 1 | Gil: 130
Steal: Remedy
Drop: Remedy

### VESPA
HP: 983 | AP: 1 | Gil: 78
Steal: Echo Screen (x2)
Drop: Antidote

### WATCHER-A
HP: 624 | AP: 1 | Gil: 0
Steal: Potion
Drop: Potion

### WATCHER-R
HP: 620 | AP: 1 | Gil: 0
Steal: Potion
Drop: Potion

### WATCHER-S
HP: 620 | AP: 1 | Gil: 0
Steal: Potion
Drop: Potion

### WILD WOLF
HP: 185 | AP: 1 | Gil: 12
Steal: Potion
Drop: Potion

### ZURVAN
HP: 583 | AP: 1 | Gil: 70
Steal: Dispel Tonic
Drop: Hi-Potion

### YOJIMBO
HP: 22000 | AP: 15 | Gil: 1500
Steal: Power Wrist
Drop: Recovery Bracer

## ITEM CHECKLIST

Ether (x3)
Sprint Shoes
Mega-Phoenix

Hi-Potion (x2)
Mega-Phoenix (x2)
White Ring

Blue Ring
Lightning Gleam
Wall Ring

Besaid Key 🅔
Tetra Master Garment Grid 🅔
Star Bracer

## MAPS

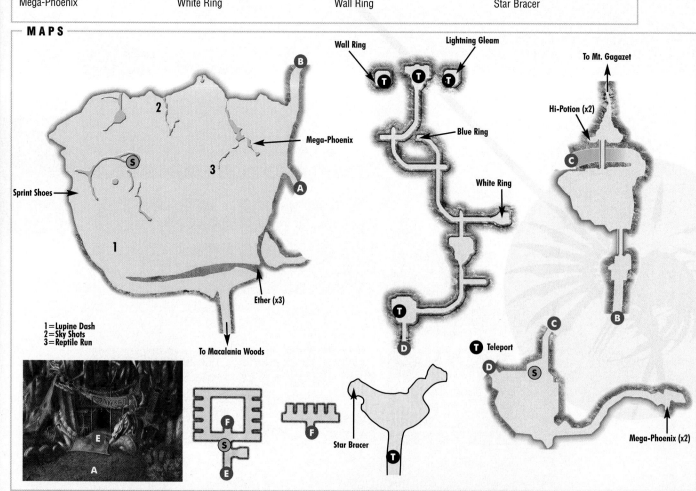

1 = Lupine Dash
2 = Sky Shots
3 = Reptile Run

# TIME TO RAISE CHOCOBOS!

When entering the Calm Lands via the airship, there's a possibility of two entry points. This entry point depends on if you completed the side quest to establish Clasko at the Chocobo Ranch. If you head to the Chocobo Ranch and Clasko isn't in the first room on the right, use the small Chocobo toy to call him back. If you ask him, Clasko will fill the party up on Gysahl, Pahsana, and Mimett greens. If you have caught any chocobos, you can raise some of them (in level) by feeding them various greens depending on what level chocobo you are trying to raise. You can also dispatch chocobos to find items for your party.

*The Chocobo Ranch becomes an even more fun place to play during Chapter 3.*

| ITEM | COST |
|------|------|
| Potion | 50 |
| Hi-Potion | 500 |
| Phoenix Down | 100 |
| Antidote | 50 |
| Eye Drops | 50 |
| Echo Screen | 50 |
| Soft | 50 |
| Holy Water | 300 |
| Titanium Bangle | 3000 |
| Gold Bracer | 4000 |
| Power Wrist | 6000 |
| Tarot Card | 6000 |

*CALM LANDS TRAVEL AGENCY (STARTING CHAPTER 3)*

# TOURIST TRAP

The other mission in this area is far more serious and tricky. Fiends are pouring out of the cave at the bottom of the gorge in the Calm Lands. There are 15 tourists trapped inside the cave. By accepting this mission, you must try and find all 15 tourists from their hiding spots and lead them to the cave entrance. However, in spite of the danger they face, the tourists all have pet peeves about group size and being in certain places in line! If your group gets too big before speaking to certain individuals, they will refuse to join the group. You can either lead the individuals out one at a time, or you can take them all out of the cave simultaneously by rescuing them in the order shown here.

*1. Proceed through the tunnel into the next large chamber. Rescue the person wearing brown who's on the cave floor.*

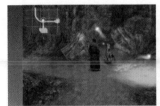

*2. Continue north and rescue the woman in blue recuperating in the small alcove. From here, head down the tunnel to the left.*

*3. Take the next left, follow the curving tunnel to the next intersection, and take another left. Search the seemingly empty chamber to find a person hiding around the corner.*

*4. Head back toward the starting point. At the previous intersection, continue east into a small alcove and rescue the person standing there.*

*5. Lead the group back toward the entrance of the cave. In the curving corridor just before the cave entrance, go down the passage on the right and rescue the person who is running frantically in circles.*

*6. Follow the tunnel north back to the second large cave, where a man in white pants is attempting to catch his breath. Rescue him and continue north in the cave.*

*7. At the first intersection to the north, head left. At the next intersection, continue north to find two people crouched near a chest containing a **Blue Ring**. This couple must be rescued together.*

*8. Proceed to the northernmost chamber and rescue the two children hiding at the top. Lead this massive group back toward the entrance.*

*9. In the small cave to the east of the first 4-way intersection from the entrance, locate a person and two children near a chest containing a **White Ring**. Lead all of these survivors out to the exit and to safety.*

Characters

1

Garment Grids & Dresspheres

2

Battle System

3

Accessories

4

Items and Item Shops

5

Walkthrough

Chapter 1
Chapter 2
Chapter 3
Chapter 4
Chapter 5

Mini-Games

7

Fiends and Enemies

8

# TELEPORT RESCUES

After escorting 13 people out of the cave, two remain. The tourists who are grateful hand over Energy Cores that power the teleportation pads at the entrance and in the last chamber. One man even relinquishes the **Besaid Key**.

*The Besaid Key is an item that unlocks a mysterious side quest on Yuna's home island.*

*If you can't figure out how to reach the two remaining victims inside the cave, speak to the gentleman standing outside to receive another Energy Core.*

*While standing on the northernmost teleport pad, turn Yuna so she faces left or right to change the destination of the device.*

Exit the cave and speak to the man dressed in green and khaki just to the right of the cave entrance. He hands over the seventh Energy Core. When you return inside the cave, use the first teleport pad to reach the last cave. Press the D-pad to the right to change the direction of the pad so that Yuna can teleport to a side chamber.

Inside the square cave, a chest contains a **Lightning Gleam**. The person here prefers to be led out of the cave alone. At the entrance, he hands over the final Energy Core. Teleport back to the last chamber of the cave and press the D-pad to the left to enter the final secret chamber. Plunder the chest for a **Wall Ring**, then lead the final tourist out of the cave. The mission isn't over until you investigate the source of the fiend uprising, however. Teleport back through the cave to the last chamber and teleport from there to the Chamber of the Fayth.

*The last two victims must be led out one at a time.*

# YOJIMBO  BOSS FIGHT

Yojimbo uses attacks that inflict Poison, so equip the entire party prior to this fight with accessories that protect against poisoning, such as Star Pendants and Glass Buckles. Since Yojimbo has several attacks that drain the characters' MP completely, you cannot rely on magic casting to overcome this awesome foe. Instead, outfit one character in a strong attacker dressphere, such as Gunner, Warrior or Dark Knight. Make another character an Alchemist with a plentiful supply of Potions and Hi-Potions to mix. Equip the Alchemist with a Haste Bangle, if possible. You may want another character to be a Thief, just so you can steal items and pilfer gil at the outset of the fight. After stealing from Yojimbo, change the Thief into a Gunner, Dark Knight, or Alchemist.

**HP:** 22000  **MP:** 9999  **EXP:** 2000  **AP:** 15

| | |
|---|---|
| **GIL DROPPED:** 1500 | **STEAL:** Normal: Power Wrist   Rare: Power Wrist |
| **PILFER GIL:** 2000 | **DROP:** Normal: Recovery Bracer   Rare: Recovery Bracer |

At this stage of the game, the best way to quickly take down Yojimbo's HP is to perform the same actions every round. Have a Gunner attack with Trigger Happy and let a Dark Knight sacrifice HP to perform Darkness. These two attacks alone should take down well over 1000 HP each. Let the Alchemist attack or heal the group with items as needed.

Watch Yojimbo carefully throughout the fight. When Yojimbo raises a finger in front of his face, he is preparing to perform his "Zanmato" attack. This is a devastating attack that reduces the entire party to 1 HP and 1 MP! If you see the monster hold one finger in front of its face, *do not command the Alchemist to perform any action until after Zanmato is executed.* If your Alchemist is equipped with a Haste Bangle, she will automatically have Haste on herself following the attack. Quickly use the Mix command to combine a Potion and a Hi-Potion to achieve the same effect as a Mega-Potion. If Yojimbo's dog, Daigoro, manages to attack and kill one or more party members, use a Mega-Phoenix or command the Alchemist to concoct one by mixing a Phoenix Down and a Hi-Potion. Repeat this strategy to stay ahead of the battle each time Yojimbo performs Zanmato. If possible, use a Chocobo Wing to cast Haste on the entire party to increase your chances of winning this fight.

## ACCESSORY LEFT BEHIND

A **Star Bracer** is contained in the chest inside Yojimbo's chamber in the cave. This item generates a constant Reflect effect, and is very useful against all magic attacks. Return to the Chamber of the Fayth and collect it before the end of Chapter 3.

Characters

Garment Grids & Dresspheres

Battle System

Accessories

Items and Item Shops

Walkthrough
Chapter 1
Chapter 2
Chapter 3
Chapter 4
Chapter 5

Mini-Games

Fiends and Enemies

# BEVELLE

COMPLETION: +0.2%

## ITEM CHECKLIST

Blood of the Beast Garment Grid ☻

If you gave the stolen sphere to New Yevon at the start of Chapter 2, then Bevelle becomes a Hotspot at the start of Chapter 3. However, the Gullwings can only watch as the members of the organization clash with each other outside the temple doors.

*Pacce and the Kinderguardians have a present for Yuna, located in the secret chamber at the bottom of Bevelle.*

Having viewed the turmoil rising in Bevelle, the Gullwings automatically return to the Celsius. Return to Bevelle and proceed through the stages. (You can claim all the items and fight the fiends listed in the second Bevelle section in the Chapter 3 portion of this walkthrough. Please refer to the checklists in that section for more details.) When you reach the room where the party fought Bahamut, the Gullwings encounter Pacce and the Kinderguardians. Whether or not you agree with Pacce that he should warn the Youth League, he hands over the **Blood of the Beast Garment Grid**. This is the *only* manner by which to obtain this Garment Grid, so those who chose to side with the Youth League at the beginning of Chapter 2 will just have to play the game differently next time around!

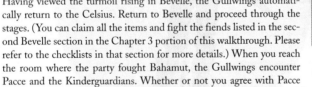

*Don't you hate it when society crumbles just because your leaders go on vacation?*

# MT. GAGAZET

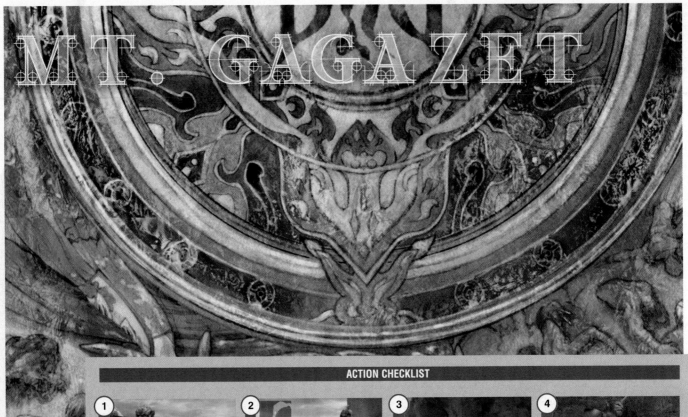

## ACTION CHECKLIST

**1** Learn of Garik's rebellion from Kimahri.

**2** Follow the marching Ronso up the mountain slopes.

**3** Activate the teleport pads along the way.

**4** Confront Garik at the summit.

COMPLETION: +0.4%

## WANDERING FIENDS

**ADAMANTOISE**
HP: 7850 | AP: 1 | Gil: 650
Steal: X-Potion
Drop: Hi-Potion (x4)

**BALIVARHA**
HP: 3688 | AP: 1 | Gil: 230
Steal: Hi-Potion (x2)
Drop: Fire Gem

**BASCINET**
HP: 1342 | AP: 1 | Gil: 110
Steal: Hi-Potion
Drop: Hi-Potion

**BICOCETTE**
HP: 182 | AP: 1 | Gil: 18
Steal: Potion
Drop: Potion

**BOLT DRAKE**
HP: 623 | AP: 1 | Gil: 130
Steal: Lightning Marble
Drop: Hi-Potion

**BORIS**
HP: 480 | AP: 1 | Gil: 300
Steal: Remedy
Drop: Star Pendant

**GEMINI**
HP: 2044 | AP: 1 | Gil: 153
Steal: Lunar Curtain (x2)
Drop: Light Curtain (x2)

**GREATER DRAKE**
HP: 1819 | AP: 1 | Gil: 140
Steal: Fire Gem
Drop: Fire Gem

**GRIM GAZE**
HP: 1720 | AP: 1 | Gil: 130
Steal: Phoenix Down
Drop: Phoenix Down

**LEUCOPHYLLA**
HP: 2234 | AP: 1 | Gil: 86
Steal: Hi-Potion
Drop: Remedy

**LUPUS**
HP: 1262 | AP: 1 | Gil: 80
Steal: Hi-Potion
Drop: Hi-Potion

**MYCOTOXIN**
HP: 810 | AP: 1 | Gil: 83
Steal: Antidote (x2)
Drop: Antidote (x2)

**QUEEN COEURL**
HP: 3270 | AP: 1 | Gil: 330
Steal: Phoenix Down
Drop: Phoenix Down (x2)

**RUKH**
HP: 12850 | AP: 1 | Gil: 530
Steal: Phoenix Down (x2)
Drop: Phoenix Down (x2)

**RHYOS**
HP: 4360 | AP: 1 | Gil: 310
Steal: Lightning Gem
Drop: Lightning Gem

**SPINE DRAKE**
HP: 2582 | AP: 1 | Gil: 127
Steal: Arctic Wind
Drop: Arctic Wind

**WATCHER-A**
HP: 624 | AP: 1 | Gil: 0
Steal: Potion
Drop: Potion

**WATCHER-R**
HP: 620 | AP: 1 | Gil: 0
Steal: Potion
Drop: Potion

**WATCHER-S**
HP: 620 | AP: 1 | Gil: 0
Steal: Potion
Drop: Potion

**VESPA**
HP: 983 | AP: 1 | Gil: 78
Steal: Echo Screen (x2)
Drop: Antidote

**RONSO YOUTH**
HP: 4060 | AP: 2 | Gil: 20
Steal: Mythril Bangle
Drop: Remedy

**GARIK RONSO**
HP: 6880 | AP: 3 | Gil: 90
Steal: Icy Gleam
Drop: Shining Bracer

## ITEM CHECKLIST

Trainer Dressphere

Characters

1

Garment Grids
& Dresspheres

2

Battle System

3

Accessories

4

Items and
Item Shops

5

Walkthrough
Chapter 1
Chapter 2
**Chapter 3**
Chapter 4
Chapter 5

Mini-Games

7

Fiends and
Enemies

8

# RONSO UPRISING

Move forward past the Save Sphere to trigger a scene with Kimahri. If you previously answered two questions for Kimahri, you can get the the **Trainer dressphere**. Garik has shut off the teleport pads, so the party must fight its way up the mountain.

*As you proceed to the summit, touch the teleport pads to reactivate them.*

# REVISITING OLD GROUNDS

At the Fayth Scar, you can climb up the cliffs the same as you did when going after the Leblanc Syndicate uniforms. Atop the rise, the artisan Ronso should now be hard at work on a statue commemorating the hero of the Ronso. If you continue to the top of this area, you can return to the Floating Ruins featured in the second mission of the game. However, don't waste time there unless you left some items behind during the timed chase of the Syndicate.

*Use the cliffs high above the hot springs cavern to reach the Floating Ruins stage from the beginning of the game.*

# GARIK RONSO, RONSO YOUTH (X2*)

**HP:** 6880  **MP:** 238  **EXP:** 380  **AP:** 3

**GIL DROPPED:** 90
**PILFER GIL:** 130

**STEAL:** Normal: Icy Gleam   Rare: Icy Gleam
**DROP:** Normal: Shining Bracer   Rare: Shining Bracer

*2 Ronso Youth appear if the Ronso concerns were answered incorrectly; 1 will appear if their concerns were answered correctly.

If you answered the Ronso's concerns incorrectly for the most part, Garik is accompanied by two Ronso Youths. Garik uses the Mighty Guard ability on himself and his followers, which is a combination of Protect, Shell, Regen, Haste, Def. Up, Magic Def. Up, and Evasion Up. Use Dispel Tonics, an Alchemist's Dispel Tonic ability, or a White Mage's Dispel spell to negate the first four of these effects. Garik attacks frequently and fiercely, so cast Haste on the party, use the Songstress's "Jitterbug" dance, or use a Chocobo Wing.

Protect the party against Darkness by equipping accessories, because Garik can cripple them with a Blind spell on a regular basis. Use a Black Mage's MP Drain ability to siphon off all of Garik's MP; this will prevent him from casting Blind. The Ronso Youth use attacks that drain MP, so don't rely too heavily on spells throughout the battle. Equip the party with dresspheres that allow swift attacks that inflict a great deal of damage quickly, such as Dark Knight, Gunner, and Warrior. Take down Garik Ronso first, then negate the Mighty Guard effects on the remaining two Ronso and defeat them as quickly as possible.

**HP:** 4060  **MP:** 170  **EXP:** 220  **AP:** 2

**GIL DROPPED:** 20
**PILFER GIL:** 60

**STEAL:** Normal: Mythril Bangle   Rare: Mythril Bangle
**DROP:** Normal: Remedy   Rare: Remedy (x2)

If, however, you answered the concerns of every Ronso during Chapters 1 and 2, Garik won't be as strong and only one Ronso Youth accompanies him during the battle, too. He doesn't use the Mighty Guard defense and instead he only casts Shell and Protect on himself on separate turns. To overcome these spells, simply drain all of his MP. Under these conditions, Garik is much easier to steal from, quite a bit easier to defeat, and his counterpart will not drain MP.

# ZANARKAND RUINS

**COMPLETION: +0.2%**

## WANDERING FIENDS

**ANOLE**
HP: 734 | AP: 1 | Gil: 70
Steal: Hi-Potion
Drop: Hi-Potion

**FLAILING OCHU**
HP: 9860 | AP: 1 | Gil: 430
Steal: Remedy
Drop: Remedy

**GUARDIAN BEAST**
HP: 2886 | AP: 1 | Gil: 200
Steal: Defense Veil
Drop: Amulet

**GUCUMATZ**
HP: 3720 | AP: 1 | Gil: 173
Steal: Soft (x2)
Drop: Soft (x2)

**IRONSIDE**
HP: 8432 | AP: 1 | Gil: 200
Steal: Shadow Gem (x2)
Drop: Stamina Tablet

**MYCOTOXIN**
HP: 810 | AP: 1 | Gil: 83
Steal: Antidote (x2)
Drop: Antidote (x2)

**WATCHER-A**
HP: 624 | AP: 1 | Gil: 0,
Steal: Potion
Drop: Potion

**WATCHER-R**
HP: 620 | AP: 1 | Gil: 0
Steal: Potion
Drop: Potion

**WATCHER-S**
HP: 620 | AP: 1 | Gil: 0
Steal: Potion
Drop: Potion

## ITEM CHECKLIST

Dispel Tonic (x2)

Phoenix Down (x3)

Hi-Potion (x3)

S-Bomb (x2)

Stamina Spring

Remedy (x2)

Lunar Curtain (x2)

Mana Spring (x2)

2000 gil

Light Curtain (x2)

Mythril Bangle

Phoenix Down (x3)

Hi-Potion (x3)

Remedy (x4)

Remedy (x3)

Ether (x3)

## MAPS

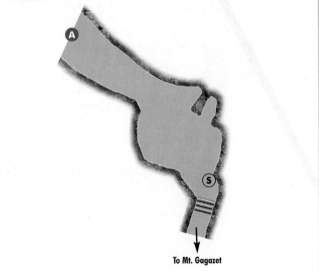

To Mt. Gagazet

ZANARKAND RUINS

176

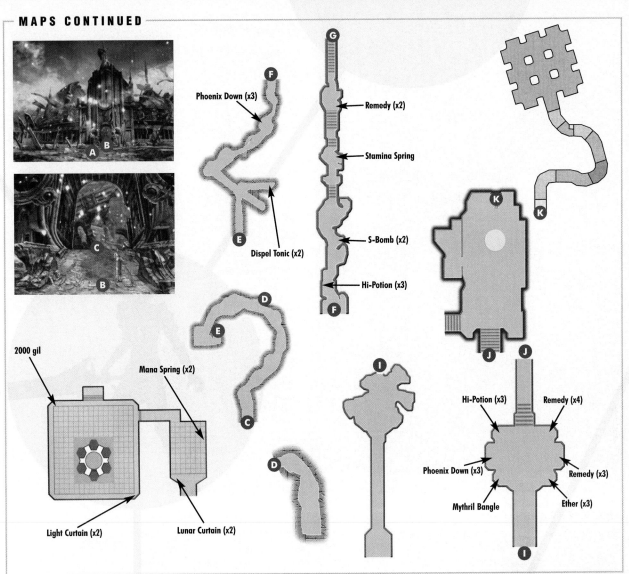

Phoenix Down (x3)

Remedy (x2)

Stamina Spring

Dispel Tonic (x2)

S-Bomb (x2)

Hi-Potion (x3)

2000 gil

Mana Spring (x2)

Light Curtain (x2)

Lunar Curtain (x2)

Hi-Potion (x3)

Remedy (x4)

Phoenix Down (x3)

Remedy (x3)

Mythril Bangle

Ether (x3)

Characters

Garment Grids
& Dресspheres

Battle System

Accessories

Items and
Item Shops

Walkthrough
Chapter 1
Chapter 2
**Chapter 3**
Chapter 4
Chapter 5

Mini-Games

Fiends and
Enemies

# MONKEY LOVE IN THE AIR

If you finished the monkey soulmate mission during Chapter 2, there is nothing more to do here than speak to Isaaru one last time as he leaves Zanarkand. If you still need to finish the monkey matchmaking side quest, do so now using the instructions contained in the Chapter 2 section. If you complete the mission in Chapter 3, exit when you're finished and speak to Isaaru outside the dome.

*Isaaru may be sad that his tourist operation has gone to the monkeys, but a sacred place shouldn't be a source of amusement.*

## DEALING WITH IRONSIDES

*A new fiend, called Ironside, appears in several locations during Chapter 3. This brute's heavy armor makes it incredibly difficult to defeat. After one or two rounds, the monster opens its chest plate to prepare a beam cannon assault. Launch your party's most devastating attacks while the chest plate is open, as this is when the monster's Defense is greatly reduced.*

| ZANARKAND DOME MERCHANT (STARTING CHAPTER 3) | |
|---|---|
| **ITEM** | **COST** |
| Potion | 50 |
| Hi-Potion | 500 |
| Phoenix Down | 100 |
| Antidote | 50 |
| Eye Drops | 50 |
| Echo Screen | 50 |
| Soft | 50 |
| Holy Water | 300 |
| Titanium Bangle | 3000 |
| Gold Bracer | 4000 *CH3+ |
| Diamond Gloves | 6000 *CH3+ |
| Mystery Veil | 6000 *CH3+ |

# BESAID ISLAND

## ACTION CHECKLIST

**1** Learn the situation from Lulu.

**2** Follow Wakka and Beclem into the temple.

**3** Speak to Beclem inside the Great Hall.

**4** Talk to Wakka inside the Cloister of Trials.

**5** Defeat Yuna's first aeon, in a much darker form.

**COMPLETION: +2.0%**

## WANDERING FIENDS

**BARBUTA**
HP: 562 | AP: 1 | Gil: 33
Steal: Lunar Curtain
Drop: Light Curtain

**CEPHALOTUS**
HP: 1830 | AP: 1 | Gil: 62
Steal: Echo Screen (x2)
Drop: Echo Screen (x2)

**CHOCOBO**
HP: 368 | AP: 0 | Gil: 0
Steal: None
Drop: None

**FLAME DRAGON**
HP: 980 | AP: 1 | Gil: 300
Steal: Hi-Potion
Drop: Red Ring

**GEMINI**
HP: 2044 | AP: 1 | Gil: 153
Steal: Lunar Curtain (x2)
Drop: Light Curtain (x2)

**HAUNT**
HP: 813 | AP: 1 | Gil: 120
Steal: Arctic Wind
Drop: Water Ring

**MALBORO**
HP: 5877 | AP: 1 | Gil: 370
Steal: Hi-Potion
Drop: Remedy (x2)

**PAIRIKA**
HP: 1130 | AP: 1 | Gil: 100
Steal: Lightning Marble
Drop: Stamina Spring

**QUEEN COEURL**
HP: 3270 | AP: 1 | Gil: 330
Steal: Phoenix Down
Drop: Phoenix Down (x2)

**SPINE DRAKE**
HP: 2582 | AP: 1 | Gil: 127
Steal: Arctic Wind
Drop: Arctic Wind

**WATCHER-A**
HP: 624 | AP: 1 | Gil: 0
Steal: Potion
Drop: Potion

**WATCHER-R**
HP: 620 | AP: 1 | Gil: 0
Steal: Potion
Drop: Potion

**WATCHER-S**
HP: 620 | AP: 1 | Gil: 0
Steal: Potion
Drop: Potion

**ZURVAN**
HP: 583 | AP: 1 | Gil: 70
Steal: Dispel Tonic
Drop: Hi-Potion

**VALEFOR**
HP: 8430 | AP: 15 | Gil: 1200
Steal: Healing Spring (x4)
Drop: Moon Bracer

## ITEM CHECKLIST

Mana Spring (x2)

Moon Bracer

Hi-Potion (x2)

X-Potion

2500 gil

Ether (x3)

Raging Giant Garment Grid

# MAPS

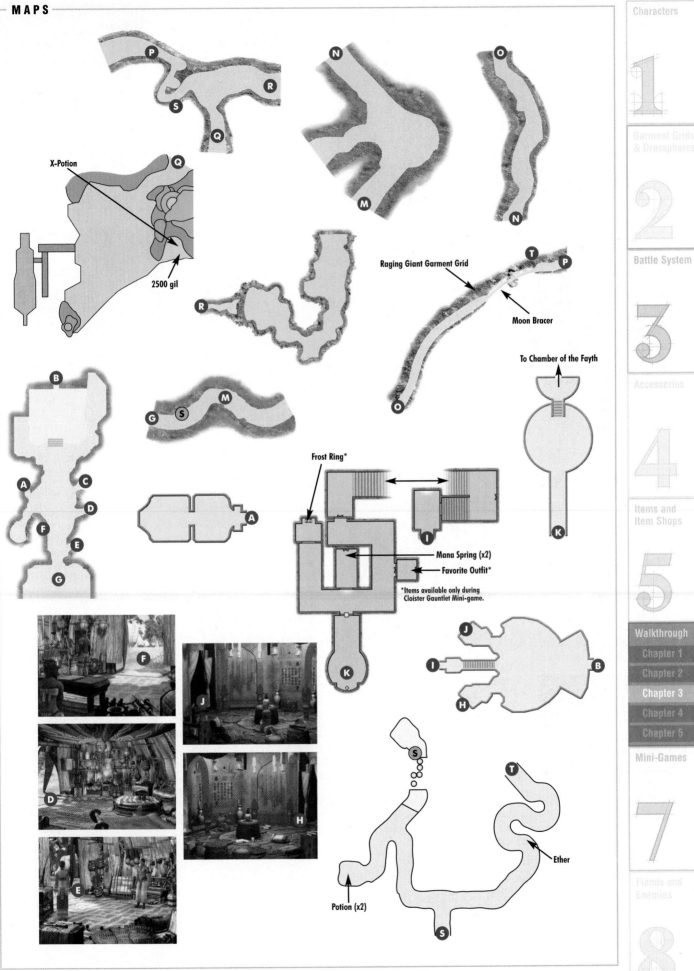

X-Potion

Q

2500 gil

Raging Giant Garment Grid

Moon Bracer

To Chamber of the Fayth

Frost Ring*

Mana Spring (x2)

Favorite Outfit*

*Items available only during
Cloister Gauntlet Mini-game.

Potion (x2)

Ether

Characters

1

Garment Grids
& Dresspheres

2

Battle System

3

Accessories

4

Items and
Item Shops

5

Walkthrough

Chapter 1

Chapter 2

Chapter 3

Chapter 4

Chapter 5

Mini-Games

7

Fiends and
Enemies

8

# CONFLICT OF COMMAND

Enter Lulu's tent on the east side of the village. After learning of the developments between Wakka and Beclem, exit the tent and follow Wakka into the temple. Ascend the center stairs and work through the trial area to the bottom level. When you reach an intersection, head right through the illusory wall to find a chest containing a **Mana Spring (x2)**. Cross the corridor to find Wakka, wounded and lying in the corridor. After Yuna and the Gullwings ride the elevator to the level below, move forward to battle another dark aeon.

*Some items in Besaid's cloister can only be obtained after the Gunner's Gauntlet.*

## VALEFOR — BOSS FIGHT

HP: 8430  MP: 9999  EXP: 1500  AP: 15

Fighting this aeon should easily remind you of the battle with Bahamut. Have a master Black Mage cast third-level elemental spells and make a Songstress decrease the frequency of Valefor's attacks with Slow Dance. Meanwhile, have a White Mage or Alchemist heal every round to keep the party on top of the battle. Valefor uses its Sonic Wings attack to drain spellcasters' MP, so make sure your Black Mage knows the MP Drain ability.

**GIL DROPPED:** 1200
**PILFER GIL:** 1500
**STEAL:** Normal: Healing Spring (x4)   Rare: Healing Spring (x6)
**DROP:** Normal: Moon Bracer   Rare: Moon Bracer

## THE SEARCH SPHERE

If you previously purchased the Besaid Key for 900,000 gil from the shop clerk in the village, or if you rescued a man in the Calm Lands gorge who rewarded you with the Besaid Key, you can now undertake a brief side quest to obtain a new Garment Grid. Use the Besaid Key to unlock the treasure chest in the north room of the temple to obtain the **Search Sphere**. To learn how to use this item, speak to the man seated in the south room inside the temple.

*Each time you enter Besaid, you must reclaim the Search Sphere from the chest inside the temple prayer room.*

*The Search Sphere helps to locate camera devices around Besaid Island, which can be used to find the second four ciphers.*

With the Search Sphere in your inventory, the device appears in the lower-right corner of the screen. Press and hold the Circle button to extend a meter from the side of the on-screen Search Sphere. As you draw closer to the location of a buried camera sphere, the meter begins to emit higher waves, rising into the red. When you're standing on the exact spot of a buried camera sphere, the sphere starts to pulsate and makes a low humming noise. Press the X button to dig up a small camera device on that spot.

## THE SECOND FOUR CIPHERS

The first of the buried camera spheres is in the village, under a small tarp erected in an area near the woods alongside the village. Hold the Circle button and move carefully under the tarp until the Search Sphere begins to flash red and make a sound, then press the X button to dig up a camera sphere. After the device is revealed, stand directly over the camera sphere and press the X button to use it. The view then switches to camera view. You can rotate the camera and cycle through a series of zoom magnifications by pressing the R1 button.

In the case of the village camera sphere, aim the device toward the roof of the temple and zoom in on the "steeple" at the top of the building. There you should find a sphere marked with a large number. The number is the first of a four-digit series of ciphers required to open the secret corridor of the cave near the beach.

*The first camera device is located under a small tent on the west side of the village.*

*Aim the camera at the top of the temple and zoom in to find the numbered sphere.*

Head along the path, and use the Search Sphere to locate the camera device buried close to one of the Besaid Aurochs near the bottom side of the path. Use the camera device to spot a glint near the middle of the nearby ridge and zoom in to find the second number written on the sphere. Get a good look, because sometimes 5s look like 6s and 1s look like 7s. The main difference between a 1 and a 7 is that the latter number has a dash through the middle.

The second camera is buried near the start of the Gunner's Gauntlet.

Pan the camera along the nearby ridge to spot a numbered sphere.

While moving up the path toward the waterfall area, use the Search Sphere to find a camera device on the right side of the path. Use this camera to zoom in on the ledge just below the second waterfall. This is the third cipher of the series.

The third camera device is located along the right side of the path, before the first bridge.

Zoom in on this rocky jut to find another numbered sphere.

For the last cipher, proceed past the cave entrance to the pond overlook area. Use the Search Sphere to detect the camera device in the left corner of the ledge over the water, and zoom across the pond to spot a lone tree high up on a hill. The sphere is set at the top of the tree. This is the last cipher in the series.

Dig up the camera device in the left corner of the overlooking edge.

Zoom in on the lone palm tree high up on the opposite cliffs.

Enter the cave and move into the short passage on the right. Input the four ciphers into the panel near the large stone block in the order in which they were discovered while traveling from the village to the pond. When the stone slab rises, proceed up the path and open the chest encountered en route for some **Ethers** (the exact number is determined by the current Chapter you are playing). Proceed to the end of the twisty passage to emerge on a hidden ledge high over the waterfall area. Move left across the screen to find a chest perched precariously on a slope. Open the chest to get the **Raging Giant Garment Grid**.

Input the ciphers in the order discovered from the village to the pond.

After obtaining the Garment Grid, move back along the ledge to the point of origin to find the cave entrance.

| BESAID ISLAND SHOP (STARTING CHAPTER 3) | |
|---|---|
| **ITEM** | **COST** |
| Potion | 50 |
| Hi-Potion | 500 |
| Phoenix Down | 100 |
| Antidote | 50 |
| Eye Drops | 50 |
| Echo Screen | 50 |
| Soft | 50 |
| Holy Water | 300 |
| Watery Gleam | 3000 |
| Blue Ring | 3000 |
| NulTide Ring | 8000 |

Characters

Garment Grids & Dresspheres

Battle System

Accessories

Items and Item Shops

Walkthrough
Chapter 1
Chapter 2
Chapter 3
Chapter 4
Chapter 5

Mini-Games

Fiends and Enemies

# KILIKA ISLAND

## ACTION CHECKLIST

**1** Conspire with Dona to sneak past the guards.

**2** Slip through the gate while Dona distracts the guard.

**3** Find the hidden path through the blockaded woods.

**4** Enter the temple and rescue Barthello from the fiend.

**5** Speak to Barthello to learn an important tip.

**6** Touch the blue flames within the temple to defeat fiends and proceed.

**7** Defeat another dark aeon in the chamber of the fayth.

**COMPLETION: +1.6%**

## WANDERING FIENDS

 **ASSASSIN BEE**
HP: 233 | AP: 1 | Gil: 48
Steal: Antidote
Drop: Antidote

**CHOCOBO**
HP: 368 | AP: 0 | Gil: 0
Steal: None
Drop: None

**DAEVA**
HP: 3230 | AP: 1 | Gil: 90
Steal: Farplane Shadow
Drop: Phoenix Down

**HAUNT**
HP: 813 | AP: 1 | Gil: 120
Steal: Arctic Wind
Drop: Water Ring

 **IRONSIDE**
HP: 8432 | AP: 1 | Gil: 200
Steal: Shadow Gem (x2)
Drop: Stamina Tablet

**LEAGUE MAGE**
HP: 1020 | AP: 1 | Gil: 130
Steal: Ether
Drop: Hi-Potion

**LEAGUE RAIDER**
HP: 293 | AP: 1 | Gil: 130
Steal: Phoenix Down
Drop: Hi-Potion

**LEAGUE WARRIOR**
HP: 422 | AP: 1 | Gil: 120
Steal: Hi-Potion
Drop: Hi-Potion

 **PAIRIKA**
HP: 1130 | AP: 1 | Gil: 100
Steal: Lightning Marble
Drop: Stamina Spring

**QUEEN COEURL**
HP: 3270 | AP: 1 | Gil: 330
Steal: Phoenix Down
Drop: Phoenix Down (x2)

**WATCHER-R**
HP: 620 | AP: 1 | Gil: 0
Steal: Potion
Drop: Potion

**WATCHER-S**
HP: 620 | AP: 1 | Gil: 0
Steal: Potion
Drop: Potion

**YEVON'S FINEST**
HP: 1722 | AP: 1 | Gil: 140
Steal: Holy Water
Drop: Hi-Potion

**YEVON STRIKER**
HP: 1730 | AP: 1 | Gil: 140
Steal: Holy Water
Drop: Hi-Potion

 **IFIRIT**
HP: 8820 | AP: 15 | Gil: 1300
Steal: Fiery Gleam
Drop: Angel Earrings

## ITEM CHECKLIST

| | | | |
|---|---|---|---|
| Turbo Ether | Eye Drops (x3) | Holy Water (x3) | 2000 gil |
| Mana Tablet (x2) | Phoenix Down (x2) | Star Curtain | Bushido Lore |
| Antidote (x3) | Light Curtain (x2) | Lunar Curtain (x2) | Samurai Dressphere |

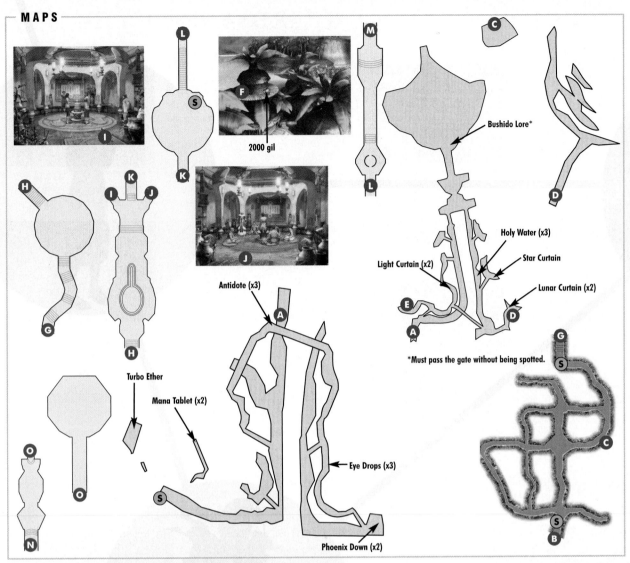

2000 gil

Bushido Lore*

Holy Water (x3)

Light Curtain (x2)

Star Curtain

Lunar Curtain (x2)

Antidote (x3)

Turbo Ether

Mana Tablet (x2)

Eye Drops (x3)

*Must pass the gate without being spotted.

Phoenix Down (x2)

Characters

1

Garment Grids & Dresspheres

2

Battle System

3

Accessories

4

Items and Item Shops

5

Walkthrough

Chapter 1
Chapter 2
Chapter 3
Chapter 4
Chapter 5

Mini-Games

7

Fiends and Enemies

8

# WORKING WITH DONA

Collect all the items in the Kilika port areas, then go to Dona's house in the second section. She and Yuna unite to distract the guards and slip through the gates into the woods. Exit Dona's house to begin the gate-rushing event. You may want to attempt a practice round to learn how to get through the gates. The key is to watch the front gate for the approach of a Youth League member. If the guard allows the person through the gate, quickly switch perspective to see if the guard with Dona is distracted or not. If the guard is facing away from Dona, wait until he turns back to her or wait until another opportunity arises.

*You get only one chance to slip through the gate unnoticed!*

*The Bushido Lore should prove to be an invaluable accessory if you have found and mastered the Samurai dressphere.*

When you enter the woods without detection, a treasure chest is waiting at the end of the bridge. When equipped, the **Bushido Lore** enables a character to use learned Bushido abilities whether she is equipped with the Samurai dressphere or not. However, if you are spotted, the mission continues and you don't get the prize.

## COLLECT YOUR MONKEY FINDING FEE

*If you found all 13 Squatter Monkeys hidden in the Kilika forest area, speak to the woman dressed in blue standing on the east side of the pier to collect your prize—the* **Chaos Maelstrom Garment Grid***.*

| KILIKA PORT MERCHANT (STARTING CHAPTER 3) | |
|---|---|
| **ITEM** | **COST** |
| Potion | 50 |
| Hi-Potion | 500 |
| Phoenix Down | 100 |
| Antidote | 50 |
| Eye Drops | 50 |
| Echo Screen | 50 |
| Soft | 50 |
| Holy Water | 300 |
| Twist Headband | 3000 |
| White Cape | 3000 |
| Silver Glasses | 3000 |
| Star Pendant | 4000 |
| Beaded Brooch | 10000 |
| Glass Buckle | 10000 |

# SCOPING OUT THE FOREST

The Youth League has erected several gates to keep people from New Yevon out. Visit all of the gates in the area, then return to the section just west of the Save Sphere. The girls remember something Dona said about a path through the trees, and leap to the bough above. Follow Rikku and Paine to the temple area.

*Visit all four barricades, then move under the curving bough to find the hidden path to the temple.*

# LAST STAND AT THE TEMPLE ENTRANCE

A shop clerk walking around the temple entrance sells only the basics. Stock up on Potions and Hi-Potions if needed, then head into the temple. A Save Sphere is tucked behind the giant machina positioned in the large round room. Use it before heading into the cloister of trials.

*Make sure an Alchemist has a large supply of Potions and Hi-Potions so you can use Mix to keep the party at optimum health. Stock up whenever the opportunity arises.*

# GUARDIANS OF THE BLUE FLAME

After being rescued, Barthello explains that the fiends are connected somehow to the blue flames. Head toward the blue flames covering the archway and another Daeva appears. After defeating the monster, the flames subside and reveal the corridor.

*You must defeat a Daeva or two each time you want to extinguish a blue flame barring your path.*

Continue into the next section and approach each of the three blue flames. Touch the flame on the right wall, then the one on the left, followed by the central blue flame on the back wall, defeating a Daeva each time.

*After fighting the Daeva duo team in the last chamber before the boss, don't overlook the **Samurai dressphere** on the ground.*

## IFRIT — BOSS FIGHT

HP: 8820  MP: 9999  EXP: 1800  AP: 15

Avoid using any attacks or spells that involve the element of fire; if you don't, Ifrit will absorb the attack and be healed rather than damaged. Ifrit is weak versus ice, so have a Black Mage cast a few Blizzaga spells to make defeating this aeon much easier. Ifrit is also vulnerable to Slow, which can reduce the frequency of its furious claw attacks.

**GIL DROPPED:** 1300
**PILFER GIL:** 1800

**STEAL:** Normal: Fiery Gleam   Rare: Fiery Gleam
**DROP:** Normal: Angel Earrings   Rare: Angel Earrings

| KILIKA ISLAND TEMPLE MERCHANT | |
|---|---|
| ITEM | COST |
| Potion | 50 |
| Hi-Potion | 500 |
| Phoenix Down | 100 |
| Antidote | 50 |
| Eye Drops | 50 |
| Echo Screen | 50 |
| Soft | 50 |
| Holy Water | 300 |

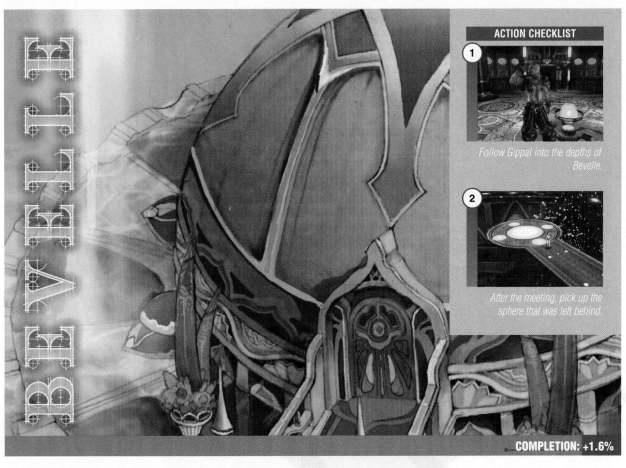

BEVELLE

Characters

1

Garment Grids & Dresspheres

2

Battle System

3

Accessories

4

Items and Item Shops

5

Walkthrough

Chapter 1

Chapter 2

**Chapter 3**

Chapter 4

Chapter 5

Mini-Games

7

Fiends and Enemies

8

## ACTION CHECKLIST

① Follow Gippal into the depths of Bevelle.

② After the meeting, pick up the sphere that was left behind.

**COMPLETION: +1.6%**

## WANDERING FIENDS

**BARONG**
HP: 2733 | AP: 1 | Gil: 138
Steal: Phoenix Down
Drop: Antidote

**DETONATOR**
HP: 1860 | AP: 1 | Gil: 98
Steal: Bomb Core
Drop: Bomb Core

**FLAN BLANCO**
HP: 625 | AP: 1 | Gil: 72
Steal: Arctic Wind
Drop: Arctic Wind

**GEORAPELLA**
HP: 4420 | AP: 1 | Gil:1000
Steal: Water Gem Drop:
NulTide Ring

**MALBORO**
HP: 5877 | AP: 1 | Gil: 370
Steal: Hi-Potion
Drop: Remedy (x2)

**PRECEPTS GUARD**
HP: 3680 | AP: 1 | Gil: 800
Steal: Mana Tablet
Drop: Regen Ring

**SKINK**
HP: 882 | AP: 1 | Gil: 78
Steal: Hi-Potion
Drop: Hi-Potion

**YAC-62**
HP: 4100 | AP: 1 | Gil: 94
Steal: Darkness Grenade
Drop: Sleep Grenade

**YAU-71**
HP: 3800 | AP: 1 | Gil: 94
Steal: Silence Grenade
Drop: Sleep Grenade

**YSLS-99**
HP: 2775 | AP: 1 | Gil: 400
Steal: Mythril Gloves
Drop: Stamina Tablet

## ITEM CHECKLIST

Electrocutioner 🅔
Hypno Crown 🅔
Remedy (x4)
Oath Veil
5000 gil
Hi-Potion (x5)
Potion (x9)
Phoenix Down (x5)
Chocobo Feather (x2)
800 gil
Faerie Earrings
Beaded Brooch
Ether (x5)
Remedy (x5)
Phoenix Down (x6)
Remedy
Crimson Sphere 1 🅔

## MAPS

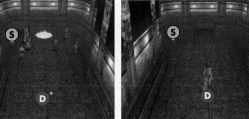

*Room Changes in Chapter 5.

Ⓐ1 Changes lift A to destination A1.
Ⓐ2 Changes lift A to destination A2.

BEVELLE

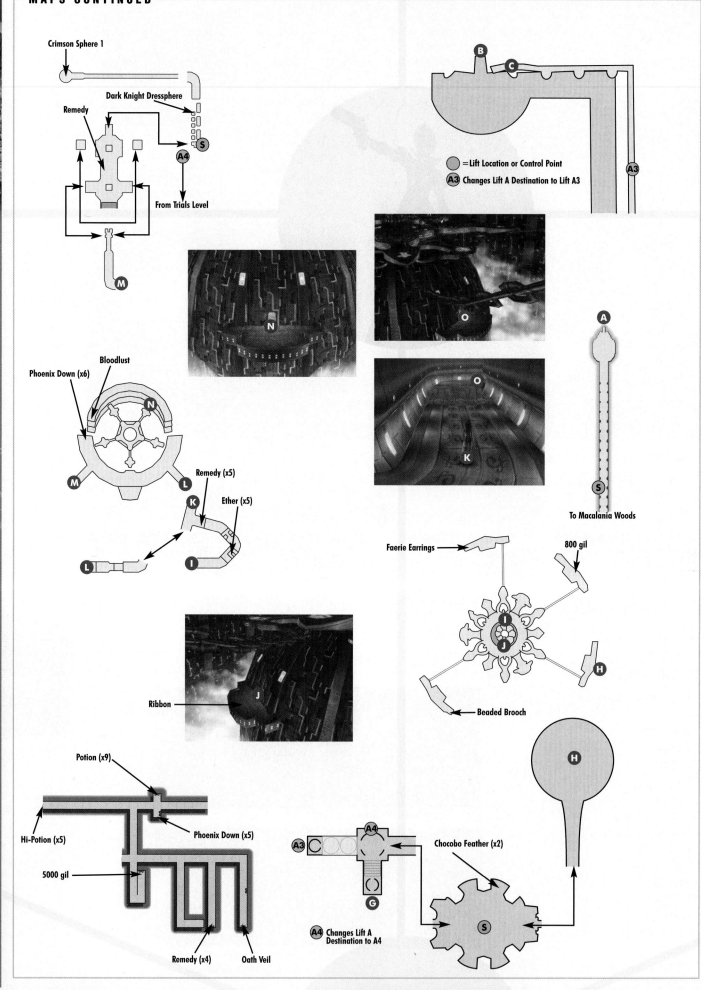

Crimson Sphere 1

Dark Knight Dressphere

Remedy

From Trials Level

A4

S

M

B

C

A3

= Lift Location or Control Point

A3 Changes Lift A Destination to Lift A3

N

O

O

K

A

S

To Macalania Woods

Bloodlust

Phoenix Down (x6)

N

M

L

K

Remedy (x5)

Ether (x5)

L

I

Faerie Earrings

800 gil

I

J

H

Beaded Brooch

Ribbon

J

H

Potion (x9)

Phoenix Down (x5)

Hi-Potion (x5)

5000 gil

Remedy (x4)

Oath Veil

A3

A4

G

A4 Changes Lift A
Destination to A4

Chocobo Feather (x2)

S

# MYSTERIOUS MEETING UNDER NEW YEVON BANNERS

Although Djose becomes a hotspot following the events in Kilika, Bevelle is now open for further exploration—even by Youth League sympathizers. Inside the temple entrance, ride the lift to the upper level and go through the open door to the outdoor balcony. Speak to the two priests walking along the rails to receive an **Electrocutioner** and a **Hypno Crown**. Return inside the temple and use the device in the west chamber to change the direction of the lift. Ride the lift down to the maze level below.

The priests on the balcony shower you with valuable gifts, but you're still not good enough to ride Baralai's private lift.

Crimson Spheres enable the Gullwings to unlock further mysteries of the past, as well as that weird door at Mushroom Rock.

Proceed through the lower areas of Bevelle to the chamber from which Vegnagun escaped. After an extended scene, a Malboro attacks. When the zone is clear, locate the **Crimson Sphere 1** on the ground. Pick it up, return to the Save Sphere in the antechamber, and board the airship. Speak to Shinra and watch "Crimson Report 1" for more revealing information.

## DJOSE TEMPLE

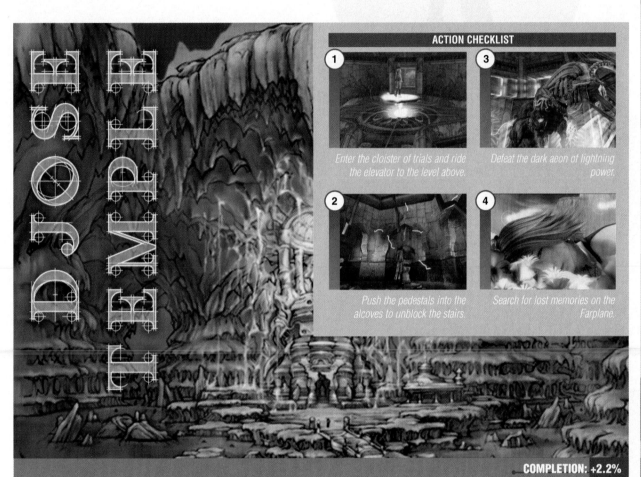

### ACTION CHECKLIST

**1** Enter the cloister of trials and ride the elevator to the level above.

**2** Push the pedestals into the alcoves to unblock the stairs.

**3** Defeat the dark aeon of lightning power.

**4** Search for lost memories on the Farplane.

COMPLETION: +2.2%

## WANDERING FIENDS

| **HAUNT** | **PAIRIKA** | **TOMB** | **IXION** |
|---|---|---|---|
| HP: 813 AP: 1 Gil: 120 | HP: 1130 AP: 1 Gil: 100 | HP: 4820 AP: 1 Gil: 130 | HP:12380 AP: 15 Gil:1800 |
| Steal: Arctic Wind | Steal: Lightning Marble | Steal: Remedy | Steal: Sprint Shoes |
| Drop: Water Ring | Drop: Stamina Spring | Drop: Remedy | Drop: Soul of Thamasa |

## ITEM CHECKLIST

*Al Bhed Primer ⓔ

Remedy

Stamina Spring

Wrist Band

Unwavering Guard Garment Grid ⓔ

**\*Only if you haven't mastered Al Bhed.**

Characters

1

Garment Grids & Dresspheres

2

Battle System

3

Accessories

4

Items and Item Shops

5

Walkthrough

Chapter 1

Chapter 2

Chapter 3

Chapter 4

Chapter 5

Mini-Games

7

Fiends and Enemies

8

# AL BHED AND OVERWHELMED

Accept the mission to clear Djose Temple and receive an **Al Bhed Primer**. Climb the center stairs and enter the Cloister of Trials. Proceed to the back of the lower level passage, and leap over the chasm filled with ruined machines to reach a chest containing a **Stamina Spring**.

This gap may be big, but Yuna can jump it.

Keep pushing pedestals into the wall until the force field is removed from the stairs.

Ride the elevator to the level above, and proceed past the guards to collect the **Wrist Band** from the chest in the circular area. Pushing one of the pedestals into its alcove in the circular area deactivates the barrier that prevents the party from ascending the stairs. The only problem is, it's impossible to say which pedestal does the trick, since the game randomly assigns one pedestal as the trigger. Fiends attack each time a pedestal, that isn't a trigger, is pushed into an alcove, so stay healthy by using items between battles and before going upstairs.

## IXION

### BOSS FIGHT

HP: 12380  MP: 9999  EXP: 2600  AP: 15

Avoid casting lightning spells or using lightning-based attacks, as these only heal Ixion. Instead, charge a master Black Mage with casting Waterga spells and have a Warrior use the Liquid Steel attack. Keep the party's HP high by healing every round, because some of Ixion's attacks can inflict between 500 to 1000 HP damage to your party members. It also employs homing missile attacks that reduce MP, so have a Black Mage use MP Drain to stay active in the battle. Like the other aeons you fought previously, the frequency of Ixion's attacks can be reduced somewhat by inflicting Slow status upon it. With diligent healing and spell casting every round, this battle shouldn't be too difficult to overcome.

| | |
|---|---|
| **GIL DROPPED:** 1800 | **STEAL:** Normal: Sprint Shoes  Rare: Sprint Shoes |
| **PILFER GIL:** 3000 | **DROP:** Normal: Soul of Thamasa  Rare: Soul of Thamasa |

## TRAPPED IN THE VOID

Following Yuna's accidental plunge into the Farplane, you will view a few scenes and then have a moment to move Yuna around a darkened space. After a few seconds, another scene begins. You have the ability to direct certain events during this scene. When Yuna says "I'm all alone," press the X button to make Yuna hear someone whistle. When the ghost disappears and Yuna is searching for it, press the X button to hear more whistling. After whistling four times, the event ends.

After Yuna is alone for a moment on the Farplane and begins to speak again, press the X button to hear a familiar whistle. Repeat this three more times to exit the Farplane. Don't hesitate, or you might lose the chance!

# AIRSHIP CELSIUS

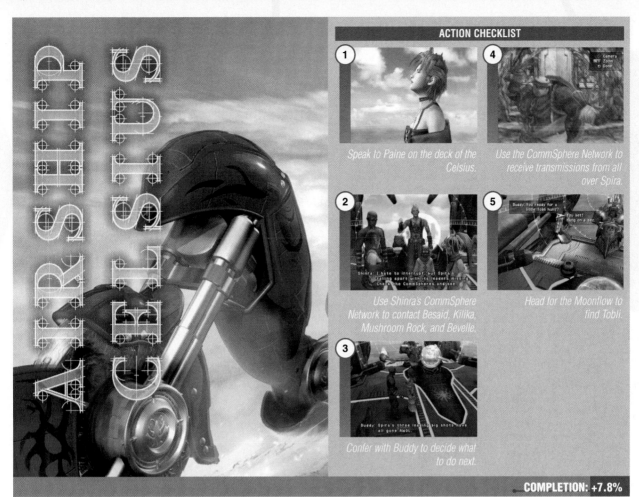

Characters

1

Garment Grids
& Dresspheres

2

Battle System

3

Accessories

4

Items and
Item Shops

5

Walkthrough

Chapter 1

Chapter 2

Chapter 3

Chapter 4

Chapter 5

Mini-Games

7

Fiends and
Enemies

8

189

## ACTION CHECKLIST

**1** Speak to Paine on the deck of the Celsius.

**2** Use Shinra's CommSphere Network to contact Besaid, Kilika, Mushroom Rock, and Bevelle.

**3** Confer with Buddy to decide what to do next.

**4** Use the CommSphere Network to receive transmissions from all over Spira.

**5** Head for the Moonflow to find Tobli.

**COMPLETION: +7.8%**

## ITEM CHECKLIST

Phoenix Down (x7)
Turbo Ether (x3)
Remedy (x6)

Hi-Potion(x8)
*Al Bhed Primer ⒠

*Only if you haven't mastered Al Bhed.

## MAPS

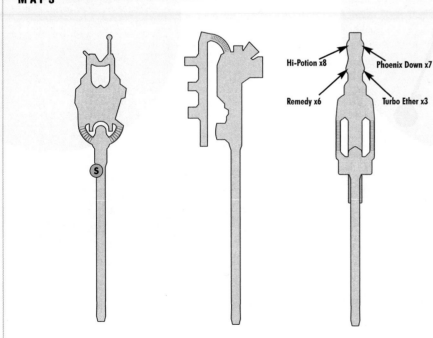

# THE COMMSPHERE NETWORK APPROACH

After the initial scene on the Bridge, head down to the Engine Room and collect the items in the four chests. After doing so, ride the elevator out to the Deck and speak to Paine. Return inside afterward and go back down to the Bridge. When Shinra asks you to check the CommSpheres, head over to his control station and speak with him again to see what's up. There is a new option at the top of Shinra's list that enables you to check the "CommSphere Network" that Shinra worked so hard to establish throughout Chapter 3. However, before dealing with the CommSpheres, remember to enter the Treasure Spheres menu and view Crimson Record 2 and Crimson Record 3.

Use the CommSphere Network to check in with people in Besaid, as well as Kilika, Bevelle, and Mushroom Rock Road.

The Gullwings opt to step back from the grim affairs tearing Spira apart at the moment. Consequently, your only means of exploring Spira during Chapter 4 is through Shinra's CommSphere Network. Only certain CommSpheres work at certain times, depending on the circumstances. For now, speak to Wakka in Besaid, then Dona in Kilika. Also, check in with Maroda at Bevelle. If you gave the Awesome Sphere to New Yevon, someone throws the CommSphere set at Mushroom Rock Road into the ocean. However, if you sided with the Youth League, Yaibal updates you on the situation when you visit Mushroom Rock Road.

You can now have conversations with the citizens of Spira remotely via Shinra's new CommSphere Network.

Although optional, viewing transmissions from the rest of Spira adds a lot of completion points to the game's overall completion total.

Sometimes you need to move the camera before someone will appear, or to trigger a scene. Be patient, because a scene may not start until up to 30 seconds after the transmission begins. Direct the CommSphere with the D-pad or Left Analog Stick, press R1 to zoom in, and press the Square button to exit if someone isn't speaking. Zooming in for a closer view of characters or areas triggers some conversations and scenes.

When all four conversations are complete, exit the CommSphere menu. Buddy is now standing patiently across from Shinra's station. Speak to him to trigger the next scene. After the Gullwings decide to look for Tobli, speak to Paine on the bridge and check the CommSphere Network for more transmissions. When you're done communicating with the people of Spira, speak with Buddy at the navigation console to head for the Moonflow in search of Tobli.

After zooming in all the way, press the R1 button again to zoom out.

# COMMUNICATING WITH SPIRA, PART ONE

Unlike the previous instance, all areas of Spira are now available for viewing through the CommSphere Network. There are several scenes you can view in each location, simply by reconnecting with each location several times. Some of these scenes are worth fractions of a completion point, but when they're all added together, they're worth well over 4 whole percentage points! Some of these scenes are quite amusing, and the CommSphere Network provides a very interesting diversion from the normal game routine of exploring and battling.

You may receive items such as Al Bhed Primers by watching some of the optional CommSphere transmissions.

The following table contains the scenes that occur in each area, in order. Fractions of a percentage point are indicated for viewing certain scenes. Do *not* use the dialog skip function; doing so will reduce the percentage you receive. Scenes may take up to 30 seconds to begin, so be patient. A scene ends when the characters stop talking, when you hear a slight rise in the background music volume, or when the CommSphere disconnects due to technical difficulty.

Some CommSphere scenes will be altered slightly by your previous actions in the game.

NOTE: The percentages listed in this section are only correct if the player watches the CommSpheres in the order listed. This applies to all the charts.

| BESAID COMMSPHERE SCENES | |
|---|---|
| **EVENT** | **%** |
| Two children play hide and seek for a while. | 0 |
| A dog sniffs around the CommSphere. | 0 |
| Wakka emerges from his tent and seems very nervous. | 0.2 |
| The Aurochs are practicing for blitzball. | 0 |
| An Auroch hits another player with a blitzball by accident, then runs off. | 0 |
| Beclem chastises the Aurochs for playing ball. | 0.2 |
| When you look away from the practicing team, one of the Aurochs hits the CommSphere with the Blitzball and Shinra gripes. | 0 |

## KILIKA TEMPLE COMMSPHERE SCENES

| EVENT | % |
|---|---|
| Wait until Barthello emerges from the temple. His lament destroys the CommSphere. | 0.2 |
| All further transmissions are distorted, because Barthello broke the CommSphere. | 0 |

## KILIKA PORT COMMSPHERE SCENES

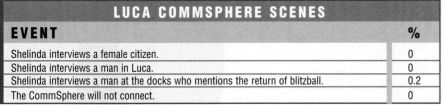

| EVENT | % |
|---|---|
| Dona talks about Rian and Ayde having stopped by on the CommSphere. | 0 |
| Transmission from Dona talking about politics and the town children. | 0 |
| The former summoner snoozes. Zoom in close to hear Dona talk in her sleep. See where Bartschella, a cactuar, is hiding. | 0 |
| Dona has left her room. | 0 |
| A view of the port area. | 0 |

## LUCA COMMSPHERE SCENES

| EVENT | % |
|---|---|
| Shelinda interviews a female citizen. | 0 |
| Shelinda interviews a man in Luca. | 0 |
| Shelinda interviews a man at the docks who mentions the return of blitzball. | 0.2 |
| The CommSphere will not connect. | 0 |

## MUSHROOM ROCK COMMSPHERE SCENES*

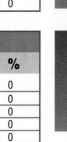

| EVENT | % |
|---|---|
| Zoom in on the face of the guard standing to the left and he gets annoyed. | 0 |
| The guard seeks to prove that the Youth League is justified. | 0 |
| The guard becomes sarcastic. | 0 |
| The guard claims the Youth League is prepared to fight. | 0 |
| The guard brags and mentions how Lucil is no longer in control. | 0 |
| The guard has a seat. | 0 |

**\*Only available if you gave the stolen sphere to the Youth League at the start of Chapter 2.**

## DJOSE TEMPLE COMMSPHERE SCENES

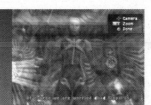

| EVENT | % |
|---|---|
| An Al Bhed technician approaches the camera. In Al Bhed, he says that in spite of the hectic situation and the disappearance of Gippal, they are holding the fort. You receive an **Al Bhed Primer**. | 0.2 |
| After a few seconds, the technician enters and relates a rumor he's heard regarding a powerful fiend in the Bikanel Desert. | 0 |
| The tech emerges from the prayer room and reports that the hole Yuna fell into was dug out from underneath, as if something "dragged the fayth into the abyss." | 0 |
| The tech speaks to the female Al Bhed on the right side of the screen about the current lack of parts, and the inability to get them from Bikanel. | 0 |
| The female tech stands in the center and tries to remember a password, which is the name of a talking cactus. You receive an **Al Bhed Primer**. | 0 |
| The female tech steals the CommSphere to repair her machine. After this scene, Shinra cannot connect to Djose for any more transmissions. | 0 |

## MOONFLOW COMMSPHERE SCENES

| EVENT | % |
|---|---|
| Yuna asks a Hypello where Tobli is, but none of the Hypello know. | 0 |
| The Hypello practice for the show. | 0 |
| Three Hypello walk in and have a private conversation. | 0 |
| The Hypello work around the wagon. | 0 |

## GUADOSALAM COMMSPHERE SCENES

| EVENT | % |
| --- | --- |
| Ormi emerges from the chateau and reveals that Leblanc is out searching for her Noojie-Woojie. | 0.2 |
| A Hypello enters and tries to sell tickets, but the guards won't pay attention. | 0 |
| The guards have an interesting conversation about Leblanc's disappearance. Shinra can't believe how much the guards like her. | 0 |
| The guards talk about how they don't have any place else to go if the Syndicate breaks up. | 0 |
| The two guards talk about what chickens they are, and how Leblanc took them in. | 0 |
| Ormi hogs a little camera time and strikes his favorite pose. | 0 |

## THUNDER PLAINS COMMSPHERE SCENES

| EVENT | % |
| --- | --- |
| Angle the camera to the right to catch a chocobo with Shinra's latest device. | 0.2 |
| During the next transmission, the ChocoPorter breaks down. | 0 |
| The signal at Thunder Plains is distorted and dark. | 0 |

## MACALANIA WOODS ENTRANCE COMMSPHERE SCENES

| EVENT | % |
| --- | --- |
| The three musicians reappear and talk about their dream of the fayth and the dying woods. | 0.2 |
| If you did *not* complete the mission to stop Garik Ronso at Mt. Gagazet during Chapter 3, the Ronso youth enter the woods and the war against the Guado begins. | 0 |
| If you did *not* complete the mission to stop Garik Ronso at Mt. Gagazet during Chapter 3, a Guado gazes at the battle in the forest. | 0 |
| If you completed the mission to stop Garik at Gagazet in Chapter 3, two Guado will appear and converse amongst themselves; no war will occur. This scene repeats each time you enter. | 0 |

## MACALANIA WOODS TRAVEL AGENCY COMMSPHERE SCENES

| EVENT | % |
| --- | --- |
| If the Al Bhed are in charge of the Agency because O'aka still has a debt, an Al Bhed woman approaches the camera and says she's leaving because there are too many fiends. You receive an **Al Bhed Primer**. | 0 |
| If you freed O'aka from debt one way or another, he will emerge from the shop for various scenes. At first he tells Yuna that business isn't too good. | 0.2 |
| If O'aka was freed from debt, he comes out and sighs that he has no customers. | 0 |
| If O'aka was freed from debt, he emerges from the Agency and complains that someone has been missing for a year. | 0 |
| If O'aka was freed from debt, he practices various sales pitches—even in Al Bhed. | 0 |
| If O'aka was freed from debt, his nephew Wantz appears and worries about having been gone so long. | 0 |
| A Barbuta attacks the Agency as a Flan Blanco slithers by. | 0 |
| A Barbuta attacks the Travel Agency. | 0 |
| A Flan Blanco slithers by. | 0 |
| There is no activity at the Travel Agency. | 0 |

## BIKANEL DESERT EXCAVATION CAMP COMMSPHERE SCENES

| EVENT | % |
| --- | --- |
| Speak to Nhadala regarding a new menace in the desert. | 0.2 |
| The diggers are hard at work. | 0 |

## BIKANEL DESERT CACTUAR NATION COMMSPHERE SCENES

| EVENT | % |
| --- | --- |
| Yuna realizes it's useless to try to communicate with the cacti without Benzo. | 0 |
| The cacti stand silent in the desert. | 0 |

## BEVELLE COMMSPHERE SCENES

| EVENT | % |
|---|---|
| If you gave the stolen sphere to the Youth League during Chapter 2, soldiers will shoot out the CommSphere. It will not work thereafter. | 0 |
| If you gave the stolen sphere to New Yevon during Chapter 2, a captain scolds his guards for letting Maroda get away. | 0 |
| The Kinderguardians defeat New Yevon soldiers and escape. | 0 |
| The Kinderguardians admire the CommSphere and bond with Shinra. | 0.2 |
| The Highbridge is empty. | 0 |

## CALM LANDS TRAVEL AGENCY SCENES

| EVENT | % |
|---|---|
| Customers can be seen coming and going. | 0 |
| Customers can be seen coming and going. | 0 |
| The young unmarried man cries, and his father consoles him. | 0 |
| The young unmarried man's father runs behind the agency and places 50000 gil in a chest. After viewing this scene, the chest becomes available in Chapter 5. | 0 |
| A fiend attacks the CommSphere and eats it. | 0 |

## CALM LANDS CHOCOBO RANCH SCENES

| EVENT | % |
|---|---|
| If you did *not* capture a chocobo before the end of Chapter 3, Clasko stands in the empty ranch and repeats over and over how hopeless he is. | 0 |
| If you captured a chocobo before the end of Chapter 3, Clasko pets the chocobo. | 0 |
| If you captured a chocobo before the end of Chapter 3, Clasko updates Yuna on his care of the chocobos. | 0.2 |
| If you captured a chocobo before the end of Chapter 3, Clasko returns with a runaway chocobo, worried about what would happen if Yuna knew. | 0 |
| If you captured a chocobo before the end of Chapter 3, Clasko pets the chocobo silently. | 0 |
| If you captured a chocobo before the end of Chapter 3, Clasko sits in the chocobo's stall. | 0 |

## MT. GAGAZET MOUNTAIN GATE SCENES

| EVENT | % |
|---|---|
| Speak with Kimahri. The conversation is slightly different depending on whether or not you stopped Garik at Mt. Gagazet during Chapter 3. | 0.2 |
| The female Ronso gives Kimahri a back massage. | 0 |

## MOUNT GAGAZET HOT SPRINGS SCENES

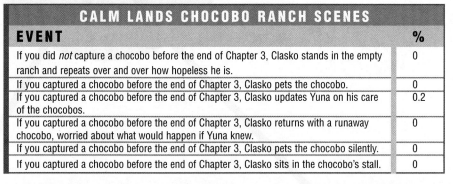

| EVENT | % |
|---|---|
| A Ronso youth lets off some steam. | 0 |
| Cactuar momentarily appears in the lower-right corner of the spring. Yuna is shocked. | 0 |
| Tobli emerges from the spring. | 0.2 |
| Zoom in on the heads floating on the surface to see a horde of Hypello. | 0 |
| Shoopufs bathe in the water. | 0 |
| A man swims alone. Yuna is disappointed. | 0 |
| Buddy gets a back massage from Barkeep. | 0.2 |
| O'aka tries new sales pitches. | 0.2 |
| Wantz spies on some girls bathing. | 0 |
| Isaaru, Maroda, and Pacce reunite. | 0.2 |
| Lucil and Elma discuss Clasko. | 0.2 |
| Maechen tries to educate a monkey. | 0.2 |
| If you captured a chocobo before the end of Chapter 3, Clasko bathes with the chocobo. If not, he bathes alone. | 0 |
| Cid, Nhadala, and Rin discuss the Al Bhed. | 0.2 |
| Dona hates bathing alone. | 0.2 |
| The hot springs are empty. | 0 |

# MYSTERY AT MI'IHEN

When the CommSphere Network is activated at Mi'ihen Highroad, Rin emerges from the Travel Agency and requests that you use the CommSpheres to help him investigate the recent strange occurrences. He's set up several CommSpheres around the Highroad area, and you can switch to the view of any CommSphere by pressing the R2 button and choosing another location. The Mi'ihen Highroad Mystery is a mini-game that you may want to start up as early as Chapter 1 and span across Chapters 4 and 5. Completing this mini-game can grant an extra item. More details are revealed in the "Mini-Games" chapter.

*Rin can't seem to figure out why the machina went crazy or why the hover crashed during Chapter 3. He needs the Gullwings' CommSphere skills and deductive ingenuity!*

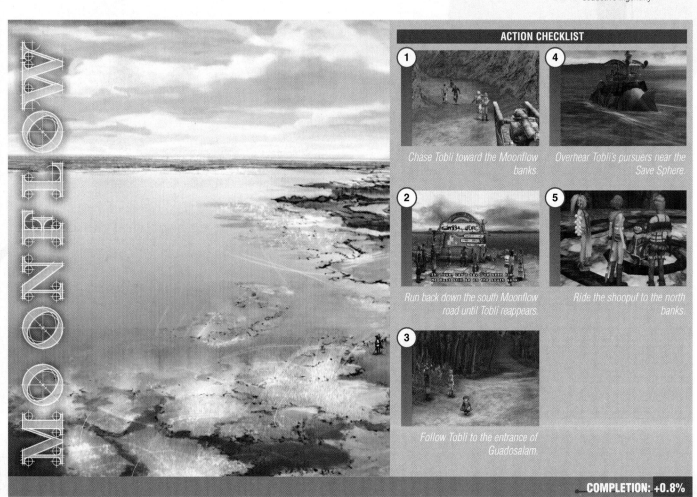

**MOONFLOW**

## ACTION CHECKLIST

**1** Chase Tobli toward the Moonflow banks.

**4** Overhear Tobli's pursuers near the Save Sphere.

**2** Run back down the south Moonflow road until Tobli reappears.

**5** Ride the shoopuf to the north banks.

**3** Follow Tobli to the entrance of Guadosalam.

**COMPLETION: +0.8%**

## WANDERING FIENDS

**AGAMA**
HP: 133 | AP: 1 | Gil: 16
Steal: Hi-Potion
Drop: Antidote

**ARCHAEOTHYRIS**
HP: 1332 | AP: 1 | Gil: 110
Steal: Eye Drops (x2)
Drop: Eye Drops (x2)

**BALIVARHA**
HP: 3688 | AP: 1 | Gil: 230
Steal: Hi-Potion (x2)
Drop: Fire Gem

**BANDIT**
HP: 132 | AP: 1 | Gil: 30
Steal: Budget Grenade
Drop: Potion

**BARBUTA**
HP: 562 | AP: 1 | Gil: 33
Steal: Lunar Curtain
Drop: Light Curtain

**BLACKGUARD**
HP: 760 | AP: 1 | Gil: 42
Steal: Phoenix
Down Drop: Potion

**CHOCOBO**
HP: 3890 | AP: 0 | Gil: 0
Steal: None
Drop: None

**FLAN BLANCO**
HP: 625 | AP: 1 | Gil: 72
Steal: Arctic Wind
Drop: Arctic Wind

**RUFFIAN**
HP: 1480 | AP: 1 | Gil: 250
Steal: Grenade
Drop: Potion (x2)

**SHELL SHOCKER**
HP: 4700 | AP: 1 | Gil: 780
Steal: Iron Bangle
Drop: Black Ring

**TAROMAITI**
HP: 1782 | AP: 1 | Gil: 280
Steal: Antidote (x2)
Drop: Star Pendant

**VARAN**
HP: 1132 | AP: 1 | Gil: 240
Steal: Dispel Tonic
Drop: Holy Water

**WATCHER-A**
HP: 624 | AP: 1 | Gil: 0
Steal: Potion
Drop: Potion

**WATCHER-R**
HP: 620 | AP: 1 | Gil: 0
Steal: Potion
Drop: Potion

**WATCHER-S**
HP: 620 | AP: 1 | Gil: 0
Steal: Potion
Drop: Potion

## ITEM CHECKLIST

Black Tabard Garment Grid **E**

# THE TOBLI CHASE!

Finding Tobli will be difficult, especially since the people he owes money to have come to collect. Head down the road just past the debt collectors, who stop and address Yuna. Tobli emerges and leads the thugs on a merry chase down the path. Follow the fleeing promoter and his pursuers to the banks of the Moonflow.

Finding Tobli is as simple as following the loan sharks who are after him.

The debt collectors block access to the shoopuf when you first arrive. You must wait for Tobli to break through their ranks before you can cross the Moonflow to find Tobli.

There's no sign of Tobli around the wagon, so continue into the passenger waiting area. One of the debt collectors confers with two guards who block the path. Retreat back through the banks area and south down the road until Yuna finds the debt collector standing on the side of the road, gasping for breath. Tobli emerges and heads south. Follow him and his pursuer until Tobli tears through the area on a scooter. Now you must run back to the banks of the Moonflow.

Tobli's scooter crashes near the wagon caravan, but there's still no sign of Tobli. The guards no longer block access to the shoopuf wharf, so ride the shoopuf across the Moonflow to the north banks. Continue following Tobli and the debt collectors up to the entrance to Guadosalam.

The debt collectors knock Tobli out of a tree. Follow Tobli up to Guadosalam's entrance to complete the mission.

## ACTION CHECKLIST

1 After Tobli's Hypello PR force deploys from the Celsius, head down to the Cabin and dance with Rikku.

2 Return to the Bridge and view CommSphere transmissions.

3 Speak with Buddy or Brother to land at the Thunder Plains.

**COMPLETION: +3.4%**

# CONCERT REHEARSAL

Following the deployment of the Hypello, you may notice that Rikku is missing from her usual position on the Bridge. Ride the elevator down to the Cabin to join Rikku in a fun mini-game, as it's time to practice some dance moves for the concert. This short challenge is worth some valuable prizes, but you only get one shot. Save your game at the Save Sphere on the Bridge before proceeding to the Cabin.

The controller buttons each play a different instrument or sound effect. Tap the button rapidly when you see it on Rikku's side of the screen.

Characters

1

Garment Grids
& Dresspheres

2

Battle System

3

Accessories

4

Items and
Item Shops

5

Walkthrough
Chapter 1
Chapter 2
Chapter 3
Chapter 4
Chapter 5

Mini-Games

7

Fiends and
Enemies

8

Upon entering the Cabin, watch Rikku's session carefully and note how the button icons appear in the lower-right corner of the screen. Each button is a different instrument or sound. Press the buttons that appear on Yuna's side of the screen. Buttons pressed at the moment the musical note in the bottom-left corner turns red score higher points.

Tap the controller buttons as rapidly as possible, even if you hit the wrong button for a second. You'll score higher if you hit the right button, but you'll also score for each button hit whether it's the right one or not. Don't let accuracy slow you down. When the song is finished, your totals for rhythm, fitness, and synch are tallied and averaged to provide a total score. Based on this result, you receive one of four prizes.

*Obtaining the best prizes for this event require a few practice attempts. Do a soft reset and try again to sharpen your skills.*

### DANCING REHEARSAL PRIZES

| TOTAL GROOVE | PRIZE |
|---|---|
| 0-49 | Pearl Necklace |
| 50-99 | Safety Bit |
| 100-149 | Sublimator |
| 150+ | Shmooth Shailing |

# COMMSPHERE WAVES, PART TWO

Before asking Buddy to go to the Thunder Plains, use Shinra's CommSphere Network to see how the concert promotion is going throughout Spira.

### BESAID COMMSPHERE SCENES

| EVENT | % |
|---|---|
| Zoom in on Beclem's head to start a conversation. | 0.2 |
| Speak with Lulu and Wakka concerning their imminent arrival. | 0.2 |
| The Aurochs talk to Yuna. | 0 |
| The Aurochs interview Wakka. | 0 |
| The Aurochs interview Wakka; it's even funnier this time. | 0 |
| Wakka paces around restlessly. This scene repeats during each transmission hereafter. | 0 |

### KILIKA PORT COMMSPHERE SCENES

| EVENT | % |
|---|---|
| Dona practices an apology. | 0.2 |
| Dona practices chastising Barthello. | 0 |
| Dona ties the CommSphere to a balloon and sends it to Kilika Temple. | 0.2 |
| Barthello receives the CommSphere, but shatters it with a mighty cry. | 0.2 |

### LUCA COMMSPHERE SCENES

| EVENT | % |
|---|---|
| Shelinda promotes Yuna's concert. | 0 |
| Luca's blitzball team practices in the square. | 0 |
| Luca's blitzball team practices on the stairs. Logos may run through the scene at some point. | 0 |
| Hypello gather Luca citizens to promote the concert. | 0 |
| Faulty transmission that repeats in a loop. | 0 |

### MUSHROOM ROCK COMMSPHERE SCENES*

| EVENT | % |
|---|---|
| Lucil assures Yuna that she will try to stop a war. | 0.2 |
| Yaibal wishes he could go to the show. | 0.2 |
| Yaibal gathers his squad for a "mission." | 0 |
| The guard standing just to the left complains that everyone is abandoning their posts. | 0 |
| The guard whines that he wants to attend the concert. | 0 |
| The guard is gone; a Hypello dances; Lucil watches with a sigh. | 0 |

**\*Only available if you gave the stolen sphere to the Youth League at the start of Chapter 2.**

### DJOSE TEMPLE COMMSPHERE SCENES

| EVENT | % |
|---|---|
| *All scenes from the first CommSphere session begin or continue. | NA |

## MOONFLOW COMMSPHERE SCENES

| EVENT | % |
|---|---|
| If you told Lian and Ayde to head to the Moonflow during Chapter 3, they will speak to Yuna. | 0 |
| A Hypello won't let Elma take her chocobo on the shoopuf. | 0.2 |
| A Hypello reports on the promotional efforts. Later, a shoopuf stomps through and smashes the CommSphere. | 0 |
| Bad reception. | 0 |

## GUADOSALAM COMMSPHERE SCENES

| EVENT | % |
|---|---|
| If you haven't spoken to Ormi previously, he emerges from the chateau and reveals that Leblanc is out searching for Nooj. | 0.2 |
| Ormi talks to Yuna about the concert. | 0.2 |
| A Hypello unsuccessfully tries to get the guards to go to the concert. | 0 |
| Two Fem-Goons emerge and talk about the concert and Leblanc. | 0 |
| Two Fem-Goons emerge and wonder if Leblanc will return and hijack the concert again. | 0 |
| Yuna or Leblanc? Leblanc's goons decide who's classier. | 0 |
| A Fem-Goon waves hello and enters the chateau. | 0 |
| A Hypello enters and tries to speak with the guards, but they don't pay attention. | 0 |
| Ormi emerges from the chateau and strikes a pose for the camera. | 0 |

## THUNDER PLAINS COMMSPHERE SCENES

| EVENT | % |
|---|---|
| People are gathering on the plains for the concert. | 0 |

## MACALANIA WOODS ENTRANCE COMMSPHERE SCENES

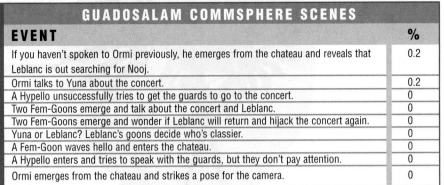

| EVENT | % |
|---|---|
| The three musicians reappear and wish Yuna well on her concert. | 0 |
| If you did *not* complete the mission to stop Garik Ronso at Mt. Gagazet during Chapter 3, the Ronso youth enter the woods and the war against the Guado will begin. This occurs here if you did not see it during the first CommSphere session. | 0 |
| Pukutak appears, waves goodbye, then disappears. | 0 |
| Donga appears, beats his drum, then waves goodbye. | 0 |
| Bayra appears, nods, then vanishes. | 0 |
| An Amorphous Gel appears. | 0 |

## MACALANIA WOODS TRAVEL AGENCY COMMSPHERE SCENES

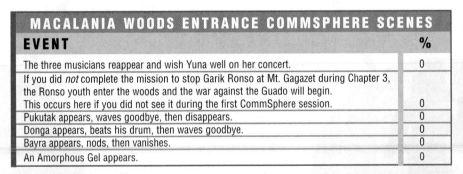

| EVENT | % |
|---|---|
| If the Al Bhed are in charge of the Agency because O'aka still has a debt, then an Al Bhed woman approaches the camera and says she's leaving because there are too many fiends. You receive an **Al Bhed Primer**. This scene occurs if you didn't see it previously. | 0 |
| If you freed O'aka from debt one way or another, he will emerge from the shop and tell Yuna that business isn't too good. This scene occurs only if is wasn't previously seen in CommSphere session one. | 0.2 |
| If you freed O'aka from debt one way or another, he will emerge from the shop and ask Yuna about the concert. He leaves the Travel Agency to head for the Thunder Plains. | 0.2 |
| A Hypello encounters fiends outside the Travel Agency and runs off. | 0 |
| A Flan Blanco appears outside the agency. | 0 |
| A Barbuta attacks the Agency as a Flan Blanco slithers by. | 0 |
| A Barbuta attacks the Travel Agency. | 0 |
| A Flan Blanco slithers by. | 0 |
| There is no activity at the Travel Agency. | 0 |

## BIKANEL DESERT EXCAVATION CAMP COMMSPHERE SCENES

| EVENT | % |
|---|---|
| Speak to Nhadala regarding their efforts to stop the fiend in the desert. An explosion wipes out the CommSphere. | 0 |

Characters

Garment Grids & Dresspheres

Battle System

Accessories

Items and Item Shops

Walkthrough
Chapter 1
Chapter 2
Chapter 3
Chapter 4
Chapter 5

Mini-Games

Fiends and Enemies

## BIKANEL DESERT CACTUAR NATION COMMSPHERE SCENES

| EVENT | % |
|---|---|
| Zoom in on the cactus named Marnella. Yuna asks Shinra if he can communicate to cacti like Benzo. | 0 |
| The cacti stand silent in the desert. | 0 |

## BEVELLE COMMSPHERE SCENES

| EVENT | % |
|---|---|
| If you gave the stolen sphere to the Youth League during Chapter 2, soldiers will shoot out the CommSphere. It will not work thereafter. This scene occurs if it wasn't seen in a previous CommSphere session. | 0 |
| If you gave the stolen sphere to New Yevon during Chapter 2, the same series of scenes involving the Kinderguardians occurs if they weren't seen in a previous CommSphere session. | NA |

## CALM LANDS TRAVEL AGENCY SCENES

| EVENT | % |
|---|---|
| *All scenes from the first CommSphere session will begin or continue. | NA |

## CALM LANDS CHOCOBO RANCH SCENES

| EVENT | % |
|---|---|
| *All scenes from the first CommSphere session will begin or continue. | NA |

## MT. GAGAZET MOUNTAIN ENTRANCE SCENES

| EVENT | % |
|---|---|
| Speak with Kimahri. The conversation is slightly different depending on whether or not you stopped Garik at Mt. Gagazet during Chapter 3. This scene occurs if it wasn't viewed during a previous CommSphere session. | 0.2 |
| If you did *not* complete the mission to stop Garik at Mt. Gagazet during Chapter 3, Ronso youths will enter and speak to the female Ronso. | 0 |
| If you did *not* complete the mission to stop Garik at Mt. Gagazet during Chapter 3, the female Ronso councils Kimahri on the departures of Garik, Lian, and Ayde. | 0 |
| If you did *not* complete the mission to stop Garik at Mt. Gagazet during Chapter 3, the female Ronso approaches the CommSphere and says not to worry about the Ronso. | 0 |
| If you completed the mission to stop Garik at Mt. Gagazet during Chapter 3, Garik will approach the CommSphere and wonder how to unite Ronso youth. | 0 |
| If you completed the mission to stop Garik at Mt. Gagazet during Chapter 3, a Ronso youth enters and tells Kimahri that he's going to the concert. | 0 |
| If you completed the mission to stop Garik at Mt. Gagazet during Chapter 3, the CommSphere is covered with snow. Move it around and a female Ronso will wipe it off. | 0 |
| If you completed the mission to stop Garik at Mt. Gagazet during Chapter 3, Kimahri swears a new oath to protect the Ronso. | 0 |
| If you completed the mission to stop Garik at Mt. Gagazet during Chapter 3, a female Ronso approaches the CommSphere and says that the Ronso now recognize Kimahri's wisdom. | 0 |
| Garik approaches the CommSphere and relates the future of the Ronso youth. | 0 |
| The female Ronso gives Kimahri a back massage. | 0 |

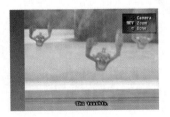

## MOUNT GAGAZET HOT SPRINGS SCENES

| EVENT | % |
|---|---|
| *All scenes from the first CommSphere session will begin or continue. | NA |

Characters

1

Garment Grids
& Dressspheres

2

Battle System

3

Accessories

4

Items and
Item Shops

5

Walkthrough
Chapter 1
Chapter 2
Chapter 3
Chapter 4
Chapter 5

Mini-Games

7

Fiends and
Enemies

8

## ZANARKAND RUINS SCENES

| EVENT | % |
|---|---|
| Isaaru speaks to Yuna about the concert. | 0.2 |
| Isaaru and Yuna talk about Maroda and the situation in Bevelle. | 0 |
| Isaaru lies behind the CommSphere and wonders what he's doing at Zanarkand. Monkeys are everywhere. | 0.2 |
| A Hypello is advertising the concert. | 0 |

# THUNDER PLAINS

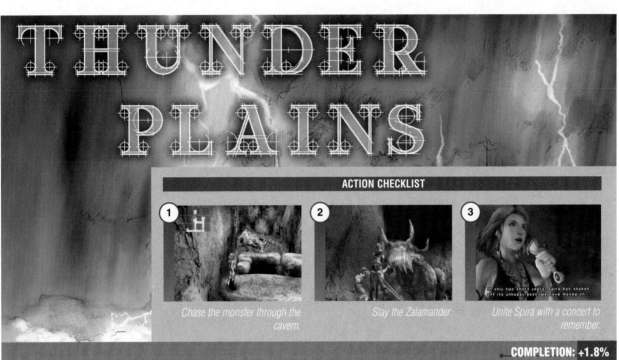

### ACTION CHECKLIST

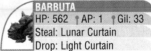

1. Chase the monster through the cavern.
2. Slay the Zalamander.
3. Unite Spira with a concert to remember.

COMPLETION: +1.8%

## WANDERING FIENDS

**AKA MANAH**
HP: 6322 AP: 1 Gil: 670
Steal: Remedy (x2)
Drop: Pretty Orb

**ANOLE**
HP: 734 AP: 1 Gil: 70
Steal: Hi-Potion
Drop: Hi-Potion

**ARCHAEOTHYRIS**
HP: 1332 AP: 1 Gil: 110
Steal: Eye Drops (x2)
Drop: Eye Drops (x2)

**ARMET**
HP: 788 AP: 1 Gil: 74
Steal: Lunar Curtain
Drop: Light Curtain

**ASSASSIN BEE**
HP: 233 AP: 1 Gil: 48
Steal: Antidote
Drop: Antidote

**BALIVARHA**
HP: 3688 AP: 1 Gil: 230
Steal: Hi-Potion (x2)
Drop: Fire Gem

**BARBUTA**
HP: 562 AP: 1 Gil: 33
Steal: Lunar Curtain
Drop: Light Curtain

**BLUE ELEMENTAL**
HP: 363 AP: 1 Gil: 180
Steal: Dragon Scale
Drop: Dragon Scale

**BOLT DRAKE**
HP: 623 AP: 1 Gil: 130
Steal: Lightning Marble
Drop: Hi-Potion

**CHOCOBO**
HP: 3890 AP: 0 Gil: 0
Steal: None
Drop: None

**FLAN ROJO**
HP: 1220 AP: 1 Gil: 125
Steal: Bomb Core
Drop: Bomb Core

**GEMINI**
HP: 2044 AP: 1 Gil: 153
Steal: Lunar Curtain (x2)
Drop: Light Curtain (x2)

**GIGAS**
HP: 2290 AP: 1 Gil: 180
Steal: Hi-Potion
Drop: None

**IRONSIDE**
HP: 8432 AP: 1 Gil: 200
Steal: Shadow Gem (x2)
Drop: Stamina Tablet

**MALBORO**
HP: 5877 AP: 1 Gil: 370
Steal: Hi-Potion
Drop: Remedy (x2)

**SPINE DRAKE**
HP: 2582 AP: 1 Gil: 127
Steal: Arctic Wind
Drop: Arctic Wind

**TAROMAITI**
HP: 1782 AP: 1 Gil: 280
Steal: Antidote (x2)
Drop: Star Pendant

**VARAN**
HP: 1132 AP: 1 Gil: 240
Steal: Dispel Tonic
Drop: Holy Water

**WATCHER-A**
HP: 624 AP: 1 Gil: 0
Steal: Potion
Drop: Potion

**WATCHER-R**
HP: 620 AP: 1 Gil: 0
Steal: Potion
Drop: Potion

**WATCHER-S**
HP: 620 AP: 1 Gil: 0
Steal: Potion
Drop: Potion

**ZALAMANDER**
HP: 12850 AP: 1 Gil: 930
Steal: Sublimator
Drop: Crimson Ring

## ITEM CHECKLIST

| | | |
|---|---|---|
| Echo Screen (x6) | Petrify Grenade (x2) | X-Potion |
| X-Potion | Turbo Ether | Elixir |
| Glass Buckle | Haste Bangle | Black Ring |
| Phoenix Down (x4) | Phoenix Down (x2) | |

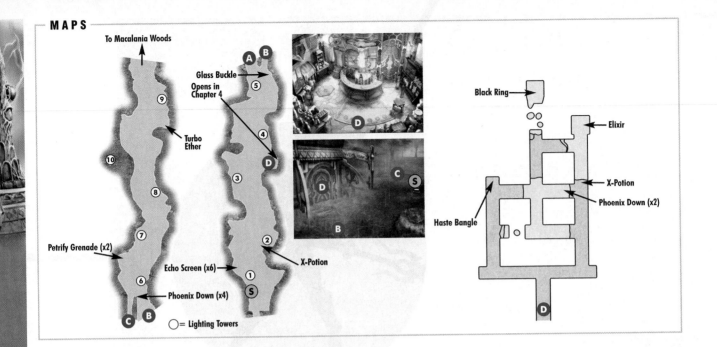

To Macalania Woods

Glass Buckle
Opens in
Chapter 4

Turbo
Ether

Black Ring

Elixir

X-Potion

Phoenix Down (x2)

Haste Bangle

Petrify Grenade (x2)

Echo Screen (x6)

X-Potion

Phoenix Down (x4)

◯ = Lighting Towers

# FEEDING ON THE CROWD

Although a large fiend is seen breaking through the rubble to a secret cavern on the Thunder Plains, there are new chests containing useful items scattered across the two main areas of the Thunder Plains. Take a trip to the north exit and back, collecting all the items.

The Zalamander waits at the back of the cave.

Inside the cave, head to the right and follow the passage north to a chest containing an **X-Potion**. From there, return to the cave entrance and continue up the west side of the cave to a chest containing a **Haste Bangle**. Head back to the first opening on the right side of the screen and climb up the rocks to the upper level. From this point, you should be able to reach the remaining two chests with ease. The Zalamander boss protects the final chest. After defeating the Zalamander, open the chest to obtain the **Black Ring** and exit the cave.

*The Hypello outside the secret cave entrance fully restores full HP and MP to your entire party when you speak to him. Make sure the party enters the cave at full strength.*

# ZALAMANDER BOSS FIGHT

The Zalamander is an overgrown lizard that benefits from a constant Null Magic effect. None of a Black Mage's spells will work, and other magic-enhanced attacks will inflict little or no damage. Therefore, your party must overcome this fiend with physical attacks.

HP: 12850   MP: 276   EXP: 1200   AP: 1

Equip powerful dresspheres such as Dark Knight, Gunner, Samurai, and Berserker to get the job done. As usual, one character should assume the role of healer by donning the Alchemist dressphere. The Zalamander can be blinded, so a Songstress can perform Darkness Dance to affect the monster's vision and Accuracy. While it will do little to protect your characters from the Zalamander's Flame Breath attack, blindness causes most of the monster's other attacks to miss. This tactic should enable you to maintain more HP between each Flame Breath attack.

GIL DROPPED: 930
PILFER GIL: 1300

STEAL: Normal: Subliminator   Rare: Subliminator
DROP: Normal: Crimson Ring   Rare: Crimson Ring

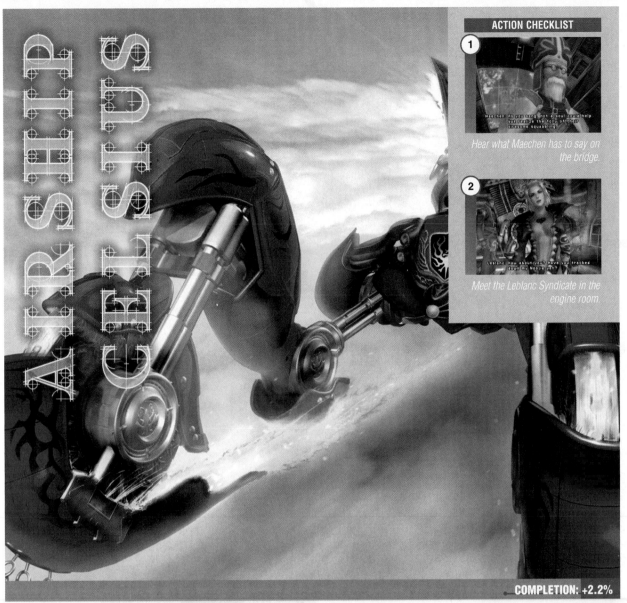

# AIRSHIP CELSIUS

Characters

1

Garment Grids & Dresspheres

2

Battle System

3

Accessories

4

Items and Item Shops

5

Walkthrough

Chapter 1

Chapter 2

Chapter 3

Chapter 4

Chapter 5

Mini-Games

7

Fiends and Enemies

8

## ACTION CHECKLIST

*Hear what Maechen has to say on the bridge.*

*Meet the Leblanc Syndicate in the engine room.*

**COMPLETION: +2.2%**

## ITEM CHECKLIST

Crimson Sphere 5

Once the concert is over and the crew is back on the Celsius, head up to the Bridge for a few historical anecdotes told by Maechen. Buddy reports that Leblanc and her henchmen are waiting in the engine room. Eventually, they hand over **Crimson Sphere 5**.

*Too bad. Now you won't get to see what's on Crimson Sphere 5 until the game's final chapter…*

## ACTION CHECKLIST

**1** Discuss entry to the Farplane.

**2** Speak to Shinra to view Crimson Report 5.

**3** Rest on the Cabin level and over-hear Brother's misery.

**4** Speak to Buddy down in the engine room.

**COMPLETION: +2.0%**

## ITEM CHECKLIST

Phoenix Down (x8)

Turbo Ether (x4)

Remedy (x7)

X-Potion (x4)

Mascot Dressphere **E**

## MAPS

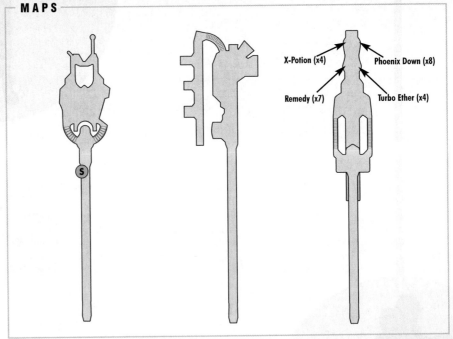

X-Potion (x4)

Phoenix Down (x8)

Remedy (x7)

Turbo Ether (x4)

# RESOLVE OF THE GULLWINGS

Any time you want to proceed to the Farplane, which is the final dungeon of the game where Vegnagun awaits, speak to Brother and tell him the location from which you would like to enter. The location you choose determines the shape of your path into the Farplane Abyss, as well as the items you can find along the route. It is strongly recommended that all of your characters reach level 60 and above before proceeding to the Farplane.

Brother will fly you to the Farplane any time you wish to go.

# "EPISODE COMPLETE" TIME

Naturally, if you skip to the Farplane now you will miss out on a ton of completion percentage. Speak to Buddy at the helm and almost every location in Spira will light up as a Hotspot. The main goal of Chapter 5 is to visit every location and obtain an "Episode Complete!" When these words appear on-screen, it means you have completed every possible mission in an area and resolved all the situations there. After obtaining an "Episode Complete" for every place in Spira except Bevelle, return to the bridge and obtain the **Mascot** dressphere. Although humorous in appearance, this is one of the best dresspheres with the broadest range of skills.

*The navigation menu starts with Hotspots in every area. Knock them all out to acquire the last dressphere.*

# CELSIUS SCENES

If you rested at the Cabin level at least once during every chapter, return to the Cabin now and rest for a final time. Upon awakening, Yuna overhears Brother complaining about his unrequited love. Following this scene, head down to the Engine Room and speak to Buddy regarding the origin of the Gullwings. These scenes are available to view if you rested at the Cabin in every chapter.

## ACTION CHECKLIST

1. View the new home of the monkeys.
2. Speak with Maechen one last time.

COMPLETION: +0.8%

## WANDERING FIENDS

**ANOLE**
HP: 734 | AP: 1 | Gil: 70
Steal: Hi-Potion
Drop: Hi-Potion

**FLAILING OCHU**
HP: 9860 | AP: 1 | Gil: 430
Steal: Remedy
Drop: Remedy

**GUARDIAN BEAST**
HP: 2886 | AP: 1 | Gil: 200
Steal: Defense Veil
Drop: Amulet

**GUCUMATZ**
HP: 3720 | AP: 1 | Gil: 173
Steal: Soft (x2)
Drop: Soft (x2)

**IRONSIDE**
HP: 8432 | AP: 1 | Gil: 200
Steal: Shadow Gem (x2)
Drop: Stamina Tablet

**MYCOTOXIN**
HP: 810 | AP: 1 | Gil: 83
Steal: Antidote (x2)
Drop: Antidote (x2)

**WATCHER-A***
HP: 624 | AP: 1 | Gil: 0
Steal: Potion
Drop: Potion

**WATCHER-R***
HP: 62, | AP: 1 | Gil: 0
Steal: Potion
Drop: Potion

**WATCHER-S***
HP: 620 | AP: 1 | Gil: 0
Steal: Potion
Drop: Potion

**\*Appears only before defeating the Machina Panzer boss on the Thunder Plains.**

## ITEM CHECKLIST

Dispel Tonic (x3)

Phoenix Down (x4)

Characters

1

Garment Grids & Dresspheres

2

Battle System

3

Accessories

4

Items and Item Shops

5

Walkthrough
Chapter 1
Chapter 2
Chapter 3
Chapter 4
Chapter 5

Mini-Games

7

Fiends and Enemies

8

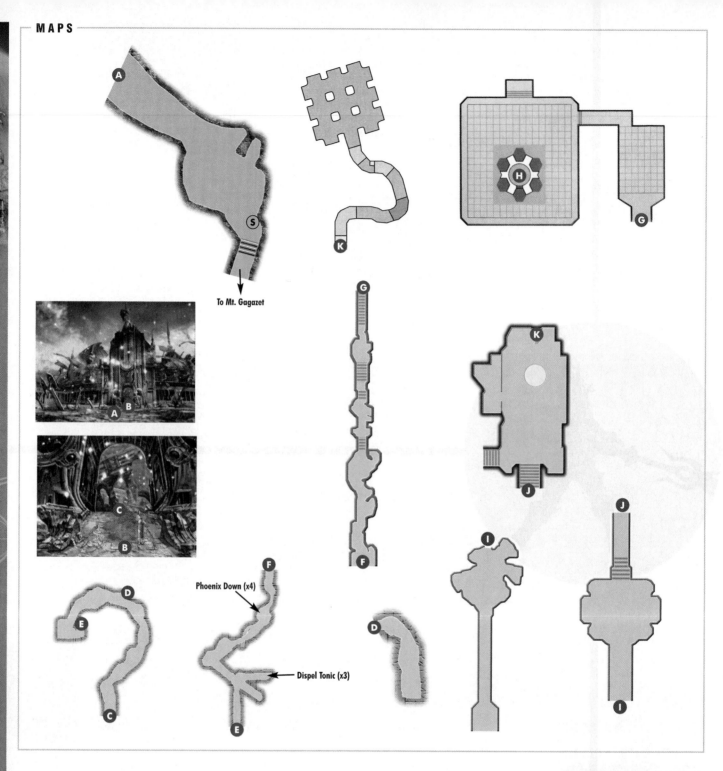

To Mt. Gagazet

Phoenix Down (x4)

Dispel Tonic (x3)

# THE NEW INHABITANTS

Zanarkand is one of the easiest areas to visit at the start of Chapter 5. Also, if you gave the sphere to New Yevon during Chapter 2, it's important that you speak to Isaaru at Zanarkand before heading to Bevelle. If you completed the monkey soulmate quest before the ending of Chapter 3, monkeys have driven off all the tourists. Episode Complete! If you were unable to complete the monkey soulmate quest, then better luck in your next game.

Maechen should be standing across from the Save Sphere. Speak to him and listen to his last story. Move toward the dome and speak with the former shopkeeper, then proceed toward the dome until you spot Isaaru on a higher ledge. Speak to Isaaru one last time. If you continue a short distance toward the dome, the party finds it sealed tight and you are offered an option to go directly back to the Save Sphere near the entrance of Zanarkand.

Monkeys have driven the tourists from the ruins, completing the game-long quest to preserve the sanctity of Zanarkand.

Isaaru finally gives up the tourist trade and decides to lead a more reverent life.

# BESAID ISLAND

Characters

1

Garment Grids & Dresspheres

2

Battle System

3

Accessories

4

Items and Item Shops

5

Walkthrough

Chapter 1

Chapter 2

Chapter 3

Chapter 4

Chapter 5

Mini-Games

7

Fiends and Enemies

8

205

## ACTION CHECKLIST

**1** Follow Wakka into the village.

**4** Give the War Buddy Sphere to Wakka.

**2** Speak to Wakka at the temple entrance.

**5** Return to the village for a celebration.

**3** Say goodbye to Beclem at the beach.

**COMPLETION: +1.8%**

## WANDERING FIENDS

**BARBUTA**
HP: 562  AP: 1  Gil: 33
Steal: Lunar Curtain
Drop: Light Curtain

**CEPHALOTUS**
HP: 1830  AP: 1  Gil: 62
Steal: Echo Screen (x2)
Drop: Echo Screen (x2)

**CHOCOBO**
HP: 3890  AP: 0  Gil: 0
Steal: None
Drop: None

**DOLMEN**
HP: 5320  AP: 1  Gil: 320
Steal: Remedy (x2)
Drop: Hi-Potion (x2)

**FLAME DRAGON**
HP: 980  AP: 1  Gil: 300
Steal: Hi-Potion
Drop: Red Ring

**GEMINI**
HP: 2044  AP: 1  Gil: 153
Steal: Lunar Curtain (x2)
Drop: Light Curtain (x2)

**MALBORO**
HP: 5877  AP: 1  Gil: 370
Steal: Hi-Potion
Drop: Remedy (x2)

**QUEEN COEURL**
HP: 3270  AP: 1  Gil: 330
Steal: Phoenix Down
Drop: Phoenix Down (x2)

**SPINE DRAKE**
HP: 2582  AP: 1  Gil: 127
Steal: Arctic Wind
Drop: Arctic Wind

**VARAN**
HP: 1132  AP: 1  Gil: 240
Steal: Dispel Tonic
Drop: Holy Water

**WATCHER-A***
HP: 624  AP: 1  Gil: 0
Steal: Potion
Drop: Potion

**WATCHER-R***
HP: 620  AP: 1  Gil: 0
Steal: Potion
Drop: Potion

**WATCHER-S***
HP: 620  AP: 1  Gil: 0
Steal: Potion
Drop: Potion

**\*Appears only before defeating the Machina Panzer boss at Thunder Plains.**

## ITEM CHECKLIST

Ether (x4)
Twilight Rain
Mega-Potion
Black Lore

War Buddy Sphere **E**
X-Potion (x2)
3500 gil

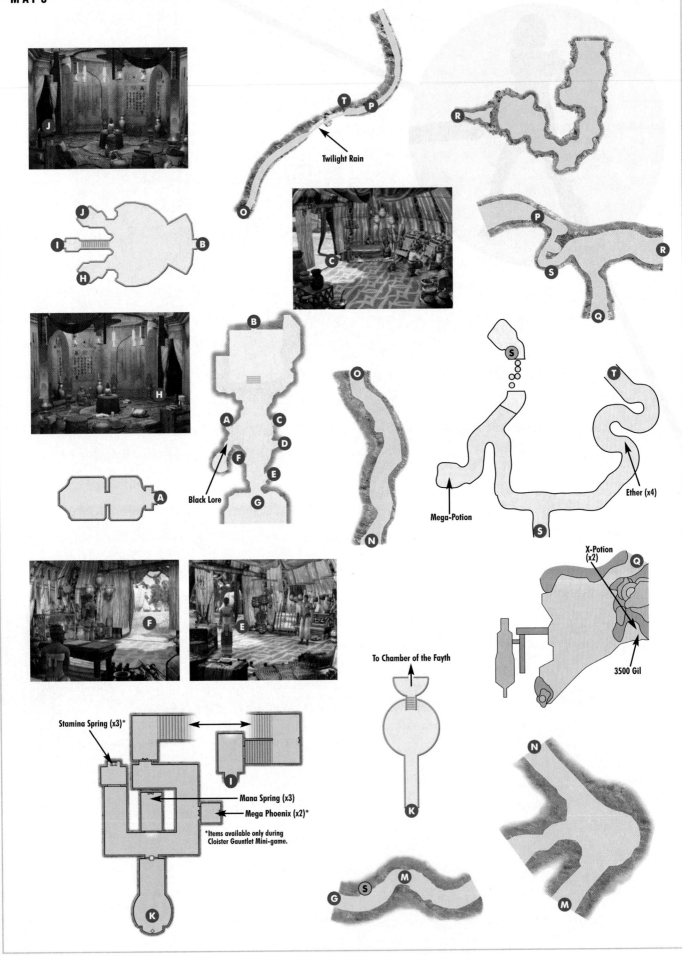

BESAID ISLAND

Twilight Rain

Black Lore

Mega-Potion

Ether (x4)

X-Potion (x2)

3500 Gil

To Chamber of the Fayth

Stamina Spring (x3)*

Mana Spring (x3)

Mega Phoenix (x2)*

*Items available only during Cloister Gauntlet Mini-game.

# WAKKA'S GIFT

Follow Wakka to the temple entrance and speak to him again there. Head to the beach and say goodbye to Beclem, who gives you the **War Buddy Sphere**. As you make your way back to the village, you'll find Wakka pacing around the statue at the highest part of the road outside Besaid. Hand the sphere to Wakka, then follow him back to the village for a celebration. Episode Complete!

*Turns out Beclem isn't such a bad guy after all.*

## KILIKA ISLAND

### ACTION CHECKLIST

1. Approach the gates at the north end of the port area.

2. Watch the citizens of Kilika reunite at the temple stairs.

**COMPLETION: +1.0%**

## WANDERING FIENDS

**ASSASSIN BEE**
HP: 233 | AP: 1 | Gil: 48
Steal: Antidote
Drop: Antidote

**CHOCOBO**
HP: 3890 | AP: 0 | Gil: 0
Steal: None
Drop: None

**DOLMEN**
HP: 5320 | AP: 1 | Gil: 320
Steal: Remedy (x2)
Drop: Hi-Potion (x2)

**IRONSIDE**
HP: 8432 | AP: 1 | Gil: 200,
Steal: Shadow Gem (x2)
Drop: Phoenix Down

**LEAGUE MAGE*2**
HP: 1020 | AP: 1 | Gil: 130
Steal: Ether
Drop: Hi-Potion

**LEAGUE MASTER*2**
HP: 1732 | AP: 1 | Gil: 140
Steal: Phoenix
Down Drop: Ether

**LEAGUE WARRIOR*2**
HP: 422 | AP: 1 | Gil: 120
Steal: Hi-Potion
Drop: Hi-Potion

**QUEEN COEURL**
HP: 3270 | AP: 1 | Gil: 330
Steal: Phoenix Down
Drop: Phoenix Down (x2)

**TAROMAITI**
HP: 1782 | AP: 1 | Gil: 280
Steal: Antidote (x2)
Drop: Star Pendant

**WATCHER-A***
HP: 624 | AP: 1 | Gil: 0
Steal: Potion
Drop: Potion

**WATCHER-R***
HP: 620 | AP: 1 | Gil: 0
Steal: Potion
Drop: Potion

**WATCHER-S***
HP: 620 | AP: 1 | Gil: 0
Steal: Potion
Drop: Potion

**YEVON'S FINEST*1**
HP: 1722 | AP: 1 | Gil: 140
Steal: Holy Water
Drop: Hi-Potion

**YEVON STRIKER*1**
HP: 1730 | AP: 1 | Gil: 140
Steal: Holy Water
Drop: Hi-Potion

**YAU 71**
HP: 3800 | AP: 1 | Gil: 94
Steal: Silence Grenade
Drop: Sleep Grenade

**\*Appears only before defeating the Machina Panzer boss at Thunder Plains.**

**\*1. Appears only if the Awesome Sphere was given to the Youth League at the start of Chapter 2.**

**\*2. Appears only if the Awesome Sphere was given to New Yevon at the start of Chapter 2.**

Characters

1

Garment Grids & Dressspheres

2

Battle System

3

Accessories

4

Items and Item Shops

5

Walkthrough 6
Chapter 1
Chapter 2
Chapter 3
Chapter 4
Chapter 5

Mini-Games

7

Fiends and Enemies

8

## ITEM CHECKLIST

Ether
Mana Tablet (x2)
Remedy
Phoenix Down (x3)
Dispel Tonic
Star Curtain (x3)
Lunar Curtain (x3)
Light Curtain (x3)

3000 gil
Arcane Lore
Tricks of the Trade Garment Grid **E**
Invincible
Georapella Coins (x5)
X-Potion
Mega-Potion
Ether

Megalixir
Wall Ring
Regen Bangle
Cat's Bell
Ether (x2)
Turbo Ether (x2) or Samurai Dressphere
Wizard Bracelet

## MAPS

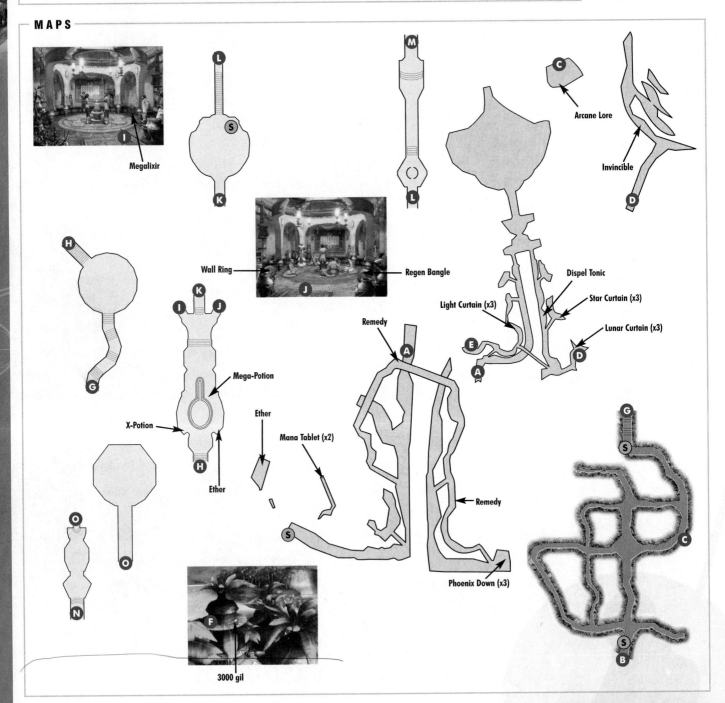

Megalixir

Arcane Lore

Invincible

Wall Ring

Regen Bangle

Dispel Tonic

Light Curtain (x3)

Star Curtain (x3)

Lunar Curtain (x3)

Remedy

Mega-Potion

X-Potion

Ether

Ether

Mana Tablet (x2)

Remedy

Phoenix Down (x3)

3000 gil

# OPENING THE GATES

Head to the second portion of the port area, where the citizens are demanding that the guard open the gate and allow access to the temple. Run through the forest to the temple stairs, where Dona and Barthello reunite. Episode Complete!

*Dona finally gets her way with Barthello.*

# KILIKA EXTRAS

There are several reasons to return to Kilika a second time after gaining the "Episode Complete." If you have not completed the quest to find the Squatter Monkeys in the woods, you may do so now. When all 13 are discovered, speak to the woman in blue standing on the east dock in the first port area to receive the **Chaos Maelstrom Garment Grid**.

The temple is full of treasure chests containing valuable items and accessories. In the last chamber just before the Chamber of the Fayth, the chest in the center of the room holds the **Samurai dressphere** if you failed to obtain it during Chapter 3. If you did pick up the Samurai Dressphere previously, the chest holds a **Turbo Ether (x2)** instead.

*Kilika Temple is now a virtual store-house of great items and accessories to collect.*

*Last chance to find those crazy monkeys!*

# INVINCIBLE

There is a secret item at Kilika that you can now obtain. During all the chapters, there is a man on the deck of the boat docked on the east side of the second port area who is observing the progress of the construction on the Youth League base with a sphere recorder. If you spoke to this man during each chapter and viewed the base through his sphere camera each time, speak to him again in Chapter 5. After viewing the base, the man offers to send you over to the base via a ferryman.

*View the base three times: Once in Chapters 1, 3 and 5 to be offered a ferry ride to the base.*

The only problem is, you must view the whole scene at the base through the lens of the sphere camera. Turn on the Guide Map if you've been playing with it off. On the guide map, you will notice a white X, which is the ferryman, who will take you back to the port when you are through. The yellow square indicates the location of a chest containing the accessory **Invincible**. This accessory enables the character wearing it to inflict more than 9999 HP damage with an attack or spell!

You may also notice a yellow X moving around the docks at the base. Run after and catch a small child, who will bribe you to go away with **5 Georapella Coins**.

*Use the Guide Map to locate the chest containing a powerful accessory.*

**ACTION CHECKLIST**

1 *Search the south side of the bridge near the exit to find a hidden moogle.*

2 *Follow the moogle back to the west dock outside Luca stadium.*

**COMPLETION: +0.6%**

**ITEM CHECKLIST**

Light Curtain (x3)

Characters

1

Garment Grids & Dresspheres

2

Battle System

3

Accessories

4

Items and Item Shops

5

Walkthrough

Chapter 1

Chapter 2

Chapter 3

Chapter 4

**Chapter 5**

Mini-Games

7

Fiends and Enemies

8

# SEASON OF THE BLITZ

Blitzball becomes available when the Gullwings enter Luca for the first time during Chapter 5. Even for those who are familiar with the game from *FINAL FANTASY X*, there are a whole lot of new things to learn. Please refer to the "Blitzball" section in the "Mini-Games" chapter for more information.

Blitzball is a challenging sport and a time-honored tradition in Luca.

# PLACE OF POIGNANCY

On the bridge leading to the exit of Luca, move toward the edge of the balcony, just below the Save Sphere, to trigger a scene where Yuna discovers a moogle that no one else can see. Follow the moogle back through Luca to the stadium, and then to the west dock where a ship is harbored. When Yuna is finished reliving her memories, Episode Complete!

The invisible moogle leads Yuna back through Luca to the docks.

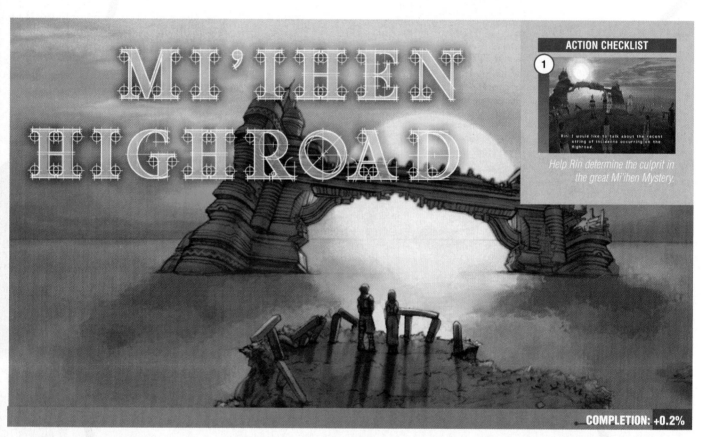

## MI'IHEN HIGHROAD

**ACTION CHECKLIST**

1. Rin: I would like to talk about the recent string of incidents occurring on the Highroad.

Help Rin determine the culprit in the great Mi'ihen Mystery.

COMPLETION: +0.2%

## WANDERING FIENDS

**AKA MANAH**
HP: 6322 | AP: 1 | Gil: 670
Steal: Remedy (x2)
Drop: Pretty Orb

**BARBUTA**
HP: 562 | AP: 1 | Gil: 33
Steal: Lunar Curtain
Drop: Light Curtain

**CEPHALOTUS**
HP: 1830 | AP: 1 | Gil: 62
Steal: Echo Screen (x2)
Drop: Echo Screen (x2)

**CREEPER**
HP: 1974 | AP: 1 | Gil: 80
Steal: Hi-Potion
Drop: S-Bomb

**EPITAPH**
HP: 17433 | AP: 1 | Gil: 330
Steal: Remedy
Drop: Remedy (x2)

**FLAN ROJO**
HP: 1220 | AP: 1 | Gil: 125
Steal: Bomb Core
Drop: Bomb Core

**HEXAPOD**
HP: 2805 | AP: 1 | Gil: 80
Steal: Hi-Potion
Drop: L-Bomb

**HUG BUG**
HP: 2350 | AP: 1 | Gil: 80
Steal: Hi-Potion
Drop: M-Bomb

**LICH**
HP: 3444 | AP: 1 | Gil: 330
Steal: Hi-Potion
Drop: None

**MYCOTOXIN**
HP: 810 | AP: 1 | Gil: 83
Steal: Antidote (x2)
Drop: Antidote (x2)

**PEREGRINE**
HP: 735 | AP: 1 | Gil: 44
Steal: Hi-Potion
Drop: Hi-Potion

**QUEEN COEURL**
HP: 3270 | AP: 1 | Gil: 330
Steal: Phoenix Down
Drop: Phoenix Down (x2)

**WATCHER-A***
HP: 624 | AP: 1 | Gil: 0
Steal: Potion
Drop: Potion

**WATCHER-R***
HP: 620 | AP: 1 | Gil: 0
Steal: Potion
Drop: Potion

**WATCHER-S***
HP: 620 | AP: 1 | Gil: 0
Steal: Potion
Drop: Potion

**ZU**
HP: 9338 | AP: 1 | Gil: 164
Steal: Phoenix Down
Drop: Phoenix Down (x2)

**KING VERMIN!**
HP: 39857 | AP: 1 | Gil: 3500
Steal: Turbo Ether
Drop: Power Gloves

*****Appears only before defeating the Machina Panzer boss at Thunder Plains.

# ITEM CHECKLIST

| | | | |
|---|---|---|---|
| Phoenix Down (x5) | Hi-Potion (x3) | Phoenix Down (x5) | Hi-Potion (x3) |
| Black Belt | Titanium Bangle | Victor Primoris | Echo Screen (x5) |
| 3000 gil | Holy Water (x6) | M-Bomb (x2) | |
| Remedy (x2) | Remedy (x2) | Soft (x5) | |

# MAPS

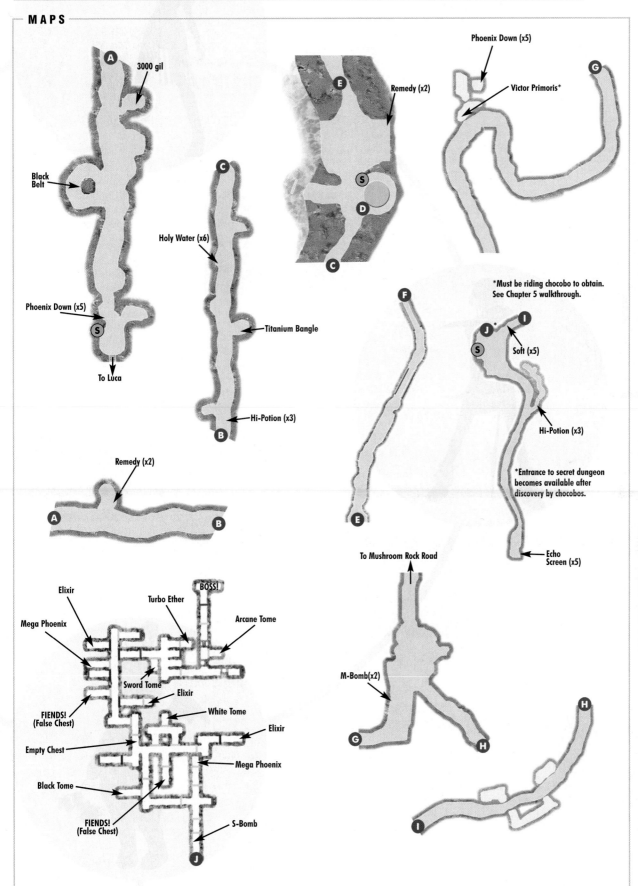

*Must be riding chocobo to obtain. See Chapter 5 walkthrough.

*Entrance to secret dungeon becomes available after discovery by chocobos.

Characters

Garment Grids & Dresspheres

Battle System

Accessories

Items and Item Shops

Walkthrough
Chapter 1
Chapter 2
Chapter 3
Chapter 4
Chapter 5

Mini-Games

Fiends and Enemies

# DETECTIVE RIN IS AT IT AGAIN!

Return to Mi'ihen via the airship or from the Luca entrance and a person will greet you. Rin is expecting you, and you can go directly to the Travel Agency. The clues you saw using the CommSpheres set up around Mi'ihen determine who's the culprit behind the recent incidents. Once Rin figures out the mystery, you can ride chocobos on the Mi'ihen Highroad. Once the scene is complete, you score an Episode Complete!

*It's fun to try and follow Rin's deductive reasoning and answer his questions correctly.*

While riding a chocobo, you can open chests by pressing the X button, and you can also continue the Publicity and Matrimony campaigns if needed by pressing the Square button when speaking with the NPCs involved.

# MI'IHEN'S FORGOTTEN TREASURES

After obtaining the Mission Complete for Mi'ihen, return to the area to gather items. Ride a chocobo through the raised road area just south of the Mushroom Rock entrance, and pause at the gap depicted in the screenshot to the left. After waiting there for a few seconds, you will gain the option to jump to a higher level where your chocobo will open a chest to obtain a **Phoenix Down (x5)**. Leave the area and return, then stand immobile in the gap for a few seconds again. This time, when you accept the option to go, the chocobo drops into the gorge to obtain the **Victor Primoris**.

*The Victor Primoris allows Paine's Full Throttle dressphere to inflict more than 9999 HP damage.*

# THE FIEND COLONY

Just when you thought you've done every task imaginable on the Mi'ihen Highroad, along comes a new challenge. There is a secret dungeon that is available at Mi'ihen during Chapter 5. However, you can only access the dungeon if you assisted Clasko in setting up the Chocobo Ranch at the Calm Lands. Visit Clasko and raise a few chocobos to level 5. When you dispatch a chocobo to search for treasure, it is more likely to return to Clasko's ranch depending on how many you have at Clasko's ranch. Dispatch one or more high-level chocobos to Mi'ihen Highroad to search for items. Check in with Clasko every once in a while to see if the chocobo you sent to Mi'ihen has returned.

*Dispatch chocobos from Clasko's place to Mi'ihen in search of the mysterious dungeon.*

When the chocobo you sent to Mi'ihen returns, Clasko reports to Yuna that a strange new portal was found near the site where the hover wrecked during Chapter 3. Return to Mi'ihen at that point to see a green cloud near the Save Sphere in the wide area at the bottom of the gorge. Enter the cloud to dive into the secret dungeon.

*The dungeon entrance appears near the Save Sphere at the bottom of the gorge.*

Next to the entrance is a chest containing **S-Bombs**. Stone walls have sealed off many of the passages in the tunnels, and you can blow them open with bombs. As you move through the passages, stand next to wall sections and watch Yuna's skirt carefully. When her skirt flaps as if rustled by a light breeze, it means you've found a wall that can be blown open. Once you find a wall to blast, you must not only choose the appropriate type of bomb, but you must plant the right number of bombs at the same time, or you will be unsuccessful at blowing through the wall. Most walls are soft enough to be destroyed by setting five S-Bombs. However, if you run out of S-Bombs, switch to M-Bombs which are more powerful, or even L-Bombs, which are the most powerful of them all. The best way to obtain more bombs is by fighting fiends in random battles. Creepers, Hug Bugs, and Hexapods all drop bombs upon defeat. If a character using the Lady Luck dressphere manages to successfully Bribe one of these monsters, you can accumulate massive amounts of various bombs.

*Set bombs on walls to open new passageways.*

*Damaging the wrong wall results in a battle with a merciless Epitaph.*

Some of the walls in the tunnel are stronger and require more firepower to blow down. Strong walls are marked in blue on the map, and the strongest walls are marked in purple. Use five S-bombs to blow down light blue walls, use five M-Bombs to blow down dark blue walls, and use nine L-Bombs to blow down purple walls. Avoid the walls marked in red, because they are trap walls. When you attempt to blow down these walls, you are forced to fight Epitaphs.

Blast through the tunnels and collect the awesome accessories located in the chests. Watch out for chests that contain fiends. It's possible that you will win extra items and bombs by blowing up walls with proficiency. The chances of obtaining items by destroying walls drops as you proceed further in the cave. Also, don't equip a Charm Bangle. Instead, fight the insect-like fiends in the area to keep your bomb supplies going. When you reach the northernmost chamber, the boss of the fiend colony appears. After defeating the monster, you return back outside the colony with all the walls reset. Collect all the items before moving on to face the boss. Defeating the monster and clearing the fiend colony completely, nets a **Font of Power Garment Grid**.

*Fantastic items await in the secret chambers behind thin walls.*

**MAP**

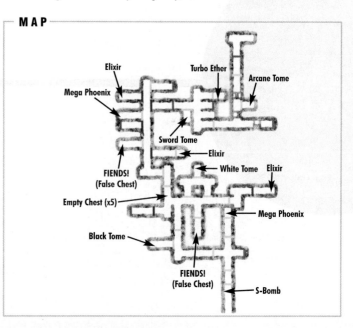

# KING VERMIN! BOSS FIGHT

The king of the colony is a creature that loves fire. It loves to use it and it loves to eat it. Equip your characters with accessories and Garment Grids with the Fire Eater ability, and King VERMIN! will handle all your healing for you whenever it tries to cast Firaga! Avoid casting fire spells or using fire-based attacks on the monster or you will heal it. King VERMIN! is not especially tough, so use your strongest Black Mage spells and a Dark Knight's Darkness attack to take it out. Keep everyone's HP high by designating one person as a White Mage or Alchemist.

**HP:** 39857  **MP:** 872  **EXP:** 5000  **AP:** 1

**GIL DROPPED:** 3500
**PILFER GIL:** 2000

**STEAL:** Normal: Turbo Ether   Rare: Turbo Ether (x2)
**DROP:** Normal: Power Gloves   Rare: Power Gloves

## MUSHROOM ROCK ROAD

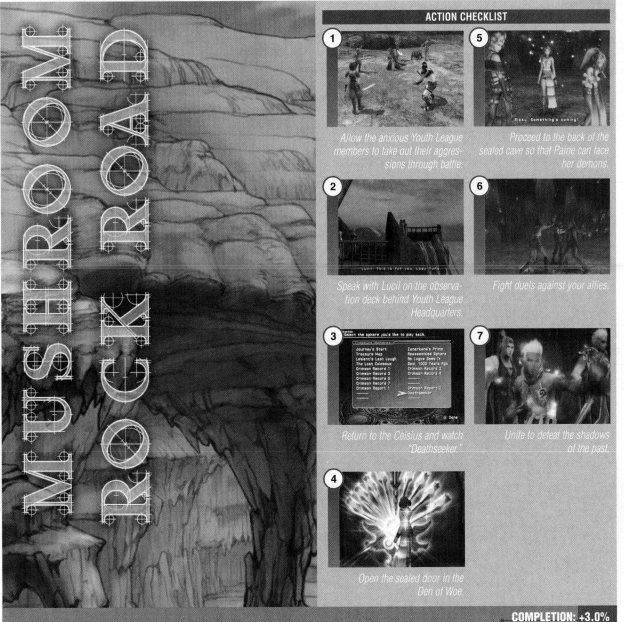

### ACTION CHECKLIST

**1** Allow the anxious Youth League members to take out their aggressions through battle.

**2** Speak with Lucil on the observation deck behind Youth League Headquarters.

**3** Return to the Celsius and watch "Deathseeker."

**4** Open the sealed door in the Den of Woe.

**5** Proceed to the back of the sealed cave so that Paine can face her demons.

**6** Fight duels against your allies.

**7** Unite to defeat the shadows of the past.

**COMPLETION: +3.0%**

## WANDERING FIENDS

**ARCHAEOTHYRIS**
HP: 1332 | AP: 1 | Gil: 110
Steal: Eye Drops (x2)
Drop: Eye Drops (x2)

**CRIMSON SHADOW**
HP: 2020 | AP: 1 | Gil: 30
Steal: Phoenix Down
Drop: Hi-Potion

**DOLMEN**
HP: 5320 | AP: 1 | Gil: 320
Steal: Remedy (x2)
Drop: Hi-Potion (x2)

**ELMA (CH5)**
HP: 4882 | AP: 2 | Gil: 500
Steal: Healing Spring (x2)
Drop: Chocobo Feather (x2)

**GUCUMATZ**
HP: 3720 | AP: 1 | Gil: 173
Steal: Soft (x2)
Drop: Soft (x2)

**LEAGUE MAGE**
HP: 1020 | AP: 1 | Gil: 130
Steal: Ether
Drop: Hi-Potion

**LEAGUE MASTER**
HP: 1732 | AP: 1 | Gil: 140
Steal: Phoenix
Down Drop: Ether

**LEAGUE SLASHER**
HP: 1650 | AP: 1 | Gil: 140
Steal: M-Bomb
Drop: Hi-Potion

**LEAGUE VETERAN**
HP: 1720 | AP: 1 | Gil: 100
Steal: M-Bomb
Drop: Hi-Potion

**LEAGUE WARRIOR**
HP: 422 | AP: 1 | Gil: 120
Steal: Hi-Potion
Drop: Hi-Potion

**LICH**
HP: 3444 | AP: 1 | Gil: 330
Steal: Hi-Potion
Drop: None

**LUPUS**
HP: 1262 | AP: 1 | Gil: 80
Steal: Hi-Potion
Drop: Hi-Potion

**SPINE DRAKE**
HP: 2582 | AP: 1 | Gil: 127
Steal: Arctic Wind
Drop: Arctic Wind

**WATCHER-A***
HP: 624 | AP: 1 | Gil: 0
Steal: Potion
Drop: Potion

**WATCHER-R***
HP: 620 | AP: 1 | Gil: 0
Steal: Potion
Drop: Potion

**WATCHER-S***
HP: 620 | AP: 1 | Gil: 0
Steal: Potion
Drop: Potion

**YAIBAL**
HP: 4330 | AP: 1 | Gil: 100
Steal: Chocobo Feather
Drop: Muscle Belt

**LUCIL**
HP: 7324 | AP: 2 | Gil: 220
Steal: Chocobo Feather
Drop: Circlet

**RIKKU**
HP: 7800 | AP: 3 | Gil: 200
Steal: Bushido Lore
Drop: Black Lore

**PAINE**
HP: 9200 | AP: 3 | Gil: 200
Steal: Sword Lore
Drop: Champion Belt

**BARALAI (CH5)**
HP: 12220 | AP: 5 | Gil: 200
Steal: Nature's Lore
Drop: Crystal Ball

**GIPPAL**
HP: 14800 | AP: 5 | Gil: 5000
Steal: White Lore
Drop: Kaiser Knuckles

**NOOJ**
HP: 23800 | AP: 10 | Gil: 30000
Steal: Arcane Lore
Drop: Magical Dances Vol. I

***Appears before defeating the Machina Panzer boss at Thunder Plains.**

## ITEM CHECKLIST

Mega-Potion
2500 gil

Turbo Ether (x3)
Elixir

Elixir
Machina Booster

Crystal Bangle
Nooj's Sphere **E**

## MAPS

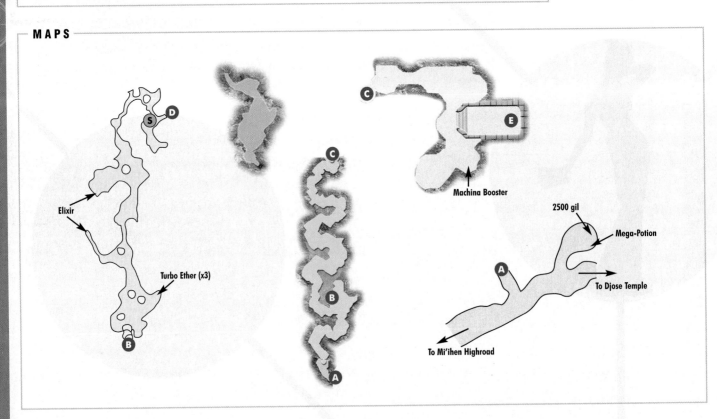

Elixir

Turbo Ether (x3)

Machina Booster

2500 gil

Mega-Potion

To Djose Temple

To Mi'ihen Highroad

# WAR: NOW FOR FUN AND EXERCISE

If you sided with the Youth League, speak to members at the entrance of Mushroom Rock Road. Restless now that the thought of impending war has subsided, the warriors desire a challenge. When ready, speak to Yaibal to accept a challenge against the first group of contenders from the Youth League. Follow Lucil through Mushroom Rock Road, encountering sets of Youth League soldiers at various points. You must fight six sets of Youth League soldiers, and Elma is in the final set. When you clear all six, you must fight Lucil. After that, Episode Complete!

*Remember to use items to recover between each set of League warriors.*

## LUCIL BOSS FIGHT

**HP:** 7324 **MP:** 370 **EXP:** 370 **AP:** 2

Lucil isn't too difficult to fight at this extremely late stage of the game. Take down her HP quickly with your strongest spells and attacks (such as a Dark Knight's Darkness ability). The real challenge is that Lucil will attempt to cast Doom on each party member in fairly rapid succession. For this reason, take her down quickly to avoid death, although an Alchemist with the Mega-Phoenix Stash ability should be able to recover the party if needed.

**GIL DROPPED:** 220
**PILFER GIL:** 3000
**STEAL:** Normal: Chocobo Feather   Rare: Chocobo Feather (x2)
**DROP:** Normal: Circlet   Rare: Circlet

## ALL ACCESS AT MUSHROOM ROCK

The Gullwings return to the Celsius automatically when the last mission at Mushroom Rock is complete. Return to the area and navigate around, collecting the items contained in the chests in the ravine as well as near the headquarters. You can now enter the headquarters and move about. Meet Lucil on the rear observatory area, and she will give you **Nooj's Sphere**. Return to the Celsius and view the recording on the sphere, titled "Deathseeker."

*With access to all parts of Youth League HQ, speak to Lucil on the rear balcony to receive a new sphere.*

## OPEN THE DEN OF WOE

Upon collecting the last two Crimson Spheres during Chapter 5, return to the Den of Woe in the gorge and examine the door. There are no items inside the Den, so proceed directly east to the large area. When the pyreflies overwhelm the party with their feelings, Yuna must take on each of her friends in separate single-character duels. Before taking on this short quest, it is strongly recommended that you equip Yuna with the Thief dressphere or the Treasure Hunt Garment Grid bearing the Mug ability, as your pyrefly-infected allies have some really good accessories to steal. Because Yuna will be fighting alone, boost her Defense by equipping accessories and Garment Grids to maximize her status.

*All 10 Crimson Spheres will open the door to the Den of Woe.*

## RIKKU BOSS FIGHT

**HP:** 7800 **MP:** 92 **EXP:** 800 **AP:** 3

Rikku fights just as hard and fast as any thief would. Snatch her valuable items and knock her down fast with your most fearsome attacks. Use Hi-Potions to recover if needed.

**GIL DROPPED:** 200
**PILFER GIL:** 3000
**STEAL:** Normal: Bushido Lore   Rare: Bushido Lore
**DROP:** Normal: Black Lore   Rare: Black Lore

Characters

1

Garment Grids & Dresspheres

2

Battle System

3

Accessories

4

Items and Item Shops

5

Walkthrough
Chapter 1
Chapter 2
Chapter 3
Chapter 4
Chapter 5

Mini-Games

7

Fiends and Enemies

8

# PAINE

BOSS FIGHT

**HP:** 9200 **MP:** 55 **EXP:** 800 **AP:** 3

Paine's attacks are slightly more powerful than Rikku's, so don't hesitate to use an X-Potion to recover if needed. Attack her quickly and mercilessly with your most powerful skills, and she should succumb almost as quickly as Rikku does.

**GIL DROPPED:** 200
**PILFER GIL:** 300

**STEAL:** Normal: Sword Lore  Rare: Sword Lore
**DROP:** Normal: Champion Belt  Rare: Champion Belt

# BARALAI

BOSS FIGHT

**HP:** 12220 **MP:** 720 **EXP:** 1200 **AP:** 5

The pyreflies have done a good job of creating an illusion of Baralai, because this battle will greatly remind you of the encounter at Bevelle. Baralai uses new attacks to drain MP and silence spellcasters, so it will be extremely difficult to rely on magic. Heal every round in preparation to survive his swinging staff attacks. Attack quickly and furiously with your best physical assaults.

**GIL DROPPED:** 200
**PILFER GIL:** 300

**STEAL:** Normal: Nature's Lore  Rare: Nature's Lore
**DROP:** Normal: Crystal Ball  Rare: Crystal Ball

# GIPPAL

BOSS FIGHT

All in all, fighting Gippal is a lot like fighting Baralai with a few exceptions. Spell-casting should prove more effective against Gippal. Although he inflicts Silence with Hush Grenade attacks, he does so infrequently. Have an Alchemist or White Mage heal on each turn, because Gippal frequently causes lots of damage to the entire party with his attacks. As his HP drops, he performs Bullseye more frequently and also causes lots of damage with Mortar. Basically, you need to take him from 5000 HP to 0 HP in as little a time as possible. Use strong attacks like Flare spells and a Dark Knight's Darkness ability. Whatever you do, pilfer gil from Gippal before the end of the battle, because nabbing up to 15000 gil in one shot is pretty nice.

**HP:** 14800 **MP:** 235 **EXP:** 1200 **AP:** 5

**GIL DROPPED:** 5000
**PILFER GIL:** 15000

**STEAL:** Normal: White Lore  Rare: White Lore
**DROP:** Normal: Magical Dances, Vol. I  Rare: Magical Dances, Vol. I

# NOOJ

**HP:** 23800  **MP:** 720  **EXP:** 1800  **AP:** 10

A healer should be working overtime yet again as you enter this battle. Nooj uses devastating gun attacks that can cause more than 1500 HP damage to a single character, and his Greedy Aura ability will siphon MP from all of your characters at once. Like the other shadows before, spell-casting will be difficult. Take down Nooj with your strongest attacks such as a Dark Knight's Darkness ability, or the regular attacks of the Samurai, Berserker, or Warrior. Also, use the Pilfer Gil ability, considering how much money you stand to make in a single swipe. Keep the entire party's HP high throughout the battle, because when Nooj drops below 3000 HP, he begins performing a rather nasty attack that can cause 5000 HP damage to your entire party. Anyone who survives this attack should use a Mega Phoenix immediately, followed by a Mega-Potion.

**GIL DROPPED:** 30000  
**PILFER GIL:** 20000

**STEAL:** Normal: Arcane Lore  Rare: Arcane Lore  
**DROP:** Normal: Magical Dances, Vol. I  Rare: Magical Dances, Vol. I

DJOSE TEMPLE

## ACTION CHECKLIST

**1** Defeat the Al Bhed's experimental new machine at reduced levels.

**2** After digging up enough parts in Bikanel Desert, fight the Experiment again at its highest levels.

**COMPLETION: +0.8%**

## WANDERING FIENDS

| | | | |
|---|---|---|---|
| **ARCHAEOTHYRIS**<br>HP: 1332  AP: 1  Gil: 110<br>Steal: Eye Drops (x2)<br>Drop: Eye Drops (x2) | **ASSASSIN BEE**<br>HP: 233  AP: 1  Gil: 48<br>Steal: Antidote<br>Drop: Antidote | **CHOCOBO**<br>HP: 3890  AP: 0  Gil: 0<br>Steal: None<br>Drop: None | **DOLMEN**<br>HP: 5320  AP: 1  Gil: 320<br>Steal: Remedy (x2)<br>Drop: Hi-Potion (x2) |
| **GREATER DRAKE**<br>HP: 1819  AP: 1  Gil: 140<br>Steal: Fire Gem<br>Drop: Fire Gem | **LEAGUE MAGE*1**<br>HP: 1020  AP: 1  Gil: 130<br>Steal: Ether<br>Drop: Hi-Potion | **LEAGUE MASTER*1**<br>HP: 1732  AP: 1  Gil: 140<br>Steal: Phoenix<br>Down Drop: Ether | **LEAGUE SLASHER*1**<br>HP: 1650  AP: 1  Gil: 140<br>Steal: M-Bomb Drop:<br>Hi-Potion |
| **LEAGUE VETERAN*1**<br>HP: 1720  AP: 1  Gil: 100<br>Steal: M-Bomb<br>Drop: Hi-Potion | **LEAGUE WARRIOR*1**<br>HP: 422  AP: 1  Gil: 120<br>Steal: Hi-Potion<br>Drop: Hi-Potion | **LICH**<br>HP: 3444  AP: 1  Gil: 330<br>Steal: Hi-Potion<br>Drop: None | **RUKH**<br>HP: 12850  AP: 1  Gil: 530<br>Steal: Phoenix Down (x2)<br>Drop: Phoenix Down (x2) |
| **TAROMAITI**<br>HP: 1782  AP: 1  Gil: 280<br>Steal: Antidote (x2)<br>Drop: Star Pendant | **WATCHER-A***<br>HP: 624  AP: 1  Gil: 0<br>Steal: Potion<br>Drop: Potion | **WATCHER-R***<br>HP: 620  AP: 1  Gil: 0<br>Steal: Potion<br>Drop: Potion | **WATCHER-S***<br>HP: 620  AP: 1  Gil: 0<br>Steal: Potion<br>Drop: Potion |

| | |
|---|---|
| **EXPERIMENT**<br>HP: 18324  AP: 40  Gil: 0<br>Steal: Turbo Ether<br>Drop: Elixir | ***Appears before defeating the Machina Panzer boss at Thunder Plains.**<br><br>***1. Appears only if the Awesome Sphere was given to New Yevon at the start of Chapter 2.** |

Characters

Garment Grids & Dresspheres

Battle System

Accessories

Items and Item Shops

Walkthrough

Chapter 1

Chapter 2

Chapter 3

Chapter 4

Chapter 5

Mini-Games

Fiends and Enemies

## ITEM CHECKLIST

Phoenix Down (x4)    Mana Spring        Hyper Wrist
X-Potion (x2)        Soul Spring        *Al Bhed Primer **Ⓔ**
Remedy (x2)          Power Wrist

**\*Only if you haven't mastered Al Bhed.**

## MAPS

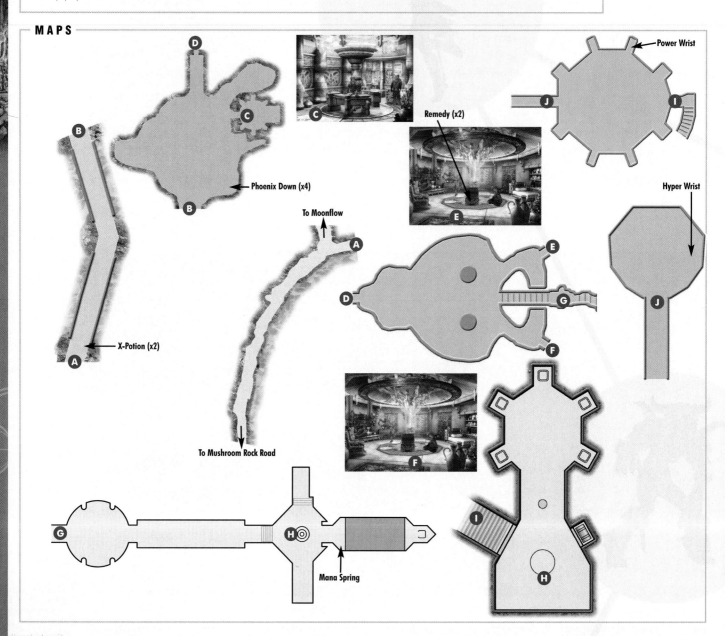

Power Wrist

Remedy (x2)

Hyper Wrist

Phoenix Down (x4)

To Moonflow

X-Potion (x2)

To Mushroom Rock Road

Mana Spring

# THE AL BHED'S TECHNICAL CHALLENGE

Enter the temple and the Al Bhed will encourage you to challenge the new machine they've assembled. To complete the episode at Djose, you must defeat the machine once at its initial levels, then defeat it again when the machine is at its highest levels. The levels of the Experiment are dependent on the number of machina assembly items excavated from Bikanel Desert. Defeat the boss at its highest level to obtain an Episode Complete and the **Magical Dances, Vol. II,** which enables a Songstress to learn Magical Masque.

The Al Bhed are just dying to find worthy adversaries to test out their new machine.

# RAISING THE EXPERIMENT'S LEVEL

As stated, the Attack, Defense and Special levels of the Experiment are dependent on the number of machina assembly items dug up in the Bikanel Desert. To obtain an Episode Complete! at Djose, fight the Experiment once in its weaker form, then fight it again when all levels have reached level 5. For this reason, it is important to not dig too often at Bikanel Desert until Chapter 5.

The technician displays the levels of the Experiment before you fight the machine in the Chamber of the Fayth.

*Remember that you can view the parts you've acquired through digging by checking the kiosk in the south chamber inside Djose Temple.*

After defeating the Experiment the first time, head to Bikanel and begin digging for Attack Assembly, Defense Assembly, and Special Assembly items of the A, S, and Z varieties. The game gives various points each time you find one of these items, and the points are each tallied to determine the level of the Experiment's Attack, Defense, and Special. For instance, if you have 1 Attack Assembly Z, 6 Attack Assembly S and 8 Attack Assembly Z, then multiply each quantity by the number of points it's worth denoted in the points table (refer to the right) to get the equation $(1 \times 5) + (6 \times 3) + 8$, which equals a total of 31 points. Referring to the status level table, you can see that 31 points brings the Experiment's Attack level up to level 4. Just find a few more parts, and the Experiment's Attack level should reach the maximum of level 5.

### POINTS PER ASSEMBLY TYPE

| TYPE | POINTS |
| --- | --- |
| Z | 5 |
| S | 3 |
| A | 1 |

### STATUS LEVEL PER POINT RANGE

| POINTS | LEVEL |
| --- | --- |
| 0 - 3 | 1 |
| 4 – 9 | 2 |
| 10 – 19 | 3 |
| 20 – 37 | 4 |
| 38+ | 5 |

## REPAIRING THE EXPERIMENT

Before you can take on the Experiment again, you must help the Al Bhed get their machine back in shape. After you defeat the Experiment once, key items called repair manuals can be found by talking to certain individuals and by searching other places around Spira. Upon obtaining a repair manual, return to the Chamber of the Fayth at Djose and give it to the technician standing next to the Experiment. The machine will be repaired immediately and you can fight it again.

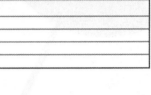

*Repair manuals enable you to take on the Experiment again, but you only get five more chances.*

Each time you want to fight the Experiment, you'll need another repair manual. Conserve your manuals wisely, because only five are available in the whole game. The repair manuals are located in the following places:

■ Speak to the man in the room with all the pedestals on the second floor of Djose Temple. When he asks for the password, enter "MARNELA". He will give you the repair manual in return.

■ Speak to the man seated on the floor in the north chamber inside Djose Temple.

■ There are three monkeys jumping up and down in the area behind the reception building outside Djose Temple. When all three monkeys jump at the exact same time, press the X button to receive a repair manual.

■ At the north end of the Mi'ihen Highroad, near the entrance to Mushroom Rock Road, there is a machina standing between Prophet and some empty wagons. Examine the machina to receive a repair manual.

■ In the secret dungeon at the Calm Lands (explained in the Calm Lands section), there is a chest that contains a repair manual at the opposite end of the dungeon from the starting point.

## EXPERIMENT

*BOSS FIGHT*

The difficulty of this boss is determined by the Attack, Defense, and Special levels listed by the Al Bhed technician before this battle. The Attack level indicates how badly the physical blows and rocket attacks of the machina will damage your characters. At level 5, these attacks are devastating but your party can quickly recover if a White Mage casts Curaga on the entire party, or if an Alchemist mixes a Mega-Potion. The Special level of the Experiment determines which attacks it will use in battle. At level 5, Lifeslicer will kill one of your characters instantly by doing damage equivalent to the character's HP. You cannot protect against this attack, but since the Experiment cannot perform it frequently, you can recover easily by using a Phoenix Down. When the Experiment's Defense is at level 5, your normal attacks and even spells will do less than half their normal damage. The best ways to damage the Experiment effectively are with a Dark Knight's Darkness ability, or with a Gunner's Cheap Shot or Tableturner ability. Therefore, the best party will include at least one Dark Knight and one Gunner, with the third person functioning as a healer. Use the listed attacks repeatedly until the Experiment finally crumbles.

HP: 18324   MP: 0   EXP: 0   AP: 40

GIL DROPPED: 0
PILFER GIL: 5000

STEAL:  Normal: Turbo Ether   Rare: Turbo Ether
DROP:  Normal: Elixir   Rare: Elixir

Characters

1

Garment Grids & Dresspheres

2

Battle System

3

Accessories

4

Items and Item Shops

5

Walkthrough
Chapter 1
Chapter 2
Chapter 3
Chapter 4
Chapter 5

Mini-Games

7

Fiends and Enemies

8

# MOONFLOW

**COMPLETION: +0.4%**

## WANDERING FIENDS

**ARCHAEOTHYRIS**
HP: 1332 | AP: 1 | Gil: 110
Steal: Eye Drops (x2)
Drop: Eye Drops (x2)

**BALIVARHA**
HP: 3688 | AP: 1 | Gil: 230
Steal: Hi-Potion (x2)
Drop: Fire Gem

**BARBUTA**
HP: 562 | AP: 1 | Gil: 33
Steal: Lunar Curtain
Drop: Light Curtain

**BLACKGUARD**
HP: 760 | AP: 1 | Gil: 42
Steal: Phoenix Down
Drop: Potion

**CHOCOBO**
HP: 3890 | AP: 0 | Gil: 0
Steal: None
Drop: None

**FLAN BLANCO**
HP: 625 | AP: 1 | Gil: 72
Steal: Arctic Wind
Drop: Arctic Wind

**RUFFIAN**
HP: 1480 | AP: 1 | Gil: 250
Steal: Grenade
Drop: Potion (x2)

**SHELL SHOCKER**
HP: 4700 | AP: 1 | Gil: 780
Steal: Iron Bangle
Drop: Black Ring

**TAROMAITI**
HP: 1782 | AP: 1 | Gil: 280
Steal: Antidote (x2)
Drop: Star Pendant

**VARAN**
HP: 1132 | AP: 1 | Gil: 240
Steal: Dispel Tonic
Drop: Holy Water

**WATCHER-A***
HP: 624 | AP: 1 | Gil: 0
Steal: Potion
Drop: Potion

**WATCHER-R***
HP: 620 | AP: 1 | Gil: 0
Steal: Potion
Drop: Potion

**WATCHER-S***
HP: 620 | AP: 1 | Gil: 0
Steal: Potion
Drop: Potion

***Appears before defeating the Machina Panzer boss at Thunder Plains.**

## MUSIC BY THE MOONFLOW BANKS

Obtaining an Episode Complete! at the Moonflow is a game-long task. If you failed to complete all of the Moonflow missions and the musician gathering mission at Macalania, all you can do is watch Tobli's final show. However, if you completed all the missions at Moonflow, sold all 10 tickets and gathered the musicians from Macalania, Tobli's show draws a larger crowd. Speak to Tobli and agree to participate in the show. While you watch, you can change the camera angle to view the girls sitting in their various positions onstage. Press the Circle button when done to see the Episode Complete! indicator.

*Check in with Tobli to see if you've done enough to deserve an Episode Complete!*

# GUADOSALAM

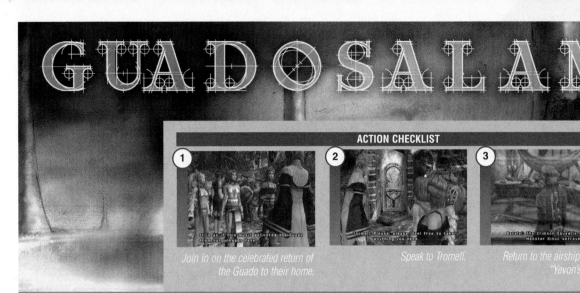

## ACTION CHECKLIST

**1** Join in on the celebrated return of the Guado to their home.

**2** Speak to Tromell.

**3** Return to the airship to watch "Yevon's Secret."

**COMPLETION: +1.2%**

## WANDERING FIENDS

**ARCHAEOTHYRIS**
HP: 1332 | AP: 1 | Gil: 110
Steal: Eye Drops (x2)
Drop: Eye Drops (x2)

**BASCINET**
HP: 1342 | AP: 1 | Gil: 110
Steal: Hi-Potion
Drop: Hi-Potion

**BLUE ELEMENTAL**
HP: 363 | AP: 1 | Gil: 180
Steal: Dragon Scale
Drop: Dragon Scale

**QUEEN COEURL**
HP: 3270 | AP: 1 | Gil: 330
Steal: Phoenix Down
Drop: Phoenix Down (x2)

## ITEM CHECKLIST

Baralai's Sphere

Key to Success, Crystal Ball or Kaiser Knuckles *

Tempered Will Garment Grid **B**

**\*Dependent upon Moonflow events.**

## RETURN OF THE GUADO

If you defeated Garik Ronso at Mt. Gagazet and gathered the musicians in Macalania Woods, the Guado will have now returned to Guadosalam. Join the troupe in the central area, and speak to Tromell a second time to receive an "Episode Complete!"

*If you succeed in helping the Guados return to their home, then it's Episode Complete! for you!*

## THE GUADO'S MEMORIES

Return to Guadosalam a second time and speak to Tromell outside the door that won't open. You can now go inside the house that has been locked throughout the entire game and speak to a Guado youth. If you previously advised Lian and Ayde on the Thunder Plains, he will speak of meeting them and turn over the **Tempered Will Garment Grid**. In a chest inside this room is **Baralai's Sphere**. Return to the Celsius and speak with Shinra to view the sphere, which contains some rather shocking revelations about the praetor.

*The Guado are finally ready to share their long-kept secrets.*

## A GIFT LEFT BY TOBLI

Inside Tobli's house, a chest contains a valuable item. The item in the chest changes depending on whether you completed all of the missions at the Moonflow perfectly, and whether you defeated Garik at Mt. Gagazet during Chapter 3. If you did not complete the mission at Gagazet during Chapter 3, but successfully competed all the Moonflow missions, the item will be the **Key to Success** accessory. If you completed the Ronso Youth uprising mission as well as all the moonflow missions, the item will be a **Kaiser Knuckles** accessory. If you defeated Garik but did not complete the Moonflow missions perfectly, the item will be a **Crystal Ball**. The Key to Success is one of the best accessories in the game, which may make you question your decision to suppress the Ronso Youth uprising.

*The item found at Tobli's house changes depending on your actions at the Moonflow and Mt. Gagazet.*

## GUADOSALAM ITEM SHOP (CHAPTER 5)

| ITEM | COST |
|---|---|
| Potion | 50 |
| Antidote | 50 |
| Eye Drops | 50 |
| Echo Screen | 50 |
| Soft | 50 |
| Holy Water | 300 |
| Pearl Necklace | 4000 |
| Favorite Outfit | 4000 |
| Angel Earrings | 5000 |
| Gold Anklet | 5000 |
| Mute Shock | 15000 |
| Dream Shock | 15000 |
| Blind Shock | 15000 |
| Venom Shock | 15000 |

Characters

1

Garment Grids & Dresspheres

2

Battle System

3

Accessories

4

Items and Item Shops

5

Walkthrough 6
Chapter 1
Chapter 2
Chapter 3
Chapter 4
Chapter 5

Mini-Games

7

Fiends and Enemies

8

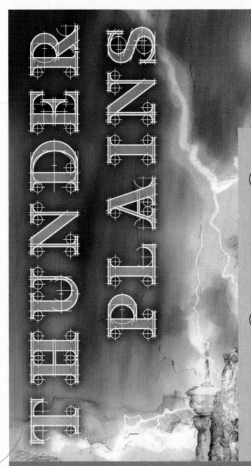
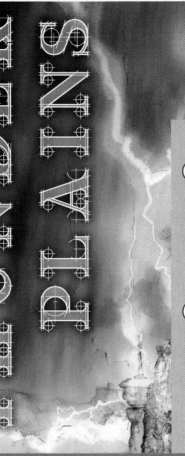
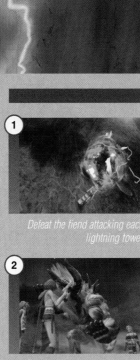

# THUNDER PLAINS

## ACTION CHECKLIST

**1**

Defeat the fiend attacking each lightning tower.

**3**

Find Cid in the secret cave.

**5**

Talk to Cid on the airship's Deck.

**2**

Survive the Humbaba's assault.

**4**

Defeat the Machina Panzer, which has been studying your moves.

**6**

Return to the Bridge to watch the confrontation between Cid and Brother.

**COMPLETION: +1.0%**

## WANDERING FIENDS

**AKA MANAH**
HP: 6322 | AP: 1 | Gil: 670
Steal: Remedy (x2)
Drop: Pretty Orb

**ANOLE**
HP: 734 | AP: 1 | Gil: 70
Steal: Hi-Potion
Drop: Hi-Potion

**ARCHAEOTHYRIS**
HP: 1332 | AP: 1 | Gil: 110
Steal: Eye Drops (x2)
Drop: Eye Drops (x2)

**ARMET**
HP: 788 | AP: 1 | Gil: 74
Steal: Lunar Curtain
Drop: Light Curtain

**ASSASSIN BEE**
HP: 233 | AP: 1 | Gil: 48
Steal: Antidote
Drop: Antidote

**BALIVARHA**
HP: 3688 | AP: 1 | Gil: 230
Steal: Hi-Potion (x2)
Drop: Fire Gem

**BARBUTA**
HP: 562 | AP: 1 | Gil: 33
Steal: Lunar Curtain
Drop: Light Curtain

**BLUE ELEMENTAL**
HP: 363 | AP: 1 | Gil: 180
Steal: Dragon Scale
Drop: Dragon Scale

**BOLT DRAKE**
HP: 623 | AP: 1 | Gil: 130
Steal: Lightning Marble
Drop: Hi-Potion

**CHOCOBO**
HP: 3890 | AP: 0 | Gil: 0
Steal: None
Drop: None

**FLAN ROJO**
HP: 1220 | AP: 1 | Gil: 125
Steal: Bomb Core
Drop: Bomb Core

**GEMINI**
HP: 2044 | AP: 1 | Gil: 153
Steal: Lunar Curtain (x2)
Drop: Light Curtain (x2)

**GIGAS**
HP: 2290 | AP: 1 | Gil: 180
Steal: Hi-Potion
Drop: None

**IRONSIDE**
HP: 8432 | AP: 1 | Gil: 200
Steal: Shadow Gem (x2)
Drop: Stamina Tablet

**MALBORO**
HP: 5877 | AP: 1 | Gil: 370
Steal: Hi-Potion
Drop: Remedy (x2)

**RHYOS**
HP: 4360 | AP: 1 | Gil: 310
Steal: Lightning Gem
Drop: Lightning Gem

**SPINE DRAKE**
HP: 2582 | AP: 1, | Gil: 127
Steal: Arctic Wind
Drop: Arctic Wind

**TAROMAITI**
HP: 1782 | AP: 1 | Gil: 280
Steal: Antidote (x2)
Drop: Star Pendant

**VARAN**
HP: 1132 | AP: 1 | Gil: 240
Steal: Dispel Tonic
Drop: Holy Water

**WATCHER-A***
HP: 624 | AP: 1 | Gil: 0
Steal: Potion
Drop: Potion

**WATCHER-R***
HP: 620 | AP: 1 | Gil: 0
Steal: Potion
Drop: Potion

**WATCHER-S***
HP: 620 | AP: 1 | Gil: 0
Steal: Potion
Drop: Potion

**ASSAULT MACHINA**
HP: 4477 | AP: 1 | Gil: 180
Steal: M-Bomb
Drop: Silence Grenade

**KILLER MACHINA**
HP: 4222 | AP: 1 | Gil: 180
Steal: M-Bomb
Drop: Darkness Grenade

**MACHINA LEADER**
HP: 2774 | AP: 1 | Gil: 120
Steal: S-Bomb
Drop: Sleep Grenade

**MACHINA SOLDIER**
HP: 3048 | AP: 1 | Gil: 120
Steal: S-Bomb
Drop: Sleep Grenade

**MACHINA STRIKER**
HP: 6722 | AP: 1 | Gil: 400
Steal: L-Bomb
Drop: L-Bomb (x3)

**HUMBABA**
HP: 27772 | AP: 1 | Gil: 550
Steal: Hi-Potion (x2)
Drop: Hi-Potion (x4)

**MACHINA PANZER**
HP: 30500 | AP: 10 | Gil: 10000
Steal: Oath Veil
Drop: Crystal Bangle

***Appears before defeating the Machina Panzer boss at Thunder Plains.**

Characters

1

Garment Grids & Dresspheres

2

Battle System

3

Accessories

4

Items and Item Shops

5

Walkthrough
Chapter 1
Chapter 2
Chapter 3
Chapter 4
Chapter 5

Mini-Games

7

Fiends and Enemies

8

## ITEM CHECKLIST

Remedy
X-Potion (x2)
Ochre Ring
Budget Grenade (x2)
Turbo Ether (x2)

Sleep Grenade (x2)
Valiant Lustre Garment Grid **E**
Diamond Gloves
Hyper Wrist
Mystery Veil

Talisman
Corpus Invictus
Nature's Lore
Salvation Promised Garment Grid
Force of Nature

## MAPS

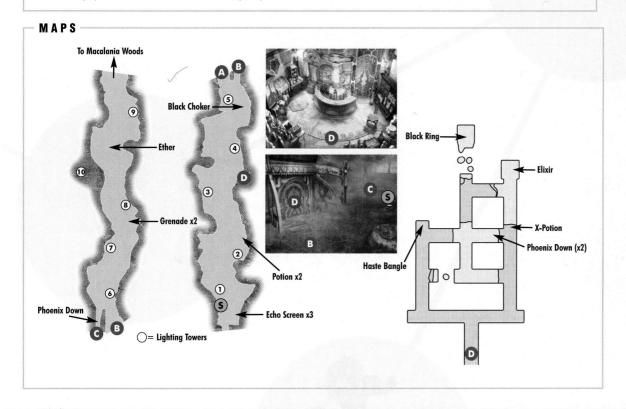

# CALIBRATION CRISIS

Fiends are attacking the lightning towers on the Thunder Plains. To complete this mission, run up to each Rhyos and engage it in battle. After defeating each creature, a treasure chest appears next to its corresponding lightning tower. The content of each chest depends on your highest score in calibrating each lightning tower during Chapters 2 and 3. For example, when you defeat the Rhyos near tower 1, the item is an Elixir if you managed to calibrate the tower with a score of 30. If your highest score is 5, you only receive an Ether. Use the table to determine what prizes are available for each chest.

*It's time to reap the rewards of your efforts in calibrating those towers.*

### LIGHTNING TOWER ITEMS FOUND IN CHESTS LEFT BY RHYOS ENEMIES

| TOWER | PRIZES PER NUMBER OF CALIBRATIONS | | | | |
|---|---|---|---|---|---|
| | 0 – 5 | 6 – 14 | 15 – 24 | 25 – 29 | 30 |
| 1 | Ether | Ether (x2) | Turbo Ether | Turbo Ether (x2) | Elixir |
| 2 | X-Potion | Mega-Potion (x2) | Elixir | Elixir | Megalixir |
| 3 | Mega Phoenix | Mega Phoenix | Elixir | Elixir | Megalixir |
| 4 | Power Wrist | Black Belt | Hyper Wrist | Power Glove | Champion Belt |
| 5 | Silver Bracer | Hypno Crown | Gold Bracer | Pixie Dust | Regal Crown |
| 6 | Yellow Ring | Lightning Gleam | NulShock Ring | Ochre Ring | Electrocutioner |
| 7 | Blue Ring | Watery Gleam | NulTide Ring | Cerulean Ring | Short Circuit |
| 8 | Red Ring | Fiery Gleam | NulBlaze Ring | Crimson Ring | Freezerburn |
| 9 | White Ring | Icy Gleam | NulFrost Ring | Snow Ring | Sublimator |
| 10 | Tetra Band | Tetra Gloves | Tetra Guard | Tetra Bracelet | Ribbon |

# LEADER OF THE PACK

When you've defeated the enemies standing next to nine of the lightning towers, the girls notice that the lighting continues to strike. There's a tenth tower across a stream on the west side of the north plains area (Tower 10 from the calibration mini-game). Run back toward the Travel Agency, moving along the west side of the area, until the Gullwings notice the tower they haven't checked yet. Make sure the party is at full HP and MP and ready to fight before checking out this tower, because a powerful boss protects it.

Move toward the red arrow on the on-screen map to locate the tenth tower.

## HUMBABA    BOSS FIGHT

The key to victory in this battle is to have one character as a White Mage and use that party member to heal, while the others use Black Mage spells or special attacks to damage the boss. A White Mage will probably need to equip an item that raises her MP substantially. Have the White Mage cast Protect and Shell to reduce both physical and magical damage. Cast Cure type spells as necessary to keep the party going. Whenever the Humbaba casts Mighty Guard, cast Dispel to remove a few of the positive effects the creature has given itself. Use Ethers as needed to keep your White Mage casting spells throughout the battle.

HP: 27772    MP: 785    EXP: 1800    AP: 1

**GIL DROPPED:** 550
**PILFER GIL:** 1800

**STEAL:** Normal: Hi-Potion (x2)    Rare: Ether
**DROP:** Normal: Hi-Potion (x4)    Rare: NulShock Ring

While your White Mage keeps everyone healthy, you'll need two characters who can cause heavy damage to the boss in spite of its raised defense. A Dark Knight and a Gunner can damage the Humbaba significantly with their Darkness and Cheap Shot abilities, respectively. Avoid the use of lightning attacks, which the fiend likes to absorb to replenish its HP. The important part of this battle is to keep everyone's HP as high as possible. When the Humbaba dies, it attempts to take your party with it by casting Meteor. If your party members' HP are low, they might die at the end of the battle.

# SECRET CAVE OF THE THUNDER PLAINS

Following the boss fight, a hole appears at the base of one of the lightning towers and an Al Bhed offers to take you into the hole. This leads to a secret cave below the Thunder Plains. First, grab the item from the chest that the Humbaba left behind, equip all your characters to protect them from Poison and Thunder magic, and then speak to the Al Bhed again.

Follow the red arrow on the on-screen map to Cid's location.

If you previously spoke to Cid at Zanarkand during Chapter 1 and told him that you were unhappy with his new business, then spoke to him again on the Thunder Plains, Cid will be in the cave. His position is represented on the on-screen map by a red arrow. Move down the long passage to the first opening on the right, and follow that passage south to the very bottom of the area. Head east and go up the next passage on the left to find Cid. Unfortunately, he is being stalked by a very powerful foe. Upon defeating this powerful foe, you receive an Episode Complete!

An Al Bhed offers to deliver you to the strange new hole that has opened on the Thunder Plains.

# MACHINA PANZER

The three Watchers appearing with the boss act as informants, relaying the information they've observed during your battles all across Spira. Using this info, the enemies will lock up your abilities to prevent you from using special attacks and abilities. The Machina Panzer will then mimic these abilities and use them to defeat your party. Watcher-A will lock any attack abilities used during battles, while Watcher-R will lock up any recovery abilities used when it was present in any battle, and Watcher-S will lock up special attacks used while it was present. However, if you maintained a steady habit of eliminating Watcher enemies first in every battle, they will have little to report and you will have an easier time using your abilities without fear of the Machina Panzer locking and mimicking them. Even if one of the Watchers can lock an action, just defeat it quickly before it gets a chance to report and scramble your abilities.

HP: 30500  MP: 1247  EXP: 4300  AP: 10

**GIL DROPPED:** 10000
**PILFER GIL:** 2500
**STEAL:** Normal: Oath Veil   Rare: Oath Veil
**DROP:** Normal: Crystal Bangle   Rare: Crystal Bangle

Even alone, without any abilities to mimic, the Machina Panzer is no slouch. Its "Gatling Gun" and "Sorcery Ray" attacks force you to heal the entire party frequently, and it will recover HP if lightning magic is used on it. The boss can be afflicted with the Slow status, so have a Songstress use the Slow Dance ability every turn. Otherwise, you should be able to strike this boss swiftly with your strongest spells.

# THUNDER PLAINS PUZZLE CAVERN

Now that you've rescued Cid, the secret cave at the Thunder Plains features a challenging puzzle. As you've probably noticed, the cave is full of tough machina and random encounters occur quite often. The cave is a place where you can level up your characters and learn abilities in no time. However, while attempting to solve the puzzle, it is in your best interests to equip a Charm Bangle to prevent random encounters. Not only will this enable you to maintain a stronger concentration, but it will also make the puzzle easier to solve.

Make notes of the key numbers provided throughout this maze.

You can only open one of the chests that appear. With any luck, the chest you choose will open the next door.

Get something to write on, because you'll need to remember and add up a lot of numbers. Upon entering the cave, a brief explanation follows. The first of many key numbers appears in the lower-right corner of the screen. The top number in yellow indicates the number of the next secret door where you can use the key number. The number in white is the first of two key numbers that you must add together to determine the password for the secret door. Make a note of the door number and the key number, because you may be asked for this information later. After the key number disappears, two chests appear. You can only open one of the chests and then both will disappear. Opening the chest either reveals a helpful hint, opens the next door, or does nothing.

After viewing a key number, the secret door that you can use it on is highlighted on the on-screen map with a red arrow. Proceed to the secret door and examine it. More key numbers will appear on-screen. This time, the key number in the upper-left corner is the second key number for the door you are standing in front of. You must add the first and second key numbers to determine the passcode. In the bottom-right corner, the first key number for the next door you can open appears. Jot down the key number, as well as the number of the door it opens. Now add the first key number and the second key number together and input the sum to open the door. Be sure to jot down the sum total before proceeding, because you may be asked for this information to open another door.

Add the two key numbers together, and input the sum when examining the proper door.

When you open a secret door, two chests appear. Again, you can open one of the chests for a chance to obtain a helpful hint or even open the next door. If you're lucky enough to open the next secret door, the passcode that would have opened the door is displayed. Make a note of this number, because you may be asked to use it to open another door somewhere else.

Characters 1

Garment Grids & Dresspheres 2

Battle System 3

Accessories 4

Items and Item Shops 5

Walkthrough 6
Chapter 1
Chapter 2
Chapter 3
Chapter 4
Chapter 5

Mini-Games

7

Fiends and Enemies

8

Sometimes when a key number is displayed, it will appear as a math problem such as $56732 + 4532$. You must add these two numbers together, then add the second key number(s) to these to open the next door. Sometimes the key numbers will not be displayed as integers. Instead of the key number, you may receive a clue such as "Amount of gil earned between entry and door 10" or "Number of battles since entry." These numbers can be looked up on the special walls in the three corners of the maze. The wall in the northeast corner keeps a record of how much gil you've earned from random battles since entering the maze. The wall in the southeast corner keeps track of the codes of every door you've opened thus far, and the one in the southwest corner keeps track of the number of battles you've fought since opening each door. However, if you enter the maze with a Charm Bangle equipped to prevent battles, then the amount of gil and the number of battles fought will always be 0. This is the best way to approach this puzzle, since it means there will be fewer numbers to remember.

Use the special walls at the four corners of the maze to track your progress.

Once you open all 16 doors, exit the cave and return for a second round. When you solve this puzzle twice, a chest appears in the north corridor that contains the **Force of Nature** accessory.

# MACALANIA WOODS

### ACTION CHECKLIST

**1** The Guado who sought shelter in these woods have returned home to Guadosalam.

*Speak to the last remaining Guado in Macalania Woods.*

**2** *Make one last visit to the spring across from the entrance to Bevelle.*

**3** *Stop by the Travel Agency near the lake to see if O'aka is back at home.*

COMPLETION: +0.6%

## WANDERING FIENDS

**AMORPHOUS GEL**
HP: 973 | AP: 1 | Gil: 380
Steal: White Ring
Drop: Blue Ring

**BARBUTA**
HP: 562 | AP: 1 | Gil: 33
Steal: Lunar Curtain
Drop: Light Curtain

**BLUE ELEMENTAL**
HP: 363 | AP: 1 | Gil: 180
Steal: Dragon Scale
Drop: Dragon Scale

**CHOCOBO**
HP: 3890 | AP: 0 | Gil: 0
Steal: None
Drop: None

**DEEP HAIZHE**
HP: 1030 | AP: 1 | Gil: 40
Steal: Gold Anklet
Drop: Hi-Potion

**DINICTUS**
HP: 1873 | AP: 1 | Gil: 88
Steal: Water Gem
Drop: Water Gem

**FLAN BLANCO**
HP: 625 | AP: 1 | Gil: 72
Steal: Arctic Wind
Drop: Arctic Wind

**LICH**
HP: 3444 | AP: 1 | Gil: 330
Steal: Hi-Potion
Drop: None

**PROTEAN GEL**
HP: 6680 | AP: 1 | Gil: 380
Steal: Blue Ring
Drop: White Ring

**TAROMAITI**
HP: 1782 | AP: 1 | Gil: 280
Steal: Antidote (x2)
Drop: Star Pendant

**TENTACLES**
HP: 2530 | AP: 1 | Gil: 95
Steal: Phoenix Down
Drop: Phoenix Down

**VARAN**
HP: 1132 | AP: 1 | Gil: 240
Steal: Dispel Tonic
Drop: Holy Water

**WATCHER-A***
HP: 624 | AP: 1 | Gil: 0
Steal: Potion
Drop: Potion

**WATCHER-R***
HP: 620 | AP: 1 | Gil: 0
Steal: Potion
Drop: Potion

**WATCHER-S***
HP: 620 | AP: 1 | Gil: 0
Steal: Potion
Drop: Potion

***Appears before defeating the Machina Panzer boss at Thunder Plains.**

Characters

1

Garment Grids & Dresspheres

2

Battle System

3

Accessories

4

Items and Item Shops

5

Walkthrough

Chapter 1
Chapter 2
Chapter 3
Chapter 4
Chapter 5

Mini-Games

7

Fiends and Enemies

8

## ITEM CHECKLIST

Snow Ring

Rune Bracer

Ray of Hope Garment Grid

Elixir

## MAPS

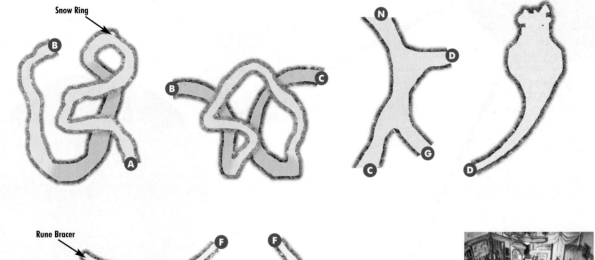

Snow Ring

Rune Bracer

To Bevelle

To Thunder Plains

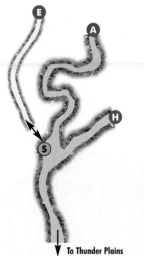

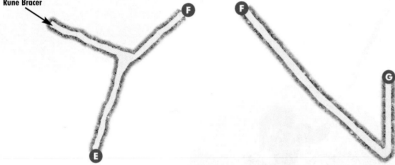

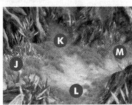

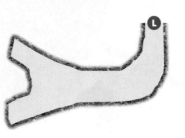

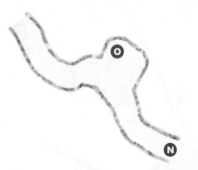

# THE FADING WOODS

Return to the Sphere Spring, where your first meeting with Tromell took place. If you previously completed the missions to defeat Garik Ronso and to gather the musicians of Macalania, only a lone Guado will be standing off to the left at the rear of the area. Speak to this person to trigger an event, then head back to the entrance of the forest, continue east, and visit the other spring. Yuna asks for a moment alone, and then you'll receive an Episode Complete! and the **Ray of Hope Garment Grid**.

Find the last remaining Guado in the forest to trigger the first of the last two events.

# O'AKA'S TRIUMPHANT RETURN

A second "Episode Complete!" is available at Macalania. If you previously rescued O'aka from debt or from his servitude in the Bikanel Desert, he will appear outside the Travel Agency with his brother. After the two argue, you'll receive an Episode Complete! Open the nearby chest for an **Elixir**, then head inside to view the awesome accessories now sold by O'aka. If anyone in Spira has a better list of items, it is probably Wantz. Each man offers a different list of items when you speak with them. Return here as soon as you have enough gil to purchase these awesome accessories!

Looks like O'aka's back in business.

| MACALANIA LAKE TRAVEL AGENCY (SPEAK TO WANTZ) | |
|---|---|
| ITEM | COST |
| Faerie Earrings | 10000 |
| Kinesis Badge | 10000 |
| Safety Bit | 10000 |
| Beaded Brooch | 10000 |
| Crimson Ring | 10000 |
| Snow Ring | 10000 |
| Ochre Ring | 10000 |
| Cerulean Ring | 10000 |
| Chaos Shock | 15000 |
| Fury Shock | 15000 |
| Lag Shock | 15000 |
| System Shock | 15000 |

| MACALANIA LAKE TRAVEL AGENCY (SPEAK TO O'AKA) | |
|---|---|
| ITEM | COST |
| Faerie Earrings | 10000 |
| Kinesis Badge | 10000 |
| Safety Bit | 10000 |
| Sword Lore | 50000 |
| Bushido Lore | 50000 |
| Arcane Lore | 50000 |
| Nature's Lore | 50000 |
| Black Lore | 50000 |
| White Lore | 50000 |
| Crimson Ring | 10000 |
| Snow Ring | 10000 |
| Ochre Ring | 10000 |
| Cerulean Ring | 10000 |

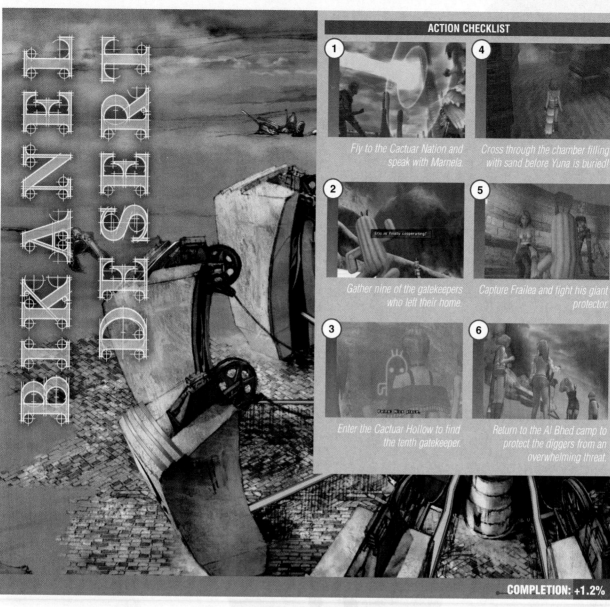

# BIKANEL DESERT

Characters

1

Garment Grids & D!spheres

2

Battle System

3

Accessories

4

Items and Item Shops

5

Walkthrough

Chapter 1

Chapter 2

Chapter 3

Chapter 4

**Chapter 5**

Mini-Games

7

Fiends and Enemies

8

## ACTION CHECKLIST

**1** Fly to the Cactuar Nation and speak with Marnela.

**2** Gather nine of the gatekeepers who left their home.

**3** Enter the Cactuar Hollow to find the tenth gatekeeper.

**4** Cross through the chamber filling with sand before Yuna is buried!

**5** Capture Frailea and fight his giant protector.

**6** Return to the Al Bhed camp to protect the diggers from an overwhelming threat.

COMPLETION: +1.2%

## WANDERING FIENDS

**ACULEATE**
HP: 776 | AP: 1 | Gil: 72
Steal: Echo Screen (x2)
Drop: Echo Screen (x2)

**AQUILA**
HP: 1897 | AP: 1 | Gil: 55
Steal: Hi-Potion
Drop: Hi-Potion

**BIG BULLY CAP**
HP: 4880 | AP: 1 | Gil: 48
Steal: Black Choker
Drop: Remedy

**BOLT DRAKE**
HP: 623 | AP: 1 | Gil: 130
Steal: Lightning Marble
Drop: Hi-Potion

**BULLY CAP**
HP: 94 | AP: 1 | Gil: 14
Steal: Eye Drops
Drop: Eye Drops

**CACTUAR**
HP: 2002 | AP: 2 | Gil: 0
Steal: None
Drop: None

**CANIS MAJOR**
HP: 943 | AP: 1 | Gil: 67
Steal: Hi-Potion
Drop: Hi-Potion

**CHOCOBO**
HP: 3890 | AP: 0 | Gil: 0
Steal: None
Drop: None

**ELDER ZURVAN**
HP: 7520 | AP: 1 | Gil: 180
Steal: Remedy
Drop: Holy Water (x2)

**FLY EYE**
HP: 258 | AP: 1 | Gil: 20
Steal: Phoenix Down
Drop: Phoenix Down

**GIGAS**
HP: 2290 | AP: 1 | Gil: 180
Steal: Hi-Potion
Drop: None

**GREAT HAUNT**
HP: 8483 | AP: 1 | Gil: 210
Steal: Mana Spring
Drop: Ether

**GUCUMATZ**
HP: 3720 | AP: 1 | Gil: 173
Steal: Soft (x2)
Drop: Soft (x2)

**GUARD MACHINA**
HP: 2460 | AP: 1 | Gil: 40
Steal: Budget Grenade
Drop: Budget Grenade

**HAUNT**
HP: 813 | AP: 1 | Gil: 120
Steal: Arctic Wind
Drop: Water Ring

**HEAVY SALLET**
HP: 11200 | AP: 1 | Gil: 110
Steal: Lunar Curtain x2
Drop: Light Curtain (x2)

**HRIMTHUR**
HP: 552 | AP: 1 | Gil: 44
Steal: Phoenix Down
Drop: Phoenix Down

**KILLER HOUND**
HP: 202 | AP: 1 | Gil: 18
Steal: Potion
Drop: Potion

**KING TAKOUBA**
HP: 18004 | AP: 1 | Gil: 300
Steal: Star Pendant
Drop: Farplane Shadow (x2)

**MACHINA HUNTER**
HP: 1780 | AP: 1 | Gil: 30
Steal: Budget Grenade
Drop: Budget Grenade

**POP FRY**
HP: 4293 | AP: 1 | Gil: 100
Steal: Sleep Grenade
Drop: Sleep Grenade

**SAHAGIN**
HP: 60 | AP: 1 | Gil: 7
Steal: Potion
Drop: Potion

**SAHAGIN PRINCE**
HP: 6430 | AP: 1 | Gil: 105
Steal: Phoenix Down (x2)
Drop: Hi-Potion (x2)

**SALLET**
HP: 60 | AP: 1 | Gil: 10
Steal: Potion
Drop: Potion

## WANDERING FIENDS CONTINUED

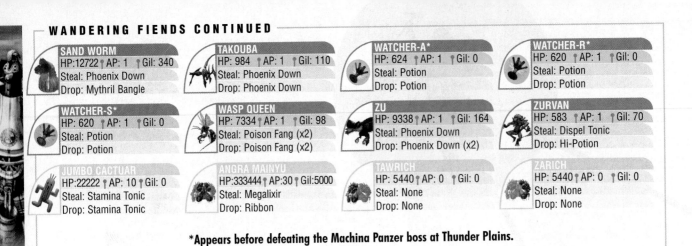

**SAND WORM**
HP:12722 AP: 1 Gil: 340
Steal: Phoenix Down
Drop: Mythril Bangle

**TAKOUBA**
HP: 984 AP: 1 Gil: 110
Steal: Phoenix Down
Drop: Phoenix Down

**WATCHER-A\***
HP: 624 AP: 1 Gil: 0
Steal: Potion
Drop: Potion

**WATCHER-R\***
HP: 620 AP: 1 Gil: 0
Steal: Potion
Drop: Potion

**WATCHER-S\***
HP: 620 AP: 1 Gil: 0
Steal: Potion
Drop: Potion

**WASP QUEEN**
HP: 7334 AP: 1 Gil: 98
Steal: Poison Fang (x2)
Drop: Poison Fang (x2)

**ZU**
HP: 9338 AP: 1 Gil: 164
Steal: Phoenix Down
Drop: Phoenix Down (x2)

**ZURVAN**
HP: 583 AP: 1 Gil: 70
Steal: Dispel Tonic
Drop: Hi-Potion

**JUMBO CACTUAR**
HP: 22222 AP: 10 Gil: 0
Steal: Stamina Tonic
Drop: Stamina Tonic

**ANGRA MAINYU**
HP:333444 AP:30 Gil:5000
Steal: Megalixir
Drop: Ribbon

**TAWRICH**
HP: 5440 AP: 0 Gil: 0
Steal: None
Drop: None

**ZARICH**
HP: 5440 AP: 0 Gil: 0
Steal: None
Drop: None

**\*Appears before defeating the Machina Panzer boss at Thunder Plains.**

## ITEM CHECKLIST

| | | | |
|---|---|---|---|
| Ether | Hi-Potion | Twist Headband | Phoenix Down |
| Faerie Earrings | Megalixir | Mute Shock | Mercurial Strike Garment Grid 🄴 |
| Mega-Phoenix | Ether | Beaded Brooch | |

## MAPS

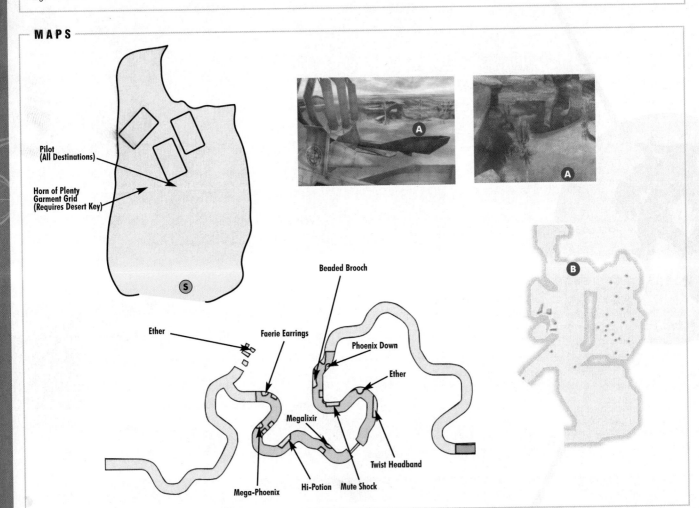

Pilot
(All Destinations)

Horn of Plenty
Garment Grid
(Requires Desert Key)

Ⓢ

Ⓐ

Ⓐ

Ⓑ

Beaded Brooch

Ether

Faerie Earrings

Phoenix Down

Ether

Megalixir

Twist Headband

Mega-Phoenix    Hi-Potion    Mute Shock

# DESERT TURMOIL

Benzo and Nhadala greet the group, then the action shifts immediately to the Cactuar Nation, where hundreds of fiends threaten to attack. To protect the Cactuar Nation, you must gather the 10 Gatekeepers hiding across Spira. To find a gatekeeper, speak to its mother. You can only speak to a gatekeeper's mother when she is awake, indicated by a green swirling around the cactus as well as a green dot on the map. The cactus will divulge clues to where her children are, and then you can set out across Spira to find them.

*Speak to the active mothers to learn clues regarding the cactuars' whereabouts.*

# TO CAPTURE A CACTUAR

Once you find a cactuar, you must complete a short "Cact-War" mini-game to make the little creature go with you. During the mini-game, the screen switches to split-focus. The picture on the left will shift between the cactuar and its two sidekicks. You must wait until the cactuar appears on-screen before you fire. Even then, a cactuar may be agile enough to dodge your shot. Sometimes the left picture will switch focus so rapidly that you must actually fire your shot when you see the sidekick right before the cactuar. If you hit a cactuar, you then have a chance to chain together additional hits by firing rapidly. Doing so enables you to rack up higher scores. If you hit one of the cactuar's sidekicks by accident, the bullet used will be subtracted from your remaining stockpile. If you are hit by the cactuar's counterattack, you will lose ammo from your current stockpile.

Cact-war is a challenging, but fun mini-game. You'll get additional chances to play it after you complete the "Ten Gatekeepers" quest.

Sometimes a cactuar will react to being shot, and it will fire its needles at Yuna. Press and hold the R1 button to dodge this attack. If you fail to dodge the cactuar's attacks, ammo will be subtracted from your stockpile. Each shot reduces the cactuar's HP by one point. If you manage to reduce the cactuar's HP to zero before running out of ammunition, you win. If you run out of ammo and the cactuar still has HP, then you lose. Either way, the cactuar will still come back to the Cactuar Nation with you. Note that in the case of Bartschella, the last of the gatekeepers exploring Spira, the two sidekicks are Magic Pots, as seen in *FINAL FANTASY X*. If you shoot one of the Magic Pots, you'll receive random items.

Once you have convinced a gatekeeper to return to the Cactuar Nation, fly back and speak to the cactuar's mother again. A new cactus will awaken and divulge clues to the location of the next gatekeeper. The 10 Gatekeepers become available to find in a specific order, and once you get the clue from their mothers, they are located in the following places:

| GATEKEEPER LOCATIONS | | | |
|---|---|---|---|
| **NO.** | **NAME** | **LOCATION** | |
| 1 | Lobivia | Bikanel Desert, Oasis | |
| 2 | Toumeya | Besaid Island, Beach | |
| 3 | Lobeira | Guadosalam Chateau, Ormi's Room | |
| 4&5 | Areg & Arroja | Calm Lands, Gagazet Entrance | |
| 6 | Islaya | Thunder Plains North, Near Tower 9 | |
| 7 | Chiapa | Kilika Island, Hidden Overlook | |
| 8 | Erio | Mt. Gagazet, Summit | |
| 9 | Bartschella | Kilika Port, Dona's House | |

Characters

Garment Grids & Dresspheres

Battle System

Accessories

Items and Item Shops

Walkthrough
Chapter 1
Chapter 2
Chapter 3
Chapter 4
Chapter 5

Mini-Games

Fiends and Enemies

# CACTUAR HOLLOW

When you have found the nine cactuars, return to the Cactuar Nation. The tenth gatekeeper in Cactuar Hollow is located at the top of the area. Proceed through the cave until you have what appears to be a randomly occurring battle. Afterwards, the Cactuars will revive and enlarge one of the monsters from your previous battle, and you must fight it again. Hereafter, the cave will be full of oversized versions of previous enemies to fight.

*A Gun Mage that has learned all the Fiend Hunter abilities will prove to be an amazing asset during these battles.*

*Race through the sands a few times to collect items, then dash through in one clear run to reach the other side.*

Proceed through the cavern and jump up the platforms near the waterfalls to obtain an **Ether**. Continue east through the passage until the chamber begins to fill with sand. You must collect the items and race through the area to the second concrete path on the other side. To obtain all the items, you must make several attempts. On your final attempt, run through the sand and reach the opposite end before Yuna is buried again. Continue from there to the end of the cave, where the tenth gatekeeper sits all alone on the ledge. After a final shootout with Frailea, the rogue cactuars unite to form a Jumbo Cactuar, and attempt to stop you from taking their friend.

## JUMBO CACTUAR, CACTUAR (X2)

BOSS FIGHT

**HP:** 22222  **MP:** 1111  **EXP:** 0  **AP:** 10

| GIL DROPPED: 0 | STEAL: | Normal: Stamina Tonic | Rare: Stamina Tonic (x2) |
| PILFER GIL: 0 | DROP: | Normal: Stamina Tonic | Rare: Rabite's Foot |

**HP:** 2002  **MP:** 120  **EXP:** 0  **AP:** 0

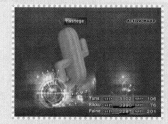

As you've probably observed while fighting in the Cactuar Hollow, these are very odd creatures to meet in combat. They offer little benefit in combat, deal exactly 1000 HP damage with their 1000 Needles attack, and oftentimes flee if the average level of the party exceeds theirs. Following in this backwards tradition, the Jumbo Cactuar seems content to do almost nothing during the battle, except casting Hastega on itself and the little cactuars. The smaller foes are the ones you really have to worry about. You'll need exceptional Accuracy to strike a Cactuar, so use special attacks like a Dark Knight's Darkness ability, and Black Mage's spells. Eliminate the two Cactuars as soon as possible, then pummel the Jumbo Cactuar at your leisure while it does… nothing. If you're unfortunate enough to kill 10 cactuars before reaching the Jumbo Cactuar (of if one of the sidekicks turns out to be the tenth), then you're in for a tougher battle with the Jumbo Cactuar's oversouled form, which uses "ga-level" magic and Flare.

| GIL DROPPED: 120 | STEAL: | Normal: None | Rare: None |
| PILFER GIL: 180 | DROP: | Normal: None | Rare: None |

# THE ANCIENT POWER

Although the threat to the Cactuar Nation has been thwarted, the desert fiend from before is now attacking the Al Bhed camp. After speaking to Nhadala, you're offered a chance to return to the airship to purchase items and equip your characters properly. Rescuing the diggers' camp means facing off against one of the toughest fiends in the game. However, once you defeat Angra Mainyu, you'll finally receive the "Episode Complete!" from Bikanel Desert.

*Nhadala and company are in trouble, and you will be too if you don't prepare adequately for the coming fight.*

# ANGRA MAINYU, TAWRICH, ZARICH

HP: 333444  MP: 9999  EXP: 5000  AP: 30

**GIL DROPPED:** 5000  **STEAL:** Normal: Megalixer  Rare: Megalixer
**PILFER GIL:** 2000  **DROP:** Normal: Ribbon  Rare: Ribbon

Equip all of your characters with accessories that enable automatic Protect and automatic Reflect, or at least the ability to cast either spell. Consider having two of your characters as Dark Knights and one as an Alchemist. Mastery of these dresspheres is not required. For the benefit of the Alchemist, enter the battle with 99 Potions and 99 Hi-Potions. Even then, make sure your Alchemist knows the Mega-Potion Stash ability. It would also be wise to equip the Alchemist with Garment Grids or accessories that bestow abilities such as Auto-Haste, SOS Haste, or the ability to cast Haste. Additionally, equip accessories or Garment Grids so that a character can perform White Mage abilities—especially Reflect.

HP: 5440  MP: 9999  EXP: 0  AP: 0

**GIL DROPPED:** 0  **STEAL:** Normal: None  Rare: None
**PILFER GIL:** 0  **DROP:** Normal: None  Rare: None

HP: 5440  MP: 9999  EXP: 0  AP: 0

**GIL DROPPED:** 0  **STEAL:** Normal: None  Rare: None
**PILFER GIL:** 0  **DROP:** Normal: None  Rare: None

Start the battle by casting Reflect and Protect on your characters as needed. The two Dark Knights should perform Darkness every round, while the Alchemist mixes a Potion and a Hi-Potion to achieve the effect of a Mega-Potion. Even if the party seems to be doing all right, mix the Mega-Potion anyway. The party must stay healthy every round, just in case Angra Mainyu performs Perdition's Flame, a devastating multi-attack that can cause up to 4000 HP damage to each character. Performing Darkness every turn, the two Dark Knights should be able to keep the sidekicks, Tawrich and Zarich, KO'ed for most of the battle. Angra Mainyu cannot perform Perdition's Flame unless the two sidekicks are alive.

While Tawrich and Zarich are inactive, Angra Mainyu must waste turns to cast Full-Life on its helpers, so cast Darkness even if the two side helpers are dead for the moment. Zarich has the ability to drain MP, so it will be difficult to cast spells for any purpose other than to reinstate Protect or Reflect spells. While Protect will reduce damage from Perdition's Flame, Reflect will protect your character from Flare spells that can cause 9999 HP damage. In fact, Reflect will bounce the spell back at Angra Mainyu, causing 9999 HP damage to the boss! Even if your characters are around level 70, winning against this boss can take a long time.

Characters

1

Garment Grids & Dresspheres

2

Battle System

3

Accessories

4

Items and Item Shops

5

**Walkthrough**
Chapter 1
Chapter 2
Chapter 3
Chapter 4
**Chapter 5**

Mini-Games

7

Fiends and Enemies

8

# BEVELLE

## ACTION CHECKLIST

**1**

View the changing of the guard in Bevelle.

**COMPLETION: +1.8%**

## WANDERING FIENDS

**BARONG**
HP: 2733 AP: 1 Gil: 138
Steal: Phoenix Down
Drop: Antidote

**DETONATOR**
HP: 1860 AP: 1 Gil: 98
Steal: Bomb Core
Drop: Bomb Core

**FLAN BLANCO**
HP: 625 AP: 1 Gil: 72
Steal: Arctic Wind
Drop: Arctic Wind

**GEORAPELLA**
HP: 4420 AP: 1 Gil:1000
Steal: Water Gem
Drop: NulTide Ring

**PRECEPTS GUARD**
HP: 3680 AP: 1 Gil: 800
Steal: Mana Tablet
Drop: Regen Ring

**SKINK**
HP: 882 AP: 1 Gil: 78
Steal: Hi-Potion
Drop: Hi-Potion

**YAC-62**
HP: 4100 AP: 1 Gil: 94
Steal: Darkness Grenade
Drop: Sleep Grenade

**YAU-71**
HP: 3800 AP: 1 Gil: 94
Steal: Silence Grenade
Drop: Sleep Grenade

**YSLS-99**
HP: 2775 AP: 1 Gil: 400
Steal: Mythril Gloves
Drop: Stamina Tablet

## ITEM CHECKLIST

| | | | |
|---|---|---|---|
| Remedy (x5) | Phoenix Down (x8) | Oath Veil | Phoenix Down (x8) |
| Crystal Gloves | Potion (x10) | White Lore | Dispel Tonic |
| 10000 gil | Chocobo Feather (x3) | Ether (x6) | Crimson Sphere 6 |
| Hi-Potion (x6) | 1200 gil | Remedy (x6) | Crimson Sphere 8 |

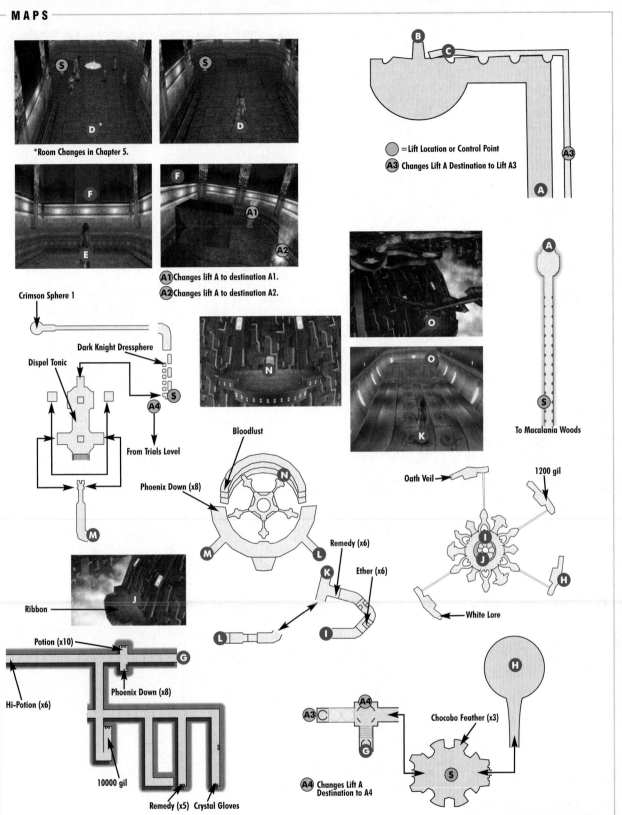

*Room Changes in Chapter 5.

= Lift Location or Control Point

**A3** Changes Lift A Destination to Lift A3

**A1** Changes lift A to destination A1.
**A2** Changes lift A to destination A2.

Crimson Sphere 1

Dark Knight Dressphere

Dispel Tonic

**A4**

From Trials Level

To Macalania Woods

Bloodlust

Phoenix Down (x8)

Ribbon

Oath Veil

1200 gil

Remedy (x6)

Ether (x6)

White Lore

Potion (x10)

Phoenix Down (x8)

Hi-Potion (x6)

Chocobo Feather (x3)

**A3**

**A4**

10000 gil

Remedy (x5)   Crystal Gloves

**A4** Changes Lift A
Destination to A4

Characters

1

Garment Grids
& Dresspheres

2

Battle System

3

Accessories

4

Items and
Item Shops

5

Walkthrough
Chapter 1
Chapter 2
Chapter 3
Chapter 4
**Chapter 5**

Mini-Games

7

Fiends and
Enemies

8

# BEVELLE FINDS ORDER

Move to the entrance of the temple. If you signed on with New Yevon, you'll receive an Episode Complete! However, if you gave the sphere to the Youth League, you'll only witness the final scene with Maroda.

*Although hardly a fitting end to Bevelle's problems, you still get enough completion points from this ending to help out.*

# VIA INFINITO

Head inside the temple and enter the east chamber. Pacce and the Kinderguardians seem to have found something of interest. Use the Save Sphere before stepping onto the teleport glyph. The teleport transports the party to a series of 101 secret levels, called "cloisters." A strange person greets the group on Cloister 0, then drops **Crimson Sphere 6**. You can view it now, if you want. To the left of the item's location is a pad that will eventually enable you to skip to the "Great Cloisters" found every 20 levels, but you must reach these special cloisters to activate this device. Straight ahead from the sphere's location is a hole in the floor, which you can drop through to Cloister 1.

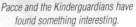
Pacce and the Kinderguardians have found something interesting.

Don't miss Crimson Sphere 6, which is left on the floor after the scene.

The layouts of the cloisters change randomly, so it's difficult to provide maps or a walkthrough for this section. Each level contains a glyph teleport that transports you back to where the Kinderguardians are gathered. Move through the level, avoiding traps if necessary. In some levels, you can actually speak to a Tonberry to obtain random items. In each cloister, find a point where you can drop into a pit, which will deposit you in the next cloister. Ideally, you should tackle this challenge with three Gun Mages in your party, because you can learn any Blue Bullet skills you might be missing. When you reach cloister 20, you must fight the Aranea boss. Boss monsters must also be fought at levels 40, 60, 80 and 100. After defeating a boss, find a teleport glyph and return to the outside world. Save your game at the Save Sphere near the labyrinth entrance, then return and skip through to the boss level where you left off.

Tonberrys are key figures in every level.

On level 20, you will fight Aranea, which drops **Crimson Sphere 8**. At level 40, you will face the Black Elemental. To have any chance of surviving in this dungeon, all your characters should be at level 99 with over 9000 HP per person to survive the bosses and monsters starting at level 40. In addition to this, you need to use limit break auto-abilities, powerful chain abilities, and Auto-Life, otherwise, the bosses will eliminate your party quickly. This is a bonus area to explore as your characters progress past normal levels and abilities.

Get ready for enemies more difficult than the final boss of the game!

## ACTION CHECKLIST

**1** The moment of truth is at hand. Now we finish this!

See who won the Publicity campaign.

**2**

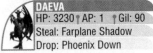
Dispatch various chocobos to uncover the Calm Land's secret dungeon.

**COMPLETION: +0.4%**

## WANDERING FIENDS

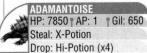
**ADAMANTOISE**
HP: 7850 | AP: 1 | Gil: 650
Steal: X-Potion
Drop: Hi-Potion (x4)

**AKA MANAH**
HP: 6322 | AP: 1 | Gil: 670
Steal: Remedy (x2)
Drop: Pretty Orb

**AMORPHOUS GEL**
HP: 973 | AP: 1 | Gil: 380
Steal: White Ring
Drop: Blue Ring

**ARMET**
HP: 788 | AP: 1 | Gil: 74
Steal: Lunar Curtain
Drop: Light Curtain

**BALIVARHA**
HP: 3688 | AP: 1, | Gil: 230
Steal: Hi-Potion (x2)
Drop: Fire Gem

**BLUE ELEMENTAL**
HP: 363 | AP: 1 | Gil: 180
Steal: Dragon Scale
Drop: Dragon Scale

**CHOCOBO**
HP: 3890 | AP: 0 | Gil: 0
Steal: None
Drop: None

**DAEVA**
HP: 3230 | AP: 1 | Gil: 90
Steal: Farplane Shadow
Drop: Phoenix Down

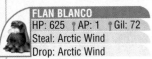
**FLAN BLANCO**
HP: 625 | AP: 1 | Gil: 72
Steal: Arctic Wind
Drop: Arctic Wind

**FLAN ROJO**
HP: 1220 | AP: 1 | Gil: 125
Steal: Bomb Core
Drop: Bomb Core

**GRIM GAZE**
HP: 1720 | AP: 1 | Gil: 130
Steal: Phoenix Down
Drop: Phoenix Down

**HAUNT**
HP: 813 | AP: 1 | Gil: 120
Steal: Arctic Wind
Drop: Water Ring

CALM LANDS

Characters

Garment Grids & Dresspheres

Battle System

Accessories

Items and Item Shops

Walkthrough
Chapter 1
Chapter 2
Chapter 3
Chapter 4
Chapter 5

Mini-Games

Fiends and Enemies

## WANDERING FIENDS CONTINUED

**LEUCOPHYLLA**
HP: 2234 | AP: 1 | Gil: 86
Steal: Hi-Potion
Drop: Remedy

**LICH**
HP: 3444 | AP: 1 | Gil: 330
Steal: Hi-Potion
Drop: None

**PAIRIKA**
HP: 1130 | AP: 1 | Gil: 100
Steal: Lightning Marble
Drop: Stamina Spring

**PEREGRINE**
HP: 735 | AP: 1 | Gil: 44
Steal: Hi-Potion
Drop: Hi-Potion

**PROTEAN GEL**
HP: 6680 | AP: 1 | Gil: 380
Steal: Blue Ring
Drop: White Ring

**QUEEN COEURL**
HP: 3270 | AP: 1 | Gil: 330
Steal: Phoenix Down
Drop: Phoenix Down (x2)

**RHYOS**
HP: 4360 | AP: 1 | Gil: 310
Steal: Lightning Gem
Drop: Lightning Gem

**SKINK**
HP: 882 | AP: 1 | Gil: 78
Steal: Hi-Potion
Drop: Hi-Potion

**TAROMAITI**
HP: 1782 | AP: 1 | Gil: 280
Steal: Antidote (x2)
Drop: Star Pendant

**TOMB**
HP: 4820 | AP: 1 | Gil: 130
Steal: Remedy
Drop: Remedy

**VARAN**
HP: 1132 | AP: 1 | Gil: 240
Steal: Dispel Tonic
Drop: Holy Water

**VESPA**
HP: 983 | AP: 1 | Gil: 78
Steal: Echo Screen (x2)
Drop: Antidote

**WATCHER-A***
HP: 624 | AP: 1 | Gil: 0
Steal: Potion
Drop: Potion

**WATCHER-R***
HP: 620 | AP: 1 | Gil: 0
Steal: Potion
Drop: Potion

**WATCHER-S***
HP: 620 | AP: 1 | Gil: 0
Steal: Potion
Drop: Potion

**ZURVAN**
HP: 583 | AP: 1 | Gil: 70
Steal: Dispel Tonic
Drop: Hi-Potion

### *Appears before defeating the Machina Panzer boss at Thunder Plains.

## ITEM CHECKLIST

| | | | |
|---|---|---|---|
| 50000 gil* | Turbo Ether | NulFrost Ring | Electrocutioner |
| Cerulean Ring | X-Potion | NulTide Ring | Aurora Rain |
| Mega Phoenix (x2) | Mega Phoenix (x2) | Defense Bracer | |

### *Depending on circumstances of CH4.

## MAPS

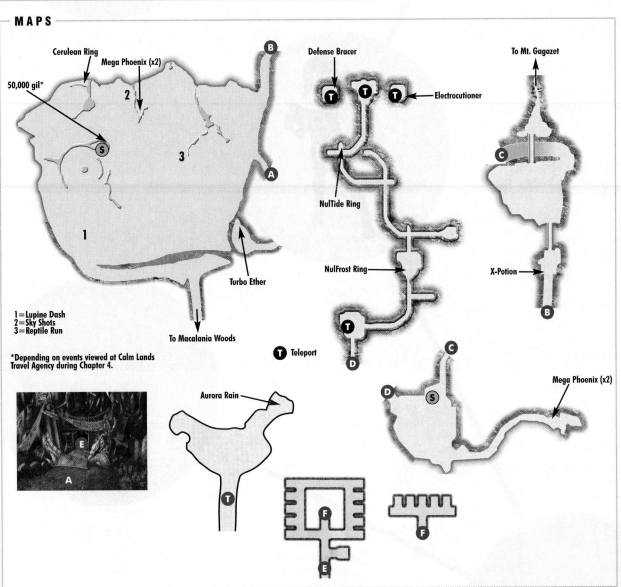

Cerulean Ring
Mega Phoenix (x2)
50,000 gil*
B
2
3
A
1
Turbo Ether
To Macalania Woods

1 = Lupine Dash
2 = Sky Shots
3 = Reptile Run

*Depending on events viewed at Calm Lands Travel Agency during Chapter 4.

Defense Bracer
T T T
Electrocutioner
NulTide Ring
NulFrost Ring
T
D
T  Teleport

To Mt. Gagazet
C
X-Potion
B

D
C
S
Mega Phoenix (x2)

Aurora Rain
T

E
A

F
E
F

# WRAPPING UP BUSINESS

If you participated in the Publicity campaign, head to the Calm Lands and after a short event where the winner is decided, you'll receive an "Episode Complete!" Speak to the man in green standing with a group inside the Travel Agency area just to the left of the shop clerk. If you helped your agency reach level 5, he'll give you the **Calm Lands Free Pass**, which allows you to ride hovers on the Calm Lands free of charge. If you failed to reach this high level but attempted the Publicity campaign anyhow, you'll obtain the **Calm Lands Discount Pass** that allows you to ride hovers at a lower fare. Speak to the man near the Travel Agency if you took up the Matrimony campaign. It's time to claim your prize for finding the young man a choice of brides! Also, if you saw the groom's father work on a treasure chest during Chapter 4, an accessory can be found in a chest behind the Travel Agency. There are all new items on the Calm Lands plains, as well as many valuable accessories and key items to be gained in the gorge cave.

*The Calm Lands in Chapter 5 are all about the rewards.*

# CLASKO'S SECRET MAZE

Yet another secret dungeon provides another challenge during Chapter 5. Dispatch three level 1 chocobos to various locations in Spira, then return to the Calm Lands later to see if any returned. If any run away, send out an equal number of replacement chocobos. If all three returned, send out three level 2 chocobos and wait for their return. Continue this process until you not only dispatch three level 3 chocobos, three level 4 chocobos, and three level 5 chocobos but have them all return safely to the Chocobo Ranch. Once this criteria is met, Clasko remarks on an amazing new dungeon that has opened up. Inside this rather challenging dungeon you'll find some useful items and accessories, including the **Machina Reactor** item, which unlocks the Break HP Limit ability for Rikku's Machina Maw special dressphere.

*You'll need to explore another area and participate in several battles while waiting for your chocobos to return to the ranch.*

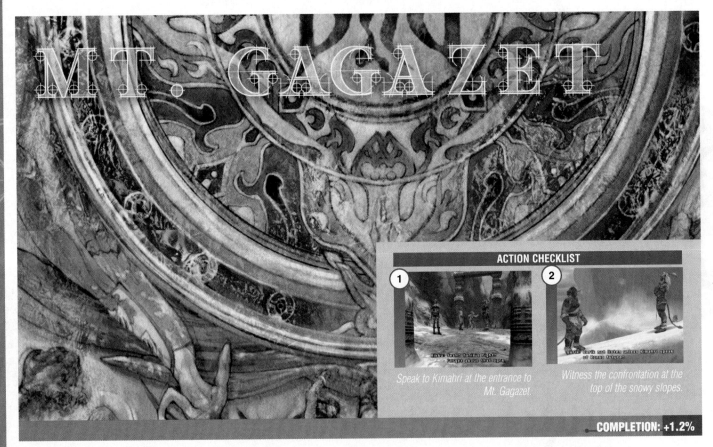

# MT. GAGAZET

### ACTION CHECKLIST

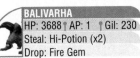

**1** Speak to Kimahri at the entrance to Mt. Gagazet.

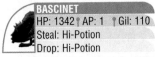

**2** Witness the confrontation at the top of the snowy slopes.

**COMPLETION: +1.2%**

## WANDERING FIENDS

**ADAMANTOISE**
HP: 7850 | AP: 1 | Gil: 650
Steal: X-Potion
Drop: Hi-Potion (x4)

**BALIVARHA**
HP: 3688 | AP: 1 | Gil: 230
Steal: Hi-Potion (x2)
Drop: Fire Gem

**BASCINET**
HP: 1342 | AP: 1 | Gil: 110
Steal: Hi-Potion
Drop: Hi-Potion

**BORIS**
HP: 480 | AP: 1 | Gil: 300
Steal: Remedy
Drop: Star Pendant

**BOLT DRAKE**
HP: 623 | AP: 1 | Gil: 130
Steal: Lightning Marble
Drop: Hi-Potion

**GEMINI**
HP: 2044 | AP: 1 | Gil: 153
Steal: Lunar Curtain (x2)
Drop: Light Curtain (x2)

**GREATER DRAKE**
HP: 1819 | AP: 1 | Gil: 140
Steal: Fire Gem
Drop: Fire Gem

**GRIM GAZE**
HP: 1720 | AP: 1 | Gil: 130
Steal: Phoenix Down
Drop: Phoenix Down

**LEUCOPHYLLALUPUS**
HP: 1262 | AP: 1 | Gil: 80
Steal: Hi-Potion
Drop: Hi-Potion

**MYCOTOXIN**
HP: 810 | AP: 1 | Gil: 83
Steal: Antidote (x2)
Drop: Antidote (x2)

**QUEEN COEURL**
HP: 3270 | AP: 1 | Gil: 330
Steal: Phoenix Down
Drop: Phoenix Down (x2)

**RUKH**
HP: 12850 | AP: 1 | Gil: 530
Steal: Phoenix Down (x2)
Drop: Phoenix Down (x2)

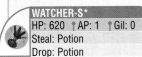

**SALLET**
HP: 60 ┃ AP: 1 ┃ Gil: 10
Steal: Potion
Drop: Potion

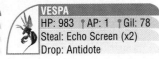

**SPINE DRAKE**
HP: 2582 ┃ AP: 1 ┃ Gil: 127
Steal: Arctic Wind
Drop: Arctic Wind

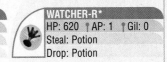

**WATCHER-A***
HP: 624 ┃ AP: 1 ┃ Gil: 0
Steal: Potion
Drop: Potion

**WATCHER-R***
HP: 620 ┃ AP: 1 ┃ Gil: 0
Steal: Potion
Drop: Potion

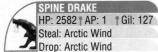

**WATCHER-S***
HP: 620 ┃ AP: 1 ┃ Gil: 0
Steal: Potion
Drop: Potion

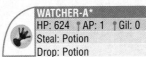

**VESPA**
HP: 983 ┃ AP: 1 ┃ Gil: 78
Steal: Echo Screen (x2)
Drop: Antidote

***Appears before defeating the Machina Panzer boss at Thunder Plains.**

## ITEM CHECKLIST

Sacred Beast Garment Grid ⓔ

# GARIK RELENTS

If you completed the mission where you defeated Garik Ronso, Garik will be complaining to Kimahri again at the entrance of Gagazet. Follow Kimahri up the snowy mountain slopes until you spot a brawl between him and Garik. Not long thereafter, you'll obtain an Episode Complete!

The final confrontation between Garik and Kimahri occurs on the snowy slopes just north of Gagazet's entrance.

# AN ODE IN STONE

The Ronso artisan on the summit has decided on a subject for her monument and begins to carve its likeness into stone. If you answered the concerns of the Ronso with the best answers during Chapters 1 and 2, the statue will turn out to be Yuna. Check back throughout Chapter 5 to view the artisan's progress. By the time you complete all the episodes in Chapter 5, the likeness should be finished.

The statue on the cliffs is starting to take shape.

Characters

1

Garment Grids & Dresspheres

2

Battle System

3

Accessories

4

Items and Item Shops

5

Walkthrough
Chapter 1
Chapter 2
Chapter 3
Chapter 4
Chapter 5

Mini-Games

7

Fiends and Enemies

8

# FARPLANE

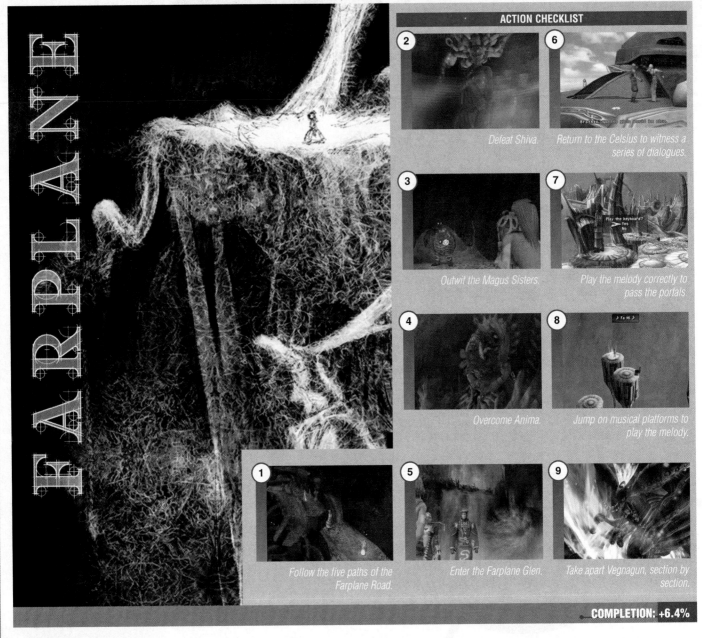

## ACTION CHECKLIST

**2** Defeat Shiva.

**6** Return to the Celsius to witness a series of dialogues.

**3** Outwit the Magus Sisters.

**7** Play the melody correctly to pass the portals.

**4** Overcome Anima.

**8** Jump on musical platforms to play the melody.

**1** Follow the five paths of the Farplane Road.

**5** Enter the Farplane Glen.

**9** Take apart Vegnagun, section by section.

**COMPLETION: +6.4%**

## WANDERING FIENDS

**AESHMA**
HP: 8788 | AP: 1 | Gil: 800
Steal: Candle of Life (x2)
Drop: Dragonfly Orb

**ADAMANTORTOISE**
HP:14580 | AP: 1 | Gil:1000
Steal: X-Potion
Drop: X-Potion

**AKA MANAH**
HP: 6322 | AP: 1 | Gil: 670
Steal: Remedy (x2)
Drop: Pretty Orb

**ARAST**
HP: 2742 | AP: 1 | Gil: 330
Steal: Dispel Tonic (x2)
Drop: Holy Water (x2)

**AZI DAHAKA**
HP:146200 | AP: 1 | Gil:1300
Steal: X-Potion
Drop: Ether

**CLARET DRAGON**
HP:17320 | AP: 1 | Gil: 780
Steal: Hi-Potion, Drop:
Hi-Potion (x2)

**DARK ELEMENTAL**
HP: 433 | AP: 1 | Gil: 410
Steal: Ice Gem (x2)
Drop: Water Gem (x2)

**DOLMEN**
HP: 5320 | AP: 1 | Gil: 320
Steal: Remedy (x2)
Drop: Hi-Potion (x2)

**EARTH WORM**
HP:36233 | AP: 1 | Gil:6000
Steal: Mega Potion
Drop: Mega Potion

**GUG**
HP: 6433 | AP: 1 | Gil: 600
Steal: Hi-Potion (x2)
Drop: Phoenix Down

**GREAT MALBORO**
HP:12988 | AP: 1 | Gil:1200
Steal: Dispel Tonic
Drop: Remedy (x2)

**JAHI**
HP: 2033 | AP: 1 | Gil: 620
Steal: Remedy (x2)
Drop: Gold Anklet

**LICH**
HP: 3444 | AP: 1 | Gil: 330
Steal: Hi-Potion
Drop: None

**OMEGA WEAPON**
HP:24200 | AP: 1 | Gil:5000
Steal: Turbo Ether
Drop: Safety Bit

**MONOLITH**
HP: 7143 | AP: 1 | Gil: 460
Steal: Phoenix Down (x2)
Drop: Hi-Potion (x3)

**TAROMAITI**
HP: 1782 | AP: 1 | Gil: 280
Steal: Antidote (x2)
Drop: Star Pendant

**TINDALOS**
HP: 3324 | AP: 1 | Gil: 315
Steal: Hi-Potion
Drop: Antidote

**VARAN**
HP: 1132 | AP: 1 | Gil: 240
Steal: Dispel Tonic
Drop: Holy Water

**VOLCANO**
HP: 6210 | AP: 1 | Gil: 330
Steal: Hi-Potion
Drop: Fire Gem (x4)

**WATCHER-A***
HP: 624 | AP: 1 | Gil: 0
Steal: Potion
Drop: Potion

## WANDERING FIENDS CONTINUED

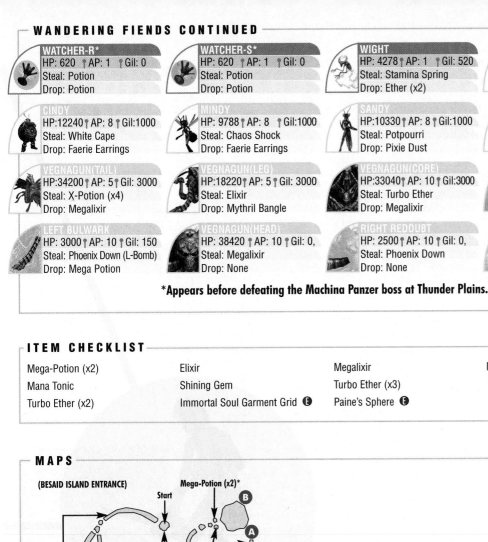

**WATCHER-R***
HP: 620 | AP: 1 | Gil: 0
Steal: Potion
Drop: Potion

**WATCHER-S***
HP: 620 | AP: 1 | Gil: 0
Steal: Potion
Drop: Potion

**WIGHT**
HP: 4278 | AP: 1 | Gil: 520
Steal: Stamina Spring
Drop: Ether (x2)

**SHIVA**
HP: 14800 | AP: 15 | Gil: 2000
Steal: Snow Ring
Drop: Crystal Gloves

**CINDY**
HP: 12240 | AP: 8 | Gil: 1000
Steal: White Cape
Drop: Faerie Earrings

**MINDY**
HP: 9788 | AP: 8 | Gil: 1000
Steal: Chaos Shock
Drop: Faerie Earrings

**SANDY**
HP: 10330 | AP: 8 | Gil: 1000
Steal: Potpourri
Drop: Pixie Dust

**ANIMA**
HP: 3600 | AP: 15 | Gil: 2000
Steal: Fury Shock
Drop: Tetra Band

**VEGNAGUN(TAIL)**
HP: 34200 | AP: 5 | Gil: 3000
Steal: X-Potion (x4)
Drop: Megalixir

**VEGNAGUN(LEG)**
HP: 18220 | AP: 5 | Gil: 3000
Steal: Elixir
Drop: Mythril Bangle

**VEGNAGUN(CORE)**
HP: 33040 | AP: 10 | Gil: 3000
Steal: Turbo Ether
Drop: Megalixir

**RIGHT BULWARK**
HP: 3000 | AP: 10 | Gil: 150
Steal: Phoenix Down (L-Bomb)
Drop: Mega Potion

**LEFT BULWARK**
HP: 3000 | AP: 10 | Gil: 150
Steal: Phoenix Down (L-Bomb)
Drop: Mega Potion

**VEGNAGUN(HEAD)**
HP: 38420 | AP: 10 | Gil: 0,
Steal: Megalixir
Drop: None

**RIGHT REDOUBT**
HP: 2500 | AP: 10 | Gil: 0,
Steal: Phoenix Down
Drop: None

**LEFT REDOUBT**
HP: 2500 | AP: 10 | Gil: 0,
Steal: Phoenix Down
Drop: None

*Appears before defeating the Machina Panzer boss at Thunder Plains.

## ITEM CHECKLIST

Mega-Potion (x2)

Mana Tonic

Turbo Ether (x2)

Elixir

Shining Gem

Immortal Soul Garment Grid ⓔ

Megalixir

Turbo Ether (x3)

Paine's Sphere ⓔ

Mega Phoenix (x2)

## MAPS

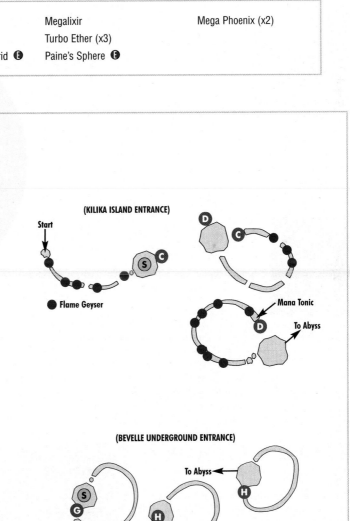

**(BESAID ISLAND ENTRANCE)**

Start

Mega-Potion (x2)*

B
A

Mega-Potion (x2)*

To Abyss

Mega-Potion (x2)

S

A

Mega-Potion (x2)

*Touch any moving rock 4 times, the item appears at next moving rock.

B

**(KILIKA ISLAND ENTRANCE)**

Start

C
S

● Flame Geyser

D
C

Mana Tonic

D

To Abyss

Start

E
S

E
F

**(DJOSE TEMPLE ENTRANCE)**

To Abyss

Turbo Ether

F

**(BEVELLE UNDERGROUND ENTRANCE)**

To Abyss

S
G

H
G

H

Start

Elixir

Characters

1

Garment Grids & D: Dressesspheres

2

Battle System

3

Accessories

4

Items and Item Shops

5

Walkthrough
Chapter 1
Chapter 2
Chapter 3
Chapter 4
Chapter 5

Mini-Games

7

Fiends and Enemies

8

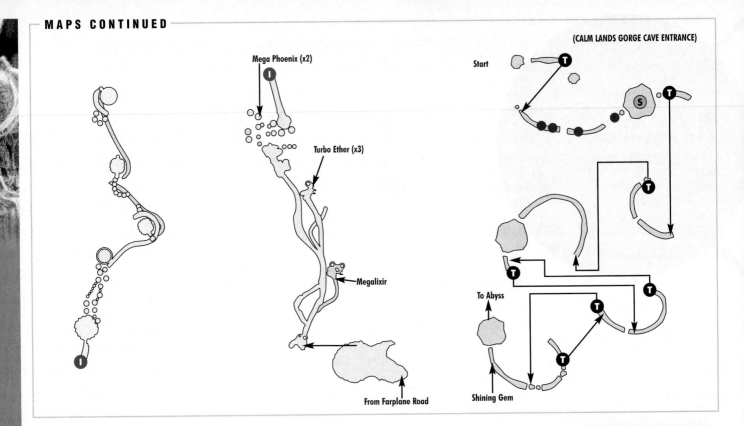

Mega Phoenix (x2)

Turbo Ether (x3)

Megalixir

From Farplane Road

(CALM LANDS GORGE CAVE ENTRANCE)

Start

To Abyss

Shining Gem

FARPLANE

# ROUTES INTO THE FARPLANE

It would be unwise to undertake the final mission at the Farplane before reaching levels 65 and above with all three characters. When you're ready to plunge into the depths of the Farplane, speak to Brother onboard the Celsius. You must choose a location from which to jump down a hole into the Farplane. There are five paths that lead from the entrance down to the Farplane Glen at the bottom. Along the routes, paths converge at three points: the larger islands where the party must fight Shiva, then the Magus Sisters, followed by Anima. Once Anima is defeated, Yuna finds herself in the Farplane Glen. Thereafter, you can travel any route into the Farplane without fighting the bosses again.

*Prepare for a boss fight as you descend to each large island that floats in space.*

*Enter the Road to the Farplane from all five points in Spira to obtain a Garment Grid.*

After choosing a location, you must proceed all the way to the bottom of the Road to the Farplane without the ablity to turn back. The path entered by dropping into the hole at Bevelle provides the easiest route, whereas the path from Djose Temple is somewhat tricky. After following one route to the Farplane Abyss, there is no reason to go back and follow the other routes. However, navigating all five routes in sequential order causes a chest to appear that contains a **Megiddo Garment Grid**.

# THE BESAID ISLAND ROUTE

When entering through the hole at Besaid, the path seems to be fairly straightforward at first. However, there is an item chest you will miss if you fail to perform a certain action. Along the route, there are four small islands that will activate when you land on them. The islands will move to a previous point on the path, depositing you there for a slight setback. After riding any of these islands four times, a chest with a **Mega-Potion (x2)** will appear at the next island.

*Ride the moving stones four times to reveal a treasure chest on the next stone you come to.*

# THE KILIKA TEMPLE ROUTE

Small flame geysers flare along the route from Kilika into the Farplane. If you touch too many of the flames in a row, you'll be teleported back to a previous location along the route. To avoid setbacks, wait until the flames die down for a brief period. Quickly run over the geyser while the fires are low to avoid setbacks.

*Wait until the flames subside before crossing.*

# THE DJOSE TEMPLE ROUTE

To cross the route leading downward from Djose Temple, you must solve a very tricky puzzle. If you continue to follow the route, you will come to a point where the islands appear to be missing. Return to the portion where the path diverges and hop across the islands to the small strip of land on the right. There are three islands anchored along this strip of land. Examine the first small island to change views. You can now see three islands in front of you that you can strike with the anchored island. Push the left island toward the island numbered 3, then push the right island toward the island numbered 1. Finally, push the center island toward the remaining island to make the islands form a path that enable you to reach the Shiva boss battle.

*Push the rocks into each other to create a path to the next area.*

*The moving rock near the end of the path delivers you to another branch.*

Further down the path, just before reaching the large island where Anima is, a small island will move Yuna to a space between the main path and a side branch. Leap from the small rock to the side branch and proceed to the end. The first treasure chest is an empty ruse, but the one at the very end of the path contains a **Turbo Ether (x2)**.

# THE BEVELLE UNDERGROUND AND CALM LAND ROUTES

The route from Bevelle into the Farplane is as straightforward as they come. Simply hop from path to path until you reach the Abyss. The Calm Land route features a tricky set of invisible teleporters that attempt to disorient you. Simply continue to head downward.

*Teleporters work to confuse your sense of direction, but just keep heading down the slopes.*

# SHIVA BOSS FIGHT

The aeon of ice is naturally weak against Fire, so use a Black Mage to exploit this weakness. Shiva's ice attacks drain HP and MP simultaneously, so make sure your Black Mage knows the MP Drain ability and can use it. Shiva can also be affected by Slow, which you should use to help you during the battle.

**HP: 14800  MP: 9999  EXP: 8000  AP: 15**

**GIL DROPPED:** 2000
**PILFER GIL:** 5000

**STEAL:** Normal: Snow Ring   Rare: Snow Ring
**DROP:** Normal: Crystal Gloves   Rare: Regal Crown

Characters

1

Garment Grids & Dresspheres

2

Battle System

3

Accessories

4

Items and Item Shops

5

Walkthrough
Chapter 1
Chapter 2
Chapter 3
Chapter 4
Chapter 5

Mini-Games

7

Fiends and Enemies

8

# THE MAGUS SISTERS

**HP:** 9788 **MP:** 9999 **EXP:** 3000 **AP:** 8

**HP:** 10330 **MP:** 9999 **EXP:** 3000 **AP:** 8

**HP:** 12240 **MP:** 9999 **EXP:** 0 **AP:** 0

**GIL DROPPED:** 1000    **STEAL:** Normal: Chaos Shock   Rare: Chaos Shock
**PILFER GIL:** 3000    **DROP:** Normal: Faerie Earrings   Rare: Faerie Earrings

This trio of sisters work together to siphon large amounts of HP from your party each round, so keep an experienced White Mage or Alchemist around and command them to heal every turn. Mindy's rapid-fire tail attacks can tie up one of your characters for almost an entire turn. Since she has the lowest HP, focus your strongest attacks on her. Have a White Mage cast Dispel, because the sisters will cast Not-So-Mighty Guard on one another, which is a misnomer. While this spell is in effect, magic will be reflected and physical attacks won't inflict as much damage. It's important to knock out one of the sisters as quickly as possible, otherwise they will perform their deadly "Delta Attack" after a few turns. Once Mindy is finished, focus your assault on Sandy followed by Cindy.

**GIL DROPPED:** 1000    **STEAL:** Normal: Potpourri   Rare: Potpourri
**PILFER GIL:** 3000    **DROP:** Normal: Pixie Dust   Rare: Crystal Gloves

**GIL DROPPED:** 0    **STEAL:** Normal: White Cape   Rare: White Cape
**PILFER GIL:** 0    **DROP:** Normal: Faerie Earrings   Rare: Pixie Dust

# ANIMA

Protect your characters from as many status ailments as possible by equipping the proper accessories before proceeding to the battle at the end of the Road to the Farplane. Anima is capable of Oblivion, a skill you may have enjoyed using in *FINAL FANTASY X*, but one you won't enjoy so much this time around. Most of Anima's other attacks will seem insignificant, but it's important for a White Mage or Alchemist to heal the party each round in preparation for major HP loss after every Oblivion attack. The creature reduces most magic damage by half, but is weak versus Holy. Employ attacks such as a Warrior's Excalibur, or Trainer Yuna's Kogoro Holy. A Dark Knight's Darkness ability will also be very useful in defeating this aeon.

**HP:** 36000 **MP:** 9999 **EXP:** 6000 **AP:** 15

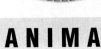

**GIL DROPPED:** 2000    **STEAL:** Normal: Fury Shock   Rare: Fury Shock
**PILFER GIL:** 4000    **DROP:** Normal: Tetra Band   Rare: Tetra Band

## UPON REACHING THE ABYSS

Surprisingly, Leblanc, Ormi and Logos are waiting for the party at the gorgeous area ironically known as the Farplane Glen. After speaking with the trio once, Leblanc will sell basic items when spoken to. A Save Sphere materializes in the corner following the scene, and you can use it to return to the Celsius. From there, you can choose another route into the Farplane to undertake more challenges and collect more items.

*Leblanc and her henchmen in the Farplane Glen.*

| FARPLANE ABYSS (LEBLANC) | |
|---|---|
| ITEM | COST |
| Potion | 50 |
| Hi-Potion | 500 |
| Phoenix Down | 100 |
| Antidote | 50 |
| Eye Drops | 50 |
| Echo Screen | 50 |
| Soft | 50 |
| Holy Water | 300 |

# THE INTERESTS OF THE GULLWINGS

*Speak to Shinra to begin a string of events involving the Celsius crew.*

After returning from the Farplane, there are several scenes possibly accessible onboard the Celsius. Speak to Shinra to learn about new data he uncovered regarding the Farplane, then ride the elevator up to the deck to overhear a conversation between Brother and Buddy. You'll need most or all of the Al Bhed Primers to understand what they are saying. Thereafter, travel down to the Cabin to witness a tense standoff between Cid and his children.

*Brother now directs traffic to the Farplane from his cockpit seat.*

When you're ready to return to the Farplane, speak to Brother in the cockpit seat. You can return directly to the Farplane Abyss where Leblanc waits, or you can follow any of the remaining routes from the temples along the Road to the Farplane.

# THE SONG OF SHUYIN

When you're ready to proceed further toward Vegnagun, walk into the glowing orange cloud just below the swirling vortex. The Gullwings enter an area filled with magical barriers. If you attempt to proceed before deactivating a barrier, you'll suffer a brutal encounter with the fiend Azi Dahakas. To deactivate the barriers properly, you must step on musical plates in the ground to learn a series of musical notes. Once you play the notes on a nearby keyboard, the barriers should drop and you can proceed.

*Step on the music plate to the left of the keyboard to reveal the notes to play.*

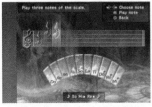

*Enter the correct notes into the instrument, mindful of stars next to certain notes.*

Move left from the starting point past the keyboard until Yuna steps onto a circle that emits light and sound. Move to the nearby keyboard and input the notes So Mi* Re*. In the case of the latter two notes, input the ones with the small stars beside them, or else it's the wrong note.

In the second area, there are three musical plates to step on before the next barrier is released. Each plate is directly under one of the electrical fields, so you must wait until the device activates and then stops before stepping onto the plate; otherwise, you'll get knocked off and may have to face a tough fiend. After stepping on all three plates, make your way up the right-hand path to the keyboard and the chest containing a **Megalixir**. Input the new notes of the series into the organ, and the next major barrier will be released.

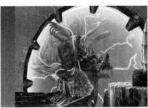

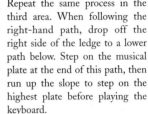

*Don't attempt to cross the barriers without entering the proper notes.*

*Drop to the lower path of the third area to find the last notes.*

Repeat the same process in the third area. When following the right-hand path, drop off the right side of the ledge to a lower path below. Step on the musical plate at the end of this path, then run up the slope to step on the highest plate before playing the keyboard.

# HOPPING MADNESS

After Paine reunites with Gippal and receives **Paine's Sphere**, you face another musical challenge. A machina will display a bird's-eye view of the area above. You must jump onto the platforms in the same order as the musical notes played previously on the keyboards. It's difficult to memorize the exact placement and order of the platforms, so refer to the map where the platforms are numbered in the correct order. After leaping on all the platforms in the correct order, proceed to the top and stand on the musical plate before the final gate. If the song plays correctly, you can proceed to Vegnagun. Between each of the following battles, use items to restore HP and move further up the path toward the head of the weapon.

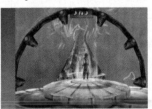

*Use moving platforms to reach the musical pads in order before approaching the gate.*

**MAPS**

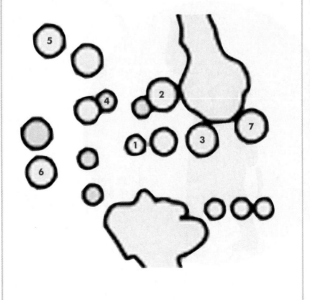

Characters

1

Garment Grids & Dresspheres

2

Battle System

3

Accessories

4

Items and Item Shops

5

Walkthrough
Chapter 1
Chapter 2
Chapter 3
Chapter 4
Chapter 5

Mini-Games

7

Fiends and Enemies

8

245

# VEGNAGUN (TAIL)

HP: 34200  MP: 9999  EXP: 5000  AP: 5

The struggle to defeat Vegnagun piece by piece unfortunately begins with one of the hardest pieces. A laser fired from the tail section will instantly knock off close to 1500 HP from one character. Use an Alchemist to mix Potions and Hi-Potions to attain the result of Mega-Potion each round. Attack the tail with strong spells and a Dark Knight's Darkness ability every turn until it is defeated.

**GIL DROPPED:** 3000  
**PILFER GIL:** 3000

**STEAL:** Normal: X-Potion (x4)   Rare: X-Potion (x6)  
**DROP:** Normal: Megalixir   Rare: Megalixir

# VEGNAGUN (LEG), NODE A, NODE B, NODE C

FARPLANE

HP: 18220  MP: 9999  EXP: 6000  AP: 5

**GIL DROPPED:** 3000  
**PILFER GIL:** 3000

**STEAL:** Normal: Elixir   Rare: Elixir (x2)  
**DROP:** Normal: Mythril Bangle   Rare: Mythril Bangle

The battle will end when the Leg is destroyed. If breezing through to the ending is your objective, then attack the leg swiftly to clear this battle and prepare for what's next. However, by examining the information in the boss boxes, you can see that by destroying the three Nodes first, you will vastly increase the amounts of EXP and gil won from this battle. You also stand a chance of receiving the exclusive **Hero's Drink** item, which is just now available. To attack a Node, you must target it with spells or ranged attacks. Even the most powerful Black Mage spells will cause only minimal damage against the nodes due to their high Magic Defense. The best method to attack the Nodes is with Ultima and Flare attacks, which are only available by equipping certain Garment Grids. Once you begin to attack the Nodes, they will react with strong spells and healing magic.

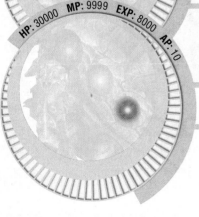

HP: 30000  MP: 9999  EXP: 8000  AP: 10

**GIL DROPPED:** 3000  
**PILFER GIL:** 10000

**STEAL:** Normal: None   Rare: None  
**DROP:** Normal: Megalixir   Rare: Hero Drink

HP: 30000  MP: 9999  EXP: 8000  AP: 10

The nodes change color after performing a certain number of actions. A green node will use recovery and support abilities, a yellow node will attack with magic, and a red node will use physical attacks. Sometimes the nodes will change color when attacked. A yellow node is immune to magical attacks and a red node is immune to physical attacks. Listening to the hints in battle reveals some of this.

**GIL DROPPED:** 3000  
**PILFER GIL:** 10000

**STEAL:** Normal: None   Rare: None  
**DROP:** Normal: Megalixir   Rare: Hero Drink

HP: 30000  MP: 9999  EXP: 8000  AP: 10

**GIL DROPPED:** 3000  
**PILFER GIL:** 10000

**STEAL:** Normal: None   Rare: None  
**DROP:** Normal: Megalixir   Rare: Hero Drink

# VEGNAGUN (CORE), RIGHT BULWARK, LEFT BULWARK

**HP:** 33040 **MP:** 9999 **EXP:** 7000 **AP:** 10

**GIL DROPPED:** 3000  **STEAL:** Normal: Turbo Ether  Rare: Turbo Ether
**PILFER GIL:** 4000  **DROP:** Normal: Megalixir  Rare: Megalixir

The Right and Left Bulwarks attempt to protect the Core by casting various protective and restorative magic, as well as some spells to disable the party. The ideal solution is for a Dark Knight to use a single Darkness attack to wipe out both Bulwarks with a single blow before they can cast Protect or Shell on the Core. This way, you can focus the full force of your attacks against the Core as it attempts to charge up a massive attack against your entire party. If you fail to defeat the Core before it fires, use a Mega-Phoenix to resurrect any dead party members. Before the Core begins its next charging session, it will revive the two Bulwarks. Destroy them again and disable the Core before you get hit again.

**HP:** 3000 **MP:** 9999 **EXP:** 200 **AP:** 10

**GIL DROPPED:** 150  **STEAL:** Normal: Phoenix Down  Rare: L-Bomb
**PILFER GIL:** 300  **DROP:** Normal: Mega-Potion  Rare: X-Potion

**HP:** 3000 **MP:** 9999 **EXP:** 200 **AP:** 10

**GIL DROPPED:** 150  **STEAL:** Normal: Phoenix Down  Rare: L-Bomb
**PILFER GIL:** 300  **DROP:** Normal: Mega-Potion  Rare: X-Potion

Characters

1

Garment Grids & Dresspheres

2

Battle System

3

Accessories

4

Items and Item Shops

5

Walkthrough

Chapter 1

Chapter 2

Chapter 3

Chapter 4

Chapter 5

Mini-Games

7

Fiends and Enemies

8

# RIGHT REDOUBT, LEFT REDOUBT, VEGNAGUN (HEAD)

**HP:** 2500 **MP:** 99999 **EXP:** 0 **AP:** 10

**GIL DROPPED:** 0    **STEAL:** Normal: Phoenix Down   Rare: Mega Phoenix
**PILFER GIL:** 350    **DROP:** Normal: None   Rare: None

**HP:** 2500 **MP:** 99999 **EXP:** 0 **AP:** 10

Although the Head section remains on the battlefield throughout the fight, you can't target it until the Redoubts are destroyed first. After doing so, you can target and attack the head. The Redoubts work together to inflict attacks on single characters that can cause up to 1500 HP damage. While the Redoubts are defeated and lie dormant, the Head will attempt to resurrect them one at a time, or poison the party with a multi-status inflicting attack. It's a good idea to equip your characters with Ribbons throughout this battle. Use your strongest attacks and spells to hit the Redoubts until they crumple, then lash out at the Head with everything you've got. You must end this battle before Shuyin speaks seven times and uses Vegnagun to fire at Spira!

**GIL DROPPED:** 0    **STEAL:** Normal: Phoenix Down   Rare: Mega Phoenix
**PILFER GIL:** 350    **DROP:** Normal: None   Rare: None

**HP:** 38420 **MP:** 99999 **EXP:** 0 **AP:** 10

**GIL DROPPED:** 0    **STEAL:** Normal: Megalixir   Rare: Megalixir
**PILFER GIL:** 8000    **DROP:** Normal: None   Rare: None

## NEW GAME PLUS DATA

Following the credits and the ending scenes, the game offers an option to allow you to save your game as a New Game Plus. When this save data is loaded, you can begin a new game with all the dressspheres, Garment Grids, accessories, items, Al Bhed primers, special dressphere upgrades, the Book of Magical Dances, and abilities gained in your previous game. However, your character levels are reset to level 1.

### ENDINGS—NO SPOILERS!

*Save the New Game Plus data to pick up another adventure where you left off in terms of advancement and item gathering.*

Upon the defeat of Vegnagun, you will proceed directly to the final battle against an adversary with very recognizable attacks. All you need do is keep your party healthy by healing every turn, and counterattack the boss to win the game.

Following that, Yuna and the Gullwings return to the Farplane Glen. This is a scene that you can alter with the controller, if you so choose. Without altering this scene, you will view the "Common" Ending of the game. The Common Ending occurs during all three endings.

However, if you press the X button during the scene at the Farplane Glen, the fayth will appear and ask Yuna if she wants to see someone. Answer "Yes" to view an extra scene after the Common Ending and the credits roll. This is called the "Good" Ending.

If you manage to accumulate 100% during one or more games, then you can view the "Perfect" Ending by pressing the X button at the Farplane Glen as described above. The "Perfect" Ending includes yet another additional scene following the Good Ending.

# 100% COMPLETION GUIDE

The purpose of this section is simple: To show that by making certain choices and completing all the missions and side quests of the game, you can achieve 100% story completion in a single game! For each Chapter, go to each location listed and perform the actions described to build up your total percentage. If you need to view a sphere, talk to Shinra on the Bridge and select the appropriate sphere. Do *not* skip any scenes or dialogue, and use the Walkthrough and Mini-Games chapters to complete the actions listed. You can get 100% all in one game and view the Perfect Ending!

## BEGINNING OF CHAPTER 1

### LUCA: +1.6%                                        TOTAL: 1.6%

Examine the moogle hiding on the second dock.

Mission Complete! (Retrieving the Garment Grid)

### AIRSHIP CELSIUS: +1.8%                             TOTAL: 3.4%

Speak with Brother, Paine, Rikku, and Shinra on the Bridge.

Speak to Barkeep in the Cabin.

Rest in the Cabin.

View Treasure Sphere: "Journey's Start"

### MT. GAGAZET, FLOATING RUINS: +2.6%     TOTAL: 6.0%

Reach the top of the floating ruins within the time limit.

Mission Complete! (Defeat the Leblanc Syndicate to the top)

### AIRSHIP CELSIUS: +0.6%                             TOTAL: 6.6%

Speak with Brother and choose "Comfort him."

### LUCA: +1.6%                                        TOTAL: 8.2%

Mission Complete! (Relive Yuna's concert events, including the Moogle healing event)

Speak with Rin in the corridor under the blitzball dome.

### MI'IHEN HIGHROAD: +0.2%                            TOTAL: 8.4%

Listen to Yuna's memories of the Mi'ihen Highroad

### MUSHROOM ROCK ROAD: +4.6%                          TOTAL: 13.0%

Speak with Yaibal and the other Youth League members.

Speak with Clasko at the entrance.

Enter the Mushroom Rock Road area to begin the "Foggy Fiend Frenzy!" mission.

Mission Complete! (Navigate through Mushroom Rock Road to the lift area)

Speak to Clasko at the entrance to Mushroom Rock Road, and allow him to come onboard the Celsius.

Outside the Youth League Headquarters entrance, speak with Lucil twice.

Outside the Youth League Headquarters, speak with Maechen without skipping or interrupting. Shake Maechen's hand when he's done.

At the Den of Woe, encounter Ormi and Logos. Speak with Maroda.

Onboard the Airship Celsius, watch the Treasure Sphere recording, "Crimson Report 1."

Speak to Clasko on the upper level of the Cabin.

Characters

1

Garment Grids & Dresspheres

2

Battle System

3

Accessories

4

Items and Item Shops

5

Walkthrough
Chapter 1
Chapter 2
Chapter 3
Chapter 4
Chapter 5

Mini-Games

7

Fiends and Enemies

8

## DJOSE TEMPLE: +1.0%

TOTAL: 14.0%

Receive the "Letter of Introduction" from Gippal.

## MOONFLOW: +0.6%

TOTAL: 14.6%

Speak to Tobli at the Moonflow South Bank.

Mission Complete! (Escort the Hypello's wagon and don't lose any cargo)

Head toward the Farplane entrance to trigger a scene.

## THUNDER PLAINS: +0.2%

TOTAL: 15.2%

Watch the entrance scene.

## MACALANIA WOODS: +2.2%

TOTAL: 17.4%

Speak to Bayra in Macalania Woods-South.

Speak to Donga at the spring area.

Speak to Pukutak in Macalania Woods-North.

Speak to Tromell four times at the sphere tree grove.

Mission Complete! ("Follow that O'aka!") Allow O'aka to board the airship.

Board the airship and speak to O'aka in the Cabin.

Before the Chapter 3 mission titled "Secure the Agency!" ends, pay off all of O'aka's debt.*

## BIKANEL DESERT: +0.8%

TOTAL: 18.2%

Mission Complete! (Dig up the machina parts before time elapses)

Watch the scene with Baralai.

## CALM LANDS: +0.2%

TOTAL: 19.0%

Watch the entrance scene.

Begin to advertise for a company. (Publicity Campaign)

## MT. GAGAZET: +0.4%

TOTAL: 19.4%

Watch the entrance scene.

## BESAID ISLAND: +2.2%

TOTAL: 21.6%

Mission Complete! (Find Wakka and defeat Flame Dragon)

## ZANARKAND RUINS: +1.8%

TOTAL: 23.4%

Inside the dome, speak with Cid and choose "You bet I do!"

Mission Complete! (Obtain the treasure sphere in the last room of Zanarkand)

## AIRSHIP CELSIUS: +0.2%

TOTAL: 23.6%

Listen to reports of an "Awesome Sphere" in Kilika.

## KILIKA ISLAND: +1.6%

TOTAL: 25.2%

Enter Dona's house and speak with her.

Mission Complete! (Reach the temple stairs and defeat YSLS-Zero)

## CHAPTER 1 COMPLETE!

# BEGINNING OF CHAPTER 2

## AIRSHIP CELSIUS: +2.4%                    TOTAL: 27.6%

Rest in the Cabin.

Speak to Brother on the Bridge and choose "Youth League." (Returning the Awesome Sphere)

## MUSHROOM ROCK ROAD: +1.0%              TOTAL: 28.6%

Give the Awesome Sphere to Nooj.

## AIRSHIP CELSIUS: +0.6%                    TOTAL: 29.2%

Begin the mission to steal three Leblanc Syndicate uniforms.

## BESAID ISLAND: +0.8%                       TOTAL: 30.0%

Mission Complete! (Run the Gunner's Gauntlet and beat Beclem's required score)

## KILIKA ISLAND: +0.2%                       TOTAL: 30.2%

Go to Kilika Island and move forward to speak with Dona and the villagers.

## LUCA: +0.8%                                 TOTAL: 31.0%

Watch the interview with Shelinda in Luca-Square.

## MI'IHEN HIGHROAD: +1.4%                 TOTAL: 32.4%

Mission Complete! (Capture a chocobo and rescue Calli within the time limit)

Speak to Clasko and Calli near the Travel Agency and let them and the chocobo board the Celsius.

## MUSHROOM ROCK ROAD: +1.0%              TOTAL: 33.4%

Outside the Youth League Headquarters, speak to Elma and Lucil.

At the Den of Woe, speak with Nooj.

Board the Celsius and speak to Shinra to watch Crimson Report 7.

## MOONFLOW: +0.2%                            TOTAL: 33.6%

Mission Complete! (Sell all 10 tickets for Tobli)

## GUADOSALAM: +0.2%                          TOTAL: 33.8%

Speak to the guards outside Leblanc's chateau.

## THUNDER PLAINS: +0.2%                     TOTAL: 34.0%

Speak to Cid in the southern portion of the Thunder Plains.

## MACALANIA WOODS: +1.4%                  TOTAL: 35.4%

Mission Complete! (Locate all three musicians for the Hypello near the entrance)

## CALM LANDS: +0.8%                          TOTAL: 36.2%

Clasko leaves the airship and runs toward the old Monster Arena.

Mission Complete! (Clear the fiends out of Clasko's Chocobo Ranch)

Capture a chocobo during a random battle before the end of Chapter 3.

Speak to Lian and Ayde at the Travel Agency.

Characters

1

Garment Grids & Dresspheres

2

Battle System

3

Accessories

4

Items and Item Shops

5

Walkthrough
Chapter 1
Chapter 2
Chapter 3
Chapter 4
Chapter 5

Mini-Games

7

Fiends and Enemies

8

## ZANARKAND RUINS: +0.4%

TOTAL: 36.6%

Speak to Isaaru just inside the dome.

Earn Mission Complete! for "Operation: Monkey!" before the end of Chapter 3.

## DJOSE TEMPLE: +0.4%

TOTAL: 37.0%

Mission Complete! (Travel down Djose Highroad to obtain a Syndicate Uniform)

## BIKANEL DESERT: +0.2%

TOTAL: 37.2%

Mission Complete! (Investigate the Oasis and defeat Logos to obtain a Syndicate Uniform)

## MT. GAGAZET MOUNTAIN: +1.0%

TOTAL: 38.2%

Speak with Kimahri twice.

Enter the hot springs from the overhanging cliff to view the complete hot springs event.

Mission Complete! (Defeat Ormi and the Fem-Goons to obtain a Syndicate Uniform)

## AIRSHIP CELSIUS: +0.2%

TOTAL: 38.4%

Watch the scene where all three Syndicate Uniforms are worn.

## GUADOSALAM: +3.4%

TOTAL: 41.8%

Mission Complete! (Steal back the stolen sphere from Leblanc)

## AIRSHIP CELSIUS: +0.4%

TOTAL: 42.2%

Watch the discussion of the mission at Bevelle.

## BEVELLE: +2.6%

TOTAL: 44.8%

Mission Complete! (Infiltrate Bevelle and defeat Bahamut)

### CHAPTER 2 COMPLETE!

### BEGINNING OF CHAPTER 3

## AIRSHIP CELSIUS: +0.8%

TOTAL: 45.6%

Initial scenes.

Rest in the Cabin.

## LUCA: +0.8%

TOTAL: 46.4%

Defeat three contestants and then Shinra to win the Sphere Break Tournament.

## MI'IHEN HIGHROAD: +0.6%

TOTAL: 47.0%

Mission Complete! (Defeat the malfunctioning machina attacking pedestrians on the Highroad.)

## MUSHROOM ROCK ROAD: +0.4%

TOTAL: 47.4%

Speak to Yaibal and Lucil near the barricade.

## DJOSE TEMPLE: +0.2%

TOTAL: 47.6%

Approach the temple to trigger a scene with Gippal.

## MOONFLOW: +0.2%

TOTAL: 47.8%

Speak to Tobli near the wagon to trigger a short scene.

## GUADOSALAM: +2.0%

TOTAL: 49.8%

Inside the chateau, speak with Logos and Ormi in the living room.

Speak with Leblanc in her upstairs bedroom.

Speak to Logos and Ormi a second time, then proceed to Logos's room.

Watch Ormi's and Logos's spheres.

Talk to Maechen.

Obtain "Crimson Sphere 4," then board the airship and watch "Crimson Report 4" at Shinra's station.

## THUNDER PLAINS: +0.2%

TOTAL: 50.0%

Speak to Lian and Ayde in the northern part of the Thunder Plains. Choose any destination.

## MACALANIA WOODS: +0.8%

TOTAL: 50.8%

After paying off O'aka's debt, head to the Travel Agency at Lake Macalania and obtain a Mission Complete! (Defend the Travel Agency from fiend attacks)

## BIKANEL DESERT: +0.4%

TOTAL: 51.2%

Speak to Marnela in the Cactuar Nation.

## CALM LANDS: +0.4%

TOTAL: 51.6%

Mission Complete! (Rescue the tourists trapped inside the cave)

Visit the Travel Agency to ensure the installation of Shinra's CommSphere.

Visit the upper floor of the Chocobo Ranch to ensure the installation of Shinra's CommSphere.

## MT. GAGAZET: +0.4%

TOTAL: 52.0%

Mission Complete! (Defeat Garik Ronso at the mountain summit to stop the Ronso from waging war)

## ZANARKAND RUINS: +0.2%

TOTAL: 52.2%

Speak to Isaaru inside the Zanarkand dome.

Complete "Operation: Monkey!" mission before the end of Chapter 3.

## BESAID ISLAND: +2.0%

TOTAL: 54.2%

Mission Complete! (Clear the temple of fiends and defeat Valefor)

## KILIKA ISLAND: +1.0%

TOTAL: 55.2%

Mission Complete! (Sneak through the port and the forest to Kilika Temple, then rescue Barthello and defeat Ifrit)

## AIRSHIP CELSIUS: +0.6%

TOTAL: 55.8%

## BEVELLE: +1.6%

TOTAL: 57.4%

Notice Gippal from the Highbridge.

Witness a scene at the Bevelle Underground.

Obtain Crimson Sphere 1, board the Celsius, and view Crimson Report 1 at Shinra's station.

## DJOSE TEMPLE: +2.2%

TOTAL: 59.6%

Mission Complete! (Defeat the fiends emanating from the temple and defeat Ixion)

When Yuna mentions "I'm all alone…" in the Farplane Abyss, press the X button to hear a distant whistle. Keep pressing the X button until you hear the whistle four times.

## CHAPTER 3 COMPLETE!

Characters

1

Garment Grids & Dresspheres

2

Battle System

3

Accessories

4

Items and Item Shops

5

Walkthrough

Chapter 1

Chapter 2

Chapter 3

Chapter 4

Chapter 5

Mini-Games

7

Fiends and Enemies

8

# BEGINNING OF CHAPTER 4

## AIRSHIP CELSIUS: +1.8%                                    TOTAL: 61.4%

Watch Crimson Report 2 and Crimson Report 3 at Shinra's station.

Rest in the Cabin.

## AIRSHIP CELSIUS:
## COMMSPHERE NETWORK: +0.8%                          TOTAL: 62.2%

View the Besaid Island CommSphere and speak to Wakka.

View the Kilika Island CommSphere and speak to Dona.

View the Mushroom Rock Road CommSphere and speak to Yaibal.

View the CommSphere in Bevelle and speak to Maroda.

## AIRSHIP CELSIUS: +0.8%                                    TOTAL: 63.0%

Ride the elevator to the Deck and speak with Paine.

## AIRSHIP CELSIUS:
## COMMSPHERE NETWORK: +4.4%                          TOTAL: 67.4%

View the Besaid Island CommSphere seven times and watch the scenes with Wakka and Beclem.

View the Kilika Island Temple CommSphere and speak to Barthello.

View the Luca CommSphere and watch all of Shelinda's interviews.

View the Mi'ihen Highroad CommSphere and view all the areas to gather evidence so that Rikku or the Chocobo Eater is the culprit.

View the Djose Temple CommSphere and watch the first scene where the Al Bhed technician approaches the CommSphere.

View the Guadosalam CommSphere; Yuna speaks to Ormi.

View the Thunder Plains CommSphere and capture the chocobo with the Choco-Porter contraption.

View the Macalania Woods Entrance CommSphere and the musicians appear and speak.

View the Macalania Woods Travel Agency CommSphere and O'aka laments the poor business.

View the Bikanel Desert Camp Area CommSphere and speak to Nhadala.

View the Calm Lands Chocobo Ranch CommSphere until you see Clasko telling the chocobo, "You're a good boy, aren't you?".

View the Mt. Gagazet Mountain Gate CommSphere and speak with Kimahri.

View the Mt. Gagazet Hot Springs CommSphere and witness the scenes involving Tobli, Buddy, Barkeep, O'aka, Isaaru, Elma & Lucil, Maechen, Cid & Nhadala, and Dona.

## MOONFLOW: +0.8%                                          TOTAL: 68.2%

Mission Complete! (Chase Tobli around the Moonflow to the entrance of Guadosalam)

## AIRSHIP CELSIUS: +1.0%                                    TOTAL: 69.2%

Rehearse for Thunder Plains concert.

## AIRSHIP CELSIUS:
## COMMSPHERE NETWORK: +2.4%                          TOTAL: 71.6%

View the Besaid Island CommSphere scenes involving Beclem and Lulu.

View the Kilika Island Port CommSphere scenes involving Dona.

View the Kilika Temple CommSphere scenes involving Barthello.

View the Mushroom Rock CommSphere scenes involving Lucil and Yaibal.

View the Moonflow CommSphere scenes involving Elma.

View the Guadosalam CommSphere scenes where Ormi speaks about the concert.

View the Macalania Woods Travel Agency CommSphere scene where O'aka leaves for the concert.

View the Zanarkand Ruins CommSphere scene with Isaaru.

## THUNDER PLAINS: +0.4%                                    TOTAL: 72.0%

Mission Complete! (Clear the fiends out of the cave and defeat Zalamander)

## AIRSHIP CELSIUS: +1.0%                    TOTAL: 73.0%

Listen in on the crowd's argument

Talk to Tobli to start the concert and watch the YRP scene that follows.

## THUNDER PLAINS: +0.4%                      TOTAL: 73.4%

Yunapalooza.

## AIRSHIP CELSIUS: +2.2%                     TOTAL: 75.6%

Speak to Maechen on the Bridge.

Speak to Leblanc in the Engine Room.

## CHAPTER 4 COMPLETE!

## BEGINNING OF CHAPTER 5

## AIRSHIP CELSIUS: +2.0%                     TOTAL: 77.6%

Watch "Crimson Report 5" at Shinra's station.

Speak to Buddy on the Bridge.

Rest in the Cabin to be awakened by Brother's rambling.

Speak to Buddy in the Engine Room.

## ZANARKAND RUINS: +0.8%                     TOTAL: 78.4%

Episode Complete!

Speak to Maechen and agree to listen about Vegnagun.

## BESAID ISLAND: +1.8%                       TOTAL: 80.2%

Episode Complete!

## KILIKA ISLAND: +1.0%                       TOTAL: 81.2%

Episode Complete!

## LUCA: +0.6%                                TOTAL: 81.8%

Mission Complete! (Follow the moogle to relive memories of *FINAL FANTASY X*) Episode Complete!

## MI'IHEN HIGHROAD: +0.2%                    TOTAL: 82.0%

Episode Complete!

## MUSHROOM ROCK ROAD: +3.0%                  TOTAL: 85.0%

Mission Complete! (Fight with the Youth League warriors and defeat Lucil) Episode Complete!

Go to the observation deck at Youth League Headquarters, and speak to Lucil to receive "Nooj's Sphere."

Board the airship and watch the Treasure Sphere movie, "Deathseeker" at Shinra's station.

Obtain all the Crimson Spheres and open the sealed door in the Den of Woe. Defeat Rikku, Paine, Baralai, Gippal and Nooj. Episode Complete!

## DJOSE TEMPLE: +0.8%                        TOTAL: 85.8%

Defeat the Experiment boss when its Attack, Defense, and Special levels are below level 5.

Repair the Experiment with the repair manual key items. Defeat Experiment boss a second time when all levels are level 5. Episode Complete!

## MOONFLOW: +0.4%                            TOTAL: 86.2%

Episode Complete!

Characters

1

Garment Grids & D!spheres

2

Battle System

3

Accessories

4

Items and Item Shops

5

Walkthrough
Chapter 1
Chapter 2
Chapter 3
Chapter 4
Chapter 5

Mini-Games

7

Fiends and Enemies

8

## GUADOSALAM: +1.2%                    TOTAL: 87.4%

Join the musical group in the central square. Episode Complete!

Return to Guadosalam and speak to Tromell outside the locked door. Enter the locked area and obtain Baralai's Sphere, then board the Celsius and watch the Yevon's Secret sphere at Shinra's station.

## THUNDER PLAINS: +1.0%                TOTAL: 88.4%

Mission Complete! (Defeat the fiends attacking the towers)

Enter the secret cave and rescue Cid. Defeat the Machina Panzer boss. Episode Complete!

Onboard the airship, speak with Cid on the outside Deck.

Return to the Bridge to view Cid's tirade.

## MACALANIA WOODS: +0.6%              TOTAL: 89.0%

View the scenes at the two springs. Episode Complete!

Trigger the scene with O'aka and Wantz near the Travel Agency. Episode Complete!

## BIKANEL DESERT: +1.2%               TOTAL: 90.2%

Mission Complete! (Locate the first nine Gatekeepers and return them to the Cactuar Nation at Bikanel)

Mission Complete! (Enter the Cactuar Hollow and defeat the Jumbo Cactuar)

Mission Complete! (Defeat Angra Mainyu) Episode Complete!

Return to the Cactuar Nation and speak with Benzo.

## BEVELLE: +1.8%                       TOTAL: 92.0%

Episode Complete!

Inside Via Infinito, the hidden dungeon at Bevelle, obtain Crimson Sphere 6 at Cloister 0. Defeat Aranea and obtain Crimson Sphere 8 at Cloister 20.

Board the Celsius and view Crimson Report 6 and Crimson Report 8 at Shinra's station.

Defeat Trema in Cloister ∞. Episode Complete!

## CALM LANDS: +0.4%                    TOTAL: 92.4

Raise the publicity level of either company to level 5 before entering the Calm Lands. Episode Complete!

Dispatch three chocobos of each level without any of them running away to reveal the Chocobo Ranch's secret dungeon. Complete the dungeon and defeat the Anything Eater. Episode Complete!

## MT. GAGAZET: +1.2%                   TOTAL: 93.6%

Episode Complete!

## AIRSHIP CELSIUS: +0.6%              TOTAL: 94.2%

After getting Episode Complete in every location, YRP is presented with the Gullwings' prized Mascot dressphere.

Talk to Brother and decide where you want to go to jump into the Farplane (any location is fine).

## FARPLANE: +0.8%                      TOTAL: 95.0%

Advance to the Farplane Abyss to find Leblanc waiting for Nooj.

## AIRSHIP CELSIUS: +2.4%              TOTAL: 96.0%

After entering the Farplane, board the Celsius and view the consecutive familiy events: Speak to Shinra on the Bridge, overhear Buddy and Brother on the Deck, view the confrontation with Cid at the Cabin area. Return from the Farplane a second time and speak with Rikku on the Deck.

## FARPLANE: +4.0%                      TOTAL: 100.0%

Defeat Vegnagun.

Defeat final boss.

## CHAPTER 5 COMPLETE!

During the scene at the Farplane Abyss, press the X button to hear whistling.

Answer the fayth "Yes!" to view the Perfect Ending.

# MINI-GAMES

Characters

Garment Grids & Dresspheres

Battle System

Accessories

Items and Item Shops

Walkthrough

Mini-Games

7

Fiends and Enemies

| When Available: | Chapters 1, 2, 3, and 5 |
| Location: | Luca |
| Objective: | A new game is all the rage among the blitzball-bereft citizens of Luca. Mathematical skills and a quick mind are what is needed to beat the Sphere Break players at their favorite game. Collect coins while digging in the Bikanel Desert or win them in matches. Come back to Luca during Chapter 3 to participate in the Sphere Break Tournament and see if you can defeat Shinra in the final match for the Lady Luck Dresssphere. |

# SPHERE BREAK OVERTAKES LUCA!

Sphere Break is one of the few mini-games that spans almost the entirety of the game. To start it, visit Luca after you see the Behind the Scenes mission explaining what Yuna was doing while Rikku and Paine were catching Leblanc at the concert. Head over to the blitzball stadium and go into the locker room on the right. There you'll meet up with Rin, the creator of Sphere Break. He'll give you some of the basics and refer you to a proctor in the other locker room.

*Clear the Behind the Scenes mission to gain unrestricted access to Luca. Head to the stadium locker rooms to start playing Sphere Break.*

Talk to the Rin's beaked asistant to get 20 entry coins and the rules of the game. During Chapter 1, you can only play against this character, so take advantage of this time to get familiar with the game and win some more coins.

The number of players you can take on increases as you proceed through the game. In Chapter 3, head back to Luca for the Sphere Break Tournament. In Chapter 5, look in the locker rooms for even stronger players and greater challenges!

*Look for this character to learn the rules of Sphere Break. His tutorial is highly recommended. In addition, he's the only player you can play in Chapter 1.*

# PLAYING SPHERE BREAK

Sphere Break is a fun game to play once you understand the rules. Basically, you're racing against the clock to create multiples of the Core Sphere's core number using combinations of 16 numbered coins.

Sphere Break takes place on a special game board that holds 16 coins and a Core Sphere. Don't worry about finding a Core Sphere of your own (you won't); just look for people who have one of their own to play with. The core sphere randomly generates a core number from 1-9 and appears as the small sphere in the center of the board. Using the 16 coins surrounding the Core Sphere, you must create a multiple of the core number to end the turn. The number of Border Coins you use in a turn is applied against the game's quota (a figure that varies depending on the Core Sphere you're playing against). When you meet the quota within the number of turns set, you win the game. If you fail to create a multiple of the core number within the time limit set or fail to meet the quota in the number of turns specified, you lose the game.

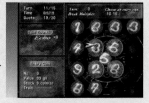

*Get used to the look of the game board so that you know where to look for information instinctively.*

*The core number on this board is 3. The Entry Coins are the ones you get at the start of the game. Their face numbers are 3, 2, 1 and 5.*

Central to Sphere Break are the two different types of coins used to create multiples of the core number. The four gold colored coins surrounding the Core Sphere are called Entry Coins, which you supply. You must have four different Entry Coins to play the game and once the game is over, they are gone for good. However, you can win more in the game or by digging in the Bikanel Desert. There are 64 different Entry Coins, each with their own base numbers from (1-9) and different traits.

Around the Entry Coins are 12 silver colored coins called Border Coins. The NPC player provides these coins. Border Coins are used in combination with the Entry Coins to create multiples of the core number. Like the Entry Coins, Border Coins are also numbered from 1-9. However, at the end of a turn, the number on the front of the remaining Border Coins increases by 1.

*The Border Coins form a ring on the outside of the board. The numbers on the coins increase by 1 at the end of each turn. Coins with the number 9 disappear at the end of a turn if they aren't used.*

The numbers on the front of both the Entry and Border Coins are used to create multiples of the core number. For example, say that the core number for a certain round is 4. You need to make a multiple of that number (4) to create a "Core Break" to end the turn. Above the game board is an information bar that indicates the current sum of the coins you've chosen and, under the heading Break Multiples, gives you the next three multiples of the core number. If you get lost, use the information bar to help close out your Core Break.

At the start of each turn, the core number is revealed and you have a set amount of time to create a multiple of that number. First, you must choose one of the Entry Coins. At the start of the mini-game, you are given four different types of coins (Coyote, Flan, Helm, and Zurvan) with the following numbers on their faces: 3, 2, 1, and 5 respectively. Let's say the core number for a turn is three. You can choose to end the turn by starting with the Coyote Entry Coin (which has a three on it), or attempt to create a larger combo by choosing one of the other Entry Coins. Since the Entry Coins you use never count directly towards the quota, you'll almost always want to use at least two coins (one Entry Coin and one or more Border Coins) to make a Core Break—otherwise, you've most likely wasted a turn.

After selecting an Entry Coin, you can choose freely from the remaining coins (both Entry and Border Coins). After choosing a coin, you cannot deselect it, so choose wisely—but quickly. Continuing the example from above, the first three multiples of the core number 4 are 4, 8, and 12. If you chose the Zurvan coin as your Entry Coin (with a face value of 5), you only have to add 3 to your current sum to create a Core Break at 8. You can combine the Zurvan coin with a Border Coin with the face value of 3 or two Border Coins with face values of 1 and 2 to create the Core Break. Whatever coins you choose, once you create a coin combination that equals a multiple of the core number, the turn ends and the number of Border Coins you used to make your Core Break are applied against the match *quota*.

When you are trying to create Break Multiples with large numbers of Border Coins, use the information bar to keep track of the sum of the coins you've chosen and the next multiples of the core number.

# ADVANCED TECHNIQUES

The terms for winning and losing a match of Sphere Break are pretty simple: To win, you must fill the Quota within the required number of turns. When you start a game of Sphere Break with one of the NPCs, these terms are clearly laid out. If you forget, look at the box in the upper-left corner of the screen for a reminder.

However, there are many ways to lose a match of Sphere Break. The most obvious way is to fail to make your quota within the set number of turns. This is easy to do at the start of your Sphere Break experience as you try to get used to the way the game works.

The core number 1 can easily derail your attempts to meet your quota, since the first Entry Coin you choose will immediately cause a Core Break. Your only chance to whittle away the quota is to go for a "Multiplier Echo."

The easiest way to lose the game is by failing to make a Core Break within the set turn time limit. Each turn has a set time limit that you have to work within. As you strive to create larger coin combinations, it is very easy to get lost within your calculations and either run out of coins or time.

Be careful when making Core Break combinations. It is very easy to panic and try to use up all of your Border Coins in one shot. Unfortunately, this urge will leave you without many options for a couple of turns and may cost you the match.

Since the Border Coins you use in a Core Break are removed from the board at the end of a turn, you should avoid using too many Border Coins for several turns until they're replenished. A 10-coin combo is nice, but there are other ways to increase the number of coins applied against your quota that don't involve using a lot of coins in one turn.

# COIN TRAITS

The majority of coins have traits associated with them that can give you prizes of items or coins, alter the gil value of your Entry Coins, or add multipliers to the number of coins applied against your quota for that turn, just to name a few. The traits assigned to Border Coins are randomly determined and vary from coin to coin. The traits associated with Entry Coins are predetermined and do not change. When choosing the four Entry Coins you're going to play with, keep their face value and traits in mind. If you can stack your deck with Entry Coins that double, triple, quadruple, or even quintuple the number of coins added toward the quota, you can reach even the largest quotas with ease!

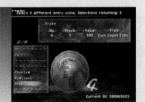

Check out an Entry Coin's traits before deciding whether to put it in the game. Use these traits to your advantage and you'll win big!

## ECHO BONUSES

There are two advanced Entry Coin traits that require special attention: Coin Count Echo and Multiplier Echo. Selecting a coin with these traits as one of your four entry coins allows you to get Coin Count Echo and Multiplier Echo bonuses during the game. Once you select these coins at the beginning of the match, you're eligible for the bonus every turn whether you select the coin on that turn or not.

You must have a coin with the "Coin Count Echo" or "Multiplier Echo" trait before you'll be able to score any Echo bonuses.

A Coin Count Echo occurs when you use the same number of coins to create a Core Break two or more in a row. The multiplier increases by one for each turn you make a Sphere Break using the same number of coins. This is a quick and easy way to tear through the quota, and you don't even have to use a large number of coins to see big results quickly. In effect, if you use 2 or 3 coins to make a Sphere Break on every turn, you can build up a large Echo Bonus without depriving yourself of Border Coins or taxing your brain. You don't have to be a math genius to figure out multipliers with three or four coins.

**Coin Count Echo Bonus = # of Border Coins Used x the # of Consecutive Echoes.**

The Multiplier Echo is a bit trickier to pull off (and the coins with this trait are harder to find). Basically, if you make a Core Break with the same multiplier twice in a row, you start a Multiplier Echo and earn bonus quota points. For example, if you have a core number of 3 and you make a core break with a sum of 6, the multiplier used in the Multiplier Echo is 2x the core number. So, in the next turn, you want to use a number that is 2x the core number to create the Core Break. If the next core number is 6, then you want to use 12 as your Core Break sum to complete the Multiplier Echo. The more turns you can keep this up, the larger the bonus.

**Multiplier Echo Bonus = Target Multiplier x # of Consecutive Echoes**

Characters

Garment Grids & Dresspheres

Battle System

Accessories

Items and Item Shops

Walkthrough

Mini-Games

Fiends and Enemies

# THE SPHERE BREAK TOURNAMENT

Visit Luca in Chapter 3 to participate in the Sphere Break Tournament. The rules for this tournament are pretty simple: You must win three matches to advance to the finals where you take on your buddy, Shinra. If you lose three matches, you are disqualified. You can't take on the same competitor twice and you must use the coins provided specicifically for the contest.

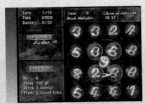

Fortunately, the coin restrictions work in your favor. The four types of coins (Ahriman, Bird, Reptile, and Wasp) aren't the greatest, but their face values (6, 5, 3, 2 respectively) are pretty useful and the Ahriman coin has the Coin Count Echo trait. Make the most of the Coin Count Echo trait by shooting for Core Breaks using the same number of coins each turn to quickly take down your opponents.

It's tournament time! Can you beat Shinra and win the Lady Luck Dresssphere?

*The Ahriman Entry Coin is the key to relatively easy victories.*

# SPHERE BREAK PLAYER INFORMATION

This section provides all of the basic information about the various Sphere Break players, including their locations and levels of difficulty. You will also find information about the types of items and coins you can win when you take them on. The lists of items and coins correspond with the information given in the following tables.

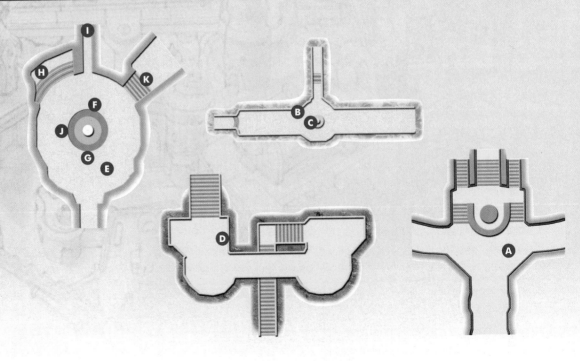

## SPHERE BREAK PLAYERS (NORMAL)

| LOC. | NAME | #TURNS | TIME LT. | QUOTA | DIFF. | ITEM | RARE ITEM | COIN | RARE COIN | AVAILABILITY |
|------|------|--------|----------|-------|-------|------|-----------|------|-----------|--------------|
| 1 | Practice Core Sphere | 15 | 60 sec | 20 | * | Item A | Rare A | Group A | Group D | Always |
| 2 | Shades Core Sphere | 15 | 60 sec | 20 | ** | Item A | Rare A | Group A | Group D | Chapters 2-5 |
| 3 | Punk Core Sphere | 20 | 45 sec | 80 | **** | Item D | Rare D | Group C | Group E | Chapters 2-5 |
| 4 | Gigolo Core Sphere | 15 | 60 sec | 30 | *** | Item B | Rare B | Group B | Group E | Chapters 3-5 |
| 5 | Dream Shop Core Sphere | 20 | 45 sec | 50 | *** | Item C | Rare B | Group B | Group E | Chapters 3-5 |
| 6 | Shoopuf Core Sphere | 20 | 45 sec | 50 | *** | Item B | Rare B | Group A | Group D | Chapter 5 |
| 7 | Pet Core Sphere | 15 | 30 sec | 50 | *** | Item P | Rare P | Group B | Group F | Chapter 5 |
| 8 | Gagazet Core Sphere | 30 | 60 sec | 100 | *** | Item C | Rare C | Group B | Group E | Chapter 5 |
| 9 | Shinra Core Sphere | 20 | 30 sec | 100 | ***** | Item S | Rare S | Group D | Group E | Chapter 5 |
| 10 | Macalania Core Sphere | 30 | 45 sec | 80 | **** | Item B | Rare C | Group B | Group D | Chapter 5 |
| 11 | Mi'ihen Core Sphere | 30 | 20 sec | 150 | ***** | Item D | Rare D | Group C | Group F | Chapter 5 |
| 12 | Bevelle Core Sphere | 30 | 30 sec | 200 | ***** | Item E | Rare E | Group D | Group G | Chapter 5 |
| 13 | Marrvelous Core Sphere | 30 | 30 sec | 300 | ***** | Item E | Rare E | Group D | Group H | Chapter 5 |

## SPHERE BREAK PLAYERS (NORMAL)

| LOC. | NAME | # TURNS | TIME LT. | QUOTA | DIFF. | ITEM | RARE ITEM | COIN | RARE COIN | AVAILABILITY |
|---|---|---|---|---|---|---|---|---|---|---|
| A | Intimidator Core Sphere | 15 | 60 sec | 20 | ** | Item A | - | - | - | Always |
| B | Slacking Guard Core Sphere | 15 | 60 sec | 20 | ** | Item A | - | - | - | Always |
| C | Grandpa Core Sphere | 15 | 45 sec | 30 | *** | Item B | - | - | - | Always |
| D | Dream Shop Core Sphere | 10 | 60 sec | 25 | ** | Item B | - | - | - | Always |
| E | Fresh Catch Core Sphere | 15 | 60 sec | 20 | ** | Item A | - | - | - | Always |
| F | Shades Core Sphere | 15 | 60 sec | 20 | ** | Item A | - | - | - | Always |
| G | Punk Core Sphere | 15 | 60 sec | 40 | *** | Item B | - | - | - | 1 Win |
| H | Gigolo Core Sphere | 15 | 60 sec | 30 | *** | Item B | - | - | - | 1 Win |
| I | Shoopuf Core Sphere | 10 | 60 sec | 20 | *** | Item B | - | - | - | 1 Win |
| J | Pet Core Sphere | 15 | 45 sec | 40 | *** | Item P | - | - | - | 2 Win |
| K | Shinra Core Sphere | 15 | 45 sec | 5 | **** | Item S | - | - | - | Final Match |

The following section lists the items given away during matches.

### ITEM A

| Hi-Potion | 60% |
|---|---|
| Remedy | 20% |
| Dispel Tonic | 20% |

### ITEM B

| Hi-Potion | 20% |
|---|---|
| Chocobo Feather | 20% |
| Lunar Curtain | 20% |
| Light Curtain | 20% |
| Star Curtain | 20% |

### ITEM C

| Hi-Potion | 20% |
|---|---|
| Ether | 20% |
| Remedy | 20% |
| Healing Spring | 20% |
| Dispel Tonic | 20% |

### ITEM D

| Mega-Potion | 20% |
|---|---|
| Healing Spring | 40% |
| Stamina Tablet | 20% |
| Mana Tablet | 20% |

### ITEM E

| Mega-Potion | 20% |
|---|---|
| Ether | 20% |
| Remedy | 20% |
| Chocobo Feather | 20% |
| Healing Spring | 20% |

### ITEM P

| *Hi-Potion | 20% |
|---|---|
| Ether | 10% |
| Remedy | 20% |
| Healing Spring | 20% |
| Dispel Tonic | 20% |
| **White Signet Garment Grid | 10% |

*Increases to 30% after winning the White Signet Garment Grid.

**Drops to 0% after winning the White Signet Garment Grid.

### ITEM S

| *Hi-Potion | 20% |
|---|---|
| Chocobo Feather | 10% |
| Lunar Curtain | 20% |
| Light Curtain | 20% |
| Star Curtain | 20% |
| **Treasure Hunt Garment Grid | 10% |

*Increases to 30% after winning the Treasure Hunt Garment Grid.

**Drops to 0% after winning the Treasure Hunt Garment Grid.

### RARE A

| X-Potion | 40% |
|---|---|
| Ether | 20% |
| Healing Spring | 20% |
| Stamina Tablet | 20% |

### RARE B

| X-Potion | 20% |
|---|---|
| Stamina Tablet | 20% |
| Mana Tablet | 20% |
| Stamina Tonic | 20% |
| Mana Tonic | 20% |

### RARE C

| Mega-Potion | 20% |
|---|---|
| Chocobo Feather | 40% |
| Chocobo Wing | 40% |

### RARE D

| X-Potion | 20% |
|---|---|
| Mega Phoenix | 20% |
| Chocobo Feather | 20% |
| Stamina Tonic | 20% |
| Mana Tonic | 20% |

### RARE E

| X-Potion | 20% |
|---|---|
| Ether | 10% |
| Mega Phoenix | 20% |
| Remedy | 10% |
| Chocobo Wing | 10% |
| Healing Spring | 10% |
| Mana Tonic | 10% |
| Twin Stars | 10% |

### RARE P

| X-Potion | 20% |
|---|---|
| Mega-Potion | 10% |
| Ether | 10% |
| Remedy | 10% |
| Chocobo Wing | 10% |
| Healing Spring | 20% |
| Mana Tonic | 10% |
| *White Signet Garment Grid | 10% |

*Becomes a Hi-Potion after winning the White Signet Garment Grid.

### RARE S

| *X-Potion | 20% |
|---|---|
| Mega Phoenix | 10% |
| Chocobo Feather | 20% |
| Chocobo Wing | 20% |
| Mana Tonic | 20% |
| **Treasure Hunt Garment Grid | 10% |

*Increases to 30% after winning the Treasure Hunt Garment Grid.

**Drops to 0% after winning the Treasure Hunt Garment Grid.

The following lists the coins given away during matches.

### GROUP A

- Ahriman Coin
- Bird Coin
- Coyote Coin
- Flan Coin
- Helm Coin
- Reptile Coin
- Wasp Coin
- Zurvan Coin

### GROUP B

- Defender Coin
- Drake Coin
- Malboro Coin
- Phantom Coin
- Purpurea Coin
- Ruminant Coin
- Worm Coin
- Zu Coin

### GROUP C

- Behemoth Coin
- Blade Coin
- Chimera Coin
- Coeurl Coin
- Elemental Coin
- Iron Giant Coin
- Ogre Coin
- Tomb Coin

### GROUP D

- Adamantoise Coin
- Bomb Coin
- Cactuar Coin
- Daeva Coin
- Kukulcan Coin
- Magic Urn Coin
- Ochu Coin
- Stalwart Coin

### GROUP E

- Arachnid Coin
- Creeper Coin
- Dragon Coin
- Fungus Coin
- Pairika Coin
- Piranha Coin
- Sahagin Coin
- Tonberry Coin

### GROUP F

- Dinictus Coin
- Eater Coin
- Evrae Coin
- Haizhe Coin
- Hermit Coin
- Omega Weapon Coin
- Tentacles Coin
- Ultima Weapon Coin

### GROUP G

- Angra Mainyu Coin
- Azi Dahaka Coin
- Chocobo Coin
- Gel Coin
- Georapella Coin
- Precepts Guard Coin
- Jumbo Cactuar Coin
- Seymour Coin

### GROUP H

- ???? Coin
- Auron Coin
- Kimahri Coin
- Lulu Coin
- Paine Coin
- Rikku Coin
- Wakka Coin
- Yuna Coin

Characters

Garment Grids & Dresspheres

Battle System

3

Accessories

Items and Item Shops

Walkthrough

Mini-Games

7

Fiends and Enemies

8

# ENTRY COIN LIST

The following table lists all of the Entry Coins you can find in the game. Most of them can be obtained through the "Let's Go Digging" mini-game. Please refer to that section to find out which coins can be found in which areas.

| COIN NAME | ENTRY NO. | TRAIT | HOW TO OBTAIN | GROUP |
|---|---|---|---|---|
| Adamantoise Coin | 3 | Item | Let's Go Digging Mini-Game | D |
| Ahriman Coin | 6 | Coin Count Echo | Sphere Break Tournament | A |
| Angra Mainyu Coin | 3 | Quota Multiplier Echo4 | - | G |
| Arachnid Coin | 1 | - | Let's Go Digging Mini-Game | E |
| Auron Coin | 9 | Quota Multiplier Echo4 | - | H |
| Azi Dahaka Coin | 7 | Rare Item | Let's Go Digging Mini-Game | G |
| Behemoth Coin, | 7 | Quota Multiplier Echo2 | Let's Go Digging Mini-Game | C |
| Bird Coin | 5 | - | Sphere Break Tournament | A |
| Blade Coin | 3 | Coin Count Echo | Let's Go Digging Mini-Game | C |
| Bomb Coin | 1 | Coin Count Echo | Let's Go Digging Mini-Game | D |
| Cactuar Coin | 2 | Coin | Let's Go Digging Mini-Game | D |
| Chimera Coin | 2 | Item | Let's Go Digging Mini-Game | C |
| Chocobo Coin | 6 | Coin | Let's Go Digging Mini-Game | G |
| Coeurl Coin | 5 | Coin Haul Multiplier Echo2 | Let's Go Digging Mini-Game | C |
| Coyote Coin | 3 | Coin | Sphere Break Tutorial | A |
| Creeper Coin | 3 | Coin Haul Multiplier Echo2 | Let's Go Digging Mini-Game | E |
| Daeva Coin | 9 | Quota Multiplier Echo2 | Let's Go Digging Mini-Game | D |
| Defender Coin | 8 | Multiplier Echo | Let's Go Digging Mini-Game | B |
| Dinictus Coin | 1 | Coin Haul Multiplier Echo2 | Let's Go Digging Mini-Game | F |
| Dragon Coin | 9 | Gil Multiplier Echo2 | Let's Go Digging Mini-Game | E |
| Drake Coin | 4 | Coin Count Echo | Let's Go Digging Mini-Game | B |
| Eater Coin | 3 | Rare Coin | Let's Go Digging Mini-Game | F |
| Elemental Coin | 9 | - | Let's Go Digging Mini-Game | C |
| Evrae Coin | 2 | Coin Haul Multiplier Echo3 | Let's Go Digging Mini-Game | F |
| Flan Coin | 2 | Item | Sphere Break Tutorial | A |
| Fungus Coin | 3 | Coin | Let's Go Digging Mini-Game | E |
| Gel Coin | 3 | - | Let's Go Digging Mini-Game | G |
| Georapella Coin | 3 | Quota Multiplier Echo4 | Speak to a person in the Youth League Base for 5 of these. | G |
| Guardian Coin | 4 | Quota Multiplier Echo3 | - | G |
| Haizhe Coin | 5 | Coin | Let's Go Digging Mini-Game | F |
| Helm Coin | 1 | - | Sphere Break Tutorial | A |
| Hermit Coin | 3 | Coin Haul Multiplier Echo2 | Let's Go Digging Mini-Game | F |
| Iron Giant Coin | 6 | Multiplier Echo | Let's Go Digging Mini-Game | C |
| Jumbo Cactuar Coin | 5 | Rare Item | - | G |
| Kimahri Coin | 9 | Rare Item | - | H |
| Kukulcan Coin | 8 | - | Let's Go Digging Mini-Game | D |
| Lulu Coin | 9 | Rare Coin | - | H |
| Magic Urn Coin | 5 | Gil Multiplier Echo2 | Let's Go Digging Mini-Game | D |
| Malboro Coin | 3 | Multiplier Echo | Let's Go Digging Mini-Game | B |
| Ochu Coin | 7 | Gil Multiplier Echo2 | Let's Go Digging Mini-Game | D |
| Ogre Coin | 4 | Coin | Let's Go Digging Mini-Game | C |
| Omega Weapon Coin | 7 | Quota Multiplier Echo3 | Let's Go Digging Mini-Game | F |
| Paine Coin | 9 | Multiplier Echo | - | H |
| Pairika Coin | 7 | Coin Count Echo | Let's Go Digging Mini-Game | E |
| Phantom Coin | 7 | Coin | Let's Go Digging Mini-Game | B |
| Piranha Coin | 6 | Multiplier Echo | Let's Go Digging Mini-Game | E |
| Purpurea Coin | 5 | - | Let's Go Digging Mini-Game | B |
| Reptile Coin | 3 | - | Sphere Break Tournament | A |
| Rikku Coin | 9 | Quota Multiplier Echo4 | - | H |
| Ruminant Coin | 1 | Item | Let's Go Digging Mini-Game | B |
| Sahagin Coin | 2 | Coin Count Echo | Let's Go Digging Mini-Game | E |
| Seymour Coin | 9 | Rare Item | - | G |
| Stalwart Coin | 4 | Multiplier Echo | Let's Go Digging Mini-Game | D |
| Tentacles Coin | 3 | Coin Count Echo | Let's Go Digging Mini-Game | F |
| Tomb Coin | 1 | - | Let's Go Digging Mini-Game | C |
| Tonberry Coin | 4 | Coin Haul Multiplier Echo2 | Let's Go Digging Mini-Game | E |
| Ultima Weapon Coin | 9 | Quota Multiplier Echo2 | Let's Go Digging Mini-Game | F |
| Wakka Coin | 9 | Rare Item | - | H |
| Wasp Coin | 2 | Item | Sphere Break Tournament | A |
| Worm Coin | 2 | Coin | Let's Go Digging Mini-Game | B |
| Yuna Coin | 9 | Coin Count Echo | - | H |
| Zu Coin | 3 | Item | Let's Go Digging Mini-Game | B |
| Zurvan Coin | 5 | - | Sphere Break Tutorial | A |
| ???? Coin | 9 | Quota Multiplier Echo5 | - | H |

Characters

1

Garment Grids
& Dresspheres

2

Battle System

3

Accessories

4

Items and
Item Shops

5

Walkthrough

6

**Mini-Games**

7

Fiends and
Enemies

8

| When Available: | Chapters 1, 2, 3, 5 |
| Location: | Bikanel Desert |
| Objective: | Help the Al Bhed search for Machina Parts hidden in the swirling sands of the Bikanel Desert. In the process, you may unearth helpful items like Al Bhed Primers and coins for Sphere Break. Digging is a great way to earn gil and EXP. |

# REGISTERING FOR THE DIG

Gippal is a bit hard to take, but you have to endure his constant flirting to get the Letter of Introduction.

In Chapter 1, visit Djose Temple and talk to Gippal to register for the desert excavation. Before you can see him, though, you must stand in line outside the office. Talk to the people waiting around the temple to make the time pass more quickly. After doing so, go inside the temple and speak to Gippal. Follow him out to the bridge in front of the temple where he'll hand over a **Letter of Introduction** to take to Nhadala at the Al Bhed outpost in the Bikanel Desert.

Go to Bikanel Island and follow Rikku to the Al Bhed camp. The journey becomes rather difficult, and eventually the Al Bhed find the Gullwings. Give Nhadala the Letter of Introduction.

If it looks like Rikku doesn't know where she's going, that's because she doesn't! Don't worry when your party collapses from dehydration; the Al Bhed will find them in plenty of time to rescue them from the harsh desert!

### WHERE'S NHADALA?

*If you visit Bikanel Desert before getting the Letter of Introduction from Gippal, you'll find the camp but you'll learn that Nhadala is out in the field working. Come back to the desert after the events with Gippal at Djose Temple to find her.*

# DIGGING 101

To start an excavation, talk to the hoverpilot and choose a location. In Chapter 1, you can only dig in the Western Expanse, but the number of locations the Al Bhed are currently excavating increases as the game progresses.

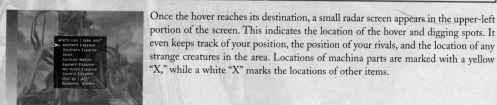

| DIGGING SPOTS IN THE BIKANEL DESERT | | |
|---|---|---|
| **LOCATION** | **CHAPTERS AVAILABLE** | **REQUIREMENTS** |
| Western Expanse | 1, 2, 3, 5 | Get the Letter of Introduction from Gippal in Chapter 1. |
| Southern Expanse | 2, 3, 5 | Complete the Oasis Mission. |
| Eastern Expanse | 3, 5 | Undertake the Cactuar Nation Mission. |
| Northern Expanse | 3, 5 | Undertake the Cactuar Nation Mission. |
| Central Expanse | 5 | Send a Chocobo from the Chocobo Ranch to Bikanel Island. (The first one you send to this area will run away.) |

You can count on this hover pilot to ferry you to the different desert locations.

Once the hover reaches its destination, a small radar screen appears in the upper-left portion of the screen. This indicates the location of the hover and digging spots. It even keeps track of your position, the position of your rivals, and the location of any strange creatures in the area. Locations of machina parts are marked with a yellow "X," while a white "X" marks the locations of other items.

To dig in the desert sand, simply stand over one of the excavation points on the radar screen. Yuna will then dig automatically.

You have 60 seconds to scavenge for treasure and get back to the hover before the heat and desert sands overwhelm the party. Keep this in mind when the radar is first revealed and plan your course appropriately. If you fail to make it back to the hover in time, the mission is automatically considered a failure!

A trip is considered successful if you manage to find the machina part in the area and return to the hover within the time limit. Make finding this item (the yellow "X") your first priority! After doing so, you can check out the other digging sites. Not only will you find items (both common and rare) under a white "X," but you may also encounter a fiend ambush! The desert is full of dangerous fiends, so be prepared for a fight.

The Gullwings can only survive for 60 seconds in the desert before help is needed!

Ambushed!

To make the excavation more interesting, the Gullwings are competing against others. Keep tabs on any rivals by looking for a grey-colored arrow on the radar screen. Occasionally, you will be alerted to the presence of a strange entity in the area. This fiend, Angra Mainyu, is marked on the radar with a purple arrow. If it appears where you are working, return to the hover as fast as possible. Angra Mainyu is next to impossible to defeat early in the game and, while it may not defeat your party, it will blast them from the desert.

Avoid Angra Mainyu at all costs until your party is strong enough to seriously wound it. This gigantic fiend has 333444 HP. And that's not including its two limbs, Tawrich and Zarich, which join the battle in Chapters 2 and 3 respectively!

# RAISING YOUR RANK

When you return from a dig, there's a chance your rank will go up. Your mad digging skills are automatically evaluated after you complete 15, 30, 60, 90, 120, 150, and 180 digs. If you have more successfull digs than failed digs when you're evaluated, your rank will go up one level. There are four ranks all together: Sandbox League, Beach Comber, Sand Blaster, and Zen Master of Digging. See if you can master the digging game before the end of Chapter 5! The ranks are just thrown in for fun and don't affect your digging wages.

# APPLY FOR PAY RAISES AT DJOSE TEMPLE!

Initially, the party earns 100 gil for each successful excavation. However, you can increase this amount by taking a simple exam at Djose Temple. Visit the temple and head straight for the room to the right of the research lab. Go up to the kiosk in the right-hand corner of the room and apply for a raise. You'll be asked your opinion of six different questions. Indicate whether you agree, disagree, or have no strong opinion about the statement asked. Each answer nets you anywhere from 2 to 0 points, depending upon how closely your opinion matches the computer's. If you score high enough, a pay raise is granted. If you fail, you must go back to the Bikanel Desert and dig for a while before you can apply again. The easiest way to pass each exam is to answer as though you love digging more than anything else in the world—including a pay raise!

Look for this kiosk inside Djose Temple. It's located in the room farthest to the right.

The exam questions are easy once you know how to answer them. Just remember to impress the computer by showing your enthusiasm for digging!

The number of points needed to pass the exam changes in each chapter, as does the maximum amount of gil you can earn in each successful mission. You can only fail the exam five times before you are no longer allowed to attempt it. In most cases, if the appropriate answer is not clear, you can expect to get at least one point by answering "No Opinion." At the start of each chapter, your previous wages are thrown out and reset to the starting wages shown in the table below.

| CHAPTER | NUMBER OF POINTS NEEDED TO PASS | STARTING WAGE | WAGE CAP |
|---|---|---|---|
| 1 | 5 points + | 100 gil | 150 gil |
| 2 | 7 points + | 150 gil | 300 gil |
| 3 | 8 points + | 200 gil | 400 gil |
| 5 | 11 points + | 300 gil | 850 gil |

Your actual wage cap depends on how high you managed to get your wages in earlier chapters. The nitty-gritty are explained in the following table, but essentially, if you want to end the game with the highest possible wages, you'll need to max out your wages before ending each chapter. If ou don't apply for any wage increases before Chapter 5, the highest wage you'll be able to get is only 500 gil!

| CHAPTER | MAX WAGE FORMULA |
|---|---|
| 1 | 150 |
| 2 | 200 + (Wage at end of Ch. 1 - 100) x2 |
| 3 | 250 + (Wage at end of Ch. 2 - 150) /3 + (Wage at end of Ch. 1 - 100) x2 |
| 5 | 500 + (Wage at end of Ch. 3 - 200) /2 + (Wage at end of Ch. 2 - 150) /3 + (Wage at end of Ch. 1 - 100) x2 |

Successful exam taking leads to higher salaries and more reasons to spend time in the desert!

MINI-GAMES

# THE OASIS AND CACTUAR NATION

| Items: | *Normal treasure chest:* Potion, Hi-Potion, Phoenix Down, Antidote; *Al Bhed treasure chest:* Hi-Potion, Mega Phoenix, Remedy |
|---|---|
| Coins: | None |

Two other areas open up when you come to Bikanel Desert to dig: the Oasis and the Cactuar Nation. The Oasis opens up in Chapter 2 when you're asked by Nhadala to check out the region for strange events. Heed the pilot's advice and make sure that you are equipped to do battle before proceeding, as strange things are afoot in the Oasis!

After completing this mission, you can return to the Oasis for a different type of treasure hunting. During visits to the Oasis, you may find a treasure chest bearing interesting stuff. Head to the Oasis in Chapters 3 and 5 and you may encounter a caravan selling lots of amazing accessories! For the low-down on the treasure available here, refer to the following tables.

## CHANCE OF VARIOUS EVENTS OCCURRING IN THE OASIS

| EVENT | PERCENTAGE |
|---|---|
| Caravan (only in Chapters 3 and 5) | 25% |
| Something appears floating in the Oasis | 70% |
| Nothing happens | 5% |

## CHANCE OF VARIOUS THINGS APPEARING IN THE OASIS

| ITEM | PERCENTAGE |
|---|---|
| Normal Treasure Chest | 20% |
| Al Bhed Treasure Chest | 30% |
| Empty Treasure Chest | 20% |
| Trash (empty bottle) | 10% |
| Trash (empty can) | 10% |
| Lost Dolphin | 10% |

*One of three things occurs when you enter the Oasis: 1. You find something floating in the Oasis; 2. You find nothing; 3. You encounter the Caravan. The Caravan only appears in Chapters 3 and 5, once you've undertaken another task for the Al Bhed.*

The Cactuar Nation is home to the cacti that have watched over Bikanel Desert for countless ages. In Chapter 3, Nhadala sends the Gullwings out with her translator, Benzo, to make contact with Marnela, the leader of the Cactuar Nation. Marnela needs your help find the Ten Gatekeepers, cactuar who've headed out into the world of Spira to learn and grow in their travles. Going to the Cactuar Nation and beginning the search for the Ten Gatekeepers opens up the Eastern and Northern Expanses for exploration. For more detailed information on the Ten Gatekeepers mini-game, read further in this chapter.

*The quest for the Ten Gatekeepers is another mini-game altogether, but speaking to Marnela opens up two more areas for digging in the desert. Just don't get distracted!*

# WESTERN EXPANSE (CHAPTERS 1-3, 5)

| Items: | Al Bhed Primer, Antidote (x2), Antidote (x5), Echo Screen (x2), Ether, Eye Drops (x2), Hi-Potion, Hi-Potion (x2), Holy Water (x2), Holy Water (x5), Potion, Phoenix Down, Potion, Remedy, Soft (x2), Soft (x5), Turbo Ether, 200 gil, 500 gil, 1000 gil, 3000 gil |
|---|---|
| Coins: | *Chapter 1,2:* Coyote Coin, Defender Coin, Drake Coin, Flan Coin, Helm Coin, Malboro Coin, Phantom Coin, Purpurea Coin, Ruminant Coin, Worm Coin, Zu Coin, ZurvanCoin; *Chapter 3, 5:* Adamantoise Coin, Behemoth Coin, Blade Coin, Chimera Coin, Coeurl Coin, Daeva Coin, Elemental Coin, Ogre Coin, Iron Giant Coin, Kukulcan Coin, Ochu Coin, Tomb Coin |

This area, the first you can excavate, is the easiest to explore. You can count on having one rival who rarely goes after the Machina part.

Characters

1

Garment Grids & D||sspheres

2

Battle System

3

Accessories

4

Items and Item Shops

5

Walkthrough

6

Mini-Games

7

Fiends and Enemies

8

# SOUTHERN EXPANSE (CHAPTERS 2, 3, 5)

| Items: | Al Bhed Primer, Antarctic Wind, Arctic Wind (x2), Bomb Core (x2), Bomb Fragment, Budget Grenade, Budget Grenade (x2), Budget Grenade (x3), Dark Grenade, Dragon Scale (x2), Electro Marble, Fish Scale, Grenade, Grenade (x2), L-Bomb (x2), Lightning Marble (x2), M-Bomb (x2), Petrify Grenade, Potion, S-Bomb (x2), Silence Grenade, 200 gil, 400 gil, 1000 gil, 4000 gil |
|---|---|
| Coins: | *Chapter 2:* Coyote Coin, Defender Coin, Drake Coin, Flan Coin, Helm Coin, Malboro Coin, Phantom Coin, Purpurea Coin, Ruminant Coin, Worm Coin, Zu Coin, Zurvan Coin; *Chapter 3, 5:* Adamantoise Coin, Behemoth Coin, Blade Coin, Chimera Coin, Coeurl Coin, Daeva Coin, Elemental Coin, Ogre Coin, Iron Giant Coin, Kukulcan Coin, Ochu Coin, Tomb Coin |

The second area to open up (starting in Chapter 2) is very similar to the first area. However, watch out for all of the shoopufs wandering around the desert, as they may block you from a digging spot. Beware, this is the first area where the swirling sands may conceal the yellow "X" that marks the location of the buried Machina parts. Keep searching, as it will eventually appear before the time limit runs out!

# EASTERN EXPANSE (CHAPTERS 3, 5)

| Items: | Al Bhed Primer, Echo Screen (x5), Ether, Eye Drops (x5), Hi-Potion, Hi-Potion (x2), Mega Phoenix, Phoenix Down, Potion, Power Gloves, Remedy, Soft (x5), 1000 gil, 5000 gil |
|---|---|
| Coins: | Arachnid Coin, Bomb Coin, Cactuar Coin, Creeper Coin, Dragon Coin, Fungus Coin, Magic Pot Coin, Pairika Coin, Piranha Coin, Sahagin Coin, Stalwart Coin, Tonberry Coin |

Watch out for the machina class monsters in this area, as they can make life tough for your party. In addition, keep an eye out for a green "X" to appear on the radar screen. When you approach this digging location, you'll find the ruins of machina scattered all over the place. When you stand in a specific position, the machina pieces rush you into a series of four battles against Machina Hunters. After this occurs, you are automatically returned to the Al Bhed camp and the green "X" never appears again.

# NORTHERN EXPANSE (CHAPTERS 3, 5)

| Items: | Al Bhed Primer, Candle of Life, Chocobo Feather, Chocobo Wing, Light Curtain, Lunar Curtain, Potion, Phoenix Tail, Silver Hourglass, Star Curtain, Twin Stars, 400 gil, 5000 gil |
|---|---|
| Coins: | Arachnid Coin, Bomb Coin, Cactuar Coin, Creeper Coin, Dragon Coin, Fungus Coin, Magic Pot Coin, Pairika Coin, Piranha Coin, Sahagin Coin, Stalwart Coin, Tonberry Coin |

Zus guard the ruins in this area, so come prepared to fight when you first travel here. You can also expect to fight them in random battles, along with Sandworms, while searching for treasure.

# CENTRAL EXPANSE (CHAPTER 5)

| Items: | Al Bhed Primer, Desert Key, Dispel Tonic, Ether, Farplane Shadow, Grenade, Hi-Potion, M-Bomb (x2), Mega-Potion, Nature's Tome, Poison Fang, Potion, S-Bomb (x2), 1000 gil, 2000 gil |
|---|---|
| Coins: | Azi Dahaka Coin, Chocobo Coin, Dinictus Coin, Eater Coin, Evrae Coin, Gel Coin, Haizhe Coin, Hermit Coin, Omega Weapon Coin, Tentacles Coin, Ultima Weapon Coin |

This area only opens up in Chapter 5 after you send a chocobo from your ranch to explore the area. Apparently, this section of the desert is so vast that you need a chocobo to explore it! Regardless, digging for buried treasure on a chocobo is a great pleasure. It makes the process much faster and riding on a chocobo protects the party from random encounters! In addition, the speed of the chocobo enables you to travel further away from the hover and return at faster speeds.

However, you must keep an eye on your rival. He also rides a chocobo and can be a fierce competitor for both treasure and the prized machina part. Since the yellow "X" rarely appears at the start of a dig here, keep an eye on the radar and make a break for it when the sands disclose its location.

Characters
1

Garment Grids & Dresspheres
2

Battle System
3

Accessories
4

Items and Item Shops
5

Walkthrough
6

Mini-Games

7

Fiends and Enemies

8

This section covers seven mini-games that occur in the Calm Lands in *FINAL FANTASY X-2*. Some are available immediately in Chapter 1, while others become available as a result of events that occur in earlier chapters. Since all these mini-games occur in this one large area, they are grouped together in this section.

# THE PUBLICITY CAMPAIGN AND "THERE GOES THE BRIDE"

| When Available: | Chapters 1, 2, 3, 5 |
|---|---|
| Location: | Calm Lands |
| Objective: | Spread the news about the Calm Lands attractions and the owner of Argent Inc.'s eligible son to the people of Spira. If you do a good enough job, you can win prizes and even trigger two new attractions to open up in Chapter 5. |

Ask about the Publicity Campaign to learn the basics and join the ranks of one of the two companies.

Two companies offer attractions in the Calm Lands: Argent, Inc. and Open Air, Inc. Each company provides their own credits and attempts to hire people to promote the games they run under their own names. They are fierce competitors, as each company tries to do their best to get the most business. When you stop by this area to try out some of their games, ask about their Publicity Campaigns, and see what you can do to help out!

Before you venture into the world of Spira to spread the gospel of either Open Air or Argent, Inc., head to the Travel Agency and talk to the head of Argent, Inc. He has a problem that you can help him with at the same time that you are promoting the area's attractions. It seems that his son is in need of a bride (or at least that's what dad thinks!), but the lad's too shy to go out and promote himself. While you're talking up the Calm Lands' games to the public, do a little matchmaking for the poor lad.

Feel like doing some matchmaking? Talk to the head of Argent, Inc. at his stand in the middle of the field to get more details!

## SPREADING THE NEWS

Playing this mini-game is easy and doesn't add much to your already heavy load of sphere hunting. All you need to do is look for people in the various towns and highways of Spira who are willing to listen to your sales pitch and matchmaking advice. The tables that follow list all of the people to whom you can make your pitch. Simply match your sales tactics to their personalities!

To initiate a conversation with someone regarding the Publicity or Matchmaking campaigns, approach someone and press the Square button. If the campaign menu appears, give that person your best pitch. If not, then you know that this character is not open to such propaganda.

Choose the right sales pitch and you'll get a pumped up response. If you fail to excite enough interest, try again in the next chapter.

Each campaign has five pitches and each one provokes various responses from NPCs. To get the most points, you must determine what line works best with each character. Talk to the character, first to get an idea of what he or she is interested in to gauge what tactic might work the best. Alternatively, you can just guess and hope that you get it right! If you fail to get the best response, you must approach that character again later on.

The Campaign Menu appears when you press the Square button while standing next to a willing participant.

## PLAYING THE PUBLICITY CAMPAIGN

Each company provides a list of their best lines. However, the responses to these lines remain the same regardless of which company you are pitching for! To get the best score, strive to get the best response ("They seem totally pumped!") and the highest point value (5) each time you speak with a NPC. In addition, you can approach the same NPC multiple times to build your score. Try making the rounds at least once a chapter for the highest total score!

Open Air and Argent, Inc. each have their own sets of sales pitches. However, once you figure out which pitch number to use, you can use the same one for the rival company.

## OPEN AIR PITCHES

1. Fun awaits you at Open Air!

2. Take to the Air. Open Air.

3. Open Air. Get your Air on.

4. I lost 30 pounds with Open Air!

5. Shee yoo at Open Air, yesh?

## ARGENT, INC. PITCHES

1. Fun awaits you at Argent!

2. Argent, at your service!

3. For a good time, call on Argent!

4. Argent. Fun you can rely on.

5. Would you like to hear about Argent, Inc.?

### RESPONSES AND POINT VALUES FOR THE PUBLICITY CAMPAIGN

| | |
|---|---|
| They seem totally pumped! | 5 points |
| They seem pretty psyched. | 3 points |
| They seem mildly intrigued. | 2 points |
| They don't seem the least bit interested. | 1 point |
| They seem put off. | 0 points |

## RAISING YOUR RANK

*You can find out your current Publicity Rating and Level by asking your local Open Air or Argent representative in the Calm Lands.*

Your score determines your rank as a PR representative. The goal is to reach Rank 5 before the end of Chapter 5. Accomplish this feat, and you'll complete the mini-game and bring fame to the winning company. Using the tables provided at the end of this section, you can rack up the points with ease. You also earn publicity points for any credits you lose while playing the mini-games in the Calm Lands region. The following tables provide the Publicity Rating needed for each Publicity Level and the conversion rate of mini-game credits to Publicity Points in each chapter.

### POINTS NEEDED TO ADVANCE PUBLICITY LEVEL

| PUBLICITY LEVEL | POINTS NEEDED |
|---|---|
| 1 | N/A |
| 2 | 60 |
| 3 | 140 |
| 4 | 260 |
| 5 | 400 |

### CONVERSION RATIO OF MINI-GAME CREDITS TO PUBLICITY POINTS

| CHAPTER # | POINT RATIO |
|---|---|
| 1 | 1 Publicity point for every 20 Mini-Game Credits |
| 2 | 1 Publicity point for every 50 Mini-Game Credits |
| 3 | 1 Publicity point for every 100 Mini-Game Credits |
| 5 | 1 Publicity point for every 200 Mini-Game Credits |

Keep in mind that your Publicity Level only grows as fast as your progress through the game. Regardless of the number of points you've accumulated, your highest rank will only be one level higher than the current chapter number. So if you pick up 283 PR points in Chapter 1, your rank at that time will max out at Level 2.

There are several gameplay aspects that are influenced by your Publicity Level advancement. They are:

■ The number of prizes available for purchase by trading in credits increases. (See the following list.)

■ New difficulty levels are added to Lupine Dash, Reptile Race, and Sky Slots.

■ The number of credits you can bet during each mini-game increases.

■ In Chapter 5, when you reach Publicity Level 5, the campaign ends. You can win up to two new mini-games based on your Publicity Level with both companies.

## SWITCHING BETWEEN COMPANIES

For the best effect, you should campaign for both companies. However, switching between Open Air and Argent, Inc. comes at a price. When switching sides, the number of points you accumulated is cut in half. If you decide to return to that side's campaign later, you start from the reduced number. For example, if you accumulate 150 points for Argent, Inc.'s campaign and decide to switch to Open Air for a while, your PR points for Argent drop to 75. When you switch back to Argent, you start back at 75 points while the points you gathered for Open Air are halved.

If you want to unlock both mini-games at the end of the campaign, you should accumulate at least 280 Publicity Points for one company during the first two chapters and then switch to the rival company. Gather the 400 points needed to bring the episode to a close in Chapter 5, and when the points are tallied at the end, you get both games.

*Before switching sides, the company representative discloses all of the point loss information so you can make an informed decision.*

MINI-GAMES

Characters

1

Garment Grids
& Dresspheres

2

Battle System

3

Accessories

4

Items and
Item Shops

5

Walkthrough

6

Mini-Games

7

Fiends and
Enemies

8

# FABULOUS PRIZES!

The items you can purchase with your game credits change based on your current Publicity Level with that company. After the companies merge in Chapter 5 (after reaching Rank 5 in one of the two companies' campaigns), the items that appear are based on the ranks you reached with each company. For example, if you reached Rank 5 for Open Air and Rank 3 for Argent, Inc., you can purchase items available for Rank 5 from the Open Air "Publicity Level (After Integration)" column and items available for Level 3 from the Argent, Inc. "Publicity Level (After Integration)" column.

*These items can only be purchased after buying the Flash of Steel Garment Grid.

You can trade in credits for valuable and sometimes rare merchandise.

## OPEN AIR

| ITEM | CREDIT | BEFORE INTEGRATION | | | | AFTER INTEGRATION | | | | |
|---|---|---|---|---|---|---|---|---|---|---|
| | | 1 | 2 | 3 | 4 | 1 | 2 | 3 | 4 | 5 |
| Potion | 10 | X | X | X | X | X | X | X | X | X |
| Phoenix Down | 30 | X | X | X | X | X | X | X | X | X |
| Budget Grenade | 50 | X | X | X | X | X | X | X | X | X |
| Hi-Potion | 150 | X | - | - | - | X | X | X | X | X |
| Charm Bangle | 500 | X | - | - | - | X | X | X | X | X |
| Grenade | 70 | - | X | X | X | - | X | X | X | X |
| Poison Fang | 100 | - | X | X | X | - | X | X | X | X |
| Remedy | 200 | - | X | X | X | - | X | X | X | X |
| Mithryl Gloves | 750 | - | X | - | - | - | X | X | X | X |
| Glass Buckle | 2500 | - | X | - | - | - | X | X | X | X |
| S-Bomb | 100 | - | - | X | X | - | - | X | X | X |
| Dark Grenade | 300 | - | - | X | X | - | - | X | X | X |
| Titanium Bangle | 500 | - | - | X | X | - | - | X | X | X |
| Power Wrist | 1500 | - | - | X | - | - | - | X | X | X |
| Black Belt | 5000 | - | - | X | - | - | - | X | X | X |
| M-Bomb | 350 | - | - | - | X | - | - | - | X | X |
| L-Bomb | 500 | - | - | - | X | - | - | - | X | X |
| Pretty Orb | 1000 | - | - | - | X | - | - | - | X | X |
| Shining Gem | 3500 | - | - | - | X | - | - | - | X | X |
| Mortal Shock | 12000 | - | - | - | X | - | - | - | X | X |
| Stamina Tablet | 1000 | - | - | - | - | - | - | - | - | X |
| Dream Shock | 3000 | - | - | - | - | - | - | - | - | X |
| Hyper Wrist | 5000 | - | - | - | - | - | - | - | - | X |
| Supreme Gem | 15000 | - | - | - | - | - | - | - | - | X |
| Tetra Gloves | 50000 | - | - | - | - | - | - | - | - | X |
| Sword Tome | 80000 | - | - | - | - | - | - | - | - | X |
| Disaster in Bloom Garment Grid | 200000 | - | - | - | - | - | - | - | - | X |
| *Bushido Tome | 100000 | - | - | - | - | - | - | - | - | X |

## ARGENT, INC.

| ITEM | CREDIT | BEFORE INTEGRATION | | | | AFTER INTEGRATION | | | | |
|---|---|---|---|---|---|---|---|---|---|---|
| | | 1 | 2 | 3 | 4 | 1 | 2 | 3 | 4 | 5 |
| Potion | 10 | X | X | X | X | X | X | X | X | X |
| Phoenix Down | 30 | X | X | X | X | X | X | X | X | X |
| Budget Grenade | 50 | X | X | X | X | X | X | X | X | X |
| Hi-Potion | 150 | X | - | - | - | X | X | X | X | X |
| Ether | 500 | X | - | - | - | X | X | X | X | X |
| Lunar Curtain | 70 | - | X | X | X | - | X | X | X | X |
| Silver Hourglass | 100 | - | X | X | X | - | X | X | X | X |
| Dispel Tonic | 200 | - | X | X | X | - | X | X | X | X |
| Defense Veil | 750 | - | X | - | - | - | X | X | X | X |
| Gold Bracer | 2500 | - | X | - | - | - | X | X | X | X |
| Farplane Shadow | 100 | - | - | X | X | - | - | X | X | X |
| Mana Spring | 300 | - | - | X | X | - | - | X | X | X |
| Soul Spring | 500 | - | - | X | X | - | - | X | X | X |
| Tarot Card | 1500 | - | - | X | - | - | - | X | X | X |
| Hypno Crown | 5000 | - | - | X | - | - | - | X | X | X |
| Stamina Spring | 350 | - | - | - | X | - | - | - | X | X |
| Gold Hourglass | 500 | - | - | - | X | - | - | - | X | X |
| Pearl Necklace | 1000 | - | - | - | X | - | - | - | X | X |
| Tetra Band | 3500 | - | - | - | X | - | - | - | X | X |
| Soul of Thamasa | 12000 | - | - | - | X | - | - | - | X | X |
| Turbo Ether | 1000 | - | - | - | - | - | - | - | - | X |
| Mana Tonic | 3000 | - | - | - | - | - | - | - | - | X |
| Pixie Dust | 5000 | - | - | - | - | - | - | - | - | X |
| Chocobo Wing | 15000 | - | - | - | - | - | - | - | - | X |
| Tetra Bracelet | 50000 | - | - | - | - | - | - | - | - | X |
| Black Tome | 80000 | - | - | - | - | - | - | - | - | X |
| Flash of Steel Garment Grid | 200000 | - | - | - | - | - | - | - | - | X |
| *White Tome | 100000 | - | - | - | - | - | - | - | - | X |

# CLOSING THE CAMPAIGN

The Publicity Campaign ends automatically in Chapter 5 upon reaching Level 5 with 400 or more points. If you want to build your campaign to that level for both companies, don't visit the Calm Lands during Chapter 5 until you are finished. During the Episode Complete event, the results of the Publicity Campaign contest are tallied and read to the anxious crowd. The company with the highest total wins.

*Now for the final tally! Which side will win?*

However, the event doesn't end there! Under the advice and leadership of Tobli, the two companies decide to join forces and create a single holding company for the Calm Land amusements, called the Calm Skies Partnership. To celebrate, the park opens up one or two new amusements based on your performance. If you get to Rank 3 for Argent, Inc., a game called "Feed the Monkey" opens up by the northern entrance. If you get to Rank 3 for Open Air, a mini-game called "Gull Force" opens at the southern entrance of the field. Get to Rank 3 or higher in both companies' campaigns to open up both mini-games at the end of the mission!

# PLAYING "HERE COMES THE BRIDE"

*Matchmaking requires a delicate touch. You don't want to risk turning off the prospective bride!*

"Here Comes the Bride" is played identically to the Publicity Campaign—after all, you are basically publicizing the son's eligibility to all of the women in Spira! As you spread the word about the Calm Lands' attractions, keep an eye out for single women who might be interested in the Argent owner's son. If you fail to illicit an excited response, try approaching the woman again later.

## MATCHMAKING PITCHES

1. Find your better half!

2. I have the perfect person for you!

3. The heir to Argent, Inc. needs a fiancée…

4. The man of your dreams awaits!

5. Do you believe in… destiny?

| RESPONSES AND POINT VALUES FOR THE PUBLICITY CAMPAIGN | |
|---|---|
| She seems really excited! | 5 points |
| You've piqued her curiosity. | 3 points |
| She doesn't seem interested. | 2 points |
| You've turned her off. | 1 point |
| You couldn't have offended her more if you tried. | 0 points |

# THE BRIDE(S) COMETH!

You can keep track of your tally by talking to the father of the groom in the Calm Lands at any time before Chapter 5. However, when you approach him in Chapter 5, he finally gives you the results of all your hard work. How many prospective brides can you persuade to look the son over?

*How many brides can you corral? It looks like the job is just starting for the Argent heir!*

| MATCHMAKING RESULTS | | |
|---|---|---|
| POINTS | # OF BRIDES | REWARD |
| 0-29 | 0 | Elixir |
| 30-49 | 1 (Frumpish Lady) | Speed Bracer |
| 50-79 | 1 | Speed Bracer |
| 80-104 | 2 | Speed Bracer |
| 105-129 | 3 | Speed Bracer |
| 130+ | 3+1 (Frumpish Lady) | Speed Bracer |

# PUBLICITY AND MATCHMAKING PARTICIPANT LOCATIONS

This section details the locations of all of the NPCs participating in the Publicity and Matchmaking Campaigns. When using these tables, refer to the accompanying maps to pinpoint the locations of the NPCs. Because some of the NPCs roam in a set course, each character's starting location is noted on the map. Also note that missions may pre-empt your ability to find or speak with a specific NPC. Look for them before or after completing a mission or event scheduled in that area.

The tables list the locations of the NPCs and the chapters in which you can find them. Some characters only appear in specific chapters or change locations from one chapter to another. The tables also provide the point value for each of the Publicity and Matchmaking pitches. Remember, a "5" indicates that you'll get the best response if you use that pitch, while a "0" indicates that you'll get the worst response.

# BESAID ISLAND

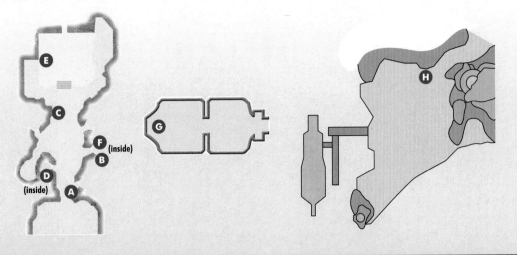

| PLACE | DESCRIPTION | CHAPTER 1 2 3 4 5 | PR PITCHES 1 2 3 4 5 | MM PITCHES 1 2 3 4 5 |
|---|---|---|---|---|
| A | Woman in blue dress. | X X - - - | 3 5 2 0 1 | 0 1 5 2 |
| B | | - - X - X | | |
| C | Girl in yellow and teal tunic walking with dog | X X X - X | 3 1 0 5 2 | 1 0 3 5 2 |
| D | Item shopkeeper | X X X - X | 2 0 3 1 5 | 3 2 5 1 0 |
| E | Boy running in and out of temple | X X X - X | 2 1 5 0 3 | - - - - - |
| F | Barechested man in first house | X X X - X | 5 0 2 1 3 | - - - - - |
| G | Keepa | X X X - - | 5 1 3 2 0 | - - - - - |
| H | | - - - - X | | |

*Table title: BESAID ISLAND*

# KILIKA ISLAND

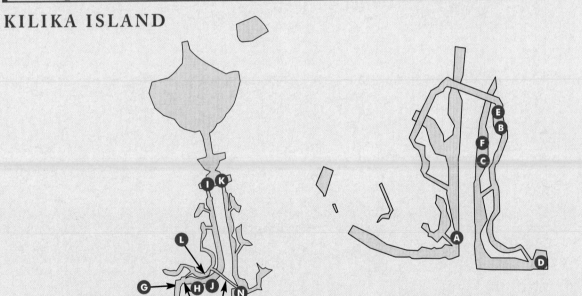

| PLACE | DESCRIPTION | CHAPTER 1 2 3 4 5 | PR PITCHES 1 2 3 4 5 | MM PITCHES 1 2 3 4 5 |
|---|---|---|---|---|
| A | Guy in red and yellow shorts | X - - - - | 1 3 0 2 5 | - - - - - |
| B | | - - X - - | | |
| C | | - - - - X | | |
| D | Man in teal shirt on dock. | X - X - X | 0 2 1 5 3 | - - - - - |
| E | Girl in white tunic talking with man. | - - X - - | 2 3 0 1 5 | 5 3 0 1 2 |
| F | | - - - - X | | |
| G | Man in green. | X - - - - | 3 2 1 5 0 | - - - - - |
| H | | - - X - - | | |
| I | | - - - - X | | |
| J | Man in teal shirt. | X - X - - | 3 1 2 0 5 | - - - - - |
| K | | - - - - X | | |
| L | Guy in red and white shorts | X - X - - | 2 3 0 1 5 | - - - - - |
| M | | - - - - X | | |
| N | Girl in white tunic by bridge | X - X - - | 0 5 3 2 1 | 3 2 5 1 0 |

*Table title: KILIKA ISLAND*

Characters
1

Garment Grids & Dresspheres
2

Battle System
3

Accessories
4

Items and Item Shops
5

Walkthrough
6

Mini-Games
7

Fiends and Enemies
8

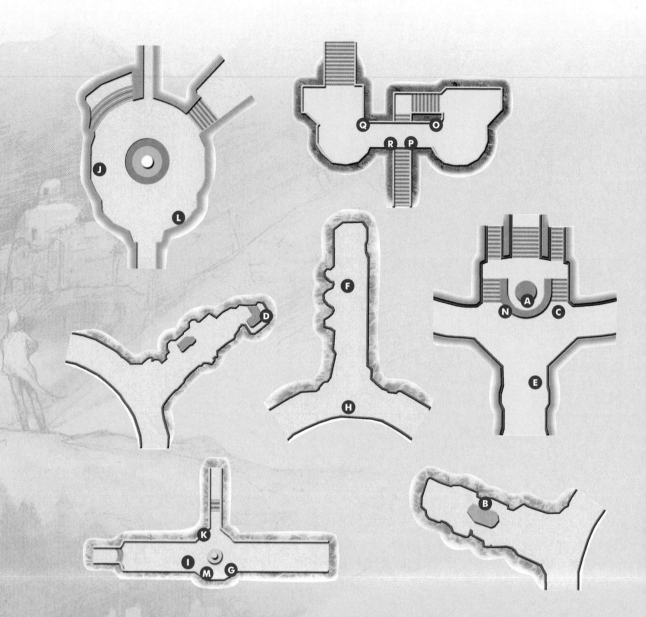

| LUCA | | | | | | | | | | | | | | | | |
|------|------|------|------|------|------|------|------|------|------|------|------|------|------|------|------|------|
| **PLACE** | **DESCRIPTION** | **CHAPTER** | | | | | **PR PITCHES** | | | | | **MM PITCHES** | | | | |
| | | 1 | 2 | 3 | 4 | 5 | 1 | 2 | 3 | 4 | 5 | 1 | 2 | 3 | 4 | 5 |
| A | Girl in white tunic | X | X | X | - | - | 3 | 5 | 2 | 0 | 1 | 0 | 5 | 1 | 3 | 2 |
| B | | - | - | - | - | X | | | | | | | | | | |
| C | Al Bhed guy in green and yellow | X | X | - | - | - | 0 | 3 | 5 | 2 | 1 | - | - | - | - | - |
| D | | - | - | - | - | X | | | | | | | | | | |
| E | Man in yellow shirt walking by entrance | - | - | X | - | - | 0 | 3 | 5 | 2 | 1 | - | - | - | - | - |
| F | Guy in grey walking in circles on dock. | X | X | - | - | X | 5 | 1 | 3 | 2 | 0 | - | - | - | - | - |
| G | Man in green outfit | - | - | X | - | - | 5 | 1 | 3 | 2 | 0 | - | - | - | - | - |
| H | Female Reporter | X | X | - | - | X | 1 | 3 | 0 | 5 | 2 | 0 | 5 | | 3 | 1 |
| I | | - | - | X | - | | - | | | | | | | | | |
| J | Man in purple robe on bench | X | X | - | - | X | 3 | 0 | 2 | 1 | 5 | - | - | - | - | - |
| K | Man in yellow shirt walking around | - | - | X | - | - | 3 | 0 | 2 | 1 | 5 | | | | | |
| L | Young boy with green bandana | X | X | - | - | - | 2 | 3 | 1 | 5 | 0 | - | - | - | - | - |
| M | | - | - | X | - | - | | | | | | | | | | |
| N | | - | - | - | - | X | | | | | | | | | | |
| O | Young girl on bench | X | X | - | - | X | 1 | 3 | 0 | 2 | 5 | 3 | 0 | 5 | 1 | 2 |
| P | Woman in red top talking to woman at R | - | - | X | - | - | 1 | 3 | 0 | 2 | 5 | 3 | 0 | 5 | 1 | 2 |
| Q | Woman on bench. | X | X | - | - | X | 1 | 2 | 5 | 3 | 0 | 0 | 5 | 1 | 2 | 3 |
| R | Woman in yellow talking to woman at P | - | - | X | - | - | 1 | 2 | 5 | 3 | 0 | 0 | 5 | 1 | 2 | 3 |

# MI'IHEN HIGHROAD

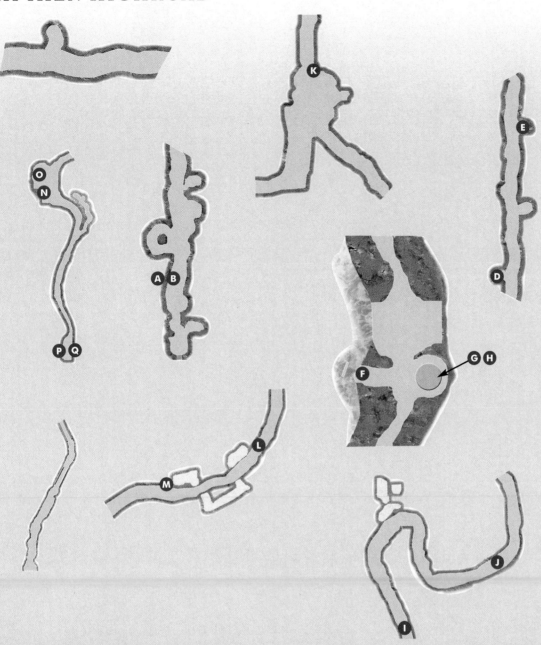

Characters

1

Garmant Grids & Dresspheres

2

Battle System

3

Accessories

4

Items and Item Shops

5

Walkthrough

6

Mini-Games

7

Fiends and Enemies

8

| MI'IHEN HIGHROAD | | | | | | | | | | | | | | | | | | |
|---|---|---|---|---|---|---|---|---|---|---|---|---|---|---|---|---|---|---|
| PLACE | DESCRIPTION | CHAPTER | | | | | PR PITCHES | | | | | MM PITCHES | | | | | | |
| | | 1 | 2 | 3 | 4 | 5 | 1 | 2 | 3 | 4 | 5 | 1 | 2 | 3 | 4 | 5 | | |
| A | Woman in blue dress | X | X | X | - | X | 5 | 1 | 0 | 3 | 2 | 5 | 1 | 2 | 3 | 0 | | |
| B | Girl in white tunic | X | X | X | - | X | 3 | 5 | 0 | 2 | 1 | 3 | 2 | 1 | 0 | 5 | | |
| C | Bare-chested man | X | X | X | - | X | 0 | 2 | 5 | 3 | 1 | - | - | - | - | - | | |
| D | Al Bhed woman | X | X | X | - | X | 2 | 1 | 0 | 5 | 3 | 1 | 5 | 0 | 3 | 2 | | |
| E | Man by Hover | X | X | X | - | X | 0 | 5 | 3 | 2 | 1 | - | - | - | - | - | | |
| F | Man looking out over the sea | X | X | X | - | X | 5 | 3 | 2 | 1 | 0 | - | - | - | - | - | | |
| G | Girl at table in Travel Agency | X | X | X | - | X | 0 | 5 | 3 | 2 | 1 | 1 | 0 | 3 | 5 | 2 | | |
| H | Boy at table in Travel Agency | X | X | X | - | X | 1 | 3 | 5 | 0 | 2 | - | - | - | - | - | | |
| I | Girl in yellow and orange. | X | X | X | - | - | 0 | 2 | 3 | 5 | 1 | 5 | 3 | 2 | 1 | 0 | | |
| J | | - | - | - | - | X | | | | | | | | | | | | |
| K | Boy by entrance to Mushroom Rock. | X | X | X | - | X | 2 | 3 | 1 | 0 | 5 | - | - | - | - | - | | |
| L | Man in purple and yellow. | X | X | X | - | - | 1 | 5 | 3 | 2 | 0 | - | - | - | - | - | | |
| M | | - | - | - | - | X | | | | | | | | | | | | |
| N | Woman in purple below bridge. | X | X | X | - | - | 2 | 3 | 1 | 5 | 0 | 5 | 3 | 2 | 1 | 0 | | |
| O | Woman in green walking back and forth under bridge | - | - | - | - | X | 2 | 3 | 1 | 5 | 0 | 5 | 3 | 2 | 1 | 0 | | |
| P | Bare-chested man | X | X | X | - | X | 3 | 0 | 5 | 2 | 1 | - | - | - | - | - | | |
| Q | Man in green shirt | X | X | X | - | X | 5 | 1 | 3 | 0 | 2 | - | - | - | - | - | | |

273

# DJOSE TEMPLE

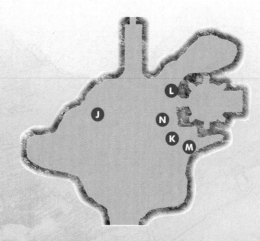

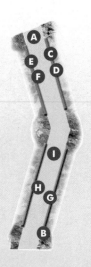

| | DJOSE TEMPLE | | | |
|---|---|---|---|---|
| **PLACE** | **DESCRIPTION** | **CHAPTER** 1 2 3 4 5 | **PR PITCHES** 1 2 3 4 5 | **MM PITCHES** 1 2 3 4 5 |
| A | Al Bhed woman in pink and red | X X - - - | 3 0 5 2 1 | 3 1 0 2 5 |
| B | | - - - - X | | |
| C | Man in green and yellow tunic | X X - - X | 5 1 0 3 2 | - - - - - |
| D | Man in yellow and blue | X X - - - | 1 0 2 5 3 | - - - - - |
| E | | - - - - X | | |
| F | Man looking at water | X X - - - | 0 1 3 2 5 | - - - - - |
| G | | - - - - X | 1 | |
| H | Old Lady in purple dress | X X - - - | 3 1 5 0 2 | 0 1 3 2 5 |
| I | | - - - - X | 2 | |
| J | Man in yellow and green | X X - - - | 2 5 0 3 1 | - - - - - |
| K | | - - - - X | | |
| L | Woman in bikini | X X - - X | 5 0 2 1 3 | 0 1 3 2 5 |
| M | Woman in yellow and orange | X X - - - | 2 1 5 0 3 | 2 0 1 5 3 |
| N | | - - - - X | | |

# MACALANIA WOODS

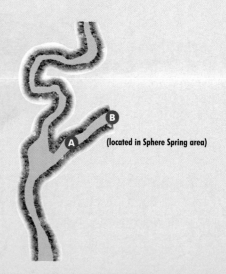

(located in Sphere Spring area)

| | MACALANIA WOODS | | | |
|---|---|---|---|---|
| **PLACE** | **DESCRIPTION** | **CHAPTER** 1 2 3 4 5 | **PR PITCHES** 1 2 3 4 5 | **MM PITCHES** 1 2 3 4 5 |
| A | Guado by tree | X X X - - | 5 0 1 2 3 | - - - - - |
| B | Guado in the woods | X X X - - | 0 3 1 5 2 | - - - - - |

# MOONFLOW

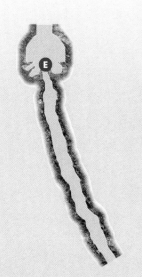

| MOONFLOW | | | | |
|---|---|---|---|---|
| PLACE | DESCRIPTION | CHAPTER<br>1 2 3 4 5 | PR PITCHES<br>1 2 3 4 5 | MM PITCHES<br>1 2 3 4 5 |
| A | Al Bhed woman | X - X X X | 3 0 5 1 2 | 5 3 2 1 0 |
| B | Al Bhed girl in coveralls | X X X X X | 0 3 1 2 5 | 0 5 3 2 1 |
| C | Boy looking at the shoopuf | X X X X X | 2 0 1 3 5 | - - - - - |
| D | Woman with red bandana | X X X X X | 0 3 2 1 5 | 2 1 0 5 3 |
| E | Old woman by Guadosalam entrance | X X X X X | 5 0 2 3 1 | 3 2 1 0 5 |

Characters

1

Garment Grids
& Dresspheres

2

Battle System

3

Accessories

4

Items and
Item Shops

5

Walkthrough

6

Mini-Games

7

Fiends and
Enemies

8

# GUADOSALAM

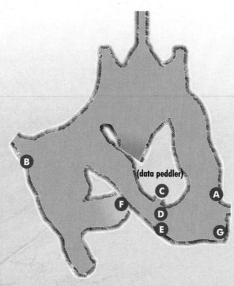

(data peddler)

| | | GUADOSALAM | | | | | | | | | | | | | | | | |
|---|---|---|---|---|---|---|---|---|---|---|---|---|---|---|---|---|---|---|
| PLACE | DESCRIPTION | CHAPTER | | | | | PR PITCHES | | | | | MM PITCHES | | | | |
| | | 1 | 2 | 3 | 4 | 5 | 1 | 2 | 3 | 4 | 5 | 1 | 2 | 3 | 4 | 5 |
| A | Hypello | X | - | - | - | X | 1 | 2 | 5 | 0 | 3 | - | - | - | - | - |
| B | | - | - | X | - | - | | | | | | | | | | |
| C | Innkeeper | X | - | X | - | X | 0 | 5 | 2 | 3 | 1 | - | - | - | - | - |
| D | Item Shopkeeper | X | - | X | - | X | 3 | 5 | 0 | 1 | 2 | - | - | - | - | - |
| E | Item shop customer | X | - | X | - | X | 0 | 3 | 2 | 5 | 1 | - | - | - | - | - |
| F | Boy in purple | X | - | X | - | - | 5 | 2 | 1 | 3 | 0 | - | - | - | - | - |
| G | | - | - | - | - | X | | | | | | | | | | |

# LUPINE DASH

| | |
|---|---|
| When Available: | Chapters 1, 2, 3, and 5 |
| Location: | Calm Lands (SW corner of field) |
| Objective: | This mini-game is the wolf equivalent of dog racing. From a field of five lupines, figure out which one is most likely to win and then place your bets! Win credits that you can use to purchase valuable and sometimes rare gifts. |

# PLACE YOUR BETS!

And the race is on! Did you bet on the right lupine?

The main objective in this game is to figure out which Lupine is most likely to win the race and place bets on him. You can choose to bet on a single winner (Win Bet) or bet on the two Lupines most likely to place 1 and 2 (Double Bet). Study their stats well and use the given odds to help you make your decision.

The odds are generated based on the Lupine's overall stats, but that doesn't always tell the whole story. When placing your bet, you can play it safe by choosing the Lupine(s) with the highest overall score and the lowest odds (and the lowest payout), or you can take a risk on an underdog.

You can place two kinds of bets. If you are lucky, at least one of them will pay off!

As your Publicity Level grows, you can bet on races with higher grades and higher stakes. These races usually provide bigger payouts, but the minimum bets are higher! On the other hand, the higher the race grade, the faster the Lupines participating in the race and the more racing fun you'll have!

| MINIMUM BETS PER RACE GRADE | |
|---|---|
| GRADE | MINIMUM BET |
| 1 | 1 |
| 2 | 5 |
| 3 | 10 |
| 4 | 25 |
| 5 | 100 |

# FIGURING OUT THE LUPINE STATS

From a field of 61 lupines, five are randomly chosen to compete in each race. You can view their stats and odds of winning when you place a bet under the Win Bet or Double Bet options. Each lupine is graded based on five stats with an overall stat used for determining the race odds. The stats indicate how well a lupine is likely to perform during a race. Ideally you want to choose a lupine with a high overall score, but sometimes you might want to take a chance on a lupine with a lower overall score but with stats that are more in line with a winner. The stats used in Lupine Dash are as follows:

| | |
|---|---|
| Speed | Speed is perhaps the greatest factor you should consider in determining a winning lupine. A (lupine's speed) changes based on the grade of the race Use the following formula in conjunction with the figure given in the Lupine stats table below to help you calculate the final sum.<br><br>Speed Stat x (Race Grade x 5 + 10) = Total Speed for the Grade entered |
| Stamina | The lupine's Stamina rating determines how long it can keep its speed up. Lupines with a high Speed rating but a low Stamin rating can run fast, but only for short distances. This is a very important modifier of a competitor's speed! |
| Rally | This describes the lupine's ability to rally its strength and speed at the very end of the race. The higher the stat, the greater the speed boost the lupine receives as it nears the goal. This stat alone can help a competitor win the race from behind. |
| Flux | This describes the probability that the lupine's starting stats will fluctuate when the race begins. The higher the Flux stat, the more easily the stats will change. |
| Luck | This stat works in conjunction with a lupine's flux stat. It determines how much the lupine's starting stats will fluctuate at the start of a race. The higher the stat, the greater the chance that its stats will change for the better. |
| Overall | This gives you the median value of the lupine's stats. The average of this stat is 50. This is used to set the odds in a race. |

*It is important to study each lupine's stats before you place your bets. Understanding how each stat works in conjunction with the others is key to winning credits!*

# REPTILE RUN

| | |
|---|---|
| **When Available:** | **Chapters 1, 2, 3, and 5** |
| **Location:** | **Calm Lands, to the left of the Chocobo Ranch** |
| **Objective:** | **To succeed at Reptile Run you must have a quick mind as well as great hand-eye coordination! This game challenges you to guide a lizard through a hazardous course to reach the finish line. The catch? You can only move forward—either in a straight vertical line or a diagonal! The faster you make it through the course, the more credits you win!** |

## HELPING THE REPTILE REACH THE GOAL LINE!

*Can you lead your lizard through a minefield of fiends without killing it?*

The goal of this game is to guide the lizard across the field, past the fiends, to the goal line within the time limit. The field is an 8x8 grid inhabited by anywhere from 10-14 fiends. Starting time limits range from 800 to 950. A horizontal row of spheres indicate when it is safe to move. A red sphere indicates certain death if you cross, while yellow and green indicate that you can pass with some safety. Get to the goal line alive to receive a payout based on the amount of remaining time on the timer.

*This game is harder than it sounds. The inability to move in multiple directions limits your ability to dodge oncoming attacks or foes!*

Naturally, the higher your Publicity Level, the more levels you can choose from. The higher the level, the more fiends you must pass and the greater the danger. However, you can also bet more, so the payout—if you win—is greater.

| MINIMUM BETS PER LEVEL | |
|---|---|
| **LEVEL** | **MINIMUM BET** |
| 1 | 1 |
| 2 | 5 |
| 3 | 10 |
| 4 | 25 |
| 5 | 100 |

Characters

1

Garment Grids & Dresspheres

2

Battle System

3

Accessories

4

Items and Item Shops

5

Walkthrough

6

Mini-Games

7

Fiends and Enemies

8

# THOSE DASTARDLY FIENDS!

Three types of fiends inhabit the field: Helms, Bombs, and Drakes. Each one has its own method and range of attack. Running into any of their attacks spells instant death for your poor lizard.

Helms can only attack the tile directly in front of them. These fiends usually walk back and forth across the field or in small repeating patterns on the same row.

Bombs spew fire in the direction they are facing. They cannot travel across the field, but they do spin in a clockwise or counterclockwise manner. Time your movements with their rotation to ensure that you don't get caught in their blast.

The Drake stampedes back and forth across the field like the Helm, but it can attack from any distance, in any of the four directions like the Bomb. Watch out for these fiends in the corners of maps!

# LAYOUT OF THE FIELDS

The layout of the field remains static for each level. Once you get to know the field, you can figure out a path through the mayhem. However, note that your starting position is randomly generated on the first row each time.

| LEVEL ONE |
|---|
| Enemies: Helm (x5), Bomb (x6)<br>Base Time Limit: 800 |

| LEVEL TWO |
|---|
| Enemies: Helm (x3), Bomb (x6), Drake (x1)<br>Base Time Limit: 850 |

| LEVEL THREE |
|---|
| Enemies: Helm (x2), Bomb (x6), Drake (x3)<br>Base Time Limit: 800 |

| LEVEL FOUR |
|---|
| Enemies: Helm (x4), Bomb (x6), Drake (x2)<br>Base Time Limit: 800 |

| LEVEL FIVE |
|---|
| Enemies: Helm (x2), Bomb (x12)<br>Base Time Limit: 950 |

# MAKING THE BIG MONEY

After successfully crossing a field, you have the option to continue on. This is the way to win or lose big. Any remaining time from the first trip is added to the time remaining after the second trip. If you make it to the end of the field the second time, your winnings are based on that larger time figure. However, if your lizard is killed by a fiend, you lose everything!

Deciding whether to continue playing is a little like playing blackjack. You might get lucky or you could lose everything!

| PAYOUT RATE BASED ON REMAINING TIME ||
|---|---|
| **TIME REMAINING** | **PAYOUT RATE** |
| 0-99 | 0 |
| 100-199 | 1.0 |
| 200-299 | 1.3 |
| 300-399 | 1.8 |
| 400-499 | 2.5 |
| 500-699 | 3.4 |
| 700-999 | 4.5 |
| 1000-1399 | 5.8 |
| 1400-1899 | 7.0 |
| 1900-2399 | 8.5 |
| 2400-2999 | 10.0 |
| 3000-3599 | 20.0 |
| 3600-4199 | 45.0 |
| 4200-4999 | 60.0 |
| 5000-5999 | 80.0 |
| 6000+ | 100.0 |

# SKY SLOTS

| When Available: | Chapters 1, 2, 3 and 5 |
| --- | --- |
| Location: | Calm Lands, north of the Travel Agency stand |
| Objective: | Win credits by playing this living version of a slot machine. As the fiends fly by, stop them in hopes of getting three in a row! |

*Sky Slots is nothing more than a living slot machine high in the sky over the Calm Lands. If you like playing the slots, then you'll love this take on the genre!*

## GETTING THREE IN A ROW

To win at Sky Slots, you must stop the spinning reels of fiends by pressing the X button to get three of the same fiend in a row. There are six fiends per reel and the number of credits you win is based on the type of fiends you line up between the two triangular marks. So, if you bet 5 credits and get three Vespa fiends in a row, you only win back your 5 credits. However, if you get three Divebeak fiends in a row, you win 500 credits! Of course, it goes without saying that the fiends with the higher multipliers are much harder to line up than the ones with lower multipliers. Use the following table to determine which fiends to aim for!

| FIENDS | MULTIPLIER |
| --- | --- |
| Divebeak | 100x |
| Peregrine | 50x |
| Death Dauber | 25x |
| Assassin Bee | 10x |
| Aculeate | 5x |
| Vespa | 1x |

| MINIMUM BETS PER LEVEL | |
| --- | --- |
| **LEVEL** | **MINIMUM BET** |
| 1 | 1 |
| 2 | 5 |
| 3 | 10 |
| 4 | 25 |
| 5 | 100 |

The amount you can bet increases as your Publicity Level increases. Of course, higher levels mean faster reels, higher stakes, and an insane amount of difficulty. However, if you are trying to win enough credits to buy something really awesome, the payout is worth it!

## TIMING IS THE KEY!

The key to winning at Sky Slots is timing. You must figure out when to press the X button so that the wheel stops on the fiend you want. The best way to do this is to memorize the order in which the fiends appear on the reels. That way, you can press the X button just before the fiend you want appears. Practice your timing on Level 1 using single credit bets until you can pull off a win. Then graduate to the next level and see if you can get the timing right on a faster reel.

*Just when you think you've got everything under control, the screen changes perspective!*

## FEED THE MONKEY

| When Available: | Chapter 5 |
| --- | --- |
| Location: | Calm Lands (north entrance) |
| Objective: | Feed the monkey on the back of the bird. If it loses too much weight, it will disappear and the bird will fly off. Feed it too much and the monkey and bird will come crashing to the ground! |

## OBTAINING THE FEED THE MONKEY MINI-GAME

Feed the Monkey is one of the two mini-games that open when the competing companies combine forces at the end of the Publicity Campaign in Chapter 5. If you get to Publicity Level 3 or higher in the Argent, Inc. campaign, this attraction opens up at the northern entrance to the Calm Lands field.

## DON'T FEED THE MONKEY TOO MUCH—OR TOO LITTLE!

In this mini-game, the challenge is to continuously feed the monkey on the bird's back while keeping its weight within a certain range. If the monkey gets too heavy or too light, it will disappear from the screen and end the game.

*Feed your monkey well to keep it from disappearing!*

Characters

1

Garment Grids & Dresspheres

2

Battle System

3

Accessories

4

Items and Item Shops

5

Walkthrough

6

Mini-Games

7

Fiends and Enemies

8

The five treasure chests on the ground are filled with a variety of fruit. Light fruit makes the monkey lighter, while heavy fruit increases its girth. Since you don't know what kind of fruit is in the closed chests, fate plays a large hand in how much weight the monkey loses or gains.

If your monkey's weight drops below 5 pounds or goes above 95, then it's game over! The info bar at the top of the screen indicates how much of each kind of fruit are in the chests. Keep an eye on its tally, because it enables you to determine the risks of opening the next treasure chest. If your monkey is on the edge of its weight range, and the chests are full of fruit you don't want, don't be afraid to end the game by pressing the Circle button.

*To continue or not? When your monkey is close to reaching its weight limit and the contents of chests aren't looking good, you're better off ending the game rather than losing your hard earned credits!*

*Calling Rikku and Paine isn't without its risks! If you see them slump their shoulders, then they've either failed to swap out the right kind of fruit, or worse yet, may have added a Forbidden Fruit to one of the chests.*

Helping out in this endeavor are Rikku and Paine. You can call upon them to fill the chests with either heavy (Rikku) or light (Paine) fruits when the tally in the window above isn't reporting what you want. At the beginning of the game you'll only be able to call each girl out twice, but as you open more chests you can earn more chances to call on them for help. Each round there's a 50% chance that opening one of the chests will give you another Rikku or Paine to call.

## THE FRUITS OF LOVE

Of course, central to this game are the fruits. To help maximize your score, memorize the information in the following table so that you know how much each piece of fruit affects your monkey's weight.

After opening 20 or more chests, the rate at which the large fruits appear in pairs increases. For this reason, try to keep your monkey's weight below 60 lbs. just to be safe. When the chest count gets close to 30, special fruits start to appear in the treasure chests. Fruits like the Plain and Balance Fruits are great things to get. However, you should beware the Forbidden Fruit. This item causes your monkey to swell up like a balloon and instantly end the game. If you see one pop up on the information bar, call on Paine or Rikku to change the fruits in the chests!

| FEED THE MONKEY FRUITS | |
|---|---|
| **FRUIT NAME** | **WEIGHT CHANGE** |
| Heavy Fruit Large | +15 |
| Heavy Fruit Medium | +10 |
| Heavy Fruit Small | +5 |
| Light Fruit Large | -15 |
| Light Fruit Medium | -10 |
| Light Fruit Small | -5 |
| Plain Fruit | +/-0 |
| Balance Fruit | Returns Monkey to original weight (45) |
| Forbidden Fruit | +150 (ends game) |

## GULL FORCE

| | | |
|---|---|---|
| **When Available:** | Chapter 5 | |
| **Location:** | Calm Lands, southern entrance | |
| **Objective:** | Try to shoot the *real* gull out of a line up of fakes! | |

## OBTAINING THE GULL FORCE MINI-GAME

Gull Force is one of the two mini-games that open when the competing companies combine forces at the end of the Publicity Campaign in Chapter 5. If you get to Publicity Level 3 or higher in the Open Air campaign, this attraction opens up at the southern entrance to the Calm Lands field.

## THE BFG (BIG FLOCKING GULLSHOT)

The rules of the game are simple. In each round, you are presented with a line of flying fiends. Depending on the level, a certain number of the fiends are real and the rest are decoys. Your job is to shoot the required number of real fiends (or more) by pressing the Square button to make it to the next stage. As you progress through the game, the stages (12 in all) get progressively harder, requiring you to shoot more targets while the number of real fiends per line decreases. You can stop the game at any point after you successfully complete a stage. The payout is based on the number of successful rounds.

*To shoot a fiend, press the Square button. You only get one shot per line of fiends.*

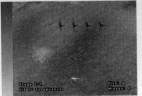

*Sometimes spinning fiends are all you have to go on!*

## SPOTTING DECOYS

Part of the job is determining which fiends are real and which ones are just decoys. In the early part of the game, it's pretty easy: all of the real fiends spin around halfway across the screen. By the mid point of the game, the real fiends are still spinning, but not all the time! In the hardest levels, the decoys start spinning too! Fortunately, they spin in the opposite direction of the real fiends.

# THE TWELVE STAGES

Each stage follows one of four patterns:

*Pattern A: Head On (Top to Bottom).*

*Pattern B: Left to Right.*

*Pattern C: Bottom to Top.*

*Pattern D: Right to Left.*

To conquer each stage, all you need is a steady hand and a good eye. The first round of stages (Stages 1-1 to 1-4) are fairly easy, because the ratio of real fiends to decoys is high and the real fiends all spin. However, the second and third rounds are where the action really kicks in. In these stages (Stages 2-1 to 2-4), the number of decoys starts to rise and the actions of the real fiends becomes more erratic. By the end of the third round (Stages 3-1 to 3-4), the ratios of real fiends to decoys is 1 to 4!

## STAGE INFORMATION

| STAGE # | # OF REAL FIENDS | SHOTS TO CLEAR | PATTERN TYPE |
|---|---|---|---|
| 1-1 | 4 | 1 | A |
| 1-2 | 4 | 2 | B |
| 1-3 | 4 | 2 | C |
| 1-4 | 3 | 3 | D |
| 2-1 | 3 | 2 | A |
| 2-2 | 3 | 2 | B |
| 2-3 | 3 | 3 | C |
| 2-4 | 3 | 3 | D |
| 3-1 | 2 | 2 | A |
| 3-2 | 2 | 3 | B |
| 3-3 | 1 | 2 | C |
| 3-4 | 1 | 3 | D |

# THE CHOCOBO RANCH

| | |
|---|---|
| When Available: | Chapters 2, 3, and 5 |
| Location: | Eastern side of the Calm Lands. |
| Objective: | The Chocobo Ranch is all about catching chocobos in the wild, taming them, and raising their levels. You can then send them to the far corners of Spira in search of items and hidden locations! |

## CLASKO AND THE CHOCOBO RANCH

Adding the Chocobo Ranch to your list of mini-games requires lots of patience and the fulfillment of several prerequisite missions. At the very least, you must ensure that you've spoken to Clasko before the end of Chapter 2 to have access to the Chocobo Ranch. Otherwise, you won't be able to play this mini-game, and Clasko will be missing-in-action for the rest of the game.

The easiest way to get the Chocobo Ranch is to participate in the following events.

*Clasko is the key to getting the Chocobo Ranch. If you see to it that he finds his way to the Calm Lands, you'll have your run of the Chocobo Ranch for sure.*

- **Step 1:** Meet Clasko during the "Foggy Fiend Frenzy!" mission at Mushroom Rock Road in Chapter 1.

- **Step 2:** After completing the "Foggy Fiend Frenzy!" mission, return to Mushroom Rock Road and invite Clasko to join the crew on the Celsius.

- **Step 3:** Participate in the "Cuckoo for Chocobos!" mission on the Mi'ihen Highroad in Chapter 2. If Clasko is onboard the Celsius, he will disembark to help you complete this mission.

- **Step 4:** After completing the "Cuckoo for Chocobos!" mission, return to the Mi'ihen Highroad and invite Clasko back onboard the Celsius. (Depending upon the outcome of the mission, you may also be able to invite Calli and her chocobo.)

- **Step 5:** With Clasko onboard, fly to the Calm Lands and help Clasko set up his stables by completing the "Clean Sweep" mission. After clearing the stables of fiends, the Chocobo Ranch is yours!

Characters
Garment Grids & Dresspheres
Battle System
Accessories
Items and Item Shops
Walkthrough
Mini-Games
Fiends and Enemies

# INSIDE THE CHOCOBO RANCH

You can find chocobos almost anywhere in Spira. After catching one, it is automatically sent to Clasko and the Chocobo Ranch. The Ranch can hold up to 14 chocobos, four Choco-Runners and 10 Choco-Reserves. When you fill the stalls, you must let one of the current chocobos go before you can catch another.

The layout of the Chocobo Ranch is fairly simple to navigate. Clasko generally hangs out in the alcove to the right of the entrance. The Choco-Reserves live in the stalls in the right and left wings on the first floor, while the Choco-Runners reside in the stalls on the second floor.

*A chocobo in its stall—what a satisfying site!*

*Clasko is the heart and soul of the Chocobo Ranch. If you need to get anything done with your chocobo, talk to him!*

Clasko handles all of the standard business in the Chocobo Ranch. If you need to check the status of your chocobos, dispatch one on a treasure hunt or feed it greens, then talk to Clasko.

# CATCHING A CHOCOBO

After cleaning out the Ranch, Clasko presents you with some Gysahl Greens to help you catch your first chocobo. Now all you have to do is find some chocobos! Wild chocobos live in virtually every part of Spira, and you encounter them in battles just like normal enemies.

If you are lucky enough to run across one that is alone, feed it some Gysahl Greens until it is tame and willingly joins your flock.

*Whether in a battle with fiends or alone, catching a chocobo is never easy.*

| AREAS WHERE CHOCOBOS NEVER APPEAR IN BATTLE |
|---|
| Bevelle |
| Lake Macalania |
| Mi'ihen Highroad |
| Mt. Gagazet |
| Mushroom Rock Road |
| Zanarkand Ruins |

*Remember, once you catch a chocobo it is automatically sent to the Ranch.*

If you run into a chocobo in a battle situation, have a party member feed it Gysahl Greens to keep it calm and interested while the other party members work on defeating the fiends. Whatever you do, do *not* attack the chocobo—even by accident! If you strike a chocobo in battle, it automatically runs off. Eliminate all of the fiends and continue to feed the chocobo until it is caught.

# INCREASING A CHOCOBO'S LEVEL

After capturing a chocobo, it's time to start raising it. Basically, you want to raise its level as high as possible. To increase a chocobo's level, you must feed it a certain number of Greens. Refer to the following table for all the pertinent information.

| LEVELING UP CHOCOBOS | | |
|---|---|---|
| LEVEL | GREENS NEEDED | # |
| 2 | Pahsana Greens | 10 |
| 3 | Mimett Greens | 10 |
| 4 | Mimett Greens | 30 |
| 5 | Sylkis Greens | 40 |

Clasko obtains new Greens while the Gullwings are out completing missions and defeating enemies. The more battles you win, the more Greens Clasko acquires. Yuna can hold 99 of each type of Green in her inventory, the rest Clasko can store in the Ranch. Since greens are essential to raising your chocobos' levels, make sure you always have a good supply on hand. Pahsana and Gysahl Greens are available from the opening of the Chocobo Ranch, while Mimett Greens appear in Chapter 3 and Sylkis Greens appear in Chapter 5. You can change the ratio of Greens that Clasko obtains by selecting the Nutritive Green option on the main menu. NOTE: You can't adjust the ratio of anything from the Junk Food Greens section.

## BREAKING DOWN THE BATTLE/GREENS RATIO

| CHAPTER | GYSAHL GREENS | PAHSANA, SYLKIS AND MIMETT GREENS |
| --- | --- | --- |
| 2 | 5 Greens for every 12 battles | 10 Greens for every 6 battles |
| 3 | 5 Greens for every 10 battles | 10 Greens for every 6 battle5 |
| 4-5 | 5 Greens for every 6 battles | 10 Greens for every 5 battles |

The higher a chocobo's level, the better the items they bring back from treasure hunts. It's a good idea to raise your chocobos' levels as high as possible!

# CHOCOBO TREASURE HUNTING

*There are many factors involved in dispatching a chocobo. Knowledge and careful reasoning is the secret to keeping a chocobo from running away.*

The main function of the chocobo is for treasure hunting. At any time, you can send a chocobo into the field to search for treasure and hidden areas that are otherwise inaccessible. However, sending a chocobo out on a treasure hunt has its risks. If a chocobo's Heart stat is low or its nature clashes with the area you send it to, there is a good chance that the chocobo will fly the coop. The more chocobos there are inside the ranch, the less likely they are to run away. Use the information provided in this section to make things easier when dispatching a chocobo.

A chocobo's Nature can be one of three types: bold, normal, or timid. A chocobo's Nature remains the same throughout the game, so if you're looking to get a chocobo with a certain Nature, you may have to capture and release several chocobos before coming across the one you're looking for. Different areas are also better for catching certain types of chocobos, as laid out in the following table:

## NATURE

| AREA | TIMID | NORMAL | BOLD |
| --- | --- | --- | --- |
| Kilika Island, Thunder Plains, Bikanel Desert | 10% | 10% | 80% |
| Djose Temple, Calm Lands | 10% | 80% | 10% |
| Besaid Island, Moonflow, Macalania Forest | 80% | 10% | 10% |

Nature is perhaps the single most important factor to consider when deciding which of your chocobos to dispatch to a given location. A chocobo whose Nature is well-suited to a location is less likely to run away, loses less Heart during the trip, and is more likely to find treasure. You want to make certain that a chocobo does its best, so make sure that you send it somewhere that suits its Nature. Refer to the following table to see where you should send your chocobos:

## MATCHING CHOCOBO NATURE WITH LOCATIONS

| DESTINATION | NATURE* | | |
| --- | --- | --- | --- |
| | TIMID | NORMAL | BOLD |
| Besaid Island | Average | Well-suited | Unsuited |
| Kilika Island | Well-suited | Unsuited | Average |
| Mi'ihen Highroad | Average | Average | Average |
| Mushroom Rock Road | Average | Average | Average |
| Djose | Unsuited | Average | Well-suited |
| Moonflow | Average | Well-suited | Unsuited |
| Thunder Plains | Well-suited | Unsuited | Average |
| Macalania | Average | Well-suited | Unsuited |
| Bikanel Island | Well-suited | Unsuited | Average |
| Calm Lands | Unsuited | Average | Well-suited |
| Mt. Gagazet | Average | Average | Average |
| Zanarkand Ruins | Average | Average | Average |

## SUITABILITY AND ITS EFFECTS

| SUITABILITY | HEART CONSUMPTION | TREASURE AMOUNT | FLEE PROBABILITY |
| --- | --- | --- | --- |
| Well-suited | 15 | More than average | Low |
| Average | 30 | Average | Average |
| Unsuited | 60 | Less than average | High |

Now that you've sent your chocobo minions out to scour Spira for you, it may be nice to know exactly what they can bring back. A chocobo's level and the location it's sent to determine what treasures it may find. Refer to the following tables for the details. The number of items the chocobo can find is determined completely by two things:

It's suitability for the area you've sent it to.

The number of Choco-Reserves currently at the Chocobo Ranch.

## GETTING THE AMAZING CHOCOBO

Dispatch level 1-5 chocobos (3 of each level) and have them come back safely (i.e. you have to dispatch AT LEAST 15 chocobos to meet this requirement; if any run away, you'll have to send out more)

All your Choco-Runners must be level 5 chocobos.

The Amazing Chocobo doesn't have a level, Nature or Heart, and it won't run away once you've got it, but it does have Fatigue ranging from 0 to 100. The Amazing Chocobo's Fatigue affects how well it can perform its tasks of "Chocobo Support" and "Exploring Spira."

Characters

1

Garment Grids & D  Dressspheres

2

Battle System

3

Accessories

4

Items and Item Shops

5

Walkthrough

6

Mini-Games

7

Fiends and Enemies

8

## CHOCOBO TREASURE HUNTING LIST

| LOCATION | CHOCOBO LEVEL | GRADE D | ITEMS IT CAN FIND GRADE C | GRADE B | GRADE A |
|----------|---------------|---------|---------|---------|---------|
| Besaid Island | Level 1 | Potion | Potion (x2) | Potion (x3) | Potion (x4) |
| | Level 2 | Hi-Potion | Phoenix Down | Ether | Turbo Ether |
| | Level 3 | Hi-Potion (x2) | Phoenix Down (x2) | Ether (x2) | Turbo Ether (x2) |
| | Level 4 | Hi-Potion (x3) | Phoenix Down (x3) | Ether (x3) | X-Potion |
| | Level 5 | Hi-Potion (x4) | Phoenix Down (x4) | Ether (x4) | Elixir |
| Kilika Island | Level 1 | Budget Grenade | Budget Grenade | Grenade | Grenade (x2) |
| | Level 2 | Grenade (x3) | M-Bomb | M-Bomb (x2) | Petrify Grenade |
| | Level 3 | Grenade (x4) | L-Bomb (x2) | L-Bomb (x2) | Petrify Grenade (x2) |
| | Level 4 | S-Bomb | L-Bomb (x3) | Sleep Grenade (x2) | Titanium Bangle |
| | Level 5 | M-Bomb | Silence Grenade (x4) | Star Pendant | Venom Shock |
| Mi'ihen Highroad | Level 1 | Soft | Soft (x2) | Soft (x4) | Soft |
| | Level 2 | Remedy | Eye Drops | Silence Grenade | Silver Bracer |
| | Level 3 | Remedy (x2) | Eye Drops (x2) | Silence Grenade (x2) | Gold Bracer |
| | Level 4 | Remedy (x3) | Eye Drops (x3) | Silence Grenade (x3) | Rune Bracer |
| | Level 5 | Remedy (x4) | Eye Drops (x4) | White Cape | Mute Shock |
| Mushroom Rock Road | Level 1 | Fish Scale | Fish Scale (x2) | Fish Scale (x3) | Fish Scale (x4) |
| | Level 2 | Dragon Scale | Water Gem | Blue Ring | Cerulean Ring |
| | Level 3 | Dragon Scale (x2) | Water Gem (x2) | Watery Gleam | Electrocutioner |
| | Level 4 | Dragon Scale (x3) | Water Gem (x3) | NulTide Ring | Short Circuit |
| | Level 5 | Dragon Scale (x4) | Water Gem (x4) | Silver Glasses | Blind Shock |
| Djose | Level 1 | Star Curtain | Star Curtain (x2) | Star Curtain (x3) | Star Curtain (x4) |
| | Level 2 | Lunar Curtain | Light Curtain | Mana Tablet | Stamina Tablet |
| | Level 3 | Lunar Curtain (x2) | Light Curtain (x2) | Mana Tablet (x2) | Stamina Tablet (x2) |
| | Level 4 | Lunar Curtain (x3) | Light Curtain (x3) | Mana Tonic | Stamina Tonic |
| | Level 5 | Lunar Curtain (x4) | Light Curtain (x4) | Twist Headband | Dream Shock |
| Moonflow | Level 1 | Antidote | Antidote (x2) | Antidote (x3) | Antidote (x4) |
| | Level 2 | Remedy | Holy Water | Healing Spring | Ether |
| | Level 3 | Remedy (x2) | Holy Water (x2) | Healing Spring (x2) | Turbo Ether |
| | Level 4 | Remedy (x3) | Holy Water (x3) | Healing Spring (x3) | Regen Bangle |
| | Level 5 | Remedy (x4) | Holy Water (x4) | Healing Spring (x4) | Recovery Bracer |
| Thunder Plains | Level 1 | Electro Marble | Electro Marble (x2) | Electro Marble (x3) | Electro Marble (x4) |
| | Level 2 | Lightning Marble | Lightning Gem | Yellow Ring | Ochre Ring |
| | Level 3 | Lightning Marble (x2) | Lightning Gem (x2) | Lightning Gleam | Short Circuit |
| | Level 4 | Lightning Marble (x3) | Lightning Gem (x3) | NulShock Ring | Electrocutioner |
| | Level 5 | Lightning Marble (x4) | Lightning Gem (x4) | Black Choker | Chaos Shock |
| Macalania | Level 1 | Potion | Potion (x2) | Potion (x3) | Potion (x4) |
| | Level 2 | Hi-Potion | Phoenix Down | Phoenix Down (x3) | Mega Phoenix |
| | Level 3 | Hi-Potion (x2) | Phoenix Down (x2) | Phoenix Down (x4) | Mega-Potion |
| | Level 4 | Hi-Potion (x3) | Phoenix Down (x3) | Mega Phoenix | Mega-Potion (x2) |
| | Level 5 | Hi-Potion (x4) | Phoenix Down (x4) | Potpourri (x2) | Fury Shock |
| Bikanel Desert | Level 1 | Bomb Fragment | Bomb Fragment (x2) | Bomb Fragment (x3) | Bomb Fragment (x4) |
| | Level 2 | Bomb Core | Fire Gem | Red Ring | Crimson Ring |
| | Level 3 | Bomb Core (x2) | Fire Gem (x2) | Fiery Gleam | Sublimator |
| | Level 4 | Bomb Core (x3) | Fire Gem (x3) | NulBlaze Ring | Freezerburn |
| | Level 5 | Bomb Core (x4) | Fire Gem (x4) | Gold Anklet | Stone Shock |
| Calm Lands | Level 1 | Potion | Potion (x2) | Potion (x3) | Potion (x4) |
| | Level 2 | Dispel Tonic | Chocobo Feather | Silver Hourglass | Gold Hourglass |
| | Level 3 | Dispel Tonic (x2) | Chocobo Feather (x2) | Silver Hourglass (x2) | Gold Hourglass (x2) |
| | Level 4 | Dispel Tonic (x3) | Chocobo Feather (x3) | Silver Hourglass (x3) | Chocobo Wing |
| | Level 5 | Dispel Tonic (x4) | Chocobo Feather (x4) | Dragonfly Orb | System Shock |
| Mt. Gagazat | Level 1 | Antarctic Wind | Antarctic Wind (x2) | Antarctic Wind (x3) | Antarctic Wind (x4) |
| | Level 2 | Arctic Wind | Ice Gem | White Ring | Snow Ring |
| | Level 3 | Arctic Wind (x2) | Ice Gem (x2) | Icy Gleam | Sublimator |
| | Level 4 | Arctic Wind (x3) | Ice Gem (x3) | NulFrost Ring | Freezerburn |
| | Level 5 | Arctic Wind (x4) | Ice Gem (x4) | Angel Earrings | Mortal Shock |
| Zanarkand Ruins | Level 1 | Echo Screen | Echo Screen (x2) | Echo Screen (x3) | Echo Screen (x4) |
| | Level 2 | Remedy | Dispel Tonic | Silver Hourglass | Ether |
| | Level 3 | Remedy (x2) | Dispel Tonic (x2) | Gold Hourglass | Turbo Ether |
| | Level 4 | Remedy (x3) | Dispel Tonic (x3) | Gold Hourglass (x2) | Kinesis Badge |
| | Level 5 | Remedy (x4) | Dispel Tonic (x4) | Pretty Orb | Lag Shock |

# SPECIAL TREASURE HUNTING EVENTS

There are a couple of special events that occur when you send a chocobo to certain locations under specific conditions. Send a chocobo to Bikanel Island in Chapter 5 and you can ride it in the Central Expanse section of the Digging mini-game. In addition, if you send out a chocobo with a Heart stat at less than 100 and it returns without finding an item, there is a chance that you'll get a Garment Grid as a consolation prize. Those Garment Grids include the following: **Mounted Assault** or **Strength of One** .

*Sending a chocobo to Bikanel Island in Chapter 5 opens up a new area in the Digging mini-game. What else might your chocobo uncover when you send it out on treasure hunts?*

# GUNNER'S GAUNLET

Characters

Garment Grids & Dresspheres

Battle System

Accessories

Items and Item Shops

Walkthrough

Mini-Games

Fiends and Enemies

| When Available: | Chapters 2, 3, and 5 |
| Location: | Besaid Island, talk to Beclem by the Save Sphere outside the city |
| Objective: | See if you can outshoot Beclem by running a gauntlet from Besaid Village to the beach, taking down dangerous fiends. Different types of ammo in limited quantities make the game even harder. But, if you beat Beclem's high score within the time limit, you can win valuable items! Strive for higher levels to get better prizes! |

## PLAYING THE GUNNER'S GAUNLET

In this mini-game, you must defeat enemies and gain enough points to beat Beclem's high score. However, it's not as easy as it sounds due to a limited amount of ammo and a multitude of fiends that appear out of thin air. You need a steady hand and a calculating mind to get the best score—shooting at will just won't cut it!

*The Gunner's Gauntlet couldn't be more fun. It's just run and shoot.*

To maximize your score, you must defeat your foes one after the other without taking any damage whatsoever! This way, your attacks turn into chains, multiplying the number of points you receive. To be successful, you must get to know the route by heart, including the starting locations of the fiends! You must also get good at switching between ammo and targets with ease.

*When surrounded by fiends, press the Square button to switch between targets and take advantage of the Volley and Dual Shot ammo to thin out the field. If all else fails, retreat!*

## HOW CHAINS WORK

Chains are at the heart of this mini-game. You will get nowhere unless you learn how to use chains to maximize your points. When you defeat a fiend, the Chain Gauge at the bottom of the screen starts to fill up. As your level goes up, your points start to multiply. The gauge has three levels: Level One provides 1x the points scored; Level Two provides 2x; while Level Three provides 3x. If you take any damage, the gauge is immediately reset and you're forced to start rebuilding the meter all over again. Learning not to get hit is crucial for building high scores!

*To keep from being ambushed, try pressing the Circle button to lock on to targets hidden by the scenery or further down the path.*

## RELOADING

Of course, in addition to all of the other challenges you face, you must integrate the reloading of your gun into your plans. You can fire up to six shots into an enemy at a time. After this, the gun must be reloaded. Naturally, you cannot fire at any approaching enemies at this time, so you are quite vulnerable to attack. During reload time, press the Circle button to search for other enemies or press the Square button to switch between targets.

*Having to reload in an ambush situation is about as dangerous as running out of ammo. Make sure that neither situation happens to you!*

## THE PRIZES

There are 10 levels in the Gunner's Gauntlet mini-game. To advance to the next level, you must defeat the level's high score. When you clear a level's high score, you also get a reward. Of course, the higher the level, the better the prize—and the more difficult the course!

| SCORE TO LEVEL UP AND PRIZES | | |
| --- | --- | --- |
| LEVEL | SCORE | PRIZE |
| Lv 1 | 501 | - |
| Lv 2 | 750 | Enigma Plate Garment Grid |
| Lv 3 | 900 | Power Wrist |
| Lv 4 | 1000 | Silver Bracer |
| Lv 5 | 1150 | Titanium Bangle |
| Lv 6 | 1300 | Mortal Coil Garment Grid |
| Lv 7 | 1400 | Beaded Brooch |
| Lv 8 | 2000 | Diamond Gloves |
| Lv 9 | 2800 | Faerie Earrings |
| Lv MAX | - | Adamantite |

# AMMO AND FIENDS LOWDOWN

Before you take on the Gunner's Gauntlet, take a moment to review the types of ammo and fiends you'll have to deal with.

## AMMO

There are four types of ammo. You start each run with a set amount of regular ammo, but you pick up refills from the treasure chests that defeated fiends drop. Each fiend drops a different type of ammo, so learn which ones drop which ammo types maximize your inventory. In addition to ammo, look for fiends that drop helpful items like Upgrades and Quick Shot.

| TYPES OF AMMO | |
| --- | --- |
| AMMO NAME | EFFECT |
| Ammo | This is the basic, garden variety ammunition. Each shot causes 1HP of damage to the targeted fiend. |
| Dual Shot | This ammo enables you to shoot at two targets at once. Each successful shot causes 1HP of damage. |
| Death | This special ammunition causes instant death. Use this type on particularly difficult fiends. |
| Volley | This rare ammunition takes out most targeted fiends on the field. |

| OTHER ITEMS | |
| --- | --- |
| ITEM NAME | EFFECT |
| Upgrade Item | There are three types of Upgrades specific to each type of ammo. This item takes two shots of ammo and turns it into one piece of ammo of the next rank. For example, using the Upgrade Item, you can turn Ammo x2 into Dual Shot x1. This only works with Ammo, Dual Shot, and Death type ammunition. |
| HP Recovery Item | This item increases Yuna's HP by 15-19 points. |
| Quick Shot Item | This item enables you to shoot at a much faster rate until your Quick Shot Gauge runs out. |

Now on to the fiends! Thirteen kinds of fiends inhabit the road between Besaid Village and the beach. You won't see all of them at once! Some only appear in the later levels!

| FIENDS IN THE GUNNER'S GAUNTLET | | | | |
| --- | --- | --- | --- | --- |
| FIEND | HP | POINTS | LV APPEARANCE | ITEM DROPPED |
| Coyote | 5 | 3 | Lv 1+ | Ammo x10-14 |
| Wild Wolf | 7 | 5 | Lv 1+ | Death x1-2 |
| Shantak | 10 | 10 | Lv 1+ | Dual Shot x10-14 |
| YSLS-99 | 17 | 15 | Lv 1+ | Death x1-2 |
| Creeper | 1 | 1 | Lv 3+ | — |
| Tomb (S) | 10 | 5 | Lv 3-5 | Volley x1 |
| Nashorn | 8 | 12 | Lv 4+ | HP Recovery x15-19 |
| Bicocette | 11 | 8 | Lv 6+ | Volley x1 |
| Tomb (M) | 16 | 8 | Lv 6-7 | Volley x2 |
| Hrimthur | 6 | 25 | Lv 7+ | Quick Shot Item |
| Divebeak | 12 | 4 | Lv 7+ | — |
| Tomb (L) | 20 | 15 | Lv 8-9 | Volley x3 |
| Tomb (XL) | 30 | 20 | Lv MAX | Volley x4 |

# GUNNER'S GAUNLET (CLOISTER OF TRIALS)

| | |
| --- | --- |
| When Available: | Chapters 3 and 5 |
| Location: | Besaid Temple, talk to the priest standing before the Cloister of Trials to start this mini-game |
| Objective: | This is a more challenging version of the regular Gunner's Gauntlet. Confined inside the Cloister of Trials, you must defeat fiends as they appear. Because this mini-game is "on rails," you only have a limited time to defeat each fiend before you move on. |

# PLAYING THE GUNNER'S GAUNTLET, CLOISTER OF TRIALS

This mini-game opens up after you defeat the aeon in Besaid Temple in the Protect Besaid Temple mission. Afterward, you can talk to the priest in front of the cloister's door to start the mini-game. This game is fairly tough, so you should only attempt it after you've gained expertise in the original Gunner's Gauntlet game!

*Talk to the priest inside Besaid Temple to start the mini-game. Beclem only provides some generic tips and hints about the Gunner's Gauntlet as a whole.*

Characters

1

Garment Grids & Dresspheres

2

Battle System

3

Accessories

4

Items and Item Shops

5

Walkthrough

6

Mini-Games

7

Fiends and Enemies

8

What could be scarier than a hallway full of creepy crawlers?

The biggest difference between this and the other Gunner's Gauntlet is the automatic scroll system, which limits your freedom of movement. Add in the first-person perspective, which requires the manipulation of the camera to find upcoming fiends, and the cloister's overall gloomy and scary feeling and you have a much more challenging game to master.

## QUICK REACTION TIMES ARE KEY

This time around, the screen constantly scrolls, taking you through the dungeon with it. Since you cannot stop or backtrack when you encounter fiends, you must get proficient at taking out fiends with ease. Use the Analog Stick to move the camera around so that you can spot fiends before they get too close. Inside the cloister, you'll face fiends that hover above your head or scurry beneath your feet, so remember to look up and down instead of just in front of you. Enemies will also try to sneak up from behind, so beware and don't get caught off guard! The new time limit is 12 minutes, so you'll have to maintain a longer attention span than before!

## PREPARE FOR TOUGHER FIENDS!

To make this task more interesting, you'll face different fiends in the cloister compared to the regular Gunner's Gauntlet. These fiends are faster and oftentimes more powerful.

Look up, look down, look all around!

| FIENDS INSIDE THE CLOISTER OF TRIALS | | | |
|---|---|---|---|
| FIEND | HP | POINTS | ITEM DROPPED |
| Coyote | 5 | 3 | Ammo x17-21 |
| Haunt | 13 | 10 | Dual Shot x10-14 |
| Death Dauber | 3-5 | 4 | — |
| Creeper | 1 | 2 | Ammo x1-4 |
| Ahriman | 7 | 15 | Quick Shot Item |
| Tomb | 80 | 20 | Death x1-2 |
| Flan Azul | 4 | 2 | HP Recovery x2-3 |
| Tonberry | 15 | 20 | Ammo x30-39 |
| Mega Tonberry | 20 | 30 | — |

## CHECKING OUT THE AREA

The way through the Cloister of Trials is fairly simple and can be divided into three parts. The first area extends from the starting point to the crossroads area. Here you need to be on the lookout for foes coming from all directions. The creepers from the Tomb are especially troubling, as they scurry across the floor. It is very easy to miss them after being distracted by a flying Death Dauber.

The Crossroads area is next. Here you'll have fiends coming from all directions as you attempt to take out a Tomb. The Tomb may not attack, but everything else will!

At the end you'll face the Tonberry Hallway, a place where Tonberry enemies attack in force. Can you handle the pressure this close to the goal line?

## LIGHTNING ROD TOWERS

| | |
|---|---|
| When Available: | Chapters 2, 3 |
| Location: | Thunder Plains |
| Objective: | Help the Al Bhed calibrate the Lightning Rod Towers on the northern and southern plains. This project starts out simple enough, but ends up being a real test of hand-eye coordination and memorization skills. If you attempted to calibrate all 10 towers and calibrate 5 of the 10 towers correctly, entering all 30 commands, you'll win the Samurai's Honor Garment Grid. |

LIGHTNING ROD TOWERS

# CALIBRATING THE LIGHTNING ROD TOWERS

When you visit the Thunder Plains in Chapters 2 and 3, you'll find Al Bhed technicians busily trying to calibrate the Lightning Rod Towers on the northern and southern plains. Talk to one of them twice and he'll ask for your help with the calibration project.

To start the Lightning Rod Tower mini-game, talk to one of the busy technicians.

If you need to confirm your progress or just get some help, speak with the technician inside the Travel Agency.

To calibrate a tower (it's recommended that you start with the first three at the southern end of the plains), you must enter a series of 30 randomly generated commands. If you miss three times, the calibration fails and you're forced to start over again. You can check your progress by talking to the technician inside the Travel Agency building between the two plains.

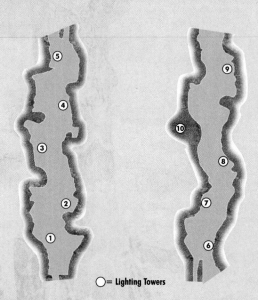

○ = Lighting Towers

# THREE TYPES OF CALIBRATIONS

Care of the Lightning Rod Towers is divided between the three girls and each one has her own style of calibration: Simple Calibration, Falling Calibration, and Memory Calibration. See if you can master these three types and calibrate all 10 of the Lightning Rod Towers.

# RIKKU AND SIMPLE CALIBRATION

At the beginning, the button commands appear directly over Rikku's head, but later on they start appearing all around the screen.

Rikku's towers use the Simple Calibration method. In this type of mini-game, button commands are flashed on the screen one at a time. You have a limited amount of time to enter the command before it is counted as a miss and another command takes it place. After the 13th command or so, the speed with which the commands appear increases, making the game more challenging. Rikku's final tower features two button commands that you must enter at the same time.

| TOWER # | ICON POSITION | MUST PRESS |
|---------|---------------|------------|
| 1 | Middle of screen | Circle, X, Triangle and Square |
| 4 | One of 13 locations on-screen | Circle, X, Triangle, Square, and D-pad |
| *7 | One of 13 locations on-screen | Circle, X, Triangle, Square, L1, R1, and D-pad |

*You must press a combination of two keys at the same time for tower 7.

# PAINE AND FALLING CALIBRATION

Paine's towers utilize the Falling Calibration method. In this case, a string of three button icons fall down the screen from the top to the bottom. Half way down, one of the icons flashes, meaning you must input the command before the line of icons hit the bottom of the screen and fall off. The speed at which the icons fall increases as the game continues.

You need to be quick at pressing buttons to succeed in Falling Calibration. Paine's towers just get harder as they go along.

| TOWER # | # OF SUCCESSFUL ENTRIES | FALL SPEED | MUST PRESS |
|---|---|---|---|
| 2 | 0-10 | Normal | Circle, X, Triangle, and Square |
| | 11-15 | Normal | Circle, X, Triangle, Square, and Up and Down on D-pad |
| | 16-25 | Normal | Circle, X, Triangle, Square, and D-pad |
| | 26-29 | Double Speed | Circle, X, Triangle, and Square |
| 5 | 0-5 | Normal | Circle, X, Triangle, and Square |
| | 6-10 | Normal | Circle, X, Triangle, Square, and D-pad |
| | 11-15 | Normal | Circle, X, Triangle, Square, L1, R1, and D-pad |
| | 16-25 | Double Speed | Circle, X, Triangle, Square, L1, R1, and D-pad |
| | 26-29 | Triple Speed | Circle, X, Triangle, Square, L1, R1, and D-pad |
| 8 | 0-5 | Normal | Circle, X, Triangle, Square, and D-pad |
| | 6-15 | Normal | Circle, X, Triangle, Square, L1, R1, and D-pad |
| | 16-25 | Double Speed | Circle, X, Triangle, Square, L1, R1, and D-pad |
| | 26-29 | Triple Speed | Circle, X, Triangle, Square, L1, R1, and D-pad |

## YUNA AND MEMORY CALIBRATION

Yuna's four towers feature the most complex form of calibration: Memory Calibration. This is divided into two procedures per round. First, during the Memory Phase, the string of button commands is presented to memorize. Then, during the Input Phase, you receive a limited amount of time to enter the string. The number of buttons you need to press increases as the towers' difficulty level increases.

*Yuna's towers really test your memorization skills!*

| TOWER # | # OF SUCCESSFUL ENTRIES | # OF COMMANDS | MUST PRESS |
|---|---|---|---|
| 3 | 0-10 | 2 | Circle, X, Triangle, and Square |
| | 11-25 | 3 | Circle, X, Triangle, and Square |
| | 26-29 | 4 | Circle, X, Triangle, and Square |
| 6 | 0-10 | 2 | Circle, X, Triangle, Square, and D-pad |
| | 11-25 | 3 | Circle, X, Triangle, Square, and D-pad |
| | 26-29 | 4 | Circle, X, Triangle, Square, and D-pad |
| 9 | 0-10 | 2 | Circle, X, Triangle, Square, L1, R1, and D-pad |
| | 11-20 | 3 | Circle, X, Triangle, Square, L1, R1, and D-pad |
| | 21-25 | 4 | Circle, X, Triangle, Square, L1, R1, and D-pad |
| | 26-29 | 5 | Circle, X, Triangle, Square, L1, R1, and D-pad |
| 10 | 0-10 | 2 | Circle, X, Triangle, Square, L1, L2, R1, R2, and D-pad |
| | 11-15 | 3 | Circle, X, Triangle, Square, L1, L2, R1, R2, and D-pad |
| | 16-20 | 4 | Circle, X, Triangle, Square, L1, L2, R1, R2, and D-pad |
| | 21-25 | 5 | Circle, X, Triangle, Square, L1, L2, R1, R2, and D-pad |
| | 26-29 | 6 | Circle, X, Triangle, Square, L1, L2, R1, R2, and D-pad |

## EVERYTHING'S COMING UP CACTUARS

| When Available: | Chapters 3 and 5 |
|---|---|
| Location: | Bikanel Desert, Cactuar Nation |
| Objective: | Search throughout Spira for 10 missing Cactuars. Convince them to return home to protect the Cactuar Nation from a great evil that arises in Chapter 5. Win the mini-game against the final Cactuar, Frailea, to receive the Covenant of Growth Garment Grid. |

# THE FLOW OF THE GAME

Cactuar Hunting is part of a larger mission that closes out the events in the Bikanel Desert. When you visit the Bikanel Desert in Chapter 3, you learn that the Al Bhed have forged a relationship with the Cactuar Nation in the midst of the desert. As a gesture of goodwill, they ask you to help their leader, Marnela, with a problem. Nhadala assigns you an Al Bhed youth, Benzo, as a translator and off you go to the Cactuar Nation.

Marnela needs you to search for 10 young cactuars that have ventured out into Spira to learn more about the world. To find out where each one is located, you must talk to their mothers. Look for a green square on the on-screen map to locate a Cactus Mother. You can only go after one cactuar at a time, so only Marnela (the guardian of the Lair of the Rogue Cactuars) and the current cactuar's mother are marked as active on the on-screen map.

*Active Cacti (i.e. those you can talk to) are marked with a green square on the on-screen map at the top-left part of the screen. They also have swirls of green that envelop them.*

*Listen closely to the Cactuar Mother's clues. Pay special attention to the highlighted words and phrases.*

After receiving the clues to a cactuar's whereabouts, it's time to head out and begin your search. The missing cactuars are scattered everywhere, from cities to mountains to plains. Try to narrow down your search to places that most resemble those in the hint, then look for a small cactuar that is just hanging out.

*That green cactuar is difficult to miss—even in the strangest locations.*

When you catch a missing cactuar, a shooting mini-game begins. Most of the Cactuars you're looking for have friends who are willing to help them defy your orders. You must shoot the cactuar from a rapidly changing display of the cactuar and its friends until its HP reaches 0.

*The faster the cactuar's speed rating, the faster the screen shifts between the cactuar and its two companions. You need great timing to shoot the fastest of the 10 Cactuars.*

You receive a set amount of ammo, so make sure your shot hits true. Additionally, when you hit a cactuar, there is a chance that it will rush and attack you. You can dodge these attacks by pressing the R1 button. If you get hit, you lose ammo and points.

*Press the R1 button to dodge the attacks of a wounded cactuar. If you get hit, you lose ammo.*

Regardless of how you fare in this mini-game, you can still persuade the cactuar to return home and fulfill its destiny. Simply return to the Cactuar Nation in the Bikanel Desert and bring the youth to his or her mother. The next cactuar's mother then awakens and you can continue your quest.

However, this does not mean that you shouldn't try to defeat each cactuar. Not only is it fun to beat your high score, it gives you good practice for when you go up against the final cactuar, Frailea.

This mini-game spans two chapters. Look for the first six Cactuar in Chapters 3 and 5. The remaining four Cactuars are accessible only in Chapter 5.

*The captured cactuar follows you around the Cactuar Nation until you return it to its mother.*

MINI-GAMES

# LET'S FIND THOSE CACTUARS!

The following section reveals the locations and statistical information for all 10 cactuars.

| #/NAME | LOCATION | |
|---|---|---|
| 1/Lobivia | In the Oasis section of the Bikanel Desert. |  |
| 2/Toumeya | Sunbathing on the beach on Besaid Island. |  |
| 3/Lobeira | Inside the Treasure Room in the secret area of Chateau Leblanc in Guadosalam. |  |
| 4&5/Areq & Arroja | Hanging out at the foot of Mt. Gagazet in the Calm Lands. |  |
| 6/Islaya | In the northern part of the Thunder Plains. |  |
| 7/Chiapa | Highest point overlooking Kilika Port and Kilika Woods. Look for a place to climb onto a ledge along the eastern path through the woods. |  |
| 8/Erio | On the snowy Mountain Trail of Mt. Gagazet. |  |
| 9/Bartschella | With Dona on Kilika Island. | |
| 10/Frailea | Inside the Cactuar Hollow. |  |

## EXTRA ITEMS

*During the fight with Lobeira, you can win extra items by shooting the treasure chests that appear with her. The same is true for the fight with Bartschella. Shoot the pots to earn some extra items!*

# RIN'S MYSTERY

| | |
|---|---|
| **When Available:** | **Chapters 4, 5** |
| **Location:** | **Celsius Bridge (use the CommSpheres) and Mi'ihen Highroad** |
| **Objective:** | **Help Rin discover the culprit behind the hover crash and the machina riot that occurred on the Mi'ihen Highroad in Chapter 3. You can win the right to ride chocobos on the Highroad or acquire some rare prizes, depending on which suspect is caught!** |

# THE SETUP

*Rin needs some assistance finding out who's responsible for the mayhem on the Mi'ihen Highroad in Chapter 3.*

Rin has his hands full searching for the person who caused the hover crash, then reprogrammed the machina on the Mi'ihen Highroad to riot. He needs someone to look for clues using the extra CommSpheres he's installed throughout the area. If you see something suspicious, or just abnormal, give him a call and he'll run over to investigate.

*Switch between the CommSpheres on the network to look for clues or just strange behavior.*

*In Chapter 5, all of your detective work is put to good use as Rin solves the case and deals with the guilty party!*

The bulk of this mini-game occurs during Chapter 4. Use the CommSphere network on the Mi'ihen Highroad to look for unusual occurrences. When you see something that looks unusual, call Rin to investigate more closely. As you locate more clues, Rin notifies you that the investigation is moving to a new level and, eventually, he'll take over the entire project himself. In Chapter 5, head over to the Mi'ihen Highroad to find out the results of your detective work.

# THE MI'IHEN HIGHROAD COMMSPHERE NETWORK

It seems that during Chapter 3, Rin added some extra CommSpheres along the Mi'ihen Highroad. While working on this mystery in Chapter 4, tap into Rin's network and use them to determine who committed the crimes in Chapter 3. There are eight CommSphere locations on the Mi'ihen Highroad. To have Shinra's CommSphere on the list, you must see the event in which Shinra drops the CommSphere after you complete the "Machina Mayhem" mission.

*The extra CommSpheres enable you to check out what's going on all around the Mi'ihen Highroad.*

| THE MI'IHEN HIGHROAD COMMSPHERE LOCATIONS |
| --- |
| Travel Agency, Front |
| Travel Agency, Back |
| Ruins |
| Newroad |
| Hover Crash Site |
| Oldroad Interior |
| Shinra's CommSphere |
| Highroad North Entrance |

## THE SUSPECTS

*Using the following information, you can deliberately skew the investigation so that Rin chooses your prime suspect.*

There are ultimately five suspects in this mystery: Rikku, Calli, the Prophet, a small Chocobo Eater, and even Rin! The culprit is determined by the clues and events you see during both the investigation in Chapter 4 and the events you witnessed on the Mi'ihen Highroad area in during Chapters 1, 2, and 3. If you don't see them all during your first run through of the game, then keep them in mind when you play through a second time.

The best part of solving Rin's Mystery is finessing who turns out to be the final culprit. You can start the process early in the game by making sure that you witness or participate in the following events:

- **Chapter 1:** Talk to the female Al Bhed technician at the southern end of the Mi'ihen Highroad.

- **Chapter 2:** Participate in the "Cuckoo for Chocobos" mission. The outcome determines whether or not Calli or Rikku are possible suspects.

- **Chapter 2:** After completing the "Cuckoo for Chocobos" mission, return to Mi'ihen Highroad and enter the Travel Agency. Look for Rin as he walks past and out the door.

- **Chapter 3:** Participate in the "Machina Mayhem" mission. To add Rin to the list of suspects, make sure that you decommission more machina than the Al Bhed (at least seven altogether). Don't miss a single machina.

- **Chapter 3:** After completing the "Machina Mayhem" mission, return to Mi'ihen Highroad and look for Shinra along the road. Watch as he installs a CommSphere in an unusual location.

Witnessing these events puts you in the position to make at least four of the five possible suspects the actual culprit. Read on to find out exactly how to stack the deck against one of the five suspects!

## FOLLOWING THE STORYLINES

The mystery is divided into three levels. The clue events you witness from the CommSpheres determine the identity of the guilty party. Therefore, it follows that if you know which clue events you need to see, then you can make any of the suspects the criminal! Before the list of clue events is revealed, let's discuss some guidelines to catching certain suspects.

## THE SMALL CHOCOBO EATER AND THE PROPHET

Setting these two characters up doesn't take much extra effort. After all, they are the most obvious suspects! Each one wants to see the chocobos return to the Mi'ihen Highroad—just for drastically different reasons!

To get the small Chocobo Eater as the criminal, make sure you see clue events 1-A, 1-D, 2-B and 2-G. To find the Prophet guilty, make sure that you witness clue event 1-C, 1-I, 2-C, 2-E, 2-F, 2-I, 2-J, 2-L, 2-M, 2-3, 3-H, and 3-I.

*The Chocobo Eater is the easiest culprit to catch.*

*The Prophet is a bit more difficult to figure out. You really have to do some detective work to uncover his trail!*

# RIKKU AND CALLI

Unfortunately, you can either add one or the other to the list. The decision point for this occurs at the end of the "Cuckoo for Chocobos" mission in Chapter 2. If you decide to invite Calli and her Chocobo to ride on the Celsius, Rikku is added to the list of suspects. If you don't let Calli and Chocobo join the Celsius crew, then Calli takes Rikku's place on the list of suspects.

To stack the deck against Calli, do the following:

■ In the "Cuckoo for Chocobos" mission in Chapter 4, make sure you see the ending in which Calli does *not* get a Chocobo.

■ Make sure you end Chapter 2 *without* inviting Calli onboard the Celsius.

■ Make sure you see clue events 1-E, 1-F, 2-A, 2-D, 3-C, and 3-E during the mystery game in Chapter 4.

To point the finger at Rikku, do the following:

■ During the "Cuckoo for Chocobos" mission in Chapter 2, make sure you see the scene in which Rikku jumps from the top of the Ruins and falls on her backside.

■ At the end of the "Cuckoo for Chocobos" mission in Chapter 2, invite Calli and her chocobo onboard the Celsius when offered the chance.

■ During your investigation in Chapter 4, make sure you witness clue event 2-K and 1-B!

Rikku's story is a fun one, although the clues Rin finds are difficult to see.

Calli's story occurs only if you fail the "Cuckoo for Chocobos" mission in Chapter 2. If you succeed, this Chocobo feather floating in the air is all you'll see of her storyline.

# RIN

Rin is doing something shady and it's up to you to find out!

Rin is the toughest suspect to corral. While it's easy enough to get him on the list of suspects, it is difficult to skew the investigation to point the finger of blame at him!

To collar Rin as the culprit, do these things:

■ In Chapter 1, make sure you talk to the female Al Bhed technician at the southern end of the Mi'ihen Highroad.

■ Once you complete the "Cuckoo for Chocobos" mission in Chapter 2, return to the area and pay a visit to the Travel Agency. You should see Rin walk by and exit the building. Wonder what he's up to?

■ In Chapter 3, defeat at least seven of the malfunctioning machina in the "Machina Mayhem" mission. Do so and you'll see Rin in the crowd of people in the scene at the end of the mission.

■ Call for Rin during clue event 1-G during the investigation.

■ Witness clue event 3-G during the investigation, then switch to the Newroad CommSphere to see clue event 3-D immediately afterward. Call Rin at that time to report what happened in 3-G.

■ After completing the previous steps, go to a place where no clue events take place and call Rin there five times. After doing so, you shouldn't be able to get Rin to come running when you call for him. End the game until Chapter 5.

# THE CLUE EVENT LIST

The following tables lists all of the clue events in the Rin's Mystery min-game. Remember that the investigation portion of the game is divided into three parts. When you hear the bell and Rin states that you are getting to the heart of the matter, move ahead to the next part of the list.

## CAUTION!
For an event to count toward the investigation, you must call Rin over to take a look.

Additionally, in each story line there are a specific number of events that you must witness before you can move on to the next part of the story. Use the following information to figure out how many you have to see for the storyline you've chosen.

| EVENTS NEEDED PER STORYLINE | | | | |
|---|---|---|---|---|
| | RIKKU | CALLI | CHOCOBO EATER | PROPHET |
| Part 1 | 2 | 3 | 3 | 3 |
| Part 2 | 2 | 3 | 3 | 4 |
| Part 3 | 2 | 3 | 2 | 3 |

Characters

Garment Grids & Dresspheres

Battle System

Accessories

Items and Item Shops

Walkthrough

Mini-Games

Fiends and Enemies

## CASE EVENTS FOR PART ONE OF THE INVESTIGATION

| EVENT | LOCATION | DESCRIPTION | REQ | PTS AWARDED | | | |
|---|---|---|---|---|---|---|---|
| | | | | RIKKU | CALLI | CHOCOBO EATER | PROPHET |
| 1-A | Travel Agency, Back | A small Chocobo Eater appears to be playing with the Drone Machina console. | None | - | - | +4 | - |
| 1-B | Ruins | The Ruins machina seems to be malfunctioning. | Must fulfill Rikku's pre-reqs. | +6 | - | - | - |
| 1-C | Newroad | The Prophet seems to be meeting with a young woman. I wonder why? | Only if you called Rin during event 1-I. | - | - | - | +4 |
| 1-D | Newroad | A small crowd is gathered at the spot where the hover went off the road. | None | +6 | +4 | +4 | +4 |
| 1-E | Hover Crash Site | A Chocobo feather floats in the air. | If going for Calli, view event 1-F first. | - | +4 | - | - |
| 1-F | Oldroad Interior | Calli appears to be looking for something. | Must fulfill Calli's pre-reqs. | - | +4 | - | - |
| 1-G | Shinra's CommSphere | Capture Rin talking to a strange Al Bhed woman. Hmmm. | None | - | - | - | - |
| 1-H | Highroad N. Entrance | The Prophet and a Chocobo Eater? What a strange pair! | Must see events 1-A or 1-C. | - | - | +4 | - |
| 1-I | Highroad N. Entrance | Who is the Prophet speaking to? | None | - | - | - | +4 |

## CASE EVENTS FOR PART TWO OF THE INVESTIGATION

| EVENT | LOCATION | DESCRIPTION | REQ | PTS AWARDED | | | |
|---|---|---|---|---|---|---|---|
| | | | | RIKKU | CALLI | CHOCOBO EATER | PROPHET |
| 2-A | Travel Agency, Front | Look for Rin and Calli in front of the hovers. | All of Calli's pre-reqs and see event 1-E. | - | +4 | - | - |
| 2-B | Travel Agency, Front | Why is that Chocobo Eater chasing a gull? | None | - | - | +4 | - |
| 2-C | Travel Agency, Back | A strange woman is checking out the computer console back there. | None | - | - | - | +3 |
| 2-D | Travel Agency, Back | Who is Calli waiting for? | All of Calli's pre-reqs. Don't call Rin at start of 2-C. | - | +4 | - | - |
| 2-E | Travel Agency, Back | An Al Bhed technician is playing with computer console. | None | - | - | +3 | - |
| 2-F | Ruins | The Prophet is having another meeting. | See event 2-E first. | - | - | - | +3 |
| 2-G | Newroad | How strange is that? A Chocobo Eater chasing a Hover. | None | - | - | +4 | - |
| 2-H | Hover Crash Site | Call Rin when you see a group of machina surround the crashed hover. | None | +6 | +4 | +4 | +3 |
| 2-I | Hover Crash Site | What is the Prophet hiding by the crash site? | See event 2-J first. | - | - | - | +3 |
| 2-J | Oldroad, Interior | The Prophet starts talking to the two guys. | See event 2-F first. | - | - | - | +3 |
| 2-K | Shinra's CommSphere | None | In "Machina Mayhem" mission, attack machina on opposite ledge. | +6 | - | - | - |
| 2-L | Highroad N. Entrance | The Prophet speaks with a young lady. | See event 2-F first. | - | - | - | +3 |
| 2-M | Highroad N. Entrance | The Prophet hides something in the ruins. | See event 2-L first. | - | - | - | +3 |
| 2-N | Highroad N. Entrance | Rin finds the item the Prophet hid. | See event 2-M first. | - | - | - | +3 |

## CASE EVENTS FOR PART THREE OF THE INVESTIGATION

| EVENT | LOCATION | DESCRIPTION | REQ | PTS AWARDED | | | |
|---|---|---|---|---|---|---|---|
| | | | | RIKKU | CALLI | CHOCOBO EATER | PROPHET |
| 3-A | Travel Agency, Front | Rin is talking to the hover driver. | See event 2-H first. | +6 | +4 | +6 | +4 |
| 3-B | Travel Agency, Back | When you call Rin a man falls from the roof. | None | +6 | - | - | - |
| 3-C | Ruins | A young woman is waiting by the ruins. | Erased when you see event 3-I first. | - | +4 | - | - |
| 3-D | Newroad | Near Hover Crash Site, you see Rin doing something strange. | See event 3-G first. This event is erased if you see another event first. | - | - | - | - |
| 3-E | Newroad | Calli tries to hide traces of something. | Complete Calli's pre-reqs. | - | +4 | - | - |
| 3-F | Hover Crash Site | Rin finds something in the Hover wreckage. | None | - | - | +6 | - |
| 3-G | Hover Crash Site | As you search the area, the CommSphere malfunctions. | None | - | - | - | - |
| 3-H | Oldroad Interior | Rin talks to the two men. | None | - | - | - | +4 |
| 3-I | Highroad N. Entrance | The Prophet and his assistant meet up. | None | - | - | - | +4 |

MINI-GAMES

# AND THE CULPRIT IS?

Without giving too much away, here's a list of pros and cons for going after each of the five suspects.

## CHOCOBO EATER

If you don't follow the advice here to make someone else the criminal, the Chocobo Eater will likely be the one caught!

**Pros:** Now that the road is safe from chocovorous fiends, you get to ride chocobos on the Mi'ihen Highroad after it's put away.

**Cons:** You don't receive any special items and your feeling of accomplishment is likely to be low.

## THE PROPHET

Hmmm… The Prophet likes chocobos so much that he'll do anything to free up the roads for them.

**Pros:** This is the funniest End of Episode scene! Done in the style of a Scooby Doo Mystery (complete with Y-R-P as the meddling kids!), this one will have you on the floor laughing.

**Cons:** You don't receive a special item and you don't get to ride chocobos on the Highroad afterward; cannot get 100% completion.

## RIKKU

Poor Rikku! She can't help being klutzy!

**Pros:** You get to ride chocobos and you get the **Ragnarok** accessory. Also, the End of Episode scene is fairly amusing.

**Cons:** Does Rikku really have to be berated for her careless and clumsy ways again!?!

## CALLI

Her love for chocobos is so strong… And so was her disappointment at not getting a chocobo in Chapter 2.

**Pros:** You still get to ride chocobos on the Highroad and you can say that you've nabbed one of the hardest-to-catch perpetrators, but…

**Cons:** You negate your chances to get the Chocobo Ranch mini-game and you fail to acquire the **Selene Guard Garment Grid** that you would have won in the "Cuckoos for Chocobos" mission.

## RIN

If you nab Rin, you're *really* good!

**Pros:** You get to ride chocobos for free on the Highroad and you win **Gippal's Sphere**.

**Cons:** Completing the pre-requisites is really tricky.

# BLITZBALL

| | |
|---|---|
| When Available: | Chapter 5 |
| Location: | Luca Stadium |
| Objective: | The Blitzball season starts in Luca during Chapter 5. Can you guide the Gullwings to victory while the Besaid Aurochs are on maternity leave? |

# A NEW AND IMPROVED BLITZBALL!

Blitzball is a game in which two teams compete in a sphere pool in a game that resembles soccer or water polo—except that it's played underwater! During each five minute match, each team attempts to take the ball from each other and score more points than the other to win the game. In this mini-game, Yuna and the Gullwings must pull together a competitive team and participate in the Spira League Tournament in place of the Besaid Aurochs. The basic rules and changes from the original Blitzball game in *FINAL FANTASY X* are discussed in this section. Keep in mind that there have been quite a few changes since Blitzball was originally introduced. The game now plays more as a coaching simulation instead of an actual game.

BLITZBALL

Characters

1

Garment Grids & Dresspheres

2

Battle System

3

Accessories

4

Items and Item Shops

5

Walkthrough

6

Mini-Games

7

Fiends and Enemies

8

# BASIC RULE #1: THE NUMBER OF PLAYERS PER TEAM

Each team has seven fielders and one goal keeper for a total of eight players. The Gullwings can also keep a maximum of four back-up players to form a team of 12 Players. You cannot increase the size of your team.

## HOW IT'S CHANGED...

The number of players on a team has increased from six to eight so that the division between the forwards and defenders is clearer. In addition, to accommodate the larger teams, the playing field has increased in size. Also, if you have backup players prepared, you can substitute them during the game.

# BASIC RULE #2: IN-GAME ACTION

The players can make a pass or a shot from any position. Also, opponents cannot steal the ball right back, even if you steal the ball by force.

## HOW IT'S CHANGED...

The ability to cause status abnormalities with one's pass or shoot is gone, but a new "injury" element has been added to the game. If a player gets injured during a match or training, then the player cannot move for the rest of the match. Special shots have now been limited to an Overhead Volley and the Corkscrew Shot.

# BASIC RULE #3: VICTORY AND DEFEAT CONDITIONS

The match lasts for five minutes and whoever scores the most goals in that time wins. In the case of a tie score, the match ends in a tie for a normal game but goes into sudden death during tournament matches.

## HOW IT'S CHANGED...

The break between the first half and the second half of the game has disappeared. Also, if either team scores seven points, then the game is called and the team with the seven points is declared the winner.

# THE FLOW OF THE GAME

When you start playing the Blitzball mini-game, you have four options: Train, Play Blitzball, Scout, or Tutorial. If you are new to the game, then familiarize yourself with the rules of the game using the Tutorial option. After doing so, you'll want to bring your team in for Training before you play your first match.

1. **Starting the Game**

There are two ways to get to the main Blitzball menu. When you first visit Luca in Chapter 5, you can agree to play when asked to participate in the tournament to start the mini-game. If you choose not to start right away, you must speak with the woman behind the ticket counter in the stadium. Here you can select between playing Blitzball or Sphere Break.

2. **Training**

Almost every member of the Gullwings team is a rank beginner at Blitzball. They all have very low stats and if you want them to have a chance at winning, you'll need a lot of training to get them to compatible levels with the rest of the teams. You can put individual players through 17 types of training regimens (at the cost of Command Points), or you can have the entire team go through group training in the different formations and types of play styles. At the start of the game, you should play in Exhibition Matches to earn the Command Points needed to raise your team members' stats

3. **Scouting**

There are a total of 99 players in Blitzball, and 35 of them are free agents who aren't attached to any one team. These free agents form a pool of talent that only the Gullwings can tap. Use the Scouting function to find and sign promising new players for your team. After all, while it's important to train the original members of the Gullwings, it is also good to scout out players who are already strong and add them to your team.

4. **Playing in a Match**

After selecting Play Blitzball on the main menu, you must select the type of match you want to play (Spira League, Tournament, and Exhibition Match). However, the game basically plays itself with you watching the action unfold in the position of coach. All you can really do is change your team's Formation and Game Play strategies and substitute players as needed. If you do not have enough players to form a team of eight, you cannot play a match.

5. **Winning Prizes and Command Points**

When the match is over, you receive prizes or Command Points based on the type of match you chose and whether or not you won. As you gain more points, your team level increases and you can win all sorts of items. At the end of a match, you have the option of continuing or returning to Luca.

# TRAINING

In *FINAL FANTASY X*, Blitzball players gained experience based on their actions during a match. In *FINAL FANTASY X-2*, experience points or levels aren't used and the players must raise their parameters through training. Since you can't directly affect a player's actions once a match starts, you must really rely on sharpening your player's skills through training.

The training method works as follows: When Blitzball begins, your current Command Points are displayed in the upper-right corner of the screen. Divide these points among the players in Training mode. While giving out lots of Command Points at one time has the biggest effect, be careful because it can lead to fatigue (FTG) and injuries. In addition to receiving various penalties, injured players can only receive limited training.

Moreover, in addition to gaining Command Points by playing matches, you can receive points (1 Command Point for every 10 seconds) just by leaving Blitzball mode and returning to the field. The default maximum points you can gain is 100 points, but that maximum number increases when the Gull Wings level up.

## FLOW OF THE TRAINING SYSTEM

1. Move the cursor to the player's name and press the X button.

2. Move the cursor to the type of training regimen you want and press the X button.

3. Allot the Command Points you want to dedicate to this training regimen (from 0-9), then press the X button to return to the main Training menu.

4. Move the cursor to Practice and press the X button. Now all of the players who have been given Command Points will receive their individualized training. In Training, the increased parameters are shown in pink and the decreased parameters are in blue.

## EXPLAINING A PLAYER'S STATS

To make the coaching simulation more realistic, the number of player stats have more than doubled. Here's a rundown on what they are and what they stand for.

The following stats can change during Training:

| | |
|---|---|
| END | Endurance: The higher the stat, the more easily the player can endure an opponent's tackle. |
| ATK | Attack: This indicates the strength of the player's tackle ability. The higher the stat, the easier it will be for the player to steal the ball when he or she sets up a tackle. |
| PAS | Pass: The higher the stat, the less likely it is that your passes will fail. |
| SHT | Shoot: The higher the stat, the more successful your shots will be. |
| BLK | Block: The higher the stat, the more likely your player will block an opponent's shots and steal the ball. |
| CAT | Catch: The higher the stat, the more likely your player is to catch shots. This stat is a must for the goal keeper. |
| RNG | Range: The higher the state, the more successful your players will be at completing shots and passes over long distances. |
| REC | Receive: The higher the stat, the easier your players can catch passes from their own team members. |

> ### TRAINING
> The list of numbers in blue that appear to the left of this first set of stats are called the Optimal Points, which indicate the amount a player can endure during training. These numbers increase or decrease by one while you are performing Training exercises. When you allot more command points than the optimal number provided, the character's Fatigue stat (FTG) rises.

The following stats don't change during Training:

| | |
|---|---|
| SPD | Speed: The higher the stat, the faster the player moves through the water. |
| RCH | Reach (extent of the player's defensive range): The higher the stat, the more easily the player discovers opponents carrying the ball and the more easily he or she can encounter them. |

The following are parameters outside of player stats:

| | |
|---|---|
| OUT | This marks the number of contracted matches the player must sit out due to injury. |
| CNT | Contract: This lists the player's number of contracted matches. When the number reaches 0, the player's contract ends. |
| GIL | Number of Command Points needed to sign a free agent to a 10-game contract with the Gullwings. |

The following are stats that change during matches:

| | |
|---|---|
| MOR | Morale: The higher this stat, the more likely your players are to use special shots and combos. |
| FTG | Fatigue: The higher this stat, the more it compromises a player's level of play and increases the likelihood that he or she will suffer an injury in training or during a match. |

Characters

Garment Grids & Dresspheres

Battle System

Accessories

Items and Item Shops

Walkthrough

Mini-Games 7

Fiends and Enemies

# CHANGING STATS THROUGH TRAINING

When you train a member of your team individually, the change in that player's stats is not just a simple reflection of the number of allotted Command Points. The rules for stat changes are shown in this section. There are a total of six stats (END, ATK, PAS, SHT, BLK, and CAT) and although they may not appear to change as a result of training, there actually have been changes to some "invisible" parameters.

Moreover, although this is not displayed on-screen, there is a maximum limit to each of the eight stats that are influenced by training. After that point, no matter how much you train, the parameter will not increase any further (unless the player receives some secret training!).

## HOW STATS ARE CHANGED BY TRAINING

■ Each of the six stats (END, ATK, PAS, SHT, BLK and CAT) is assigned a hidden value between 1-8 (the default value is 4). When you train a player, the allotted command points are added to these hidden values and, when the hidden value exceeds 8, 1 point is added to the actual parameter.

■ The stats RNG and REC do not have any hidden values. Their values are raised by the same value as the allotted command points.

■ If a player participates in a training regimen that lowers a certain stat, then in the case of stats with hidden values (END- CAT), the command points are subtracted from the hidden value and the total stat is decreased as necessary. In the case of a stat without hidden values (i.e. RNG and REC), the stat is decreased based on the number of command points subtracted from the previous total.

■ When the hidden value drops below 1, the stat is lowered by 1 and the hidden value starts again at 7.

| MENU OPTION | RAISES | LOWERS | EFFECT |
|---|---|---|---|
| **TRAINING REGIMENS FOR SINGLE PLAYERS** | | | |
| Downtime | - | FTG | Decreases the player's 1-2 points per Command Point allotted. |
| Iron Man | END | BLK | See previous section for explanation of how this works. |
| Sandbagging | ATK | CAT | See previous section for explanation of how this works |
| Passing | PAS | END | See previous section for explanation of how this works |
| Shooting | SHT | REC | See previous section for explanation of how this works |
| Blocking | BLK | RNG | See previous section for explanation of how this works |
| Goalkeeping | CAT | PAS | See previous section for explanation of how this works |
| Receiving | REC | SHT | See previous section for explanation of how this works |
| Throwing Arm | RNG | ATK | See previous section for explanation of how this works |
| Pep Talk | MOR | - | May raise Morale (MOR) to max (99 points). Probability is based on (# of Command Points allotted x 10)%. |
| Counseling | Optimal Points | - | May max out the player's Optimal Points for END-REC. Probability is based on (# of Command Points allotted x 10)%. |
| Teamwork | - | - | Raises the combination points between two players on your team |

# PREPARING FOR A MATCH

How a player moves during a match is affected by the combination of their position, formation, and play style. By understanding these characteristics, you can find the kind of combination you want for your own strategy.

| POSITION | JOB |
|---|---|
| **PLAYER POSITIONS IN FORMATIONS** | |
| FW | Forward.: Takes up residence closest to the opposition's goal. Largely responsible for aiming shots. |
| MF | Middle Fielder: Hangs out in mid-field and controls the match. |
| DF | Defender: Largely responsible for stealing the ball from attacking opponents. |
| GL | Goalkeeper: Repels opponent's shots from the goal. |

# LIST OF FORMATIONS

### 4-2-1

A formation that places an emphasis on a strong defensive line in front of its own goal. With this, even a weak team can defend its own goal. This is the Gullwings' default formation.

### 4-1-2

Moving one of the mid-fielders up from the "4-2-1" formation creates two forwards. Although it strengthens the offense, it may make it easier for the opposing team to score a goal.

### 3-3-1

With three players in the midfield and three on defense, it is a strong defensive formation, but rather difficult to score a goal with. It's a good formation for doing a counter attack.

### 3-2-2

A formation with very few holes. It may look like it's balanced, but if the players don't have high parameters, then there is a danger of both attack and defense being mediocre.

### 3-1-3

While taking the risk of having only one MF, this formation has a strong defensive and offensive line. The stronger the DF ability of your players, the easier it is to perform a counter attack.

## 2-4-1

With four MF, it is easy to control the midfield with this formation. However, it is then necessary for the MF to play both offense and defense. This formation is best for teams that have strong midfielders.

## 2-3-2

With five players able to move to offense, this formation is best for offensive attacks. Although this is strong during attack periods, since there are only 2 DF, it is vulnerable to attacks and counter attacks.

## 2-2-3

By moving one of the mid-fielders up from the 2-3-2 formation, this formation improves offense. With a FW with a strong END parameter, you can mount a strong attack but the defensive line remains somewhat weak.

# LIST OF PLAY STYLES

## CENTER ATTACK

Recommended Formations: 4-2-1 and 3-2-2
This style enables you to break through the opposing defense using a combination of short passes. This is the default Play Style for the Gullwings.

## RIGHT SIDE

Recommended Formations: 2-4-1 and 3-3-1
This formation uses aggressive dribbling to drive up the right side of the field deep into the opponent's territory. With a FW stationed in front of the opponent's goal, you are just a pass and a shot away from a scoring opportunity.

## LEFT SIDE

Recommended Formations: 2-4-1 and 3-3-1
Almost identical to the Right Side style, this uses aggressive dribbling to drive up the left side of the field deep into the opponent's territory.

## POST PLAY

**Recommended Formations:** 3-1-3 and 2-2-3
Pass the ball to the center FW and create scoring opportunities for the offensive line. With formations skewed toward offensive players, this style enables your teammates to pass the ball back and forth until there is a scoring opportunity.

## SHORT PASS

**Recommended Formations:** 4-1-2 and 3-2-2
In this style, team members pass the ball quickly around the field to take advantage of holes in the opponent's defense.

## LONG FEED

**Recommended Formations:** 4-2-1 and 3-3-1
This style relies of long passes between DF players and the FW to create scoring opportunities. Make sure that your key players have a good range before attempting this style.

# SCOUTING HIDDEN TALENTS

There are 35 players who are listed as free agents. You can use Command Points to scout and hire any of these new players. The Free Agents that you can scout are determined by the Gullwings' scout level. You can scout other players if you increase the team's level by winning games. Use the following information to determine what your team level needs to be before your scout level increases.

There are seven Free Agents for each Scout Level, but only a maximum of four players are shown on-screen each time you search for player information. If the player who you want to scout is not on-screen, search again until the player appears. Keep in mind that each search costs 10 Command Points.

| COMMAND POINTS NEEDED FOR SCOUTING | | | | | |
|---|---|---|---|---|---|
| HOW TO USE COMMAND POINTS | | | SCOUT LV | | |
| | 1 | 2 | 3 | 4 | MAX |
| Acquiring Player data | 10 | 10 | 10 | 10 | 10 |
| Sign Contract with Player | 10 | 15 | 20 | 30 | 40 |

| SCOUT LV AND TEAM LV RELATIONSHIP | |
|---|---|
| SCOUT LV | TEAM LV |
| 1 | 1 (0 wins) |
| 2 | 5 (8 wins) |
| 3 | 10 (18 wins) |
| 4 | 20 (38 wins) |
| MAX | 30 (58 wins) |

Characters
1

Garment Grids & Dresspheres
2

Battle System
3

Accessories
4

Items and Item Shops
5

Walkthrough
6

Mini-Games
7

Fiends and Enemies
8

# RECOMMENDED FREE AGENTS

The following are the best Free Agents for the Gullwings at each Scout Level.

## SCOUT LEVEL 1: SHUU AND ROPP

Shuu has high END and SHT stats that make her a perfect choice as a FW. She can also pull off the Overhead Volley move, which can be very effective as your team learns the ropes. Ropp, on the other hand, is a born DF player with his high ATK and BLK stats. Put him on your defensive line and let him do his stuff.

## SCOUT LEVEL 2: MEP

Mep is the same type of player as Miyu. He has high END and SHT stats and can be used much the same way as you would use Miyu.

## SCOUT LEVEL 3: SHAAMI

Shaami has decent stats that should be in line with the rest of your team. What she has that others might not is the Corkscrew Shot.

## SCOUT LEVEL 4: KWINN

Only Kwinn's CAT stat grows steadily as he advances, making him a great GL for your team. With a max CAT of 94, he's a good investment until you can scout Yuyui.

## SCOUT LEVEL MAX: LUCIL AND YUYUI

Yuyui's stats max out at the highest levels possible (99 for END-CAT and 255 for both RND and REC). This makes her great at any position! Lucil, on the other hand, is a bit of a step down. Her stats max out at 77 for END-CAT and 177 for RND and REC. Not as great as Yuyui, but not a bad addition to your team as a whole.

# CONTROLLING THE TEAM AS MANAGER

The flow of a Blitzball game is described in this section. After you decide upon the match type and the camera angle you want to use during the match, the game proceeds virtually on autopilot. However, during the match, you can interrupt play by pressing the Triangle button. A menu appears after a team makes a successful goal and you can change formations, play style, and even switch out players. During the game, you can zoom in on the action by pressing the Square button and press the R1 and L1 buttons to boost or lower the team's Adrenaline Gauge.

# TYPES OF MATCHES

There are three types of Blitzball matches: Spira League, Tournament, and Exhibition. At the start of the game, you should stick with Exhibition matches to build up your Command Points and train your characters until their stats are compatible with the other teams.

## RULES FOR THE SPIRA LEAGUE

- Six teams compete in the tournament. Each team plays the others twice for a total of 10 matches.
- Each match lasts five minutes. The winner is determined by who scores the most points within the time limit. In case of a tie score, a tie game is called.
- The winner of the tournament is the team with the highest number of points. A win nets you 3 points, a tie 1 point, and a loss 0.
- At the end of all of the matches, the points are tallied and a winner is declared. The teams placing first, second, and third win prizes.

## RULES FOR A TOURNAMENT

- Six teams battle until one wins. Your opponent is chosen randomly.
- Each match lasts five minutes. The winner is determined by who scores the most points within the time limit. In case of a tie score, the game goes into Sudden Death overtime. Periods of 30 seconds each are called until one team scores.

## EXHIBITION

- Play a single practice match.
- Choose your opponent from among five teams.

| SPIRA LEAGUE AND TOURNAMENT PRIZES | | | |
|---|---|---|---|
| FIRST PLACE | SECOND PLACE | THIRD PLACE | EXHIBITION |
| Crystal Bangle | Mythril Bangle | X-Potion (x2) | X-Potion (x2) |
| Rune Bracer | Gold Bracer | Mega-Potion (x2) | Mega Potion (x2) |
| Moon Bracer | Power Gloves | Ether (x2) | Ether (x2) |
| Shining Bracer | Diamond Gloves | Turbo Ether | Mega Phoenix (x2) |
| Star Bracer | Pixie Dust | Mega Phoenix (x2) | - |
| Recovery Bracer | Mystery Veil | Mythril Bangle | - |
| Sprint Shoes | Crimson Ring | Hyper Wrist | - |
| Charm Bangle | Snow Ring | Diamond Gloves | - |
| Gold Hairpin | Ochre Ring | Talisman | - |
| AP Egg | Cerulean Ring | Mystery Veil | - |

# BLITZBALL PLAYER STATS

This section contains all of the stats for every player on each team, including the free agents. Use this information to help decide which players to scout or trade for.

# READING THE PLAYER STATS ENTRIES

| | |
|---|---|
| Scout Level | Indicates the stage at which the player can be scouted. This does not pertain to players on established teams. |
| Contract Duration | Indicates the maximum number of games for which a player can be contracted during one signing period (equal to the CNT stat). |
| CP Needed to Sign | Lists the number of Command Points (CP) needed to sign a player or renew their contract. |
| Special Shot | Shows a player's type of Special Shot. |
| Stats | Indicates the player's Starting Stats, their Maximum Stats, and the Optimal Points assigned to the stats. Remember, these only apply to the first eight stats, which can be changed through Training. |

# GULLWINGS

Characters

1

Garment Grids & Dancespheres

2

Battle System

3

Accessories

4

Items and Item Shops

5

Walkthrough

6

Mini-Games

7

Fiends and Enemies

8

## PAINE

| Scout Level: | 1 |
|---|---|
| Contract Duration: | 99 |
| CP Needed to Sign: | 3 |
| Special Shot: | N/A |

| STAT | START | MAX | OPT PTS |
|---|---|---|---|
| END | 3 | 48 | 7 |
| ATK | 2 | 20 | 5 |
| PAS | 2 | 30 | 5 |
| SHT | 5 | 92 | 9 |
| BLK | 2 | 20 | 5 |
| CAT | 1 | 10 | 4 |
| RNG | 70 | 130 | 8 |
| REC | 50 | 135 | 9 |
| SPD | 30 | - | - |
| RCH | 50 | - | - |

## WEDGE

| Scout Level: | 1 |
|---|---|
| Contract Duration: | 15 |
| CP Needed to Sign: | 3 |
| Special Shot: | N/A |

| STAT | START | MAX | OPT PTS |
|---|---|---|---|
| END | 2 | 33 | 4 |
| ATK | 4 | 57 | 6 |
| PAS | 3 | 60 | 8 |
| SHT | 1 | 20 | 4 |
| BLK | 3 | 40 | 8 |
| CAT | 1 | 10 | 4 |
| RNG | 27 | 95 | 8 |
| REC | 32 | 82 | 8 |
| SPD | 30 | - | - |
| RCH | 60 | - | - |

## YUNA

| Scout Level: | 1 |
|---|---|
| Contract Duration: | 99 |
| CP Needed to Sign: | 3 |
| Special Shot: | N/A |

| STAT | START | MAX | OPT PTS |
|---|---|---|---|
| END | 3 | 41 | 7 |
| ATK | 3 | 28 | 4 |
| PAS | 4 | 84 | 9 |
| SHT | 2 | 42 | 8 |
| BLK | 3 | 73 | 5 |
| CAT | 1 | 65 | 4 |
| RNG | 39 | 119 | 8 |
| REC | 45 | 154 | 9 |
| SPD | 30 | - | - |
| RCH | 50 | - | - |

## BUDDY

| Scout Level: | 1 |
|---|---|
| Contract Duration: | 20 |
| CP Needed to Sign: | 3 |
| Special Shot: | N/A |

| STAT | START | MAX | OPT PTS |
|---|---|---|---|
| END | 3 | 38 | 5 |
| ATK | 4 | 61 | 5 |
| PAS | 4 | 63 | 7 |
| SHT | 1 | 32 | 4 |
| BLK | 2 | 40 | 8 |
| CAT | 1 | 10 | 5 |
| RNG | 46 | 120 | 8 |
| REC | 30 | 105 | 9 |
| SPD | 30 | - | - |
| RCH | 65 | - | - |

## BIGGS

| Scout Level: | 1 |
|---|---|
| Contract Duration: | 10 |
| CP Needed to Sign: | 3 |
| Special Shot: | N/A |

| STAT | START | MAX | OPT PTS |
|---|---|---|---|
| END | 3 | 33 | 5 |
| ATK | 2 | 10 | 5 |
| PAS | 3 | 71 | 8 |
| SHT | 3 | 42 | 5 |
| BLK | 4 | 21 | 5 |
| CAT | 1 | 10 | 4 |
| RNG | 39 | 88 | 8 |
| REC | 45 | 95 | 7 |
| SPD | 30 | - | - |
| RCH | 60 | - | - |

## BROTHER

| Scout Level: | 1 |
|---|---|
| Contract Duration: | 40 |
| CP Needed to Sign: | 3 |
| Special Shot: | N/A |

| STAT | START | MAX | OPT PTS |
|---|---|---|---|
| END | 4 | 42 | 7 |
| ATK | 2 | 12 | 5 |
| PAS | 2 | 43 | 8 |
| SHT | 1 | 51 | 9 |
| BLK | 4 | 21 | 6 |
| CAT | 1 | 10 | 5 |
| RNG | 36 | 115 | 8 |
| REC | 4 | 200 | 9 |
| SPD | 40 | - | - |
| RCH | 60 | - | - |

## RIKKU

| Scout Level: | 1 |
|---|---|
| Contract Duration: | 99 |
| CP Needed to Sign: | 3 |
| Special Shot: | N/A |

| STAT | START | MAX | OPT PTS |
|---|---|---|---|
| END | 2 | 43 | 6 |
| ATK | 2 | 22 | 5 |
| PAS | 4 | 78 | 9 |
| SHT | 2 | 45 | 6 |
| BLK | 4 | 82 | 9 |
| CAT | 1 | 34 | 7 |
| RNG | 38 | 89 | 8 |
| REC | 28 | 190 | 8 |
| SPD | 35 | - | - |
| RCH | 65 | - | - |

## SHINRA

| Scout Level: | 1 |
|---|---|
| Contract Duration: | 30 |
| CP Needed to Sign: | 3 |
| Special Shot: | N/A |

| STAT | START | MAX | OPT PTS |
|---|---|---|---|
| END | 1 | 44 | 5 |
| ATK | 3 | 20 | 5 |
| PAS | 3 | 11 | 5 |
| SHT | 2 | 5 | 5 |
| BLK | 1 | 42 | 5 |
| CAT | 3 | 79 | 3 |
| RNG | 37 | 72 | 5 |
| REC | 11 | 26 | 5 |
| SPD | 33 | - | - |
| RCH | 70 | - | - |

## BICKSON

| | |
|---|---|
| Scout Level: | - |
| Contract Duration: | 10 |
| CP Needed to Sign: | 40 |
| Special Shot: | N/A |

| STAT | START | MAX | OPT PTS |
|---|---|---|---|
| END | 20 | 55 | 7 |
| ATK | 13 | 37 | 4 |
| PAS | 11 | 41 | 4 |
| SHT | 30 | 52 | 8 |
| BLK | 14 | 38 | 5 |
| CAT | 2 | 19 | 3 |
| RNG | 105 | 120 | 8 |
| REC | 105 | 112 | 8 |
| SPD | 40 | - | - |
| RCH | 55 | - | - |

## GRAAV

| | |
|---|---|
| Scout Level: | - |
| Contract Duration: | 10 |
| CP Needed to Sign: | 40 |
| Special Shot: | N/A |

| SPECIAL SHOT: | N/A | | |
|---|---|---|---|
| STAT | START | MAX | OPT PTS |
| END | 23 | 51 | 7 |
| ATK | 11 | 42 | 6 |
| PAS | 30 | 54 | 9 |
| SHT | 15 | 55 | 5 |
| BLK | 14 | 41 | 5 |
| CAT | 3 | 19 | 4 |
| RNG | 100 | 122 | 7 |
| REC | 106 | 120 | 8 |
| SPD | 35 | - | - |

## BALGERDA

| | |
|---|---|
| Scout Level: | - |
| Contract Duration: | 10 |
| CP Needed to Sign: | 40 |
| Special Shot: | N/A |

| STAT | START | MAX | OPT PTS |
|---|---|---|---|
| END | 9 | 41 | 4 |
| ATK | 25 | 52 | 7 |
| PAS | 17 | 52 | 8 |
| SHT | 3 | 26 | 4 |
| BLK | 19 | 29 | 4 |
| CAT | 6 | 28 | 3 |
| RNG | 72 | 92 | 6 |
| REC | 95 | 140 | 7 |
| SPD | 30 | - | - |
| RCH | 65 | - | - |

## PRETUS

| | |
|---|---|
| Scout Level: | - |
| Contract Duration: | 10 |
| CP Needed to Sign: | 40 |
| Special Shot: | N/A |

| STAT | START | MAX | OPT PTS |
|---|---|---|---|
| END | 25 | 48 | 4 |
| ATK | 12 | 77 | 7 |
| PAS | 20 | 53 | 5 |
| SHT | 2 | 11 | 3 |
| BLK | 20 | 51 | 5 |
| CAT | 2 | 13 | 2 |
| RNG | 130 | 142 | 6 |
| REC | 95 | 105 | 7 |
| SPD | 40 | - | - |
| RCH | 65 | - | - |

## ABUS

| | |
|---|---|
| Scout Level: | - |
| Contract Duration: | 10 |
| CP Needed to Sign: | 40 |
| Special Shot: | N/A |

| STAT | START | MAX | OPT PTS |
|---|---|---|---|
| END | 15 | 41 | 5 |
| ATK | 3 | 18 | 3 |
| PAS | 16 | 41 | 7 |
| SHT | 21 | 45 | 8 |
| BLK | 11 | 38 | 4 |
| CAT | 5 | 17 | 3 |
| RNG | 105 | 118 | 6 |
| REC | 110 | 158 | 7 |
| SPD | 35 | - | - |
| RCH | 50 | - | - |

## DORAM

| | |
|---|---|
| Scout Level: | - |
| Contract Duration: | 10 |
| CP Needed to Sign: | 40 |
| Special Shot: | N/A |

| STAT | START | MAX | OPT PTS |
|---|---|---|---|
| END | 15 | 54 | 6 |
| ATK | 18 | 38 | 8 |
| PAS | 27 | 51 | 9 |
| SHT | 3 | 30 | 5 |
| BLK | 10 | 75 | 4 |
| CAT | 7 | 28 | 3 |
| RNG | 120 | 130 | 8 |
| REC | 99 | 110 | 8 |
| SPD | 40 | - | - |
| RCH | 55 | - | - |

## BOWER

| | |
|---|---|
| Scout Level: | 1 |
| Contract Duration: | 10 |
| CP Needed to Sign: | 40 |
| Special Shot: | N/A |

| STAT | START | MAX | OPT PTS |
|---|---|---|---|
| END | 16 | 30 | 5 |
| ATK | 21 | 51 | 7 |
| PAS | 18 | 37 | 5 |
| SHT | 6 | 18 | 4 |
| BLK | 17 | 42 | 7 |
| CAT | 1 | 10 | 3 |
| RNG | 90 | 100 | 7 |
| REC | 88 | 130 | 8 |
| SPD | 30 | - | - |
| RCH | 80 | - | - |

## RAUDY

| | |
|---|---|
| Scout Level: | 1 |
| Contract Duration: | 10 |
| CP Needed to Sign: | 40 |
| Special Shot: | N/A |

| STAT | START | MAX | OPT PTS |
|---|---|---|---|
| END | 1 | 11 | 2 |
| ATK | 2 | 11 | 3 |
| PAS | 1 | 13 | 3 |
| SHT | 1 | 26 | 2 |
| BLK | 9 | 26 | 2 |
| CAT | 22 | 52 | 6 |
| RNG | 30 | 70 | 5 |
| REC | 37 | 37 | 4 |
| SPD | 30 | - | - |
| RCH | 60 | - | - |

# KILIKA BEASTS

## LARBEIGHT

| | |
|---|---|
| Scout Level: | - |
| Contract Duration: | 10 |
| CP Needed to Sign: | 12 |
| Special Shot: | N/A |

| STAT | START | MAX | OPT PTS |
|---|---|---|---|
| END | 3 | 45 | 5 |
| ATK | 2 | 30 | 3 |
| PAS | 2 | 22 | 4 |
| SHT | 4 | 54 | 9 |
| BLK | 4 | 10 | 4 |
| CAT | 2 | 10 | 3 |
| RNG | 71 | 104 | 8 |
| REC | 85 | 89 | 9 |
| SPD | 30 | - | - |
| RCH | 50 | - | - |

## VUROJA

| | |
|---|---|
| Scout Level: | - |
| Contract Duration: | 10 |
| CP Needed to Sign: | 12 |
| Special Shot: | N/A |

| STAT | START | MAX | OPT PTS |
|---|---|---|---|
| END | 4 | 56 | 7 |
| ATK | 3 | 30 | 4 |
| PAS | 5 | 76 | 9 |
| SHT | 1 | 21 | 4 |
| BLK | 4 | 20 | 4 |
| CAT | 1 | 92 | 5 |
| RNG | 61 | 88 | 8 |
| REC | 81 | 95 | 9 |
| SPD | 30 | - | - |
| RCH | 40 | - | - |

## DEIM

| | |
|---|---|
| Scout Level: | - |
| Contract Duration: | 10 |
| CP Needed to Sign: | 12 |
| Special Shot: | N/A |

| STAT | START | MAX | OPT PTS |
|---|---|---|---|
| END | 2 | 20 | 4 |
| ATK | 3 | 52 | 7 |
| PAS | 4 | 77 | 8 |
| SHT | 2 | 10 | 3 |
| BLK | 3 | 20 | 5 |
| CAT | 1 | 10 | 2 |
| RNG | 60 | 87 | 6 |
| REC | 66 | 70 | 6 |
| SPD | 30 | - | - |
| RCH | 30 | - | - |

## ZANDA

| | |
|---|---|
| Scout Level: | - |
| Contract Duration: | 10 |
| CP Needed to Sign: | 12 |
| Special Shot: | N/A |

| STAT | START | MAX | OPT PTS |
|---|---|---|---|
| END | 4 | 22 | 4 |
| ATK | 3 | 77 | 9 |
| PAS | 2 | 40 | 5 |
| SHT | 1 | 10 | 4 |
| BLK | 3 | 10 | 5 |
| CAT | 1 | 10 | 3 |
| RNG | 65 | 85 | 6 |
| REC | 43 | 78 | 8 |
| SPD | 30 | - | - |
| RCH | 45 | - | - |

## ISKEN

| | |
|---|---|
| Scout Level: | - |
| Contract Duration: | 10 |
| CP Needed to Sign: | 12 |
| Special Shot: | N/A |

| STAT | START | MAX | OPT PTS |
|---|---|---|---|
| END | 4 | 41 | 5 |
| ATK | 3 | 10 | 3 |
| PAS | 3 | 45 | 6 |
| SHT | 3 | 55 | 5 |
| BLK | 5 | 10 | 3 |
| CAT | 1 | 10 | 3 |
| RNG | 78 | 104 | 6 |
| REC | 72 | 92 | 6 |
| SPD | 30 | - | - |
| RCH | 50 | - | - |

## KULUKAN

| | |
|---|---|
| Scout Level: | - |
| Contract Duration: | 10 |
| CP Needed to Sign: | 12 |
| Special Shot: | N/A |

| STAT | START | MAX | OPT PTS |
|---|---|---|---|
| END | 3 | 29 | 5 |
| ATK | 3 | 51 | 5 |
| PAS | 4 | 92 | 8 |
| SHT | 3 | 30 | 4 |
| BLK | 3 | 55 | 4 |
| CAT | 1 | 10 | 3 |
| RNG | 65 | 130 | 9 |
| REC | 56 | 100 | 8 |
| SPD | 36 | - | - |
| RCH | 40 | - | - |

## ENKROY

| | |
|---|---|
| Scout Level: | - |
| Contract Duration: | 10 |
| CP Needed to Sign: | 12 |
| Special Shot: | N/A |

| STAT | START | MAX | OPT PTS |
|---|---|---|---|
| END | 3 | 20 | 4 |
| ATK | 2 | 93 | 8 |
| PAS | 4 | 40 | 5 |
| SHT | | 18 | 4 |
| BLK | 2 | 20 | 4 |
| CAT | 1 | 10 | 3 |
| RNG | 62 | 78 | 6 |
| REC | 57 | 85 | 7 |
| SPD | 28 | - | - |
| RCH | 45 | - | - |

## NIZARUT

| | |
|---|---|
| Scout Level: | - |
| Contract Duration: | 10 |
| CP Needed to Sign: | 12 |
| Special Shot: | N/A |

| STAT | START | MAX | OPT PTS |
|---|---|---|---|
| END | 2 | 43 | 4 |
| ATK | 2 | 30 | 5 |
| PAS | 3 | 30 | 3 |
| SHT | 1 | 8 | 2 |
| BLK | 3 | 10 | 3 |
| CAT | 2 | 52 | 3 |
| RNG | 40 | 88 | 7 |
| REC | 35 | 52 | 7 |
| SPD | 30 | - | - |
| RCH | 30 | - | - |

Characters

1

Garment Grids & Dresspheres

2

Battle System

3

Accessories

4

Items and Item Shops

5

Walkthrough

6

**Mini-Games**

7

Fiends and Enemies

8

# AL BHED PSYCHES

## EIGAAR

| | |
|---|---|
| Scout Level: | - |
| Contract Duration: | 10 |
| CP Needed to Sign: | 70 |
| Special Shot: | Overhead Volley, Corkscrew Shot |

| STAT | START | MAX | OPT PTS |
|---|---|---|---|
| END | 31 | 73 | 4 |
| ATK | 20 | 52 | 4 |
| PAS | 25 | 54 | 3 |
| SHT | 35 | 71 | 6 |
| BLK | 11 | 52 | 4 |
| CAT | 2 | 18 | 3 |
| RNG | 130 | 150 | 8 |
| REC | 155 | 178 | 6 |
| SPD | 33 | - | - |
| RCH | 45 | - | - |

## BERRIK

| | |
|---|---|
| Scout Level: | - |
| Contract Duration: | 10 |
| CP Needed to Sign: | 70 |
| Special Shot: | Overhead Volley, Corkscrew Shot |

| STAT | START | MAX | OPT PTS |
|---|---|---|---|
| END | 28 | 71 | 6 |
| ATK | 10 | 40 | 4 |
| PAS | 21 | 51 | 9 |
| SHT | 36 | 72 | 6 |
| BLK | 13 | 56 | 4 |
| CAT | 2 | 51 | 2 |
| RNG | 118 | 122 | 8 |
| REC | 128 | 158 | 7 |
| SPD | 35 | - | - |
| RCH | 55 | - | - |

## LAKKAM

| | |
|---|---|
| Scout Level: | - |
| Contract Duration: | 10 |
| CP Needed to Sign: | 70 |
| Special Shot: | Corkscrew Shot |

| STAT | START | MAX | OPT PTS |
|---|---|---|---|
| END | 10 | 27 | 6 |
| ATK | 28 | 93 | 9 |
| PAS | 41 | 69 | 4 |
| SHT | 2 | 12 | 3 |
| BLK | 16 | 54 | 5 |
| CAT | 3 | 20 | 4 |
| RNG | 72 | 104 | 4 |
| REC | 100 | 115 | 8 |
| SPD | 30 | - | - |
| RCH | 90 | - | - |

## NOMMA

| | |
|---|---|
| Scout Level: | - |
| Contract Duration: | 10 |
| CP Needed to Sign: | 70 |
| Special Shot: | Corkscrew Shot |

| STAT | START | MAX | OPT PTS |
|---|---|---|---|
| END | 12 | 54 | 6 |
| ATK | 33 | 71 | 8 |
| PAS | 27 | 42 | 9 |
| SHT | 1 | 18 | 4 |
| BLK | 34 | 72 | 7 |
| CAT | 2 | 19 | 4 |
| RNG | 82 | 113 | 8 |
| REC | 99 | 115 | 9 |
| SPD | 30 | - | - |
| RCH | 70 | - | - |

## BLAPPA

| | |
|---|---|
| Scout Level: | - |
| Contract Duration: | 10 |
| CP Needed to Sign: | 70 |
| Special Shot: | Overhead Volley, Corkscrew Shot |

| STAT | START | MAX | OPT PTS |
|---|---|---|---|
| END | 41 | 82 | 5 |
| ATK | 10 | 41 | 4 |
| PAS | 18 | 72 | 6 |
| SHT | 33 | 90 | 7 |
| BLK | 21 | 37 | 3 |
| CAT | 9 | 11 | 3 |
| RNG | 120 | 132 | 9 |
| REC | 160 | 190 | 9 |
| SPD | 35 | - | - |
| RCH | 30 | - | - |

## JUDDA

| | |
|---|---|
| Scout Level: | - |
| Contract Duration: | 10 |
| CP Needed to Sign: | 70 |
| Special Shot: | Corkscrew Shot |

| STAT | START | MAX | OPT PTS |
|---|---|---|---|
| END | 21 | 51 | 3 |
| ATK | 21 | 52 | 4 |
| PAS | 37 | 76 | 6 |
| SHT | 19 | 51 | 6 |
| BLK | 14 | 37 | 6 |
| CAT | 2 | 54 | 4 |
| RNG | 104 | 120 | 7 |
| REC | 110 | 153 | 4 |
| SPD | 35 | - | - |
| RCH | 40 | - | - |

## KEPPEL

| | |
|---|---|
| Scout Level: | - |
| Contract Duration: | 10 |
| CP Needed to Sign: | 70 |
| Special Shot: | N/A |

| STAT | START | MAX | OPT PTS |
|---|---|---|---|
| END | 14 | 39 | 5 |
| ATK | 39 | 72 | 7 |
| PAS | 17 | 51 | 6 |
| SHT | 4 | 17 | 4 |
| BLK | 30 | 40 | 7 |
| CAT | 2 | 17 | 3 |
| RNG | 88 | 115 | 7 |
| REC | 120 | 151 | 6 |
| SPD | 30 | - | - |
| RCH | 80 | - | - |

## NIMROOK

| | |
|---|---|
| Scout Level: | - |
| Contract Duration: | 10 |
| CP Needed to Sign: | 70 |
| Special Shot: | Corkscrew Shot |

| STAT | START | MAX | OPT PTS |
|---|---|---|---|
| END | 19 | 72 | 6 |
| ATK | 10 | 27 | 5 |
| PAS | 12 | 27 | 7 |
| SHT | 8 | 38 | 7 |
| BLK | 16 | 73 | 7 |
| CAT | 32 | 73 | 9 |
| RNG | 34 | 114 | 3 |
| REC | 113 | 155 | 4 |
| SPD | 30 | - | - |
| RCH | 60 | - | - |

# RONSO FANGS

## BASIK RONSO

| Scout Level: | - |
|---|---|
| Contract Duration: | 10 |
| CP Needed to Sign: | 30 |
| Special Shot: | Overhead Volley |

| STAT | START | MAX | OPT PTS |
|---|---|---|---|
| END | 33 | 93 | 8 |
| ATK | 9 | 41 | 8 |
| PAS | 10 | 37 | 4 |
| SHT | 16 | 54 | 6 |
| BLK | 9 | 39 | 4 |
| CAT | 2 | 10 | 3 |
| RNG | 100 | 190 | 8 |
| REC | 135 | 155 | 9 |
| SPD | 30 | - | - |
| RCH | 50 | - | - |

## GAZNA RONSO

| Scout Level: | - |
|---|---|
| Contract Duration: | 10 |
| CP Needed to Sign: | 30 |
| Special Shot: | Overhead Volley |

| STAT | START | MAX | OPT PTS |
|---|---|---|---|
| END | 28 | 91 | 8 |
| ATK | 15 | 56 | 4 |
| PAS | 17 | 73 | 5 |
| SHT | 11 | 37 | 4 |
| BLK | 6 | 39 | 4 |
| CAT | 4 | 21 | 6 |
| RNG | 71 | 101 | 5 |
| REC | 125 | 164 | 8 |
| SPD | 30 | - | - |
| RCH | 55 | - | - |

## IRGA RONSO

| Scout Level: | - |
|---|---|
| Contract Duration: | 10 |
| CP Needed to Sign: | 30 |
| Special Shot: | N/A |

| STAT | START | MAX | OPT PTS |
|---|---|---|---|
| END | 41 | 71 | 7 |
| ATK | 16 | 52 | 8 |
| PAS | 19 | 54 | 9 |
| SHT | 6 | 37 | 4 |
| BLK | 17 | 54 | 6 |
| CAT | 10 | 28 | 8 |
| RNG | 53 | 110 | 8 |
| REC | 136 | 172 | 9 |
| SPD | 30 | - | - |
| RCH | 60 | - | - |

## DARGA RONSO

| Scout Level: | - |
|---|---|
| Contract Duration: | 10 |
| CP Needed to Sign: | 30 |
| Special Shot: | N/A |

| STAT | START | MAX | OPT PTS |
|---|---|---|---|
| END | 41 | 75 | 9 |
| ATK | 20 | 55 | 7 |
| PAS | 17 | 55 | 6 |
| SHT | 3 | 18 | 4 |
| BLK | 17 | 53 | 4 |
| CAT | 3 | 30 | 2 |
| RNG | 93 | 123 | 8 |
| REC | 108 | 152 | 8 |
| SPD | 30 | - | - |
| RCH | 60 | - | - |

## ARGAI RONSO

| Scout Level: | - |
|---|---|
| Contract Duration: | 10 |
| CP Needed to Sign: | 30 |
| Special Shot: | N/A |

| STAT | START | MAX | OPT PTS |
|---|---|---|---|
| END | 43 | 71 | 9 |
| ATK | 10 | 27 | 8 |
| PAS | 9 | 30 | 6 |
| SHT | 17 | 53 | 7 |
| BLK | 11 | 73 | 7 |
| CAT | 5 | 31 | 5 |
| RNG | 110 | 120 | 8 |
| REC | 157 | 178 | 6 |
| SPD | 30 | - | - |
| RCH | 50 | - | - |

## NUVY RONSO

| Scout Level: | - |
|---|---|
| Contract Duration: | 10 |
| CP Needed to Sign: | 30 |
| Special Shot: | N/A |

| STAT | START | MAX | OPT PTS |
|---|---|---|---|
| END | 31 | 95 | 8 |
| ATK | 11 | 52 | 6 |
| PAS | 21 | 55 | 5 |
| SHT | 9 | 40 | 5 |
| BLK | 9 | 30 | 4 |
| CAT | 4 | 31 | 4 |
| RNG | 53 | 109 | 8 |
| REC | 125 | 135 | 8 |
| SPD | 30 | - | - |
| RCH | 60 | - | - |

## ZONDI RONSO

| Scout Level: | - |
|---|---|
| Contract Duration: | 10 |
| CP Needed to Sign: | 30 |
| Special Shot: | N/A |

| STAT | START | MAX | OPT PTS |
|---|---|---|---|
| END | 35 | 93 | 9 |
| ATK | 20 | 56 | 7 |
| PAS | 12 | 39 | 6 |
| SHT | 9 | 29 | 5 |
| BLK | 21 | 40 | 4 |
| CAT | 6 | 31 | 5 |
| RNG | 72 | 118 | 7 |
| REC | 141 | 153 | 8 |
| SPD | 30 | - | - |
| RCH | 60 | - | - |

## ZAMZI RONSO

| Scout Level: | - |
|---|---|
| Contract Duration: | 10 |
| CP Needed to Sign: | 30 |
| Special Shot: | N/A |

| STAT | START | MAX | OPT PTS |
|---|---|---|---|
| END | 31 | 95 | 8 |
| ATK | 26 | 54 | 7 |
| PAS | 12 | 42 | 8 |
| SHT | 1 | 27 | 4 |
| BLK | 11 | 39 | 7 |
| CAT | 4 | 19 | 3 |
| RNG | 56 | 107 | 8 |
| REC | 73 | 111 | 8 |
| SPD | 30 | - | - |
| RCH | 60 | - | - |

Characters

Garment Grids & D:esspheres

Battle System

Accessories

Items and Item Shops

Walkthrough

Mini-Games

Fiends and Enemies

# GUADO GLORIES

## GIERA GUADO

| Scout Level: | - |
|---|---|
| Contract Duration: | 10 |
| CP Needed to Sign: | 30 |
| Special Shot: | Overhead Volley |

| STAT | START | MAX | OPT PTS |
|---|---|---|---|
| END | 5 | 31 | 5 |
| ATK | 4 | 31 | 5 |
| PAS | 29 | 72 | 7 |
| SHT | 6 | 41 | 8 |
| BLK | 4 | 28 | 4 |
| CAT | 5 | 30 | 4 |
| RNG | 180 | 200 | 9 |
| REC | 190 | 250 | 9 |
| SPD | 27 | - | - |
| RCH | 55 | - | - |

## NAV GUADO

| Scout Level: | - |
|---|---|
| Contract Duration: | 10 |
| CP Needed to Sign: | 30 |
| Special Shot: | N/A |

| STAT | START | MAX | OPT PTS |
|---|---|---|---|
| END | 4 | 27 | 5 |
| ATK | 3 | 30 | 4 |
| PAS | 26 | 92 | 9 |
| SHT | 5 | 42 | 4 |
| BLK | 7 | 38 | 5 |
| CAT | 1 | 10 | 3 |
| RNG | 220 | 230 | 9 |
| REC | 175 | 223 | 9 |
| SPD | 28 | - | - |
| RCH | 55 | - | - |

## PAH GUADO

| Scout Level: | - |
|---|---|
| Contract Duration: | 10 |
| CP Needed to Sign: | 30 |
| Special Shot: | N/A |

| STAT | START | MAX | OPT PTS |
|---|---|---|---|
| END | 5 | 12 | 4 |
| ATK | 7 | 37 | 6 |
| PAS | 42 | 73 | 8 |
| SHT | 1 | 3 | 3 |
| BLK | 7 | 40 | 7 |
| CAT | 2 | 21 | 6 |
| RNG | 131 | 165 | 9 |
| REC | 200 | 250 | 9 |
| SPD | 24 | - | - |
| RCH | 70 | - | - |

## WON GUADO

| Scout Level: | - |
|---|---|
| Contract Duration: | 10 |
| CP Needed to Sign: | 30 |
| Special Shot: | Overhead Volley |

| STAT | START | MAX | OPT PTS |
|---|---|---|---|
| END | 4 | 12 | 6 |
| ATK | 8 | 54 | 4 |
| PAS | 55 | 93 | 8 |
| SHT | 3 | 11 | 3 |
| BLK | 9 | 73 | 7 |
| CAT | 1 | 11 | 3 |
| RNG | 235 | 250 | 8 |
| REC | 120 | 187 | 9 |
| SPD | 27 | - | - |
| RCH | 60 | - | - |

## ZAZI GUADO

| Scout Level: | - |
|---|---|
| Contract Duration: | 10 |
| CP Needed to Sign: | 30 |
| Special Shot: | Overhead Volley |

| STAT | START | MAX | OPT PTS |
|---|---|---|---|
| END | 3 | 31 | 4 |
| ATK | 6 | 41 | 6 |
| PAS | 38 | 74 | 8 |
| SHT | 6 | 55 | 7 |
| BLK | 8 | 37 | 4 |
| CAT | 3 | 30 | 4 |
| RNG | 195 | 220 | 8 |
| REC | 195 | 250 | 9 |
| SPD | 28 | - | - |
| RCH | 55 | - | - |

## AUDA GUADO

| Scout Level: | - |
|---|---|
| Contract Duration: | 10 |
| CP Needed to Sign: | 30 |
| Special Shot: | Corkscrew Shot |

| STAT | START | MAX | OPT PTS |
|---|---|---|---|
| END | 4 | 41 | 5 |
| ATK | 6 | 52 | 7 |
| PAS | 53 | 93 | 9 |
| SHT | 4 | 28 | 4 |
| BLK | 8 | 54 | 7 |
| CAT | 5 | 10 | 3 |
| RNG | 240 | 150 | 6 |
| REC | 170 | 195 | 6 |
| SPD | 28 | - | - |
| RCH | 60 | - | - |

## YIL GUADO

| Scout Level: | - |
|---|---|
| Contract Duration: | 10 |
| CP Needed to Sign: | 30 |
| Special Shot: | N/A |

| STAT | START | MAX | OPT PTS |
|---|---|---|---|
| END | 6 | 11 | 3 |
| ATK | 8 | 55 | 5 |
| PAS | 60 | 91 | 9 |
| SHT | 1 | 10 | 4 |
| BLK | 5 | 51 | 7 |
| CAT | 3 | 17 | 7 |
| RNG | 185 | 220 | 8 |
| REC | 150 | 168 | 8 |
| SPD | 25 | - | - |
| RCH | 60 | - | - |

## NOY GUADO

| Scout Level: | - |
|---|---|
| Contract Duration: | 10 |
| CP Needed to Sign: | 30 |
| Special Shot: | N/A |

| STAT | START | MAX | OPT PTS |
|---|---|---|---|
| END | 2 | 43 | 4 |
| ATK | 5 | 38 | 5 |
| PAS | 20 | 53 | 7 |
| SHT | 2 | 12 | 4 |
| BLK | 3 | 10 | 3 |
| CAT | 4 | 52 | 9 |
| RNG | 90 | 109 | 7 |
| REC | 120 | 220 | 9 |
| SPD | 25 | - | - |
| RCH | 60 | - | - |

# BESAID AUROCHS

## BECLEM

| | | |
|---|---|---|
| Scout Level: | - | |
| Contract Duration: | 10 | |
| CP Needed to Sign: | 60 | |
| Special Shot: | Overhead Volley. Corkscrew Shot | |

| STAT | START | MAX | OPT PTS |
|---|---|---|---|
| END | 38 | 56 | 9 |
| ATK | 21 | 38 | 4 |
| PAS | 29 | 40 | 6 |
| SHT | 42 | 75 | 9 |
| BLK | 9 | 16 | 4 |
| CAT | 1 | 11 | 3 |
| RNG | 120 | 125 | 9 |
| REC | 190 | 187 | 9 |
| SPD | 30 | - | - |
| RCH | 50 | - | - |

## LETTY

| | | |
|---|---|---|
| Scout Level: | - | |
| Contract Duration: | 10 | |
| CP Needed to Sign: | 60 | |
| Special Shot: | N/A | |

| STAT | START | MAX | OPT PTS |
|---|---|---|---|
| END | 22 | 56 | 4 |
| ATK | 20 | 41 | 5 |
| PAS | 45 | 92 | 9 |
| SHT | 25 | 31 | 5 |
| BLK | 9 | 73 | 7 |
| CAT | 2 | 17 | 3 |
| RNG | 80 | 89 | 8 |
| REC | 120 | 198 | 9 |
| SPD | 30 | - | - |
| RCH | 60 | - | - |

## JASSU

| | | |
|---|---|---|
| Scout Level: | - | |
| Contract Duration: | 10 | |
| CP Needed to Sign: | 60 | |
| Special Shot: | N/A | |

| STAT | START | MAX | OPT PTS |
|---|---|---|---|
| END | 18 | 38 | 6 |
| ATK | 48 | 62 | 9 |
| PAS | 21 | 52 | 7 |
| SHT | 10 | 37 | 4 |
| BLK | 24 | 75 | 6 |
| CAT | 1 | 20 | 3 |
| RNG | 80 | 91 | 8 |
| REC | 175 | 188 | 7 |
| SPD | 30 | - | - |
| RCH | 65 | - | - |

## VILUCHA

| | | |
|---|---|---|
| Scout Level: | - | |
| Contract Duration: | 10 | |
| CP Needed to Sign: | 60 | |
| Special Shot: | N/A | |

| STAT | START | MAX | OPT PTS |
|---|---|---|---|
| END | 24 | 53 | 6 |
| ATK | 25 | 92 | 9 |
| PAS | 32 | 30 | 7 |
| SHT | 1 | 92 | 5 |
| BLK | 12 | 29 | 5 |
| CAT | 1 | 38 | 3 |
| RNG | 107 | 120 | 6 |
| REC | 114 | 124 | 5 |
| SPD | 33 | - | - |
| RCH | 60 | - | - |

## WAKKA

| | | |
|---|---|---|
| Scout Level: | - | |
| Contract Duration: | 10 | |
| CP Needed to Sign: | 60 | |
| Special Shot: | Overhead Volley | |

| STAT | START | MAX | OPT PTS |
|---|---|---|---|
| END | 35 | 72 | 9 |
| ATK | 6 | 39 | 4 |
| PAS | 10 | 27 | 6 |
| SHT | 48 | 74 | 8 |
| BLK | 7 | 40 | 5 |
| CAT | 2 | 16 | 3 |
| RNG | 130 | 134 | 8 |
| REC | 180 | 190 | 8 |
| SPD | 30 | - | - |
| RCH | 50 | - | - |

## DATTO

| | | |
|---|---|---|
| Scout Level: | - | |
| Contract Duration: | 10 | |
| CP Needed to Sign: | 60 | |
| Special Shot: | N/A | |

| STAT | START | MAX | OPT PTS |
|---|---|---|---|
| END | 31 | 95 | 8 |
| ATK | 22 | 51 | 5 |
| PAS | 24 | 74 | 6 |
| SHT | 4 | 37 | 5 |
| BLK | 22 | 40 | 4 |
| CAT | 3 | 19 | 3 |
| RNG | 85 | 87 | 7 |
| REC | 110 | 140 | 7 |
| SPD | 40 | - | - |
| RCH | 60 | - | - |

## BOTTA

| | | |
|---|---|---|
| Scout Level: | - | |
| Contract Duration: | 10 | |
| CP Needed to Sign: | 60 | |
| Special Shot: | N/A | |

| STAT | START | MAX | OPT PTS |
|---|---|---|---|
| END | 22 | 52 | 5 |
| ATK | 48 | 72 | 8 |
| PAS | 19 | 53 | 9 |
| SHT | 3 | 12 | 5 |
| BLK | 19 | 39 | 4 |
| CAT | 3 | 10 | 3 |
| RNG | 52 | 83 | 5 |
| REC | 124 | 131 | 6 |
| SPD | 30 | - | - |
| RCH | 65 | - | - |

## KEEPA

| | | |
|---|---|---|
| Scout Level: | - | |
| Contract Duration: | 10 | |
| CP Needed to Sign: | 60 | |
| Special Shot: | N/A | |

| STAT | START | MAX | OPT PTS |
|---|---|---|---|
| END | 3 | 16 | 4 |
| ATK | 5 | 21 | 4 |
| PAS | 4 | 19 | 4 |
| SHT | 1 | 99 | 2 |
| BLK | 4 | 18 | 4 |
| CAT | 39 | 74 | 7 |
| RNG | 60 | 67 | 5 |
| REC | 87 | 99 | 5 |
| SPD | 40 | - | - |
| RCH | 40 | - | - |

Characters

Garment Grids
& Dresspheres

Battle System

Accessories

Items and
Item Shops

Walkthrough

Mini-Games

Fiends and
Enemies

# ZANARKAND ABES

## KIRYL

| | |
|---|---|
| Scout Level: | - |
| Contract Duration: | 10 |
| CP Needed to Sign: | 90 |
| Special Shot: | Overhead Volley |

| STAT | START | MAX | OPT PTS |
|---|---|---|---|
| END | 43 | 75 | 7 |
| ATK | 23 | 26 | 4 |
| PAS | 31 | 59 | 5 |
| SHT | 63 | 95 | 9 |
| BLK | 20 | 42 | 4 |
| CAT | 8 | 13 | 3 |
| RNG | 180 | 190 | 9 |
| REC | 155 | 190 | 9 |
| SPD | 30 | - | - |
| RCH | 30 | - | - |

## TOMA

| | |
|---|---|
| Scout Level: | - |
| Contract Duration: | 10 |
| CP Needed to Sign: | 90 |
| Special Shot: | Overhead Volley |

| STAT | START | MAX | OPT PTS |
|---|---|---|---|
| END | 30 | 55 | 6 |
| ATK | 21 | 38 | 4 |
| PAS | 27 | 52 | 4 |
| SHT | 68 | 71 | 8 |
| BLK | 19 | 39 | 4 |
| CAT | 8 | 10 | 3 |
| RNG | 140 | 145 | 7 |
| REC | 135 | 159 | 9 |
| SPD | 38 | - | - |
| RCH | 30 | - | - |

## NAYA

| | |
|---|---|
| Scout Level: | - |
| Contract Duration: | 10 |
| CP Needed to Sign: | 90 |
| Special Shot: | Overhead Volley, Corkscrew Shot |

| STAT | START | MAX | OPT PTS |
|---|---|---|---|
| END | 51 | 99 | 4 |
| ATK | 30 | 39 | 5 |
| PAS | 41 | 53 | 9 |
| SHT | 29 | 35 | 5 |
| BLK | 48 | 53 | 9 |
| CAT | 10 | 19 | 3 |
| RNG | 200 | 230 | 6 |
| REC | 121 | 154 | 8 |
| SPD | 35 | - | - |
| RCH | 60 | - | - |

## LUPERIS

| | |
|---|---|
| Scout Level: | - |
| Contract Duration: | 10 |
| CP Needed to Sign: | 90 |
| Special Shot: | Corkscrew Shot |

| STAT | START | MAX | OPT PTS |
|---|---|---|---|
| END | 30 | 53 | 6 |
| ATK | 54 | 92 | 8 |
| PAS | 32 | 55 | 6 |
| SHT | 2 | 28 | 4 |
| BLK | 28 | 31 | 4 |
| CAT | 9 | 10 | 3 |
| RNG | 34 | 67 | 6 |
| REC | 90 | 113 | 7 |
| SPD | 30 | - | - |
| RCH | 70 | - | - |

## STAR PLAYER

| | |
|---|---|
| Scout Level: | - |
| Contract Duration: | 10 |
| CP Needed to Sign: | 90 |
| Special Shot: | Overhead Volley, Corkscrew Shot |

| STAT | START | MAX | OPT PTS |
|---|---|---|---|
| END | 47 | 92 | 7 |
| ATK | 27 | 36 | 4 |
| PAS | 30 | 73 | 4 |
| SHT | 98 | 99 | 9 |
| BLK | 10 | 42 | 4 |
| CAT | 2 | 13 | 3 |
| RNG | 190 | 199 | 7 |
| REC | 174 | 250 | 6 |
| SPD | 32 | - | - |
| RCH | 50 | - | - |

## SHAFT

| | |
|---|---|
| Scout Level: | - |
| Contract Duration: | 10 |
| CP Needed to Sign: | 90 |
| Special Shot: | Overhead Volley |

| STAT | START | MAX | OPT PTS |
|---|---|---|---|
| END | 37 | 74 | 4 |
| ATK | 30 | 40 | 6 |
| PAS | 51 | 74 | 9 |
| SHT | 32 | 34 | 4 |
| BLK | 41 | 58 | 4 |
| CAT | 12 | 20 | 3 |
| RNG | 102 | 116 | 8 |
| REC | 120 | 160 | 7 |
| SPD | 40 | - | - |
| RCH | 50 | - | - |

## SUZAM

| | |
|---|---|
| Scout Level: | - |
| Contract Duration: | 10 |
| CP Needed to Sign: | 90 |
| Special Shot: | N/A |

| STAT | START | MAX | OPT PTS |
|---|---|---|---|
| END | 30 | 40 | 5 |
| ATK | 61 | 99 | 8 |
| PAS | 31 | 39 | 5 |
| SHT | 12 | 13 | 4 |
| BLK | 41 | 55 | 6 |
| CAT | 3 | 17 | 5 |
| RNG | 90 | 100 | 7 |
| REC | 98 | 116 | 8 |
| SPD | 30 | - | - |
| RCH | 80 | - | - |

## CETAN

| | |
|---|---|
| Scout Level: | - |
| Contract Duration: | 10 |
| CP Needed to Sign: | 90 |
| Special Shot: | N/A |

| STAT | START | MAX | OPT PTS |
|---|---|---|---|
| END | 11 | 38 | 4 |
| ATK | 30 | 30 | 4 |
| PAS | 5 | 72 | 8 |
| SHT | 2 | 20 | 3 |
| BLK | 18 | 71 | 7 |
| CAT | 54 | 93 | 9 |
| RNG | 90 | 120 | 8 |
| REC | 21 | 36 | 8 |
| SPD | 30 | - | - |
| RCH | 30 | - | - |

# FREE AGENTS

## UKYOU

| | |
|---|---|
| Scout Level: | 1 |
| Contract Duration: | 10 |
| CP Needed to Sign: | 10 |
| Special Shot: | N/A |

| STAT | START | MAX | OPT PTS |
|---|---|---|---|
| END | 10 | 61 | 9 |
| ATK | 3 | 16 | 5 |
| PAS | 5 | 26 | 7 |
| SHT | 4 | 31 | 4 |
| BLK | 5 | 28 | 6 |
| CAT | 1 | 11 | 4 |
| RNG | 38 | 78 | 7 |
| REC | 55 | 132 | 9 |
| SPD | 30 | - | - |
| RCH | 55 | - | - |

## SULYA

| | |
|---|---|
| Scout Level: | 1 |
| Contract Duration: | 10 |
| CP Needed to Sign: | 10 |
| Special Shot: | N/A |

| STAT | START | MAX | OPT PTS |
|---|---|---|---|
| END | 1 | 39 | 4 |
| ATK | 3 | 30 | 5 |
| PAS | 1 | 10 | 3 |
| SHT | 1 | 13 | 3 |
| BLK | 3 | 30 | 6 |
| CAT | 8 | 57 | 3 |
| RNG | 36 | 80 | 8 |
| REC | 65 | 72 | 6 |
| SPD | 30 | - | - |
| RCH | 60 | - | - |

## BALKAI

| | |
|---|---|
| Scout Level: | 1 |
| Contract Duration: | 10 |
| CP Needed to Sign: | 10 |
| Special Shot: | N/A |

| STAT | START | MAX | OPT PTS |
|---|---|---|---|
| END | 6 | 33 | 4 |
| ATK | 9 | 74 | 6 |
| PAS | 3 | 60 | 5 |
| SHT | 2 | 20 | 4 |
| BLK | 13 | 53 | 6 |
| CAT | 1 | 17 | 2 |
| RNG | 50 | 73 | 8 |
| REC | 64 | 99 | 8 |
| SPD | 30 | - | - |
| RCH | 60 | - | - |

## ROPP

| | |
|---|---|
| Scout Level: | 1 |
| Contract Duration: | 10 |
| CP Needed to Sign: | 10 |
| Special Shot: | N/A |

| STAT | START | MAX | OPT PTS |
|---|---|---|---|
| END | 3 | 28 | 4 |
| ATK | 12 | 40 | 6 |
| PAS | 6 | 26 | 4 |
| SHT | 2 | 19 | 3 |
| BLK | 11 | 60 | 7 |
| CAT | 1 | 26 | 3 |
| RNG | 48 | 81 | 7 |
| REC | 45 | 78 | 7 |
| SPD | 30 | - | - |
| RCH | 60 | - | - |

## SHUU

| | |
|---|---|
| Scout Level: | 1 |
| Contract Duration: | 10 |
| CP Needed to Sign: | 10 |
| Special Shot: | Overhead Volley |

| STAT | START | MAX | OPT PTS |
|---|---|---|---|
| END | 7 | 62 | 7 |
| ATK | 2 | 37 | 5 |
| PAS | 2 | 39 | 4 |
| SHT | 9 | 45 | 6 |
| BLK | 1 | 19 | 4 |
| CAT | 2 | 16 | 3 |
| RNG | 51 | 102 | 8 |
| REC | 58 | 112 | 8 |
| SPD | 30 | - | - |
| RCH | 60 | - | - |

## NEDUS

| | |
|---|---|
| Scout Level: | 1 |
| Contract Duration: | 10 |
| CP Needed to Sign: | 10 |
| Special Shot: | N/A |

| STAT | START | MAX | OPT PTS |
|---|---|---|---|
| END | 4 | 41 | 4 |
| ATK | 4 | 40 | 4 |
| PAS | 8 | 58 | 7 |
| SHT | 2 | 27 | 4 |
| BLK | 9 | 56 | 8 |
| CAT | 3 | 57 | 3 |
| RNG | 41 | 75 | 8 |
| REC | 56 | 105 | 9 |
| SPD | 30 | - | - |
| RCH | 60 | - | - |

## HILDI

| | |
|---|---|
| Scout Level: | 1 |
| Contract Duration: | 10 |
| CP Needed to Sign: | 10 |
| Special Shot: | N/A |

| STAT | START | MAX | OPT PTS |
|---|---|---|---|
| END | 6 | 40 | 4 |
| ATK | 8 | 21 | 3 |
| PAS | 10 | 38 | 4 |
| SHT | 5 | 53 | 7 |
| BLK | 3 | 42 | 6 |
| CAT | 3 | 51 | 2 |
| RNG | 51 | 89 | 7 |
| REC | 71 | 113 | 8 |
| SPD | 30 | - | - |
| RCH | 60 | - | - |

Characters

Garment Grids & Dresspheres

Battle System

Accessories

Items and Item Shops

Walkthrough

Mini-Games

Fiends and Enemies

# FREE AGENTS

## ZALITZ

| Scout Level: | 2 |
|---|---|
| Contract Duration: | 10 |
| CP Needed to Sign: | 15 |
| Special Shot: | N/A |

| STAT | START | MAX | OPT PTS |
|---|---|---|---|
| END | 18 | 52 | 6 |
| ATK | 7 | 42 | 5 |
| PAS | 6 | 56 | 8 |
| SHT | 2 | 28 | 4 |
| BLK | 15 | 72 | 4 |
| CAT | 4 | 39 | 3 |
| RNG | 51 | 91 | 7 |
| REC | 78 | 150 | 8 |
| SPD | 38 | - | - |
| RCH | 60 | - | - |

## SVANDA

| Scout Level: | 2 |
|---|---|
| Contract Duration: | 10 |
| CP Needed to Sign: | 15 |
| Special Shot: | N/A |

| STAT | START | MAX | OPT PTS |
|---|---|---|---|
| END | 1 | 26 | 6 |
| ATK | 4 | 19 | 4 |
| PAS | 14 | 72 | 9 |
| SHT | 2 | 11 | 3 |
| BLK | 7 | 26 | 7 |
| CAT | 11 | 71 | 5 |
| RNG | 51 | 111 | 7 |
| REC | 81 | 132 | 8 |
| SPD | 35 | - | - |
| RCH | 70 | - | - |

## NHADALA

| Scout Level: | 2 |
|---|---|
| Contract Duration: | 10 |
| CP Needed to Sign: | 15 |
| Special Shot: | N/A |

| STAT | START | MAX | OPT PTS |
|---|---|---|---|
| END | 8 | 26 | 5 |
| ATK | 5 | 26 | 5 |
| PAS | 15 | 71 | 8 |
| SHT | 4 | 17 | 4 |
| BLK | 1 | 30 | 4 |
| CAT | 4 | 28 | 4 |
| RNG | 60 | 120 | 9 |
| REC | 67 | 155 | 9 |
| SPD | 30 | - | - |
| RCH | 60 | - | - |

## MEP

| Scout Level: | 2 |
|---|---|
| Contract Duration: | 10 |
| CP Needed to Sign: | 15 |
| Special Shot: | Overhead Volley |

| STAT | START | MAX | OPT PTS |
|---|---|---|---|
| END | 14 | 54 | 6 |
| ATK | 6 | 55 | 4 |
| PAS | 3 | 55 | 4 |
| SHT | 13 | 75 | 8 |
| BLK | 1 | 54 | 4 |
| CAT | 3 | 29 | 2 |
| RNG | 71 | 98 | 7 |
| REC | 68 | 115 | 8 |
| SPD | 30 | - | - |
| RCH | 60 | - | - |

## JUMAL

| Scout Level: | 2 |
|---|---|
| Contract Duration: | 10 |
| CP Needed to Sign: | 15 |
| Special Shot: | N/A |

| STAT | START | MAX | OPT PTS |
|---|---|---|---|
| END | 9 | 44 | 8 |
| ATK | 15 | 94 | 9 |
| PAS | 9 | 11 | 4 |
| SHT | 4 | 6 | 3 |
| BLK | 6 | 60 | 4 |
| CAT | 5 | 57 | 3 |
| RNG | 43 | 100 | 8 |
| REC | 50 | 70 | 7 |
| SPD | 30 | - | - |
| RCH | 60 | - | - |

## DURREN

| Scout Level: | 2 |
|---|---|
| Contract Duration: | 10 |
| CP Needed to Sign: | 15 |
| Special Shot: | N/A |

| STAT | START | MAX | OPT PTS |
|---|---|---|---|
| END | 3 | 51 | 6 |
| ATK | 3 | 31 | 4 |
| PAS | 16 | 53 | 8 |
| SHT | 4 | 37 | 4 |
| BLK | 15 | 79 | 9 |
| CAT | 5 | 39 | 3 |
| RNG | 64 | 120 | 9 |
| REC | 61 | 154 | 9 |
| SPD | 30 | - | - |
| RCH | 60 | - | - |

## NAIDA

| Scout Level: | 2 |
|---|---|
| Contract Duration: | 10 |
| CP Needed to Sign: | 15 |
| Special Shot: | N/A |

| STAT | START | MAX | OPT PTS |
|---|---|---|---|
| END | 1 | 75 | 3 |
| ATK | 3 | 20 | 4 |
| PAS | 10 | 56 | 8 |
| SHT | 12 | 54 | 7 |
| BLK | 3 | 42 | 5 |
| CAT | 5 | 28 | 4 |
| RNG | 54 | 118 | 8 |
| REC | 70 | 130 | 9 |
| SPD | 30 | - | - |
| RCH | 60 | - | - |

# FREE AGENTS

## SCOUT LEVEL: 3

### KIYURI

| | |
|---|---|
| Scout Level: | 3 |
| Contract Duration: | 10 |
| CP Needed to Sign: | 20 |
| Special Shot: | N/A |

| STAT | START | MAX | OPT PTS |
|---|---|---|---|
| END | 15 | 55 | 6 |
| ATK | 26 | 95 | 9 |
| PAS | 9 | 42 | 4 |
| SHT | 11 | 20 | 5 |
| BLK | 12 | 21 | 4 |
| CAT | 8 | 16 | 4 |
| RNG | 85 | 110 | 7 |
| REC | 95 | 136 | 9 |
| SPD | 30 | - | - |
| RCH | 60 | - | - |

### ZEV RONSO

| | |
|---|---|
| Scout Level: | 3 |
| Contract Duration: | 10 |
| CP Needed to Sign: | 20 |
| Special Shot: | N/A |

| STAT | START | MAX | OPT PTS |
|---|---|---|---|
| END | 12 | 31 | 4 |
| ATK | 18 | 64 | 9 |
| PAS | 11 | 39 | 4 |
| SHT | 9 | 42 | 5 |
| BLK | 24 | 68 | 9 |
| CAT | 18 | 56 | 7 |
| RNG | 70 | 92 | 7 |
| REC | 90 | 175 | 9 |
| SPD | 30 | - | - |
| RCH | 60 | - | - |

### JAIALAI

| | |
|---|---|
| Scout Level: | 3 |
| Contract Duration: | 10 |
| CP Needed to Sign: | 20 |
| Special Shot: | N/A |

| STAT | START | MAX | OPT PTS |
|---|---|---|---|
| END | 12 | 38 | 4 |
| ATK | 25 | 75 | 9 |
| PAS | 23 | 40 | 8 |
| SHT | 11 | 16 | 4 |
| BLK | 12 | 30 | 6 |
| CAT | 9 | 30 | 5 |
| RNG | 70 | 130 | 8 |
| REC | 80 | 110 | 8 |
| SPD | 38 | - | - |
| RCH | 60 | - | - |

### YUMA GUADO

| | |
|---|---|
| Scout Level: | 3 |
| Contract Duration: | 10 |
| CP Needed to Sign: | 20 |
| Special Shot: | N/A |

| STAT | START | MAX | OPT PTS |
|---|---|---|---|
| END | 13 | 39 | 5 |
| ATK | 11 | 21 | 3 |
| PAS | 11 | 37 | 4 |
| SHT | 6 | 5 | 2 |
| BLK | 27 | 73 | 9 |
| CAT | 5 | 40 | 3 |
| RNG | 56 | 115 | 8 |
| REC | 74 | 114 | 8 |
| SPD | 30 | - | - |
| RCH | 60 | - | - |

### SHAAMI

| | |
|---|---|
| Scout Level: | 3 |
| Contract Duration: | 10 |
| CP Needed to Sign: | 20 |
| Special Shot: | Corkscrew Shot |

| STAT | START | MAX | OPT PTS |
|---|---|---|---|
| END | 20 | 53 | 8 |
| ATK | 17 | 39 | 6 |
| PAS | 11 | 29 | 4 |
| SHT | 28 | 72 | 9 |
| BLK | 12 | 31 | 4 |
| CAT | 8 | 19 | 3 |
| RNG | 81 | 125 | 8 |
| REC | 78 | 171 | 9 |
| SPD | 30 | - | - |
| RCH | 60 | - | - |

### NEFFE

| | |
|---|---|
| Scout Level: | 3 |
| Contract Duration: | 10 |
| CP Needed to Sign: | 20 |
| Special Shot: | N/A |

| STAT | START | MAX | OPT PTS |
|---|---|---|---|
| END | 22 | 73 | 9 |
| ATK | 11 | 56 | 7 |
| PAS | 10 | 51 | 5 |
| SHT | 21 | 73 | 7 |
| BLK | 11 | 41 | 5 |
| CAT | 8 | 31 | 4 |
| RNG | 70 | 120 | 9 |
| REC | 70 | 156 | 9 |
| SPD | 30 | - | - |
| RCH | 60 | - | - |

### MIFUREY

| | |
|---|---|
| Scout Level: | 3 |
| Contract Duration: | 10 |
| CP Needed to Sign: | 20 |
| Special Shot: | Overhead Volley |

| STAT | START | MAX | OPT PTS |
|---|---|---|---|
| END | 20 | 31 | 6 |
| ATK | 3 | 28 | 4 |
| PAS | 3 | 26 | 4 |
| SHT | 2 | 16 | 3 |
| BLK | 1 | 18 | 7 |
| CAT | 29 | 73 | 9 |
| RNG | 64 | 70 | 6 |
| REC | 77 | 192 | 8 |
| SPD | 30 | - | - |
| RCH | 60 | - | - |

Characters

Garment Grids & Dressspheres

Battle System

Accessories

Items and Item Shops

Walkthrough

**Mini-Games**

Fiends and Enemies

# FREE AGENTS

## ADDA

| Scout Level: | 4 |
|---|---|
| Contract Duration: | 10 |
| CP Needed to Sign: | 30 |
| Special Shot: | N/A |

| STAT | START | MAX | OPT PTS |
|---|---|---|---|
| END | 1 | 28 | 6 |
| ATK | 27 | 56 | 7 |
| PAS | 1 | 93 | 9 |
| SHT | 1 | 29 | 5 |
| BLK | 3 | 40 | 7 |
| CAT | 5 | 10 | 3 |
| RNG | 58 | 110 | 8 |
| REC | 110 | 174 | 9 |
| SPD | 30 | - | - |
| RCH | 60 | - | - |

## KWINN

| Scout Level: | 4 |
|---|---|
| Contract Duration: | 10 |
| CP Needed to Sign: | 30 |
| Special Shot: | Corkscrew Shot |

| STAT | START | MAX | OPT PTS |
|---|---|---|---|
| END | 1 | 3 | 2 |
| ATK | 3 | 4 | 2 |
| PAS | 3 | 5 | 2 |
| SHT | 2 | 4 | 2 |
| BLK | 1 | 2 | 2 |
| CAT | 24 | 94 | 2 |
| RNG | 93 | 95 | 5 |
| REC | 10 | 23 | 4 |
| SPD | 30 | - | - |
| RCH | 60 | - | - |

## FOBBI

| Scout Level: | 4 |
|---|---|
| Contract Duration: | 10 |
| CP Needed to Sign: | 30 |
| Special Shot: | N/A |

| STAT | START | MAX | OPT PTS |
|---|---|---|---|
| END | 19 | 22 | 4 |
| ATK | 11 | 31 | 6 |
| PAS | 14 | 51 | 8 |
| SHT | 2 | 3 | 2 |
| BLK | 31 | 93 | 9 |
| CAT | 9 | 72 | 5 |
| RNG | 72 | 104 | 7 |
| REC | 145 | 168 | 8 |
| SPD | 30 | - | - |
| RCH | 60 | - | - |

## RIN

| Scout Level: | 4 |
|---|---|
| Contract Duration: | 10 |
| CP Needed to Sign: | 30 |
| Special Shot: | N/A |

| STAT | START | MAX | OPT PTS |
|---|---|---|---|
| END | 19 | 53 | 9 |
| ATK | 11 | 27 | 5 |
| PAS | 19 | 52 | 7 |
| SHT | 35 | 73 | 9 |
| BLK | 15 | 52 | 4 |
| CAT | 7 | 27 | 3 |
| RNG | 93 | 135 | 8 |
| REC | 91 | 152 | 8 |
| SPD | 30 | - | - |
| RCH | 60 | - | - |

## CAHHAN

| Scout Level: | 4 |
|---|---|
| Contract Duration: | 10 |
| CP Needed to Sign: | 30 |
| Special Shot: | N/A |

| STAT | START | MAX | OPT PTS |
|---|---|---|---|
| END | 18 | 38 | 5 |
| ATK | 22 | 51 | 7 |
| PAS | 31 | 76 | 9 |
| SHT | 11 | 30 | 6 |
| BLK | 24 | 74 | 9 |
| CAT | 5 | 28 | 4 |
| RNG | 120 | 132 | 9 |
| REC | 72 | 200 | 8 |
| SPD | 30 | - | - |
| RCH | 60 | - | - |

## TATTS

| Scout Level: | 4 |
|---|---|
| Contract Duration: | 10 |
| CP Needed to Sign: | 30 |
| Special Shot: | Overhead Volley |

| STAT | START | MAX | OPT PTS |
|---|---|---|---|
| END | 25 | 55 | 6 |
| ATK | 15 | 42 | 7 |
| PAS | 18 | 39 | 5 |
| SHT | 32 | 92 | 9 |
| BLK | 15 | 96 | 9 |
| CAT | 2 | 41 | 3 |
| RNG | 100 | 121 | 7 |
| REC | 100 | 188 | 7 |
| SPD | 30 | - | - |
| RCH | 60 | - | - |

## MIYU

| Scout Level: | 4 |
|---|---|
| Contract Duration: | 10 |
| CP Needed to Sign: | 30 |
| Special Shot: | Overhead Volley, Corkscrew Shot |

| STAT | START | MAX | OPT PTS |
|---|---|---|---|
| END | 24 | 54 | 5 |
| ATK | 21 | 41 | 5 |
| PAS | 16 | 41 | 5 |
| SHT | 32 | 83 | 9 |
| BLK | 16 | 39 | 6 |
| CAT | 9 | 38 | 6 |
| RNG | 72 | 110 | 8 |
| REC | 82 | 210 | 9 |
| SPD | 30 | - | - |
| RCH | 60 | - | - |

# FREE AGENTS

## SCOUT LEVEL: MAX

### ISAARU

| Scout Level: | MAX |
|---|---|
| Contract Duration: | 10 |
| CP Needed to Sign: | 40 |
| Special Shot: | N/A |

| STAT | START | MAX | OPT PTS |
|---|---|---|---|
| END | 35 | 92 | 5 |
| ATK | 2 | 10 | 5 |
| PAS | 42 | 96 | 5 |
| SHT | 1 | 12 | 5 |
| BLK | 39 | 96 | 5 |
| CAT | 1 | 10 | 5 |
| RNG | 11 | 22 | 5 |
| REC | 130 | 210 | 5 |
| SPD | 30 | – | – |
| RCH | 60 | – | – |

### DONA

| Scout Level: | MAX |
|---|---|
| Contract Duration: | 10 |
| CP Needed to Sign: | 40 |
| Special Shot: | N/A |

| STAT | START | MAX | OPT PTS |
|---|---|---|---|
| END | 25 | 52 | 5 |
| ATK | 25 | 52 | 5 |
| PAS | 25 | 51 | 5 |
| SHT | 24 | 54 | 5 |
| BLK | 26 | 52 | 5 |
| CAT | 25 | 54 | 5 |
| RNG | 73 | 84 | 5 |
| REC | 73 | 84 | 5 |
| SPD | 28 | – | – |
| RCH | 60 | – | – |

### MARODA

| Scout Level: | MAX |
|---|---|
| Contract Duration: | 10 |
| CP Needed to Sign: | 40 |
| Special Shot: | N/A |

| STAT | START | MAX | OPT PTS |
|---|---|---|---|
| END | 8 | 41 | 5 |
| ATK | 18 | 27 | 7 |
| PAS | 31 | 92 | 9 |
| SHT | 17 | 19 | 7 |
| BLK | 11 | 29 | 5 |
| CAT | 10 | 40 | 7 |
| RNG | 90 | 105 | 6 |
| REC | 135 | 158 | 9 |
| SPD | 30 | – | – |
| RCH | 60 | – | – |

### LUCIL

| Scout Level: | MAX |
|---|---|
| Contract Duration: | 10 |
| CP Needed to Sign: | 40 |
| Special Shot: | Overhead Volley; Corkscrew Shot |

| STAT | START | MAX | OPT PTS |
|---|---|---|---|
| END | 7 | 77 | 7 |
| ATK | 7 | 77 | 7 |
| PAS | 7 | 77 | 7 |
| SHT | 7 | 77 | 7 |
| BLK | 7 | 77 | 7 |
| CAT | 7 | 77 | 7 |
| RNG | 77 | 177 | 7 |
| REC | 77 | 177 | 7 |
| SPD | 30 | – | – |
| RCH | 77 | – | – |

### AUBORINE

| Scout Level: | MAX |
|---|---|
| Contract Duration: | 10 |
| CP Needed to Sign: | 40 |
| Special Shot: | N/A |

| STAT | START | MAX | OPT PTS |
|---|---|---|---|
| END | 1 | 2 | 2 |
| ATK | 3 | 4 | 2 |
| PAS | 3 | 4 | 2 |
| SHT | 99 | 99 | 3 |
| BLK | 1 | 2 | 2 |
| CAT | 5 | 6 | 2 |
| RNG | 10 | 11 | 2 |
| REC | 10 | 11 | 2 |
| SPD | 60 | – | – |
| RCH | 60 | – | – |

### BARTHELLO

| Scout Level: | MAX |
|---|---|
| Contract Duration: | 10 |
| CP Needed to Sign: | 40 |
| Special Shot: | Corkscrew Shot |

| STAT | START | MAX | OPT PTS |
|---|---|---|---|
| END | 4 | 42 | 7 |
| ATK | 3 | 20 | 5 |
| PAS | 6 | 18 | 4 |
| SHT | 39 | 94 | 9 |
| BLK | 4 | 31 | 7 |
| CAT | 41 | 92 | 5 |
| RNG | 5 | 71 | 6 |
| REC | 33 | 90 | 5 |
| SPD | 30 | – | – |
| RCH | 60 | – | – |

### YUYUI

| Scout Level: | MAX |
|---|---|
| Contract Duration: | 10 |
| CP Needed to Sign: | 40 |
| Special Shot: | N/A |

| STAT | START | MAX | OPT PTS |
|---|---|---|---|
| END | 1 | 99 | 1 |
| ATK | 1 | 99 | 1 |
| PAS | 1 | 99 | 1 |
| SHT | 1 | 99 | 1 |
| BLK | 1 | 99 | 1 |
| CAT | 1 | 99 | 1 |
| RNG | 1 | 255 | 1 |
| REC | 1 | 255 | 1 |
| SPD | 30 | – | – |
| RCH | 60 | – | – |

Characters

Garment Grids & Dresspheres

Battle System

Accessories

Items and Item Shops

Walkthrough

Mini-Games

Fiends and Enemies

# LEARNING THE AL BHED LANGUAGE

| | |
|---|---|
| **When Available:** | Chapters 1, 2, 3, 4, and 5 |
| **Location:** | Throughout Spira |
| **Objective:** | Collect all 26 primers to master the Al Bhed language. |

If you played *FINAL FANTASY X*, then you should know that the only way to learn the Al Bhed language is to acquire all of the Al Bhed Primers and learn each letter. After acquiring some of the Primers, you'll notice that when someone speaks to you in Al Bhed, some of the letters appear pink in color. There are 26 volumes of the Primers and each one teaches you a different letter. After collecting all of the Primers, you'll find that you can understand Al Bhed perfectly!

## SO THAT'S WHAT THEY WERE SAYING!

*If scouring Spira for Primers isn't for you, wait until you play the game a second time with the "New Game Plus" file. This file enables you to start the game with all the Al Bhed primers you previously collected and allows you to search the game for the ones you missed.*

## OBTAINING THE AL BHED PRIMERS

The following table indicates how to acquire all 26 volumes of the Al Bhed Primer. Now you have no excuse not to get them all!

| LOCATION | CH # 1 | 2 | 3 | 4 | 5 | # OF COPIES | HOW TO OBTAIN |
|---|---|---|---|---|---|---|---|
| Bikanel Desert | X | X | X | - | X | 6 | During the Digging mini-game, you can find Al Bhed Primers scattered throughout the desert. |
| Celsius | X | - | - | - | - | 3 | After finishing the first mission, talk to Brother. You can get up to three volumes. |
| Celsius | X | - | - | - | - | 1 | After finishing the first mission, and before you hear Brother's broadcast, talk to Buddy. |
| Djose Temple | X | X | - | - | - | 1 | Sign up for the Digging mini-game with Gippal at Djose Temple; he will relinquish one volume. |
| Lake Macalania | X | X | - | - | - | 1 | Speak to the Al Bhed woman in front of the Travel Agency before the "Follow That O'aka" mission begins. |
| Bikanel Desert | X | - | - | - | - | 1 | You get this volume on your first visit to Bikanel Desert. |
| Luca | X | - | - | - | - | 1 | After finishing the mission "Behind the Scenes" in Luca, look for Rin in the locker room area of Luca Stadium. |
| Celsius | - | X | - | - | - | 1 | Speak with Shinra at the start of Chapter 2. |
| Djose Temple | - | X | - | - | - | 1 | Speak to Gippal at the Temple. |
| Djose Temple | - | - | X | - | - | 1 | Before the Hotspot link to Djose Temple appears in Chapter 2, go to the Temple and speak with Gippal. |
| Djose Temple | - | - | X | - | - | 1 | Start the "No Way, Djose" mission. |
| Lake Macalania | - | - | X | - | - | 1 | Complete the "Secure the Agency" mission. |
| Celsius | - | - | - | X | - | 1 | At the start of Chapter 4, talk to Paine on the deck of the Celsius and return to the bridge. |
| Djose Temple (CommSphere) | - | - | - | X | - | 1 | Watch the first event through the Djose Temple CommSphere. |
| Djose Temple (CommSphere) | - | - | - | X | - | 1 | Watch the sixth event through the Djose Temple CommSphere. |
| Macalania Woods (CommSphere) | - | - | - | X | - | 1 | Watch the first event through the Macalania CommSphere. |
| Djose Temple | - | - | - | - | X | 1 | You win this one when you defeat the Experiment in the "Masterpiece Theatre" mission inside Djose Temple. |
| Thunder Plains | - | - | - | - | X | 1 | Complete the "A Fallen Genius" mission in Thunder Plains by rescuing Cid. |
| Celsius | | | | | X | 1 | Watch the scene in which Buddy and Brother talk on the deck of the Celsius. |

# FIENDS & ENEMIES

Characters

1

Garment Grids & Dresspheres

2

Battle System

3

Accessories

4

Items and Item Shops

5

Walkthrough

6

Mini Games

7

Fiends and Enemies

8

## LEGEND

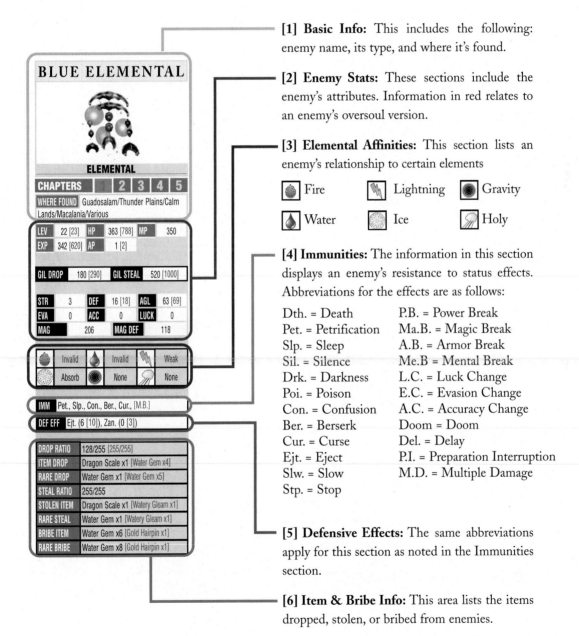

**BLUE ELEMENTAL**

ELEMENTAL

| CHAPTERS | | 2 | 3 | 4 | 5 |
| --- | --- | --- | --- | --- | --- |

| WHERE FOUND | Guadosalam/Thunder Plains/Calm Lands/Macalania/Various |
| --- | --- |

| LEV | 22 [23] | HP | 363 [788] | MP | 350 |
| --- | --- | --- | --- | --- | --- |
| EXP | 342 [620] | AP | 1 [2] | | |

| GIL DROP | 180 [290] | GIL STEAL | 520 [1000] |
| --- | --- | --- | --- |

| STR | 3 | DEF | 16 [18] | AGL | 63 [69] |
| --- | --- | --- | --- | --- | --- |
| EVA | 0 | ACC | 0 | LUCK | 0 |
| MAG | 206 | MAG DEF | 118 | | |

| | Invalid | | Invalid | | Weak |
| --- | --- | --- | --- | --- | --- |
| | Absorb | | None | | None |

| IMM | Pet., Slp., Con., Ber., Cur., [M.B.] |
| --- | --- |

| DEF EFF | Ejt. (6 [10]), Zan. (0 [3]) |
| --- | --- |

| DROP RATIO | 128/255 [255/255] |
| --- | --- |
| ITEM DROP | Dragon Scale x1 [Water Gem x4] |
| RARE DROP | Water Gem x1 [Water Gem x5] |
| STEAL RATIO | 255/255 |
| STOLEN ITEM | Dragon Scale x1 [Watery Gleam x1] |
| RARE STEAL | Water Gem x1 [Watery Gleam x1] |
| BRIBE ITEM | Water Gem x6 [Gold Hairpin x1] |
| RARE BRIBE | Water Gem x8 [Gold Hairpin x1] |

**[1] Basic Info:** This includes the following: enemy name, its type, and where it's found.

**[2] Enemy Stats:** These sections include the enemy's attributes. Information in red relates to an enemy's oversoul version.

**[3] Elemental Affinities:** This section lists an enemy's relationship to certain elements

 Fire     Lightning     Gravity

 Water    Ice    Holy

**[4] Immunities:** The information in this section displays an enemy's resistance to status effects. Abbreviations for the effects are as follows:

Dth. = Death
Pet. = Petrification
Slp. = Sleep
Sil. = Silence
Drk. = Darkness
Poi. = Poison
Con. = Confusion
Ber. = Berserk
Cur. = Curse
Ejt. = Eject
Slw. = Slow
Stp. = Stop

P.B. = Power Break
Ma.B. = Magic Break
A.B. = Armor Break
Me.B = Mental Break
L.C. = Luck Change
E.C. = Evasion Change
A.C. = Accuracy Change
Doom = Doom
Del. = Delay
P.I. = Preparation Interruption
M.D. = Multiple Damage

**[5] Defensive Effects:** The same abbreviations apply for this section as noted in the Immunities section.

**[6] Item & Bribe Info:** This area lists the items dropped, stolen, or bribed from enemies.

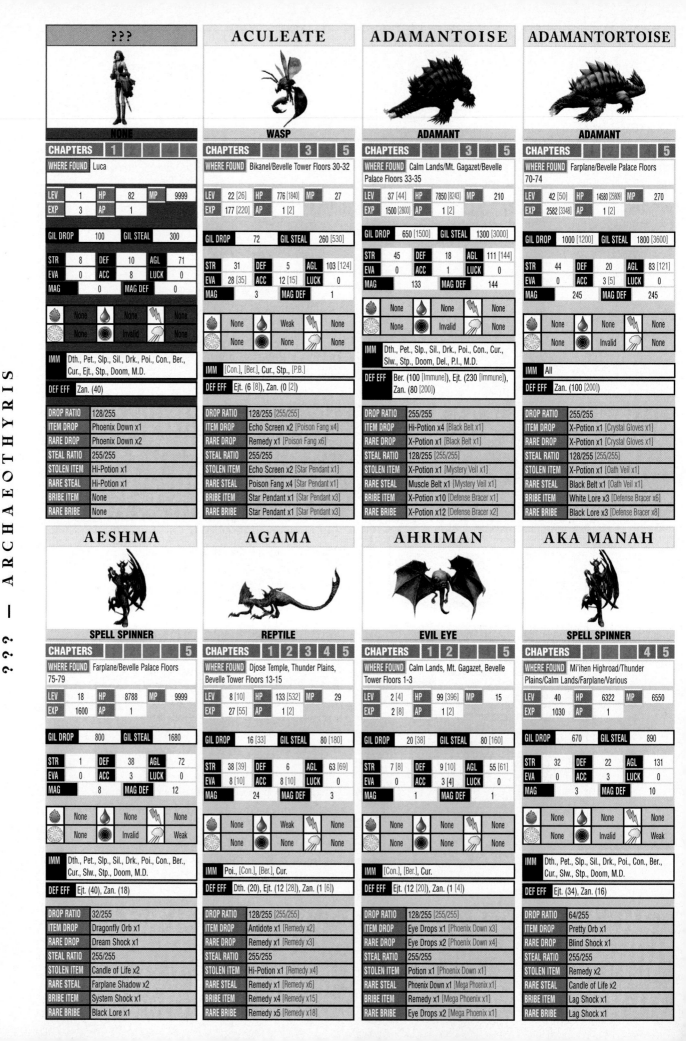

## ??? 

**NONE**

| CHAPTERS | 1 | | | |
|---|---|---|---|---|

**WHERE FOUND** Luca

| LEV | 1 | HP | 82 | MP | 9999 |
|---|---|---|---|---|---|
| EXP | 3 | AP | 1 | | |

| GIL DROP | 100 | GIL STEAL | 300 |
|---|---|---|---|

| STR | 8 | DEF | 10 | AGL | 71 |
|---|---|---|---|---|---|
| EVA | 0 | ACC | 8 | LUCK | 0 |
| MAG | 0 | MAG DEF | 0 | | |

Fire None / Water None / Thunder None / Ice None / Holy Invalid / Gravity None

IMM Dth., Pet., Slp., Sil., Drk., Poi., Con., Ber., Cur., Ejt., Stp., Doom, M.D.

DEF EFF Zan. (40)

| DROP RATIO | 128/255 |
|---|---|
| ITEM DROP | Phoenix Down x1 |
| RARE DROP | Phoenix Down x2 |
| STEAL RATIO | 255/255 |
| STOLEN ITEM | Hi-Potion x1 |
| RARE STEAL | Hi-Potion x1 |
| BRIBE ITEM | None |
| RARE BRIBE | None |

## ACULEATE

**WASP**

| CHAPTERS | | | 3 | | 5 |
|---|---|---|---|---|---|

**WHERE FOUND** Bikanel/Bevelle Tower Floors 30-32

| LEV | 22 [26] | HP | 776 [1840] | MP | 27 |
|---|---|---|---|---|---|
| EXP | 177 [220] | AP | 1 [2] | | |

| GIL DROP | 72 | GIL STEAL | 260 [530] |
|---|---|---|---|

| STR | 31 | DEF | 5 | AGL | 103 [124] |
|---|---|---|---|---|---|
| EVA | 28 [35] | ACC | 12 [15] | LUCK | 0 |
| MAG | 3 | MAG DEF | 1 | | |

Fire None / Water Weak / Thunder None / Ice None / Holy None / Gravity None

IMM [Con.], [Ber.], Cur., Stp., [P.B.]

DEF EFF Ejt. (6 [8]), Zan. (0 [2])

| DROP RATIO | 128/255 [255/255] |
|---|---|
| ITEM DROP | Echo Screen x2 [Poison Fang x4] |
| RARE DROP | Remedy x1 [Poison Fang x6] |
| STEAL RATIO | 255/255 |
| STOLEN ITEM | Echo Screen x2 [Star Pendant x1] |
| RARE STEAL | Poison Fang x4 [Star Pendant x1] |
| BRIBE ITEM | Star Pendant x1 [Star Pendant x3] |
| RARE BRIBE | Star Pendant x1 [Star Pendant x3] |

## ADAMANTOISE

**ADAMANT**

| CHAPTERS | | | 3 | | 5 |
|---|---|---|---|---|---|

**WHERE FOUND** Calm Lands/Mt. Gagazet/Bevelle Palace Floors 33-35

| LEV | 37 [44] | HP | 7850 [8243] | MP | 210 |
|---|---|---|---|---|---|
| EXP | 1500 [2800] | AP | 1 [2] | | |

| GIL DROP | 650 [1500] | GIL STEAL | 1300 [3000] |
|---|---|---|---|

| STR | 45 | DEF | 18 | AGL | 111 [144] |
|---|---|---|---|---|---|
| EVA | 0 | ACC | 1 | LUCK | 0 |
| MAG | 133 | MAG DEF | 144 | | |

Fire None / Water None / Thunder None / Ice None / Holy Invalid / Gravity None

IMM Dth., Pet., Slp., Sil., Drk., Poi., Con., Cur., Slw., Stp., Doom, Del., P.I., M.D.

DEF EFF Ber. (100 [Immune]), Ejt. (230 [Immune]), Zan. (80 [200])

| DROP RATIO | 255/255 |
|---|---|
| ITEM DROP | Hi-Potion x4 [Black Belt x1] |
| RARE DROP | X-Potion x1 [Black Belt x1] |
| STEAL RATIO | 128/255 [255/255] |
| STOLEN ITEM | X-Potion x1 [Mystery Veil x1] |
| RARE STEAL | Muscle Belt x1 [Mystery Veil x1] |
| BRIBE ITEM | X-Potion x10 [Defense Bracer x1] |
| RARE BRIBE | X-Potion x12 [Defense Bracer x2] |

## ADAMANTORTOISE

**ADAMANT**

| CHAPTERS | | | | | 5 |
|---|---|---|---|---|---|

**WHERE FOUND** Farplane/Bevelle Palace Floors 70-74

| LEV | 42 [50] | HP | 14580 [25809] | MP | 270 |
|---|---|---|---|---|---|
| EXP | 2582 [3348] | AP | 1 [2] | | |

| GIL DROP | 1000 [1200] | GIL STEAL | 1800 [3600] |
|---|---|---|---|

| STR | 44 | DEF | 20 | AGL | 83 [121] |
|---|---|---|---|---|---|
| EVA | 0 | ACC | 3 [5] | LUCK | 0 |
| MAG | 245 | MAG DEF | 245 | | |

Fire None / Water None / Thunder None / Ice None / Holy Invalid / Gravity None

IMM All

DEF EFF Zan. (100 [200])

| DROP RATIO | 255/255 |
|---|---|
| ITEM DROP | X-Potion x1 [Crystal Gloves x1] |
| RARE DROP | X-Potion x1 [Crystal Gloves x1] |
| STEAL RATIO | 128/255 [255/255] |
| STOLEN ITEM | X-Potion x1 [Oath Veil x1] |
| RARE STEAL | Black Belt x1 [Oath Veil x1] |
| BRIBE ITEM | White Lore x3 [Defense Bracer x6] |
| RARE BRIBE | Black Lore x3 [Defense Bracer x8] |

## AESHMA

**SPELL SPINNER**

| CHAPTERS | | | | | 5 |
|---|---|---|---|---|---|

**WHERE FOUND** Farplane/Bevelle Palace Floors 75-79

| LEV | 18 | HP | 8788 | MP | 9999 |
|---|---|---|---|---|---|
| EXP | 1600 | AP | 1 | | |

| GIL DROP | 800 | GIL STEAL | 1680 |
|---|---|---|---|

| STR | 1 | DEF | 38 | AGL | 72 |
|---|---|---|---|---|---|
| EVA | 0 | ACC | 3 | LUCK | 0 |
| MAG | 8 | MAG DEF | 12 | | |

Fire None / Water None / Thunder None / Ice None / Holy Invalid / Gravity Weak

IMM Dth., Pet., Slp., Sil., Drk., Poi., Con., Ber., Cur., Slw., Stp., Doom, M.D.

DEF EFF Ejt. (40), Zan. (18)

| DROP RATIO | 32/255 |
|---|---|
| ITEM DROP | Dragonfly Orb x1 |
| RARE DROP | Dream Shock x1 |
| STEAL RATIO | 255/255 |
| STOLEN ITEM | Candle of Life x2 |
| RARE STEAL | Farplane Shadow x2 |
| BRIBE ITEM | System Shock x1 |
| RARE BRIBE | Black Lore x1 |

## AGAMA

**REPTILE**

| CHAPTERS | 1 | 2 | 3 | 4 | 5 |
|---|---|---|---|---|---|

**WHERE FOUND** Djose Temple, Thunder Plains, Bevelle Tower Floors 13-15

| LEV | 8 [10] | HP | 133 [532] | MP | 29 |
|---|---|---|---|---|---|
| EXP | 27 [55] | AP | 1 [2] | | |

| GIL DROP | 16 [33] | GIL STEAL | 80 [180] |
|---|---|---|---|

| STR | 38 [39] | DEF | 6 | AGL | 63 [69] |
|---|---|---|---|---|---|
| EVA | 8 [10] | ACC | 8 [10] | LUCK | 0 |
| MAG | 24 | MAG DEF | 3 | | |

Fire None / Water Weak / Thunder None / Ice None / Holy None / Gravity None

IMM Poi., [Con.], [Ber.], Cur.

DEF EFF Dth. (20), Ejt. (12 [28]), Zan. (1 [6])

| DROP RATIO | 128/255 [255/255] |
|---|---|
| ITEM DROP | Antidote x1 [Remedy x2] |
| RARE DROP | Remedy x1 [Remedy x3] |
| STEAL RATIO | 255/255 |
| STOLEN ITEM | Hi-Potion x1 [Remedy x4] |
| RARE STEAL | Remedy x1 [Remedy x6] |
| BRIBE ITEM | Remedy x4 [Remedy x15] |
| RARE BRIBE | Remedy x5 [Remedy x18] |

## AHRIMAN

**EVIL EYE**

| CHAPTERS | 1 | 2 | | | 5 |
|---|---|---|---|---|---|

**WHERE FOUND** Calm Lands, Mt. Gagazet, Bevelle Tower Floors 1-3

| LEV | 2 [4] | HP | 99 [396] | MP | 15 |
|---|---|---|---|---|---|
| EXP | 2 [8] | AP | 1 [2] | | |

| GIL DROP | 20 [38] | GIL STEAL | 80 [160] |
|---|---|---|---|

| STR | 7 [8] | DEF | 9 [10] | AGL | 55 [61] |
|---|---|---|---|---|---|
| EVA | 0 | ACC | 3 [4] | LUCK | 0 |
| MAG | 1 | MAG DEF | 1 | | |

Fire None / Water None / Thunder None / Ice None / Holy None / Gravity None

IMM [Con.], [Ber.], Cur.

DEF EFF Ejt. (12 [20]), Zan. (1 [4])

| DROP RATIO | 128/255 [255/255] |
|---|---|
| ITEM DROP | Eye Drops x1 [Phoenix Down x3] |
| RARE DROP | Eye Drops x2 [Phoenix Down x4] |
| STEAL RATIO | 255/255 |
| STOLEN ITEM | Potion x1 [Phoenix Down x1] |
| RARE STEAL | Phoenix Down x1 [Mega Phoenix x1] |
| BRIBE ITEM | Remedy x1 [Mega Phoenix x1] |
| RARE BRIBE | Eye Drops x2 [Mega Phoenix x1] |

## AKA MANAH

**SPELL SPINNER**

| CHAPTERS | | | | 4 | 5 |
|---|---|---|---|---|---|

**WHERE FOUND** Mi'ihen Highroad/Thunder Plains/Calm Lands/Farplane/Various

| LEV | 40 | HP | 6322 | MP | 6550 |
|---|---|---|---|---|---|
| EXP | 1030 | AP | 1 | | |

| GIL DROP | 670 | GIL STEAL | 890 |
|---|---|---|---|

| STR | 32 | DEF | 22 | AGL | 131 |
|---|---|---|---|---|---|
| EVA | 0 | ACC | 3 | LUCK | 0 |
| MAG | 3 | MAG DEF | 10 | | |

Fire None / Water None / Thunder None / Ice None / Holy Invalid / Gravity Weak

IMM Dth., Pet., Slp., Sil., Drk., Poi., Con., Ber., Cur., Slw., Stp., Doom, M.D.

DEF EFF Ejt. (34), Zan. (16)

| DROP RATIO | 64/255 |
|---|---|
| ITEM DROP | Pretty Orb x1 |
| RARE DROP | Blind Shock x1 |
| STEAL RATIO | 255/255 |
| STOLEN ITEM | Remedy x2 |
| RARE STEAL | Candle of Life x2 |
| BRIBE ITEM | Lag Shock x1 |
| RARE BRIBE | Lag Shock x1 |

Characters

1

Garment Grids & Dressspheres

2

Battle System

3

Accessories

4

Items and Item Shops

5

Walkthrough

6

Mini Games

7

Fiends and Enemies

8

# AMORPHOUS GEL

**GEL**

| CHAPTERS | 1 | 2 | 3 | | 5 |
|---|---|---|---|---|---|
| WHERE FOUND | Macalania/Calm Lands/Bevelle Tower Floors 27-29 | | | | |

| LEV | 28 [34] | HP | 973 [2333] | MP | 999 |
|---|---|---|---|---|---|
| EXP | 480 [780] | AP | 1 [2] | | |

| GIL DROP | 380 [520] | GIL STEAL | 720 [1430] |
|---|---|---|---|

| STR | 18 | DEF | 58 | AGL | 82 [98] |
|---|---|---|---|---|---|
| EVA | 0 | ACC | 4 [5] | LUCK | 0 |
| MAG | 255 | MAG DEF | 0 | | |

| | Absorb | | Weak | | Invalid |
|---|---|---|---|---|---|
| | Invalid | | Invalid | | None |

| IMM | All *but* Ejt., P.B., M.B., A.B., M.B. |
|---|---|
| DEF EFF | Ejt. (180 [Immune]), Zan. (20 [25]) |

| DROP RATIO | 128/255 [255/255] |
|---|---|
| ITEM DROP | Blue Ring x1 [Cerulean Ring x1] |
| RARE DROP | Blue Ring x1 [Cerulean Ring] |
| STEAL RATIO | 64/255 [255/255] |
| STOLEN ITEM | White Ring x1 [Water Gem x3] |
| RARE STEAL | White Ring x1 [Water Gem x4] |
| BRIBE ITEM | Blue Ring x1 [Cerulean Ring x1] |
| RARE BRIBE | Blue Ring x1 [Short Circuit x1] |

# ANGRA MAINYU

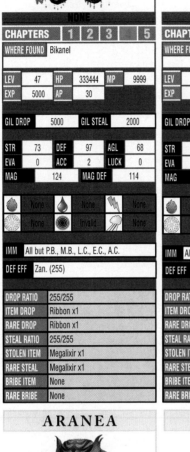

**NONE**

| CHAPTERS | 1 | 2 | 3 | | 5 |
|---|---|---|---|---|---|
| WHERE FOUND | Bikanel | | | | |

| LEV | 47 | HP | 333444 | MP | 9999 |
|---|---|---|---|---|---|
| EXP | 5000 | AP | 30 | | |

| GIL DROP | 5000 | GIL STEAL | 2000 |
|---|---|---|---|

| STR | 73 | DEF | 97 | AGL | 68 |
|---|---|---|---|---|---|
| EVA | 0 | ACC | 2 | LUCK | 0 |
| MAG | 124 | MAG DEF | 114 | | |

| | None | | None | | None |
|---|---|---|---|---|---|
| | None | | Invalid | | None |

| IMM | All but P.B., M.B., L.C., E.C., A.C. |
|---|---|
| DEF EFF | Zan. (255) |

| DROP RATIO | 255/255 |
|---|---|
| ITEM DROP | Ribbon x1 |
| RARE DROP | Ribbon x1 |
| STEAL RATIO | 255/255 |
| STOLEN ITEM | Megalixir x1 |
| RARE STEAL | Megalixir x1 |
| BRIBE ITEM | None |
| RARE BRIBE | None |

# ANIMA

**NONE**

| CHAPTERS | | | | | 5 |
|---|---|---|---|---|---|
| WHERE FOUND | Farplane | | | | |

| LEV | 43 | HP | 3600 | MP | 9999 |
|---|---|---|---|---|---|
| EXP | 6000 | AP | 15 | | |

| GIL DROP | 2000 | GIL STEAL | 4000 |
|---|---|---|---|

| STR | 32 | DEF | 33 | AGL | 133 |
|---|---|---|---|---|---|
| EVA | 0 | ACC | 5 | LUCK | 0 |
| MAG | 84 | MAG DEF | 42 | | |

| | Half | | Half | | Half |
|---|---|---|---|---|---|
| | Half | | Absorb | | Weak |

| IMM | All |
|---|---|
| DEF EFF | Zan. (110) |

| DROP RATIO | 255/255 |
|---|---|
| ITEM DROP | Tetra Band x1 |
| RARE DROP | Tetra Band x1 |
| STEAL RATIO | 128/255 |
| STOLEN ITEM | Fury Shock x1 |
| RARE STEAL | Fury Shock x1 |
| BRIBE ITEM | None |
| RARE BRIBE | None |

# ANYTHING EATER

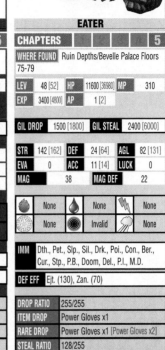

**EATER**

| CHAPTERS | | | | | 5 |
|---|---|---|---|---|---|
| WHERE FOUND | Ruin Depths/Bevelle Palace Floors 75-79 | | | | |

| LEV | 48 [52] | HP | 11600 [36980] | MP | 310 |
|---|---|---|---|---|---|
| EXP | 3400 [4800] | AP | 1 [2] | | |

| GIL DROP | 1500 [1800] | GIL STEAL | 2400 [6000] |
|---|---|---|---|

| STR | 142 [162] | DEF | 24 [64] | AGL | 82 [131] |
|---|---|---|---|---|---|
| EVA | 0 | ACC | 11 [14] | LUCK | 0 |
| MAG | 38 | MAG DEF | 22 | | |

| | None | | None | | None |
|---|---|---|---|---|---|
| | None | | Invalid | | None |

| IMM | Dth., Pet., Slp., Sil., Drk., Poi., Con., Ber., Cur., Stp., P.B., Doom, Del., P.I., M.D. |
|---|---|
| DEF EFF | Ejt. (130), Zan. (70) |

| DROP RATIO | 255/255 |
|---|---|
| ITEM DROP | Power Gloves x1 |
| RARE DROP | Power Gloves x1 [Power Gloves x2] |
| STEAL RATIO | 128/255 |
| STOLEN ITEM | Mega Potion x1 |
| RARE STEAL | Mega Potion x2 [Elixir x1] |
| BRIBE ITEM | White Lore x3 [Kaiser Knuckles x1] |
| RARE BRIBE | White Lore x4 [Kaiser Knuckles x1] |

# AQUILA

**BIRD**

| CHAPTERS | | | 3 | | 5 |
|---|---|---|---|---|---|
| WHERE FOUND | Bikanel, Bevelle Tower Floors 44-46 | | | | |

| LEV | 22 [26] | HP | 1897 [4843] | MP | 42 |
|---|---|---|---|---|---|
| EXP | 102 [130] | AP | 1 [2] | | |

| GIL DROP | 55 [85] | GIL STEAL | 240 [448] |
|---|---|---|---|

| STR | 44 | DEF | 24 | AGL | 130 [156] |
|---|---|---|---|---|---|
| EVA | 56 [74] | ACC | 16 [20] | LUCK | 0 |
| MAG | 4 | MAG DEF | 6 | | |

| | None | | None | | None |
|---|---|---|---|---|---|
| | None | | None | | None |

| IMM | [Con.], [Ber.], Cur. |
|---|---|
| DEF EFF | Ejt. (8 [12]), Zan. (0 [3]) |

| DROP RATIO | 128/255 [255/255] |
|---|---|
| ITEM DROP | Hi-Potion x1 [Hi-Potion x4] |
| RARE DROP | Hi-Potion x2 [Hi-Potion x6] |
| STEAL RATIO | 255/255 |
| STOLEN ITEM | Hi-Potion x1 [Mega Potion x1] |
| RARE STEAL | Hi-Potion x2 [Mega Potion x2] |
| BRIBE ITEM | Hi-Potion x20 [X-Potion x12] |
| RARE BRIBE | Hi-Potion x24 [X-Potion x16] |

# ARANEA

**ARACHNID**

| CHAPTERS | | | | | 5 |
|---|---|---|---|---|---|
| WHERE FOUND | Bevelle Tower Floors 20, 81-99 | | | | |

| LEV | 52 [62] | HP | 18280 [33394] | MP | 178 |
|---|---|---|---|---|---|
| EXP | 4000 [7500] | AP | 1 [2] | | |

| GIL DROP | 800 [2500] | GIL STEAL | 2200 [4200] |
|---|---|---|---|

| STR | 74 [104] | DEF | 63 [93] | AGL | 72 [115] |
|---|---|---|---|---|---|
| EVA | 0 | ACC | 16 [20] | LUCK | 0 |
| MAG | 44 | MAG DEF | 12 | | |

| | None | | None | | None |
|---|---|---|---|---|---|
| | None | | Invalid | | None |

| IMM | All *but* Ejt. |
|---|---|
| DEF EFF | Ejt. (100 [110]), Zan. (80 [100]) |

| DROP RATIO | 255/255 |
|---|---|
| ITEM DROP | Stamina Tonic x1 [Stamina Tonic x2] |
| RARE DROP | Mythril Bangle x1 [Crystal Bangle x1] |
| STEAL RATIO | 64/255 [32/255] |
| STOLEN ITEM | Turbo Ether x1 [Turbo Ether 2] |
| RARE STEAL | Kinesis Badge x1 [Kinesis Badge x2] |
| BRIBE ITEM | Black Lore x5 [Sword Tome x10] |
| RARE BRIBE | Sword Tome x8 [Sword Tome x16] |

# ARAST

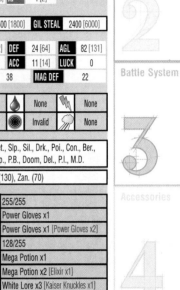

**IMP**

| CHAPTERS | | | | | 5 |
|---|---|---|---|---|---|
| WHERE FOUND | Farplane/Bevelle Palace Floors 65-69 | | | | |

| LEV | 29 | HP | 2742 | MP | 650 |
|---|---|---|---|---|---|
| EXP | 880 | AP | 1 | | |

| GIL DROP | 330 | GIL STEAL | 880 |
|---|---|---|---|

| STR | 21 | DEF | 44 | AGL | 64 |
|---|---|---|---|---|---|
| EVA | 36 | ACC | 0 | LUCK | 0 |
| MAG | 24 | MAG DEF | 223 | | |

| | Weak | | Invalid | | Invalid |
|---|---|---|---|---|---|
| | Invalid | | None | | None |

| IMM | Sil., Con., Ber., Cur., Slw., Stp., M.B., Doom |
|---|---|
| DEF EFF | Dth. (100), Pet. (70), Slp. (60), Drk. (40), Poi. (60), Ejt. (20), Zan. (2) |

| DROP RATIO | 128/255 |
|---|---|
| ITEM DROP | Holy Water x2 |
| RARE DROP | Holy Water x3 |
| STEAL RATIO | 255/255 |
| STOLEN ITEM | Dispel Tonic x2 |
| RARE STEAL | Dispel Tonic x3 |
| BRIBE ITEM | Turbo Ether x6 |
| RARE BRIBE | Turbo Ether x8 |

# ARCHAEOTHYRIS

**REPTILE**

| CHAPTERS | | | 3 | 4 | 5 |
|---|---|---|---|---|---|
| WHERE FOUND | Mushroom Rock/Djose Temple/Guadosalam/Thunder Plains/Others | | | | |

| LEV | 32 [38] | HP | 1332 [3230] | MP | 58 |
|---|---|---|---|---|---|
| EXP | 188 [334] | AP | 1 [2] | | |

| GIL DROP | 110 [198] | GIL STEAL | 420 [780] |
|---|---|---|---|

| STR | 36 | DEF | 17 | AGL | 85 [102] |
|---|---|---|---|---|---|
| EVA | 35 [44] | ACC | 8 [10] | LUCK | 0 |
| MAG | 33 [44] | MAG DEF | 5 | | |

| | None | | Weak | | None |
|---|---|---|---|---|---|
| | None | | None | | None |

| IMM | Poi., [Con.], [Ber.], Cur. |
|---|---|
| DEF EFF | Ejt. (14 [29]), Zan. (1 [7]) |

| DROP RATIO | 128/255 [255/255] |
|---|---|
| ITEM DROP | Eye Drops x2 [Remedy x2] |
| RARE DROP | Remedy x1 [Remedy x3] |
| STEAL RATIO | 255/255 |
| STOLEN ITEM | Eye Drops x2 [Remedy x3] |
| RARE STEAL | Remedy x2 [Remedy x8] |
| BRIBE ITEM | Star Pendant x1 [Haste Ring x2] |
| RARE BRIBE | Star Pendant x2 [Haste Ring x3] |

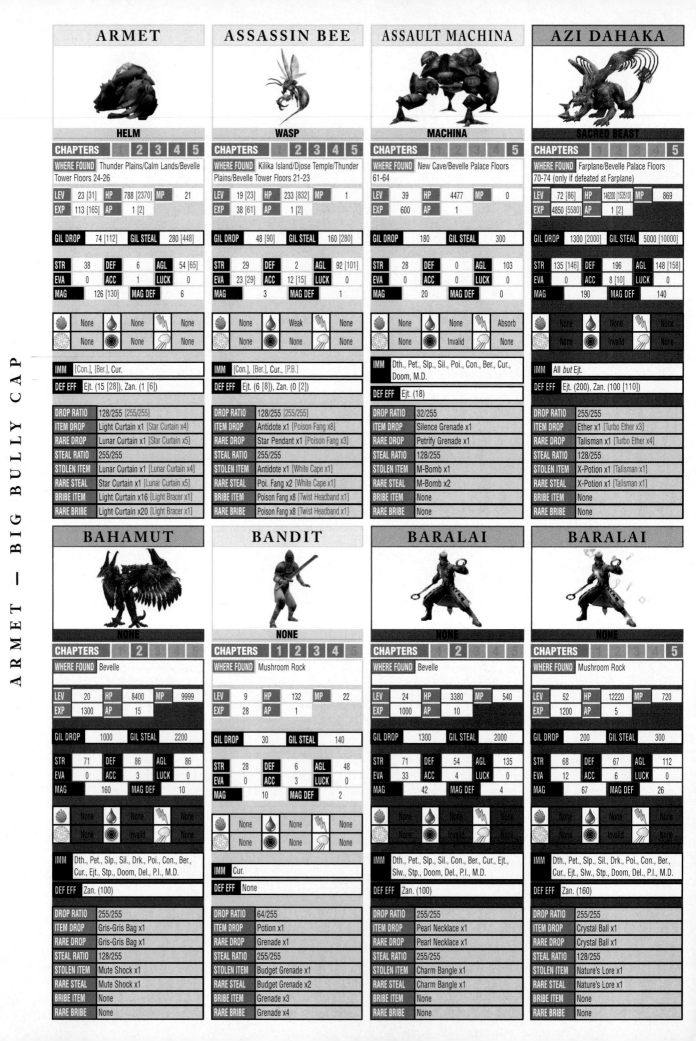

## ARMET

**HELM**

| CHAPTERS | 1 | 2 | 3 | 4 | 5 |
|---|---|---|---|---|---|

**WHERE FOUND** Thunder Plains/Calm Lands/Bevelle Tower Floors 24-26

| LEV | 23 [31] | HP | 788 [2370] | MP | 21 |
|---|---|---|---|---|---|
| EXP | 113 [165] | AP | 1 [2] | | |

| GIL DROP | 74 [112] | GIL STEAL | 280 [448] |
|---|---|---|---|

| STR | 38 | DEF | 6 | AGL | 54 [65] |
|---|---|---|---|---|---|
| EVA | 0 | ACC | 1 | LUCK | 0 |
| MAG | 126 [130] | MAG DEF | 6 | | |

| | None | | None | | None |
|---|---|---|---|---|---|
| | None | | None | | None |

**IMM** [Con.], [Ber.], Cur.

**DEF EFF** Ejt. (15 [28]), Zan. (1 [6])

| DROP RATIO | 128/255 [255/255] |
|---|---|
| ITEM DROP | Light Curtain x1 [Star Curtain x4] |
| RARE DROP | Lunar Curtain x1 [Star Curtain x5] |
| STEAL RATIO | 255/255 |
| STOLEN ITEM | Lunar Curtain x1 [Lunar Curtain x4] |
| RARE STEAL | Star Curtain x1 [Lunar Curtain x5] |
| BRIBE ITEM | Light Curtain x16 [Light Bracer x1] |
| RARE BRIBE | Light Curtain x20 [Light Bracer x1] |

## ASSASSIN BEE

**WASP**

| CHAPTERS | 1 | 2 | 3 | 4 | 5 |
|---|---|---|---|---|---|

**WHERE FOUND** Kilika Island/Djose Temple/Thunder Plains/Bevelle Tower Floors 21-23

| LEV | 19 [23] | HP | 233 [832] | MP | 1 |
|---|---|---|---|---|---|
| EXP | 38 [61] | AP | 1 [2] | | |

| GIL DROP | 48 [90] | GIL STEAL | 160 [280] |
|---|---|---|---|

| STR | 29 | DEF | 2 | AGL | 92 [101] |
|---|---|---|---|---|---|
| EVA | 23 [29] | ACC | 12 [15] | LUCK | 0 |
| MAG | 3 | MAG DEF | 1 | | |

| | None | | Weak | | None |
|---|---|---|---|---|---|
| | None | | None | | None |

**IMM** [Con.], [Ber.], Cur., [P.B.]

**DEF EFF** Ejt. (6 [8]), Zan. (0 [2])

| DROP RATIO | 128/255 [255/255] |
|---|---|
| ITEM DROP | Antidote x1 [Poison Fang x8] |
| RARE DROP | Star Pendant x1 [Poison Fang x3] |
| STEAL RATIO | 255/255 |
| STOLEN ITEM | Antidote x1 [White Cape x1] |
| RARE STEAL | Poi. Fang x2 [White Cape x1] |
| BRIBE ITEM | Poison Fang x8 [Twist Headband x1] |
| RARE BRIBE | Poison Fang x8 [Twist Headband x1] |

## ASSAULT MACHINA

**MACHINA**

| CHAPTERS | 1 | 2 | 3 | 4 | 5 |
|---|---|---|---|---|---|

**WHERE FOUND** New Cave/Bevelle Palace Floors 61-64

| LEV | 39 | HP | 4477 | MP | 0 |
|---|---|---|---|---|---|
| EXP | 600 | AP | 1 | | |

| GIL DROP | 180 | GIL STEAL | 300 |
|---|---|---|---|

| STR | 28 | DEF | 0 | AGL | 103 |
|---|---|---|---|---|---|
| EVA | 0 | ACC | 0 | LUCK | 0 |
| MAG | 20 | MAG DEF | 0 | | |

| | None | | None | | Absorb |
|---|---|---|---|---|---|
| | None | | Invalid | | None |

**IMM** Dth., Pet., Slp., Sil., Poi., Con., Ber., Cur., Doom, M.D.

**DEF EFF** Ejt. (18)

| DROP RATIO | 32/255 |
|---|---|
| ITEM DROP | Silence Grenade x1 |
| RARE DROP | Petrify Grenade x1 |
| STEAL RATIO | 128/255 |
| STOLEN ITEM | M-Bomb x1 |
| RARE STEAL | M-Bomb x2 |
| BRIBE ITEM | None |
| RARE BRIBE | None |

## AZI DAHAKA

**SACRED BEAST**

| CHAPTERS | 1 | 2 | 3 | 4 | 5 |
|---|---|---|---|---|---|

**WHERE FOUND** Farplane/Bevelle Palace Floors 70-74 (only if defeated at Farplane)

| LEV | 72 [86] | HP | 146200 [153510] | MP | 869 |
|---|---|---|---|---|---|
| EXP | 4850 [5580] | AP | 1 [2] | | |

| GIL DROP | 1300 [2000] | GIL STEAL | 5000 [10000] |
|---|---|---|---|

| STR | 135 [146] | DEF | 196 | AGL | 148 [158] |
|---|---|---|---|---|---|
| EVA | 0 | ACC | 8 [10] | LUCK | 0 |
| MAG | 190 | MAG DEF | 140 | | |

| | None | | None | | None |
|---|---|---|---|---|---|
| | None | | Invalid | | None |

**IMM** All but Ejt.

**DEF EFF** Ejt. (200), Zan. (100 [110])

| DROP RATIO | 255/255 |
|---|---|
| ITEM DROP | Ether x1 [Turbo Ether x3] |
| RARE DROP | Talisman x1 [Turbo Ether x4] |
| STEAL RATIO | 128/255 |
| STOLEN ITEM | X-Potion x1 [Talisman x1] |
| RARE STEAL | X-Potion x1 [Talisman x1] |
| BRIBE ITEM | None |
| RARE BRIBE | None |

## BAHAMUT

**NONE**

| CHAPTERS | 1 | 2 | 3 | 4 | 5 |
|---|---|---|---|---|---|

**WHERE FOUND** Bevelle

| LEV | 20 | HP | 8400 | MP | 9999 |
|---|---|---|---|---|---|
| EXP | 1300 | AP | 15 | | |

| GIL DROP | 1000 | GIL STEAL | 2200 |
|---|---|---|---|

| STR | 71 | DEF | 86 | AGL | 86 |
|---|---|---|---|---|---|
| EVA | 0 | ACC | 3 | LUCK | 0 |
| MAG | 160 | MAG DEF | 10 | | |

| | None | | None | | None |
|---|---|---|---|---|---|
| | None | | Invalid | | None |

**IMM** Dth., Pet., Slp., Sil., Drk., Poi., Con., Ber., Cur., Ejt., Stp., Doom, Del., P.I., M.D.

**DEF EFF** Zan. (100)

| DROP RATIO | 255/255 |
|---|---|
| ITEM DROP | Gris-Gris Bag x1 |
| RARE DROP | Gris-Gris Bag x1 |
| STEAL RATIO | 128/255 |
| STOLEN ITEM | Mute Shock x1 |
| RARE STEAL | Mute Shock x1 |
| BRIBE ITEM | None |
| RARE BRIBE | None |

## BANDIT

**NONE**

| CHAPTERS | 1 | 2 | 3 | 4 | 5 |
|---|---|---|---|---|---|

**WHERE FOUND** Mushroom Rock

| LEV | 9 | HP | 132 | MP | 22 |
|---|---|---|---|---|---|
| EXP | 28 | AP | 1 | | |

| GIL DROP | 30 | GIL STEAL | 140 |
|---|---|---|---|

| STR | 28 | DEF | 6 | AGL | 48 |
|---|---|---|---|---|---|
| EVA | 0 | ACC | 3 | LUCK | 0 |
| MAG | 10 | MAG DEF | 2 | | |

| | None | | None | | None |
|---|---|---|---|---|---|
| | None | | None | | None |

**IMM** Cur.

**DEF EFF** None

| DROP RATIO | 64/255 |
|---|---|
| ITEM DROP | Potion x1 |
| RARE DROP | Grenade x1 |
| STEAL RATIO | 255/255 |
| STOLEN ITEM | Budget Grenade x1 |
| RARE STEAL | Budget Grenade x2 |
| BRIBE ITEM | Grenade x3 |
| RARE BRIBE | Grenade x4 |

## BARALAI

**NONE**

| CHAPTERS | 1 | 2 | 3 | 4 | 5 |
|---|---|---|---|---|---|

**WHERE FOUND** Bevelle

| LEV | 24 | HP | 3380 | MP | 540 |
|---|---|---|---|---|---|
| EXP | 1000 | AP | 10 | | |

| GIL DROP | 1300 | GIL STEAL | 2000 |
|---|---|---|---|

| STR | 71 | DEF | 54 | AGL | 135 |
|---|---|---|---|---|---|
| EVA | 33 | ACC | 4 | LUCK | 0 |
| MAG | 42 | MAG DEF | 4 | | |

| | None | | None | | None |
|---|---|---|---|---|---|
| | None | | Invalid | | None |

**IMM** Dth., Pet., Slp., Sil., Con., Ber., Cur., Ejt., Slw., Stp., Doom, Del., P.I., M.D.

**DEF EFF** Zan. (100)

| DROP RATIO | 255/255 |
|---|---|
| ITEM DROP | Pearl Necklace x1 |
| RARE DROP | Pearl Necklace x1 |
| STEAL RATIO | 255/255 |
| STOLEN ITEM | Charm Bangle x1 |
| RARE STEAL | Charm Bangle x1 |
| BRIBE ITEM | None |
| RARE BRIBE | None |

## BARALAI

**NONE**

| CHAPTERS | 1 | 2 | 3 | 4 | 5 |
|---|---|---|---|---|---|

**WHERE FOUND** Mushroom Rock

| LEV | 52 | HP | 12220 | MP | 720 |
|---|---|---|---|---|---|
| EXP | 1200 | AP | 5 | | |

| GIL DROP | 200 | GIL STEAL | 300 |
|---|---|---|---|

| STR | 68 | DEF | 67 | AGL | 112 |
|---|---|---|---|---|---|
| EVA | 12 | ACC | 6 | LUCK | 0 |
| MAG | 67 | MAG DEF | 26 | | |

| | None | | None | | None |
|---|---|---|---|---|---|
| | None | | Invalid | | None |

**IMM** Dth., Pet., Slp., Sil., Drk., Poi., Con., Ber., Cur., Ejt., Slw., Stp., Doom, Del., P.I., M.D.

**DEF EFF** Zan. (160)

| DROP RATIO | 255/255 |
|---|---|
| ITEM DROP | Crystal Ball x1 |
| RARE DROP | Crystal Ball x1 |
| STEAL RATIO | 128/255 |
| STOLEN ITEM | Nature's Lore x1 |
| RARE STEAL | Nature's Lore x1 |
| BRIBE ITEM | None |
| RARE BRIBE | None |

Characters

Garment Grids & Dressspheres

Battle System

Accessories

Items and Item Shops

Walkthrough

Mini Games

Fiends and Enemies

1 2 3 4 5 6 7 8

## BARBUTA

**HELM**

| CHAPTERS | | 2 | 3 | 4 | 5 |
|---|---|---|---|---|---|

**WHERE FOUND** Besaid/Mi'ihen Highroad/Thunder Plains/Macalania/Others

| LEV | 22 [26] | HP | 562 [2144] | MP | 13 |
|---|---|---|---|---|---|
| EXP | 42 [75] | AP | 1 [2] | | |

| GIL DROP | 33 [72] | GIL STEAL | 130 [270] |
|---|---|---|---|

| STR | 31 | DEF | 5 | AGL | 52[57] |
|---|---|---|---|---|---|
| EVA | 0 | ACC | 1 | LUCK | 0 |
| MAG | 124 [127] | MAG DEF | 5 | | |

| | None | | None | | Weak |
|---|---|---|---|---|---|
| | None | | None | | None |

**IMM** [Con.], [Ber.], Cur.

**DEF EFF** Ejt. (14[26]), Zan. (1[6])

| DROP RATIO | 128/255 [255/255] |
|---|---|
| ITEM DROP | Light Curtain x1 [Lunar Curtain x3] |
| RARE DROP | Light Curtain x2 [Wall Ring x1] |
| STEAL RATIO | 255/255 |
| STOLEN ITEM | Lunar Curtain x1 [Light Curtain x6] |
| RARE STEAL | Star Curtain x2 [Light Curtain x8] |
| BRIBE ITEM | Lunar Curtain x12 [Star Bracer x1] |
| RARE BRIBE | Lunar Curtain x15 [Star Bracer x1] |

## BARIIVARUHA

**RUMINANT**

| CHAPTERS | | | 3 | 4 | 5 |
|---|---|---|---|---|---|

**WHERE FOUND** Thunder Plains/Calm Lands/Mt. Gagazet/Others

| LEV | 28 [34] | HP | 3688 [8758] | MP | 0 |
|---|---|---|---|---|---|
| EXP | 460 [710] | AP | 1 [2] | | |

| GIL DROP | 230 [320] | GIL STEAL | 520 [1250] |
|---|---|---|---|

| STR | 47 [48] | DEF | 36 | AGL | 78 [90] |
|---|---|---|---|---|---|
| EVA | 0 | ACC | 8 [10] | LUCK | 0 |
| MAG | 61 [72] | MAG DEF | 2 | | |

| | Absorb | | None | | None |
|---|---|---|---|---|---|
| | None | | None | | None |

**IMM** Poi., [Con.], Cur., Doom

**DEF EFF** Ejt. (22 [32]), Zan. (6 [7])

| DROP RATIO | 64/255 [255/255] |
|---|---|
| ITEM DROP | Fire Gem x1 [Fiery Gleam x1] |
| RARE DROP | Fiery Gleam x1 |
| STEAL RATIO | 255/255 |
| STOLEN ITEM | Hi-Potion x2 [Crimson Ring x1] |
| RARE STEAL | Fire Gem x2 [Crimson Ring x1] |
| BRIBE ITEM | NulBlaze Ring x1 [Crystal Bangle x1] |
| RARE BRIBE | Crimson Ring x1 [Crimson Bangle x1] |

## BARONG

**BLADE**

| CHAPTERS | | | 3 | | 5 |
|---|---|---|---|---|---|

**WHERE FOUND** Bevelle, Bevelle Tower Floors 47-49

| LEV | 33 [41] | HP | 2733 [6833] | MP | 0 |
|---|---|---|---|---|---|
| EXP | 270 [260] | AP | 1 [2] | | |

| GIL DROP | 138 [240] | GIL STEAL | 430 [830] |
|---|---|---|---|

| STR | 43 [48] | DEF | 0 | AGL | 95 [114] |
|---|---|---|---|---|---|
| EVA | 24 [38] | ACC | 3 [4] | LUCK | 0 |
| MAG | 8 | MAG DEF | 4 | | |

| | Weak | | None | | None |
|---|---|---|---|---|---|
| | None | | Invalid | | None |

**IMM** Slp., Sil., Poi., [Con.], [Ber.], Cur., Slw., A.B., M.B., Doom, M.D.

**DEF EFF** Drk. (40 [0]), Ejt. (24 [30]), Zan. (5 [8])

| DROP RATIO | 64/255 [255/255] |
|---|---|
| ITEM DROP | Antidote x1 [Angel Earrings x1] |
| RARE DROP | Angel Earrings x1 |
| STEAL RATIO | 255/255 [64/255] |
| STOLEN ITEM | Phoenix Down x1 [Mortal Shock x1] |
| RARE STEAL | Phoenix Down x2 [Mortal Shock x1] |
| BRIBE ITEM | Angle Earrings x1 [Elixir x5] |
| RARE BRIBE | Angle Earrings x2 [Elixir x6] |

## BASCINET

**HELM**

| CHAPTERS | | | 3 | | 5 |
|---|---|---|---|---|---|

**WHERE FOUND** Guadosalam/Mt. Gagazet/Bevelle Tower Floors 41-43

| LEV | 33 [41] | HP | 1342 [3355] | MP | 27 |
|---|---|---|---|---|---|
| EXP | 210 [270] | AP | 1 [2] | | |

| GIL DROP | 110 [188] | GIL STEAL | 260 [483] |
|---|---|---|---|

| STR | 44 | DEF | 7 | AGL | 67 [80] |
|---|---|---|---|---|---|
| EVA | 0 | ACC | 1 | LUCK | 0 |
| MAG | 128 [134] | MAG DEF | 8 | | |

| | None | | None | | None |
|---|---|---|---|---|---|
| | None | | None | | None |

**IMM** [Con.], [Ber.], Cur.

**DEF EFF** Ejt. (16[30]), Zan. (1[6])

| DROP RATIO | 128/255 |
|---|---|
| ITEM DROP | Hi-Potion [Star Curtain (x4)] |
| RARE DROP | Hi-Potion (x2) [Star Curtain (x5)] |
| STEAL RATIO | 255/255 |
| STOLEN ITEM | Hi-Potion [Star Curtain (x2)] |
| RARE STEAL | Hi-Potion (x2) [Star Curtain (x3)] |
| BRIBE ITEM | Wall Ring [Moon Bangle] |
| RARE BRIBE | Wall Ring [Moon Bangle] |

## BATTLESNAKE

**BANDOLEER**

| CHAPTERS | | 2 | | | 5 |
|---|---|---|---|---|---|

**WHERE FOUND** Guadosalam/Bevelle Palace Floors 13-15

| LEV | 20 | HP | 252 | MP | 0 |
|---|---|---|---|---|---|
| EXP | 12 | AP | 1 | | |

| GIL DROP | 40 | GIL STEAL | 80 |
|---|---|---|---|

| STR | 32 | DEF | 0 | AGL | 74 |
|---|---|---|---|---|---|
| EVA | 0 | ACC | 1 | LUCK | 0 |
| MAG | 2 | MAG DEF | 0 | | |

| | None | | None | | None |
|---|---|---|---|---|---|
| | None | | None | | None |

**IMM** Dth., Pet., Slp., Sil., Poi., Cur., Doom

**DEF EFF** None

| DROP RATIO | 128/255 |
|---|---|
| ITEM DROP | Potion x1 |
| RARE DROP | Hi-Potion x1 |
| STEAL RATIO | 255/255 |
| STOLEN ITEM | Phoenix Down x1 |
| RARE STEAL | Phoenix Down x1 |
| BRIBE ITEM | None |
| RARE BRIBE | None |

## BEHEMOTH

**BEHEMOTH**

| CHAPTERS | 1 | 2 | | | 5 |
|---|---|---|---|---|---|

**WHERE FOUND** Zanarkand Ruins/Bevelle Tower Floors 7-9

| LEV | 28 [34] | HP | 1420 [1491] | MP | 280 |
|---|---|---|---|---|---|
| EXP | 102 [180] | AP | 1 [2] | | |

| GIL DROP | 80 [152] | GIL STEAL | 340 [780] |
|---|---|---|---|

| STR | 48 | DEF | 85 | AGL | 68 [88] |
|---|---|---|---|---|---|
| EVA | 0 | ACC | 6 [8] | LUCK | 0 |
| MAG | 4 | MAG DEF | 2 | | |

| | None | | None | | Absorb |
|---|---|---|---|---|---|
| | None | | Invalid | | None |

**IMM** All but Pet., Ejt. Slw., P.B., M.B., A.B., L.C., E.C., A.C.

**DEF EFF** Pet. (50), Ejt. (32 [40]), Zan. (30 [36])

| DROP RATIO | 32/255 [255/255] |
|---|---|
| ITEM DROP | Circlet x1 [Yellow Ring x1] |
| RARE DROP | Yellow Ring x1 |
| STEAL RATIO | 255/255 |
| STOLEN ITEM | Phoenix Down x1 [Circlet x1] |
| RARE STEAL | Electro Marble x2 [Circlet x1] [Short Circuit x1] |
| BRIBE ITEM | Hypno Crown x1 [Ochre Ring x1] |
| RARE BRIBE | Hypno Crown x1 [Ochre Ring x1] |

## BICOCETTE

**HELM**

| CHAPTERS | 1 | 2 | 3 | | 5 |
|---|---|---|---|---|---|

**WHERE FOUND** Thunder Plains, Mt. Gagazet/Bevelle Tower Floors 10-12

| LEV | 8 [10] | HP | 182 [738] | MP | 10 |
|---|---|---|---|---|---|
| EXP | 44 [82] | AP | 1 [2] | | |

| GIL DROP | 18 [34] | GIL STEAL | 120 [224] |
|---|---|---|---|

| STR | 22 [23] | DEF | 2 | AGL | 48 [53] |
|---|---|---|---|---|---|
| EVA | 0 | ACC | 1 | LUCK | 0 |
| MAG | 123 [124] | MAG DEF | 3 | | |

| | None | | None | | None |
|---|---|---|---|---|---|
| | None | | None | | None |

**IMM** [Con.], [Ber.], Cur.

**DEF EFF** Ejt. (13[24]), Zan. (1[5])

| DROP RATIO | 128/255 [255/255] |
|---|---|
| ITEM DROP | Potion x1 [Light Curtain x2] |
| RARE DROP | Light Curtain x1 [Light Curtain x3] |
| STEAL RATIO | 255/255 |
| STOLEN ITEM | Potion x1 [Wall Ring x1] |
| RARE STEAL | Light Curtain x1 [Wall Ring x1] |
| BRIBE ITEM | Light Curtain x3 [Light Curtain x12] |
| RARE BRIBE | Light Curtain x6 [Light Curtain x16] |

## BIG BULLY CAP

**FUNGUS**

| CHAPTERS | | | | | 5 |
|---|---|---|---|---|---|

**WHERE FOUND** Bikanel/Bevelle Tower Floors 50-59

| LEV | 51 [52] | HP | 4880 [5124] | MP | 128 |
|---|---|---|---|---|---|
| EXP | 180 [372] | AP | 1 [2] | | |

| GIL DROP | 48 [98] | GIL STEAL | 180 [380] |
|---|---|---|---|

| STR | 5 | DEF | 38 [46] | AGL | 38 [48] |
|---|---|---|---|---|---|
| EVA | 0 | ACC | 1 | LUCK | 0 |
| MAG | 114 | MAG DEF | 82 | | |

| | Weak | | None | | None |
|---|---|---|---|---|---|
| | Absorb | | Invalid | | None |

**IMM** Pet., Slp., Sil., Drk., Poi., Con., Ber. ([0]), Cur., Stp., Doom ([0]), Del., P.I., M.D.

**DEF EFF** Dth. (20), Ejt. (32 [52]), Zan. (15 [22])

| DROP RATIO | 128/255 [255/255] |
|---|---|
| ITEM DROP | Remedy x1 [Remedy x3] |
| RARE DROP | Remedy x1 [Remedy x5] |
| STEAL RATIO | 128/255 [16/255] |
| STOLEN ITEM | Black Choker x1 |
| RARE STEAL | Potpourri x1 |
| BRIBE ITEM | Potpourri x1 [Potpourri x3] |
| RARE BRIBE | Potpourri x2 [Potpourri x4] |

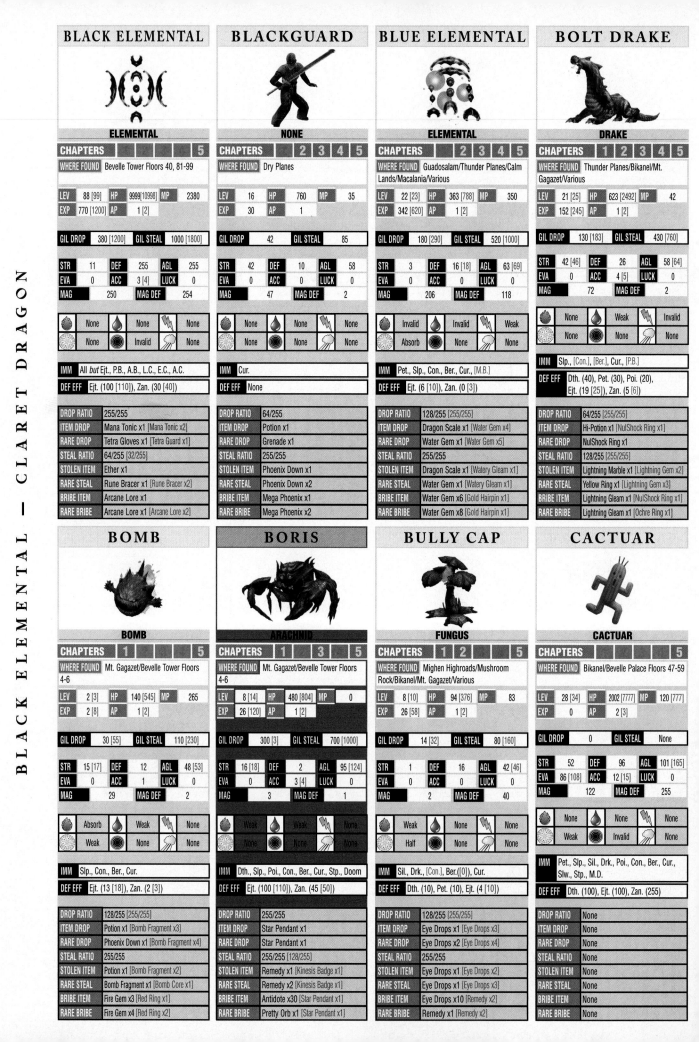

## BLACK ELEMENTAL

**ELEMENTAL**

CHAPTERS: 5

WHERE FOUND: Bevelle Tower Floors 40, 81-99

| | | |
|---|---|---|
| LEV 88 [99] | HP 9999[10998] | MP 2380 |
| EXP 770 [1200] | AP 1 [2] | |

GIL DROP 380 [1200] — GIL STEAL 1000 [1800]

| STR 11 | DEF 255 | AGL 255 |
|---|---|---|
| EVA 0 | ACC 3 [4] | LUCK 0 |
| MAG 250 | MAG DEF 254 | |

Elements: None / None / None / None / Invalid / None

IMM All *but* Ejt., P.B., A.B., L.C., E.C., A.C.

DEF EFF Ejt. (100 [110]), Zan. (30 [40])

| DROP RATIO | 255/255 |
|---|---|
| ITEM DROP | Mana Tonic x1 [Mana Tonic x2] |
| RARE DROP | Tetra Gloves x1 [Tetra Guard x1] |
| STEAL RATIO | 64/255 [32/255] |
| STOLEN ITEM | Ether x1 |
| RARE STEAL | Rune Bracer x1 [Rune Bracer x2] |
| BRIBE ITEM | Arcane Lore x1 |
| RARE BRIBE | Arcane Lore x1 [Arcane Lore x2] |

## BLACKGUARD

**NONE**

CHAPTERS: 2 3 4 5

WHERE FOUND: Dry Plains

| | | |
|---|---|---|
| LEV 16 | HP 760 | MP 35 |
| EXP 30 | AP 1 | |

GIL DROP 42 — GIL STEAL 85

| STR 42 | DEF 10 | AGL 58 |
|---|---|---|
| EVA 0 | ACC 0 | LUCK 0 |
| MAG 47 | MAG DEF 2 | |

Elements: None / None / None / None / None / None

IMM Cur.

DEF EFF None

| DROP RATIO | 64/255 |
|---|---|
| ITEM DROP | Potion x1 |
| RARE DROP | Grenade x1 |
| STEAL RATIO | 255/255 |
| STOLEN ITEM | Phoenix Down x1 |
| RARE STEAL | Phoenix Down x2 |
| BRIBE ITEM | Mega Phoenix x1 |
| RARE BRIBE | Mega Phoenix x2 |

## BLUE ELEMENTAL

**ELEMENTAL**

CHAPTERS: 2 3 4 5

WHERE FOUND: Guadosalam/Thunder Plains/Calm Lands/Macalania/Various

| | | |
|---|---|---|
| LEV 22 [23] | HP 363 [788] | MP 350 |
| EXP 342 [620] | AP 1 [2] | |

GIL DROP 180 [290] — GIL STEAL 520 [1000]

| STR 3 | DEF 16 [18] | AGL 63 [69] |
|---|---|---|
| EVA 0 | ACC 0 | LUCK 0 |
| MAG 206 | MAG DEF 118 | |

Elements: Invalid / Invalid / Weak / Absorb / None / None

IMM Pet., Slp., Con., Ber., Cur., [M.B.]

DEF EFF Ejt. (6 [10]), Zan. (0 [3])

| DROP RATIO | 128/255 [255/255] |
|---|---|
| ITEM DROP | Dragon Scale x1 [Water Gem x4] |
| RARE DROP | Water Gem x1 [Water Gem x5] |
| STEAL RATIO | 255/255 |
| STOLEN ITEM | Dragon Scale x1 [Watery Gleam x1] |
| RARE STEAL | Water Gem x1 [Watery Gleam x1] |
| BRIBE ITEM | Water Gem x6 [Gold Hairpin x1] |
| RARE BRIBE | Water Gem x8 [Gold Hairpin x1] |

## BOLT DRAKE

**DRAKE**

CHAPTERS: 1 2 3 4 5

WHERE FOUND: Thunder Plains/Bikanel/Mt. Gagazet/Various

| | | |
|---|---|---|
| LEV 21 [25] | HP 623 [2492] | MP 42 |
| EXP 152 [245] | AP 1 [2] | |

GIL DROP 130 [183] — GIL STEAL 430 [760]

| STR 42 [46] | DEF 26 | AGL 58 [64] |
|---|---|---|
| EVA 0 | ACC 4 [5] | LUCK 0 |
| MAG 72 | MAG DEF 2 | |

Elements: None / Weak / Invalid / None / None / None

IMM Slp., [Con.], [Ber.], Cur., [P.B.]

DEF EFF Dth. (40), Pet. (30), Poi. (20), Ejt. (19 [25]), Zan. (5 [6])

| DROP RATIO | 64/255 [255/255] |
|---|---|
| ITEM DROP | Hi-Potion x1 [NulShock Ring x1] |
| RARE DROP | NulShock Ring x1 |
| STEAL RATIO | 128/255 [255/255] |
| STOLEN ITEM | Lightning Marble x1 [Lightning Gem x2] |
| RARE STEAL | Yellow Ring x1 [Lightning Gem x3] |
| BRIBE ITEM | Lightning Gleam x1 [NulShock Ring x1] |
| RARE BRIBE | Lightning Gleam x1 [Ochre Ring x1] |

## BOMB

**BOMB**

CHAPTERS: 1 5

WHERE FOUND: Mt. Gagazet/Bevelle Tower Floors 4-6

| | | |
|---|---|---|
| LEV 2 [3] | HP 140 [545] | MP 265 |
| EXP 2 [8] | AP 1 [2] | |

GIL DROP 30 [55] — GIL STEAL 110 [230]

| STR 15 [17] | DEF 12 | AGL 48 [53] |
|---|---|---|
| EVA 0 | ACC 1 | LUCK 0 |
| MAG 29 | MAG DEF 2 | |

Elements: Absorb / Weak / None / Weak / None / None

IMM Slp., Con., Ber., Cur.

DEF EFF Ejt. (13 [18]), Zan. (2 [3])

| DROP RATIO | 128/255 [255/255] |
|---|---|
| ITEM DROP | Potion x1 [Bomb Fragment x3] |
| RARE DROP | Phoenix Down x1 [Bomb Fragment x4] |
| STEAL RATIO | 255/255 |
| STOLEN ITEM | Potion x1 [Bomb Fragment x2] |
| RARE STEAL | Bomb Fragment x1 [Bomb Core x1] |
| BRIBE ITEM | Fire Gem x3 [Red Ring x1] |
| RARE BRIBE | Fire Gem x4 [Red Ring x2] |

## BORIS

**ARACHNID**

CHAPTERS: 1 3 5

WHERE FOUND: Mt. Gagazet/Bevelle Tower Floors 4-6

| | | |
|---|---|---|
| LEV 8 [14] | HP 480 [804] | MP 0 |
| EXP 26 [120] | AP 1 [2] | |

GIL DROP 300 [3] — GIL STEAL 700 [1000]

| STR 16 [18] | DEF 2 | AGL 95 [124] |
|---|---|---|
| EVA 0 | ACC 3 [4] | LUCK 0 |
| MAG 3 | MAG DEF 1 | |

Elements: Weak / Weak / None / None / None / None

IMM Dth., Slp., Poi., Con., Ber., Cur., Stp., Doom

DEF EFF Ejt. (100 [110]), Zan. (45 [50])

| DROP RATIO | 255/255 |
|---|---|
| ITEM DROP | Star Pendant x1 |
| RARE DROP | Star Pendant x1 |
| STEAL RATIO | 255/255 [128/255] |
| STOLEN ITEM | Remedy x1 [Kinesis Badge x1] |
| RARE STEAL | Remedy x2 [Kinesis Badge x1] |
| BRIBE ITEM | Antidote x30 [Star Pendant x1] |
| RARE BRIBE | Pretty Orb x1 [Star Pendant x1] |

## BULLY CAP

**FUNGUS**

CHAPTERS: 1 2 5

WHERE FOUND: Mighen Highroads/Mushroom Rock/Bikanel/Mt. Gagazet/Various

| | | |
|---|---|---|
| LEV 8 [10] | HP 94 [376] | MP 83 |
| EXP 26 [58] | AP 1 [2] | |

GIL DROP 14 [32] — GIL STEAL 80 [160]

| STR 1 | DEF 16 | AGL 42 [46] |
|---|---|---|
| EVA 0 | ACC 0 | LUCK 0 |
| MAG 2 | MAG DEF 40 | |

Elements: Weak / None / None / Half / None / None

IMM Sil., Drk., [Con.], Ber.([0]), Cur.

DEF EFF Dth. (10), Pet. (10), Ejt. (4 [10])

| DROP RATIO | 128/255 [255/255] |
|---|---|
| ITEM DROP | Eye Drops x1 [Eye Drops x3] |
| RARE DROP | Eye Drops x2 [Eye Drops x4] |
| STEAL RATIO | 255/255 |
| STOLEN ITEM | Eye Drops x1 [Eye Drops x2] |
| RARE STEAL | Eye Drops x1 [Eye Drops x3] |
| BRIBE ITEM | Eye Drops x10 [Remedy x2] |
| RARE BRIBE | Remedy x1 [Remedy x2] |

## CACTUAR

**CACTUAR**

CHAPTERS: 5

WHERE FOUND: Bikanel/Bevelle Palace Floors 47-59

| | | |
|---|---|---|
| LEV 28 [34] | HP 2002 [7777] | MP 120 [777] |
| EXP 0 | AP 2 [3] | |

GIL DROP 0 — GIL STEAL None

| STR 52 | DEF 96 | AGL 101 [165] |
|---|---|---|
| EVA 86 [108] | ACC 12 [15] | LUCK 0 |
| MAG 122 | MAG DEF 255 | |

Elements: None / None / None / Weak / Invalid / None

IMM Pet., Slp., Sil., Drk., Poi., Con., Ber., Cur., Slw., Stp., M.D.

DEF EFF Dth. (100), Ejt. (100), Zan. (255)

| DROP RATIO | None |
|---|---|
| ITEM DROP | None |
| RARE DROP | None |
| STEAL RATIO | None |
| STOLEN ITEM | None |
| RARE STEAL | None |
| BRIBE ITEM | None |
| RARE BRIBE | None |

Characters

1

Garment Grids
& Dresspheres

2

Battle System

3

Accessories

4

Items and
Item Shops

5

Walkthrough

6

Mini Games

7

Fiends and
Enemies

8

# CANIS MAJOR

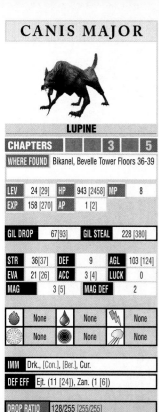

**LUPINE**

| CHAPTERS | | 3 | | 5 |
|---|---|---|---|---|

| WHERE FOUND | Bikanel, Bevelle Tower Floors 36-39 |
|---|---|

| LEV | 24 [29] | HP | 943 [2458] | MP | 8 |
|---|---|---|---|---|---|
| EXP | 158 [270] | AP | 1 [2] | | |

| GIL DROP | 67[93] | GIL STEAL | 228 [380] |
|---|---|---|---|

| STR | 36[37] | DEF | 9 | AGL | 103 [124] |
|---|---|---|---|---|---|
| EVA | 21 [26] | ACC | 3 [4] | LUCK | 0 |
| MAG | 3 [5] | MAG DEF | 2 | | |

| | None | | None | | None |
|---|---|---|---|---|---|
| | None | | None | | None |

| IMM | Drk., [Con.], [Ber.], Cur. |
|---|---|
| DEF EFF | Ejt. (11 [24]), Zan. (1 [6]) |

| DROP RATIO | 128/255 [255/255] |
|---|---|
| ITEM DROP | Hi Potion x1 [Hi Potion x4] |
| RARE DROP | Hi Potion x2 [Hi Potion x6] |
| STEAL RATIO | 255/255 |
| STOLEN ITEM | Hi Potion x1 [Hi Potion x4] |
| RARE STEAL | Hi Potion x2 [Hi Potion x5] |
| BRIBE ITEM | Hi Potion x8 [Haste Ring x1] |
| RARE BRIBE | Hi Potion x10 [Haste Ring x1] |

# CEPHALOTUS

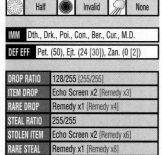

**PLANT**

| CHAPTERS | | 3 | | 5 |
|---|---|---|---|---|

| WHERE FOUND | Besaid/Mi'ihen Highroad/Bevelle Tower Floors 30-32 |
|---|---|

| LEV | 23 [25] | HP | 1830 [6075] | MP | 0 |
|---|---|---|---|---|---|
| EXP | 213 [347] | AP | 1 [2] | | |

| GIL DROP | 62 [111] | GIL STEAL | 220 [450] |
|---|---|---|---|

| STR | 44 [57] | DEF | 0 | AGL | 71 [76] |
|---|---|---|---|---|---|
| EVA | 0 | ACC | 1 | LUCK | 0 |
| MAG | 82 [97] | MAG DEF | 4 | | |

| | Weak | | None | | None |
|---|---|---|---|---|---|
| | Half | | Invalid | | None |

| IMM | Dth., Drk., Poi., Con., Ber., Cur., M.D. |
|---|---|
| DEF EFF | Pet. (50), Ejt. (24 [30]), Zan. (0 [2]) |

| DROP RATIO | 128/255 [255/255] |
|---|---|
| ITEM DROP | Echo Screen x2 [Remedy x3] |
| RARE DROP | Remedy x1 [Remedy x4] |
| STEAL RATIO | 255/255 |
| STOLEN ITEM | Echo Screen x2 [Remedy x6] |
| RARE STEAL | Remedy x1 [Remedy x8] |
| BRIBE ITEM | White Cape x2 [Remedy x80] |
| RARE BRIBE | White Cape x3 [Remedy x99] |

# CHAC

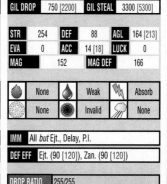

**BASILISK**

| CHAPTERS | | | | 5 |
|---|---|---|---|---|

| WHERE FOUND | Bevelle Tower Floors 80-84 |
|---|---|

| LEV | 98 [99] | HP | 437850 [459743] | MP | 820 |
|---|---|---|---|---|---|
| EXP | 2200 [950] | AP | 1 [2] | | |

| GIL DROP | 750 [2200] | GIL STEAL | 3300 [5300] |
|---|---|---|---|

| STR | 254 | DEF | 88 | AGL | 164 [213] |
|---|---|---|---|---|---|
| EVA | 0 | ACC | 14 [18] | LUCK | 0 |
| MAG | 152 | MAG DEF | 166 | | |

| | None | | Weak | | Absorb |
|---|---|---|---|---|---|
| | None | | Invalid | | None |

| IMM | All but Ejt., Delay, P.I. |
|---|---|
| DEF EFF | Ejt. (90 [120]), Zan. (90 [120]) |

| DROP RATIO | 255/255 |
|---|---|
| ITEM DROP | Shining Gem x1 [Shining Gem x2] |
| RARE DROP | Pixie Dust x1 [Crystal Ball x1] |
| STEAL RATIO | 64/255 [32/255] |
| STOLEN ITEM | Ether x1 |
| RARE STEAL | Ether x2 |
| BRIBE ITEM | Supreme Gem x3 [Supreme Gem x10] |
| RARE BRIBE | Supreme Gem x6 [Supreme Gem x12] |

# CHOCOBO

**NONE**

| CHAPTERS | 1 | 2 | | |
|---|---|---|---|---|

| WHERE FOUND | Besaid/Kilika Island/Djose Highlands/Dry Planes/Thunder Planes/Various |
|---|---|

| LEV | 5 | HP | 368 | MP | 0 |
|---|---|---|---|---|---|
| EXP | 0 | AP | 0 | | |

| GIL DROP | 0 | GIL STEAL | None |
|---|---|---|---|

| STR | 32 | DEF | 24 | AGL | 53 |
|---|---|---|---|---|---|
| EVA | 0 | ACC | 12 | LUCK | 0 |
| MAG | 9 | MAG DEF | 9 | | |

| | None | | None | | None |
|---|---|---|---|---|---|
| | None | | Invalid | | None |

| IMM | Dth., Pet., Slp., Sil., Drk., Poi., Con., Ber., Cur., Slw., Stp., Doom, Del., P.I., M.D. |
|---|---|
| DEF EFF | Ejt. (100), Zan. (30) |

| DROP RATIO | None |
|---|---|
| ITEM DROP | None |
| RARE DROP | None |
| STEAL RATIO | None |
| STOLEN ITEM | None |
| RARE STEAL | None |
| BRIBE ITEM | Chocobo Feather x1 |
| RARE BRIBE | Chocobo Wing x1 |

# CHOCOBO

**NONE**

| CHAPTERS | | | 3 | 4 | 5 |
|---|---|---|---|---|---|

| WHERE FOUND | Besaid/Kilika Island/Djose Highlands/Dry Planes/Thunder Planes/Various |
|---|---|

| LEV | 34 | HP | 3890 | MP | 0 |
|---|---|---|---|---|---|
| EXP | 0 | AP | 0 | | |

| GIL DROP | 0 | GIL STEAL | 0 |
|---|---|---|---|

| STR | 38 | DEF | 52 | AGL | 72 |
|---|---|---|---|---|---|
| EVA | 33 | ACC | 28 | LUCK | 0 |
| MAG | 11 | MAG DEF | 11 | | |

| | None | | None | | None |
|---|---|---|---|---|---|
| | None | | Invalid | | None |

| IMM | All but Drk., Con., Ejt. |
|---|---|
| DEF EFF | Con. (120), Ejt. (100), Zan. (30) |

| DROP RATIO | None |
|---|---|
| ITEM DROP | None |
| RARE DROP | None |
| STEAL RATIO | None |
| STOLEN ITEM | None |
| RARE STEAL | None |
| BRIBE ITEM | Chocobo Feather x12 |
| RARE BRIBE | Chocobo Wing x4 |

# CHOCOBO EATER

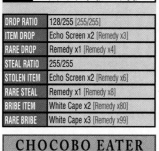

**EATER**

| CHAPTERS | | 2 | | 5 |
|---|---|---|---|---|

| WHERE FOUND | Mi'ihen Highroad/Bevelle Palace Floors 16-19 (only if defeated at Mi'ihen Highroad) |
|---|---|

| LEV | 11 [16] | HP | 2350 [2993] | MP | 230 |
|---|---|---|---|---|---|
| EXP | 350 [680] | AP | 1 [2] | | |

| GIL DROP | 500 [700] | GIL STEAL | 2000 [3000] |
|---|---|---|---|

| STR | 92 [101] | DEF | 27 | AGL | 72 [94] |
|---|---|---|---|---|---|
| EVA | 0 | ACC | 8 [10] | LUCK | 0 |
| MAG | 4 | MAG DEF | 4 | | |

| | Weak | | None | | None |
|---|---|---|---|---|---|
| | None | | Invalid | | None |

| IMM | Dth., Pet., Slp., Drk., Poi., Con., Ber., Cur., Stp., P.B., Doom, Del., P.I., M.D. |
|---|---|
| DEF EFF | Ejt. (100 [110]), Zan. (60) |

| DROP RATIO | 255/255 |
|---|---|
| ITEM DROP | Wall Ring x1 [X-Potion x3] |
| RARE DROP | Wall Ring x1 [X-Potion x5] |
| STEAL RATIO | 128/255 |
| STOLEN ITEM | X-Potion x1 [Shining Bracer x1] |
| RARE STEAL | X-Potion x2 [Shining Bracer x2] |
| BRIBE ITEM | None |
| RARE BRIBE | None |

# CINDY

**NONE**

| CHAPTERS | | | | 5 |
|---|---|---|---|---|

| WHERE FOUND | Farplane |
|---|---|

| LEV | 46 | HP | 12240 | MP | 9999 |
|---|---|---|---|---|---|
| EXP | 3000 | AP | 8 | | |

| GIL DROP | 1000 | GIL STEAL | 3000 |
|---|---|---|---|

| STR | 38 | DEF | 9 | AGL | 72 |
|---|---|---|---|---|---|
| EVA | 4 | ACC | 4 | LUCK | 0 |
| MAG | 172 | MAG DEF | 133 | | |

| | None | | None | | None |
|---|---|---|---|---|---|
| | None | | Invalid | | None |

| IMM | All |
|---|---|
| DEF EFF | Zan. (150) |

| DROP RATIO | 255/255 |
|---|---|
| ITEM DROP | Faerie Earrings x1 |
| RARE DROP | Pixie Dust x1 |
| STEAL RATIO | 128/255 |
| STOLEN ITEM | White CAPe x1 |
| RARE STEAL | White CAPe x1 |
| BRIBE ITEM | None |
| RARE BRIBE | None |

# CLARET DRAGON

**DRAGON**

| CHAPTERS | | | | 5 |
|---|---|---|---|---|

| WHERE FOUND | Farplane/Bevelle Tower Floors 61-64 |
|---|---|

| LEV | 45 [52] | HP | 17320 [18186] | MP | 378 |
|---|---|---|---|---|---|
| EXP | 1280 [2213] | AP | 1 [2] | | |

| GIL DROP | 780 [1300] | GIL STEAL | 1830 [1020] |
|---|---|---|---|

| STR | 140 [158] | DEF | 60 [71] | AGL | 107 [139] |
|---|---|---|---|---|---|
| EVA | 0 | ACC | 4 [5] | LUCK | 0 |
| MAG | 103 [133] | MAG DEF | 94 | | |

| | Absorb | | Absorb | | Absorb |
|---|---|---|---|---|---|
| | Absorb | | Absorb | | Absorb |

| IMM | All but Doom |
|---|---|
| DEF EFF | Ejt. (50 [60]), Zan. (15 [25]) |

| DROP RATIO | 255/255 |
|---|---|
| ITEM DROP | Hi Potion x2 [Sublimator x1] |
| RARE DROP | Hi-Potion x3 [Sublimator x1] |
| STEAL RATIO | 128/255 |
| STOLEN ITEM | Hi-Potion x1 [Ether x2] |
| RARE STEAL | Ether x1 [Ether x3] |
| BRIBE ITEM | Sublimator x2 [Black Tome x1] |
| RARE BRIBE | Sublimator x3 [Black Tome x2] |

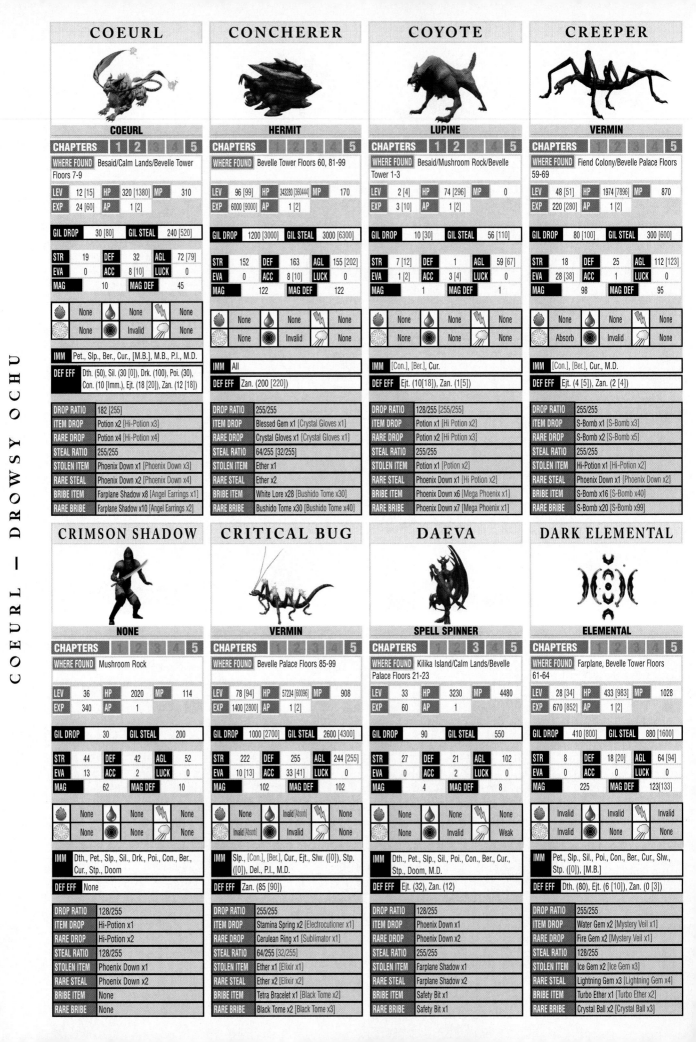

# COEURL

**COEURL**

| CHAPTERS | 1 | 2 | 3 | 4 | 5 |
|---|---|---|---|---|---|

**WHERE FOUND** Besaid/Calm Lands/Bevelle Tower Floors 7-9

| LEV | 12 [15] | HP | 320 [1380] | MP | 310 |
|---|---|---|---|---|---|
| EXP | 24 [60] | AP | 1 [2] | | |

| GIL DROP | 30 [80] | GIL STEAL | 240 [520] |
|---|---|---|---|

| STR | 19 | DEF | 32 | AGL | 72 [79] |
|---|---|---|---|---|---|
| EVA | 0 | ACC | 8 [10] | LUCK | 0 |
| MAG | 10 | MAG DEF | 45 | | |

| | None | | None | | None |
|---|---|---|---|---|---|
| | None | | Invalid | | None |

**IMM** Pet., Slp., Ber., Cur., [M.B.], M.B., P.I., M.D.

**DEF EFF** Dth. (50), Sil. (30 [0]), Drk. (100), Poi. (30), Con. (10 [Imm.]), Ejt. (18 [20]), Zan. (12 [18])

| DROP RATIO | 182 [255] |
|---|---|
| ITEM DROP | Potion x2 [Hi-Potion x3] |
| RARE DROP | Potion x4 [Hi-Potion x4] |
| STEAL RATIO | 255/255 |
| STOLEN ITEM | Phoenix Down x1 [Phoenix Down x3] |
| RARE STEAL | Phoenix Down x2 [Phoenix Down x4] |
| BRIBE ITEM | Farplane Shadow x8 [Angel Earrings x1] |
| RARE BRIBE | Farplane Shadow x10 [Angel Earrings x2] |

# CONCHERER

**HERMIT**

| CHAPTERS | 1 | 2 | 3 | 4 | 5 |
|---|---|---|---|---|---|

**WHERE FOUND** Bevelle Tower Floors 60, 81-99

| LEV | 96 [99] | HP | 343280 [360444] | MP | 170 |
|---|---|---|---|---|---|
| EXP | 6000 [9000] | AP | 1 [2] | | |

| GIL DROP | 1200 [3000] | GIL STEAL | 3000 [6300] |
|---|---|---|---|

| STR | 152 | DEF | 163 | AGL | 155 [202] |
|---|---|---|---|---|---|
| EVA | 0 | ACC | 8 [10] | LUCK | 0 |
| MAG | 122 | MAG DEF | 122 | | |

| | None | | None | | None |
|---|---|---|---|---|---|
| | None | | Invalid | | None |

**IMM** All

**DEF EFF** Zan. (200 [220])

| DROP RATIO | 255/255 |
|---|---|
| ITEM DROP | Blessed Gem x1 [Crystal Gloves x1] |
| RARE DROP | Crystal Gloves x1 [Crystal Gloves x1] |
| STEAL RATIO | 64/255 [32/255] |
| STOLEN ITEM | Ether x1 |
| RARE STEAL | Ether x2 |
| BRIBE ITEM | White Lore x28 [Bushido Tome x30] |
| RARE BRIBE | Bushido Tome x30 [Bushido Tome x40] |

# COYOTE

**LUPINE**

| CHAPTERS | 1 | 2 | 3 | 4 | 5 |
|---|---|---|---|---|---|

**WHERE FOUND** Besaid/Mushroom Rock/Bevelle Tower 1-3

| LEV | 2 [4] | HP | 74 [296] | MP | 0 |
|---|---|---|---|---|---|
| EXP | 3 [10] | AP | 1 [2] | | |

| GIL DROP | 10 [30] | GIL STEAL | 56 [110] |
|---|---|---|---|

| STR | 7 [12] | DEF | 1 | AGL | 59 [67] |
|---|---|---|---|---|---|
| EVA | 1 [2] | ACC | 3 [4] | LUCK | 0 |
| MAG | 1 | MAG DEF | 1 | | |

| | None | | None | | None |
|---|---|---|---|---|---|
| | None | | None | | None |

**IMM** [Con.], [Ber.], Cur.

**DEF EFF** Ejt. (10[18]), Zan. (1[5])

| DROP RATIO | 128/255 [255/255] |
|---|---|
| ITEM DROP | Potion x1 [Hi Potion x2] |
| RARE DROP | Potion x2 [Hi Potion x3] |
| STEAL RATIO | 255/255 |
| STOLEN ITEM | Potion x1 [Potion x2] |
| RARE STEAL | Phoenix Down x1 [Hi Potion x2] |
| BRIBE ITEM | Phoenix Down x6 [Mega Phoenix x1] |
| RARE BRIBE | Phoenix Down x7 [Mega Phoenix x1] |

# CREEPER

**VERMIN**

| CHAPTERS | 1 | 2 | 3 | 4 | 5 |
|---|---|---|---|---|---|

**WHERE FOUND** Fiend Colony/Bevelle Palace Floors 59-69

| LEV | 48 [51] | HP | 1974 [7896] | MP | 870 |
|---|---|---|---|---|---|
| EXP | 220 [280] | AP | 1 [2] | | |

| GIL DROP | 80 [100] | GIL STEAL | 300 [600] |
|---|---|---|---|

| STR | 18 | DEF | 25 | AGL | 112 [123] |
|---|---|---|---|---|---|
| EVA | 28 [38] | ACC | 1 | LUCK | 0 |
| MAG | 98 | MAG DEF | 95 | | |

| | None | | None | | None |
|---|---|---|---|---|---|
| | Absorb | | Invalid | | None |

**IMM** [Con.], [Ber.], Cur., M.D.

**DEF EFF** Ejt. (4 [5]), Zan. (2 [4])

| DROP RATIO | 255/255 |
|---|---|
| ITEM DROP | S-Bomb x1 [S-Bomb x3] |
| RARE DROP | S-Bomb x2 [S-Bomb x5] |
| STEAL RATIO | 255/255 |
| STOLEN ITEM | Hi-Potion x1 [Hi-Potion x2] |
| RARE STEAL | Phoenix Down x1 [Phoenix Down x2] |
| BRIBE ITEM | S-Bomb x16 [S-Bomb x40] |
| RARE BRIBE | S-Bomb x20 [S-Bomb x99] |

# CRIMSON SHADOW

**NONE**

| CHAPTERS | 1 | 2 | 3 | 4 | 5 |
|---|---|---|---|---|---|

**WHERE FOUND** Mushroom Rock

| LEV | 36 | HP | 2020 | MP | 114 |
|---|---|---|---|---|---|
| EXP | 340 | AP | 1 | | |

| GIL DROP | 30 | GIL STEAL | 200 |
|---|---|---|---|

| STR | 44 | DEF | 42 | AGL | 52 |
|---|---|---|---|---|---|
| EVA | 13 | ACC | 2 | LUCK | 0 |
| MAG | 62 | MAG DEF | 10 | | |

| | None | | None | | None |
|---|---|---|---|---|---|
| | None | | None | | None |

**IMM** Dth., Pet., Slp., Sil., Drk., Poi., Con., Ber., Cur., Stp., Doom

**DEF EFF** None

| DROP RATIO | 128/255 |
|---|---|
| ITEM DROP | Hi-Potion x1 |
| RARE DROP | Hi-Potion x2 |
| STEAL RATIO | 128/255 |
| STOLEN ITEM | Phoenix Down x1 |
| RARE STEAL | Phoenix Down x2 |
| BRIBE ITEM | None |
| RARE BRIBE | None |

# CRITICAL BUG

**VERMIN**

| CHAPTERS | 1 | 2 | 3 | 4 | 5 |
|---|---|---|---|---|---|

**WHERE FOUND** Bevelle Palace Floors 85-99

| LEV | 78 [94] | HP | 57234 [60096] | MP | 908 |
|---|---|---|---|---|---|
| EXP | 1400 [2800] | AP | 1 [2] | | |

| GIL DROP | 1000 [2700] | GIL STEAL | 2600 [4300] |
|---|---|---|---|

| STR | 222 | DEF | 255 | AGL | 244 [255] |
|---|---|---|---|---|---|
| EVA | 10 [13] | ACC | 33 [41] | LUCK | 0 |
| MAG | 102 | MAG DEF | 102 | | |

| | None | | Invalid [Absorb] | | None |
|---|---|---|---|---|---|
| | Invalid [Absorb] | | Invalid | | None |

**IMM** Slp., [Con.], [Ber.], Cur., Ejt., Slw. ([0]), Stp. ([0]), Del., P.I., M.D.

**DEF EFF** Zan. (85 [90])

| DROP RATIO | 255/255 |
|---|---|
| ITEM DROP | Stamina Spring x2 [Electrocutioner x1] |
| RARE DROP | Cerulean Ring x1 [Sublimator x1] |
| STEAL RATIO | 64/255 [32/255] |
| STOLEN ITEM | Ether x1 [Elixir x1] |
| RARE STEAL | Ether x2 [Elixir x2] |
| BRIBE ITEM | Tetra Bracelet x1 [Black Tome x2] |
| RARE BRIBE | Black Tome x2 [Black Tome x3] |

# DAEVA

**SPELL SPINNER**

| CHAPTERS | 1 | 2 | 3 | 4 | 5 |
|---|---|---|---|---|---|

**WHERE FOUND** Kilika Island/Calm Lands/Bevelle Palace Floors 21-23

| LEV | 33 | HP | 3230 | MP | 4480 |
|---|---|---|---|---|---|
| EXP | 60 | AP | 1 | | |

| GIL DROP | 90 | GIL STEAL | 550 |
|---|---|---|---|

| STR | 27 | DEF | 21 | AGL | 102 |
|---|---|---|---|---|---|
| EVA | 2 | ACC | 2 | LUCK | 0 |
| MAG | 4 | MAG DEF | 8 | | |

| | None | | None | | None |
|---|---|---|---|---|---|
| | None | | Invalid | | Weak |

**IMM** Dth., Pet., Slp., Sil., Poi., Con., Ber., Cur., Stp., Doom, M.D.

**DEF EFF** Ejt. (32), Zan. (12)

| DROP RATIO | 128/255 |
|---|---|
| ITEM DROP | Phoenix Down x1 |
| RARE DROP | Phoenix Down x2 |
| STEAL RATIO | 255/255 |
| STOLEN ITEM | Farplane Shadow x1 |
| RARE STEAL | Farplane Shadow x2 |
| BRIBE ITEM | Safety Bit x1 |
| RARE BRIBE | Safety Bit x1 |

# DARK ELEMENTAL

**ELEMENTAL**

| CHAPTERS | 1 | 2 | 3 | 4 | 5 |
|---|---|---|---|---|---|

**WHERE FOUND** Farplane, Bevelle Tower Floors 61-64

| LEV | 28 [34] | HP | 433 [983] | MP | 1028 |
|---|---|---|---|---|---|
| EXP | 670 [852] | AP | 1 [2] | | |

| GIL DROP | 410 [800] | GIL STEAL | 880 [1600] |
|---|---|---|---|

| STR | 8 | DEF | 18 [20] | AGL | 64 [94] |
|---|---|---|---|---|---|
| EVA | 0 | ACC | 1 | LUCK | 0 |
| MAG | 225 | MAG DEF | 123[133] | | |

| | Invalid | | Invalid | | Invalid |
|---|---|---|---|---|---|
| | Invalid | | None | | None |

**IMM** Pet., Slp., Sil., Poi., Con., Ber., Cur., Slw., Stp. ([0]), [M.B.]

**DEF EFF** Dth. (80), Ejt. (6 [10]), Zan. (0 [3])

| DROP RATIO | 255/255 |
|---|---|
| ITEM DROP | Water Gem x2 [Mystery Veil x1] |
| RARE DROP | Fire Gem x2 [Mystery Veil x1] |
| STEAL RATIO | 128/255 |
| STOLEN ITEM | Ice Gem x2 [Ice Gem x3] |
| RARE STEAL | Lightning Gem x3 [Lightning Gem x4] |
| BRIBE ITEM | Turbo Ether x1 [Turbo Ether x2] |
| RARE BRIBE | Crystal Ball x2 [Crystal Ball x3] |

# DEATH DAUBER

**WASP**

| CHAPTERS | 1 | 2 | 3 | 4 | 5 |
|---|---|---|---|---|---|

**WHERE FOUND** Kilika Island/Djose Temple/Bikanel/Calm Lands/Others

| LEV | 5 [6] | HP | 78 [312] | MP | 1 |
|---|---|---|---|---|---|
| EXP | 18 [32] | AP | 1 [2] | | |

| GIL DROP | 12 [18] | GIL STEAL | 70 [130] |
|---|---|---|---|

| STR | 18 | DEF | 1 | AGL | 133 [146] |
|---|---|---|---|---|---|
| EVA | 21 [26] | ACC | 12 [15] | LUCK | 0 |
| MAG | 2 | MAG DEF | 1 | | |

| Fire | Water | Lightning |
|---|---|---|
| Weak | Weak | None |
| Earth | Gravity | Holy |
| None | None | None |

**IMM** [Con.], [Ber.], Cur., [P.B.]

**DEF EFF** Ejt. (6 [8]), Zan. (0 [2])

| DROP RATIO | 128/255 [255/255] |
|---|---|
| ITEM DROP | Potion x1 [Phoenix Down x2] |
| RARE DROP | Potion x2 [Phoenix Down x3] |
| STEAL RATIO | 255/255 |
| STOLEN ITEM | Potion x1 [Phoenix Down x2] |
| RARE STEAL | Phoenix Down x1 [Phoenix Down x3] |
| BRIBE ITEM | Remedy x2 |
| RARE BRIBE | Silver Glasses x1 [Remedy x2] |

# DEEP HAIZHE

**HAIZHE**

| CHAPTERS | 1 | 2 | 3 | 4 | 5 |
|---|---|---|---|---|---|

**WHERE FOUND** Macalania/Bevelle Tower Floors 24-26

| LEV | 20 [24] | HP | 1030 [4119] | MP | 122 |
|---|---|---|---|---|---|
| EXP | 133 [188] | AP | 1 [2] | | |

| GIL DROP | 40 [83] | GIL STEAL | 152 [300] |
|---|---|---|---|

| STR | 18 | DEF | 26 | AGL | 56 [62] |
|---|---|---|---|---|---|
| EVA | 0 | ACC | 3 [4] | LUCK | 0 |
| MAG | 72 | MAG DEF | 22 | | |

| Fire | Water | Lightning |
|---|---|---|
| None | None | Weak |
| Earth | Gravity | Holy |
| None | Weak | None |

**IMM** Pet., Slp., Sil., Con., [Ber.], Cur., M.B., M.B.

**DEF EFF** Poi. (10 [0]), Ejt. (22 [30]), Zan. (3 [6])

| DROP RATIO | 128/255 [255/255] |
|---|---|
| ITEM DROP | Hi-Potion x1 [Dragonfly Orb x1] |
| RARE DROP | Hi-Potion x1 [Dragonfly Orb x1] |
| STEAL RATIO | 128/255 [255/255] |
| STOLEN ITEM | Gold Anklet x1 [Gold Hourglass x1] |
| RARE STEAL | Dragonfly Orb x1 [Gold Hourglass x1] |
| BRIBE ITEM | Dragonfly Orb x1 [Kinesis Badge x1] |
| RARE BRIBE | Dragonfly Orb x1 [Kinesis Badge x2] |

# DETONATOR

**BOMB**

| CHAPTERS | 1 | 2 | 3 | 4 | 5 |
|---|---|---|---|---|---|

**WHERE FOUND** Bevelle/Bevelle Tower Floors 24-26

| LEV | 24 [29] | HP | 1860 [7220] | MP | 423 |
|---|---|---|---|---|---|
| EXP | 132 [220] | AP | 1 [2] | | |

| GIL DROP | 98 [190] | GIL STEAL | 330 [650] |
|---|---|---|---|

| STR | 31 | DEF | 21 | AGL | 58 [64] |
|---|---|---|---|---|---|
| EVA | 0 | ACC | 1 | LUCK | 0 |
| MAG | 52 | MAG DEF | 3 | | |

| Fire | Water | Lightning |
|---|---|---|
| Absorb | Weak | None |
| Earth | Gravity | Holy |
| None | Invalid | None |

**IMM** Slp., Sil., Con., Ber., Cur., Del., M.D.

**DEF EFF** Dth. (50), Pet. (70), Ejt. (13 [18]), Zan. (2 [3])

| DROP RATIO | 128/255 [255/255] |
|---|---|
| ITEM DROP | Bomb Core x1 [Candle of Life x4] |
| RARE DROP | Fire Gem x1 [Candle of Life x6] |
| STEAL RATIO | 255/255 |
| STOLEN ITEM | Bomb Core x1 [Fire Gem x2] |
| RARE STEAL | Candle of Life x1 [Fire Gem x2] |
| BRIBE ITEM | Candle of Life x80 [Soul of Thamasa x1] |
| RARE BRIBE | Candle of Life x99 [Soul of Thamasa x1] |

# DINICTUS

**DINOFISH**

| CHAPTERS | 1 | 2 | 3 | 4 | 5 |
|---|---|---|---|---|---|

**WHERE FOUND** Macalania/Ruin Depths/Bevelle Tower Floors 41-43

| LEV | 24 [32] | HP | 1873 [7792] | MP | 0 |
|---|---|---|---|---|---|
| EXP | 187 [370] | AP | 1 [2] | | |

| GIL DROP | 88 [140] | GIL STEAL | 280 [590] |
|---|---|---|---|

| STR | 78 [84] | DEF | 22 | AGL | 68 [78] |
|---|---|---|---|---|---|
| EVA | 0 | ACC | 5 [6] | LUCK | 0 |
| MAG | 114 | MAG DEF | 3 | | |

| Fire | Water | Lightning |
|---|---|---|
| None | None | Weak |
| Earth | Gravity | Holy |
| Invalid | Weak | None |

**IMM** Pet., Slp., [Con.], [Ber.], Cur.

**DEF EFF** Drk. (80 [0]), Poi. (10 [0]), Ejt. (14 [18]), Zan. (3 [5])

| DROP RATIO | 128/255 [255/255] |
|---|---|
| ITEM DROP | Water Gem x1 [Water Gem x3] |
| RARE DROP | Water Gem x2 [Water Gem x4] |
| STEAL RATIO | 128/255 |
| STOLEN ITEM | Water Gem x1 [Short Circuit x1] |
| RARE STEAL | Water Gem x2 [Short Circuit x1] |
| BRIBE ITEM | Blue Ring x1 [Short Circuit x1] |
| RARE BRIBE | Cerulean Ring x1 [Short Circuit x2] |

# DIVEBEAK

**BIRD**

| CHAPTERS | 1 | 2 | 3 | 4 | 5 |
|---|---|---|---|---|---|

**WHERE FOUND** Mi'ihen Highroad/Calm Lands/Gagazet Island/Others

| LEV | 1 [5] | HP | 10 [72] | MP | 2 |
|---|---|---|---|---|---|
| EXP | 2 [8] | AP | 1 [2] | | |

| GIL DROP | 12 [28] | GIL STEAL | 60 [180] |
|---|---|---|---|

| STR | 4 [7] | DEF | 1 | AGL | 82 [110] |
|---|---|---|---|---|---|
| EVA | 33 [41] | ACC | 16 [20] | LUCK | 0 |
| MAG | 1 | MAG DEF | 2 | | |

| Fire | Water | Lightning |
|---|---|---|
| None | None | None |
| Earth | Gravity | Holy |
| None | None | None |

**IMM** [Con.], [Ber.], Cur.

**DEF EFF** Ejt. (8 [12]), Zan. (0 [3])

| DROP RATIO | 96/255 [255/255] |
|---|---|
| ITEM DROP | Antidote x1 [Ether x2] |
| RARE DROP | Antidote x2 [Ether x3] |
| STEAL RATIO | 255/255 |
| STOLEN ITEM | Potion x1 [Ether x1] |
| RARE STEAL | Ether x1 [Ether x2] |
| BRIBE ITEM | Antidote x1 [Ether x1] |
| RARE BRIBE | Ether x1 |

# DOLMEN

**DOOMSTONE**

| CHAPTERS | 1 | 2 | 3 | 4 | 5 |
|---|---|---|---|---|---|

**WHERE FOUND** Besaid/Kilika Island/Mushroom Rock/Djose Highland/Farplane/Various

| LEV | 32 | HP | 5320 | MP | 9999 |
|---|---|---|---|---|---|
| EXP | 1130 | AP | 1 | | |

| GIL DROP | 320 | GIL STEAL | 680 |
|---|---|---|---|

| STR | 37 | DEF | 40 | AGL | 79 |
|---|---|---|---|---|---|
| EVA | 0 | ACC | 3 | LUCK | 0 |
| MAG | 68 | MAG DEF | 1 | | |

| Fire | Water | Lightning |
|---|---|---|
| Half | Half | Half |
| Earth | Gravity | Holy |
| Weak | Invalid | Weak |

**IMM** Dth., Pet., Slp., Sil., Drk., Poi., Con., Cur., Slw., Stp., Doom, M.D.

**DEF EFF** Ejt. (34), Zan. (14)

| DROP RATIO | 128/255 |
|---|---|
| ITEM DROP | Hi-Potion x2 |
| RARE DROP | Gris-Gris Bag |
| STEAL RATIO | 255/255 |
| STOLEN ITEM | Remedy x2 |
| RARE STEAL | Remedy x3 |
| BRIBE ITEM | Gris-Gris-Bag x2 |
| RARE BRIBE | Black Lore x1 |

# DR. GOON

**NONE**

| CHAPTERS | 1 | 2 | 3 | 4 | 5 |
|---|---|---|---|---|---|

**WHERE FOUND** Djose Highlands/Guadosalam/Mt. Gagazet

| LEV | 14 | HP | 232 | MP | 41 |
|---|---|---|---|---|---|
| EXP | 10 | AP | 1 | | |

| GIL DROP | 50 | GIL STEAL | 160 |
|---|---|---|---|

| STR | 35 | DEF | 10 | AGL | 56 |
|---|---|---|---|---|---|
| EVA | 0 | ACC | 3 | LUCK | 0 |
| MAG | 6 | MAG DEF | 6 | | |

| Fire | Water | Lightning |
|---|---|---|
| None | None | None |
| Earth | Gravity | Holy |
| None | None | None |

**IMM** Cur.

**DEF EFF** None

| DROP RATIO | 128/255 |
|---|---|
| ITEM DROP | Potion x1 |
| RARE DROP | Grenade x1 |
| STEAL RATIO | 255/255 |
| STOLEN ITEM | Budget Grenade x1 |
| RARE STEAL | Grenade x1 |
| BRIBE ITEM | S-Bomb x4 |
| RARE BRIBE | M-Bomb x4 |

# DROWSY OCHU

**OCHU**

| CHAPTERS | 1 | 2 | 3 | 4 | 5 |
|---|---|---|---|---|---|

**WHERE FOUND** Mushroom Rock/Bevelle Tower Floors 27-29

| LEV | 18 [26] | HP | 2484 [2608] | MP | 103 |
|---|---|---|---|---|---|
| EXP | 280 [480] | AP | 1 [2] | | |

| GIL DROP | 180 [310] | GIL STEAL | 700 [1120] |
|---|---|---|---|

| STR | 36 [42] | DEF | 38 | AGL | 42 [55] |
|---|---|---|---|---|---|
| EVA | 0 | ACC | 1 | LUCK | 0 |
| MAG | 17 | MAG DEF | 13 | | |

| Fire | Water | Lightning |
|---|---|---|
| Weak | None | None |
| Earth | Gravity | Holy |
| Half | Invalid | None |

**IMM** Dth., Pet., Sil., Drk., Poi., Con., Ber., Cur., Slw., Stp., Doom, Del., P.I., M.D.

**DEF EFF** Ejt. (32 [34]), Zan. (5 [10])

| DROP RATIO | 255/255 |
|---|---|
| ITEM DROP | Remedy x2 [Remedy x4] |
| RARE DROP | Remedy x3 [Remedy x6] |
| STEAL RATIO | 128/255 [64/255] |
| STOLEN ITEM | Remedy x1 [Beaded Broch x1] |
| RARE STEAL | Remedy x2 [Beaded Broch x1] |
| BRIBE ITEM | None |
| RARE BRIBE | None |

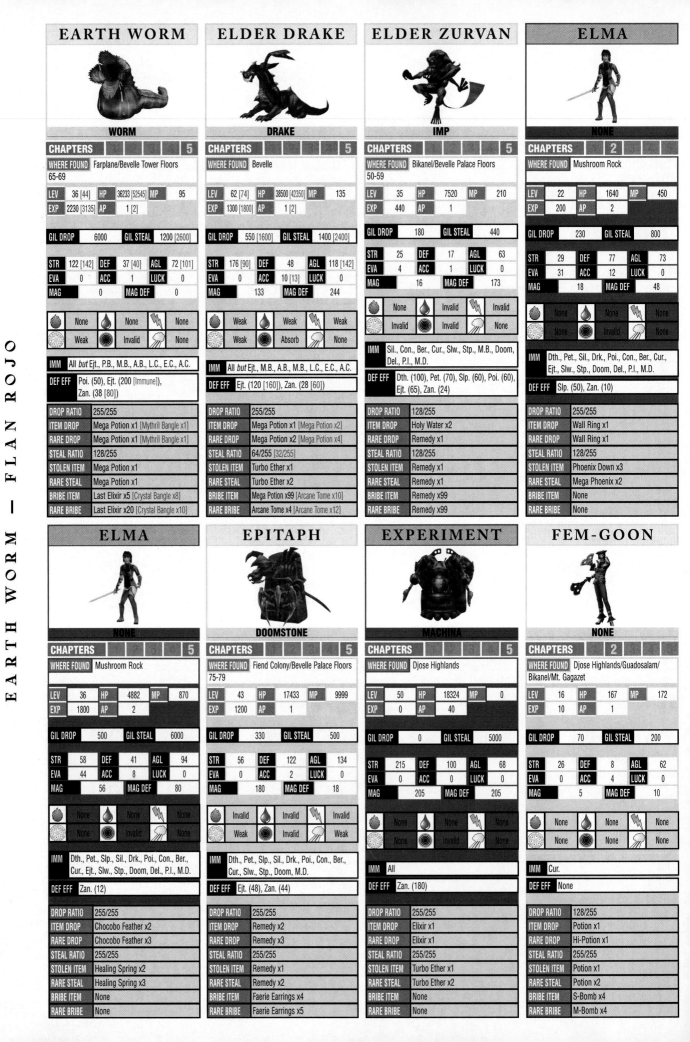

## EARTH WORM

**WORM**

CHAPTERS ▢▢▢▢5

| WHERE FOUND | Farplane/Bevelle Tower Floors 65-69 |

| LEV | 36 [44] | HP | 36233 [52545] | MP | 95 |
| EXP | 2230 [3135] | AP | 1 [2] | | |

| GIL DROP | 6000 | GIL STEAL | 1200 [2600] |

| STR | 122 [142] | DEF | 37 [40] | AGL | 72 [101] |
| EVA | 0 | ACC | 1 | LUCK | 0 |
| MAG | 0 | MAG DEF | 0 | | |

Fire: None | Water: None | Lightning: None
Holy: Weak | Gravity: Invalid | Ice: None

| IMM | All *but* Ejt., P.B., M.B., A.B., L.C., E.C., A.C. |
| DEF EFF | Poi. (50), Ejt. (200 [Immune]), Zan. (38 [80]) |

| DROP RATIO | 255/255 |
| ITEM DROP | Mega Potion x1 [Mythril Bangle x1] |
| RARE DROP | Mega Potion x1 [Mythril Bangle x1] |
| STEAL RATIO | 128/255 |
| STOLEN ITEM | Mega Potion x1 |
| RARE STEAL | Mega Potion x1 |
| BRIBE ITEM | Last Elixir x5 [Crystal Bangle x8] |
| RARE BRIBE | Last Elixir x20 [Crystal Bangle x10] |

## ELDER DRAKE

**DRAKE**

CHAPTERS ▢▢▢▢5

| WHERE FOUND | Bevelle |

| LEV | 62 [74] | HP | 38500 [42350] | MP | 135 |
| EXP | 1300 [1800] | AP | 1 [2] | | |

| GIL DROP | 550 [1600] | GIL STEAL | 1400 [2400] |

| STR | 176 [90] | DEF | 48 | AGL | 118 [142] |
| EVA | 0 | ACC | 10 [13] | LUCK | 0 |
| MAG | 133 | MAG DEF | 244 | | |

Fire: Weak | Water: Weak | Lightning: Weak
Holy: Weak | Gravity: Absorb | Ice: None

| IMM | All *but* Ejt., M.B., A.B., M.B., L.C., E.C., A.C. |
| DEF EFF | Ejt. (120 [160]), Zan. (28 [60]) |

| DROP RATIO | 255/255 |
| ITEM DROP | Mega Potion x1 [Mega Potion x2] |
| RARE DROP | Mega Potion x2 [Mega Potion x4] |
| STEAL RATIO | 64/255 [32/255] |
| STOLEN ITEM | Turbo Ether x1 |
| RARE STEAL | Turbo Ether x2 |
| BRIBE ITEM | Mega Potion x99 [Arcane Tome x10] |
| RARE BRIBE | Arcane Tome x4 [Arcane Tome x12] |

## ELDER ZURVAN

**IMP**

CHAPTERS ▢▢▢▢5

| WHERE FOUND | Bikanel/Bevelle Palace Floors 50-59 |

| LEV | 35 | HP | 7520 | MP | 210 |
| EXP | 440 | AP | 1 | | |

| GIL DROP | 180 | GIL STEAL | 440 |

| STR | 25 | DEF | 17 | AGL | 63 |
| EVA | 4 | ACC | 1 | LUCK | 0 |
| MAG | 16 | MAG DEF | 173 | | |

Fire: None | Water: Invalid | Lightning: Invalid
Holy: Invalid | Gravity: Invalid | Ice: None

| IMM | Sil., Con., Ber., Cur., Slw., Stp., M.B., Doom, Del., P.I., M.D. |
| DEF EFF | Dth. (100), Pet. (70), Slp. (60), Poi. (60), Ejt. (65), Zan. (24) |

| DROP RATIO | 128/255 |
| ITEM DROP | Holy Water x2 |
| RARE DROP | Remedy x1 |
| STEAL RATIO | 128/255 |
| STOLEN ITEM | Remedy x1 |
| RARE STEAL | Remedy x1 |
| BRIBE ITEM | Remedy x99 |
| RARE BRIBE | Remedy x99 |

## ELMA

**NONE**

CHAPTERS ▢2▢▢

| WHERE FOUND | Mushroom Rock |

| LEV | 22 | HP | 1640 | MP | 450 |
| EXP | 200 | AP | 2 | | |

| GIL DROP | 230 | GIL STEAL | 800 |

| STR | 29 | DEF | 77 | AGL | 73 |
| EVA | 31 | ACC | 12 | LUCK | 0 |
| MAG | 18 | MAG DEF | 48 | | |

Fire: None | Water: None | Lightning: None
Holy: None | Gravity: Invalid | Ice: None

| IMM | Dth., Pet., Sil., Drk., Poi., Con., Ber., Cur., Ejt., Slw., Stp., Doom, Del., P.I., M.D. |
| DEF EFF | Slp. (50), Zan. (10) |

| DROP RATIO | 255/255 |
| ITEM DROP | Wall Ring x1 |
| RARE DROP | Wall Ring x1 |
| STEAL RATIO | 128/255 |
| STOLEN ITEM | Phoenix Down x3 |
| RARE STEAL | Mega Phoenix x2 |
| BRIBE ITEM | None |
| RARE BRIBE | None |

## ELMA

**NONE**

CHAPTERS ▢▢▢▢5

| WHERE FOUND | Mushroom Rock |

| LEV | 36 | HP | 4882 | MP | 870 |
| EXP | 1800 | AP | 2 | | |

| GIL DROP | 500 | GIL STEAL | 6000 |

| STR | 58 | DEF | 41 | AGL | 94 |
| EVA | 44 | ACC | 8 | LUCK | 0 |
| MAG | 56 | MAG DEF | 80 | | |

Fire: None | Water: None | Lightning: None
Holy: None | Gravity: Invalid | Ice: None

| IMM | Dth., Pet., Slp., Sil., Drk., Poi., Con., Ber., Cur., Ejt., Slw., Stp., Doom, Del., P.I., M.D. |
| DEF EFF | Zan. (12) |

| DROP RATIO | 255/255 |
| ITEM DROP | Chocobo Feather x2 |
| RARE DROP | Chocobo Feather x3 |
| STEAL RATIO | 255/255 |
| STOLEN ITEM | Healing Spring x2 |
| RARE STEAL | Healing Spring x3 |
| BRIBE ITEM | None |
| RARE BRIBE | None |

## EPITAPH

**DOOMSTONE**

CHAPTERS ▢▢▢▢5

| WHERE FOUND | Fiend Colony/Bevelle Palace Floors 75-79 |

| LEV | 43 | HP | 17433 | MP | 9999 |
| EXP | 1200 | AP | 1 | | |

| GIL DROP | 330 | GIL STEAL | 500 |

| STR | 56 | DEF | 122 | AGL | 134 |
| EVA | 0 | ACC | 2 | LUCK | 0 |
| MAG | 180 | MAG DEF | 18 | | |

Fire: Invalid | Water: Invalid | Lightning: Invalid
Holy: Weak | Gravity: Invalid | Ice: Weak

| IMM | Dth., Pet., Slp., Sil., Drk., Poi., Con., Ber., Cur., Ejt., Slw., Stp., Doom, M.D. |
| DEF EFF | Ejt. (48), Zan. (44) |

| DROP RATIO | 255/255 |
| ITEM DROP | Remedy x2 |
| RARE DROP | Remedy x3 |
| STEAL RATIO | 255/255 |
| STOLEN ITEM | Remedy x1 |
| RARE STEAL | Remedy x2 |
| BRIBE ITEM | Faerie Earrings x4 |
| RARE BRIBE | Faerie Earrings x5 |

## EXPERIMENT

**MACHINA**

CHAPTERS ▢▢▢▢5

| WHERE FOUND | Djose Highlands |

| LEV | 50 | HP | 18324 | MP | 0 |
| EXP | 0 | AP | 40 | | |

| GIL DROP | 0 | GIL STEAL | 5000 |

| STR | 215 | DEF | 100 | AGL | 68 |
| EVA | 0 | ACC | 0 | LUCK | 0 |
| MAG | 205 | MAG DEF | 205 | | |

Fire: None | Water: None | Lightning: None
Holy: None | Gravity: Invalid | Ice: None

| IMM | All |
| DEF EFF | Zan. (180) |

| DROP RATIO | 255/255 |
| ITEM DROP | Elixir x1 |
| RARE DROP | Elixir x1 |
| STEAL RATIO | 255/255 |
| STOLEN ITEM | Turbo Ether x1 |
| RARE STEAL | Turbo Ether x2 |
| BRIBE ITEM | None |
| RARE BRIBE | None |

## FEM-GOON

**NONE**

CHAPTERS ▢2▢▢

| WHERE FOUND | Djose Highlands/Guadosalam/Bikanel/Mt. Gagazet |

| LEV | 16 | HP | 167 | MP | 172 |
| EXP | 10 | AP | 1 | | |

| GIL DROP | 70 | GIL STEAL | 200 |

| STR | 26 | DEF | 8 | AGL | 62 |
| EVA | 0 | ACC | 4 | LUCK | 0 |
| MAG | 5 | MAG DEF | 10 | | |

Fire: None | Water: None | Lightning: None
Holy: None | Gravity: None | Ice: None

| IMM | Cur. |
| DEF EFF | None |

| DROP RATIO | 128/255 |
| ITEM DROP | Potion x1 |
| RARE DROP | Hi-Potion x1 |
| STEAL RATIO | 255/255 |
| STOLEN ITEM | Potion x1 |
| RARE STEAL | Potion x2 |
| BRIBE ITEM | S-Bomb x4 |
| RARE BRIBE | M-Bomb x4 |

Characters

1

Garment Grids & Dressspheres

2

Battle System

3

Accessories

4

Items and Item Shops

5

Walkthrough

6

Mini Games

7

Fiends and Enemies

8

# FLAILING OCHU

**OCHU**

| CHAPTERS | | | 3 | | 5 |
|---|---|---|---|---|---|

**WHERE FOUND** Zanarkand Ruins/Bevelle Tower Floors 47-49

| LEV | 36 [43] | HP | 9860 [24650] | MP | 85 |
|---|---|---|---|---|---|
| EXP | 977 [1600] | AP | 1 [2] | | |

| GIL DROP | 430 | GIL STEAL | 630 [1212] |
|---|---|---|---|

| STR | 57 [63] | DEF | 58 | AGL | 83 [100] |
|---|---|---|---|---|---|
| EVA | 0 | ACC | 9 [11] | LUCK | 0 |
| MAG | 58 | MAG DEF | 57 | | |

| | | | | | |
|---|---|---|---|---|---|
| Fire | Weak | Water | None | Lightning | None |
| Ice | Half | Holy | Invalid | Wind | None |

**IMM** All but Sil., Drk., Poi., Ejt., Slw., P.B., M.B., A.B.

**DEF EFF** Sil. (80 [0]), Drk. (100 [0]), Poi. (254), Ejt. (30 [32]), Zan. (4 [7])

| DROP RATIO | 128/255 [255/255] |
|---|---|
| ITEM DROP | Remedy x1 [White Cape x1] |
| RARE DROP | Ether x1 [White Cape x1] |
| STEAL RATIO | 128/255 [255/255] |
| STOLEN ITEM | Remedy x1 [Mute Shock x1] |
| RARE STEAL | White Cape x1 [Mute Shock x1] |
| BRIBE ITEM | Beaded Brooch x1 [Faerie Earrings] |
| RARE BRIBE | Beaded Brooch x1 [Ribbon x1] |

# FLAK PYTHON

**BANDOLEER**

| CHAPTERS | 1 | | | | 5 |
|---|---|---|---|---|---|

**WHERE FOUND** Zanarkand Ruins/Bevelle Palace Floors 13-15

| LEV | 7 | HP | 152 | MP | 0 |
|---|---|---|---|---|---|
| EXP | 8 | AP | 1 | | |

| GIL DROP | 10 | GIL STEAL | 80 |
|---|---|---|---|

| STR | 18 | DEF | 0 | AGL | 42 |
|---|---|---|---|---|---|
| EVA | 0 | ACC | 1 | LUCK | 0 |
| MAG | 0 | MAG DEF | 0 | | |

| | | | | | |
|---|---|---|---|---|---|
| Fire | None | Water | None | Lightning | None |
| Ice | None | Holy | None | Wind | None |

**IMM** Dth., Pet., Slp., Sil., Poi., Cur., Doom

**DEF EFF** None

| DROP RATIO | 128/255 |
|---|---|
| ITEM DROP | Potion x1 |
| RARE DROP | Phoenix Down x1 |
| STEAL RATIO | 255/255 |
| STOLEN ITEM | Budget Grenade x1 |
| RARE STEAL | Budget Grenade x2 |
| BRIBE ITEM | None |
| RARE BRIBE | None |

# FLAME DRAGON

**DRAGON**

| CHAPTERS | 1 | | 3 | | 5 |
|---|---|---|---|---|---|

**WHERE FOUND** Besaid/Bevelle Tower Floors 7-9

| LEV | 16 [21] | HP | 980 [1883] | MP | 84 |
|---|---|---|---|---|---|
| EXP | 60 [180] | AP | 1 [2] | | |

| GIL DROP | 300 [350] | GIL STEAL | 800 [1600] |
|---|---|---|---|

| STR | 37 | DEF | 48 | AGL | 78 [107] |
|---|---|---|---|---|---|
| EVA | 0 | ACC | 4 [5] | LUCK | 0 |
| MAG | 38 | MAG DEF | 1 | | |

| | | | | | |
|---|---|---|---|---|---|
| Fire | Half | Water | Weak | Lightning | None |
| Ice | None | Holy | Invalid | Wind | None |

**IMM** All but Drk., Poi., Ejt., Slw., P.B., M.B., A.B., M.B., L.C., E.C., Doom.

**DEF EFF** Drk. (50), Ejt. (40 [50]), Zan. (15 [25])

| DROP RATIO | 255/255 |
|---|---|
| ITEM DROP | Red Ring x1 |
| RARE DROP | Red Ring x1 |
| STEAL RATIO | 255/255 |
| STOLEN ITEM | Hi-Potion x1 [Hi-Potion x4] |
| RARE STEAL | Hi-Potion x2 [Hi-Potion x4] |
| BRIBE ITEM | Fire Gem x30 [NulBlaze Ring x1] |
| RARE BRIBE | Fire Gem x40 [Crimson Ring x1] |

# FLAN AMARILLO

**FLAN**

| CHAPTERS | | 2 | | | 5 |
|---|---|---|---|---|---|

**WHERE FOUND** Bevelle/Mt. Gagazet/Bevelle Tower Floors 10-12

| LEV | 18 | HP | 303 [1172] | MP | 322 |
|---|---|---|---|---|---|
| EXP | 82 [152] | AP | 1 [2] | | |

| GIL DROP | 42 [72] | GIL STEAL | 130 [223] |
|---|---|---|---|

| STR | 14 | DEF | 14 [17] | AGL | 56 [62] |
|---|---|---|---|---|---|
| EVA | 0 | ACC | 4 [5] | LUCK | 0 |
| MAG | 110 | MAG DEF | 5 | | |

| | | | | | |
|---|---|---|---|---|---|
| Fire | Half | Water | Half | Lightning | Absorb |
| Ice | Weak | Holy | None | Wind | None |

**IMM** [Con.], Ber., Cur., [M.B.]

**DEF EFF** Ejt. (12 [18]), Stp. (20), Zan. (2 [4])

| DROP RATIO | 128/255 [255/255] |
|---|---|
| ITEM DROP | Electro Marble x2 [Lightning Gem x2] |
| RARE DROP | Lightning Marble x1 [Lightning Gem x3] |
| STEAL RATIO | 255/255 |
| STOLEN ITEM | Electro Marble x2 [Lightning Gem x2] |
| RARE STEAL | Lightning Marble x1 [Lightning Gem x3] |
| BRIBE ITEM | Lightning Gem x3 [NulShock Ring x1] |
| RARE BRIBE | Lightning Gem x4 [NulShock Ring x1] |

# FLAN AZABACHE

**FLAN**

| CHAPTERS | | | | | 5 |
|---|---|---|---|---|---|

**WHERE FOUND** Ruin Depths/Bevelle Tower Floors 65-69

| LEV | 47 [56] | HP | 7730 [9667] | MP | 999 |
|---|---|---|---|---|---|
| EXP | 380 [650] | AP | 1 [2] | | |

| GIL DROP | 98 [230] | GIL STEAL | 630 [1300] |
|---|---|---|---|

| STR | 203 | DEF | 34 | AGL | 82 [107] |
|---|---|---|---|---|---|
| EVA | 0 | ACC | 4 [5] | LUCK | 0 |
| MAG | 222 | MAG DEF | 222 | | |

| | | | | | |
|---|---|---|---|---|---|
| Fire | Invalid | Water | Invalid | Lightning | Invalid |
| Ice | Invalid | Holy | Absorb [None] | Wind | Invalid |

**IMM** Dth., Pet., Slp., Sil., Drk., Con., Ber., Cur., Slw. ([0]), Stp. ([0]), [M.B.], Doom, M.D. ([0])

**DEF EFF** Poi. (100 [0]), Ejt. (44 [38]), Zan. (10 [20])

| DROP RATIO | 255/255 |
|---|---|
| ITEM DROP | Ether x1 [Ether x3] |
| RARE DROP | Ether x2 [Ether x4] |
| STEAL RATIO | 128/255 |
| STOLEN ITEM | Ether x1 |
| RARE STEAL | Ether x1 |
| BRIBE ITEM | Ether x99 [Turbo Ether x60] |
| RARE BRIBE | Turbo Ether x40 [Turbo Ether x60] |

# FLAN AZUL

**FLAN**

| CHAPTERS | 1 | 2 | | | 5 |
|---|---|---|---|---|---|

**WHERE FOUND** Besaid/Dry Plains/Macalania, Others

| LEV | 4 [7] | HP | 55 [220] | MP | 87 |
|---|---|---|---|---|---|
| EXP | 5 [24] | AP | 1 [2] | | |

| GIL DROP | 20 [63] | GIL STEAL | 104 [200] |
|---|---|---|---|

| STR | 4 | DEF | 10 [14] | AGL | 53 [58] |
|---|---|---|---|---|---|
| EVA | 0 | ACC | 4 [5] | LUCK | 0 |
| MAG | 98 | MAG DEF | 2 | | |

| | | | | | |
|---|---|---|---|---|---|
| Fire | Half | Water | Half | Lightning | Weak |
| Ice | Absorb | Holy | None | Wind | None |

**IMM** [Con.], [Ber.], Cur., [M.B.]

**DEF EFF** Ejt. (12 [18]), Zan. (2 [4])

| DROP RATIO | 128/255 [255/255] |
|---|---|
| ITEM DROP | Potion x1 [Fish Scale x2] |
| RARE DROP | Fish Scale x1 [Fish Scale x3] |
| STEAL RATIO | 255/255 |
| STOLEN ITEM | Potion x1 [Fish Scale x2] |
| RARE STEAL | Fish Scale x1 [Dragon Scale x2] |
| BRIBE ITEM | Fish Scale x2 [Water Gem x2] |
| RARE BRIBE | Fish Scale x3 [Water Gem x2] |

# FLAN PALIDO

**FLAN**

| CHAPTERS | 1 | 2 | | | 5 |
|---|---|---|---|---|---|

**WHERE FOUND** Mi'ihen Highroad/Mt. Gagazet/Bevelle Tower Floors 13-15

| LEV | 12 [15] | HP | 188 [851] | MP | 222 |
|---|---|---|---|---|---|
| EXP | 24 [73] | AP | 1 [2] | | |

| GIL DROP | 30 [82] | GIL STEAL | 160 [260] |
|---|---|---|---|

| STR | 3 | DEF | 21 [23] | AGL | 54 [59] |
|---|---|---|---|---|---|
| EVA | 0 | ACC | 4 [5] | LUCK | 0 |
| MAG | 102 | MAG DEF | 4 | | |

| | | | | | |
|---|---|---|---|---|---|
| Fire | Weak | Water | Absorb | Lightning | Half |
| Ice | Half | Holy | None | Wind | None |

**IMM** [Con.], Ber., Cur., [M.B.]

**DEF EFF** Ejt. (12 [18]), Zan. (2 [4])

| DROP RATIO | 128/255 [255/255] |
|---|---|
| ITEM DROP | Potion x1 [Hi-Potion x3] |
| RARE DROP | Antarctic Wind x1 [Antarctic Wind x4] |
| STEAL RATIO | 255/255 |
| STOLEN ITEM | Potion x1 [Hi-Potion x2] |
| RARE STEAL | Antarctic Wind x1 [Arctic Wind x3] |
| BRIBE ITEM | Antarctic Wind x8 [Ice Gem x6] |
| RARE BRIBE | Antarctic Wind x8 [Ice Gem x8] |

# FLAN ROJO

**FLAN**

| CHAPTERS | | | 3 | 4 | 5 |
|---|---|---|---|---|---|

**WHERE FOUND** Mi'ihen Highroad/Thunder Plains/Calm Lands/Bevelle Tower Floors 36-39

| LEV | 28 [34] | HP | 1220 [3050] | MP | 674 |
|---|---|---|---|---|---|
| EXP | 320 [520] | AP | 1 [2] | | |

| GIL DROP | 125 [520] | GIL STEAL | 330 [600] |
|---|---|---|---|

| STR | 11 | DEF | 1 [5] | AGL | 56 [67] |
|---|---|---|---|---|---|
| EVA | 0 | ACC | 4 [5] | LUCK | 0 |
| MAG | 104 | MAG DEF | 10 | | |

| | | | | | |
|---|---|---|---|---|---|
| Fire | Absorb | Water | Weak | Lightning | Half |
| Ice | Half | Holy | Half | Wind | Half |

**IMM** [Con.], Ber., Cur., [M.B.]

**DEF EFF** Ejt. (14 [22]), Stp. (40), Zan. (2 [4])

| DROP RATIO | 128/255 [255/255] |
|---|---|
| ITEM DROP | Bomb Core x1 [Fire Gem x3] |
| RARE DROP | Fire Gem x1 [Fire Gem x4] |
| STEAL RATIO | 255/255 |
| STOLEN ITEM | Bomb Core x1 [Red Ring x1] |
| RARE STEAL | Fire Gem x1 [Red Ring x1] |
| BRIBE ITEM | Fire Gem x12 [Crimson Ring x1] |
| RARE BRIBE | Fire Gem x14 [Crimson Ring x1] |

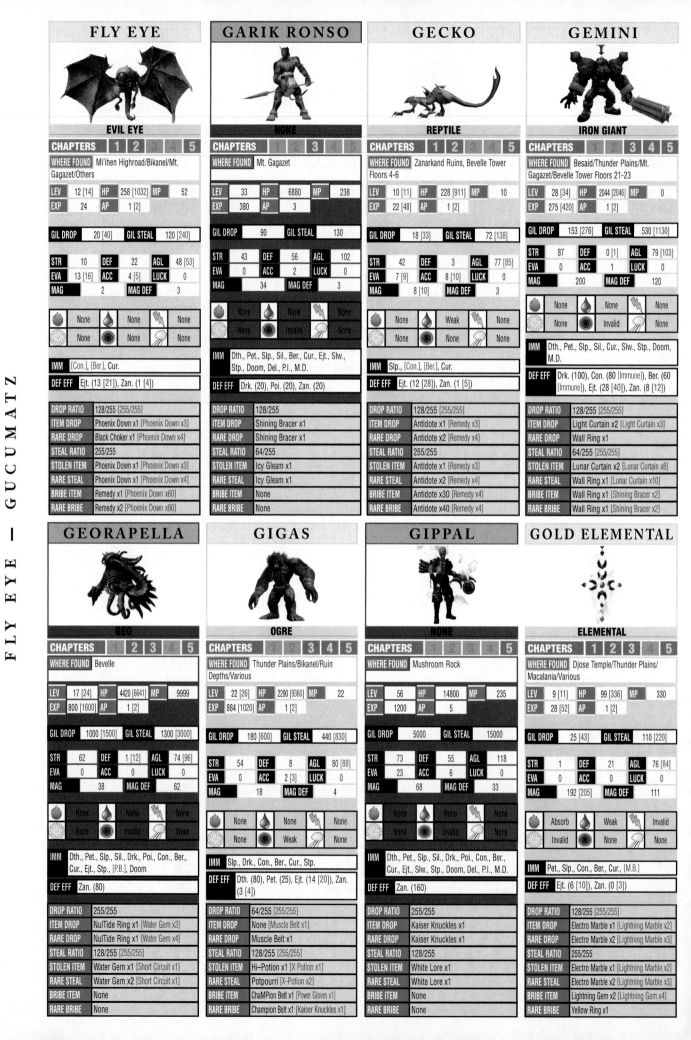

## FLY EYE
### EVIL EYE

| CHAPTERS | 1 | 2 | 3 | 4 | 5 |
|---|---|---|---|---|---|

WHERE FOUND: Mi'ihen Highroad/Bikanel/Mt. Gagazet/Others

| LEV | 12 [14] | HP | 258 [1032] | MP | 52 |
|---|---|---|---|---|---|
| EXP | 24 | AP | 1 [2] | | |

| GIL DROP | 20 [40] | GIL STEAL | 120 [240] |
|---|---|---|---|

| STR | 10 | DEF | 22 | AGL | 48 [53] |
|---|---|---|---|---|---|
| EVA | 13 [16] | ACC | 4 [5] | LUCK | 0 |
| MAG | 2 | MAG DEF | 3 | | |

| | None | | None | | None | | None |
|---|---|---|---|---|---|---|---|
| | None | | None | | None | | None |

IMM: [Con.], [Ber.], Cur.

DEF EFF: Ejt. (13 [21]), Zan. (1 [4])

| DROP RATIO | 128/255 [255/255] |
|---|---|
| ITEM DROP | Phoenix Down x1 [Phoenix Down x3] |
| RARE DROP | Black Choker x1 [Phoenix Down x4] |
| STEAL RATIO | 255/255 |
| STOLEN ITEM | Phoenix Down x1 [Phoenix Down x3] |
| RARE STEAL | Phoenix Down x1 [Phoenix Down x4] |
| BRIBE ITEM | Remedy x1 [Phoenix Down x60] |
| RARE BRIBE | Remedy x2 [Phoenix Down x80] |

## GARIK RONSO
### NONE

| CHAPTERS | 1 | 2 | 3 | 4 | 5 |
|---|---|---|---|---|---|

WHERE FOUND: Mt. Gagazet

| LEV | 33 | HP | 6880 | MP | 238 |
|---|---|---|---|---|---|
| EXP | 380 | AP | 3 | | |

| GIL DROP | 90 | GIL STEAL | 130 |
|---|---|---|---|

| STR | 43 | DEF | 56 | AGL | 102 |
|---|---|---|---|---|---|
| EVA | 0 | ACC | 2 | LUCK | 0 |
| MAG | 34 | MAG DEF | 3 | | |

| | None | | None | | None | | None |
|---|---|---|---|---|---|---|---|
| | None | | None | | Invalid | | None |

IMM: Dth., Pet., Slp., Sil., Ber., Cur., Ejt., Slw., Stp., Doom, Del., P.l., M.D.

DEF EFF: Drk. (20), Poi. (20), Zan. (20)

| DROP RATIO | 128/255 |
|---|---|
| ITEM DROP | Shining Bracer x1 |
| RARE DROP | Shining Bracer x1 |
| STEAL RATIO | 64/255 |
| STOLEN ITEM | Icy Gleam x1 |
| RARE STEAL | Icy Gleam x1 |
| BRIBE ITEM | None |
| RARE BRIBE | None |

## GECKO
### REPTILE

| CHAPTERS | 1 | 2 | 3 | 4 | 5 |
|---|---|---|---|---|---|

WHERE FOUND: Zanarkand Ruins, Bevelle Tower Floors 4-6

| LEV | 10 [11] | HP | 228 [911] | MP | 10 |
|---|---|---|---|---|---|
| EXP | 22 [48] | AP | 1 [2] | | |

| GIL DROP | 18 [33] | GIL STEAL | 72 [138] |
|---|---|---|---|

| STR | 42 | DEF | 3 | AGL | 77 [85] |
|---|---|---|---|---|---|
| EVA | 7 [9] | ACC | 8 [10] | LUCK | 0 |
| MAG | 8 [10] | MAG DEF | 3 | | |

| | None | | None | | Weak | | None |
|---|---|---|---|---|---|---|---|
| | None | | None | | None | | None |

IMM: Slp., [Con.], [Ber.], Cur.

DEF EFF: Ejt. (12 [28]), Zan. (1 [5])

| DROP RATIO | 128/255 [255/255] |
|---|---|
| ITEM DROP | Antidote x1 [Remedy x3] |
| RARE DROP | Antidote x2 [Remedy x4] |
| STEAL RATIO | 255/255 |
| STOLEN ITEM | Antidote x1 [Remedy x3] |
| RARE STEAL | Antidote x2 [Remedy x4] |
| BRIBE ITEM | Antidote x30 [Remedy x4] |
| RARE BRIBE | Antidote x40 [Remedy x4] |

## GEMINI
### IRON GIANT

| CHAPTERS | 1 | 2 | 3 | 4 | 5 |
|---|---|---|---|---|---|

WHERE FOUND: Besaid/Thunder Plains/Mt. Gagazet/Bevelle Tower Floors 21-23

| LEV | 28 [34] | HP | 2044 [2046] | MP | 0 |
|---|---|---|---|---|---|
| EXP | 275 [420] | AP | 1 [2] | | |

| GIL DROP | 153 [276] | GIL STEAL | 530 [1130] |
|---|---|---|---|

| STR | 87 | DEF | 0 [1] | AGL | 79 [103] |
|---|---|---|---|---|---|
| EVA | 0 | ACC | 1 | LUCK | 0 |
| MAG | 200 | MAG DEF | 120 | | |

| | None | | None | | None | | None |
|---|---|---|---|---|---|---|---|
| | None | | None | | Invalid | | None |

IMM: Dth., Pet., Slp., Sil., Cur., Slw., Stp., Doom, M.D.

DEF EFF: Drk. (100), Con. (80 [Immune]), Ber. (60 [Immune]), Ejt. (28 [40]), Zan. (8 [12])

| DROP RATIO | 128/255 [255/255] |
|---|---|
| ITEM DROP | Light Curtain x2 [Light Curtain x3] |
| RARE DROP | Wall Ring x1 |
| STEAL RATIO | 64/255 [255/255] |
| STOLEN ITEM | Lunar Curtain x2 [Lunar Curtain x8] |
| RARE STEAL | Wall Ring x1 [Lunar Curtain x10] |
| BRIBE ITEM | Wall Ring x1 [Shining Bracer x2] |
| RARE BRIBE | Wall Ring x1 [Shining Bracer x2] |

## GEORAPELLA
### GEO

| CHAPTERS | 1 | 2 | 3 | 4 | 5 |
|---|---|---|---|---|---|

WHERE FOUND: Bevelle

| LEV | 17 [24] | HP | 4420 [6641] | MP | 9999 |
|---|---|---|---|---|---|
| EXP | 800 [1600] | AP | 1 [2] | | |

| GIL DROP | 1000 [1500] | GIL STEAL | 1300 [3000] |
|---|---|---|---|

| STR | 62 | DEF | 1 [12] | AGL | 74 [96] |
|---|---|---|---|---|---|
| EVA | 0 | ACC | 0 | LUCK | 0 |
| MAG | 38 | MAG DEF | 62 | | |

| | None | | None | | None | | None |
|---|---|---|---|---|---|---|---|
| | None | | None | | Invalid | | Weak |

IMM: Dth., Pet., Slp., Sil., Drk., Poi., Con., Ber., Cur., Ejt., Stp., [P.B.], Doom

DEF EFF: Zan. (80)

| DROP RATIO | 255/255 |
|---|---|
| ITEM DROP | NulTide Ring x1 [Water Gem x3] |
| RARE DROP | NulTide Ring x1 [Water Gem x4] |
| STEAL RATIO | 128/255 [255/255] |
| STOLEN ITEM | Water Gem x1 [Short Circuit x1] |
| RARE STEAL | Water Gem x2 [Short Circuit x1] |
| BRIBE ITEM | None |
| RARE BRIBE | None |

## GIGAS
### OGRE

| CHAPTERS | 1 | 2 | 3 | 4 | 5 |
|---|---|---|---|---|---|

WHERE FOUND: Thunder Plains/Bikanel/Ruin Depths/Various

| LEV | 22 [26] | HP | 2290 [9360] | MP | 22 |
|---|---|---|---|---|---|
| EXP | 884 [1020] | AP | 1 [2] | | |

| GIL DROP | 180 [600] | GIL STEAL | 440 [830] |
|---|---|---|---|

| STR | 54 | DEF | 8 | AGL | 80 [88] |
|---|---|---|---|---|---|
| EVA | 0 | ACC | 2 [3] | LUCK | 0 |
| MAG | 18 | MAG DEF | 4 | | |

| | None | | None | | None | | None |
|---|---|---|---|---|---|---|---|
| | None | | None | | Weak | | None |

IMM: Slp., Drk., Con., Ber., Cur., Stp.

DEF EFF: Dth. (80), Pet. (25), Ejt. (14 [20]), Zan. (3 [4])

| DROP RATIO | 64/255 [255/255] |
|---|---|
| ITEM DROP | None [Muscle Belt x1] |
| RARE DROP | Muscle Belt x1 |
| STEAL RATIO | 128/255 [255/255] |
| STOLEN ITEM | Hi–Potion x1 [X Potion x1] |
| RARE STEAL | Potpourri [X-Potion x2] |
| BRIBE ITEM | ChaMpion Belt x1 [Power Gloves x1] |
| RARE BRIBE | Champion Belt x1 [Kaiser Knuckles x1] |

## GIPPAL
### NONE

| CHAPTERS | 1 | 2 | 3 | 4 | 5 |
|---|---|---|---|---|---|

WHERE FOUND: Mushroom Rock

| LEV | 56 | HP | 14800 | MP | 235 |
|---|---|---|---|---|---|
| EXP | 1200 | AP | 5 | | |

| GIL DROP | 5000 | GIL STEAL | 15000 |
|---|---|---|---|

| STR | 73 | DEF | 55 | AGL | 118 |
|---|---|---|---|---|---|
| EVA | 23 | ACC | 6 | LUCK | 0 |
| MAG | 68 | MAG DEF | 33 | | |

| | None | | None | | None | | None |
|---|---|---|---|---|---|---|---|
| | None | | None | | Invalid | | None |

IMM: Dth., Pet., Slp., Sil., Drk., Poi., Con., Ber., Cur., Ejt., Slw., Stp., Doom, Del., P.l., M.D.

DEF EFF: Zan. (160)

| DROP RATIO | 255/255 |
|---|---|
| ITEM DROP | Kaiser Knuckles x1 |
| RARE DROP | Kaiser Knuckles x1 |
| STEAL RATIO | 128/255 |
| STOLEN ITEM | White Lore x1 |
| RARE STEAL | White Lore x1 |
| BRIBE ITEM | None |
| RARE BRIBE | None |

## GOLD ELEMENTAL
### ELEMENTAL

| CHAPTERS | 1 | 2 | 3 | 4 | 5 |
|---|---|---|---|---|---|

WHERE FOUND: Djose Temple/Thunder Plains/Macalania/Various

| LEV | 9 [11] | HP | 99 [336] | MP | 330 |
|---|---|---|---|---|---|
| EXP | 28 [52] | AP | 1 [2] | | |

| GIL DROP | 25 [43] | GIL STEAL | 110 [220] |
|---|---|---|---|

| STR | 1 | DEF | 21 | AGL | 76 [84] |
|---|---|---|---|---|---|
| EVA | 0 | ACC | 0 | LUCK | 0 |
| MAG | 192 [205] | MAG DEF | 111 | | |

| | Absorb | | Weak | | Invalid |
|---|---|---|---|---|---|
| | Invalid | | None | | None |

IMM: Pet., Slp., Con., Ber., Cur., [M.B.]

DEF EFF: Ejt. (6 [10]), Zan. (0 [3])

| DROP RATIO | 128/255 [255/255] |
|---|---|
| ITEM DROP | Electro Marble x1 [Lightning Marble x2] |
| RARE DROP | Electro Marble x2 [Lightning Marble x2] |
| STEAL RATIO | 255/255 |
| STOLEN ITEM | Electro Marble x1 [Lightning Marble x2] |
| RARE STEAL | Electro Marble x2 [Lightning Marble x2] |
| BRIBE ITEM | Lightning Gem x2 [Lightning Gem x4] |
| RARE BRIBE | Yellow Ring x1 |

# GOON

**NONE**

CHAPTERS: 1

| WHERE FOUND | Luca, Mt. Gagazet |
|---|---|

| LEV | 1 | HP | 13 (29 Luca） | MP | 8 |
|---|---|---|---|---|---|
| EXP | 1 | AP | 1 | | |

| GIL DROP | 30 | GIL STEAL | 200 |
|---|---|---|---|

| STR | 7 | DEF | 1 | AGL | 47 |
|---|---|---|---|---|---|
| EVA | 0 | ACC | 3 | LUCK | 0 |
| MAG | 4 | MAG DEF | 4 | | |

Elements: None / None / None / None / None / None

| IMM | Cur. |
|---|---|
| DEF EFF | None |

| DROP RATIO | 128/255 |
|---|---|
| ITEM DROP | Potion x1 |
| RARE DROP | Phoenix Down x1 |
| STEAL RATIO | 255/255 |
| STOLEN ITEM | Budget Grenade x1 |
| RARE STEAL | Phoenix Down x1 |
| BRIBE ITEM | Budget Grenade x1 |
| RARE BRIBE | Phoenix Down x1 |

---

# GREAT HAUNT

**REVENANT**

CHAPTERS: 5

| WHERE FOUND | Bikanel/Bevelle Palace Floors 50-59 |
|---|---|

| LEV | 46 | HP | 8483 | MP | 720 |
|---|---|---|---|---|---|
| EXP | 120 | AP | 1 | | |

| GIL DROP | 210 | GIL STEAL | 600 |
|---|---|---|---|

| STR | 26 | DEF | 55 | AGL | 61 |
|---|---|---|---|---|---|
| EVA | 0 | ACC | 1 | LUCK | 0 |
| MAG | 142 | MAG DEF | 2 | | |

Elements: Varies / Varies / Varies / Varies / Invalid / Weak

| IMM | Dth., Pet., Slp., Sil., Drk., Poi., Con., Ber., Cur., Stp., Doom, Del., P.l., M.D. |
|---|---|
| DEF EFF | Ejt. (30), Zan. (10) |

| DROP RATIO | 128/255 |
|---|---|
| ITEM DROP | Ether x1 |
| RARE DROP | Ether x1 |
| STEAL RATIO | 128/255 |
| STOLEN ITEM | Mana Spring x1 |
| RARE STEAL | Soul Spring x1 |
| BRIBE ITEM | Gold Hairpin x3 |
| RARE BRIBE | Gold Hairpin x3 |

---

# GREAT MALBORO

**MALBORO**

CHAPTERS: 5

| WHERE FOUND | Farplane/Bevelle Tower Floors 70-74 |
|---|---|

| LEV | 42 [51] | HP | 12988 [19937] | MP | 152 |
|---|---|---|---|---|---|
| EXP | 2235 [3860] | AP | 1 [2] | | |

| GIL DROP | 1200 [1500] | GIL STEAL | 1600 [3300] |
|---|---|---|---|

| STR | 53 | DEF | 68 | AGL | 81 [105] |
|---|---|---|---|---|---|
| EVA | 0 | ACC | 3 [4] | LUCK | 0 |
| MAG | 16 | MAG DEF | 12 | | |

Elements: None / None / None / None / Invalid / None

| IMM | Dth., Pet., Slp., Sil., Drk., Poi., Con., Ber., Cur., Slw., Stp., Doom, Del., P.l., M.D. |
|---|---|
| DEF EFF | Ejt. (40 [44]), Zan. (46 [55]) |

| DROP RATIO | 255/255 |
|---|---|
| ITEM DROP | Remedy x2 [Beaded Brooch x1] |
| RARE DROP | Remedy x3 [Beaded Brooch x1] |
| STEAL RATIO | 128/255 |
| STOLEN ITEM | Dispel Tonic x1 [Remedy x2] |
| RARE STEAL | Dispel Tonic x1 [Remedy x3] |
| BRIBE ITEM | White Lore x2 [White Tome x2] |
| RARE BRIBE | White Lore x2 [White Tome x2] |

---

# GREATER DRAKE

**DRAKE**

CHAPTERS: 3, 5

| WHERE FOUND | Djose Temple/Mt. Gagazet/Ruin Depths/Various |
|---|---|

| LEV | 23 [27] | HP | 1819 [6658] | MP | 103 [107] |
|---|---|---|---|---|---|
| EXP | 320 [470] | AP | 1 [2] | | |

| GIL DROP | 140 [210] | GIL STEAL | 630 [1300] |
|---|---|---|---|

| STR | 47 [48] | DEF | 36 [90] | AGL | 72 [80] |
|---|---|---|---|---|---|
| EVA | 0 | ACC | 4 [5] | LUCK | 0 |
| MAG | 88 [102] | MAG DEF | 3 [37] | | |

Elements: Invalid / Weak / None / None / None / None

| IMM | Slp., Sil., Drk., Poi., Con., Ber., Cur., Slw., [P.B.] |
|---|---|
| DEF EFF | Dth. (50), Pet. (30), Ejt. (19 [25]), Zan. (5 [6]) |

| DROP RATIO | 64/255 [255/255] |
|---|---|
| ITEM DROP | Fire Gem x1 [NulBlaze Ring x1] |
| RARE DROP | NulBlaze Ring x1 |
| STEAL RATIO | 255/255 |
| STOLEN ITEM | Fire Gem x1 [Fire Gem x3] |
| RARE STEAL | Fire Gem x2 [Fire Gem x10] |
| BRIBE ITEM | NulBlaze Ring x1 [Subliminator x2] |
| RARE BRIBE | NulBlaze Ring x1 [Subliminator x3] |

---

# GRIM GAZE

**EVIL EYE**

CHAPTERS: 3, 4, 5

| WHERE FOUND | Calm Lands/Mt. Gagazet/Bevelle Tower Floors 41-43 |
|---|---|

| LEV | 33 [41] | HP | 1720 [4223] | MP | 388 |
|---|---|---|---|---|---|
| EXP | 244 [380] | AP | 1 [2] | | |

| GIL DROP | 130 [220] | GIL STEAL | 330 [650] |
|---|---|---|---|

| STR | 31 | DEF | 21 | AGL | 62 [79] |
|---|---|---|---|---|---|
| EVA | 27 [59] | ACC | 4 [5] | LUCK | 0 |
| MAG | 5 | MAG DEF | 8 | | |

Elements: None / None / None / None / None / Invalid / None

| IMM | Con., Ber., Cur., Slw. ([0]), Stp. ([0]), M.D. |
|---|---|
| DEF EFF | Ejt. (15 [23]), Zan. (1 [4]) |

| DROP RATIO | 128/255 [255/255] |
|---|---|
| ITEM DROP | Phoenix Down x1 [Remedy x3] |
| RARE DROP | Holy Water x1 [Remedy x4] |
| STEAL RATIO | 255/255 |
| STOLEN ITEM | Phoenix Down x1 [Pixie Dust x1] |
| RARE STEAL | Remedy x1 [Pixie Dust x1] |
| BRIBE ITEM | Silver Glasses x1 [Elixir x4] |
| RARE BRIBE | Silver Glasses x1 [Elixir x4] |

---

# GUARD MACHINA

**MACHINA**

CHAPTERS: 3

| WHERE FOUND | Bikanel/Bevelle Palace Floors 27-29 |
|---|---|

| LEV | 24 | HP | 2460 | MP | 0 |
|---|---|---|---|---|---|
| EXP | 85 | AP | 1 | | |

| GIL DROP | 40 | GIL STEAL | 80 |
|---|---|---|---|

| STR | 25 | DEF | 0 | AGL | 50 |
|---|---|---|---|---|---|
| EVA | 0 | ACC | 0 | LUCK | 0 |
| MAG | 20 | MAG DEF | 0 | | |

Elements: None / None / None / Absorb / None / None / None

| IMM | Dth., Pet., Slp., Sil., Poi., Con., Ber., Cur., Doom |
|---|---|
| DEF EFF | Ejt. (18) |

| DROP RATIO | 128/255 |
|---|---|
| ITEM DROP | Budget Grenade x1 |
| RARE DROP | Darkness Grenade x1 |
| STEAL RATIO | 128/255 |
| STOLEN ITEM | Budget Grenade x1 |
| RARE STEAL | Darkness Grenade x1 |
| BRIBE ITEM | None |
| RARE BRIBE | None |

---

# GUARDIAN BEAST

**SACRED BEAST**

CHAPTERS: 1, 3, 5

| WHERE FOUND | Zanarkand Ruins/Bevelle Palace Floors 7-9 |
|---|---|

| LEV | 18 [26] | HP | 2886 [4030] | MP | 1000 |
|---|---|---|---|---|---|
| EXP | 170 [380] | AP | 1 [2] | | |

| GIL DROP | 200 [380] | GIL STEAL | 1500 [3200] |
|---|---|---|---|

| STR | 65 [75] | DEF | 46 | AGL | 112 [146] |
|---|---|---|---|---|---|
| EVA | 0 | ACC | 6 [8] | LUCK | 0 |
| MAG | 60 | MAG DEF | 3 | | |

Elements: Weak / Weak / Weak / Weak / Invalid / Weak

| IMM | Dth., Pet., Slp., Sil., Poi., Con., Cur., Stp., Doom ([0]), Del., P.l., M.D. |
|---|---|
| DEF EFF | Drk. (50), Ber. (60 [Immune]), Ejt. (200), Zan. (80 [100]) |

| DROP RATIO | 255/255 |
|---|---|
| ITEM DROP | Amulet x1 [Pixie Dust x1] |
| RARE DROP | Amulet x1 [Pixie Dust x1] |
| STEAL RATIO | 128/255 [255/255] |
| STOLEN ITEM | Defense Veil x1 [Mystery Veil x1] |
| RARE STEAL | Defense Veil x1 [Mystery Veil x1] |
| BRIBE ITEM | Oath Veil x1 |
| RARE BRIBE | Oath Veil x1 [Oath Veil x2] |

---

# GUCUMATZ

**BASILISK**

CHAPTERS: 3, 5

| WHERE FOUND | Mushroom Rock/Thunder Plains/Bikanel/Zanarkand Ruins/Various |
|---|---|

| LEV | 34 [41] | HP | 3720 [13820] | MP | 140 |
|---|---|---|---|---|---|
| EXP | 410 [780] | AP | 1 [2] | | |

| GIL DROP | 173 [340] | GIL STEAL | 680 [1000] |
|---|---|---|---|

| STR | 46 | DEF | 10 [53] | AGL | 67 [74] |
|---|---|---|---|---|---|
| EVA | 0 | ACC | 3 [4] | LUCK | 0 |
| MAG | 93 | MAG DEF | 32 | | |

Elements: None / Weak / None / None / Invalid / None

| IMM | Dth., Pet., Slp., Poi., Con., Cur., Slw., P.B., M.B., Doom, M.D. |
|---|---|
| DEF EFF | Ber. (60 [Immune]), Ejt. (25 [30]), Zan. (7 [8]) |

| DROP RATIO | 128/255 [255/255] |
|---|---|
| ITEM DROP | Soft x2 [Gold Anklet x1] |
| RARE DROP | Soft x4 [Gold Anklet x1] |
| STEAL RATIO | 128/255 [255/255] |
| STOLEN ITEM | Soft x2 [Mana Tablet x2] |
| RARE STEAL | Gold Anklet x4 [Mana Tablet x3] |
| BRIBE ITEM | Stone Shock x1 [Stone Shock x6] |
| RARE BRIBE | Stone Shock x1 [Stone Shock x8] |

Characters

1

Garment Grids & Dressspheres

2

Battle System

3

Accessories

4

Items and Item Shops

5

Walkthrough

6

Mini Games

7

Fiends and Enemies

8

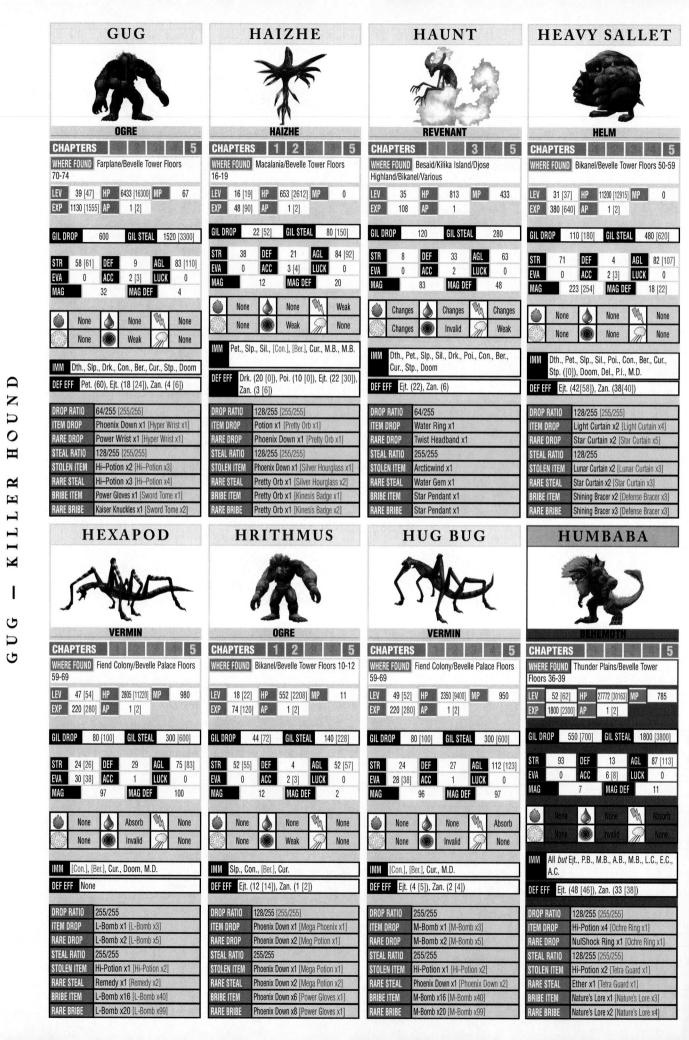

## GUG

**OGRE**

| CHAPTERS | | | | | 5 |
|---|---|---|---|---|---|

**WHERE FOUND** Farplane/Bevelle Tower Floors 70-74

| LEV | 39 [47] | HP | 6433 [16300] | MP | 67 |
|---|---|---|---|---|---|
| EXP | 1130 [1555] | AP | 1 [2] | | |

| GIL DROP | 600 | GIL STEAL | 1520 [3300] |
|---|---|---|---|

| STR | 58 [61] | DEF | 9 | AGL | 83 [110] |
|---|---|---|---|---|---|
| EVA | 0 | ACC | 2 [3] | LUCK | 0 |
| MAG | 32 | MAG DEF | 4 | | |

| | None | | None | | None |
|---|---|---|---|---|---|
| | None | | Weak | | None |

**IMM** Dth., Slp., Drk., Con., Ber., Cur., Stp., Doom

**DEF EFF** Pet. (60), Ejt. (18 [24]), Zan. (4 [6])

| DROP RATIO | 64/255 [255/255] |
|---|---|
| ITEM DROP | Phoenix Down x1 [Hyper Wrist x1] |
| RARE DROP | Power Wrist x1 [Hyper Wrist x1] |
| STEAL RATIO | 128/255 [255/255] |
| STOLEN ITEM | Hi-Potion x2 [Hi-Potion x3] |
| RARE STEAL | Hi-Potion x3 [Hi-Potion x4] |
| BRIBE ITEM | Power Gloves x1 [Sword Tome x1] |
| RARE BRIBE | Kaiser Knuckles x1 [Sword Tome x2] |

## HAIZHE

**HAIZHE**

| CHAPTERS | 1 | 2 | | | 5 |
|---|---|---|---|---|---|

**WHERE FOUND** Macalania/Bevelle Tower Floors 16-19

| LEV | 16 [19] | HP | 653 [2612] | MP | 0 |
|---|---|---|---|---|---|
| EXP | 48 [90] | AP | 1 [2] | | |

| GIL DROP | 22 [52] | GIL STEAL | 80 [150] |
|---|---|---|---|

| STR | 38 | DEF | 21 | AGL | 84 [92] |
|---|---|---|---|---|---|
| EVA | 0 | ACC | 3 [4] | LUCK | 0 |
| MAG | 12 | MAG DEF | 20 | | |

| | None | | None | | Weak |
|---|---|---|---|---|---|
| | None | | Weak | | None |

**IMM** Pet., Slp., Sil., [Con.], [Ber.], Cur., M.B., M.B.

**DEF EFF** Drk. (20 [0]), Poi. (10 [0]), Ejt. (22 [30]), Zan. (3 [6])

| DROP RATIO | 128/255 [255/255] |
|---|---|
| ITEM DROP | Potion x1 [Pretty Orb x1] |
| RARE DROP | Phoenix Down x1 [Pretty Orb x1] |
| STEAL RATIO | 128/255 [255/255] |
| STOLEN ITEM | Phoenix Down x1 [Silver Hourglass x1] |
| RARE STEAL | Pretty Orb x1 [Silver Hourglass x2] |
| BRIBE ITEM | Pretty Orb x1 [Kinesis Badge x1] |
| RARE BRIBE | Pretty Orb x1 [Kinesis Badge x2] |

## HAUNT

**REVENANT**

| CHAPTERS | | | 3 | | 5 |
|---|---|---|---|---|---|

**WHERE FOUND** Besaid/Kilika Island/Djose Highland/Bikanel/Various

| LEV | 35 | HP | 813 | MP | 433 |
|---|---|---|---|---|---|
| EXP | 108 | AP | 1 | | |

| GIL DROP | 120 | GIL STEAL | 280 |
|---|---|---|---|

| STR | 8 | DEF | 33 | AGL | 63 |
|---|---|---|---|---|---|
| EVA | 0 | ACC | 2 | LUCK | 0 |
| MAG | 83 | MAG DEF | 48 | | |

| | Changes | | Changes | | Changes |
|---|---|---|---|---|---|
| | Changes | | Invalid | | Weak |

**IMM** Dth., Pet., Slp., Sil., Drk., Poi., Con., Ber., Cur., Stp., Doom

**DEF EFF** Ejt. (22), Zan. (6)

| DROP RATIO | 64/255 |
|---|---|
| ITEM DROP | Water Ring x1 |
| RARE DROP | Twist Headband x1 |
| STEAL RATIO | 255/255 |
| STOLEN ITEM | Arcticwind x1 |
| RARE STEAL | Water Gem x1 |
| BRIBE ITEM | Star Pendant x1 |
| RARE BRIBE | Star Pendant x1 |

## HEAVY SALLET

**HELM**

| CHAPTERS | | | | | 5 |
|---|---|---|---|---|---|

**WHERE FOUND** Bikanel/Bevelle Tower Floors 50-59

| LEV | 31 [37] | HP | 11200 [12915] | MP | 0 |
|---|---|---|---|---|---|
| EXP | 380 [640] | AP | 1 [2] | | |

| GIL DROP | 110 [180] | GIL STEAL | 480 [620] |
|---|---|---|---|

| STR | 71 | DEF | 4 | AGL | 82 [107] |
|---|---|---|---|---|---|
| EVA | 0 | ACC | 2 [3] | LUCK | 0 |
| MAG | 223 [254] | MAG DEF | 18 [22] | | |

| | None | | None | | None |
|---|---|---|---|---|---|
| | None | | None | | None |

**IMM** Dth., Pet., Slp., Sil., Poi., Con., Ber., Cur., Stp. ([0]), Doom, Del., P.I., M.D.

**DEF EFF** Ejt. (42[58]), Zan. (38[40])

| DROP RATIO | 128/255 [255/255] |
|---|---|
| ITEM DROP | Light Curtain x2 [Light Curtain x4] |
| RARE DROP | Star Curtain x2 [Star Curtain x5] |
| STEAL RATIO | 128/255 |
| STOLEN ITEM | Lunar Curtain x2 [Lunar Curtain x3] |
| RARE STEAL | Star Curtain x2 [Star Curtain x3] |
| BRIBE ITEM | Shining Bracer x2 [Defense Bracer x3] |
| RARE BRIBE | Shining Bracer x3 [Defense Bracer x3] |

## HEXAPOD

**VERMIN**

| CHAPTERS | | | | | 5 |
|---|---|---|---|---|---|

**WHERE FOUND** Fiend Colony/Bevelle Palace Floors 59-69

| LEV | 47 [54] | HP | 2805 [11220] | MP | 980 |
|---|---|---|---|---|---|
| EXP | 220 [280] | AP | 1 [2] | | |

| GIL DROP | 80 [100] | GIL STEAL | 300 [600] |
|---|---|---|---|

| STR | 24 [26] | DEF | 29 | AGL | 75 [83] |
|---|---|---|---|---|---|
| EVA | 30 [38] | ACC | 1 | LUCK | 0 |
| MAG | 97 | MAG DEF | 100 | | |

| | None | | Absorb | | None |
|---|---|---|---|---|---|
| | None | | Invalid | | None |

**IMM** [Con.], [Ber.], Cur., Doom, M.D.

**DEF EFF** None

| DROP RATIO | 255/255 |
|---|---|
| ITEM DROP | L-Bomb x1 [L-Bomb x3] |
| RARE DROP | L-Bomb x2 [L-Bomb x5] |
| STEAL RATIO | 255/255 |
| STOLEN ITEM | Hi-Potion x1 [Hi-Potion x2] |
| RARE STEAL | Remedy x1 [Remedy x2] |
| BRIBE ITEM | L-Bomb x16 [L-Bomb x40] |
| RARE BRIBE | L-Bomb x20 [L-Bomb x99] |

## HRITHMUS

**OGRE**

| CHAPTERS | 1 | 2 | | | 5 |
|---|---|---|---|---|---|

**WHERE FOUND** Bikanel/Bevelle Tower Floors 10-12

| LEV | 18 [22] | HP | 552 [2208] | MP | 11 |
|---|---|---|---|---|---|
| EXP | 74 [120] | AP | 1 [2] | | |

| GIL DROP | 44 [72] | GIL STEAL | 140 [228] |
|---|---|---|---|

| STR | 52 [55] | DEF | 4 | AGL | 52 [57] |
|---|---|---|---|---|---|
| EVA | 0 | ACC | 2 [3] | LUCK | 0 |
| MAG | 12 | MAG DEF | 2 | | |

| | None | | None | | None |
|---|---|---|---|---|---|
| | None | | Weak | | None |

**IMM** Slp., Con., [Ber.], Cur.

**DEF EFF** Ejt. (12 [14]), Zan. (1 [2])

| DROP RATIO | 128/255 [255/255] |
|---|---|
| ITEM DROP | Phoenix Down x1 [Mega Phoenix x1] |
| RARE DROP | Phoenix Down x2 [Meg Potion x1] |
| STEAL RATIO | 255/255 |
| STOLEN ITEM | Phoenix Down x1 [Mega Potion x1] |
| RARE STEAL | Phoenix Down x2 [Mega Potion x2] |
| BRIBE ITEM | Phoenix Down x6 [Power Gloves x1] |
| RARE BRIBE | Phoenix Down x8 [Power Gloves x1] |

## HUG BUG

**VERMIN**

| CHAPTERS | | | | | 5 |
|---|---|---|---|---|---|

**WHERE FOUND** Fiend Colony/Bevelle Palace Floors 59-69

| LEV | 49 [52] | HP | 2350 [9400] | MP | 950 |
|---|---|---|---|---|---|
| EXP | 220 [280] | AP | 1 [2] | | |

| GIL DROP | 80 [100] | GIL STEAL | 300 [600] |
|---|---|---|---|

| STR | 24 | DEF | 27 | AGL | 112 [123] |
|---|---|---|---|---|---|
| EVA | 28 [38] | ACC | 1 | LUCK | 0 |
| MAG | 96 | MAG DEF | 97 | | |

| | None | | None | | Absorb |
|---|---|---|---|---|---|
| | None | | Invalid | | None |

**IMM** [Con.], [Ber.], Cur., M.D.

**DEF EFF** Ejt. (4 [5]), Zan. (2 [4])

| DROP RATIO | 255/255 |
|---|---|
| ITEM DROP | M-Bomb x1 [M-Bomb x3] |
| RARE DROP | M-Bomb x2 [M-Bomb x5] |
| STEAL RATIO | 255/255 |
| STOLEN ITEM | Hi-Potion x1 [Hi-Potion x2] |
| RARE STEAL | Phoenix Down x1 [Phoenix Down x2] |
| BRIBE ITEM | M-Bomb x16 [M-Bomb x40] |
| RARE BRIBE | M-Bomb x20 [M-Bomb x99] |

## HUMBABA

**BEHEMOTH**

| CHAPTERS | | | | | 5 |
|---|---|---|---|---|---|

**WHERE FOUND** Thunder Plains/Bevelle Tower Floors 36-39

| LEV | 52 [62] | HP | 27772 [30163] | MP | 785 |
|---|---|---|---|---|---|
| EXP | 1800 [2300] | AP | 1 [2] | | |

| GIL DROP | 550 [700] | GIL STEAL | 1800 [3800] |
|---|---|---|---|

| STR | 93 | DEF | 13 | AGL | 87 [113] |
|---|---|---|---|---|---|
| EVA | 0 | ACC | 6 [8] | LUCK | 0 |
| MAG | 7 | MAG DEF | 11 | | |

| | None | | None | | Absorb |
|---|---|---|---|---|---|
| | None | | Invalid | | None |

**IMM** All but Ejt., P.B., M.B., A.B., M.B., L.C., E.C., A.C.

**DEF EFF** Ejt. (48 [46]), Zan. (33 [38])

| DROP RATIO | 128/255 [255/255] |
|---|---|
| ITEM DROP | Hi-Potion x4 [Ochre Ring x1] |
| RARE DROP | NulShock Ring x1 [Ochre Ring x1] |
| STEAL RATIO | 128/255 [255/255] |
| STOLEN ITEM | Hi-Potion x2 [Tetra Guard x1] |
| RARE STEAL | Ether x1 [Tetra Guard x1] |
| BRIBE ITEM | Nature's Lore x1 [Nature's Lore x3] |
| RARE BRIBE | Nature's Lore x2 [Nature's Lore x3] |

Characters 1
Garment Grids & Dresspheres 2
Battle System 3
Accessories 4
Items and Item Shops 5
Walkthrough 6
Mini Games 7
Fiends and Enemies 8

# IFRIT

**NONE**

**CHAPTERS:** 3
**WHERE FOUND:** Kilika Island

| LEV | 23 | HP | 8820 | MP | 9999 |
|---|---|---|---|---|---|
| EXP | 1800 | AP | 15 | | |

| GIL DROP | 1300 | GIL STEAL | 1800 |
|---|---|---|---|

| STR | 82 | DEF | 22 | AGL | 114 |
|---|---|---|---|---|---|
| EVA | 14 | ACC | 2 | LUCK | 0 |
| MAG | 98 | MAG DEF | 49 | | |

Elements: Fire Absorb, Water Weak, Lightning None, Ice None, Holy None, Gravity Invalid, Water(Arcane) None

**IMM** Dth., Pet., Slp., Sil., Drk., Poi., Con., Ber., Cur., Ejt., Stp., Doom, Del., P.I., M.D.
**DEF EFF** Zan. (80)

| DROP RATIO | 255/255 |
|---|---|
| ITEM DROP | Angel Earrings x1 |
| RARE DROP | Angel Earrings x1 |
| STEAL RATIO | 128/255 |
| STOLEN ITEM | Fiery Gleam x1 |
| RARE STEAL | Fiery Gleam x1 |
| BRIBE ITEM | None |
| RARE BRIBE | None |

# INSECT MATRIARCH

**VERMIN**

**CHAPTERS:** 5
**WHERE FOUND:** Bevelle Palace Floors 85-99

| LEV | 78 [94] | HP | 48796 [51236] | MP | 868 |
|---|---|---|---|---|---|
| EXP | 1200 [2200] | AP | 1 [2] | | |

| GIL DROP | 1000 [2700] | GIL STEAL | 2600 [4300] |
|---|---|---|---|

| STR | 222 | DEF | 255 | AGL | 244 [255] |
|---|---|---|---|---|---|
| EVA | 10 [13] | ACC | 33 [41] | LUCK | 0 |
| MAG | 90 | MAG DEF | 98 | | |

Elements: Fire None, Water None, Lightning Invalid, Ice None, Holy None, Gravity Invalid, Water(Arcane) None

**IMM** Slp., [Con.], [Ber.], Cur., Ejt., Slw. ([0]), Stp. ([0]), Del., P.I., M.D.
**DEF EFF** Zan. (85 [90])

| DROP RATIO | 255/255 |
|---|---|
| ITEM DROP | Mana Spring x2 [Freezerburn x1] |
| RARE DROP | Snow Ring x1 [Sublimator x1] |
| STEAL RATIO | 64/255 [32/255] |
| STOLEN ITEM | Ether x1 [Elixir x1] |
| RARE STEAL | Ether x2 [Elixir x2] |
| BRIBE ITEM | Tetra Gloves x1 [White Tome x2] |
| RARE BRIBE | White Tome x2 [White Tome x3] |

# IRON GIANT

**IRON GIANT**

**CHAPTERS:** 1 2 5
**WHERE FOUND:** Besaid/Mi'ihen Highroads/Bevelle Tower Floors 1-3

| LEV | 7 [8] | HP | 222 [233] | MP | 0 |
|---|---|---|---|---|---|
| EXP | 20 [100] | AP | 1 [2] | | |

| GIL DROP | 40 [110] | GIL STEAL | 233 [510] |
|---|---|---|---|

| STR | 48 | DEF | 1 [4] | AGL | 93 [121] |
|---|---|---|---|---|---|
| EVA | 0 | ACC | 1 | LUCK | 0 |
| MAG | 152 [155] | MAG DEF | 2 | | |

Elements: Fire None, Water None, Lightning None, Ice None, Holy None, Gravity Invalid, Water(Arcane) None

**IMM** Pet., Sil., Poi., [Con.], [Ber.], Cur., Stp., P.I., M.D.
**DEF EFF** Dth. (100), Ejt. (26 [37]), Zan. (8 [12])

| DROP RATIO | 128/255 [255/255] |
|---|---|
| ITEM DROP | Budget Grenade x1 [Grenade x2] |
| RARE DROP | Grenade x1 [Grenade x3] |
| STEAL RATIO | 255/255 |
| STOLEN ITEM | Budget Grenade x1 [M-Bomb x2] |
| RARE STEAL | Grenade x1 [M-Bomb x4] |
| BRIBE ITEM | Grenade x18 [Mythril Gloves x1] |
| RARE BRIBE | Grenade x20 [Mythril Gloves x1] |

# IRONSIDE

**ARMOR**

**CHAPTERS:** 3 4 5
**WHERE FOUND:** Kilika Island/Thunder Plains/Zanarkand Ruins/Various

| LEV | 34 [40] | HP | 8432 [12154] | MP | 1400 |
|---|---|---|---|---|---|
| EXP | 660 [940] | AP | 1 [2] | | |

| GIL DROP | 200 [340] | GIL STEAL | 800 [1500] |
|---|---|---|---|

| STR | 72 [88] | DEF | 94 | AGL | 74 [101] |
|---|---|---|---|---|---|
| EVA | 0 | ACC | 2 [3] | LUCK | 0 |
| MAG | 223 [233] | MAG DEF | 173 [233] | | |

Elements: Fire None, Water None, Lightning None, Ice None, Holy None, Gravity Invalid, Water(Arcane) None

**IMM** All *but* Ejt.
**DEF EFF** Ejt. (33 [40]), Zan. (15)

| DROP RATIO | 64/255 [255/255] |
|---|---|
| ITEM DROP | Stamina Tablet x1 [Shadow Gem x6] |
| RARE DROP | Stamina Tablet x1 [Shadow Gem x8] |
| STEAL RATIO | 255/255 |
| STOLEN ITEM | Shadow Gem x2 [Stamina Tablet x6] |
| RARE STEAL | Shadow Gem x3 [Stamina Tablet x8] |
| BRIBE ITEM | Shining Gem x16 [Shining Gem x30] |
| RARE BRIBE | Shining Gem x20 [Shining Gem x40] |

# IXION

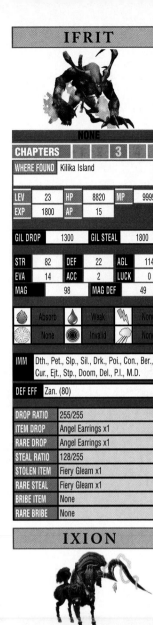

**NONE**

**CHAPTERS:** 3
**WHERE FOUND:** Djose Highlands

| LEV | 28 | HP | 12380 | MP | 9999 |
|---|---|---|---|---|---|
| EXP | 2600 | AP | 15 | | |

| GIL DROP | 1800 | GIL STEAL | 3000 |
|---|---|---|---|

| STR | 62 | DEF | 21 | AGL | 138 |
|---|---|---|---|---|---|
| EVA | 35 | ACC | 4 | LUCK | 0 |
| MAG | 106 | MAG DEF | 82 | | |

Elements: Fire None, Water None, Lightning Absorb, Ice Weak, Holy Invalid, Gravity None

**IMM** Dth., Pet., Slp., Sil., Drk., Poi., Con., Ber., Cur., Ejt., Stp., Doom, Del., P.I., M.D.
**DEF EFF** Zan. (80)

| DROP RATIO | 255/255 |
|---|---|
| ITEM DROP | Soul of Thamasa x1 |
| RARE DROP | Soul of Thamasa x1 |
| STEAL RATIO | 128/255 |
| STOLEN ITEM | Sprint Shoes x1 |
| RARE STEAL | Sprint Shoes x1 |
| BRIBE ITEM | None |
| RARE BRIBE | None |

# JAHI

**LARVA**

**CHAPTERS:** 5
**WHERE FOUND:** Farplane/Bevelle Palace Floors 75-79

| LEV | 46 | HP | 2033 | MP | 360 |
|---|---|---|---|---|---|
| EXP | 1200 | AP | 1 | | |

| GIL DROP | 620 | GIL STEAL | 1020 |
|---|---|---|---|

| STR | 39 | DEF | 52 | AGL | 68 |
|---|---|---|---|---|---|
| EVA | 0 | ACC | 2 | LUCK | 0 |
| MAG | 84 | MAG DEF | 86 | | |

Elements: Fire None, Water None, Lightning Absorb, Ice Invalid, Holy None, Gravity Weak

**IMM** Dth., Pet., Slp., Sil., Con., Ber., Cur., Stp., Doom, M.D.
**DEF EFF** Ejt. (26), Zan. (6)

| DROP RATIO | 32/255 |
|---|---|
| ITEM DROP | Gold Anklet x1 |
| RARE DROP | Gold Anklet x1 |
| STEAL RATIO | 255/255 |
| STOLEN ITEM | Remedy x2 |
| RARE STEAL | Mana Spring x2 |
| BRIBE ITEM | Mana Spring x30 |
| RARE BRIBE | Mana Spring x40 |

# JUMBO CACTUAR

**CACTUAR**

**CHAPTERS:** 5
**WHERE FOUND:** Bikanel/Bevelle Palace Floors 50-59 (only if defeated at Bikanel)

| LEV | 42 [50] | HP | 22222 [33333] | MP | 1111 |
|---|---|---|---|---|---|
| EXP | 0 | AP | 10 [15] | | |

| GIL DROP | 0 | GIL STEAL | None |
|---|---|---|---|

| STR | 73 | DEF | 74 | AGL | 254 [85] |
|---|---|---|---|---|---|
| EVA | 0 | ACC | 7 [9] | LUCK | 0 |
| MAG | 4 | MAG DEF | 4 | | |

Elements: Fire None, Water None, Lightning None, Ice None, Holy None, Gravity Invalid

**IMM** All
**DEF EFF** Zan. (200 [255])

| DROP RATIO | 255/255 |
|---|---|
| ITEM DROP | Stamina Tonic x1 [Rabite's Foot x1] |
| RARE DROP | Rabite's Foot x1 |
| STEAL RATIO | 255/255 |
| STOLEN ITEM | Stamina Tonic x1 [Stamina Tonic x3] |
| RARE STEAL | Stamina Tonic x2 [Stamina Tonic x5] |
| BRIBE ITEM | None |
| RARE BRIBE | None |

# KILLER HOUND

**LUPINE**

**CHAPTERS:** 1 2 3 5
**WHERE FOUND:** Bikanel/Bevelle Tower Floors 13-15

| LEV | 12 [14] | HP | 202 [818] | MP | 0 |
|---|---|---|---|---|---|
| EXP | 36 [68] | AP | 1 [2] | | |

| GIL DROP | 18 [34] | GIL STEAL | 82 [143] |
|---|---|---|---|

| STR | 28 | DEF | 8 | AGL | 62 [68] |
|---|---|---|---|---|---|
| EVA | 5 [6] | ACC | 3 [4] | LUCK | 0 |
| MAG | 2 [3] | MAG DEF | 1 | | |

Elements: Fire None, Water None, Lightning None, Ice None, Holy None, Gravity None

**IMM** [Con.], [Ber.], Cur.
**DEF EFF** Ejt. (11 [22]), Zan. (1 [5])

| DROP RATIO | 128/255 [255/255] |
|---|---|
| ITEM DROP | Potion x1 [Hi-Potion x3] |
| RARE DROP | Hi-Potion x1 [Hi-Potion x4] |
| STEAL RATIO | 255/255 |
| STOLEN ITEM | Potion x1 [Hi-Potion x2] |
| RARE STEAL | Phoenix Down x1 [Hi-Potion x3] |
| BRIBE ITEM | Hi-Potion x2 [Chocobo Feather x4] |
| RARE BRIBE | Hi-Potion x2 [Chocobo Feather x5] |

## KILLER MACHINA — MACHINA

CHAPTERS 1 2 3 4 **5**

WHERE FOUND: New Cave/Bevelle Palace Floors 70-74

| LEV | 48 | HP | 4222 | MP | 0 |
|---|---|---|---|---|---|
| EXP | 600 | AP | 1 | | |

GIL DROP 180 — GIL STEAL 300

| STR | 36 | DEF | 0 | AGL | 68 |
|---|---|---|---|---|---|
| EVA | 0 | ACC | 0 | LUCK | 0 |
| MAG | 0 | MAG DEF | 0 | | |

Fire None | Water None | Lightning Absorb
Holy/Earth None | Shell Invalid | Gravity None

IMM: Dth., Pet., Slp., Sil., Poi., Con., Ber., Cur., Slw., Stp., Doom, M.D.
DEF EFF: Ejt. (18)

| DROP RATIO | 32/255 |
|---|---|
| ITEM DROP | Darkness Grenade x1 |
| RARE DROP | Petrify Grenade x1 |
| STEAL RATIO | 128/255 |
| STOLEN ITEM | M-Bomb x1 |
| RARE STEAL | M-Bomb x2 |
| BRIBE ITEM | None |
| RARE BRIBE | None |

## KING TAKOUBA — BLADE

CHAPTERS 1 2 3 4 **5**

WHERE FOUND: Bikanel, Bevelle Tower Floors 50-59

| LEV | 48 [56] | HP | 18004 [22104] | MP | 0 |
|---|---|---|---|---|---|
| EXP | 485 [963] | AP | 1 [2] | | |

GIL DROP 300 [735] — GIL STEAL 800 [1800]

| STR | 71 [72] | DEF | 14 | AGL | 75 [98] |
|---|---|---|---|---|---|
| EVA | 27 [34] | ACC | 1 | LUCK | 0 |
| MAG | 43 [48] | MAG DEF | 22 | | |

Fire Weak | Water None | Lightning None
None | Holy Invalid | Gravity None

IMM: All but Dth., Ejt., P.B., M.B., L.C., E.C., A.C.
DEF EFF: Dth. (30), Ejt. (48 [70]), Zan. (26 [38])

| DROP RATIO | 128/255 [255/255] |
|---|---|
| ITEM DROP | Farplane Shadow x2 [Farplane Shadow x4] |
| RARE DROP | Candle of Life x2 [Farplane Shadow x5] |
| STEAL RATIO | 128/255 [16/255] |
| STOLEN ITEM | Star Pendant x1 [Glass Buckle x1] |
| RARE STEAL | Angel Earrings x1 |
| BRIBE ITEM | Angel Earrings x6 [Glass Buckle x10] |
| RARE BRIBE | Angel Earrings x10 [Glass Buckle x12] |

## KING VERMIN! — VERMIN

CHAPTERS 1 2 3 4 **5**

WHERE FOUND: Fiend Colony/Bevelle Palace Floors 59-69 (only if defeated at Fiend Colony)

| LEV | 54 [58] | HP | 39857 [41850] | MP | 872 |
|---|---|---|---|---|---|
| EXP | 5000 [7200] | AP | 1 [2] | | |

GIL DROP 3500 [3800] — GIL STEAL 2000 [3000]

| STR | 46 [48] | DEF | 46 | AGL | None [173] |
|---|---|---|---|---|---|
| EVA | 8 [13] | ACC | 1 | LUCK | 0 |
| MAG | 88 | MAG DEF | 60 | | |

Fire Absorb | Water None | Lightning None
None | Holy Invalid | Gravity None

IMM: Dth., Pet., Slp., Sil., Drk., Poi., Con., Ber., Cur., Ejt., Slw., Stp., Doom, Del., P.I., M.D.
DEF EFF: Zan. (60)

| DROP RATIO | 255/255 |
|---|---|
| ITEM DROP | Power Gloves x1 [Champion Belt x1] |
| RARE DROP | Power Gloves x1 [Champion Belt x1] |
| STEAL RATIO | 128/255 [255/255] |
| STOLEN ITEM | Turbo Ether x1 [Turbo Ether x2] |
| RARE STEAL | Turbo Ether x2 |
| BRIBE ITEM | Turbo Ether x80 [Elixir x24] |
| RARE BRIBE | Turbo Ether x99 [Elixir x30] |

## KUKULCAN — BASILISK

CHAPTERS 1 **2** 3 4 5

WHERE FOUND: Bevelle/Bevelle Tower Floors 16-19

| LEV | 23 [28] | HP | 3220 [9480] | MP | 85 |
|---|---|---|---|---|---|
| EXP | 135 [233] | AP | 1 [2] | | |

GIL DROP 86 [140] — GIL STEAL 550 [1100]

| STR | 44 | DEF | 3 | AGL | 78 [86] |
|---|---|---|---|---|---|
| EVA | 0 | ACC | 2 [3] | LUCK | 0 |
| MAG | 92 | MAG DEF | 30 | | |

Fire None | Water Weak | Lightning None
None | Holy None | Gravity None

IMM: Dth., Pet., Slp., Poi., Con., [Ber.], Cur., Slw., P.B., M.B.
DEF EFF: Ejt. (24 [28]), Zan. (7 [8])

| DROP RATIO | 128/255 [255/255] |
|---|---|
| ITEM DROP | Soft x2 [Gold Anklet x1] |
| RARE DROP | Gold Anklet x1 |
| STEAL RATIO | 255/255 |
| STOLEN ITEM | Soft x2 [Remedy x8] |
| RARE STEAL | Remedy x1 [Remedy x10] |
| BRIBE ITEM | Stone Shock x1 [Stone Shock x4] |
| RARE BRIBE | Stone Shock x1 [Stone Shock x6] |

## LEAGUE FIGHTER — NONE

CHAPTERS **1** **2** 3 4 5

WHERE FOUND: Kilika Island/Djose Highlands

| LEV | 6 | HP | 168 | MP | 14 |
|---|---|---|---|---|---|
| EXP | 10 | AP | 1 | | |

GIL DROP 50 — GIL STEAL 150

| STR | 31 | DEF | 3 | AGL | 55 |
|---|---|---|---|---|---|
| EVA | 0 | ACC | 3 | LUCK | 0 |
| MAG | 48 | MAG DEF | 1 | | |

All None

IMM: Cur.
DEF EFF: None

| DROP RATIO | 128/255 |
|---|---|
| ITEM DROP | Budget Grenade x1 |
| RARE DROP | Grenade x1 |
| STEAL RATIO | 255/255 |
| STOLEN ITEM | Potion x1 |
| RARE STEAL | Phoenix Down x1 |
| BRIBE ITEM | Phoenix Down x12 |
| RARE BRIBE | Phoenix Down x16 |

## LEAGUE MAGE — NONE

CHAPTERS 1 2 **3** 4 **5**

WHERE FOUND: Kilika Island/Mushroom Rock/Djose Highland

| LEV | 23 | HP | 1020 | MP | 420 |
|---|---|---|---|---|---|
| EXP | 70 | AP | 1 | | |

GIL DROP 130 — GIL STEAL 450

| STR | 29 | DEF | 22 | AGL | 73 |
|---|---|---|---|---|---|
| EVA | 0 | ACC | 5 | LUCK | 0 |
| MAG | 2 | MAG DEF | 52 | | |

All None

IMM: Cur.
DEF EFF: None

| DROP RATIO | 128/255 |
|---|---|
| ITEM DROP | Hi-Potion x1 |
| RARE DROP | Phoenix Down x1 |
| STEAL RATIO | 255/255 |
| STOLEN ITEM | Ether x1 |
| RARE STEAL | Amulet x1 |
| BRIBE ITEM | Talisman x1 |
| RARE BRIBE | Talisman x1 |

## LEAGUE MASTER — NONE

CHAPTERS 1 2 3 4 **5**

WHERE FOUND: Kilika Island/Mushroom Rock/Djose Highlands

| LEV | 32 | HP | 1732 | MP | 670 |
|---|---|---|---|---|---|
| EXP | 160 | AP | 1 | | |

GIL DROP 140 — GIL STEAL 550

| STR | 32 | DEF | 43 | AGL | 76 |
|---|---|---|---|---|---|
| EVA | 0 | ACC | 5 | LUCK | 0 |
| MAG | 18 | MAG DEF | 56 | | |

All None

IMM: Cur.
DEF EFF: Dth. (50), Pet. (50)

| DROP RATIO | 64/255 |
|---|---|
| ITEM DROP | Ether x1 |
| RARE DROP | Ether x1 |
| STEAL RATIO | 255/255 |
| STOLEN ITEM | Phoenix Down x1 |
| RARE STEAL | Phoenix Down x2 |
| BRIBE ITEM | Ether x12 |
| RARE BRIBE | Ether x14 |

## LEAGUE RAIDER — NONE

CHAPTERS 1 **2** **3** 4 5

WHERE FOUND: Kilika Island/Mushroom Rock/Djose Highlands

| LEV | 16 | HP | 293 | MP | 30 |
|---|---|---|---|---|---|
| EXP | 70 | AP | 1 | | |

GIL DROP 130 — GIL STEAL 380

| STR | 37 | DEF | 13 | AGL | 64 |
|---|---|---|---|---|---|
| EVA | 0 | ACC | 8 | LUCK | 0 |
| MAG | 34 | MAG DEF | 13 | | |

All None

IMM: Drk., Cur.
DEF EFF: None

| DROP RATIO | 128/255 |
|---|---|
| ITEM DROP | Hi-Potion x1 |
| RARE DROP | Grenade x2 |
| STEAL RATIO | 255/255 |
| STOLEN ITEM | Phoenix Down x1 |
| RARE STEAL | Phoenix Down x2 |
| BRIBE ITEM | Phoenix Down x16 |
| RARE BRIBE | Phoenix Down x24 |

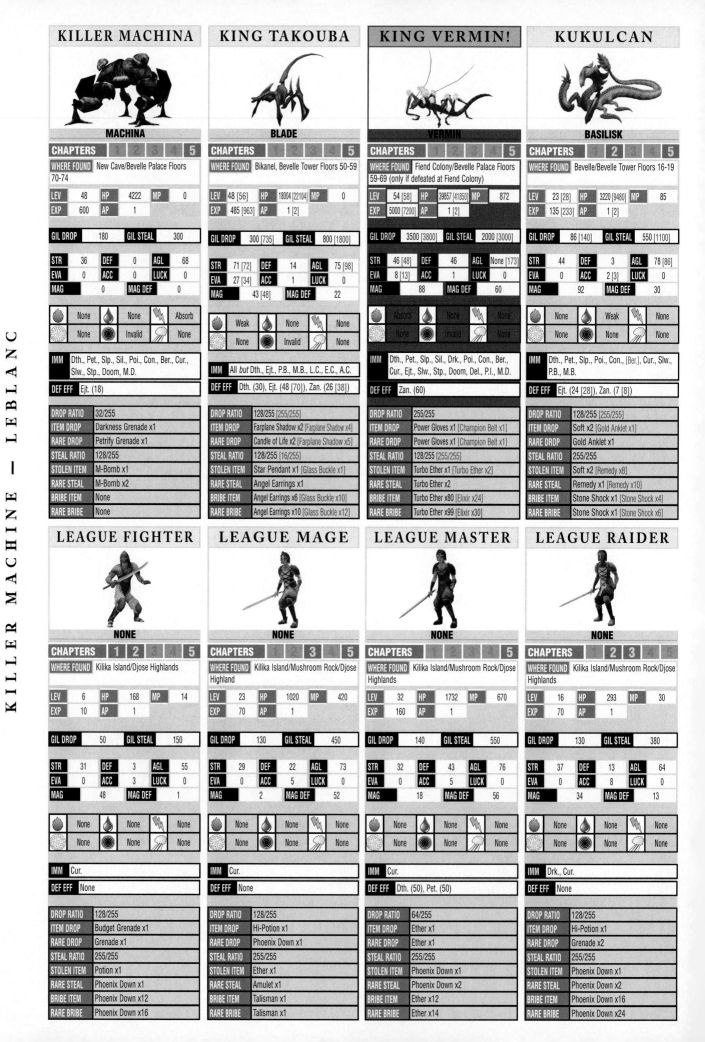

Characters

1

Garment Grids & Dresspheres

2

Battle System

3

Accessories

4

Items and Item Shops

5

Walkthrough

6

Mini Games

7

Fiends and Enemies

8

# LEAGUE RANGER

NONE

| CHAPTERS | 1 | 2 | 3 | 4 | 5 |
|---|---|---|---|---|---|

**WHERE FOUND** Mushroom Rock/Djose Highlands

| LEV | 16 | HP | 230 | MP | 180 |
|---|---|---|---|---|---|
| EXP | 10 | AP | 1 | | |

| GIL DROP | 80 | GIL STEAL | 320 |
|---|---|---|---|

| STR | 18 | DEF | 83 | AGL | 66 |
|---|---|---|---|---|---|
| EVA | 0 | ACC | 3 | LUCK | 0 |
| MAG | 2 | MAG DEF | 50 | | |

| | None | | None | | None |
|---|---|---|---|---|---|
| | None | | None | | None |

**IMM** Cur.

**DEF EFF** None

| DROP RATIO | 128/255 |
|---|---|
| ITEM DROP | Potion x1 |
| RARE DROP | Phoenix Down x1 |
| STEAL RATIO | 255/255 |
| STOLEN ITEM | Phoenix Down x1 |
| RARE STEAL | Phoenix Down x1 |
| BRIBE ITEM | S-Bomb x2 |
| RARE BRIBE | Ether x1 |

# LEAGUE SCOUT

NONE

| CHAPTERS | 1 | 2 | 3 | 4 | 5 |
|---|---|---|---|---|---|

**WHERE FOUND** Kilika Island/Djose Highlands

| LEV | 6 | HP | 128 | MP | 18 |
|---|---|---|---|---|---|
| EXP | 10 | AP | 1 | | |

| GIL DROP | 60 | GIL STEAL | 300 |
|---|---|---|---|

| STR | 27 | DEF | 4 | AGL | 62 |
|---|---|---|---|---|---|
| EVA | 0 | ACC | 8 | LUCK | 0 |
| MAG | 33 | MAG DEF | 12 | | |

| | None | | None | | None |
|---|---|---|---|---|---|
| | None | | None | | None |

**IMM** Drk., Cur.

**DEF EFF** None

| DROP RATIO | 128/255 |
|---|---|
| ITEM DROP | Budget Grenade x1 |
| RARE DROP | Hi-Potion x1 |
| STEAL RATIO | 255/255 |
| STOLEN ITEM | Potion x1 |
| RARE STEAL | Phoenix Down x1 |
| BRIBE ITEM | Phoenix Down x10 |
| RARE BRIBE | Mega Potion x1 |

# LEAGUE SLASHER

NONE

| CHAPTERS | 1 | 2 | 3 | 4 | 5 |
|---|---|---|---|---|---|

**WHERE FOUND** Kilika Island/Mushroom Rock/Djose Highlands

| LEV | 30 | HP | 1650 | MP | 58 |
|---|---|---|---|---|---|
| EXP | 160 | AP | 1 | | |

| GIL DROP | 140 | GIL STEAL | 550 |
|---|---|---|---|

| STR | 38 | DEF | 16 | AGL | 82 |
|---|---|---|---|---|---|
| EVA | 0 | ACC | 8 | LUCK | 0 |
| MAG | 30 | MAG DEF | 0 | | |

| | None | | None | | None |
|---|---|---|---|---|---|
| | None | | None | | None |

**IMM** Sil., Cur.

**DEF EFF** None

| DROP RATIO | 128/255 |
|---|---|
| ITEM DROP | Hi-Potion x1 |
| RARE DROP | Hi-Potion x2 |
| STEAL RATIO | 64/255 |
| STOLEN ITEM | M-Bomb x1 |
| RARE STEAL | L-Bomb x1 |
| BRIBE ITEM | Ether x16 |
| RARE BRIBE | Ether x20 |

# LEAGUE SOLDIER

NONE

| CHAPTERS | 1 | 2 | 3 | 4 | 5 |
|---|---|---|---|---|---|

**WHERE FOUND** Mushroom Rock, Djose Highlands

| LEV | 14 | HP | 178 | MP | 28 |
|---|---|---|---|---|---|
| EXP | 10 | AP | 1 | | |

| GIL DROP | 80 | GIL STEAL | 300 |
|---|---|---|---|

| STR | 34 | DEF | 12 | AGL | 58 |
|---|---|---|---|---|---|
| EVA | 0 | ACC | 8 | LUCK | 0 |
| MAG | 28 | MAG DEF | 10 | | |

| | None | | None | | None |
|---|---|---|---|---|---|
| | None | | None | | None |

**IMM** Drk., Curse

**DEF EFF** None

| DROP RATIO | 128/255 |
|---|---|
| ITEM DROP | Grenade x1 |
| RARE DROP | Grenade x2 |
| STEAL RATIO | 255/255 |
| STOLEN ITEM | Grenade x1 |
| RARE STEAL | Grenade x2 |
| BRIBE ITEM | S-Bomb x2 |
| RARE BRIBE | M-Bomb x2 |

# LEAGUE TROOPER

NONE

| CHAPTERS | 1 | 2 | 3 | 4 | 5 |
|---|---|---|---|---|---|

**WHERE FOUND** Mushroom Rock/Djose Highlands

| LEV | 13 | HP | 244 | MP | 16 |
|---|---|---|---|---|---|
| EXP | 10 | AP | 1 | | |

| GIL DROP | 60 | GIL STEAL | 160 |
|---|---|---|---|

| STR | 41 | DEF | 6 | AGL | 56 |
|---|---|---|---|---|---|
| EVA | 0 | ACC | 0 | LUCK | 0 |
| MAG | 52 | MAG DEF | 2 | | |

| | None | | None | | None |
|---|---|---|---|---|---|
| | None | | None | | None |

**IMM** Slp., Sil., Cur.

**DEF EFF** None

| DROP RATIO | 128/255 |
|---|---|
| ITEM DROP | Grenade x1 |
| RARE DROP | Phoenix Down x1 |
| STEAL RATIO | 255/255 |
| STOLEN ITEM | Grenade x1 |
| RARE STEAL | Grenade x1 |
| BRIBE ITEM | S-Bomb x2 |
| RARE BRIBE | M-Bomb x2 |

# LEAGUE VETERAN

NONE

| CHAPTERS | 1 | 2 | 3 | 4 | 5 |
|---|---|---|---|---|---|

**WHERE FOUND** Kilika Island/Mushroom Rock/Djose Highlands

| LEV | 33 | HP | 1720 | MP | 42 |
|---|---|---|---|---|---|
| EXP | 160 | AP | 1 | | |

| GIL DROP | 100 | GIL STEAL | 300 |
|---|---|---|---|

| STR | 42 | DEF | 17 | AGL | 68 |
|---|---|---|---|---|---|
| EVA | 0 | ACC | 4 | LUCK | 0 |
| MAG | 54 | MAG DEF | 6 | | |

| | None | | None | | None |
|---|---|---|---|---|---|
| | None | | None | | None |

**IMM** Cur.

**DEF EFF** Dth. (50), Pet. (50)

| DROP RATIO | 128/255 |
|---|---|
| ITEM DROP | Hi-Potion x1 |
| RARE DROP | Hi-Potion x2 |
| STEAL RATIO | 64/255 |
| STOLEN ITEM | M-Bomb x1 |
| RARE STEAL | L-Bomb x1 |
| BRIBE ITEM | L-Bomb x14 |
| RARE BRIBE | L-Bomb x20 |

# LEAGUE WARRIOR

NONE

| CHAPTERS | 1 | 2 | 3 | 4 | 5 |
|---|---|---|---|---|---|

**WHERE FOUND** Kilika Island/Mushroom Rock/Djose Highlands

| LEV | 24 | HP | 422 | MP | 26 |
|---|---|---|---|---|---|
| EXP | 70 | AP | 1 | | |

| GIL DROP | 120 | GIL STEAL | 180 |
|---|---|---|---|

| STR | 41 | DEF | 12 | AGL | 58 |
|---|---|---|---|---|---|
| EVA | 0 | ACC | 4 | LUCK | 0 |
| MAG | 53 | MAG DEF | 3 | | |

| | None | | None | | None |
|---|---|---|---|---|---|
| | None | | None | | None |

**IMM** Slp., Cur.

**DEF EFF** None

| DROP RATIO | 128/255 |
|---|---|
| ITEM DROP | Hi-Potion x1 |
| RARE DROP | Grenade x2 |
| STEAL RATIO | 255/255 |
| STOLEN ITEM | Hi-Potion x1 |
| RARE STEAL | Grenade x2 |
| BRIBE ITEM | M-Bomb x4 |
| RARE BRIBE | M-Bomb x5 |

# LEBLANC

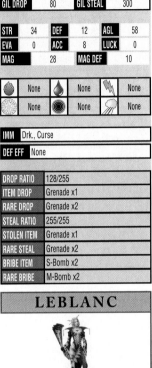

NONE

| CHAPTERS | 1 | 2 | 3 | 4 | 5 |
|---|---|---|---|---|---|

**WHERE FOUND** Mt. Gagazet

| LEV | 5 | HP | 120 | MP | 320 |
|---|---|---|---|---|---|
| EXP | 20 | AP | 2 | | |

| GIL DROP | 250 | GIL STEAL | 700 |
|---|---|---|---|

| STR | 15 | DEF | 26 | AGL | 52 |
|---|---|---|---|---|---|
| EVA | 20 | ACC | 16 | LUCK | 0 |
| MAG | 8 | MAG DEF | 55 | | |

| | None | | None | | None |
|---|---|---|---|---|---|
| | None | | Invalid | | None |

**IMM** Dth., Pet., Sil., Con., Ber., Cur., Ejt., Stp., P.B., A.B., L.C., Doom, M.D.

**DEF EFF** Poi. (70), Zan. (60)

| DROP RATIO | 128/255 |
|---|---|
| ITEM DROP | Hi-Potion x1 |
| RARE DROP | Hi-Potion x2 |
| STEAL RATIO | 192/255 |
| STOLEN ITEM | Tiara x1 |
| RARE STEAL | Tiara x1 |
| BRIBE ITEM | None |
| RARE BRIBE | None |

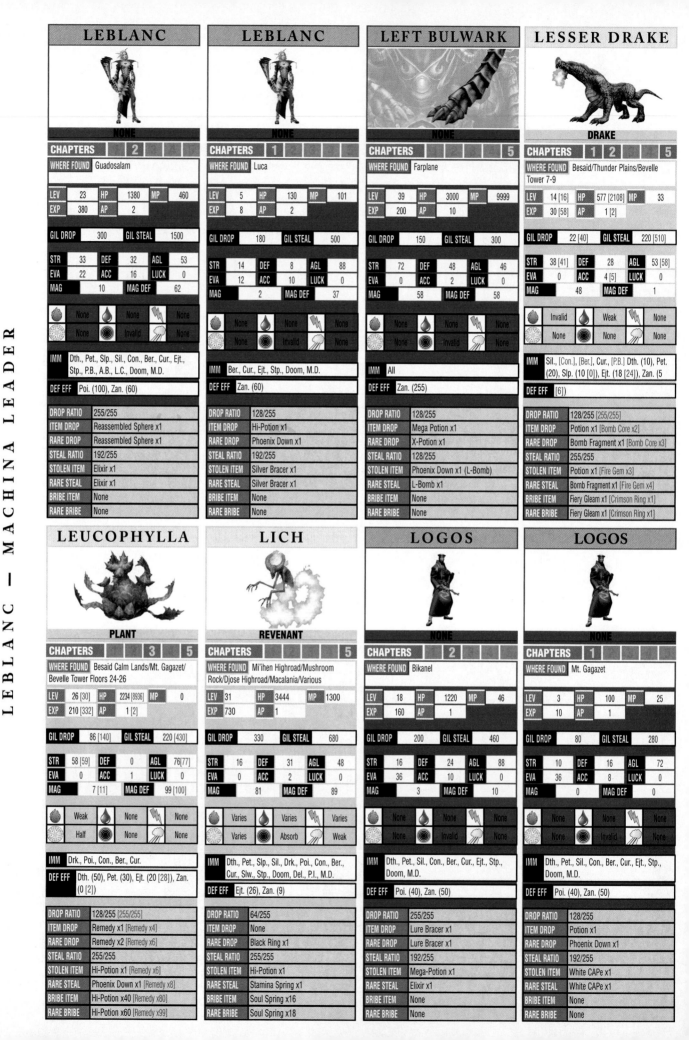

## LEBLANC

**NONE**

| | |
|---|---|
| CHAPTERS | 2 |
| WHERE FOUND | Guadosalam |

| LEV | 23 | HP | 1380 | MP | 460 |
|---|---|---|---|---|---|
| EXP | 380 | AP | 2 | | |

| GIL DROP | 300 | GIL STEAL | 1500 |
|---|---|---|---|

| STR | 33 | DEF | 32 | AGL | 53 |
|---|---|---|---|---|---|
| EVA | 22 | ACC | 16 | LUCK | 0 |
| MAG | 10 | MAG DEF | 62 | | |

Fire: None / Water: None / Lightning: None / Ice: None / Gravity: Invalid / Holy: None

| IMM | Dth., Pet., Slp., Sil., Con., Ber., Cur., Ejt., Stp., P.B., A.B., L.C., Doom, M.D. |
|---|---|
| DEF EFF | Poi. (100), Zan. (60) |

| DROP RATIO | 255/255 |
|---|---|
| ITEM DROP | Reassembled Sphere x1 |
| RARE DROP | Reassembled Sphere x1 |
| STEAL RATIO | 192/255 |
| STOLEN ITEM | Elixir x1 |
| RARE STEAL | Elixir x1 |
| BRIBE ITEM | None |
| RARE BRIBE | None |

## LEBLANC

**NONE**

| | |
|---|---|
| CHAPTERS | 1 |
| WHERE FOUND | Luca |

| LEV | 5 | HP | 130 | MP | 101 |
|---|---|---|---|---|---|
| EXP | 8 | AP | 2 | | |

| GIL DROP | 180 | GIL STEAL | 500 |
|---|---|---|---|

| STR | 14 | DEF | 8 | AGL | 88 |
|---|---|---|---|---|---|
| EVA | 12 | ACC | 10 | LUCK | 0 |
| MAG | 2 | MAG DEF | 37 | | |

Fire: None / Water: None / Lightning: None / Ice: None / Gravity: Invalid / Holy: None

| IMM | Ber., Cur., Ejt., Stp., Doom, M.D. |
|---|---|
| DEF EFF | Zan. (60) |

| DROP RATIO | 128/255 |
|---|---|
| ITEM DROP | Hi-Potion x1 |
| RARE DROP | Phoenix Down x1 |
| STEAL RATIO | 192/255 |
| STOLEN ITEM | Silver Bracer x1 |
| RARE STEAL | Silver Bracer x1 |
| BRIBE ITEM | None |
| RARE BRIBE | None |

## LEFT BULWARK

**NONE**

| | |
|---|---|
| CHAPTERS | 5 |
| WHERE FOUND | Farplane |

| LEV | 39 | HP | 3000 | MP | 9999 |
|---|---|---|---|---|---|
| EXP | 200 | AP | 10 | | |

| GIL DROP | 150 | GIL STEAL | 300 |
|---|---|---|---|

| STR | 72 | DEF | 48 | AGL | 46 |
|---|---|---|---|---|---|
| EVA | 0 | ACC | 2 | LUCK | 0 |
| MAG | 58 | MAG DEF | 58 | | |

Fire: None / Water: None / Lightning: None / Ice: None / Gravity: Invalid / Holy: None

| IMM | All |
|---|---|
| DEF EFF | Zan. (255) |

| DROP RATIO | 128/255 |
|---|---|
| ITEM DROP | Mega Potion x1 |
| RARE DROP | X-Potion x1 |
| STEAL RATIO | 128/255 |
| STOLEN ITEM | Phoenix Down x1 (L-Bomb) |
| RARE STEAL | L-Bomb x1 |
| BRIBE ITEM | None |
| RARE BRIBE | None |

## LESSER DRAKE

**DRAKE**

| | |
|---|---|
| CHAPTERS | 1 2 5 |
| WHERE FOUND | Besaid/Thunder Plains/Bevelle Tower 7-9 |

| LEV | 14 [16] | HP | 577 [2108] | MP | 33 |
|---|---|---|---|---|---|
| EXP | 30 [58] | AP | 1 [2] | | |

| GIL DROP | 22 [40] | GIL STEAL | 220 [510] |
|---|---|---|---|

| STR | 38 [41] | DEF | 28 | AGL | 53 [58] |
|---|---|---|---|---|---|
| EVA | 0 | ACC | 4 [5] | LUCK | 0 |
| MAG | 48 | MAG DEF | 1 | | |

Fire: Invalid / Water: Weak / Lightning: None / Ice: None / Gravity: None / Holy: None

| IMM | Sil., [Con.], [Ber.], Cur., [P.B.] Dth. (10), Pet. (20), Slp. (10 [0]), Ejt. (18 [24]), Zan. (5 |
|---|---|
| DEF EFF | [6] |

| DROP RATIO | 128/255 [255/255] |
|---|---|
| ITEM DROP | Potion x1 [Bomb Core x2] |
| RARE DROP | Bomb Fragment x1 [Bomb Core x3] |
| STEAL RATIO | 255/255 |
| STOLEN ITEM | Potion x1 [Fire Gem x3] |
| RARE STEAL | Bomb Fragment x1 [Fire Gem x4] |
| BRIBE ITEM | Fiery Gleam x1 [Crimson Ring x1] |
| RARE BRIBE | Fiery Gleam x1 [Crimson Ring x1] |

## LEUCOPHYLLA

**PLANT**

| | |
|---|---|
| CHAPTERS | 3 5 |
| WHERE FOUND | Besaid Calm Lands/Mt. Gagazet/Bevelle Tower Floors 24-26 |

| LEV | 26 [30] | HP | 2234 [8936] | MP | 0 |
|---|---|---|---|---|---|
| EXP | 210 [332] | AP | 1 [2] | | |

| GIL DROP | 86 [140] | GIL STEAL | 220 [430] |
|---|---|---|---|

| STR | 58 [59] | DEF | 0 | AGL | 76 [77] |
|---|---|---|---|---|---|
| EVA | 0 | ACC | 1 | LUCK | 0 |
| MAG | 7 [11] | MAG DEF | 99 [100] | | |

Fire: Weak / Water: None / Lightning: None / Ice: Half / Gravity: None / Holy: None

| IMM | Drk., Poi., Con., Ber., Cur. |
|---|---|
| DEF EFF | Dth. (50), Pet. (30), Ejt. (20 [28]), Zan. (0 [2]) |

| DROP RATIO | 128/255 [255/255] |
|---|---|
| ITEM DROP | Remedy x1 [Remedy x4] |
| RARE DROP | Remedy x2 [Remedy x6] |
| STEAL RATIO | 255/255 |
| STOLEN ITEM | Hi-Potion x1 [Remedy x6] |
| RARE STEAL | Phoenix Down x1 [Remedy x8] |
| BRIBE ITEM | Hi-Potion x40 [Remedy x80] |
| RARE BRIBE | Hi-Potion x60 [Remedy x99] |

## LICH

**REVENANT**

| | |
|---|---|
| CHAPTERS | 5 |
| WHERE FOUND | Mi'ihen Highroad/Mushroom Rock/Djose Highroad/Macalania/Various |

| LEV | 31 | HP | 3444 | MP | 1300 |
|---|---|---|---|---|---|
| EXP | 730 | AP | 1 | | |

| GIL DROP | 330 | GIL STEAL | 680 |
|---|---|---|---|

| STR | 16 | DEF | 31 | AGL | 48 |
|---|---|---|---|---|---|
| EVA | 0 | ACC | 2 | LUCK | 0 |
| MAG | 81 | MAG DEF | 89 | | |

Fire: Varies / Water: Varies / Lightning: Varies / Ice: Varies / Gravity: Absorb / Holy: Weak

| IMM | Dth., Pet., Slp., Sil., Drk., Poi., Con., Ber., Cur., Slw., Stp., Doom, Del., P.I., M.D. |
|---|---|
| DEF EFF | Ejt. (26), Zan. (9) |

| DROP RATIO | 64/255 |
|---|---|
| ITEM DROP | None |
| RARE DROP | Black Ring x1 |
| STEAL RATIO | 255/255 |
| STOLEN ITEM | Hi-Potion x1 |
| RARE STEAL | Stamina Spring x1 |
| BRIBE ITEM | Soul Spring x16 |
| RARE BRIBE | Soul Spring x18 |

## LOGOS

**NONE**

| | |
|---|---|
| CHAPTERS | 2 |
| WHERE FOUND | Bikanel |

| LEV | 18 | HP | 1220 | MP | 46 |
|---|---|---|---|---|---|
| EXP | 160 | AP | 1 | | |

| GIL DROP | 200 | GIL STEAL | 460 |
|---|---|---|---|

| STR | 16 | DEF | 24 | AGL | 88 |
|---|---|---|---|---|---|
| EVA | 36 | ACC | 10 | LUCK | 0 |
| MAG | 3 | MAG DEF | 10 | | |

Fire: None / Water: None / Lightning: None / Ice: None / Gravity: Invalid / Holy: None

| IMM | Dth., Pet., Sil., Con., Ber., Cur., Ejt., Stp., Doom, M.D. |
|---|---|
| DEF EFF | Poi. (40), Zan. (50) |

| DROP RATIO | 255/255 |
|---|---|
| ITEM DROP | Lure Bracer x1 |
| RARE DROP | Lure Bracer x1 |
| STEAL RATIO | 192/255 |
| STOLEN ITEM | Mega-Potion x1 |
| RARE STEAL | Elixir x1 |
| BRIBE ITEM | None |
| RARE BRIBE | None |

## LOGOS

**NONE**

| | |
|---|---|
| CHAPTERS | 1 |
| WHERE FOUND | Mt. Gagazet |

| LEV | 3 | HP | 100 | MP | 25 |
|---|---|---|---|---|---|
| EXP | 10 | AP | 1 | | |

| GIL DROP | 80 | GIL STEAL | 280 |
|---|---|---|---|

| STR | 10 | DEF | 16 | AGL | 72 |
|---|---|---|---|---|---|
| EVA | 36 | ACC | 8 | LUCK | 0 |
| MAG | 0 | MAG DEF | 0 | | |

Fire: None / Water: None / Lightning: None / Ice: None / Gravity: Invalid / Holy: None

| IMM | Dth., Pet., Sil., Con., Ber., Cur., Ejt., Stp., Doom, M.D. |
|---|---|
| DEF EFF | Poi. (40), Zan. (50) |

| DROP RATIO | 128/255 |
|---|---|
| ITEM DROP | Potion x1 |
| RARE DROP | Phoenix Down x1 |
| STEAL RATIO | 192/255 |
| STOLEN ITEM | White CAPe x1 |
| RARE STEAL | White CAPe x1 |
| BRIBE ITEM | None |
| RARE BRIBE | None |

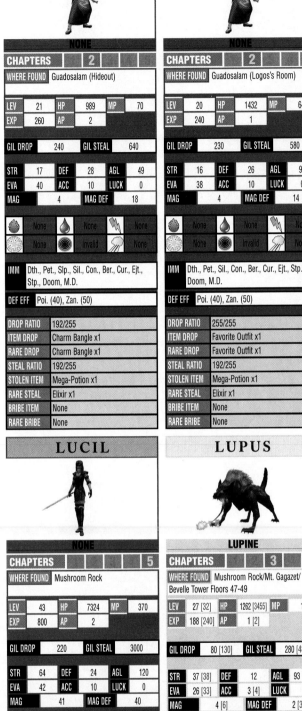
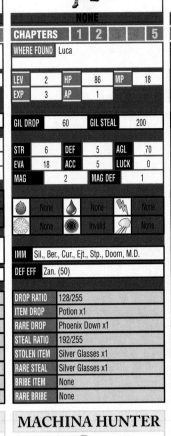
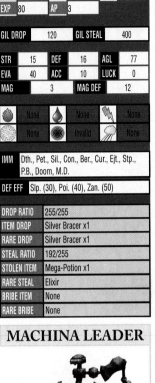
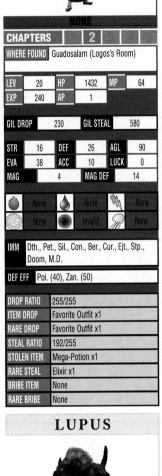

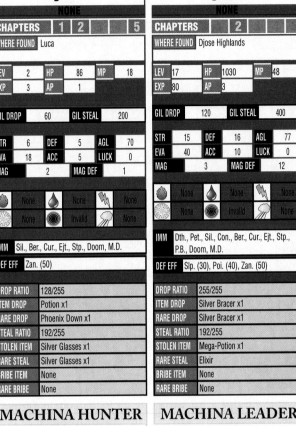
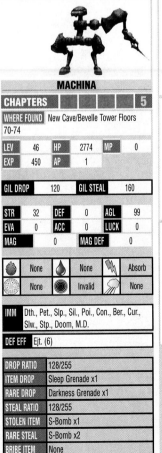

Characters

Garment Grids & Dresspheres

Battle System

Accessories

Items and Item Shops

Walkthrough

Mini Games

Fiends and Enemies

## LOGOS

**NONE**

**CHAPTERS** | 2

**WHERE FOUND** Guadosalam (Hideout)

| LEV | 21 | HP | 989 | MP | 70 |
|---|---|---|---|---|---|
| EXP | 260 | AP | 2 | | |

| GIL DROP | 240 | GIL STEAL | 640 |
|---|---|---|---|

| STR | 17 | DEF | 28 | AGL | 49 |
|---|---|---|---|---|---|
| EVA | 40 | ACC | 10 | LUCK | 0 |
| MAG | 4 | MAG DEF | 18 | | |

Fire None · Water None · Lightning None · Holy None · Gravity None · Water(target) Invalid · Wind None

**IMM** Dth., Pet., Slp., Sil., Con., Ber., Cur., Ejt., Stp., Doom, M.D.

**DEF EFF** Poi. (40), Zan. (50)

| DROP RATIO | 192/255 |
|---|---|
| ITEM DROP | Charm Bangle x1 |
| RARE DROP | Charm Bangle x1 |
| STEAL RATIO | 192/255 |
| STOLEN ITEM | Mega-Potion x1 |
| RARE STEAL | Elixir x1 |
| BRIBE ITEM | None |
| RARE BRIBE | None |

## LOGOS

**NONE**

**CHAPTERS** | 2

**WHERE FOUND** Guadosalam (Logos's Room)

| LEV | 20 | HP | 1432 | MP | 64 |
|---|---|---|---|---|---|
| EXP | 240 | AP | 1 | | |

| GIL DROP | 230 | GIL STEAL | 580 |
|---|---|---|---|

| STR | 16 | DEF | 26 | AGL | 90 |
|---|---|---|---|---|---|
| EVA | 38 | ACC | 10 | LUCK | 0 |
| MAG | 4 | MAG DEF | 14 | | |

Fire None · Water None · Lightning None · Holy None · Gravity None · Water(target) Invalid · Wind None

**IMM** Dth., Pet., Sil., Con., Ber., Cur., Ejt., Stp., Doom, M.D.

**DEF EFF** Poi. (40), Zan. (50)

| DROP RATIO | 255/255 |
|---|---|
| ITEM DROP | Favorite Outfit x1 |
| RARE DROP | Favorite Outfit x1 |
| STEAL RATIO | 192/255 |
| STOLEN ITEM | Mega-Potion x1 |
| RARE STEAL | Elixir x1 |
| BRIBE ITEM | None |
| RARE BRIBE | None |

## LOGOS

**NONE**

**CHAPTERS** | 1 | 2 | | | 5

**WHERE FOUND** Luca

| LEV | 2 | HP | 86 | MP | 18 |
|---|---|---|---|---|---|
| EXP | 3 | AP | 1 | | |

| GIL DROP | 60 | GIL STEAL | 200 |
|---|---|---|---|

| STR | 6 | DEF | 5 | AGL | 70 |
|---|---|---|---|---|---|
| EVA | 18 | ACC | 5 | LUCK | 0 |
| MAG | 2 | MAG DEF | 1 | | |

Fire None · Water None · Lightning None · Holy None · Gravity None · Water(target) Invalid · Wind None

**IMM** Sil., Ber., Cur., Ejt., Stp., Doom, M.D.

**DEF EFF** Zan. (50)

| DROP RATIO | 128/255 |
|---|---|
| ITEM DROP | Potion x1 |
| RARE DROP | Phoenix Down x1 |
| STEAL RATIO | 192/255 |
| STOLEN ITEM | Silver Glasses x1 |
| RARE STEAL | Silver Glasses x1 |
| BRIBE ITEM | None |
| RARE BRIBE | None |

## LOGOS

**NONE**

**CHAPTERS** | 2

**WHERE FOUND** Djose Highlands

| LEV | 17 | HP | 1030 | MP | 48 |
|---|---|---|---|---|---|
| EXP | 80 | AP | 3 | | |

| GIL DROP | 120 | GIL STEAL | 400 |
|---|---|---|---|

| STR | 15 | DEF | 16 | AGL | 77 |
|---|---|---|---|---|---|
| EVA | 40 | ACC | 10 | LUCK | 0 |
| MAG | 3 | MAG DEF | 12 | | |

Fire None · Water None · Lightning None · Holy None · Gravity None · Water(target) Invalid · Wind None

**IMM** Dth., Pet., Sil., Con., Ber., Cur., Ejt., Stp., P.B., Doom, M.D.

**DEF EFF** Slp. (30), Poi. (40), Zan. (50)

| DROP RATIO | 255/255 |
|---|---|
| ITEM DROP | Silver Bracer x1 |
| RARE DROP | Silver Bracer x1 |
| STEAL RATIO | 192/255 |
| STOLEN ITEM | Mega-Potion x1 |
| RARE STEAL | Elixir |
| BRIBE ITEM | None |
| RARE BRIBE | None |

## LUCIL

**NONE**

**CHAPTERS** | | | | 5

**WHERE FOUND** Mushroom Rock

| LEV | 43 | HP | 7324 | MP | 370 |
|---|---|---|---|---|---|
| EXP | 800 | AP | 2 | | |

| GIL DROP | 220 | GIL STEAL | 3000 |
|---|---|---|---|

| STR | 64 | DEF | 24 | AGL | 120 |
|---|---|---|---|---|---|
| EVA | 42 | ACC | 10 | LUCK | 0 |
| MAG | 41 | MAG DEF | 40 | | |

Fire None · Water None · Lightning None · Holy None · Gravity None · Water(target) Invalid · Wind None

**IMM** Dth., Pet., Slp., Sil., Drk., Poi., Con., Ber., Cur., Ejt., Slw., Stp., Doom, Del., P.I., M.D.

**DEF EFF** Zan. (10)

| DROP RATIO | 255/255 |
|---|---|
| ITEM DROP | Circlet x1 |
| RARE DROP | Circlet x1 |
| STEAL RATIO | 255/255 |
| STOLEN ITEM | Chocobo Feather x1 |
| RARE STEAL | Chocobo Feather x2 |
| BRIBE ITEM | None |
| RARE BRIBE | None |

## LUPUS

**LUPINE**

**CHAPTERS** | | | 3 | | 5

**WHERE FOUND** Mushroom Rock/Mt. Gagazet/ Bevelle Tower Floors 47-49

| LEV | 27 [32] | HP | 1262 [3455] | MP | 10 |
|---|---|---|---|---|---|
| EXP | 188 [240] | AP | 1 [2] | | |

| GIL DROP | 80 [130] | GIL STEAL | 280 [480] |
|---|---|---|---|

| STR | 37 [38] | DEF | 12 | AGL | 93 [112] |
|---|---|---|---|---|---|
| EVA | 26 [33] | ACC | 3 [4] | LUCK | 0 |
| MAG | 4 [6] | MAG DEF | 2 [3] | | |

Fire None · Water None · Lightning None · Holy None · Gravity None · Water(target) None · Wind None

**IMM** [Con.], [Ber.], Cur.

**DEF EFF** Dth. (50) Ejt. (12 [26]), Zan. (1 [6])

| DROP RATIO | 128/255 [255/255] |
|---|---|
| ITEM DROP | Hi-Potion x1 [Hi-Potion x4] |
| RARE DROP | Hi-Potion x2 [Hi-Potion x5] |
| STEAL RATIO | 255/255 |
| STOLEN ITEM | Hi-Potion x1 [Hi-Potion x3] |
| RARE STEAL | Hi-Potion x2 [Potion x4] |
| BRIBE ITEM | X-Potion x3 [Haste Ring x2] |
| RARE BRIBE | X-Potion x3 [Haste Ring x3] |

## MACHINA HUNTER

**MACHINA**

**CHAPTERS** | | | 3 | | 5

**WHERE FOUND** Bikanel/Bevelle Tower Floors 27-29

| LEV | 19 | HP | 1780 | MP | 0 |
|---|---|---|---|---|---|
| EXP | 63 | AP | 1 | | |

| GIL DROP | 30 | GIL STEAL | 60 |
|---|---|---|---|

| STR | 23 | DEF | 0 | AGL | 71 |
|---|---|---|---|---|---|
| EVA | 0 | ACC | 0 | LUCK | 0 |
| MAG | 20 | MAG DEF | 0 | | |

Fire None · Water None · Lightning Absorb · Holy None · Gravity None · Water(target) None · Wind None

**IMM** Dth., Pet., Slp., Sil., Poi., Con., Ber., Cur., Doom

**DEF EFF** Ejt. (6)

| DROP RATIO | Budget Grenade x1 |
|---|---|
| ITEM DROP | Silence Grenade x1 |
| RARE DROP | 128/255 |
| STEAL RATIO | Budget Grenade x1 |
| STOLEN ITEM | Silence Grenade x1 |
| RARE STEAL | None |
| BRIBE ITEM | None |
| RARE BRIBE | None |

## MACHINA LEADER

**MACHINA**

**CHAPTERS** | | | | | 5

**WHERE FOUND** New Cave/Bevelle Tower Floors 70-74

| LEV | 46 | HP | 2774 | MP | 0 |
|---|---|---|---|---|---|
| EXP | 450 | AP | 1 | | |

| GIL DROP | 120 | GIL STEAL | 160 |
|---|---|---|---|

| STR | 32 | DEF | 0 | AGL | 99 |
|---|---|---|---|---|---|
| EVA | 0 | ACC | 0 | LUCK | 0 |
| MAG | | MAG DEF | 0 | | |

Fire None · Water None · Lightning Absorb · Holy None · Gravity None · Water(target) Invalid · Wind None

**IMM** Dth., Pet., Slp., Sil., Poi., Con., Ber., Cur., Slw., Stp., Doom, M.D.

**DEF EFF** Ejt. (6)

| DROP RATIO | 128/255 |
|---|---|
| ITEM DROP | Sleep Grenade x1 |
| RARE DROP | Darkness Grenade x1 |
| STEAL RATIO | 128/255 |
| STOLEN ITEM | S-Bomb x1 |
| RARE STEAL | S-Bomb x2 |
| BRIBE ITEM | None |
| RARE BRIBE | None |

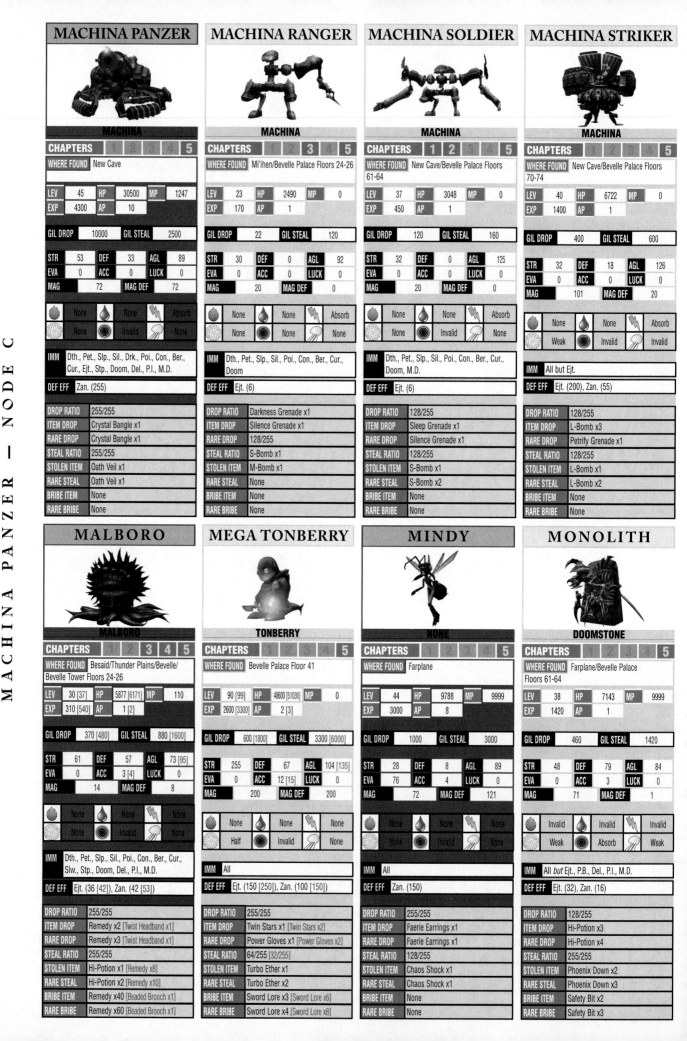

# MACHINA PANZER

**MACHINA**

| CHAPTERS | 1 | 2 | 3 | 4 | 5 |
|---|---|---|---|---|---|

| WHERE FOUND | New Cave |
|---|---|

| LEV | 45 | HP | 30500 | MP | 1247 |
|---|---|---|---|---|---|
| EXP | 4300 | AP | 10 | | |

| GIL DROP | 10000 | GIL STEAL | 2500 |
|---|---|---|---|

| STR | 53 | DEF | 33 | AGL | 89 |
|---|---|---|---|---|---|
| EVA | 0 | ACC | 0 | LUCK | 0 |
| MAG | 72 | | MAG DEF | 72 | |

| | Fire | Water | Lightning | Ice |
|---|---|---|---|---|
| | None | None | Absorb | None |
| | None | Invalid | None | |

| IMM | Dth., Pet., Slp., Sil., Drk., Poi., Con., Ber., Cur., Ejt., Stp., Doom, Del., P.I., M.D. |
|---|---|

| DEF EFF | Zan. (255) |
|---|---|

| DROP RATIO | 255/255 |
|---|---|
| ITEM DROP | Crystal Bangle x1 |
| RARE DROP | Crystal Bangle x1 |
| STEAL RATIO | 255/255 |
| STOLEN ITEM | Oath Veil x1 |
| RARE STEAL | Oath Veil x1 |
| BRIBE ITEM | None |
| RARE BRIBE | None |

# MACHINA RANGER

**MACHINA**

| CHAPTERS | 1 | 2 | 3 | 4 | 5 |
|---|---|---|---|---|---|

| WHERE FOUND | Mi'ihen/Bevelle Palace Floors 24-26 |
|---|---|

| LEV | 23 | HP | 2490 | MP | 0 |
|---|---|---|---|---|---|
| EXP | 170 | AP | 1 | | |

| GIL DROP | 22 | GIL STEAL | 120 |
|---|---|---|---|

| STR | 30 | DEF | 0 | AGL | 92 |
|---|---|---|---|---|---|
| EVA | 0 | ACC | 0 | LUCK | 0 |
| MAG | 20 | | MAG DEF | 0 | |

| | Fire | Water | Lightning | Ice |
|---|---|---|---|---|
| | None | None | None | Absorb |
| | None | None | None | None |

| IMM | Dth., Pet., Slp., Sil., Poi., Con., Ber., Cur., Doom |
|---|---|

| DEF EFF | Ejt. (6) |
|---|---|

| DROP RATIO | Darkness Grenade x1 |
|---|---|
| ITEM DROP | Silence Grenade x1 |
| RARE DROP | 128/255 |
| STEAL RATIO | S-Bomb x1 |
| STOLEN ITEM | M-Bomb x1 |
| RARE STEAL | None |
| BRIBE ITEM | None |
| RARE BRIBE | None |

# MACHINA SOLDIER

**MACHINA**

| CHAPTERS | 1 | 2 | 3 | 4 | 5 |
|---|---|---|---|---|---|

| WHERE FOUND | New Cave/Bevelle Palace Floors 61-64 |
|---|---|

| LEV | 37 | HP | 3048 | MP | 0 |
|---|---|---|---|---|---|
| EXP | 450 | AP | 1 | | |

| GIL DROP | 120 | GIL STEAL | 160 |
|---|---|---|---|

| STR | 32 | DEF | 0 | AGL | 125 |
|---|---|---|---|---|---|
| EVA | 0 | ACC | 0 | LUCK | 0 |
| MAG | 20 | | MAG DEF | 0 | |

| | Fire | Water | Lightning | Ice |
|---|---|---|---|---|
| | None | None | None | Absorb |
| | None | Invalid | None | |

| IMM | Dth., Pet., Slp., Sil., Poi., Con., Ber., Cur., Doom, M.D. |
|---|---|

| DEF EFF | Ejt. (6) |
|---|---|

| DROP RATIO | 128/255 |
|---|---|
| ITEM DROP | Sleep Grenade x1 |
| RARE DROP | Silence Grenade x1 |
| STEAL RATIO | 128/255 |
| STOLEN ITEM | S-Bomb x1 |
| RARE STEAL | S-Bomb x2 |
| BRIBE ITEM | None |
| RARE BRIBE | None |

# MACHINA STRIKER

**MACHINA**

| CHAPTERS | 1 | 2 | 3 | 4 | 5 |
|---|---|---|---|---|---|

| WHERE FOUND | New Cave/Bevelle Palace Floors 70-74 |
|---|---|

| LEV | 40 | HP | 6722 | MP | 0 |
|---|---|---|---|---|---|
| EXP | 1400 | AP | 1 | | |

| GIL DROP | 400 | GIL STEAL | 600 |
|---|---|---|---|

| STR | 32 | DEF | 18 | AGL | 126 |
|---|---|---|---|---|---|
| EVA | 0 | ACC | 0 | LUCK | 0 |
| MAG | 101 | | MAG DEF | 20 | |

| | Fire | Water | Lightning | Ice |
|---|---|---|---|---|
| | None | None | Absorb | None |
| | Weak | Invalid | Invalid | |

| IMM | All but Ejt. |
|---|---|

| DEF EFF | Ejt. (200), Zan. (55) |
|---|---|

| DROP RATIO | 128/255 |
|---|---|
| ITEM DROP | L-Bomb x3 |
| RARE DROP | Petrify Grenade x1 |
| STEAL RATIO | 128/255 |
| STOLEN ITEM | L-Bomb x1 |
| RARE STEAL | L-Bomb x2 |
| BRIBE ITEM | None |
| RARE BRIBE | None |

# MALBORO

**MALBORO**

| CHAPTERS | 1 | 2 | 3 | 4 | 5 |
|---|---|---|---|---|---|

| WHERE FOUND | Besaid/Thunder Plains/Bevelle/Bevelle Tower Floors 24-26 |
|---|---|

| LEV | 30 [37] | HP | 5877 [6171] | MP | 110 |
|---|---|---|---|---|---|
| EXP | 310 [540] | AP | 1 [2] | | |

| GIL DROP | 370 [480] | GIL STEAL | 880 [1600] |
|---|---|---|---|

| STR | 61 | DEF | 57 | AGL | 73 [95] |
|---|---|---|---|---|---|
| EVA | 0 | ACC | 3 [4] | LUCK | 0 |
| MAG | 14 | | MAG DEF | 8 | |

| | Fire | Water | Lightning | Ice |
|---|---|---|---|---|
| | None | None | None | None |
| | None | Invalid | None | |

| IMM | Dth., Pet., Slp., Sil., Poi., Con., Ber., Cur., Slw., Stp., Doom, Del., P.I., M.D. |
|---|---|

| DEF EFF | Ejt. (36 [42]), Zan. (42 [53]) |
|---|---|

| DROP RATIO | 255/255 |
|---|---|
| ITEM DROP | Remedy x2 [Twist Headband x1] |
| RARE DROP | Remedy x3 [Twist Headband x1] |
| STEAL RATIO | 255/255 |
| STOLEN ITEM | Hi-Potion x1 [Remedy x8] |
| RARE STEAL | Hi-Potion x2 [Remedy x10] |
| BRIBE ITEM | Remedy x40 [Beaded Brooch x1] |
| RARE BRIBE | Remedy x60 [Beaded Brooch x1] |

# MEGA TONBERRY

**TONBERRY**

| CHAPTERS | 1 | 2 | 3 | 4 | 5 |
|---|---|---|---|---|---|

| WHERE FOUND | Bevelle Palace Floor 41 |
|---|---|

| LEV | 90 [99] | HP | 48600 [51030] | MP | 0 |
|---|---|---|---|---|---|
| EXP | 2600 [3300] | AP | 2 [3] | | |

| GIL DROP | 600 [1800] | GIL STEAL | 3300 [6000] |
|---|---|---|---|

| STR | 255 | DEF | 67 | AGL | 104 [135] |
|---|---|---|---|---|---|
| EVA | 0 | ACC | 12 [15] | LUCK | 0 |
| MAG | 200 | | MAG DEF | 200 | |

| | Fire | Water | Lightning | Ice |
|---|---|---|---|---|
| | None | None | None | None |
| | Half | Invalid | None | |

| IMM | All |
|---|---|

| DEF EFF | Ejt. (150 [250]), Zan. (100 [150]) |
|---|---|

| DROP RATIO | 255/255 |
|---|---|
| ITEM DROP | Twin Stars x1 [Twin Stars x2] |
| RARE DROP | Power Gloves x1 [Power Gloves x2] |
| STEAL RATIO | 64/255 [32/255] |
| STOLEN ITEM | Turbo Ether x1 |
| RARE STEAL | Turbo Ether x2 |
| BRIBE ITEM | Sword Lore x3 [Sword Lore x6] |
| RARE BRIBE | Sword Lore x4 [Sword Lore x8] |

# MINDY

**NONE**

| CHAPTERS | 1 | 2 | 3 | 4 | 5 |
|---|---|---|---|---|---|

| WHERE FOUND | Farplane |
|---|---|

| LEV | 44 | HP | 9788 | MP | 9999 |
|---|---|---|---|---|---|
| EXP | 3000 | AP | 8 | | |

| GIL DROP | 1000 | GIL STEAL | 3000 |
|---|---|---|---|

| STR | 28 | DEF | 8 | AGL | 89 |
|---|---|---|---|---|---|
| EVA | 76 | ACC | 4 | LUCK | 0 |
| MAG | 72 | | MAG DEF | 121 | |

| | Fire | Water | Lightning | Ice |
|---|---|---|---|---|
| | None | None | None | None |
| | None | Invalid | None | |

| IMM | All |
|---|---|

| DEF EFF | Zan. (150) |
|---|---|

| DROP RATIO | 255/255 |
|---|---|
| ITEM DROP | Faerie Earrings x1 |
| RARE DROP | Faerie Earrings x1 |
| STEAL RATIO | 128/255 |
| STOLEN ITEM | Chaos Shock x1 |
| RARE STEAL | Chaos Shock x1 |
| BRIBE ITEM | None |
| RARE BRIBE | None |

# MONOLITH

**DOOMSTONE**

| CHAPTERS | 1 | 2 | 3 | 4 | 5 |
|---|---|---|---|---|---|

| WHERE FOUND | Farplane/Bevelle Palace Floors 61-64 |
|---|---|

| LEV | 38 | HP | 7143 | MP | 9999 |
|---|---|---|---|---|---|
| EXP | 1420 | AP | 1 | | |

| GIL DROP | 460 | GIL STEAL | 1420 |
|---|---|---|---|

| STR | 48 | DEF | 79 | AGL | 84 |
|---|---|---|---|---|---|
| EVA | 0 | ACC | 3 | LUCK | 0 |
| MAG | 71 | | MAG DEF | 1 | |

| | Fire | Water | Lightning | Ice |
|---|---|---|---|---|
| | Invalid | Invalid | Invalid | Invalid |
| | Weak | Absorb | Weak | |

| IMM | All but Ejt., P.B., Del., P.I., M.D. |
|---|---|

| DEF EFF | Ejt. (32), Zan. (16) |
|---|---|

| DROP RATIO | 128/255 |
|---|---|
| ITEM DROP | Hi-Potion x3 |
| RARE DROP | Hi-Potion x4 |
| STEAL RATIO | 255/255 |
| STOLEN ITEM | Phoenix Down x2 |
| RARE STEAL | Phoenix Down x3 |
| BRIBE ITEM | Safety Bit x2 |
| RARE BRIBE | Safety Bit x3 |

# MR. GOON

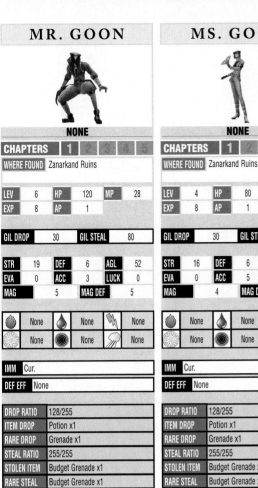

**NONE**

| CHAPTERS | 1 | 2 | 3 | 4 | 5 |
|---|---|---|---|---|---|

| WHERE FOUND | Zanarkand Ruins |
|---|---|

| LEV | 6 | HP | 120 | MP | 28 |
|---|---|---|---|---|---|
| EXP | 8 | AP | 1 | | |

| GIL DROP | 30 | GIL STEAL | 80 |
|---|---|---|---|

| STR | 19 | DEF | 6 | AGL | 52 |
|---|---|---|---|---|---|
| EVA | 0 | ACC | 3 | LUCK | 0 |
| MAG | 5 | MAG DEF | 5 | | |

| 🔥 | None | 💧 | None | ⚡ | None |
|---|---|---|---|---|---|
| ❄ | None | ◎ | None | 🌀 | None |

| IMM | Cur. |
|---|---|
| DEF EFF | None |

| DROP RATIO | 128/255 |
|---|---|
| ITEM DROP | Potion x1 |
| RARE DROP | Grenade x1 |
| STEAL RATIO | 255/255 |
| STOLEN ITEM | Budget Grenade x1 |
| RARE STEAL | Budget Grenade x1 |
| BRIBE ITEM | Grenade x2 |
| RARE BRIBE | S-Bomb x2 |

# MS. GOON

**NONE**

| CHAPTERS | 1 | 2 | 3 | 4 | 5 |
|---|---|---|---|---|---|

| WHERE FOUND | Zanarkand Ruins |
|---|---|

| LEV | 4 | HP | 80 | MP | 85 |
|---|---|---|---|---|---|
| EXP | 8 | AP | 1 | | |

| GIL DROP | 30 | GIL STEAL | 80 |
|---|---|---|---|

| STR | 16 | DEF | 6 | AGL | 60 |
|---|---|---|---|---|---|
| EVA | 0 | ACC | 5 | LUCK | 0 |
| MAG | 4 | MAG DEF | 8 | | |

| 🔥 | None | 💧 | None | ⚡ | None |
|---|---|---|---|---|---|
| ❄ | None | ◎ | None | 🌀 | None |

| IMM | Cur. |
|---|---|
| DEF EFF | None |

| DROP RATIO | 128/255 |
|---|---|
| ITEM DROP | Potion x1 |
| RARE DROP | Grenade x1 |
| STEAL RATIO | 255/255 |
| STOLEN ITEM | Budget Grenade x1 |
| RARE STEAL | Budget Grenade x2 |
| BRIBE ITEM | Grenade x2 |
| RARE BRIBE | S-Bomb x2 |

# MUSHROOM CLOUD

**FUNGUS**

| CHAPTERS | 1 | 2 | 3 | 4 | 5 |
|---|---|---|---|---|---|

| WHERE FOUND | Bikanel/Bevelle Tower Floors 50-59 |
|---|---|

| LEV | 81 [97] | HP | 9999 [10998] | MP | 270 |
|---|---|---|---|---|---|
| EXP | 1100 [2000] | AP | 1 [2] | | |

| GIL DROP | 320 [1000] | GIL STEAL | 520 [1000] |
|---|---|---|---|

| STR | 1 | DEF | 32 [82] | AGL | 78 [94] |
|---|---|---|---|---|---|
| EVA | 0 | ACC | 7 [9] | LUCK | 0 |
| MAG | 138 | MAG DEF | 240 | | |

| 🔥 | Weak | 💧 | None | ⚡ | None |
|---|---|---|---|---|---|
| ❄ | Half | ◎ | Invalid | 🌀 | None |

| IMM | Dth., Pet., Slp., Sil., Drk., Poi., Con., Ber. ([0]), Cur., Slw., Stp., Doom, Del., P.I., M.D. |
|---|---|
| DEF EFF | Ejt. (85 [100]), Zan. (40 [50]) |

| DROP RATIO | 255/255 |
|---|---|
| ITEM DROP | Mana Tonic x1 [Remedy x2] |
| RARE DROP | Remedy x2 [Remedy x4] |
| STEAL RATIO | 64/255 [32/255] |
| STOLEN ITEM | Ether x1 |
| RARE STEAL | Ether x2 |
| BRIBE ITEM | Regal Crown x7 [Nature's Tome x2] |
| RARE BRIBE | Nature's Tome x1 [Nature's Tome x2] |

# MYCOTOXIN

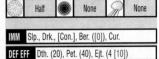

**FUNGUS**

| CHAPTERS | 1 | 2 | 3 | 4 | 5 |
|---|---|---|---|---|---|

| WHERE FOUND | Mi'ihen Highroad/Mt. Gagazet/Zanarkand Ruins/Various |
|---|---|

| LEV | 29 [34] | HP | 810 [3240] | MP | 120 |
|---|---|---|---|---|---|
| EXP | 212 [276] | AP | 1 [2] | | |

| GIL DROP | 83 [152] | GIL STEAL | 280 [550] |
|---|---|---|---|

| STR | 1 | DEF | 20 [21] | AGL | 43 [47] |
|---|---|---|---|---|---|
| EVA | 0 | ACC | 0 | LUCK | 0 |
| MAG | 4 | MAG DEF | 42 | | |

| 🔥 | Weak | 💧 | None | ⚡ | None |
|---|---|---|---|---|---|
| ❄ | Half | ◎ | None | 🌀 | None |

| IMM | Slp., Drk., [Con.], Ber. ([0]), Cur. |
|---|---|
| DEF EFF | Dth. (20), Pet. (40), Ejt. (4 [10]) |

| DROP RATIO | 64/255 [255/255] |
|---|---|
| ITEM DROP | Antidote x2 [Antidote x4] |
| RARE DROP | NulTide Ring x1 [Antidote x6] |
| STEAL RATIO | 255/255 |
| STOLEN ITEM | Antidote x2 [NulTide Ring x1] |
| RARE STEAL | Antidote x3 [NulTide Ring x1] |
| BRIBE ITEM | Star Pendant x1 [Star Pendant x3] |
| RARE BRIBE | Star Pendant x1 [Star Pendant x4] |

# NASHORN

**RUMINANT**

| CHAPTERS | 1 | 2 | 3 | 4 | 5 |
|---|---|---|---|---|---|

| WHERE FOUND | Bikanel/Calm Lands/Zanarkand Ruins/Others |
|---|---|

| LEV | 10 [12] | HP | 482 [1928] | MP | 0 |
|---|---|---|---|---|---|
| EXP | 33 [63] | AP | 1 [2] | | |

| GIL DROP | 22 [53] | GIL STEAL | 85 [180] |
|---|---|---|---|

| STR | 72 | DEF | 10 | AGL | 65 [72] |
|---|---|---|---|---|---|
| EVA | 0 | ACC | 8 [10] | LUCK | 0 |
| MAG | 2 | MAG DEF | 3 | | |

| 🔥 | None | 💧 | None | ⚡ | None |
|---|---|---|---|---|---|
| ❄ | None | ◎ | None | 🌀 | None |

| IMM | Slp., Poi., [Con.], Cur., Doom |
|---|---|
| DEF EFF | Ejt. (20 [28]), Zan. (6 [7]) |

| DROP RATIO | 196/255 [255/255] |
|---|---|
| ITEM DROP | Potion x1 [Hi-Potion x3] |
| RARE DROP | Phoenix Down x1 [Hi-Potion x4] |
| STEAL RATIO | 255/255 |
| STOLEN ITEM | Potion x1 [Mega Phoenix x2] |
| RARE STEAL | Phoenix Down x1 [Mega Phoenix x2] |
| BRIBE ITEM | Hi-Potion x6 [NulBlaze Ring x1] |
| RARE BRIBE | Hi-Potion x6 [Crimson Ring x1] |

# NODE A

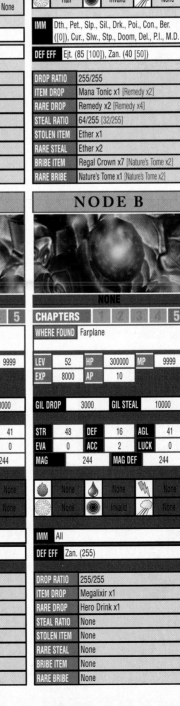

**NONE**

| CHAPTERS | 1 | 2 | 3 | 4 | 5 |
|---|---|---|---|---|---|

| WHERE FOUND | Farplane |
|---|---|

| LEV | 52 | HP | 300000 | MP | 9999 |
|---|---|---|---|---|---|
| EXP | 8000 | AP | 10 | | |

| GIL DROP | 3000 | GIL STEAL | 10000 |
|---|---|---|---|

| STR | 48 | DEF | 16 | AGL | 41 |
|---|---|---|---|---|---|
| EVA | 0 | ACC | 2 | LUCK | 0 |
| MAG | 244 | MAG DEF | 244 | | |

| 🔥 | None | 💧 | None | ⚡ | None |
|---|---|---|---|---|---|
| ❄ | None | ◎ | Invalid | 🌀 | None |

| IMM | All |
|---|---|
| DEF EFF | Zan. (255) |

| DROP RATIO | 255/255 |
|---|---|
| ITEM DROP | Megalixir x1 |
| RARE DROP | Hero Drink x1 |
| STEAL RATIO | None |
| STOLEN ITEM | None |
| RARE STEAL | None |
| BRIBE ITEM | None |
| RARE BRIBE | None |

# NODE B

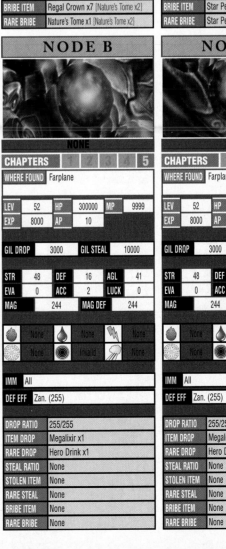

**NONE**

| CHAPTERS | 1 | 2 | 3 | 4 | 5 |
|---|---|---|---|---|---|

| WHERE FOUND | Farplane |
|---|---|

| LEV | 52 | HP | 300000 | MP | 9999 |
|---|---|---|---|---|---|
| EXP | 8000 | AP | 10 | | |

| GIL DROP | 3000 | GIL STEAL | 10000 |
|---|---|---|---|

| STR | 48 | DEF | 16 | AGL | 41 |
|---|---|---|---|---|---|
| EVA | 0 | ACC | 2 | LUCK | 0 |
| MAG | 244 | MAG DEF | 244 | | |

| 🔥 | None | 💧 | None | ⚡ | None |
|---|---|---|---|---|---|
| ❄ | None | ◎ | Invalid | 🌀 | None |

| IMM | All |
|---|---|
| DEF EFF | Zan. (255) |

| DROP RATIO | 255/255 |
|---|---|
| ITEM DROP | Megalixir x1 |
| RARE DROP | Hero Drink x1 |
| STEAL RATIO | None |
| STOLEN ITEM | None |
| RARE STEAL | None |
| BRIBE ITEM | None |
| RARE BRIBE | None |

# NODE C

**NONE**

| CHAPTERS | 1 | 2 | 3 | 4 | 5 |
|---|---|---|---|---|---|

| WHERE FOUND | Farplane |
|---|---|

| LEV | 52 | HP | 300000 | MP | 9999 |
|---|---|---|---|---|---|
| EXP | 8000 | AP | 10 | | |

| GIL DROP | 3000 | GIL STEAL | 10000 |
|---|---|---|---|

| STR | 48 | DEF | 16 | AGL | 41 |
|---|---|---|---|---|---|
| EVA | 0 | ACC | 2 | LUCK | 0 |
| MAG | 244 | MAG DEF | 244 | | |

| 🔥 | None | 💧 | None | ⚡ | None |
|---|---|---|---|---|---|
| ❄ | None | ◎ | Invalid | 🌀 | None |

| IMM | All |
|---|---|
| DEF EFF | Zan. (255) |

| DROP RATIO | 255/255 |
|---|---|
| ITEM DROP | Megalixir x1 |
| RARE DROP | Hero Drink x1 |
| STEAL RATIO | None |
| STOLEN ITEM | None |
| RARE STEAL | None |
| BRIBE ITEM | None |
| RARE BRIBE | None |

Characters

Garment Grids & Dresspheres

Battle System

Accessories

Items and Item Shops

Walkthrough

Mini Games

Fiends and Enemies

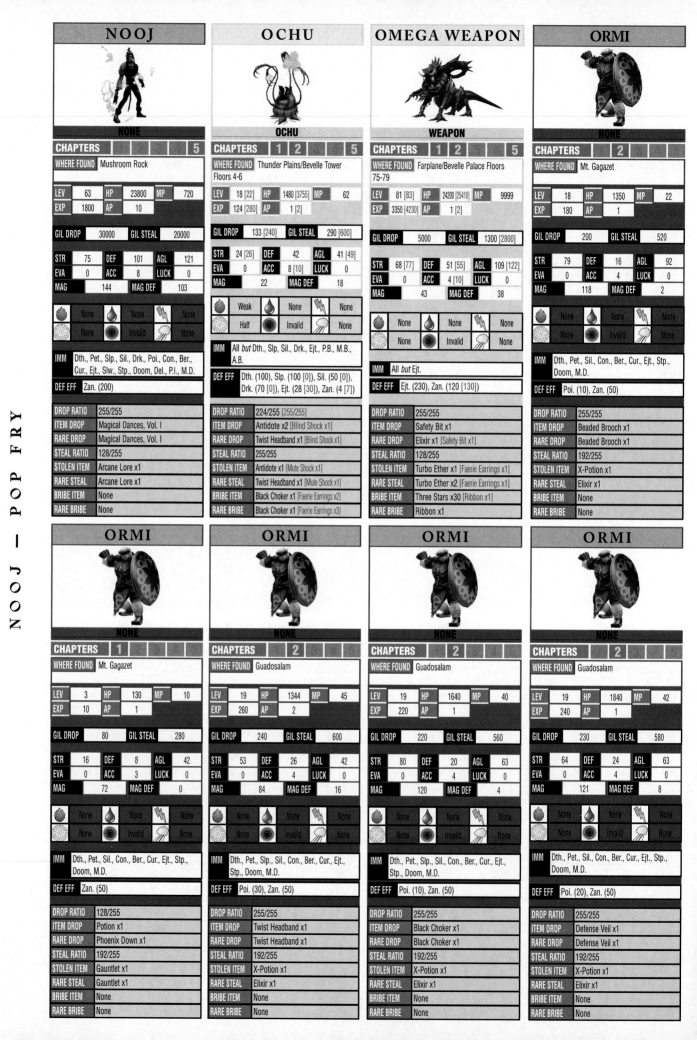

## NOOJ

NONE

| CHAPTERS | | | | | 5 |
|---|---|---|---|---|---|

**WHERE FOUND** Mushroom Rock

| LEV | 63 | HP | 23800 | MP | 720 |
|---|---|---|---|---|---|
| EXP | 1800 | AP | 10 | | |

| GIL DROP | 30000 | GIL STEAL | 20000 |
|---|---|---|---|

| STR | 75 | DEF | 101 | AGL | 121 |
|---|---|---|---|---|---|
| EVA | 0 | ACC | 8 | LUCK | 0 |
| MAG | | 144 | MAG DEF | | 103 |

| | None | | None | | None |
|---|---|---|---|---|---|
| | None | | Invalid | | None |

**IMM** Dth., Pet., Slp., Sil., Drk., Poi., Con., Ber., Cur., Ejt., Slw., Stp., Doom, Del., P.I., M.D.

**DEF EFF** Zan. (200)

| DROP RATIO | 255/255 |
|---|---|
| ITEM DROP | Magical Dances, Vol. I |
| RARE DROP | Magical Dances, Vol. I |
| STEAL RATIO | 128/255 |
| STOLEN ITEM | Arcane Lore x1 |
| RARE STEAL | Arcane Lore x1 |
| BRIBE ITEM | None |
| RARE BRIBE | None |

## OCHU

OCHU

| CHAPTERS | 1 | 2 | | | 5 |
|---|---|---|---|---|---|

**WHERE FOUND** Thunder Plains/Bevelle Tower Floors 4-6

| LEV | 18 [22] | HP | 1480 [3755] | MP | 62 |
|---|---|---|---|---|---|
| EXP | 124 [280] | AP | 1 [2] | | |

| GIL DROP | 133 [240] | GIL STEAL | 290 [600] |
|---|---|---|---|

| STR | 24 [26] | DEF | 42 | AGL | 41 [49] |
|---|---|---|---|---|---|
| EVA | 0 | ACC | 8 [10] | LUCK | 0 |
| MAG | | 22 | MAG DEF | | 18 |

| | Weak | | None | | None |
|---|---|---|---|---|---|
| | Half | | Invalid | | None |

**IMM** All *but* Dth., Slp., Sil., Drk., Ejt., P.B., M.B., A.B.

**DEF EFF** Dth. (100), Slp. (100 [0]), Sil. (50 [0]), Drk. (70 [0]), Ejt. (28 [30]), Zan. (4 [7])

| DROP RATIO | 224/255 [255/255] |
|---|---|
| ITEM DROP | Antidote x2 [Blind Shock x1] |
| RARE DROP | Twist Headband x1 [Blind Shock x1] |
| STEAL RATIO | 255/255 |
| STOLEN ITEM | Antidote x1 [Mute Shock x1] |
| RARE STEAL | Twist Headband x1 [Mute Shock x1] |
| BRIBE ITEM | Black Choker x1 [Faerie Earrings x2] |
| RARE BRIBE | Black Choker x1 [Faerie Earrings x3] |

## OMEGA WEAPON

WEAPON

| CHAPTERS | 1 | 2 | | | 5 |
|---|---|---|---|---|---|

**WHERE FOUND** Farplane/Bevelle Palace Floors 75-79

| LEV | 81 [83] | HP | 24200 [25410] | MP | 9999 |
|---|---|---|---|---|---|
| EXP | 3350 [4230] | AP | 1 [2] | | |

| GIL DROP | 5000 | GIL STEAL | 1300 [2800] |
|---|---|---|---|

| STR | 68 [77] | DEF | 51 [55] | AGL | 109 [122] |
|---|---|---|---|---|---|
| EVA | 0 | ACC | 4 [10] | LUCK | 0 |
| MAG | | 43 | MAG DEF | | 38 |

| | None | | None | | None |
|---|---|---|---|---|---|
| | None | | Invalid | | None |

**IMM** All *but* Ejt.

**DEF EFF** Ejt. (230), Zan. (120 [130])

| DROP RATIO | 255/255 |
|---|---|
| ITEM DROP | Safety Bit x1 |
| RARE DROP | Elixir x1 [Safety Bit x1] |
| STEAL RATIO | 128/255 |
| STOLEN ITEM | Turbo Ether x1 [Faerie Earrings x1] |
| RARE STEAL | Turbo Ether x2 [Faerie Earrings x1] |
| BRIBE ITEM | Three Stars x30 [Ribbon x1] |
| RARE BRIBE | Ribbon x1 |

## ORMI

NONE

| CHAPTERS | | | 2 | | |
|---|---|---|---|---|---|

**WHERE FOUND** Mt. Gagazet

| LEV | 18 | HP | 1350 | MP | 22 |
|---|---|---|---|---|---|
| EXP | 180 | AP | 1 | | |

| GIL DROP | 200 | GIL STEAL | 520 |
|---|---|---|---|

| STR | 79 | DEF | 16 | AGL | 92 |
|---|---|---|---|---|---|
| EVA | 0 | ACC | 4 | LUCK | 0 |
| MAG | | 118 | MAG DEF | | 2 |

| | None | | None | | None |
|---|---|---|---|---|---|
| | None | | Invalid | | None |

**IMM** Dth., Pet., Sil., Con., Ber., Cur., Ejt., Stp., Doom, M.D.

**DEF EFF** Poi. (10), Zan. (50)

| DROP RATIO | 255/255 |
|---|---|
| ITEM DROP | Beaded Brooch x1 |
| RARE DROP | Beaded Brooch x1 |
| STEAL RATIO | 192/255 |
| STOLEN ITEM | X-Potion x1 |
| RARE STEAL | Elixir x1 |
| BRIBE ITEM | None |
| RARE BRIBE | None |

## ORMI

NONE

| CHAPTERS | 1 | | | | |
|---|---|---|---|---|---|

**WHERE FOUND** Mt. Gagazet

| LEV | 3 | HP | 130 | MP | 10 |
|---|---|---|---|---|---|
| EXP | 10 | AP | 1 | | |

| GIL DROP | 80 | GIL STEAL | 280 |
|---|---|---|---|

| STR | 16 | DEF | 8 | AGL | 42 |
|---|---|---|---|---|---|
| EVA | 0 | ACC | 3 | LUCK | 0 |
| MAG | | 72 | MAG DEF | | 0 |

| | None | | None | | None |
|---|---|---|---|---|---|
| | None | | Invalid | | None |

**IMM** Dth., Pet., Sil., Con., Ber., Cur., Ejt., Stp., Doom, M.D.

**DEF EFF** Zan. (50)

| DROP RATIO | 128/255 |
|---|---|
| ITEM DROP | Potion x1 |
| RARE DROP | Phoenix Down x1 |
| STEAL RATIO | 192/255 |
| STOLEN ITEM | Gauntlet x1 |
| RARE STEAL | Gauntlet x1 |
| BRIBE ITEM | None |
| RARE BRIBE | None |

## ORMI

NONE

| CHAPTERS | | 2 | | | |
|---|---|---|---|---|---|

**WHERE FOUND** Guadosalam

| LEV | 19 | HP | 1344 | MP | 45 |
|---|---|---|---|---|---|
| EXP | 260 | AP | 2 | | |

| GIL DROP | 240 | GIL STEAL | 600 |
|---|---|---|---|

| STR | 53 | DEF | 26 | AGL | 42 |
|---|---|---|---|---|---|
| EVA | 0 | ACC | 4 | LUCK | 0 |
| MAG | | 84 | MAG DEF | | 16 |

| | None | | None | | None |
|---|---|---|---|---|---|
| | None | | Invalid | | None |

**IMM** Dth., Pet., Slp., Sil., Con., Ber., Cur., Ejt., Stp., Doom, M.D.

**DEF EFF** Poi. (30), Zan. (50)

| DROP RATIO | 255/255 |
|---|---|
| ITEM DROP | Twist Headband x1 |
| RARE DROP | Twist Headband x1 |
| STEAL RATIO | 192/255 |
| STOLEN ITEM | X-Potion x1 |
| RARE STEAL | Elixir x1 |
| BRIBE ITEM | None |
| RARE BRIBE | None |

## ORMI

NONE

| CHAPTERS | | 2 | | | |
|---|---|---|---|---|---|

**WHERE FOUND** Guadosalam

| LEV | 19 | HP | 1640 | MP | 40 |
|---|---|---|---|---|---|
| EXP | 220 | AP | 1 | | |

| GIL DROP | 220 | GIL STEAL | 560 |
|---|---|---|---|

| STR | 80 | DEF | 20 | AGL | 63 |
|---|---|---|---|---|---|
| EVA | 0 | ACC | 4 | LUCK | 0 |
| MAG | | 120 | MAG DEF | | 4 |

| | None | | None | | None |
|---|---|---|---|---|---|
| | None | | Invalid | | None |

**IMM** Dth., Pet., Slp., Sil., Con., Ber., Cur., Ejt., Stp., Doom, M.D.

**DEF EFF** Poi. (10), Zan. (50)

| DROP RATIO | 255/255 |
|---|---|
| ITEM DROP | Black Choker x1 |
| RARE DROP | Black Choker x1 |
| STEAL RATIO | 192/255 |
| STOLEN ITEM | X-Potion x1 |
| RARE STEAL | Elixir x1 |
| BRIBE ITEM | None |
| RARE BRIBE | None |

## ORMI

NONE

| CHAPTERS | | 2 | | | |
|---|---|---|---|---|---|

**WHERE FOUND** Guadosalam

| LEV | 19 | HP | 1840 | MP | 42 |
|---|---|---|---|---|---|
| EXP | 240 | AP | 1 | | |

| GIL DROP | 230 | GIL STEAL | 580 |
|---|---|---|---|

| STR | 64 | DEF | 24 | AGL | 63 |
|---|---|---|---|---|---|
| EVA | 0 | ACC | 4 | LUCK | 0 |
| MAG | | 121 | MAG DEF | | 8 |

| | None | | None | | None |
|---|---|---|---|---|---|
| | None | | Invalid | | None |

**IMM** Dth., Pet., Sil., Con., Ber., Cur., Ejt., Stp., Doom, M.D.

**DEF EFF** Poi. (20), Zan. (50)

| DROP RATIO | 255/255 |
|---|---|
| ITEM DROP | Defense Veil x1 |
| RARE DROP | Defense Veil x1 |
| STEAL RATIO | 192/255 |
| STOLEN ITEM | X-Potion x1 |
| RARE STEAL | Elixir x1 |
| BRIBE ITEM | None |
| RARE BRIBE | None |

Characters

1

Garment Grids & Dresspheres

2

Battle System

3

Accessories

4

Items and Item Shops

5

Walkthrough

6

Mini Games

7

Fiends and Enemies

8

## ORMI

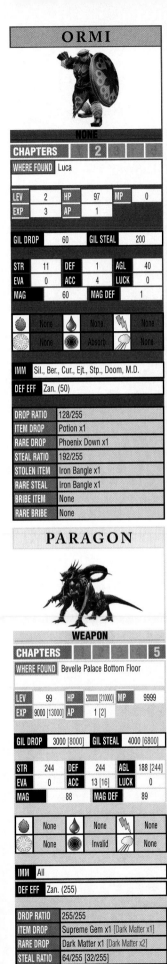

**NONE**

| CHAPTERS | 2 | | |
|---|---|---|---|

**WHERE FOUND** Luca

| LEV | 2 | HP | 97 | MP | 0 |
|---|---|---|---|---|---|
| EXP | 3 | AP | 1 | | |

| GIL DROP | 60 | GIL STEAL | 200 |
|---|---|---|---|

| STR | 11 | DEF | 1 | AGL | 40 |
|---|---|---|---|---|---|
| EVA | 0 | ACC | 4 | LUCK | 0 |
| MAG | 60 | MAG DEF | 1 | | |

| | None | | None | | None |
|---|---|---|---|---|---|
| | None | | Absorb | | None |

**IMM** Sil., Ber., Cur., Ejt., Stp., Doom, M.D.

**DEF EFF** Zan. (50)

| DROP RATIO | 128/255 |
|---|---|
| ITEM DROP | Potion x1 |
| RARE DROP | Phoenix Down x1 |
| STEAL RATIO | 192/255 |
| STOLEN ITEM | Iron Bangle x1 |
| RARE STEAL | Iron Bangle x1 |
| BRIBE ITEM | None |
| RARE BRIBE | None |

## ORMI

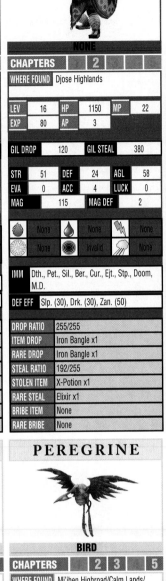

**NONE**

| CHAPTERS | 2 | | |
|---|---|---|---|

**WHERE FOUND** Djose Highlands

| LEV | 16 | HP | 1150 | MP | 22 |
|---|---|---|---|---|---|
| EXP | 80 | AP | 3 | | |

| GIL DROP | 120 | GIL STEAL | 380 |
|---|---|---|---|

| STR | 51 | DEF | 24 | AGL | 58 |
|---|---|---|---|---|---|
| EVA | 0 | ACC | 4 | LUCK | 0 |
| MAG | 115 | MAG DEF | 2 | | |

| | None | | None | | None |
|---|---|---|---|---|---|
| | None | | Invalid | | None |

**IMM** Dth., Pet., Sil., Ber., Cur., Ejt., Stp., Doom, M.D.

**DEF EFF** Slp. (30), Drk. (30), Zan. (50)

| DROP RATIO | 255/255 |
|---|---|
| ITEM DROP | Iron Bangle x1 |
| RARE DROP | Iron Bangle x1 |
| STEAL RATIO | 192/255 |
| STOLEN ITEM | X-Potion x1 |
| RARE STEAL | Elixir x1 |
| BRIBE ITEM | None |
| RARE BRIBE | None |

## PAINE

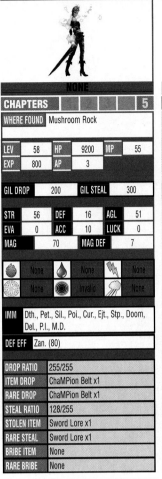

**NONE**

| CHAPTERS | | | 5 |
|---|---|---|---|

**WHERE FOUND** Mushroom Rock

| LEV | 58 | HP | 9200 | MP | 55 |
|---|---|---|---|---|---|
| EXP | 800 | AP | 3 | | |

| GIL DROP | 200 | GIL STEAL | 300 |
|---|---|---|---|

| STR | 56 | DEF | 16 | AGL | 51 |
|---|---|---|---|---|---|
| EVA | 0 | ACC | 10 | LUCK | 0 |
| MAG | 70 | MAG DEF | 7 | | |

| | None | | None | | None |
|---|---|---|---|---|---|
| | None | | Invalid | | None |

**IMM** Dth., Pet., Sil., Poi., Cur., Ejt., Stp., Doom, Del., P.I., M.D.

**DEF EFF** Zan. (80)

| DROP RATIO | 255/255 |
|---|---|
| ITEM DROP | ChaMPion Belt x1 |
| RARE DROP | ChaMPion Belt x1 |
| STEAL RATIO | 128/255 |
| STOLEN ITEM | Sword Lore x1 |
| RARE STEAL | Sword Lore x1 |
| BRIBE ITEM | None |
| RARE BRIBE | None |

## PAIRIKA

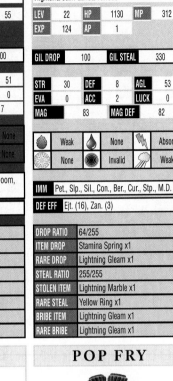

**LARVA**

| CHAPTERS | | 3 | 5 |
|---|---|---|---|

**WHERE FOUND** Besaid/Kilika Island/Djose Highland/Calm Lands/Various

| LEV | 22 | HP | 1130 | MP | 312 |
|---|---|---|---|---|---|
| EXP | 124 | AP | 1 | | |

| GIL DROP | 100 | GIL STEAL | 330 |
|---|---|---|---|

| STR | 30 | DEF | 8 | AGL | 53 |
|---|---|---|---|---|---|
| EVA | 0 | ACC | 2 | LUCK | 0 |
| MAG | 83 | MAG DEF | 82 | | |

| | Weak | | None | | Absorb |
|---|---|---|---|---|---|
| | None | | Invalid | | Weak |

**IMM** Pet., Slp., Sil., Con., Ber., Cur., Stp., M.D.

**DEF EFF** Ejt. (16), Zan. (3)

| DROP RATIO | 64/255 |
|---|---|
| ITEM DROP | Stamina Spring x1 |
| RARE DROP | Lightning Gleam x1 |
| STEAL RATIO | 255/255 |
| STOLEN ITEM | Lightning Marble x1 |
| RARE STEAL | Yellow Ring x1 |
| BRIBE ITEM | Lightning Gleam x1 |
| RARE BRIBE | Lightning Gleam x1 |

## PARAGON

**WEAPON**

| CHAPTERS | | | 5 |
|---|---|---|---|

**WHERE FOUND** Bevelle Palace Bottom Floor

| LEV | 99 | HP | 200000 [210000] | MP | 9999 |
|---|---|---|---|---|---|
| EXP | 9000 [13000] | AP | 1 [2] | | |

| GIL DROP | 3000 [8000] | GIL STEAL | 4000 [6800] |
|---|---|---|---|

| STR | 244 | DEF | 244 | AGL | 188 [244] |
|---|---|---|---|---|---|
| EVA | 0 | ACC | 13 [16] | LUCK | 0 |
| MAG | 88 | MAG DEF | 89 | | |

| | None | | None | | None |
|---|---|---|---|---|---|
| | None | | Invalid | | None |

**IMM** All

**DEF EFF** Zan. (255)

| DROP RATIO | 255/255 |
|---|---|
| ITEM DROP | Supreme Gem x1 [Dark Matter x1] |
| RARE DROP | Dark Matter x1 [Dark Matter x2] |
| STEAL RATIO | 64/255 [32/255] |
| STOLEN ITEM | Supreme Gem x1 |
| RARE STEAL | Supreme Gem x2 |
| BRIBE ITEM | Dark Matter x10 [Dark Matter x24] |
| RARE BRIBE | Dark Matter x20 [Dark Matter x30] |

## PEREGRINE

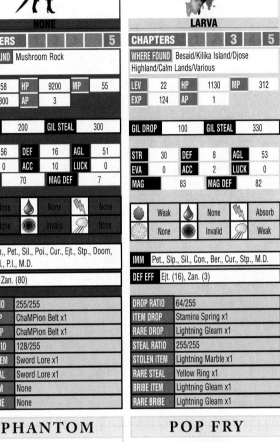

**BIRD**

| CHAPTERS | | 2 | 3 | 5 |
|---|---|---|---|---|

**WHERE FOUND** Mi'ihen Highroad/Calm Lands/Bevelle Tower Floors 21-23

| LEV | 12 [14] | HP | 735 [3040] | MP | 28 |
|---|---|---|---|---|---|
| EXP | 70 [110] | AP | 1 [2] | | |

| GIL DROP | 44 [83] | GIL STEAL | 175 [360] |
|---|---|---|---|

| STR | 39[40] | DEF | 16 | AGL | 113 [124] |
|---|---|---|---|---|---|
| EVA | 48 [63] | ACC | 16 [20] | LUCK | 0 |
| MAG | 3 | MAG DEF | 4 | | |

| | None | | None | | None |
|---|---|---|---|---|---|
| | None | | None | | None |

**IMM** [Con.], [Ber.], Cur.

**DEF EFF** Ejt. (8 [12]), Zan. (0 [3])

| DROP RATIO | 128/255 [255/255] |
|---|---|
| ITEM DROP | Hi-Potion x1 [Mega Phoenix x1] |
| RARE DROP | Hi-Potion x2 [Mega Phoenix x2] |
| STEAL RATIO | 255/255 |
| STOLEN ITEM | Hi-Potion x1 [Mega Phoenix x1] |
| RARE STEAL | Phoenix Down x3 [Mega Phoenix x2] |
| BRIBE ITEM | Phoenix Down x36 [Mega Phoenix x8] |
| RARE BRIBE | Phoenix Down x40 [Mega Potion x10] |

## PHANTOM

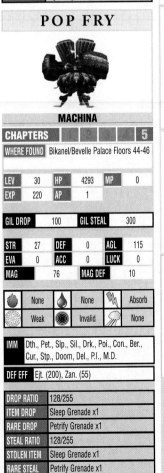

**REVENANT**

| CHAPTERS | | | 5 |
|---|---|---|---|

**WHERE FOUND** Ruin Depths/Bevelle Palace Floors 70-74

| LEV | 44 | HP | 1755 | MP | 852 |
|---|---|---|---|---|---|
| EXP | 950 | AP | 1 | | |

| GIL DROP | 140 | GIL STEAL | 700 |
|---|---|---|---|

| STR | 33 | DEF | 25 | AGL | 73 |
|---|---|---|---|---|---|
| EVA | 0 | ACC | 2 | LUCK | 0 |
| MAG | 84 | MAG DEF | 62 | | |

| | Weak | | None | | None |
|---|---|---|---|---|---|
| | None | | Absorb | | Weak |

**IMM** Dth., Pet., Slp., Sil., Drk., Poi., Con., Ber., Cur., Stp., Del., P.I., M.D.

**DEF EFF** Ejt. (30), Zan. (15)

| DROP RATIO | 255/255 |
|---|---|
| ITEM DROP | Phoenix Down x1 |
| RARE DROP | Phoenix Down x2 |
| STEAL RATIO | 128/255 |
| STOLEN ITEM | Hi-Potion x1 |
| RARE STEAL | Hi-Potion x2 |
| BRIBE ITEM | Mega Potion x5 |
| RARE BRIBE | Mega Potion x6 |

## POP FRY

**MACHINA**

| CHAPTERS | | | 5 |
|---|---|---|---|

**WHERE FOUND** Bikanel/Bevelle Palace Floors 44-46

| LEV | 30 | HP | 4293 | MP | 0 |
|---|---|---|---|---|---|
| EXP | 220 | AP | 1 | | |

| GIL DROP | 100 | GIL STEAL | 300 |
|---|---|---|---|

| STR | 27 | DEF | 0 | AGL | 115 |
|---|---|---|---|---|---|
| EVA | 0 | ACC | 0 | LUCK | 0 |
| MAG | 76 | MAG DEF | 10 | | |

| | None | | None | | Absorb |
|---|---|---|---|---|---|
| | Weak | | Invalid | | None |

**IMM** Dth., Pet., Slp., Sil., Drk., Poi., Con., Ber., Cur., Stp., Doom, Del., P.I., M.D.

**DEF EFF** Ejt. (200), Zan. (55)

| DROP RATIO | 128/255 |
|---|---|
| ITEM DROP | Sleep Grenade x1 |
| RARE DROP | Petrify Grenade x1 |
| STEAL RATIO | 128/255 |
| STOLEN ITEM | Sleep Grenade x1 |
| RARE STEAL | Petrify Grenade x1 |
| BRIBE ITEM | None |
| RARE BRIBE | None |

## PRECEPTS GUARD
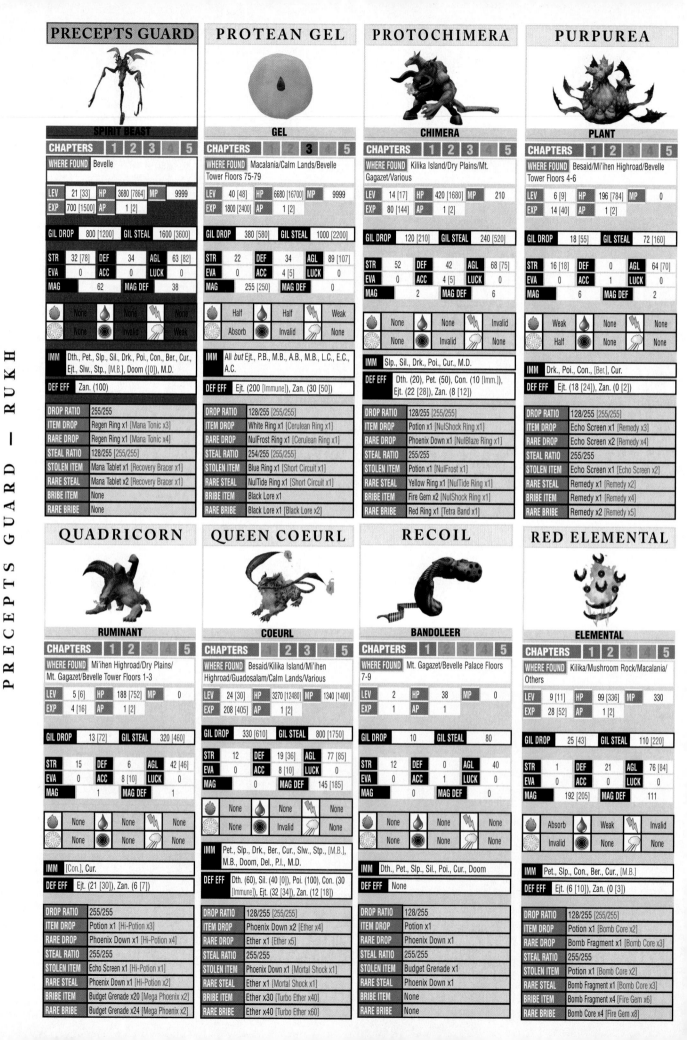

**SPIRIT BEAST**

| CHAPTERS | 1 | 2 | 3 | 4 | 5 |
|---|---|---|---|---|---|

WHERE FOUND: Bevelle

| LEV | 21 [33] | HP | 3680 [7864] | MP | 9999 |
| EXP | 700 [1500] | AP | 1 [2] | | |

| GIL DROP | 800 [1200] | GIL STEAL | 1600 [3600] |

| STR | 32 [78] | DEF | 34 | AGL | 63 [82] |
| EVA | 0 | ACC | 0 | LUCK | 0 |
| MAG | 62 | MAG DEF | 38 | | |

| | None | | None | | None |
| | None | | Invalid | | Weak |

IMM: Dth., Pet., Slp., Sil., Drk., Poi., Con., Ber., Cur., Ejt., Slw., Stp., [M.B.], Doom ([0]), M.D.

DEF EFF: Zan. (100)

| DROP RATIO | 255/255 |
| ITEM DROP | Regen Ring x1 [Mana Tonic x3] |
| RARE DROP | Regen Ring x1 [Mana Tonic x4] |
| STEAL RATIO | 128/255 [255/255] |
| STOLEN ITEM | Mana Tablet x1 [Recovery Bracer x1] |
| RARE STEAL | Mana Tablet x2 [Recovery Bracer x1] |
| BRIBE ITEM | None |
| RARE BRIBE | None |

## PROTEAN GEL

**GEL**

| CHAPTERS | 1 | 2 | 3 | 4 | 5 |
|---|---|---|---|---|---|

WHERE FOUND: Macalania/Calm Lands/Bevelle Tower Floors 75-79

| LEV | 40 [48] | HP | 6680 [16700] | MP | 9999 |
| EXP | 1800 [2400] | AP | 1 [2] | | |

| GIL DROP | 380 [580] | GIL STEAL | 1000 [2200] |

| STR | 22 | DEF | 34 | AGL | 89 [107] |
| EVA | 0 | ACC | 4 [5] | LUCK | 0 |
| MAG | 255 [250] | MAG DEF | 0 | | |

| | Half | | Half | | Weak |
| | Absorb | | Invalid | | None |

IMM: All *but* Ejt., P.B., M.B., A.B., M.B., L.C., E.C., A.C.

DEF EFF: Ejt. (200 [Immune]), Zan. (30 [50])

| DROP RATIO | 128/255 [255/255] |
| ITEM DROP | White Ring x1 [Cerulean Ring x1] |
| RARE DROP | NulFrost Ring x1 [Cerulean Ring x1] |
| STEAL RATIO | 254/255 [255/255] |
| STOLEN ITEM | Blue Ring x1 [Short Circuit x1] |
| RARE STEAL | NulTide Ring x1 [Short Circuit x1] |
| BRIBE ITEM | Black Lore x1 |
| RARE BRIBE | Black Lore x1 [Black Lore x2] |

## PROTOCHIMERA

**CHIMERA**

| CHAPTERS | 1 | 2 | 3 | 4 | 5 |
|---|---|---|---|---|---|

WHERE FOUND: Kilika Island/Dry Plains/Mt. Gagazet/Various

| LEV | 14 [17] | HP | 420 [1680] | MP | 210 |
| EXP | 80 [144] | AP | 1 [2] | | |

| GIL DROP | 120 [210] | GIL STEAL | 240 [520] |

| STR | 52 | DEF | 42 | AGL | 68 [75] |
| EVA | 0 | ACC | 4 [5] | LUCK | 0 |
| MAG | 2 | MAG DEF | 6 | | |

| | None | | None | | Invalid |
| | None | | Invalid | | None |

IMM: Slp., Sil., Drk., Poi., Cur., M.D.

DEF EFF: Dth. (20), Pet. (50), Con. (10 [Imm.]), Ejt. (22 [28]), Zan. (8 [12])

| DROP RATIO | 128/255 [255/255] |
| ITEM DROP | Potion x1 [NulShock Ring x1] |
| RARE DROP | Phoenix Down x1 [NulBlaze Ring x1] |
| STEAL RATIO | 255/255 |
| STOLEN ITEM | Potion x1 [NulFrost x1] |
| RARE STEAL | Yellow Ring x1 [NulTide Ring x1] |
| BRIBE ITEM | Fire Gem x2 [NulShock Ring x1] |
| RARE BRIBE | Red Ring x1 [Tetra Band x1] |

## PURPUREA

**PLANT**

| CHAPTERS | 1 | 2 | 3 | 4 | 5 |
|---|---|---|---|---|---|

WHERE FOUND: Besaid/Mi'ihen Highroad/Bevelle Tower Floors 4-6

| LEV | 6 [9] | HP | 196 [784] | MP | 0 |
| EXP | 14 [40] | AP | 1 [2] | | |

| GIL DROP | 18 [55] | GIL STEAL | 72 [160] |

| STR | 16 [18] | DEF | 0 | AGL | 64 [70] |
| EVA | 0 | ACC | 1 | LUCK | 0 |
| MAG | 6 | MAG DEF | 2 | | |

| | Weak | | None | | None |
| | Half | | None | | None |

IMM: Drk., Poi., Con., [Ber.], Cur.

DEF EFF: Ejt. (18 [24]), Zan. (0 [2])

| DROP RATIO | 128/255 [255/255] |
| ITEM DROP | Echo Screen x1 [Remedy x3] |
| RARE DROP | Echo Screen x2 [Remedy x4] |
| STEAL RATIO | 255/255 |
| STOLEN ITEM | Echo Screen x1 [Echo Screen x2] |
| RARE STEAL | Remedy x1 [Remedy x2] |
| BRIBE ITEM | Remedy x1 [Remedy x4] |
| RARE BRIBE | Remedy x2 [Remedy x5] |

## QUADRICORN

**RUMINANT**

| CHAPTERS | 1 | 2 | 3 | 4 | 5 |
|---|---|---|---|---|---|

WHERE FOUND: Mi'ihen Highroad/Dry Plains/Mt. Gagazet/Bevelle Tower Floors 1-3

| LEV | 5 [6] | HP | 188 [752] | MP | 0 |
| EXP | 4 [16] | AP | 1 [2] | | |

| GIL DROP | 13 [72] | GIL STEAL | 320 [460] |

| STR | 15 | DEF | 6 | AGL | 42 [46] |
| EVA | 0 | ACC | 8 [10] | LUCK | 0 |
| MAG | 1 | MAG DEF | 1 | | |

| | None | | None | | None |
| | None | | None | | None |

IMM: [Con.], Cur.

DEF EFF: Ejt. (21 [30]), Zan. (6 [7])

| DROP RATIO | 255/255 |
| ITEM DROP | Potion x1 [Hi-Potion x3] |
| RARE DROP | Phoenix Down x1 [Hi-Potion x4] |
| STEAL RATIO | 255/255 |
| STOLEN ITEM | Echo Screen x1 [Hi-Potion x1] |
| RARE STEAL | Phoenix Down x1 [Hi-Potion x2] |
| BRIBE ITEM | Budget Grenade x20 [Mega Phoenix x2] |
| RARE BRIBE | Budget Grenade x24 [Mega Phoenix x2] |

## QUEEN COEURL

**COEURL**

| CHAPTERS | 1 | 2 | 3 | 4 | 5 |
|---|---|---|---|---|---|

WHERE FOUND: Besaid/Kilika Island/Mi'ihen Highroad/Guadosalam/Calm Lands/Various

| LEV | 24 [30] | HP | 3270 [12480] | MP | 1340 [1400] |
| EXP | 208 [405] | AP | 1 [2] | | |

| GIL DROP | 330 [610] | GIL STEAL | 800 [1750] |

| STR | 12 | DEF | 19 [36] | AGL | 77 [85] |
| EVA | 0 | ACC | 8 [10] | LUCK | 0 |
| MAG | 0 | MAG DEF | 145 [185] | | |

| | None | | None | | None |
| | None | | Invalid | | None |

IMM: Pet., Slp., Drk., Ber., Cur., Slw., Stp., [M.B.], M.B., Doom, Del., P.I., M.D.

DEF EFF: Dth. (60), Sil. (40 [0]), Poi. (100), Con. (30 [Immune]), Ejt. (32 [34]), Zan. (12 [18])

| DROP RATIO | 128/255 [255/255] |
| ITEM DROP | Phoenix Down x2 [Ether x4] |
| RARE DROP | Ether x1 [Ether x5] |
| STEAL RATIO | 255/255 |
| STOLEN ITEM | Phoenix Down x1 [Mortal Shock x1] |
| RARE STEAL | Ether x1 [Mortal Shock x1] |
| BRIBE ITEM | Ether x30 [Turbo Ether x40] |
| RARE BRIBE | Ether x40 [Turbo Ether x60] |

## RECOIL

**BANDOLEER**

| CHAPTERS | 1 | 2 | 3 | 4 | 5 |
|---|---|---|---|---|---|

WHERE FOUND: Mt. Gagazet/Bevelle Palace Floors 7-9

| LEV | 2 | HP | 38 | MP | 0 |
| EXP | 1 | AP | 1 | | |

| GIL DROP | 10 | GIL STEAL | 80 |

| STR | 12 | DEF | 0 | AGL | 40 |
| EVA | 0 | ACC | 1 | LUCK | 0 |
| MAG | 0 | MAG DEF | 0 | | |

| | None | | None | | None |
| | None | | None | | None |

IMM: Dth., Pet., Slp., Sil., Poi., Cur., Doom

DEF EFF: None

| DROP RATIO | 128/255 |
| ITEM DROP | Potion x1 |
| RARE DROP | Phoenix Down x1 |
| STEAL RATIO | 255/255 |
| STOLEN ITEM | Budget Grenade x1 |
| RARE STEAL | Phoenix Down x1 |
| BRIBE ITEM | None |
| RARE BRIBE | None |

## RED ELEMENTAL

**ELEMENTAL**

| CHAPTERS | 1 | 2 | 3 | 4 | 5 |
|---|---|---|---|---|---|

WHERE FOUND: Kilika/Mushroom Rock/Macalania/Others

| LEV | 9 [11] | HP | 99 [336] | MP | 330 |
| EXP | 28 [52] | AP | 1 [2] | | |

| GIL DROP | 25 [43] | GIL STEAL | 110 [220] |

| STR | 1 | DEF | 21 | AGL | 76 [84] |
| EVA | 0 | ACC | 0 | LUCK | 0 |
| MAG | 192 [205] | MAG DEF | 111 | | |

| | Absorb | | Weak | | Invalid |
| | Invalid | | None | | None |

IMM: Pet., Slp., Con., Ber., Cur., [M.B.]

DEF EFF: Ejt. (6 [10]), Zan. (0 [3])

| DROP RATIO | 128/255 [255/255] |
| ITEM DROP | Potion x1 [Bomb Core x2] |
| RARE DROP | Bomb Fragment x1 [Bomb Core x3] |
| STEAL RATIO | 255/255 |
| STOLEN ITEM | Potion x1 [Bomb Core x2] |
| RARE STEAL | Bomb Fragment x1 [Bomb Core x3] |
| BRIBE ITEM | Bomb Fragment x4 [Fire Gem x6] |
| RARE BRIBE | Bomb Core x4 [Fire Gem x8] |

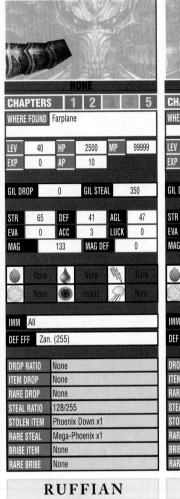
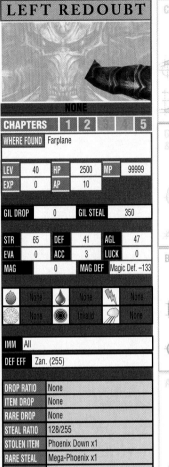

## RHYOS — CHIMERA

CHAPTERS: 3 5

WHERE FOUND: Thunder Plains/Macalania/Calm Lands/Mt. Gagazet/Various

| | | | |
|---|---|---|---|
| LEV | 31 [34] | HP | 4360 [14440] | MP | 485 |
| EXP | 650 [1000] | AP | 1 [2] | | |

GIL DROP 310 [550] · GIL STEAL 558 [1305]

| STR | 37 [38] | DEF | 45 [46] | AGL | 93 [108] |
|---|---|---|---|---|---|
| EVA | 0 | ACC | 4 [5] | LUCK | 0 |
| MAG | 46 [48] | | MAG DEF | 50 | |

Fire: Half · Water: None · Lightning: Invalid · Ice: Half · Gravity: Invalid · Holy: None

IMM: Dth., Slp., Sil., Drk., Poi., Cur., Stp., Doom, M.D.

DEF EFF: Pet. (60), Con. (60 [Imm.]), Ejt. (24 [30]), Zan. (8 [12])

| DROP RATIO | 128/255 [255/255] |
|---|---|
| ITEM DROP | Lightning Gem x1, [NulTide Ring x1] |
| RARE DROP | Watery Gleam x1 [NulTide Ring x1] |
| STEAL RATIO | 128/255 [255/255] |
| STOLEN ITEM | Lightning Gem x1 [Lightning Gleam x1] |
| RARE STEAL | Lightning Gleam x1 |
| BRIBE ITEM | Electrocutioner x1 [Tetra Gloves x2] |
| RARE BRIBE | Electrocutioner x1 [Tetra Gloves x3] |

## RIGHT BULWARK — NONE

CHAPTERS: 5

WHERE FOUND: Farplane

| | | | |
|---|---|---|---|
| LEV | 39 | HP | 3000 | MP | 9999 |
| EXP | 200 | AP | 10 | | |

GIL DROP 150 · GIL STEAL 300

| STR | 72 | DEF | 48 | AGL | 46 |
|---|---|---|---|---|---|
| EVA | 0 | ACC | 2 | LUCK | 0 |
| MAG | 58 | | MAG DEF | 58 | |

Fire: None · Water: None · Lightning: None · Ice: None · Gravity: Invalid · Holy: None

IMM: All

DEF EFF: Zan. (255)

| DROP RATIO | 128/255 |
|---|---|
| ITEM DROP | Mega Potion x1 |
| RARE DROP | X-Potion x1 |
| STEAL RATIO | 128/255 |
| STOLEN ITEM | Phoenix Down x1 (L-Bomb) |
| RARE STEAL | L-Bomb x1 |
| BRIBE ITEM | None |
| RARE BRIBE | None |

## RIGHT REDOUBT — NONE

CHAPTERS: 5

WHERE FOUND: Farplane

| | | | |
|---|---|---|---|
| LEV | 40 | HP | 2500 | MP | 99999 |
| EXP | 0 | AP | 10 | | |

GIL DROP 0 · GIL STEAL 350

| STR | 65 | DEF | 41 | AGL | 47 |
|---|---|---|---|---|---|
| EVA | 0 | ACC | 3 | LUCK | 0 |
| MAG | 133 | | MAG DEF | 0 | |

Fire: None · Water: None · Lightning: None · Ice: None · Gravity: Invalid · Holy: None

IMM: All

DEF EFF: Zan. (255)

| DROP RATIO | None |
|---|---|
| ITEM DROP | None |
| RARE DROP | None |
| STEAL RATIO | 128/255 |
| STOLEN ITEM | Phoenix Down x1 |
| RARE STEAL | Mega-Phoenix x1 |
| BRIBE ITEM | None |
| RARE BRIBE | None |

## LEFT REDOUBT — NONE

CHAPTERS: 5

WHERE FOUND: Farplane

| | | | |
|---|---|---|---|
| LEV | 40 | HP | 2500 | MP | 99999 |
| EXP | 0 | AP | 10 | | |

GIL DROP 0 · GIL STEAL 350

| STR | 65 | DEF | 41 | AGL | 47 |
|---|---|---|---|---|---|
| EVA | 0 | ACC | 3 | LUCK | 0 |
| MAG | | | MAG DEF | Magic Def. –133 | |

Fire: None · Water: None · Lightning: None · Ice: None · Gravity: Invalid · Holy: None

IMM: All

DEF EFF: Zan. (255)

| DROP RATIO | None |
|---|---|
| ITEM DROP | None |
| RARE DROP | None |
| STEAL RATIO | 128/255 |
| STOLEN ITEM | Phoenix Down x1 |
| RARE STEAL | Mega-Phoenix x1 |
| BRIBE ITEM | None |
| RARE BRIBE | None |

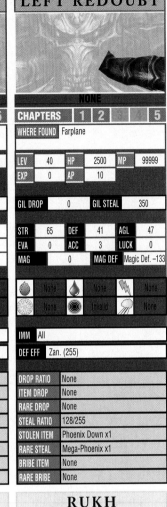

## RIKKU — NONE

CHAPTERS: 1 2 3 4 5

WHERE FOUND: Mushroom Rock

| | | | |
|---|---|---|---|
| LEV | 53 | HP | 7800 | MP | 92 |
| EXP | 800 | AP | 3 | | |

GIL DROP 200 · GIL STEAL 300

| STR | 42 | DEF | 39 | AGL | 82 |
|---|---|---|---|---|---|
| EVA | 18 | ACC | 12 | LUCK | 0 |
| MAG | 31 | | MAG DEF | 82 | |

Fire: None · Water: None · Lightning: None · Ice: None · Gravity: Invalid · Holy: None

IMM: Dth., Pet., Sil., Poi., Cur., Ejt., Stp., Doom, Del., P.I., M.D.

DEF EFF: Zan. (80)

| DROP RATIO | 255/255 |
|---|---|
| ITEM DROP | Black Lore x1 |
| RARE DROP | Black Lore x1 |
| STEAL RATIO | 128/255 |
| STOLEN ITEM | Bushido Lore x1 |
| RARE STEAL | Bushido Lore x1 |
| BRIBE ITEM | None |
| RARE BRIBE | None |

## RONSO YOUTH — NONE

CHAPTERS: 3

WHERE FOUND: Mt. Gagazet

| | | | |
|---|---|---|---|
| LEV | 24 | HP | 4060 | MP | 170 |
| EXP | 220 | AP | 2 | | |

GIL DROP 20 · GIL STEAL 80

| STR | 51 | DEF | 48 | AGL | 78 |
|---|---|---|---|---|---|
| EVA | 0 | ACC | 2 | LUCK | 0 |
| MAG | 23 | | MAG DEF | 3 | |

Fire: None · Water: None · Lightning: None · Ice: None · Gravity: Invalid · Holy: None

IMM: Dth., Pet., Slp., Sil., Cur., Doom, M.D.

DEF EFF: Drk. (20)

| DROP RATIO | 155/255 |
|---|---|
| ITEM DROP | Remedy x1 |
| RARE DROP | Remedy x2 |
| STEAL RATIO | 64/255 |
| STOLEN ITEM | Mythril Bangle x1 |
| RARE STEAL | Mythril Bangle x1 |
| BRIBE ITEM | None |
| RARE BRIBE | None |

## RUFFIAN — NONE

CHAPTERS: 3 4 5

WHERE FOUND: Dry Plains

| | | | |
|---|---|---|---|
| LEV | 26 | HP | 1480 | MP | 45 |
| EXP | 90 | AP | 1 | | |

GIL DROP 250 · GIL STEAL 480

| STR | 33 | DEF | 37 | AGL | 68 |
|---|---|---|---|---|---|
| EVA | 0 | ACC | 3 | LUCK | 0 |
| MAG | 50 | | MAG DEF | 3 | |

Fire: None · Water: None · Lightning: None · Ice: None · Gravity: None · Holy: None

IMM: Cur.

DEF EFF: None

| DROP RATIO | 18/255 |
|---|---|
| ITEM DROP | Potion x2 |
| RARE DROP | Ether x1 |
| STEAL RATIO | 255/255 |
| STOLEN ITEM | Grenade x1 |
| RARE STEAL | S-Bomb x1 |
| BRIBE ITEM | Mega Phoenix x3 |
| RARE BRIBE | Mega Phoenix x3 |

## RUKH — ROC

CHAPTERS: 3 4 5

WHERE FOUND: Djose Highlands/Mt. Gagazet/Bevelle Tower Floors 50-59

| | | | |
|---|---|---|---|
| LEV | 36 [43] | HP | 12850 [16493] | MP | 112 |
| EXP | 1220 [2130] | AP | 1 [2] | | |

GIL DROP 530 [840] · GIL STEAL 1000 [2000]

| STR | 98 | DEF | 28 | AGL | 66 [86] |
|---|---|---|---|---|---|
| EVA | 23 [38] | ACC | 3 [4] | LUCK | 0 |
| MAG | 44 | | MAG DEF | 255 | |

Fire: None · Water: None · Lightning: None · Ice: None · Gravity: Invalid · Holy: None

IMM: All but Ejt.

DEF EFF: Ejt. (42 [60]), Zan. (18 [28])

| DROP RATIO | 64/255 [255/255] |
|---|---|
| ITEM DROP | Phoenix Down x2 [Mega Phoenix x2] |
| RARE DROP | Angel Earrings x1 [Mega Phoenix x2] |
| STEAL RATIO | 128/255 [255/255] |
| STOLEN ITEM | Phoenix Down x2 [Angel Earrings x1] |
| RARE STEAL | Ether [Angel Earrings x1] |
| BRIBE ITEM | Mega Phoenix x30 |
| RARE BRIBE | Mega Phoenix x35 [Mega Phoenix x40] |

Characters — 1

Garment Grids & Dresspheres — 2

Battle System — 3

Accessories — 4

Items and Item Shops — 5

Walkthrough — 6

Mini Games — 7

Fiends and Enemies — 8

339

SAHAGIN – TAROMAITI

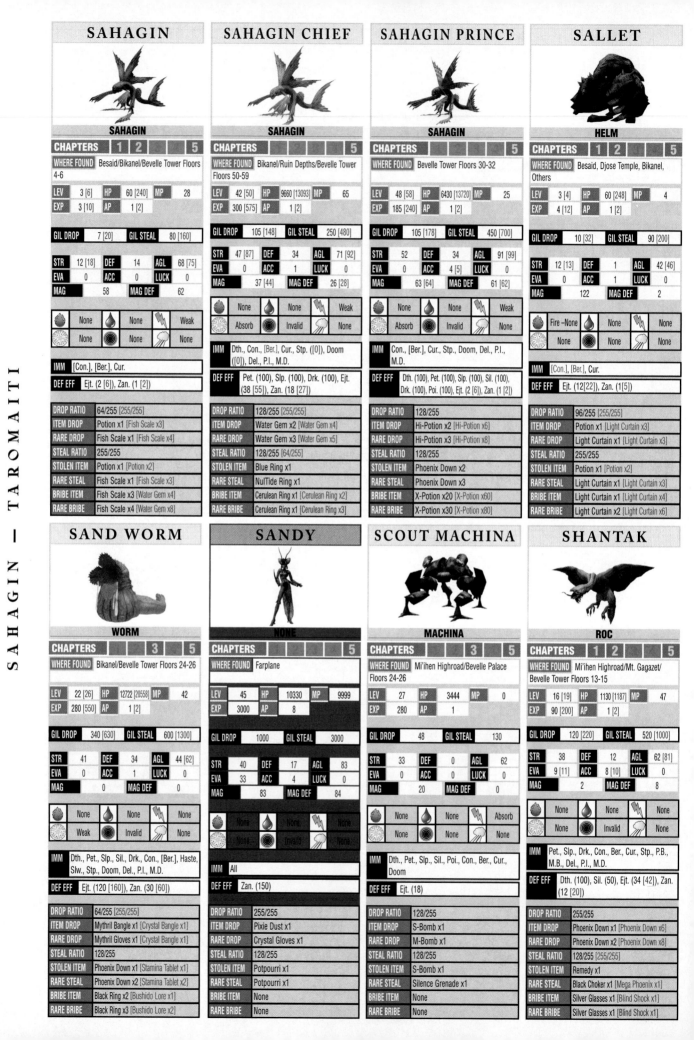

## SAHAGIN

SAHAGIN

| CHAPTERS | 1 | 2 | | | 5 |
|---|---|---|---|---|---|

WHERE FOUND: Besaid/Bikanel/Bevelle Tower Floors 4-6

| LEV | 3 [6] | HP | 60 [240] | MP | 28 |
|---|---|---|---|---|---|
| EXP | 3 [10] | AP | 1 [2] | | |

| GIL DROP | 7 [20] | GIL STEAL | 80 [160] |
|---|---|---|---|

| STR | 12 [18] | DEF | 14 | AGL | 68 [75] |
|---|---|---|---|---|---|
| EVA | 0 | ACC | 0 | LUCK | 0 |
| MAG | 58 | MAG DEF | 62 | | |

| | None | | None | | Weak |
|---|---|---|---|---|---|
| | None | | None | | None |

IMM: [Con.], [Ber.], Cur.

DEF EFF: Ejt. (2 [6]), Zan. (1 [2])

| DROP RATIO | 64/255 [255/255] |
|---|---|
| ITEM DROP | Potion x1 [Fish Scale x3] |
| RARE DROP | Fish Scale x1 [Fish Scale x4] |
| STEAL RATIO | 255/255 |
| STOLEN ITEM | Potion x1 [Potion x2] |
| RARE STEAL | Fish Scale x1 [Fish Scale x3] |
| BRIBE ITEM | Fish Scale x3 [Water Gem x4] |
| RARE BRIBE | Fish Scale x4 [Water Gem x8] |

## SAHAGIN CHIEF

SAHAGIN

| CHAPTERS | | | | | 5 |
|---|---|---|---|---|---|

WHERE FOUND: Bikanel/Ruin Depths/Bevelle Tower Floors 50-59

| LEV | 42 [50] | HP | 9660 [13093] | MP | 65 |
|---|---|---|---|---|---|
| EXP | 300 [575] | AP | 1 [2] | | |

| GIL DROP | 105 [148] | GIL STEAL | 250 [480] |
|---|---|---|---|

| STR | 47 [87] | DEF | 34 | AGL | 71 [92] |
|---|---|---|---|---|---|
| EVA | 0 | ACC | 1 | LUCK | 0 |
| MAG | 37 [44] | MAG DEF | 26 [28] | | |

| | None | | None | | Weak |
|---|---|---|---|---|---|
| | Absorb | | Invalid | | None |

IMM: Dth., Con., [Ber.], Cur., Stp. ([0]), Doom ([0]), Del., P.I., M.D.

DEF EFF: Pet. (100), Slp. (100), Drk. (100), Ejt. (38 [55]), Zan. (18 [27])

| DROP RATIO | 128/255 [255/255] |
|---|---|
| ITEM DROP | Water Gem x2 [Water Gem x4] |
| RARE DROP | Water Gem x3 [Water Gem x5] |
| STEAL RATIO | 128/255 [64/255] |
| STOLEN ITEM | Blue Ring x1 |
| RARE STEAL | NulTide Ring x1 |
| BRIBE ITEM | Cerulean Ring x1 [Cerulean Ring x2] |
| RARE BRIBE | Cerulean Ring x1 [Cerulean Ring x3] |

## SAHAGIN PRINCE

SAHAGIN

| CHAPTERS | | | | | 5 |
|---|---|---|---|---|---|

WHERE FOUND: Bevelle Tower Floors 30-32

| LEV | 48 [58] | HP | 6430 [13720] | MP | 25 |
|---|---|---|---|---|---|
| EXP | 185 [240] | AP | 1 [2] | | |

| GIL DROP | 105 [178] | GIL STEAL | 450 [700] |
|---|---|---|---|

| STR | 52 | DEF | 34 | AGL | 91 [99] |
|---|---|---|---|---|---|
| EVA | 0 | ACC | 4 [5] | LUCK | 0 |
| MAG | 63 [64] | MAG DEF | 61 [62] | | |

| | None | | None | | Weak |
|---|---|---|---|---|---|
| | Absorb | | Invalid | | None |

IMM: Con., [Ber.], Cur., Stp., Doom, Del., M.D.

DEF EFF: Dth. (100), Pet. (100), Slp. (100), Sil. (100), Drk. (100), Poi. (100), Ejt. (2 [6]), Zan. (1 [2])

| DROP RATIO | 128/255 |
|---|---|
| ITEM DROP | Hi-Potion x2 [Hi-Potion x6] |
| RARE DROP | Hi-Potion x3 [Hi-Potion x8] |
| STEAL RATIO | 128/255 |
| STOLEN ITEM | Phoenix Down x2 |
| RARE STEAL | Phoenix Down x3 |
| BRIBE ITEM | X-Potion x20 [X-Potion x60] |
| RARE BRIBE | X-Potion x30 [X-Potion x80] |

## SALLET

HELM

| CHAPTERS | 1 | 2 | | | 5 |
|---|---|---|---|---|---|

WHERE FOUND: Besaid, Djose Temple, Bikanel, Others

| LEV | 3 [4] | HP | 60 [248] | MP | 4 |
|---|---|---|---|---|---|
| EXP | 4 [12] | AP | 1 [2] | | |

| GIL DROP | 10 [32] | GIL STEAL | 90 [200] |
|---|---|---|---|

| STR | 12 [13] | DEF | 1 | AGL | 42 [46] |
|---|---|---|---|---|---|
| EVA | 0 | ACC | 1 | LUCK | 0 |
| MAG | 122 | MAG DEF | 2 | | |

| | Fire –None | | None | | None |
|---|---|---|---|---|---|
| | None | | None | | None |

IMM: [Con.], [Ber.], Cur.

DEF EFF: Ejt. (12[22]), Zan. (1[5])

| DROP RATIO | 96/255 [255/255] |
|---|---|
| ITEM DROP | Potion x1 [Light Curtain x3] |
| RARE DROP | Light Curtain x1 [Light Curtain x3] |
| STEAL RATIO | 255/255 |
| STOLEN ITEM | Potion x1 [Potion x2] |
| RARE STEAL | Light Curtain x1 [Light Curtain x3] |
| BRIBE ITEM | Light Curtain x1 [Light Curtain x4] |
| RARE BRIBE | Light Curtain x2 [Light Curtain x6] |

## SAND WORM

WORM

| CHAPTERS | | | 3 | | 5 |
|---|---|---|---|---|---|

WHERE FOUND: Bikanel/Bevelle Tower Floors 24-26

| LEV | 22 [26] | HP | 12722 [20558] | MP | 42 |
|---|---|---|---|---|---|
| EXP | 280 [550] | AP | 1 [2] | | |

| GIL DROP | 340 [630] | GIL STEAL | 600 [1300] |
|---|---|---|---|

| STR | 41 | DEF | 34 | AGL | 44 [62] |
|---|---|---|---|---|---|
| EVA | 0 | ACC | 1 | LUCK | 0 |
| MAG | 0 | MAG DEF | 0 | | |

| | None | | None | | None |
|---|---|---|---|---|---|
| | Weak | | Invalid | | None |

IMM: Dth., Pet., Slp., Sil., Drk., Con., [Ber.], Haste, Slw., Stp., Doom, Del., P.I., M.D.

DEF EFF: Ejt. (120 [160]), Zan. (30 [60])

| DROP RATIO | 64/255 [255/255] |
|---|---|
| ITEM DROP | Mythril Bangle x1 [Crystal Bangle x1] |
| RARE DROP | Mythril Gloves x1 [Crystal Bangle x1] |
| STEAL RATIO | 128/255 |
| STOLEN ITEM | Phoenix Down x1 [Stamina Tablet x1] |
| RARE STEAL | Phoenix Down x2 [Stamina Tablet x2] |
| BRIBE ITEM | Black Ring x2 [Bushido Lore x1] |
| RARE BRIBE | Black Ring x3 [Bushido Lore x2] |

## SANDY

NONE

| CHAPTERS | | | | | 5 |
|---|---|---|---|---|---|

WHERE FOUND: Farplane

| LEV | 45 | HP | 10330 | MP | 9999 |
|---|---|---|---|---|---|
| EXP | 3000 | AP | 8 | | |

| GIL DROP | 1000 | GIL STEAL | 3000 |
|---|---|---|---|

| STR | 40 | DEF | 17 | AGL | 83 |
|---|---|---|---|---|---|
| EVA | 33 | ACC | 4 | LUCK | 0 |
| MAG | 83 | MAG DEF | 84 | | |

| | None | | None | | None |
|---|---|---|---|---|---|
| | None | | Invalid | | None |

IMM: All

DEF EFF: Zan. (150)

| DROP RATIO | 255/255 |
|---|---|
| ITEM DROP | Pixie Dust x1 |
| RARE DROP | Crystal Gloves x1 |
| STEAL RATIO | 128/255 |
| STOLEN ITEM | Potpourri x1 |
| RARE STEAL | Potpourri x1 |
| BRIBE ITEM | None |
| RARE BRIBE | None |

## SCOUT MACHINA

MACHINA

| CHAPTERS | | | 3 | | 5 |
|---|---|---|---|---|---|

WHERE FOUND: Mi'ihen Highroad/Bevelle Palace Floors 24-26

| LEV | 27 | HP | 3444 | MP | 0 |
|---|---|---|---|---|---|
| EXP | 280 | AP | 1 | | |

| GIL DROP | 48 | GIL STEAL | 130 |
|---|---|---|---|

| STR | 33 | DEF | 0 | AGL | 62 |
|---|---|---|---|---|---|
| EVA | 0 | ACC | 0 | LUCK | 0 |
| MAG | 20 | MAG DEF | 0 | | |

| | None | | None | | Absorb |
|---|---|---|---|---|---|
| | None | | None | | None |

IMM: Dth., Pet., Slp., Sil., Poi., Con., Ber., Cur., Doom

DEF EFF: Ejt. (18)

| DROP RATIO | 128/255 |
|---|---|
| ITEM DROP | S-Bomb x1 |
| RARE DROP | M-Bomb x1 |
| STEAL RATIO | 128/255 |
| STOLEN ITEM | S-Bomb x1 |
| RARE STEAL | Silence Grenade x1 |
| BRIBE ITEM | None |
| RARE BRIBE | None |

## SHANTAK

ROC

| CHAPTERS | 1 | 2 | | | 5 |
|---|---|---|---|---|---|

WHERE FOUND: Mi'ihen Highroad/Mt. Gagazet/Bevelle Tower Floors 13-15

| LEV | 16 [19] | HP | 1130 [1187] | MP | 47 |
|---|---|---|---|---|---|
| EXP | 90 [200] | AP | 1 [2] | | |

| GIL DROP | 120 [220] | GIL STEAL | 520 [1000] |
|---|---|---|---|

| STR | 38 | DEF | 12 | AGL | 62 [81] |
|---|---|---|---|---|---|
| EVA | 9 [11] | ACC | 8 [10] | LUCK | 0 |
| MAG | 2 | MAG DEF | 8 | | |

| | None | | None | | None |
|---|---|---|---|---|---|
| | None | | Invalid | | None |

IMM: Pet., Slp., Drk., Con., Ber., Cur., Stp., P.B., M.B., Del., P.I., M.D.

DEF EFF: Dth. (100), Sil. (50), Ejt. (34 [42]), Zan. (12 [20])

| DROP RATIO | 255/255 |
|---|---|
| ITEM DROP | Phoenix Down x1 [Phoenix Down x6] |
| RARE DROP | Phoenix Down x2 [Phoenix Down x8] |
| STEAL RATIO | 128/255 [255/255] |
| STOLEN ITEM | Remedy x1 |
| RARE STEAL | Black Choker x1 [Mega Phoenix x1] |
| BRIBE ITEM | Silver Glasses x1 [Blind Shock x1] |
| RARE BRIBE | Silver Glasses x1 [Blind Shock x1] |

Characters

Garment Grids & Dresspheres

Battle System

Accessories

Items and Item Shops

Walkthrough

Mini Games

Fiends and Enemies

## SHE GOON

**NONE**

| CHAPTERS | 1 | | | | |
|---|---|---|---|---|---|

WHERE FOUND: Luca/Mt. Gagazet

| LEV | 1 | HP | 7 | MP | 38 |
|---|---|---|---|---|---|
| EXP | 1 | AP | 1 | | |

| GIL DROP | 30 | GIL STEAL | 80 |
|---|---|---|---|

| STR | 4 | DEF | 3 | AGL | 58 |
|---|---|---|---|---|---|
| EVA | 0 | ACC | 4 | LUCK | 0 |
| MAG | | 3 | MAG DEF | 6 | |

| | | | | | |
|---|---|---|---|---|---|
| 🔥 | None | 💧 | None | ⚡ | None |
| ◔ | None | ◎ | None | 🌀 | None |

IMM: Cur.

DEF EFF: None

| DROP RATIO | 128/255 |
|---|---|
| ITEM DROP | Potion x1 |
| RARE DROP | Phoenix Down x1 |
| STEAL RATIO | 255/255 |
| STOLEN ITEM | Budget Grenade x1 |
| RARE STEAL | Phoenix Down x1 |
| BRIBE ITEM | Budget Grenade x1 |
| RARE BRIBE | Phoenix Down x1 |

## SHELL SHOCKER

**HERMIT**

| CHAPTERS | 1 | 2 | 3 | 4 | 5 |
|---|---|---|---|---|---|

WHERE FOUND: Dry Plains, Bevelle Tower Floors 27-29

| LEV | 24 [31] | HP | 4700 [4935] | MP | 82 |
|---|---|---|---|---|---|
| EXP | 860 [1380] | AP | 1 [2] | | |

| GIL DROP | 780 [1500] | GIL STEAL | 1300 [2500] |
|---|---|---|---|

| STR | 71 [78] | DEF | 68 | AGL | 72 [94] |
|---|---|---|---|---|---|
| EVA | 0 | ACC | 3 [4] | LUCK | 0 |
| MAG | | 72 | MAG DEF | 46 | |

| | | | | | |
|---|---|---|---|---|---|
| 🔥 | None | 💧 | None | ⚡ | None |
| ◔ | None | ◎ | Invalid | 🌀 | None |

IMM: Dth., Pet., Slp., Sil., Drk., Poi., Con., Ber., Cur., Slw., Stp., A.B., M.B., Doom, M.D.

DEF EFF: Ejt. (240 [Immune]), Zan. (80 [100])

| DROP RATIO | 32/255 [255/255] |
|---|---|
| ITEM DROP | Black Ring x1 [Tetra Band x1] |
| RARE DROP | Titanium Bangle x1 [Tetra Band x1] |
| STEAL RATIO | 32/255 [255/255] |
| STOLEN ITEM | Iron Bangle x1 [Mythril Bangle x1] |
| RARE STEAL | Mythril Gloves x1 [Mythril Bangle x1] |
| BRIBE ITEM | Black Ring x1 [Tetra Guard x1] |
| RARE BRIBE | Black Ring x2 [Tetra Guard x1] |

## SHIVA

**NONE**

| CHAPTERS | | | | | 5 |
|---|---|---|---|---|---|

WHERE FOUND: Farplane

| LEV | 41 | HP | 14800 | MP | 9999 |
|---|---|---|---|---|---|
| EXP | 8000 | AP | 15 | | |

| GIL DROP | 2000 | GIL STEAL | 5000 |
|---|---|---|---|

| STR | 69 | DEF | 58 | AGL | 124 |
|---|---|---|---|---|---|
| EVA | 58 | ACC | 6 | LUCK | 0 |
| MAG | | 74 | MAG DEF | 183 | |

| | | | | | |
|---|---|---|---|---|---|
| 🔥 | Weak | 💧 | Absorb | ⚡ | None |
| ◔ | None | ◎ | Invalid | 🌀 | None |

IMM: Dth., Pet., Slp., Sil., Drk., Poi., Con., Ber., Cur., Ejt., Stp., Doom, Del., P.I., M.D.

DEF EFF: Zan. (80)

| DROP RATIO | 255/255 |
|---|---|
| ITEM DROP | Crystal Gloves x1 |
| RARE DROP | Regal Crown x1 |
| STEAL RATIO | 128/255 |
| STOLEN ITEM | Snow Ring x1 |
| RARE STEAL | Snow Ring x1 |
| BRIBE ITEM | None |
| RARE BRIBE | None |

## SKINK

**REPTILE**

| CHAPTERS | | 2 | 3 | | 5 |
|---|---|---|---|---|---|

WHERE FOUND: Djose Temple/Bevelle/Calm Lands/Bevelle Tower Floors 21-23

| LEV | 25 [33] | HP | 882 [2328] | MP | 44 [46] |
|---|---|---|---|---|---|
| EXP | 108 [188] | AP | 1 [2] | | |

| GIL DROP | 78 [133] | GIL STEAL | 330 [680] |
|---|---|---|---|

| STR | 26 [31] | DEF | 13 | AGL | 73 [78] |
|---|---|---|---|---|---|
| EVA | 11 [14] | ACC | 8 [10] | LUCK | 0 |
| MAG | | 28 [34] | MAG DEF | 4 | |

| | | | | | |
|---|---|---|---|---|---|
| 🔥 | None | 💧 | Weak | ⚡ | None |
| ◔ | None | ◎ | None | 🌀 | None |

IMM: Poi., [Con.], [Ber.], Cur.

DEF EFF: Dth. (30), Pet. (50), Ejt. (13 [29]), Zan. (1 [7])

| DROP RATIO | 64/255 [255/255] |
|---|---|
| ITEM DROP | Hi-Potion x1 [Dispel Tonic x3] |
| RARE DROP | Pretty Orb x1 [Dispel Tonic x4] |
| STEAL RATIO | 255/255 |
| STOLEN ITEM | Hi-Potion x1 [Dispel Tonic x4] |
| RARE STEAL | Dispel Tonic x1 [Dispel Tonic x6] |
| BRIBE ITEM | Dispel Tonic x20 [Chocobo Wing x12] |
| RARE BRIBE | Dispel Tonic x24 [Chocobo Wing x14] |

## SPINE DRAKE

**DRAKE**

| CHAPTERS | | | 3 | 4 | 5 |
|---|---|---|---|---|---|

WHERE FOUND: Besaid/Mushroom Rock/Thunder Plains/Mt. Gagazet/Various

| LEV | 26 [32] | HP | 2582 [8826] | MP | 82 [103] |
|---|---|---|---|---|---|
| EXP | 226 [378] | AP | 1 [2] | | |

| GIL DROP | 127 [208] | GIL STEAL | 333 [650] |
|---|---|---|---|

| STR | 46 [47] | DEF | 38 [40] | AGL | 64 [74] |
|---|---|---|---|---|---|
| EVA | 0 | ACC | 4 [5] | LUCK | 0 |
| MAG | | 92 [104] | MAG DEF | 4 [5] | |

| | | | | | |
|---|---|---|---|---|---|
| 🔥 | None | 💧 | Invalid | ⚡ | None |
| ◔ | None | ◎ | None | 🌀 | None |

IMM: Slp., Drk., Poi., [Con.], [Ber.], Cur., Slw., [P.B.]

DEF EFF: Dth. (40), Pet. (30), Ejt. (18 [24]), Zan. (5 [6])

| DROP RATIO | 64/255 [255/255] |
|---|---|
| ITEM DROP | Arctic Wind x1 [Ice Gem x3] |
| RARE DROP | NulFrost Ring x1 [Ice Gem x4] |
| STEAL RATIO | 255/255 |
| STOLEN ITEM | Arctic Wind x1 [NulFrost Ring x1] |
| RARE STEAL | Ice Gem x1 [NulFrost Ring x1] |
| BRIBE ITEM | NulFrost Ring x1 [Snow Ring x1] |
| RARE BRIBE | NulFrost Ring x1 [Snow Ring x2] |

## STALWART

**ARMOR**

| CHAPTERS | 1 | 2 | | | 5 |
|---|---|---|---|---|---|

WHERE FOUND: Kilika Island/Thunder Plains/Bevelle Tower Floors 4-6

| LEV | 30 [36] | HP | 1240 [1312] | MP | 175 |
|---|---|---|---|---|---|
| EXP | 122 [202] | AP | 1 [2] | | |

| GIL DROP | 100 [210] | GIL STEAL | 630 [980] |
|---|---|---|---|

| STR | 75 | DEF | 42 | AGL | 36 [46] |
|---|---|---|---|---|---|
| EVA | 0 | ACC | 8 | LUCK | 0 |
| MAG | | 142 | MAG DEF | 13 | |

| | | | | | |
|---|---|---|---|---|---|
| 🔥 | None | 💧 | None | ⚡ | None |
| ◔ | None | ◎ | Invalid | 🌀 | None |

IMM: All but Pet., Con., Ejt., P.B., L.C., E.C., A.C.

DEF EFF: Pet. (100), Con. (50 [Immune]), Ejt. (32 [38]), Zan. (15)

| DROP RATIO | 186/255 [255/255] |
|---|---|
| ITEM DROP | Phoenix Down x2 [Black Ring x1] |
| RARE DROP | Shadow Gem x1 [Black Ring x1] |
| STEAL RATIO | 255/255 |
| STOLEN ITEM | Phoenix Down x1 [Diamond Gloves x1] |
| RARE STEAL | Gauntlets x1 [Diamond Gloves x1] |
| BRIBE ITEM | Shadow Gem x30 |
| RARE BRIBE | Shadow Gem x40 [Black Ring x1] |

## TAKOUBA

**BLADE**

| CHAPTERS | 1 | 2 | | | 5 |
|---|---|---|---|---|---|

WHERE FOUND: Dry Plains, Bikanel, Mt. Gagazet, Bevelle Tower Floors 7-9

| LEV | 16 [19] | HP | 984 [3936] | MP | 0 |
|---|---|---|---|---|---|
| EXP | 75 [122] | AP | 1 [2] | | |

| GIL DROP | 110 [185] | GIL STEAL | 320 [530] |
|---|---|---|---|

| STR | 33 | DEF | 0 | AGL | 112 [123] |
|---|---|---|---|---|---|
| EVA | 0 | ACC | 3 [4] | LUCK | 0 |
| MAG | | 5 | MAG DEF | 4 | |

| | | | | | |
|---|---|---|---|---|---|
| 🔥 | Weak | 💧 | None | ⚡ | None |
| ◔ | None | ◎ | Invalid | 🌀 | None |

IMM: Slp., Sil., [Con.], [Ber.], Cur., A.B., M.B., M.D.

DEF EFF: Dth. (30), Pet. (50), Drk. (30 [0]), Ejt. (20 [28]), Zan. (4 [7])

| DROP RATIO | 178/255 [255/255] |
|---|---|
| ITEM DROP | Phoenix Down x1 [Candle of Life x3] |
| RARE DROP | Phoenix Down x1 [Candle of Life x4] |
| STEAL RATIO | 255/255 |
| STOLEN ITEM | Phoenix Down x1 [Candle of Life x4] |
| RARE STEAL | Candle of Life x2 [Candle of Life x5] |
| BRIBE ITEM | Candle of Life x30 [Safety Bit x1] |
| RARE BRIBE | Candle of Life x40 [Safety Bit x2] |

## TAROMAITI

**LARVA**

| CHAPTERS | | | | 4 | 5 |
|---|---|---|---|---|---|

WHERE FOUND: Kilika Island/Djose Highland/Dry Plains/Thunder Plains/Macalania/Various

| LEV | 35 | HP | 1782 | MP | 999 |
|---|---|---|---|---|---|
| EXP | 650 | AP | 1 | | |

| GIL DROP | 280 | GIL STEAL | 520 |
|---|---|---|---|

| STR | 16 | DEF | 32 | AGL | 64 |
|---|---|---|---|---|---|
| EVA | 0 | ACC | 2 | LUCK | 0 |
| MAG | | 72 | MAG DEF | 66 | |

| | | | | | |
|---|---|---|---|---|---|
| 🔥 | Weak | 💧 | None | ⚡ | Absorb |
| ◔ | None | ◎ | Invalid | 🌀 | Weak |

IMM: Dth., Pet., Slp., Sil., Drk., Poi., Con., Ber., Cur., Stp., Doom, M.D.

DEF EFF: Ejt. (16), Zan. (3)

| DROP RATIO | 64/255 |
|---|---|
| ITEM DROP | Star Pendant x1 |
| RARE DROP | Venom Shock x1 |
| STEAL RATIO | 255/255 |
| STOLEN ITEM | Antidote x2 |
| RARE STEAL | Stamina Spring x1 |
| BRIBE ITEM | Stamina Spring x60 |
| RARE BRIBE | Stamina Spring x99 |

## TAWRICH — NONE

| | | |
|---|---|---|
| **CHAPTERS** | 1 2 3 4 5 | |
| **WHERE FOUND** | Bikanel | |
| LEV 38 | HP 5440 | MP 9999 |
| EXP 0 | AP 0 | |
| GIL DROP 0 | GIL STEAL None | |
| STR 85 | DEF 42 | AGL 113 |
| EVA 0 | ACC 1 | LUCK 0 |
| MAG 99 | MAG DEF 0 | |

Elements: None / None / None / None / None / Invalid / None

**IMM** P.B., M.B., L.C., E.C., A.C.
**DEF EFF** Zan. (255)

| | |
|---|---|
| DROP RATIO | None |
| ITEM DROP | None |
| RARE DROP | None |
| STEAL RATIO | None |
| STOLEN ITEM | None |
| RARE STEAL | None |
| BRIBE ITEM | None |
| RARE BRIBE | None |

## TENTACLES — CEPHALOPOD

| | | |
|---|---|---|
| **CHAPTERS** | 1 2 3 4 5 | |
| **WHERE FOUND** | Macalania, Bevelle Tower Floors 36-39 | |
| LEV 35 [38] | HP 2530 [10120] | MP 64 |
| EXP 143 [220] | AP 1 [2] | |
| GIL DROP 95 [180] | GIL STEAL 380 [760] | |
| STR 44 [46] | DEF 34 | AGL 61 [77] |
| EVA 0 | ACC 6 [8] | LUCK 0 |
| MAG 38 | MAG DEF 47 | |

Elements: None / None / None / None; Absorb / Absorb / None / None

**IMM** Pet., Slp., Cur., Stp., M.D.
**DEF EFF** Dth. (80), Sil. (80 [0]), Poi. (30 [0]), Con. (50 [Res.]), Ber. (100 [Res.]), Ejt. (12 [22]), Zan. (4 [10])

| | |
|---|---|
| DROP RATIO | 128/255 [255/255] |
| ITEM DROP | Phoenix Down x1 [Phoenix Down x4] |
| RARE DROP | Phoenix Down x2 [Phoenix Down x5] |
| STEAL RATIO | 128/255 [255/255] |
| STOLEN ITEM | Phoenix Down x1 [Mega Phoenix x2] |
| RARE STEAL | Blue Ring x1 [Mega Phoenix x3] |
| BRIBE ITEM | Blue Ring x1 [Mega Phoenix x16] |
| RARE BRIBE | Cerulean Ring x1 [Mega Phoenix x20] |

## TINDALOS — LUPINE

| | | |
|---|---|---|
| **CHAPTERS** | 1 2 3 4 5 | |
| **WHERE FOUND** | Farplane, Bevelle Tower Floors 61-64 | |
| LEV 30 [36] | HP 3324 [7330] | MP 12 |
| EXP 900 [985] | AP 1 [2] | |
| GIL DROP 315 [550] | GIL STEAL 660 [1200] | |
| STR 40 | DEF 19 | AGL 135 [152] |
| EVA 33 [41] | ACC 3 [4] | LUCK 0 |
| MAG 4 [8] | MAG DEF 3 [4] | |

Elements: None / None / None / None; None / None / None / None

**IMM** Slp., [Con.], [Ber.], Cur., Stp. ([0]), M.D.
**DEF EFF** Dth. (80) Ejt. (13 [26]), Zan. (1 [6])

| | |
|---|---|
| DROP RATIO | 128/255 [255/255] |
| ITEM DROP | Antidote x1 [Sprint Shoes x1] |
| RARE DROP | Hi-Potion x2 [Sprint Shoes x1] |
| STEAL RATIO | 255/255 [128/255] |
| STOLEN ITEM | Hi-Potion x1 [Chocobo Feather x1] |
| RARE STEAL | Hi-Potion x1 [Chocobo Feather x1] |
| BRIBE ITEM | Chocobo Feather x20 [Chocobo Wing x30] |
| RARE BRIBE | Chocobo Feather x30 [Chocobo Wing x40] |

## TOMB — DOOMSTONE

| | | |
|---|---|---|
| **CHAPTERS** | 1 2 3 4 5 | |
| **WHERE FOUND** | Djose Highlands/Calm Lands/Bevelle Palace Floors 27-29 | |
| LEV 27 | HP 4820 | MP 999 |
| EXP 480 | AP 1 | |
| GIL DROP 130 | GIL STEAL 380 | |
| STR 34 | DEF 66 | AGL 85 |
| EVA 0 | ACC 3 | LUCK 0 |
| MAG 64 | MAG DEF 1 | |

Elements: Half / Half / Half; Weak / Invalid / Weak

**IMM** Dth., Pet., Slp., Sil., Cur., Slw., Stp., Doom, M.D.
**DEF EFF** Drk. (100), Poi. (100), Con. (100), Ber. (50), Ejt. (24), Zan. (7)

| | |
|---|---|
| DROP RATIO | 128/255 |
| ITEM DROP | Remedy x1 |
| RARE DROP | White Cape x1 |
| STEAL RATIO | 128/255 |
| STOLEN ITEM | Remedy x1 |
| RARE STEAL | Black Choker x1 |
| BRIBE ITEM | Faerie Earrings x1 |
| RARE BRIBE | Faerie Earrings x1 |

## TONBERRY — TONBERRY

| | | |
|---|---|---|
| **CHAPTERS** | 1 2 3 4 5 | |
| **WHERE FOUND** | Mushroom Rock/Bevelle Palace | |
| LEV 21 [25] | HP 9999 [39996] | MP 0 |
| EXP 120 [250] | AP 2 [3] | |
| GIL DROP 300 [600] | GIL STEAL 1500 [3000] | |
| STR 16 | DEF 46 | AGL 71 [78] |
| EVA 0 | ACC 4 [5] | LUCK 0 |
| MAG 3 | MAG DEF 4 | |

Elements: None / None / None / None; Half / Invalid / None

**IMM** All
**DEF EFF** Ejt. (100 [200]), Zan. (60 [110])

| | |
|---|---|
| DROP RATIO | 128/255 [255/255] |
| ITEM DROP | Hi-Potion x1 [Turbo Ether x2] |
| RARE DROP | Ether x1 [Turbo Ether x2] |
| STEAL RATIO | 64/255 |
| STOLEN ITEM | Ether x1 [Turbo Ether x1] |
| RARE STEAL | Ether x1 [Turbo Ether x1] |
| BRIBE ITEM | Ether x99 [Sword Lore x3] |
| RARE BRIBE | Ether x99 [Sword Lore x4] |

## TREMA — NONE

| | | |
|---|---|---|
| **CHAPTERS** | 5 | |
| **WHERE FOUND** | Bevelle Palace Bottom Floor | |
| LEV 99 | HP 999999 | MP 999 |
| EXP 10000 | AP 50 | |
| GIL DROP 10000 | GIL STEAL 300 | |
| STR 255 | DEF 255 | AGL 128 |
| EVA 99 | ACC 26 | LUCK 0 |
| MAG 255 | MAG DEF 255 | |

Elements: None / None / None / None; None / Invalid / None

**IMM** All
**DEF EFF** Zan. (255)

| | |
|---|---|
| DROP RATIO | 255/255 |
| ITEM DROP | Dark Matter x1 |
| RARE DROP | Dark Matter x2 |
| STEAL RATIO | 128/255 |
| STOLEN ITEM | Ether x1 |
| RARE STEAL | Turbo Ether x2 |
| BRIBE ITEM | None |
| RARE BRIBE | None |

## ULTIMA WEAPON — TYPE –WEAPON

| | | |
|---|---|---|
| **CHAPTERS** | 1 2 3 4 5 | |
| **WHERE FOUND** | Ruin Depths/Bevelle Palace Floors 47-49 | |
| LEV 82 [86] | HP 34300 [67515] | MP 9999 |
| EXP 3350 [4230] | AP 1 [2] | |
| GIL DROP 3000 [4200] | GIL STEAL 3000 [6000] | |
| STR 74 [86] | DEF 53 [63] | AGL 112 [155] |
| EVA 0 | ACC 4 [10] | LUCK 0 |
| MAG 32 [82] | MAG DEF 33 [83] | |

Elements: None / None / None / None; None / Invalid / None

**IMM** All *but* Ejt.
**DEF EFF** Ejt. (200 [220]), Zan. (100 [120])

| | |
|---|---|
| DROP RATIO | 255/255 |
| ITEM DROP | Safety Bit x1 [Rune Bracer x1] |
| RARE DROP | Rune Bracer x1 [Crystal Bangle x1] |
| STEAL RATIO | 128/255 |
| STOLEN ITEM | Supreme Gem x1 |
| RARE STEAL | Supreme Gem x2 |
| BRIBE ITEM | Defense Bracer x8 [Ribbon x3] |
| RARE BRIBE | Ribbon x1 [Ribbon x3] |

## VALEFOR — NONE

| | | |
|---|---|---|
| **CHAPTERS** | 1 2 3 4 5 | |
| **WHERE FOUND** | Besaid | |
| LEV 22 | HP 8430 | MP 9999 |
| EXP 1500 | AP 15 | |
| GIL DROP 1200 | GIL STEAL 1500 | |
| STR 97 | DEF 11 | AGL 125 |
| EVA 25 | ACC 3 | LUCK 0 |
| MAG 76 | MAG DEF 20 | |

Elements: None / None / None / None; None / Invalid / None

**IMM** Dth., Pet., Slp., Sil., Drk., Poi., Con., Ber., Cur., Ejt., Stp., Doom, Del., P.I., M.D.
**DEF EFF** Zan. (80)

| | |
|---|---|
| DROP RATIO | 255/255 |
| ITEM DROP | Moon Bracer x1 |
| RARE DROP | Moon Bracer x1 |
| STEAL RATIO | 128/255 |
| STOLEN ITEM | Healing Spring x4 |
| RARE STEAL | Healing Spring x6 |
| BRIBE ITEM | None |
| RARE BRIBE | None |

Characters

1

Garment Grids & Dresspheres

2

Battle System

3

Accessories

4

Items and Item Shops

5

Walkthrough

6

Mini Games

7

Fiends and Enemies

8

## VARAN

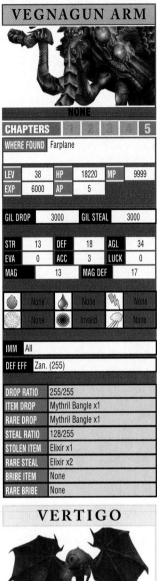

**IMP**

| CHAPTERS | 1 | 2 | 3 | 4 | 5 |
|---|---|---|---|---|---|

| WHERE FOUND | Besaid/Dry Plains/Thunder Plains/Macalania/Calm Lands/Various |
|---|---|

| LEV | 28 | HP | 1132 | MP | 480 |
|---|---|---|---|---|---|
| EXP | 410 | AP | 1 | | |

| GIL DROP | 240 | GIL STEAL | 443 |
|---|---|---|---|

| STR | 6 | DEF | 43 | AGL | 84 |
|---|---|---|---|---|---|
| EVA | 42 | ACC | 0 | LUCK | 0 |
| MAG | 22 | MAG DEF | 214 | | |

Weak / None / None
None / None / None

| IMM | Sil., Con., Cur., Slw., Stp., M.B., Doom |
|---|---|

| DEF EFF | Dth. (70), Pet. (50), Slp. (60), Drk. (30), Poi. (60), Ber. (30), Ejt. (12), Zan. (1) |
|---|---|

| DROP RATIO | 128/255 |
|---|---|
| ITEM DROP | Holy Water x1 |
| RARE DROP | Holy Water x2 |
| STEAL RATIO | 255/255 |
| STOLEN ITEM | Dispel Tonic x1 |
| RARE STEAL | Dispel Tonic x2 |
| BRIBE ITEM | Dispel Tonic x24 |
| RARE BRIBE | Dispel Tonic x30 |

## VEGNAGUN ARM

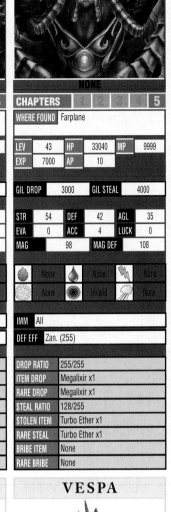

**NONE**

| CHAPTERS | 1 | 2 | 3 | 4 | 5 |
|---|---|---|---|---|---|

| WHERE FOUND | Farplane |
|---|---|

| LEV | 38 | HP | 18220 | MP | 9999 |
|---|---|---|---|---|---|
| EXP | 6000 | AP | 5 | | |

| GIL DROP | 3000 | GIL STEAL | 3000 |
|---|---|---|---|

| STR | 13 | DEF | 18 | AGL | 34 |
|---|---|---|---|---|---|
| EVA | 0 | ACC | 3 | LUCK | 0 |
| MAG | 13 | MAG DEF | 17 | | |

None / None / None
None / Invalid / None

| IMM | All |
|---|---|

| DEF EFF | Zan. (255) |
|---|---|

| DROP RATIO | 255/255 |
|---|---|
| ITEM DROP | Mythril Bangle x1 |
| RARE DROP | Mythril Bangle x1 |
| STEAL RATIO | 128/255 |
| STOLEN ITEM | Elixir x1 |
| RARE STEAL | Elixir x2 |
| BRIBE ITEM | None |
| RARE BRIBE | None |

## VEGNAGUN CORE

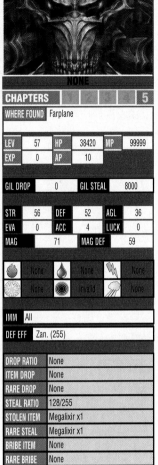

**NONE**

| CHAPTERS | 1 | 2 | 3 | 4 | 5 |
|---|---|---|---|---|---|

| WHERE FOUND | Farplane |
|---|---|

| LEV | 43 | HP | 33040 | MP | 9999 |
|---|---|---|---|---|---|
| EXP | 7000 | AP | 10 | | |

| GIL DROP | 3000 | GIL STEAL | 4000 |
|---|---|---|---|

| STR | 54 | DEF | 42 | AGL | 35 |
|---|---|---|---|---|---|
| EVA | 0 | ACC | 4 | LUCK | 0 |
| MAG | 98 | MAG DEF | 108 | | |

None / None / None
None / Invalid / None

| IMM | All |
|---|---|

| DEF EFF | Zan. (255) |
|---|---|

| DROP RATIO | 255/255 |
|---|---|
| ITEM DROP | Megalixir x1 |
| RARE DROP | Megalixir x1 |
| STEAL RATIO | 128/255 |
| STOLEN ITEM | Turbo Ether x1 |
| RARE STEAL | Turbo Ether x1 |
| BRIBE ITEM | None |
| RARE BRIBE | None |

## VEGNAGUN FACE

**NONE**

| CHAPTERS | 1 | 2 | 3 | 4 | 5 |
|---|---|---|---|---|---|

| WHERE FOUND | Farplane |
|---|---|

| LEV | 57 | HP | 38420 | MP | 99999 |
|---|---|---|---|---|---|
| EXP | 0 | AP | 10 | | |

| GIL DROP | 0 | GIL STEAL | 8000 |
|---|---|---|---|

| STR | 56 | DEF | 52 | AGL | 36 |
|---|---|---|---|---|---|
| EVA | 0 | ACC | 4 | LUCK | 0 |
| MAG | 71 | MAG DEF | 59 | | |

None / None / None
None / Invalid / None

| IMM | All |
|---|---|

| DEF EFF | Zan. (255) |
|---|---|

| DROP RATIO | None |
|---|---|
| ITEM DROP | None |
| RARE DROP | None |
| STEAL RATIO | 128/255 |
| STOLEN ITEM | Megalixir x1 |
| RARE STEAL | Megalixir x1 |
| BRIBE ITEM | None |
| RARE BRIBE | None |

## VEGNAGUN TAIL

**NONE**

| CHAPTERS | 1 | 2 | 3 | 4 | 5 |
|---|---|---|---|---|---|

| WHERE FOUND | Farplane |
|---|---|

| LEV | 41 | HP | 34200 | MP | 9999 |
|---|---|---|---|---|---|
| EXP | 5000 | AP | 5 | | |

| GIL DROP | 3000 | GIL STEAL | 3000 |
|---|---|---|---|

| STR | 77 | DEF | 72 | AGL | 115 |
|---|---|---|---|---|---|
| EVA | 0 | ACC | 3 | LUCK | 0 |
| MAG | 82 | MAG DEF | 76 | | |

None / None / None
None / Invalid / None

| IMM | All |
|---|---|

| DEF EFF | Zan. (255) |
|---|---|

| DROP RATIO | 255/255 |
|---|---|
| ITEM DROP | Megalixir x1 |
| RARE DROP | Megalixir x1 |
| STEAL RATIO | 128/255 |
| STOLEN ITEM | X-Potion x4 |
| RARE STEAL | X-Potion x6 |
| BRIBE ITEM | None |
| RARE BRIBE | None |

## VERTIGO

**EVIL EYE**

| CHAPTERS | 1 | 2 | 3 | 4 | 5 |
|---|---|---|---|---|---|

| WHERE FOUND | Bevelle/Bevelle Tower Floors 13-15 |
|---|---|

| LEV | 18 [22] | HP | 688 [2352] | MP | 57 |
|---|---|---|---|---|---|
| EXP | 65 [108] | AP | 1 [2] | | |

| GIL DROP | 36 [78] | GIL STEAL | 130 [270] |
|---|---|---|---|

| STR | 24 | DEF | 31 | AGL | 58 [64] |
|---|---|---|---|---|---|
| EVA | 14 [18] | ACC | 4 [5] | LUCK | 0 |
| MAG | 3 | MAG DEF | 7 | | |

None / None / None
None / None / None

| IMM | [Con.], [Ber.], Cur., Slw. ([0]) |
|---|---|

| DEF EFF | Ejt. (14 [22]), Zan. (1 [4]) |
|---|---|

| DROP RATIO | 128/255 [255/255] |
|---|---|
| ITEM DROP | Antidote x1 [Remedy x3] |
| RARE DROP | Holy Water x1 [Remedy x4] |
| STEAL RATIO | 255/255 |
| STOLEN ITEM | Antidote x2 [Tarot Card x1] |
| RARE STEAL | Antidote x3 [Tarot Card x1] |
| BRIBE ITEM | Silver Glasses x1 [Elixir x2] |
| RARE BRIBE | Silver Glasses x1 [Elixir x2] |

## VESPA

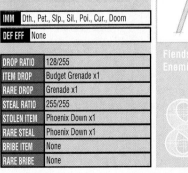

**WASP**

| CHAPTERS | 1 | 2 | 3 | 4 | 5 |
|---|---|---|---|---|---|

| WHERE FOUND | Calm Lands/Mt. Gagazet/Bevelle Tower Floors 36-39 |
|---|---|

| LEV | 25 [28] | HP | 983 [2758] | MP | 32 |
|---|---|---|---|---|---|
| EXP | 185 [294] | AP | 1 [2] | | |

| GIL DROP | 78 [124] | GIL STEAL | 244 [460] |
|---|---|---|---|

| STR | 36 [37] | DEF | 6 | AGL | 101 [168] |
|---|---|---|---|---|---|
| EVA | 37 [47] | ACC | 12 [15] | LUCK | 0 |
| MAG | 4 | MAG DEF | 2 | | |

Fire -None / Weak / None
None / None / None

| IMM | [Con.], [Ber.], Cur., Stp. ([0]), [P.B.] |
|---|---|

| DEF EFF | Ejt. (6 [8]), Zan. (0 [2]) |
|---|---|

| DROP RATIO | 128/255 [255/255] |
|---|---|
| ITEM DROP | Antidote x2 [Poison Fang x4] |
| RARE DROP | Remedy x1 [Poison Fang x6] |
| STEAL RATIO | 255/255 |
| STOLEN ITEM | Echo Screen x2 [Star Pendant x1] |
| RARE STEAL | Poison Fang x1 [Star Pendant x1] |
| BRIBE ITEM | Remedy x5 [Faerie Earrings x1] |
| RARE BRIBE | Remedy x6 [Faerie Earrings x1] |

## VIPER SNIPER

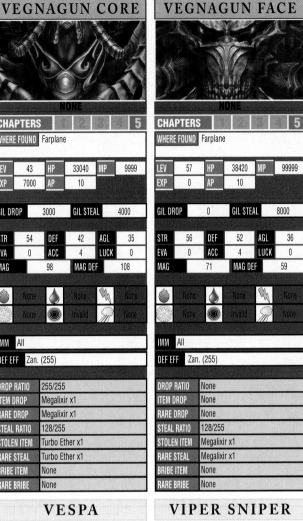

**BANDOLEER**

| CHAPTERS | 1 | 2 | 3 | 4 | 5 |
|---|---|---|---|---|---|

| WHERE FOUND | Mt. Gagazet/Bevelle Tower Floors 13-15 |
|---|---|

| LEV | 18 | HP | 256 | MP | 0 |
|---|---|---|---|---|---|
| EXP | 10 | AP | 1 | | |

| GIL DROP | 20 | GIL STEAL | 60 |
|---|---|---|---|

| STR | 32 | DEF | 0 | AGL | 73 |
|---|---|---|---|---|---|
| EVA | 0 | ACC | 1 | LUCK | 0 |
| MAG | 0 | MAG DEF | 0 | | |

None / None / None
None / None / None

| IMM | Dth., Pet., Slp., Sil., Poi., Cur., Doom |
|---|---|

| DEF EFF | None |
|---|---|

| DROP RATIO | 128/255 |
|---|---|
| ITEM DROP | Budget Grenade x1 |
| RARE DROP | Grenade x1 |
| STEAL RATIO | 255/255 |
| STOLEN ITEM | Phoenix Down x1 |
| RARE STEAL | Phoenix Down x1 |
| BRIBE ITEM | None |
| RARE BRIBE | None |

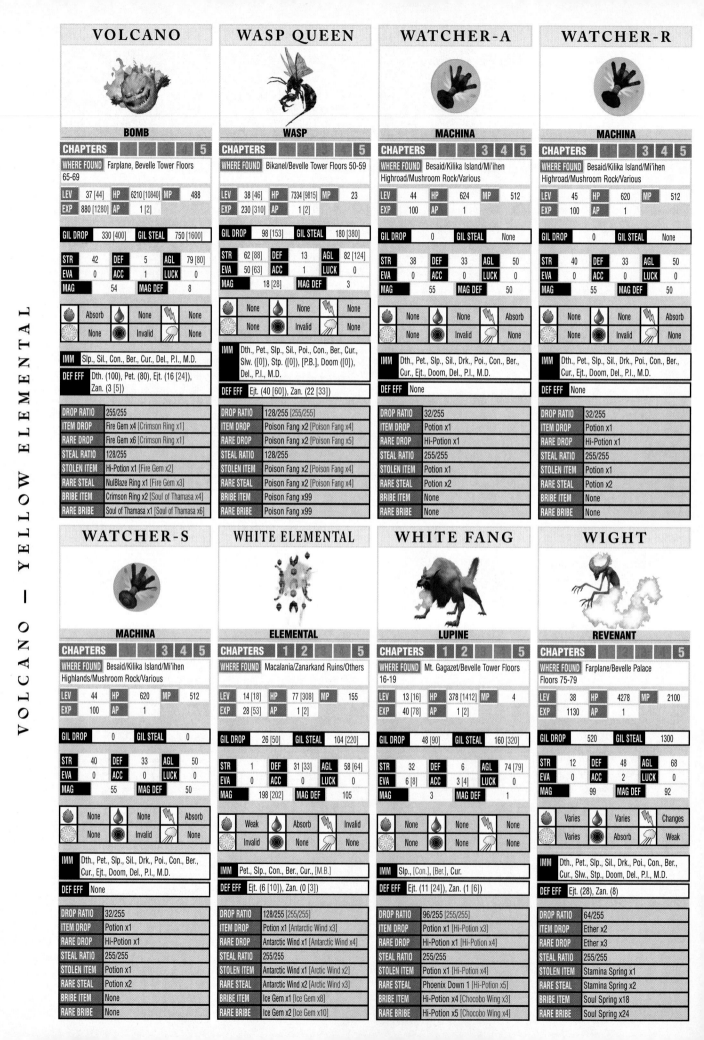

## VOLCANO

**BOMB**

| CHAPTERS | | | | | 5 |
|---|---|---|---|---|---|

**WHERE FOUND** Farplane, Bevelle Tower Floors 65-69

| LEV | 37 [44] | HP | 6210 [10840] | MP | 488 |
|---|---|---|---|---|---|
| EXP | 880 [1280] | AP | 1 [2] | | |

| GIL DROP | 330 [400] | GIL STEAL | 750 [1600] |
|---|---|---|---|

| STR | 42 | DEF | 5 | AGL | 79 [80] |
|---|---|---|---|---|---|
| EVA | 0 | ACC | 1 | LUCK | 0 |
| MAG | | 54 | MAG DEF | | 8 |

| | | | | | |
|---|---|---|---|---|---|
| Absorb | | None | | None | |
| None | | Invalid | | None | |

**IMM** Slp., Sil., Con., Ber., Cur., Del., P.I., M.D.

**DEF EFF** Dth. (100), Pet. (80), Ejt. (16 [24]), Zan. (3 [5])

| DROP RATIO | 255/255 |
|---|---|
| ITEM DROP | Fire Gem x4 [Crimson Ring x1] |
| RARE DROP | Fire Gem x6 [Crimson Ring x1] |
| STEAL RATIO | 128/255 |
| STOLEN ITEM | Hi-Potion x1 [Fire Gem x2] |
| RARE STEAL | NulBlaze Ring x1 [Fire Gem x3] |
| BRIBE ITEM | Crimson Ring x2 [Soul of Thamasa x4] |
| RARE BRIBE | Soul of Thamasa x1 [Soul of Thamasa x6] |

## WASP QUEEN

**WASP**

| CHAPTERS | | | | | 5 |
|---|---|---|---|---|---|

**WHERE FOUND** Bikanel/Bevelle Tower Floors 50-59

| LEV | 38 [46] | HP | 7334 [9815] | MP | 23 |
|---|---|---|---|---|---|
| EXP | 230 [310] | AP | 1 [2] | | |

| GIL DROP | 98 [153] | GIL STEAL | 180 [380] |
|---|---|---|---|

| STR | 62 [88] | DEF | 13 | AGL | 82 [124] |
|---|---|---|---|---|---|
| EVA | 50 [63] | ACC | 1 | LUCK | 0 |
| MAG | | 18 [28] | MAG DEF | | 3 |

| | | | | | |
|---|---|---|---|---|---|
| None | | None | | None | |
| None | | Invalid | | None | |

**IMM** Dth., Pet., Slp., Sil., Poi., Con., Ber., Cur., Slw. ([0]), Stp. ([0]), [P.B.], Doom ([0]), Del., P.I., M.D.

**DEF EFF** Ejt. (40 [60]), Zan. (22 [33])

| DROP RATIO | 128/255 [255/255] |
|---|---|
| ITEM DROP | Poison Fang x2 [Poison Fang x4] |
| RARE DROP | Poison Fang x2 [Poison Fang x5] |
| STEAL RATIO | 128/255 |
| STOLEN ITEM | Poison Fang x2 [Poison Fang x4] |
| RARE STEAL | Poison Fang x2 [Poison Fang x4] |
| BRIBE ITEM | Poison Fang x99 |
| RARE BRIBE | Poison Fang x99 |

## WATCHER-A

**MACHINA**

| CHAPTERS | | | 3 | 4 | 5 |
|---|---|---|---|---|---|

**WHERE FOUND** Besaid/Kilika Island/Mi'ihen Highroad/Mushroom Rock/Various

| LEV | 44 | HP | 624 | MP | 512 |
|---|---|---|---|---|---|
| EXP | 100 | AP | 1 | | |

| GIL DROP | 0 | GIL STEAL | None |
|---|---|---|---|

| STR | 38 | DEF | 33 | AGL | 50 |
|---|---|---|---|---|---|
| EVA | 0 | ACC | 0 | LUCK | 0 |
| MAG | | 55 | MAG DEF | | 50 |

| | | | | | |
|---|---|---|---|---|---|
| None | | None | | Absorb | |
| None | | Invalid | | None | |

**IMM** Dth., Pet., Slp., Sil., Drk., Poi., Con., Ber., Cur., Ejt., Doom, Del., P.I., M.D.

**DEF EFF** None

| DROP RATIO | 32/255 |
|---|---|
| ITEM DROP | Potion x1 |
| RARE DROP | Hi-Potion x1 |
| STEAL RATIO | 255/255 |
| STOLEN ITEM | Potion x1 |
| RARE STEAL | Potion x2 |
| BRIBE ITEM | None |
| RARE BRIBE | None |

## WATCHER-R

**MACHINA**

| CHAPTERS | | | 3 | 4 | 5 |
|---|---|---|---|---|---|

**WHERE FOUND** Besaid/Kilika Island/Mi'ihen Highroad/Mushroom Rock/Various

| LEV | 45 | HP | 620 | MP | 512 |
|---|---|---|---|---|---|
| EXP | 100 | AP | 1 | | |

| GIL DROP | 0 | GIL STEAL | None |
|---|---|---|---|

| STR | 40 | DEF | 33 | AGL | 50 |
|---|---|---|---|---|---|
| EVA | 0 | ACC | 0 | LUCK | 0 |
| MAG | | 55 | MAG DEF | | 50 |

| | | | | | |
|---|---|---|---|---|---|
| None | | None | | Absorb | |
| None | | Invalid | | None | |

**IMM** Dth., Pet., Slp., Sil., Drk., Poi., Con., Ber., Cur., Ejt., Doom, Del., P.I., M.D.

**DEF EFF** None

| DROP RATIO | 32/255 |
|---|---|
| ITEM DROP | Potion x1 |
| RARE DROP | Hi-Potion x1 |
| STEAL RATIO | 255/255 |
| STOLEN ITEM | Potion x1 |
| RARE STEAL | Potion x2 |
| BRIBE ITEM | None |
| RARE BRIBE | None |

## WATCHER-S

**MACHINA**

| CHAPTERS | | | 3 | 4 | 5 |
|---|---|---|---|---|---|

**WHERE FOUND** Besaid/Kilika Island/Mi'ihen Highlands/Mushroom Rock/Various

| LEV | 44 | HP | 620 | MP | 512 |
|---|---|---|---|---|---|
| EXP | 100 | AP | 1 | | |

| GIL DROP | 0 | GIL STEAL | 0 |
|---|---|---|---|

| STR | 40 | DEF | 33 | AGL | 50 |
|---|---|---|---|---|---|
| EVA | 0 | ACC | 0 | LUCK | 0 |
| MAG | | 55 | MAG DEF | | 50 |

| | | | | | |
|---|---|---|---|---|---|
| None | | None | | Absorb | |
| None | | Invalid | | None | |

**IMM** Dth., Pet., Slp., Sil., Drk., Poi., Con., Ber., Cur., Ejt., Doom, Del., P.I., M.D.

**DEF EFF** None

| DROP RATIO | 32/255 |
|---|---|
| ITEM DROP | Potion x1 |
| RARE DROP | Hi-Potion x1 |
| STEAL RATIO | 255/255 |
| STOLEN ITEM | Potion x1 |
| RARE STEAL | Potion x2 |
| BRIBE ITEM | None |
| RARE BRIBE | None |

## WHITE ELEMENTAL

**ELEMENTAL**

| CHAPTERS | 1 | 2 | | | 5 |
|---|---|---|---|---|---|

**WHERE FOUND** Macalania/Zanarkand Ruins/Others

| LEV | 14 [18] | HP | 77 [308] | MP | 155 |
|---|---|---|---|---|---|
| EXP | 28 [53] | AP | 1 [2] | | |

| GIL DROP | 26 [50] | GIL STEAL | 104 [220] |
|---|---|---|---|

| STR | 1 | DEF | 31 [33] | AGL | 58 [64] |
|---|---|---|---|---|---|
| EVA | 0 | ACC | 0 | LUCK | 0 |
| MAG | | 198 [202] | MAG DEF | | 105 |

| | | | | | |
|---|---|---|---|---|---|
| Weak | | Absorb | | Invalid | |
| Invalid | | None | | None | |

**IMM** Pet., Slp., Con., Ber., Cur., [M.B.]

**DEF EFF** Ejt. (6 [10]), Zan. (0 [3])

| DROP RATIO | 128/255 [255/255] |
|---|---|
| ITEM DROP | Potion x1 [Antarctic Wind x3] |
| RARE DROP | Antarctic Wind x1 [Antarctic Wind x4] |
| STEAL RATIO | 255/255 |
| STOLEN ITEM | Antarctic Wind x2 [Arctic Wind x2] |
| RARE STEAL | Antarctic Wind x2 [Arctic Wind x3] |
| BRIBE ITEM | Ice Gem x1 [Ice Gem x8] |
| RARE BRIBE | Ice Gem x2 [Ice Gem x10] |

## WHITE FANG

**LUPINE**

| CHAPTERS | 1 | 2 | | | 5 |
|---|---|---|---|---|---|

**WHERE FOUND** Mt. Gagazet/Bevelle Tower Floors 16-19

| LEV | 13 [16] | HP | 378 [1412] | MP | 4 |
|---|---|---|---|---|---|
| EXP | 40 [78] | AP | 1 [2] | | |

| GIL DROP | 48 [90] | GIL STEAL | 160 [320] |
|---|---|---|---|

| STR | 32 | DEF | 6 | AGL | 74 [79] |
|---|---|---|---|---|---|
| EVA | 6 [8] | ACC | 3 [4] | LUCK | 0 |
| MAG | | 3 | MAG DEF | | 1 |

| | | | | | |
|---|---|---|---|---|---|
| None | | None | | None | |
| None | | None | | None | |

**IMM** Slp., [Con.], [Ber.], Cur.

**DEF EFF** Ejt. (11 [24]), Zan. (1 [6])

| DROP RATIO | 96/255 [255/255] |
|---|---|
| ITEM DROP | Potion x1 [Hi-Potion x3] |
| RARE DROP | Hi-Potion x1 [Hi-Potion x4] |
| STEAL RATIO | 255/255 |
| STOLEN ITEM | Potion x1 [Hi-Potion x4] |
| RARE STEAL | Phoenix Down 1 [Hi-Potion x5] |
| BRIBE ITEM | Hi-Potion x4 [Chocobo Wing x3] |
| RARE BRIBE | Hi-Potion x5 [Chocobo Wing x4] |

## WIGHT

**REVENANT**

| CHAPTERS | | | | | 5 |
|---|---|---|---|---|---|

**WHERE FOUND** Farplane/Bevelle Palace Floors 75-79

| LEV | 38 | HP | 4278 | MP | 2100 |
|---|---|---|---|---|---|
| EXP | 1130 | AP | 1 | | |

| GIL DROP | 520 | GIL STEAL | 1300 |
|---|---|---|---|

| STR | 12 | DEF | 48 | AGL | 68 |
|---|---|---|---|---|---|
| EVA | 0 | ACC | 2 | LUCK | 0 |
| MAG | | 99 | MAG DEF | | 92 |

| | | | | | |
|---|---|---|---|---|---|
| Varies | | Varies | | Changes | |
| Varies | | Absorb | | Weak | |

**IMM** Dth., Pet., Sil., Drk., Poi., Con., Ber., Cur., Slw., Stp., Doom, Del., P.I., M.D.

**DEF EFF** Ejt. (28), Zan. (8)

| DROP RATIO | 64/255 |
|---|---|
| ITEM DROP | Ether x2 |
| RARE DROP | Ether x3 |
| STEAL RATIO | 255/255 |
| STOLEN ITEM | Stamina Spring x1 |
| RARE STEAL | Stamina Spring x2 |
| BRIBE ITEM | Soul Spring x18 |
| RARE BRIBE | Soul Spring x24 |

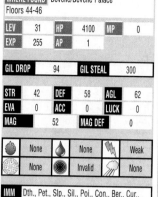

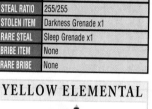

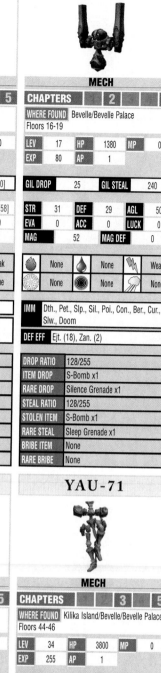
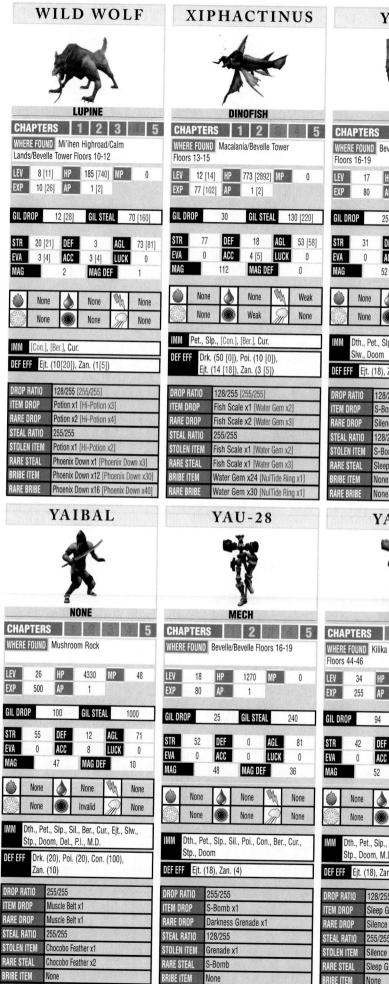
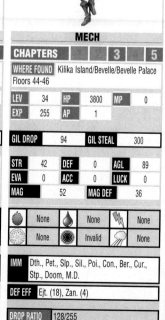
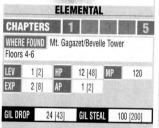

## WILD WOLF

**LUPINE**

| CHAPTERS | 1 | 2 | 3 | | 5 |
|---|---|---|---|---|---|

**WHERE FOUND** Mi'ihen Highroad/Calm Lands/Bevelle Tower Floors 10-12

| LEV | 8 [11] | HP | 185 [740] | MP | 0 |
|---|---|---|---|---|---|
| EXP | 10 [26] | AP | 1 [2] | | |

| GIL DROP | 12 [28] | GIL STEAL | 70 [160] |
|---|---|---|---|

| STR | 20 [21] | DEF | 3 | AGL | 73 [81] |
|---|---|---|---|---|---|
| EVA | 3 [4] | ACC | 3 [4] | LUCK | 0 |
| MAG | 2 | MAG DEF | 1 | | |

| | None | | None | | None |
|---|---|---|---|---|---|
| | None | | None | | None |

**IMM** [Con.], [Ber.], Cur.

**DEF EFF** Ejt. (10[20]), Zan. (1[5])

| DROP RATIO | 128/255 [255/255] |
|---|---|
| ITEM DROP | Potion x1 [Hi-Potion x3] |
| RARE DROP | Potion x2 [Hi-Potion x4] |
| STEAL RATIO | 255/255 |
| STOLEN ITEM | Potion x1 [Hi-Potion x2] |
| RARE STEAL | Phoenix Down x1 [Phoenix Down x3] |
| BRIBE ITEM | Phoenix Down x12 [Phoenix Down x30] |
| RARE BRIBE | Phoenix Down x16 [Phoenix Down x40] |

## XIPHACTINUS

**DINOFISH**

| CHAPTERS | 1 | 2 | | 5 |
|---|---|---|---|---|

**WHERE FOUND** Macalania/Bevelle Tower Floors 13-15

| LEV | 12 [14] | HP | 773 [2892] | MP | 0 |
|---|---|---|---|---|---|
| EXP | 77 [102] | AP | 1 [2] | | |

| GIL DROP | 30 | GIL STEAL | 130 [220] |
|---|---|---|---|

| STR | 77 | DEF | 18 | AGL | 53 [58] |
|---|---|---|---|---|---|
| EVA | 0 | ACC | 4 [5] | LUCK | 0 |
| MAG | 112 | MAG DEF | 0 | | |

| | None | | None | | Weak |
|---|---|---|---|---|---|
| | None | | Weak | | None |

**IMM** Pet., Slp., [Con.], [Ber.], Cur.

**DEF EFF** Drk. (50 [0]), Poi. (10 [0]), Ejt. (14 [18]), Zan. (3 [5])

| DROP RATIO | 128/255 [255/255] |
|---|---|
| ITEM DROP | Fish Scale x1 [Water Gem x2] |
| RARE DROP | Fish Scale x2 [Water Gem x3] |
| STEAL RATIO | 255/255 |
| STOLEN ITEM | Fish Scale x1 [Water Gem x2] |
| RARE STEAL | Fish Scale x1 [Water Gem x3] |
| BRIBE ITEM | Water Gem x24 [NulTide Ring x1] |
| RARE BRIBE | Water Gem x30 [NulTide Ring x1] |

## YAC-13

**MECH**

| CHAPTERS | | 2 | | 5 |
|---|---|---|---|---|

**WHERE FOUND** Bevelle/Bevelle Palace Floors 16-19

| LEV | 17 | HP | 1380 | MP | 0 |
|---|---|---|---|---|---|
| EXP | 80 | AP | 1 | | |

| GIL DROP | 25 | GIL STEAL | 240 |
|---|---|---|---|

| STR | 31 | DEF | 29 | AGL | 50 |
|---|---|---|---|---|---|
| EVA | 0 | ACC | 0 | LUCK | 0 |
| MAG | 52 | MAG DEF | 0 | | |

| | None | | None | | Weak |
|---|---|---|---|---|---|
| | None | | None | | None |

**IMM** Dth., Pet., Slp., Sil., Poi., Con., Ber., Cur., Slw., Doom

**DEF EFF** Ejt. (18), Zan. (2)

| DROP RATIO | 128/255 |
|---|---|
| ITEM DROP | S-Bomb x1 |
| RARE DROP | Silence Grenade x1 |
| STEAL RATIO | 128/255 |
| STOLEN ITEM | S-Bomb x1 |
| RARE STEAL | Sleep Grenade x1 |
| BRIBE ITEM | None |
| RARE BRIBE | None |

## YAC-62

**MECH**

| CHAPTERS | | | 3 | | 5 |
|---|---|---|---|---|---|

**WHERE FOUND** Bevelle/Bevelle Palace Floors 44-46

| LEV | 31 | HP | 4100 | MP | 0 |
|---|---|---|---|---|---|
| EXP | 255 | AP | 1 | | |

| GIL DROP | 94 | GIL STEAL | 300 |
|---|---|---|---|

| STR | 42 | DEF | 58 | AGL | 62 |
|---|---|---|---|---|---|
| EVA | 0 | ACC | 0 | LUCK | 0 |
| MAG | 52 | MAG DEF | 0 | | |

| | None | | None | | Weak |
|---|---|---|---|---|---|
| | None | | Invalid | | None |

**IMM** Dth., Pet., Slp., Sil., Poi., Con., Ber., Cur., Stp., Doom, M.D.

**DEF EFF** Ejt. (18), Zan. (2)

| DROP RATIO | 128/255 |
|---|---|
| ITEM DROP | Sleep Grenade x1 |
| RARE DROP | Darkness Grenade x1 |
| STEAL RATIO | 255/255 |
| STOLEN ITEM | Darkness Grenade x1 |
| RARE STEAL | Sleep Grenade x1 |
| BRIBE ITEM | None |
| RARE BRIBE | None |

## YAIBAL

**NONE**

| CHAPTERS | | | | | 5 |
|---|---|---|---|---|---|

**WHERE FOUND** Mushroom Rock

| LEV | 26 | HP | 4330 | MP | 48 |
|---|---|---|---|---|---|
| EXP | 500 | AP | 1 | | |

| GIL DROP | 100 | GIL STEAL | 1000 |
|---|---|---|---|

| STR | 55 | DEF | 12 | AGL | 71 |
|---|---|---|---|---|---|
| EVA | 0 | ACC | 8 | LUCK | 0 |
| MAG | 47 | MAG DEF | 10 | | |

| | None | | None | | None |
|---|---|---|---|---|---|
| | None | | Invalid | | None |

**IMM** Dth., Pet., Slp., Sil., Ber., Cur., Ejt., Slw., Stp., Doom, Del., P.I., M.D.

**DEF EFF** Drk. (20), Poi. (20), Con. (100), Zan. (10)

| DROP RATIO | 255/255 |
|---|---|
| ITEM DROP | Muscle Belt x1 |
| RARE DROP | Muscle Belt x1 |
| STEAL RATIO | 255/255 |
| STOLEN ITEM | Chocobo Feather x1 |
| RARE STEAL | Chocobo Feather x2 |
| BRIBE ITEM | None |
| RARE BRIBE | None |

## YAU-28

**MECH**

| CHAPTERS | | 2 | | 5 |
|---|---|---|---|---|

**WHERE FOUND** Bevelle/Bevelle Floors 16-19

| LEV | 18 | HP | 1270 | MP | 0 |
|---|---|---|---|---|---|
| EXP | 80 | AP | 1 | | |

| GIL DROP | 25 | GIL STEAL | 240 |
|---|---|---|---|

| STR | 52 | DEF | 0 | AGL | 81 |
|---|---|---|---|---|---|
| EVA | 0 | ACC | 0 | LUCK | 0 |
| MAG | 48 | MAG DEF | 36 | | |

| | None | | None | | None |
|---|---|---|---|---|---|
| | None | | None | | None |

**IMM** Dth., Pet., Slp., Sil., Poi., Con., Ber., Cur., Stp., Doom

**DEF EFF** Ejt. (18), Zan. (4)

| DROP RATIO | 255/255 |
|---|---|
| ITEM DROP | S-Bomb x1 |
| RARE DROP | Darkness Grenade x1 |
| STEAL RATIO | 128/255 |
| STOLEN ITEM | Grenade x1 |
| RARE STEAL | S-Bomb |
| BRIBE ITEM | None |
| RARE BRIBE | None |

## YAU-71

**MECH**

| CHAPTERS | | | 3 | | 5 |
|---|---|---|---|---|---|

**WHERE FOUND** Kilika Island/Bevelle/Bevelle Palace Floors 44-46

| LEV | 34 | HP | 3800 | MP | 0 |
|---|---|---|---|---|---|
| EXP | 255 | AP | 1 | | |

| GIL DROP | 94 | GIL STEAL | 300 |
|---|---|---|---|

| STR | 42 | DEF | 0 | AGL | 89 |
|---|---|---|---|---|---|
| EVA | 0 | ACC | 0 | LUCK | 0 |
| MAG | 52 | MAG DEF | 36 | | |

| | None | | None | | None |
|---|---|---|---|---|---|
| | None | | Invalid | | None |

**IMM** Dth., Pet., Slp., Sil., Poi., Con., Ber., Cur., Stp., Doom, M.D.

**DEF EFF** Ejt. (18), Zan. (4)

| DROP RATIO | 128/255 |
|---|---|
| ITEM DROP | Sleep Grenade x1 |
| RARE DROP | Silence Grenade x1 |
| STEAL RATIO | 255/255 |
| STOLEN ITEM | Silence Grenade x1 |
| RARE STEAL | Sleep Grenade x1 |
| BRIBE ITEM | None |
| RARE BRIBE | None |

## YELLOW ELEMENTAL

**ELEMENTAL**

| CHAPTERS | 1 | | | | 5 |
|---|---|---|---|---|---|

**WHERE FOUND** Mt. Gagazet/Bevelle Tower Floors 4-6

| LEV | 1 [2] | HP | 12 [48] | MP | 120 |
|---|---|---|---|---|---|
| EXP | 2 [8] | AP | 1 [2] | | |

| GIL DROP | 24 [43] | GIL STEAL | 100 [200] |
|---|---|---|---|

| STR | 2 | DEF | 5 | AGL | 62 [68] |
|---|---|---|---|---|---|
| EVA | 0 | ACC | 0 | LUCK | 0 |
| MAG | 188 | MAG DEF | 100 | | |

| | Invalid | | Invalid | | Absorb |
|---|---|---|---|---|---|
| | Weak | | None | | None |

**IMM** Pet., Slp., Con., Ber., Cur., [M.B.]

**DEF EFF** Ejt. (6 [10]), Zan. (0 [3])

| DROP RATIO | 128/255 [255/255] |
|---|---|
| ITEM DROP | Potion x1 [Electro Marble x3] |
| RARE DROP | Phoenix Down x1 [Electro Marble x4] |
| STEAL RATIO | 255/255 |
| STOLEN ITEM | Potion x1 [Electro Marble x1] |
| RARE STEAL | Electro Marble x1 [Lightning Marble x1] |
| BRIBE ITEM | Electro Marble x1 [Lightning Marble x2] |
| RARE BRIBE | Lightning Marble x1 [Lightning Marble x2] |

Characters

1

Garment Grids & Dresspheres

2

Battle System

3

Accessories

4

Items and Item Shops

5

Walkthrough

6

Mini Games

7

Fiends and Enemies

8

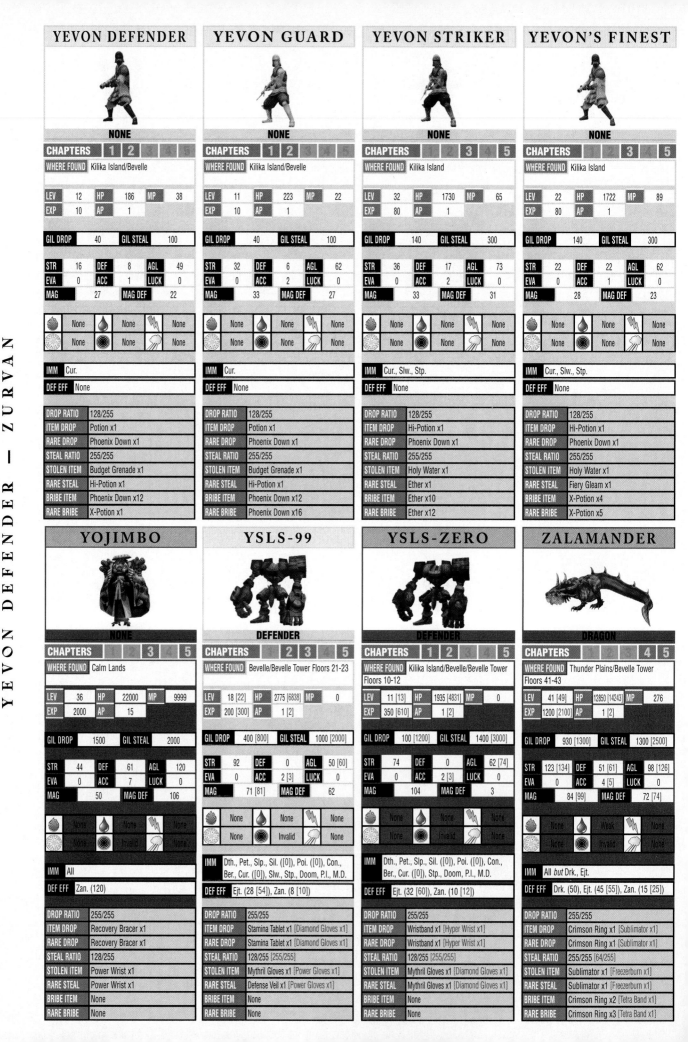

## YEVON DEFENDER

**NONE**

| CHAPTERS | 1 | 2 | 3 | 4 | 5 |
|---|---|---|---|---|---|
| WHERE FOUND | Kilika Island/Bevelle | | | | |

| LEV | 12 | HP | 186 | MP | 38 |
|---|---|---|---|---|---|
| EXP | 10 | AP | 1 | | |

| GIL DROP | 40 | GIL STEAL | 100 |
|---|---|---|---|

| STR | 16 | DEF | 8 | AGL | 49 |
|---|---|---|---|---|---|
| EVA | 0 | ACC | 1 | LUCK | 0 |
| MAG | 27 | MAG DEF | 22 | | |

| Fire | None | Water | None | Lightning | None |
|---|---|---|---|---|---|
| Holy | None | Gravity | None | Ice | None |

| IMM | Cur. |
|---|---|
| DEF EFF | None |

| DROP RATIO | 128/255 |
|---|---|
| ITEM DROP | Potion x1 |
| RARE DROP | Phoenix Down x1 |
| STEAL RATIO | 255/255 |
| STOLEN ITEM | Budget Grenade x1 |
| RARE STEAL | Hi-Potion x1 |
| BRIBE ITEM | Phoenix Down x12 |
| RARE BRIBE | X-Potion x1 |

## YEVON GUARD

**NONE**

| CHAPTERS | 1 | 2 | 3 | 4 | 5 |
|---|---|---|---|---|---|
| WHERE FOUND | Kilika Island/Bevelle | | | | |

| LEV | 11 | HP | 223 | MP | 22 |
|---|---|---|---|---|---|
| EXP | 10 | AP | 1 | | |

| GIL DROP | 40 | GIL STEAL | 100 |
|---|---|---|---|

| STR | 32 | DEF | 6 | AGL | 62 |
|---|---|---|---|---|---|
| EVA | 0 | ACC | 2 | LUCK | 0 |
| MAG | 33 | MAG DEF | 27 | | |

| Fire | None | Water | None | Lightning | None |
|---|---|---|---|---|---|
| Holy | None | Gravity | None | Ice | None |

| IMM | Cur. |
|---|---|
| DEF EFF | None |

| DROP RATIO | 128/255 |
|---|---|
| ITEM DROP | Potion x1 |
| RARE DROP | Phoenix Down x1 |
| STEAL RATIO | 255/255 |
| STOLEN ITEM | Budget Grenade x1 |
| RARE STEAL | Hi-Potion x1 |
| BRIBE ITEM | Phoenix Down x12 |
| RARE BRIBE | Phoenix Down x16 |

## YEVON STRIKER

**NONE**

| CHAPTERS | 1 | 2 | 3 | 4 | 5 |
|---|---|---|---|---|---|
| WHERE FOUND | Kilika Island | | | | |

| LEV | 32 | HP | 1730 | MP | 65 |
|---|---|---|---|---|---|
| EXP | 80 | AP | 1 | | |

| GIL DROP | 140 | GIL STEAL | 300 |
|---|---|---|---|

| STR | 36 | DEF | 17 | AGL | 73 |
|---|---|---|---|---|---|
| EVA | 0 | ACC | 2 | LUCK | 0 |
| MAG | 33 | MAG DEF | 31 | | |

| Fire | None | Water | None | Lightning | None |
|---|---|---|---|---|---|
| Holy | None | Gravity | None | Ice | None |

| IMM | Cur., Slw., Stp. |
|---|---|
| DEF EFF | None |

| DROP RATIO | 128/255 |
|---|---|
| ITEM DROP | Hi-Potion x1 |
| RARE DROP | Phoenix Down x1 |
| STEAL RATIO | 255/255 |
| STOLEN ITEM | Holy Water x1 |
| RARE STEAL | Ether x1 |
| BRIBE ITEM | Ether x10 |
| RARE BRIBE | Ether x12 |

## YEVON'S FINEST

**NONE**

| CHAPTERS | 1 | 2 | 3 | 4 | 5 |
|---|---|---|---|---|---|
| WHERE FOUND | Kilika Island | | | | |

| LEV | 22 | HP | 1722 | MP | 89 |
|---|---|---|---|---|---|
| EXP | 80 | AP | 1 | | |

| GIL DROP | 140 | GIL STEAL | 300 |
|---|---|---|---|

| STR | 22 | DEF | 22 | AGL | 62 |
|---|---|---|---|---|---|
| EVA | 0 | ACC | 1 | LUCK | 0 |
| MAG | 28 | MAG DEF | 23 | | |

| Fire | None | Water | None | Lightning | None |
|---|---|---|---|---|---|
| Holy | None | Gravity | None | Ice | None |

| IMM | Cur., Slw., Stp. |
|---|---|
| DEF EFF | None |

| DROP RATIO | 128/255 |
|---|---|
| ITEM DROP | Hi-Potion x1 |
| RARE DROP | Phoenix Down x1 |
| STEAL RATIO | 255/255 |
| STOLEN ITEM | Holy Water x1 |
| RARE STEAL | Fiery Gleam x1 |
| BRIBE ITEM | X-Potion x4 |
| RARE BRIBE | X-Potion x5 |

## YOJIMBO

**NONE**

| CHAPTERS | 1 | 2 | 3 | 4 | 5 |
|---|---|---|---|---|---|
| WHERE FOUND | Calm Lands | | | | |

| LEV | 36 | HP | 22000 | MP | 9999 |
|---|---|---|---|---|---|
| EXP | 2000 | AP | 15 | | |

| GIL DROP | 1500 | GIL STEAL | 2000 |
|---|---|---|---|

| STR | 44 | DEF | 61 | AGL | 120 |
|---|---|---|---|---|---|
| EVA | 0 | ACC | 7 | LUCK | 0 |
| MAG | 50 | MAG DEF | 106 | | |

| Fire | None | Water | None | Lightning | None |
|---|---|---|---|---|---|
| Holy | None | Gravity | Invalid | Ice | None |

| IMM | All |
|---|---|
| DEF EFF | Zan. (120) |

| DROP RATIO | 255/255 |
|---|---|
| ITEM DROP | Recovery Bracer x1 |
| RARE DROP | Recovery Bracer x1 |
| STEAL RATIO | 128/255 |
| STOLEN ITEM | Power Wrist x1 |
| RARE STEAL | Power Wrist x1 |
| BRIBE ITEM | None |
| RARE BRIBE | None |

## YSLS-99

**DEFENDER**

| CHAPTERS | 1 | 2 | 3 | 4 | 5 |
|---|---|---|---|---|---|
| WHERE FOUND | Bevelle/Bevelle Tower Floors 21-23 | | | | |

| LEV | 18 [22] | HP | 2775 [6838] | MP | 0 |
|---|---|---|---|---|---|
| EXP | 200 [300] | AP | 1 [2] | | |

| GIL DROP | 400 [800] | GIL STEAL | 1000 [2000] |
|---|---|---|---|

| STR | 92 | DEF | 0 | AGL | 50 [60] |
|---|---|---|---|---|---|
| EVA | 0 | ACC | 2 [3] | LUCK | 0 |
| MAG | 71 [81] | MAG DEF | 62 | | |

| Fire | None | Water | None | Lightning | None |
|---|---|---|---|---|---|
| Holy | None | Gravity | Invalid | Ice | None |

| IMM | Dth., Pet., Slp., Sil. ([0]), Poi. ([0]), Con., Ber., Cur. ([0]), Slw., Stp., Doom, P.I., M.D. |
|---|---|
| DEF EFF | Ejt. (28 [54]), Zan. (8 [10]) |

| DROP RATIO | 255/255 |
|---|---|
| ITEM DROP | Stamina Tablet x1 [Diamond Gloves x1] |
| RARE DROP | Stamina Tablet x1 [Diamond Gloves x1] |
| STEAL RATIO | 128/255 [255/255] |
| STOLEN ITEM | Mythril Gloves x1 [Power Gloves x1] |
| RARE STEAL | Defense Veil x1 [Power Gloves x1] |
| BRIBE ITEM | None |
| RARE BRIBE | None |

## YSLS-ZERO

**DEFENDER**

| CHAPTERS | 1 | 2 | 3 | 4 | 5 |
|---|---|---|---|---|---|
| WHERE FOUND | Kilika Island/Bevelle/Bevelle Tower Floors 10-12 | | | | |

| LEV | 11 [13] | HP | 1935 [4831] | MP | 0 |
|---|---|---|---|---|---|
| EXP | 350 [610] | AP | 1 [2] | | |

| GIL DROP | 100 [1200] | GIL STEAL | 1400 [3000] |
|---|---|---|---|

| STR | 74 | DEF | 0 | AGL | 62 [74] |
|---|---|---|---|---|---|
| EVA | 0 | ACC | 2 [3] | LUCK | 0 |
| MAG | 104 | MAG DEF | 3 | | |

| Fire | None | Water | None | Lightning | None |
|---|---|---|---|---|---|
| Holy | None | Gravity | Invalid | Ice | None |

| IMM | Dth., Pet., Slp., Sil. ([0]), Poi. ([0]), Con., Ber., Cur. ([0]), Stp., Doom, P.I., M.D. |
|---|---|
| DEF EFF | Ejt. (32 [60]), Zan. (10 [12]) |

| DROP RATIO | 255/255 |
|---|---|
| ITEM DROP | Wristband x1 [Hyper Wrist x1] |
| RARE DROP | Wristband x1 [Hyper Wrist x1] |
| STEAL RATIO | 128/255 [255/255] |
| STOLEN ITEM | Mythril Gloves x1 [Diamond Gloves x1] |
| RARE STEAL | Mythril Gloves x1 [Diamond Gloves x1] |
| BRIBE ITEM | None |
| RARE BRIBE | None |

## ZALAMANDER

**DRAGON**

| CHAPTERS | 1 | 2 | 3 | 4 | 5 |
|---|---|---|---|---|---|
| WHERE FOUND | Thunder Plains/Bevelle Tower Floors 41-43 | | | | |

| LEV | 41 [49] | HP | 12850 [14243] | MP | 276 |
|---|---|---|---|---|---|
| EXP | 1200 [2100] | AP | 1 [2] | | |

| GIL DROP | 930 [1300] | GIL STEAL | 1300 [2500] |
|---|---|---|---|

| STR | 123 [134] | DEF | 51 [61] | AGL | 98 [126] |
|---|---|---|---|---|---|
| EVA | 0 | ACC | 4 [5] | LUCK | 0 |
| MAG | 84 [99] | MAG DEF | 72 [74] | | |

| Fire | None | Water | Weak | Lightning | None |
|---|---|---|---|---|---|
| Holy | None | Gravity | Invalid | Ice | None |

| IMM | All but Drk., Ejt. |
|---|---|
| DEF EFF | Drk. (50), Ejt. (45 [55]), Zan. (15 [25]) |

| DROP RATIO | 255/255 |
|---|---|
| ITEM DROP | Crimson Ring x1 [Sublimator x1] |
| RARE DROP | Crimson Ring x1 [Sublimator x1] |
| STEAL RATIO | 255/255 [64/255] |
| STOLEN ITEM | Sublimator x1 [Freezerburn x1] |
| RARE STEAL | Sublimator x1 [Freezerburn x1] |
| BRIBE ITEM | Crimson Ring x2 [Tetra Band x1] |
| RARE BRIBE | Crimson Ring x3 [Tetra Band x1] |

## ZARICH

**NONE**

| CHAPTERS | 1 | 2 | **3** | 4 | **5** |
|---|---|---|---|---|---|

| WHERE FOUND | Bikanel |
|---|---|

| LEV | 36 | HP | 5440 | MP | 9999 |
|---|---|---|---|---|---|
| EXP | 0 | AP | 0 | | |

| GIL DROP | 0 | GIL STEAL | None |
|---|---|---|---|

| STR | 70 | DEF | 25 | AGL | 82 |
|---|---|---|---|---|---|
| EVA | 0 | ACC | 1 | LUCK | 0 |
| MAG | 0 | MAG DEF | 99 | | |

|  | Half |  | Half |  | Half |
|---|---|---|---|---|---|
|  | Half |  | Invalid |  | Half |

| IMM | P.B., M.B., L.C., E.C., A.C. |
|---|---|

| DEF EFF | Zan. (255) |
|---|---|

| DROP RATIO | None |
|---|---|
| ITEM DROP | None |
| RARE DROP | None |
| STEAL RATIO | None |
| STOLEN ITEM | None |
| RARE STEAL | None |
| BRIBE ITEM | None |
| RARE BRIBE | None |

## ZU

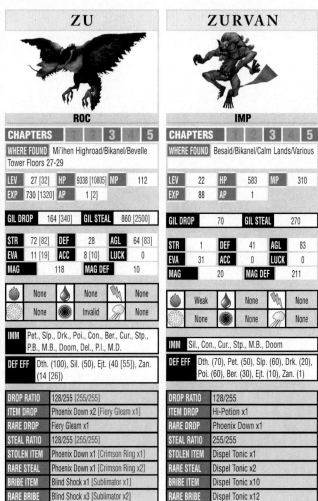

**ROC**

| CHAPTERS | 1 | 2 | **3** | 4 | **5** |
|---|---|---|---|---|---|

| WHERE FOUND | Mi'ihen Highroad/Bikanel/Bevelle Tower Floors 27-29 |
|---|---|

| LEV | 27 [32] | HP | 9338 [10805] | MP | 112 |
|---|---|---|---|---|---|
| EXP | 730 [1320] | AP | 1 [2] | | |

| GIL DROP | 164 [340] | GIL STEAL | 860 [2500] |
|---|---|---|---|

| STR | 72 [82] | DEF | 28 | AGL | 64 [83] |
|---|---|---|---|---|---|
| EVA | 11 [19] | ACC | 8 [10] | LUCK | 0 |
| MAG | 118 | MAG DEF | 10 | | |

|  | None |  | None |  | None |
|---|---|---|---|---|---|
|  | None |  | Invalid |  | None |

| IMM | Pet., Slp., Drk., Poi., Con., Ber., Cur., Stp., P.B., M.B., Doom, Del., P.I., M.D. |
|---|---|

| DEF EFF | Dth. (100), Sil. (50), Ejt. (40 [55]), Zan. (14 [26]) |
|---|---|

| DROP RATIO | 128/255 [255/255] |
|---|---|
| ITEM DROP | Phoenix Down x2 [Fiery Gleam x1] |
| RARE DROP | Fiery Gleam x1 |
| STEAL RATIO | 128/255 [255/255] |
| STOLEN ITEM | Phoenix Down x1 [Crimson Ring x1] |
| RARE STEAL | Phoenix Down x1 [Crimson Ring x2] |
| BRIBE ITEM | Blind Shock x1 [Sublimator x1] |
| RARE BRIBE | Blind Shock x3 [Sublimator x2] |

## ZURVAN

**IMP**

| CHAPTERS | 1 | 2 | **3** | 4 | **5** |
|---|---|---|---|---|---|

| WHERE FOUND | Besaid/Bikanel/Calm Lands/Various |
|---|---|

| LEV | 22 | HP | 583 | MP | 310 |
|---|---|---|---|---|---|
| EXP | 88 | AP | 1 | | |

| GIL DROP | 70 | GIL STEAL | 270 |
|---|---|---|---|

| STR | 1 | DEF | 41 | AGL | 83 |
|---|---|---|---|---|---|
| EVA | 31 | ACC | 0 | LUCK | 0 |
| MAG | 20 | MAG DEF | 211 | | |

|  | Weak |  | None |  | None |
|---|---|---|---|---|---|
|  | None |  | None |  | None |

| IMM | Sil., Con., Cur., Stp., M.B., Doom |
|---|---|

| DEF EFF | Dth. (70), Pet. (50), Slp. (60), Drk. (20), Poi. (60), Ber. (30), Ejt. (10), Zan. (1) |
|---|---|

| DROP RATIO | 128/255 |
|---|---|
| ITEM DROP | Hi-Potion x1 |
| RARE DROP | Phoenix Down x1 |
| STEAL RATIO | 255/255 |
| STOLEN ITEM | Dispel Tonic x1 |
| RARE STEAL | Dispel Tonic x2 |
| BRIBE ITEM | Dispel Tonic x10 |
| RARE BRIBE | Dispel Tonic x12 |

Characters

Garment Grids & Dresspheres

Battle System

Accessories

Items and Item Shops

Walkthrough

Mini Games

Fiends and Enemies

347

# Don't walk. Speed.

## AOL TopSpeed™ Technology

letsyoudownloadwebpagesquickerthaneverbefore. Phew.

### To order call 1-800-383-3176

Life needs a faster way.

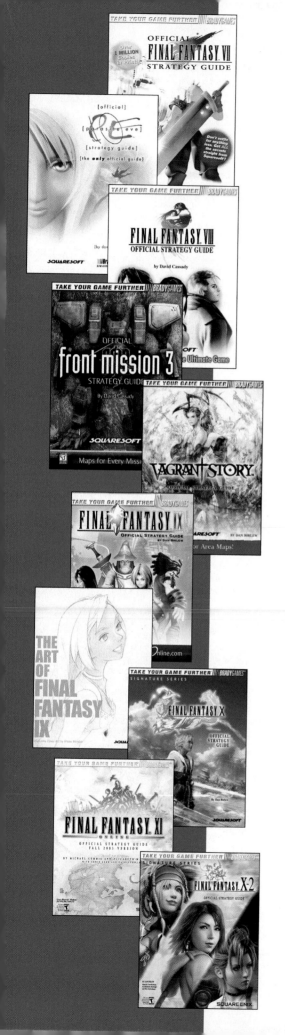

# BRADYGAMES®

# TENTH ANNIVERSARY

BradyGAMES published its first strategy guide in November of 1993, and every year since then, we've made great efforts to give you the best guides possible. Now celebrating our 10th anniversary, we'd like to take this opportunity to say a few things and extend a special invitation to you—our readers.

First of all, THANK YOU! Whether you're a long-time customer, or this is your first BradyGAMES guide, we appreciate your support. We hope that our guides have enhanced your overall experience when playing games. These days, completing a game isn't just about how quickly you finish. It's about uncovering absolutely everything a game has to offer: side quests, mini-games, secret characters, and multiple endings just to name a few. That's what the *TAKE YOUR GAME FURTHER*® banner at the top of our guides is all about.

Many games deserve more than just a standard strategy guide, and we recognize that. Our guides are produced with the highest quality standards and are tailored specifically for the games they cover. With the introduction of our Signature Series and Limited Edition guides, we raised the bar even higher.

Now for the "invitation" part. Although we constantly challenge ourselves to improve our guides, we'd like your help too. You're formally invited to tell us what you think about our guides. Like something we do? Let us know. Think something we've done is totally lame? *Please* let us know. We want your feedback no matter if it's good, bad, or just plain ugly. You can write or e-mail us at the addresses below, and we *will* read what you send. Your opinions are important to us, and may influence the direction for our guides in the future.

Write to:
BradyGAMES
800 E. 96th Street, 3rd Floor
Indianapolis, IN 46240

Send e-mail to:
feedback@bradygames.com

For now, we hope you enjoy this guide. Thanks again for choosing BradyGAMES.

# FINAL FANTASY X-2
## OFFICIAL STRATEGY GUIDE

Dan Birlew

With Special Contributions by
Elizabeth Hollinger & Wes Ehrlichman

©2004 Pearson Education

BradyGAMES® is a registered trademark of Pearson Education, Inc.

All rights reserved, including the right of reproduction in whole or in part in any form.

**BradyGAMES® Publishing**

An Imprint of Pearson Education
800 East 96th Street, Third Floor
Indianapolis, Indiana 46240

ISBN: 0-7440-0285-0

Library of Congress Catalog No.: 2003114153

Printing Code: The rightmost double-digit number is the year of the book's printing; the rightmost single-digit number is the number of the book's printing. For example, 03-1 shows that the first printing of the book occurred in 2003.

06 05 04 03          4 3 2 1

Manufactured in the United States of America.

## BRADYGAMES STAFF

**Publisher**
David Waybright

**Editor-In-Chief**
H. Leigh Davis

**Marketing Manager**
Janet Eshenour

**Creative Director**
Robin Lasek

**Licensing Manager**
Mike Degler

**Assistant Marketing Manager**
Susie Nieman

### CREDITS

**Title Manager**
Tim Cox

**Screenshot Editor**
Michael Owen

**Book Designers**
Ann-Marie Deets
Doug Wilkins

**Poster & Cover Designer**
Dan Caparo

**Production Designers**
Wil Cruz
Bob Klunder
Chris Luckenbill
Tracy Wehmeyer

## ACKNOWLEDGMENTS

Dan Birlew would like to thank the following people, without whom this book would have been impossible: Tim Cox, for leading this project like a well-honed drill sergeant; David Waybright, Mike Degler and Leigh Davis, for obtaining this project and assigning it to me; my co-authors Beth Hollinger and Wes Erlichman, for picking up the slack and helping us wrestle down this huge game in such a wickedly short amount of time; Jeremy Blaustein, for some excellent and fast translations; my brother Tom and Shannon, for spending all their time with us while they were visiting; and most importantly, my wife Laura, for allowing me to put everything else in our life on hold while I worked on this amazing project.

## ABOUT THE AUTHOR

Dan Birlew is the author of 30 videogame books, including expert strategy guides on other Squaresoft and Enix titles such as *Kingdom Hearts*, *FINAL FANTASY X*, *FINAL FANTASY Chronicles*, and *The Bouncer*, to name a few. He is a graduate of the University of Texas, still cheers for the Horns every weekend, and spends his spare time beta testing software for several companies. He has been married for 10 years.